AF600274

Motif-Index of Folk-Literature

Vol. 6.1

MOTIF-INDEX
OF
FOLK-LITERATURE

A Classification of Narrative Elements in Folktales, Ballads, Myths, Fables, Mediaeval Romances, Exempla, Fabliaux, Jest-Books, and Local Legends

REVISED AND ENLARGED EDITION BY

STITH THOMPSON

Indiana University

VOLUME 6.1
INDEX
(A-K)

INDIANA UNIVERSITY PRESS

BLOOMINGTON AND INDIANAPOLIS

This book is a publication of

Indiana University Press
601 North Morton Street
Bloomington, IN 47404-3797 USA

http://iupress.indiana.edu

Telephone orders 800-842-6796
Fax orders 812-855-7931
Orders by e-mail iuporder@indiana.edu

Manufactured in the United States of America

Cataloging information is available from the Library of Congress.

Volume 6.1 ISBN: 0-253-34089-6
Volume 6.2 ISBN: 0-253-34091-8

ALPHABETICAL INDEX[1]

An asterisk before a number indicates that cross-references to related matters will be found immediately following the item. Numbers followed by "ff." indicate that the item is general and introduces specific examples not always recorded in this index. Plurals always immediately follow the singular number of nouns.

Aaron's censer (pistol) J1446; rod F971.1. — Miracles cease at A's death F900.3.1.

Abandoned castle F771.4.3; child aided by seagulls, doe, angel T611.7; child joins parents in game (recognition) H151.9; child receives magic sight D1821.6; child rescued by dog B549.3; children accidentally discovered N768; or murdered children S300—399; maiden helped by nurse P361.5; queen entertains in forest, recognized H155; son exposed to tiger H105.5.4; souls feed on spiders E752.7.1; wife recognized H152.3. — Child born of woman a. in pit T581.2; father reinstates a. son N731.3; ghost of one a. by lover E334.3; girl a. in tree H151.14.1; girl rescued, then a. R111.6; parent seeks famine relief from a. child H154; rescue of a. persons R130ff.; waves break caul of a. child N655.

Abandoning. — Mortal a. world to live in fairyland F373; mother a. beautiful baby F575.1.1.

Abandonment to avoid fulfillment of prophecy M371.0.1; on cliff submerged at high tide (punishment) Q466.2; and exposures S140ff.; in forest as punishment Q435; of hero at birth A511.2.1; of hero in lower world *K1931.2; of integrity brings devil G303.6.2.5; on stretching tree K1113; in water *S142. — Step-sisters cause girl's a. in jungle K2129.3.

Abandonments and exposures S140ff.

Abbess caught in sin permits nuns to sin K1274; secretly delivered of her child by Virgin T401.1; and washerwoman (flea and fever) J612.1. — Nun hidden by a. from pursuing knight betrays own hiding place V465.1.2.1; nun rewarded, made a. Q87.3.

Abbey. — Ghost prevents box's removal from a. E299.2; looking for keys of a. J703.1.

Abbot burns mouth, excuses crying J1478.1; caught in sin permits monks to sin K1274; escapes from paramour's husband K521.6; and king

[1] For invaluable aid in the preparation of this index I am indebted to Miss Clara L. Little and Mrs. Sue Lena Hickam. The new and enlarged index had the expert help of Mrs. Nancy MacClintock and Mrs. Marjorie Congram, and was prepared under special grants of the American Philosophical Society and Indiana University. For all this I am most grateful.

H561.2; cannot find needle J1651; receives guest in rags J916. — Angel chastizes a. V235.3; fat a. cured by starving K1955.1.1; fire consumes woman slandering a. Q552.13.3; God as surety: a. pays J1559.2; luxury of a. and cardinal J1263.4.1; monk who did not ask for the position made a. Q61.1; self-righteous monk rebuked by a. L435.1.1; sham a. K1961.5; thievish a. to be eaten by wolves Q556.12.1; virgin becomes monastery a. K1837.7.

Abdicating. — Father a. in son's favor P16.1.4; king a. after queen's adultery P16.1.2.

Abducted bride hidden in fairyland F322.4; wife brought back by fakir R165.3; wife leaves needle sign H119.2. — Druid discovers a. wife D1816.5.1; girl a. by fairy F324; girl a. by fairy accidentally drowns N339.9; hero's wife a. N391.0.1; man a. by devil G303.9.5.6; quest as punishment by a. girl's father H1219.3; sacrifice for return of a. person V17.7; statue left instead of a. queen K661.4; thieves carry a. woman on bier, drown out her wailings K419.8; woman a. by giving medicine K1364; youth a. by fairy F325.

Abduction *R10ff.; by animal for breaking tabu C986; of Christianized fairy F389.2; by devil *G303.9.5; to fairyland *F320; by man disguised as woman K1321.2; by masking as husband K755.1; by mountain-men *F460.4.4.1; by ogre G440ff.; punished Q213; by taking aboard ship to inspect wares K1332. — Banishment for a. of bride Q431.5.2.

Abducting child by calling self "her husband" K361.1.1; woman after asking her for fire K762. — Demons a. men G302.9.2; fairy a. men with whom in love F302.3.1.4; fairy a. mortal's wife F301.6; false accusation of a. wife K2127.1; king a. woman P19.2.1; lover a. beloved K1371.4; lover in disguise for a. K1831.2.2; moon a. woman A753.1.1; ogre a. new-born babe G442.1.

Abductor in disguise R24; induces magic sleep D1964.3; pretends lover sent him to princess K1914. — Burning to punish a. Q414.0.4.2; lover rescues his lady from a. R161.1; magic sleep induced by a. D1964.3.

Abel slain with camel bone F839.3. — Animals refuse to avenge murder of A. B591.0.1; Cain drinks blood of A. D1812.3.3.7; cry of blood of A. A1344.1.

Abersetus as guardian of door of heaven A661.0.1.4.

Abiding. — Vow on a. laws M185.

Ability. — God dislikes offerings beyond one's a. V10.2; person transformed to animal recognized by a. to read H62.2; recognition by unique a. H31; reward for a. to keep secrets Q62; test of a. *H500; test of wife's a. to keep secret H472ff.

Abnormal features or growth of changeling F321.1.2.1.

Abnormally born child has unusual powers T550.2.

Aboard. — Capture by taking a. ship K775.1; man magically appears a. ship D2121.11.

Abode, see also **Dwelling, Home;** of the dead *E480ff.; of devil (between

hoofs of swine) G303.8.7; of evil spirits (north) G633; of unpromising hero (heroine) L130ff.

Abortion T572.2; placed in innocent woman's bed K2112.2.4. — Ghost of a. E225.1; origin of a. A1351.2; punishment for a. Q251.1.

Above. — Creator from a. A21; deceptive crop division: a. the ground, below the ground K171.1; dwarfs have homes a. the ground F451.4.2ff.; emergence of gods from a. A115.5; the Lord a., the lord below K1525; region a. the three worlds A651.1.1.2; vehicle travels a. and below ground *D1533.2ff.

Abraham learns to worship God (cumulative tale) Z42.2; as prophet M301.7.3. — Angel's visit to A. H828.

Abraham's — Land of dead in A's bosom E489.10.

Abridgement of freedom as punishment Q430ff.

Abroad. — Do not marry a girl from a. J21.4; wild hunt a. until cock-crow *E501.11.1.2.

Abscess breaks when patient laughs at foolish diagnosis N641. — Birth from a. T541.2; tigress grateful for opening of a. B386.

Absence. — Feigned a. tests wife H466.1; in god's a. his function ceases A173.1; obedient husband given leave of a. J2523.

Absent person seems to be present K1881. — Why certain animals are a. from countries A2434.2; bending bow of woman's a. husband (suitor contest) H331.4.2; cannibals advised to be a. while hero is being cooked K619.1; present servant girl preferred to a. mistress J326; sleeper not to be awakened, since soul is a. E721.1.1; body in trance while soul is a. E721.2; wraith looks after a. person E723.4.6; youth a. when entire family wiped out N659.2.

Absent-minded nurse puts child down well J2175.3.

Absent-mindedness, absurd J2000—J2049.

Absolution. — Unquiet dead sinner taken to priest for a. E411.0.2.

Absorption in charms of beloved causes cut finger T26.1.

Abstinence from wine by deer after breaking leg J133.3.

Abstract. — Wanting to see a. quality J2488.

Abstractions, gods of A460ff.; personified Z110ff.

Absurd contest won by deception K60ff.; tasks H1010—H1049ff.; truth discredits husband J1151.1.2. — King makes a. statement J817.3; wife agrees with husband's a. statements H474.

Absurdities based upon false assumptions J2210ff.; cause fool to laugh U1.5; rebuke another absurdity *J1530ff.; of tight-rope walker's performance J156.2. — Lies: logical a. X1700.

Absurdum, reductio ad (of judgment) J1191, (task) H952, (riddle: stallions of Babylon) H572.

Abundance in otherworld F169.8. — Fairy promises a. to mortal F349.4.

Abuse of dwarfs by mortals F451.5.11; of fairy gifts tabu F348.7.1; of hospitality punished Q292.3; of live stock by fairies F366; of mother punished (devils carry off girl) Q281.1.1; of property by witch *G265;

of stepchildren punished by return of dead mother *E221.2.1; of women, children tabu C867.1. — Ears stopped to avoid hearing a. J672.2.

Abuses. — Repartee concerning clerical a. J1263ff.; twelve a. of world Z71.8.2.

Abused and pampered horses B316; son becomes hero L10.2; stepdaughter L55.1; youngest daughter L52.

Abusive speeches drive ogres away G571. — Woman's a. lover T232.4.

Abyss at end of Milky Way A778.10. — Bodies of water in primitive a. sink A910.3; tree appears to save saint from a. V222.10.

Access to lower world F90ff.; to other world F150ff.; to upper world *F50ff.

Accident. — Animal warns against a. B521.2; ghost haunts a. scene E275, E334.2.2; injury from reënacting a. J2133.14; knockers' appearance as a. warning F456.1.2.2.4; luring victim by feigning a. K833; magic object protects from a. on journey D1384; mountains from a. to primeval lizard A 961.3; plant characteristics from a. to original plant A2741; sounds of a. reënact tragedy E337.1.2; treasure discovered by a. N534; who is guilty of a.? Z49.11.

Accidents. — Birds fight, cause series of a. Z49.6.1; bungling fool has succession of a. J2661; lucky a. *N400ff.; unlucky a. N300ff.

Accidental action of ancient animal produces animal characteristics A2211; arrival in lower world *F102; calling on god's name held to outweigh a life of wickedness V91; cannibalism (man eats the dried meat of a Jew on shipboard) X21; death of woman scorned in love T71.1; discharge of gun kills much game X1124.3; discovery of crime N610ff.; discovery of riddle answer H575; drinking of love philtre produces mutual love *T21; encounters N700—N799; and intentional fire J1175.2; killing as bad omen D1812.5.1.23; success in hunting or fishing N620ff. — Detection by a. remark N275.2; recognition through a. encounter H152; victim of a. death cannot rest in grave E411.10.

Accidentally. — Bride wounded a. on way home T152; cobold a. acquired F481.0.1.4; hasty condemnation of man who a. becomes suspected of crime N342; magic a. found D841; objects a. picked up used to overawe ogre N691; princess defeated in repartee by means of objects a. picked up H507.1.0.1; sham wise man a. unmasks robbers K1956.1; villain a. killed by own order K1612.1; youth a. knocks old woman over M301.2.1.

Acclamation of saint by miraculous manifestation *V222.

Accompanying. — Animal a. man on journey B579.1; marvelous light a. saint V222.1; sea dragon in serpent form a. hero D659.4.2.

Accomplishment of quests H1230ff.; of tasks D753, H950ff.; of vigilance test H1480ff.

Account book of dead E481.8.1; book of mistakes J1371; of common experiences demanded as identity-test H15. — Giving a. of what happened in princess's bedchamber H344.1.

Accounts squared by shaving the wife J2082; straightened by ignorant steward L144.1. — Cutting paper of a. J2489.4.
Accountants. — God's a. tally human acts A189.8.
Accounting to be given afterward J1627.
Accoutrements. — Disguise by carrying other's a. K1810.1.
Accursed, see also **Cursed;** dancers C94.1.1. — What are most a. things? H659.18.
Accusation admitted and accuser discomfited J1162; admitted but fool pleads mistakes in the details J2499.3; of murder from blood smeared on innocent person K2155.1. — Bishop's nose bitten off for false a. Q451.5.3; criminal in church mistakes service as a. N275.5; quilty man sentenced for false a. J1141.12; reductio ad absurdum of a. J1191.5.
Accusations, false *K2100—K2199.
Accused. — Benefactor falsely a. of theft W154.13; criminal confesses because he thinks himself a. N275; congregation a. of sins by devil G303.24.1; falsely a. maiden dies F1041.1.3.1; falsely a. man's suicide N347.6; foster brother falsely a. of seduction P273.2.3; heavenly voice test: lying for a. H216.2.
Accuser, envious J1351.2. — Proverb on winning over a. J171.3.2.
Accusing conspirators to confiscate their estates K487. — Thief a. companion of mutual theft K401.0.1.
Accustomed. — Longing for a. living V135.
Achikar *H561.5.
Achilles, see *K1836; heel Z311.
Acid bath for unwelcome lover K1227.4.1.
Acknowledgement of son brings disenchantment of monster D741.1.
Acorn crop (payment to be made at harvest of first crop) K221.
Acorns. — Magic a. D985.4, D1667.2; pseudo-magic a.: protect pigs K119.2.
Acquisition of culture A1400—A1499; of familiar spirit F403.2.1; of helpful animal B310; of food supply for human race A1420ff.; of magic objects D810ff.; of magic powers *D1720ff.; of magic strength D1835; of strength by strong hero F611.3; of extraordinary skill by brothers *F660.1; of treasure or money (accidental) N630ff.; of wisdom (knowledge) J0—J199.
Act of truth H252. — Respite from death until performance of certain a. *K551.
Acts of charity bring forgiveness for sin Q171.1; performed for changing luck *N131. — Clever a. J1100ff.; short-sighted a. J2050ff.
Acteon transformed to deer and eaten by dogs Q415.1.1.
Action. — Confession induced by bringing unjust a. against accused J1141.1; continuous a. started by breaking tabu C916; extraordinary a. explained H591; inappropriate a. from misunderstanding J1820ff.; magic statue of archer put into a. by picking up precious object from ground D1620.1.5.1.

Actor *P471; forgets and speaks in his own person J2041ff.
Adam names all animals A2571.0.1 named from first letters of four stars A1577.1; learns animal languages from Eve B217.8; names male animals, Eve, female A2571.0.2; at first nameless A1281.6; spat on tobacco plant A2854; story false since skeleton has all his ribs J1262.8. — First walk by A. A1392; five devils created by A. create other devils in same manner G303.1.5; God sends A. to earth to father mankind A1285.1.1.; Mother Earth pregnant with A. A401.1; ravens show A. how to bury dead D2223.7; riddles concerning A. H706, H812, H813; Satan jealous of A. A63.5.1; souls presented to A. E755.0.3; tears of A. and Eve leaving paradise become trees A2612.1; why Eve not made with A. A1275.8.
Adam's Apple, origin of A1319.1; body made of eight things A1260.1.3; burial place N774.3.1; clothes of light F821.7; corpse talks with God E545.22; disobedience blamed H1557.2; tears of repentance bring flood A1012.1; wisdom D1811.0.1; work destroyed by devil by night G303.14.1.1. — Earth created from A's body A831.9; fairies not A's children F251.10; heavenly bodies mourn A's death F961.0.3.1; tree from Christ's crucifixion planted by A's son A2632.2.
Adaptability J800ff.
Adder grows in heart of man F559.7.2; kills bird hunter just as he is shooting bird N335.1; transformed to blindworm *A2145.5.
Adder's — Why a's tail tastes like liver A2378.9.4.
Adders in hell A671.2.1.1.
Address of fool (a big high house) J1742.2. — Modesty has no a. J91.
Addressing the dead E545.19; saints to win contest K18.1.2; spirit compels it to speak F404.1; woman in verse betrays changeling's maturity F321.1.1.3. — Pardon for a. courtier as king P15.1.2; use of second plural in a. anyone A1599.5.
Adhesion of blood test of paternity H486.1; for breaking tabu C994. — Magic a. *D2171ff.; (to object as punishment) Q551.2.1.
Adhesive stone (magic) D1413.17.
Admiration of beautiful things causes thief's capture J2136.5.1.
Admirers. — Poet vaults away from a. J1224.1.
Admission of accusation discomfits accuser J1162; of theft by many, real thief concealed K415.1; to heaven Q172; to heaven (faultfinding forbidden) *F13; denied to both heaven and hell *Q565, A1942.1; of sale of kisses provoked by rival's overstrict conduct K1275.1; to woman's bed brings disenchantment of animal D734; to woman's room bought T45. — Test for a. to warrior band H1566.
Adopted son plots parents' death S22.1.1. — Abandoned child a. by queen S354.1; hill as a. child A969.6; mermaid ruins her a. daughter's seducer B81.13.9; mortal god's a. son A189.11.
Adoption of children J21.27, *T670ff.; as sister by dwarfs F451.5.1.2; by fairies F311; of hero by king *N836.1; by old couple N825.1; of

own son by king N731.1.1; by rich man K2015; by transforming self to child D646.2.

Adrift. — Ghost sets boats a. E299.5; imposter casts foster brother a. on seas K1931.1.1; punishment: setting a. in boat Q466.0.2.

Adult transformed to child D55.2.5.

Adulterer can't rest in grave E411.2; causes sun to stand still D2146.1.1.2; killed Q411.0.1.1; punished by madness Q555.2. — Magic cup sticks to a. H411.4.2.

Adulteress betrayed by child J125.2; blackmailed by lover K1582; charges pair of shoes as fee, prepares for old age J761.3; chooses loathly paramour T232.2; on death-bed reveals children's illegitimacy T238; discredits scorned suitor's testimony J1151.4; ejected into street clad only in shirt Q432.2; escapes in old-woman's disguise K521.4.5; explains child born by suggestion J2338; feigns unusual sensitiveness K2051; forced to wear symbolic dress Q487; hurled from high rock escapes injury: she may not be punished again J1184.1; kills lover K2231.1; lures husband to his death K778.5; outwits husband K1510ff.; and paramour outwitted by husband *K1550ff.; and paramour outwitted by trickster K1570ff.; and paramour plot against her stepson S31.1; persuades husband she has not been away J2315.1; plots own abduction R10.2; rebuked for absurdity J1532; tells lover, "I can see whole world" K1271.4; tricks husband into killing lover K2111.4. — Animal as confederate of a. B598; "chaste" woman an a. K2063; paramour exposes a. naked K1213.1; veiled a. flees with paramour K1821.3.1; wife as a. K1500ff.; woman slandered as a. K2112; woman slandered as a. is thrown into lion pit: lions do not harm her B522.3.

Adulterous love changed into chaste one T372; person cannot rest in grave E411.2; wife plots own abduction R10.2. — Animal as confederate of a. wife B598; coarse living sends a. king back to wife V146.1; devil as messenger to the a. G303.9.4.5.2; god from a. union A112.8; whimbrel's a. mate sent to death K813.1.

Adultery *T230, *T481ff., see also **Infidelity;** among the gods A164.2; betrayed by riddling answers H582.2; detected by spit marks J1142.3; in primeval family A1556.3; punished *Q241ff.; revealed by child in mother's womb T575.1.1.2; tests H400ff.; tabu C115. — Animal reveals mistress's a. *A2237.1, J551.1; the bag of lies: threat to tell of queen's a. K1271.1.1; deception connected with a. *K1500ff.; fairy banished for a. F252.4.1; fairies commit a. F254.5; father causes death of son innocent of a. N344.2; fool discloses woman's a.; killed J2365; foster son commits a. with foster father's wife P275.1; husband as God behind tree forces his wife to confess a. *K1971.5; husband refuses to believe in wife's a. J2342; husband relates wife's a. in dream J1147.1; husband takes wife's place and receives punishment for her a. T261.1; husband's jealousy forces wife to a. T257.7; king abdicates after queen's a. P16.1.2; man dies at wife's a. F1041.1.3.5; overlooking a. for reputa-

tion's sake J221.1.1; princess disguised as man accused of a. with queen K2113; queen commits a. with husband's foster son P29.2; rich woman accuses ascetic of a. K2113.2; senator overlooks wife's a. rather than impair his reputation J221.1.1; sun-god commits a. A220.0.1; unwitting a. with blood-brother's wife N766; wife's a. to aid husband in battle T455.2.1.

Advancement. — Worshipping devil to secure a. V55.

Advantage temporarily gained by pretending to yield in combat K2378.

Advent. — Time of Messiah's a. tabu C428.

Adventure told as dream J1155. — Animal cries recall ancient a. A2275.4; casting lots for a. N126.1; going home before a. completed tabu C756.3; quest for a. H1221; vow not to eat before hearing of a. M151.

Adventures, experiences leading to N770ff.; of kings P15ff.; related by old robber frees his three sons R153.3.3; result from promise to dying father M258.1; of thumbling F535.1.1. — Clever wife advises husband how to succeed on a. J1112.3.

Adventurers, twin T685.1.

Adversary pushed into ground F942.2.1. — Animal overcomes man's a. B524; ground cut from under a. F942.2; quest for strong a. H1225.

Adversity genius appears to king C14; personified Z135. — Spirit of a. brings bad luck N134.1.4; sultan tries to avoid a. J2488.2.

Advice, see also **Counsel;** from animals *B560ff.; from bird B122.1; from bodily members D1312.1; to bride T137.1; of cock proves disastrous to himself K1633; from dead mother E323.4; from dervish J152.2; of devil to human beings G303.9.7; from distant sage H1393; from dream D1814.2; from druid P427.3; of your enemy to be disregarded J646; after event valueless J756; from excrements *D1312.1.1; from fairy F347; from God D1814.3; from grateful objects D1658.3.1; from magic object D1312; to marry own daughter secured from priest by unnatural father T411.1.1; sought by Palamides from Ulysses who has injured him J646.1; from supernaturals seen in dreams K2035; from thief for owner to go away K343; from wife behind tree K1971.4.1; of wife scorned leads to disaster J155.3; from a woman in bed T453. — Brother's false a. causes death K991.1; "don't take woman's a." J21.37; giant gives reward for a. Q111.5; god gives king a. A182.3.4.1; hero gets a. from peasant P411.4; king sends wise man to give rival a. K1944; magic a. *D1814; prostitute gets a. from customer T453.2; reward for good a. Q113.1; saint gives a. V223.1; spendthrift's a. to thrifty J1363; taking woman's a. tabu C195.

Adviser. — Beware of following an interested a. J758; creator's a. A40ff.; foster brother as a. P273.1.3; gifts made to a. Q114.0.1; wife as a. J155.4.

Advising. — Animals a. men B569ff.; god a. mortal A182.3.5; heads of slain a. hero E545.21; mortal a. fairy F394.1; trickster a. intercourse K1354.1.1; wife a. husband J1112.3.

Advocate, devil as G303.22.11, M215.

Adze. — Magic a. D1601.14.2, origin of a. A1446.4.

Aegeus and Theseus N344.

Aerial journey, seduction on K1334.

Aesculapius as magician D1711.6.2.

Aesop with lantern J1303; with unbent bow J553.1.

Affection shown by frightened wife so rare that husband pardons robber T284.

Affiancing. See **Betrothals, Engagements.**

Afire, see also **Fire.** — Building with enemies inside set a. K925.1; dupe's house set a. K812.1; enemies' forest set a. K2364.1; house seems a. K1889.1; magic object sets things a. D1566.1; murder by setting house a. S113.2.3.

Aforesaid as title J1749.1.

Afraid, see also **Fear.** — Sun a. to wander at night A722.6.

African. — Origin of A. tribes A1611.3.

Africans. — Why A. have bad feet A1665.1.

After. — Advice a. event valueless J756; before, during, and a. J1343.2; dead returns third day a. burial E586.2; devil works with man who continues to work a. night G303.22.9; devil appears when woman looks at herself in mirror a. sunset G303.6.1.4; dwarfs come a. giants have almost died out F451.1.3; ogres powerless a. cockcrow G636; peace before rather than a. war J156.1; prophecy: death a. certain time M341.1.6; tabu: action a. certain time C752ff.; wandering a. death as punishment Q503, E501.3.7; whistling a. sunset brings devil G303.16.18.

Afterbirth. See **Placenta.**

Afterworld. Creator goes to make a. A78.

Again. — "Shall I tell it a.?" Z49.4.

Agaria are cultivators A1689.10; eat rats A1681.4; not afraid of fire A1689.2.

Agartree a transformed magician A2731.4.

Agates. — Water becomes a. D475.4.8.

Age of dwarfs F451.3.11; of giants F531.6.4; of owl causes it to be killed K1985; is relative J1352.2; of trolls F455.2.10; and youth in love T91.4. — Adulteress prepares for old a. J761.3; changeling calculates his a. by age of forest F321.1.1.5; changeling deceived into betraying a. F321.1.1; effects of a. and size absurdly applied J2212; god of a. A474.2; gods' great a. A191.1; guessing unknown propounder's a. H521.1; finding a. of monster C821; magic change in a. D56; magic object produces immunity from old a. D1349.2; magic peach gives immunity from a. (eternal youth) D1338.3.2; man claims same a. for many years J1218; old a. personified Z114; old a. must be planned for J761; in old a. spirits become gods A117.3; secret a. overheard by eavesdropper N475.1;

suffering in youth or old a. J214; trees of extraordinary a. F811.21; youth and a. are alike J2214.2.

Ages of animals B841.2; of the world (four) A1101.

Aged, see also **Old;** man as hero L101.1; people abandoned S140.1; people killed in famine S110.1; person eaten G76. — Disenchanted children a. D799.1.

Aging retarded D1338.0.1. — Magic a. D1890ff.; premature a. F126, Q551.12.

"**Agnus dei**" as a prayer for money J1741.2.

Agreeing. — Flatterer always a. with king J814.2; wife a. with all husband's statements H474.

Agreement, see also **Bargain.** — Deceptive a. to kill wives K944; marital continence by mutual a. T315.1; refusal to perform part in mutual a. K231.1.

Agriculture. — Acquisition of a. A1441; god of a. A432, A541.2; goddess of a. A432.1; sacrificial rite for a. S274.

"**Ah me!**" (ogre's name) C21.

Aid, see also **Help;** of animal summoned by using part of its body as talisman *B501; to children brought by dead mother *E323.2; from deer, opossum, and snake J461.4; from ghost to living E363ff.; of God not used in creating devil G303.1.3; of hidden informant in solving riddle H573.1; to ogre brings about hero's capture G411; from ogre's relative G530ff.; of owner's daughter to capture castle K781; of supporting forces not asked J1169.3; to thief by owner J1392; from wild man released from captivity G671. — Asking king for military a. H1224; call for a. heard from distance D1827.2; fairy offers a. for marriage F302.3.2.1.

Ailments, see also **Diseases.** — Eclipses due to sun's a. A737.11.

Air fragrant at Nativity V211.1.1; magically made fragrant D1599.2. — Angels fill a. above druid's grave V238.4; castle in a. F771.2.1, H1133.2; climbing into a. on magic rope D1582; dupe takes prisoner's place in a. K842.1; eagles carry castle in a. F982.1, F771.2.1.2; extraordinary flights through a. F1021ff., (by magic) *D2135, (on animal) B542ff., (on geese — lying tale) X1258.1, (dwarf on wooden horse) F451.6.2.2, (inflated giant) F531.6.17.2, (god on wind-swift horse) A171.1, (girl being rescued) *R111.3.1, (mountain-folk on horses) F460.2.2, (Wild Hunt) E501.14.1; fairies take persons into a. F329.3; fairies travel through a. F282; god rides through a. A171.1; god of the a. A216; gods nourished by a. A153.9; image flies through a. D1626; object magically raised in a. D2135.0.2; object rises into a. *F1083; object thrown into a. causes enemies to fight over it K1082.2; magic shears clip garments from a. D1601.12.1; paradise in a. over mountain F132.1.1; refuge in a. R324; same a. at home as abroad J2274.2; spirits in a. E587.4, F407.2, F411.2, F418, F966; voices from the a. F966; witch rides through a. G241.3.2.

Air-castles J2060ff.

Airship. — Magic a. *D1118; person killed from magic a. K988.

Aladdin D845, D1662.2, D1470.1.16.

Alarm by cackling geese B521.3.2; from bells rung backward P651.3; given by captured animal which asks respite K551.7; given by magic bell *D1317.7; of king by flea's bite B521.3.3; raised in order to cheat *K484; raised puts cheater out of countenance J1216; raised by stolen magic object D1612.5ff.; sounded foolishly J2199.1.

Alba. — Prophecy: death between Erin and A. M341.3.2.

Albatross. — Bad luck follows killing a. C841.10.1, N250.1; mythical white a. B30.1.

Albino twins cannibals G11.11.1.

Alcestis dies so that husband's death may be postponed T211.1. — Death postponed if substitute can be found for A. *D1855.2; Hercules fights with "Death" and rescues A. R185.

Alchemist K1966; fox as B121.2.

Alder. — Magic a. tree D950.11.

Ale, magic D1045.1; serves itself D1601.23. — Acquisition of a. A1426.3; brewing a. from milk H1021.10; consecrated a. as magic cure D1500.1.10.5; inexhaustible barrel of a. is fairy gift F348.9; making a. from single grain H1022.6.1; poison flows from a. vessel F1092; saint purifies poisoned a. V229.6.2; transformation: water to a. D478.2; wives compete in a.-brewing T145.3.

Alehouses. — Devil sings in a. G303.13.4; tabu for chief to enter a. C564.1.

Alexander carried by two birds B552.1; drinks cup poisoned by friend P317.1; orders feast for those who have not known sorrow N135.3.1. —Cynic praises reason to A. J1442.1.1.

Alexius K1815.1.1.

Alfred the Great (bakes cakes) K521.4.1.2, (punished for late rising) P15.1.

Ali Baba and the forty thieves K312.

Alibi by thief who plays all night for dance K411. — Thief cuts off own arm as a. K407.2.1.

Alike. — Brothers so a. wrong one killed P251.5.2; twins look exactly a. T685.3.

Alive. — Dead made to appear a. K1885; dog buried a. to prevent ghosts from walking E431.8; hero still a. A570ff.; hero taken to heaven a. D1856.1; man kept a. by consecrated sword E163; marriage to man a. only at night T113; person dead during day, a. at night E155.4.

All depends on how you take it J555.1, H588. — Cruel father puts to death a. children S11.3.4; murderers kill a. coming to certain spot S110.5; queen copulating with a. men T492; treasure finders must not take a. money N553.3; tree bearing a. fruits F811.7.

All Saints' Day. — Death for worshipping idols on A. A558.12.

Allah. — Escaping A. by moving away from Moslem land J1823.4.

Allegorical quests H1376ff.; riddles H767; visions V515. — Prophetic dream a. D1812.3.3.5.

Allegory, see **Symbolism, Symbolic.**

Allerleirauh K1815.

Allies erroneously slain at night N349.1; and possessions of the devil G303.10ff. — Animal a. B267ff.; demigods fight as mortals' a. A536; foolishness of attacking real a. J683; foxes desert their a., the hares J682.1.

Alligator. — Enmity of jackal and a. A2494.5.4; friendship of jackal and a. A2493.11.1; man becomes a. D194.1; prophecy: death by a. M341.2.24.

Alligator's rough back A2356.2.11; scales A2315.2; stripes A2413.5; short tongue A2344.1.2.

Ally. — Former a. helps king in disguise K1812.18; mortal as a. of gods A189.1ff.

Almond tree, transformation to D215.7.

Alms obtained thrice by disguised ubiquitous beggar K1982; to be returned hundredfold so parishoner steals them J1262.5. — Arm grows from giving a. F1095; ghost asks a. as before death E599.4; giving a. in God's name brings tenfold return J1262.5.1; man to marry first woman giving him a. T62.1; nurse begs a. to keep child R131.0.1; poor people given a. H152.1; pupils eat a. given master W125.4; refusal to accept a. from barren woman V436; saint refuses pearls as a. V462.2.2.1; seven to whom a. are given Z71.5.6.11; tabu misuse of money in a. box C51.1.4; tabu not to give a. to Brahmins C94.1.2; three reasons for not giving a. J2225; women giving a. to each other reincarnated as wells H1292.1.1; wager: woman can be forced to give a. N67.

Almsgiving. — Practical retorts connected with a. J1580ff.; reward for a. Q44; saint saves a. king from hell V229.15.

Aloes, island of F732.2.

Aloft, magic object bears person *D1532ff.

Alone. — Animals that live a. A2433.2.3; animal or object expected to go a. J1881; are you a. at home? H583.1.1; bathe a. and not in common bathing place J21.33; "don't go a. on journey" J21.36; "don't rob women a." J647.2; eating a. tabu C284; escaping sin by living a. J495; hero fights whole army a. F614.10; husband frightened into sleeping a. K1514.17.2; king's traveling a. tabu C563.1; "I am not a.!" W211.3; magic sight by standing a. D1821.10; rescue a. from shipwreck chosen over drowning with goods J222; sleeping children not left a. A1579.1; symbolism shows not good to fight a. Z161; why leopard walks a. A2433.2.3.1; woman a. in house makes Indians think men are home K548.1.

Aloof. — Jews keep a. A1689.13.

Alp (nightmare) F471.1.

Alphabet to be said to restrain anger J571.1; written on cake learned

by eating it D1819.4.2. — Magic a. D1273.6; origin of a. A1484.2; reading without learning the a. F695.1.

Altar V116; as best of stones H659.3.1; bleeding F991.4.1; casts away host with louse baked in it V31.4; cloths F962.12.2, V135; floats in air F1083.0.1.1; magic D1166; in otherworld F166.5; as refuge R325; shakes at unworthy F1009.3; smoke from sacrifice tabu for chief C564.5. — Celibacy at the a. J1264.2; chalice on a. tests guilt H233.1; devil won't stoop to a. V298; drop must not fall on a. C51.1.8; false swearer not allowed to approach a. M101.1; Jinns frequent sacrificial a. F499.3.3; leaf falls on a. F962.12.5; olive branch laid on a. of Mercy V15; Satan entangles ram's horns on a. G303.9.9.20; tabu: using a. for secular purposes C51.1.1; transformation: man to a. D261.

Altarcloths V135; from heaven F962.12.2.

Altered letter of execution gives princess to hero *K1355.

Alternate biting and caressing of hares by dog K2031; punishments of sinners in hell Q562. — Fairies become birds in a. years D624.2.

Amalekites as magicians D1711.10.6.

Amaranth. — Contest between rose and a. J242.1.

Amazon bride T173.1; overcomes enemies singly K778.1; sets task for hero H1149.5.

Amazon's curse M411.11.1; daughter loves hero T91.6.4.1.2.

Amazons F565; control river issuing from cave D915.5; kill all male children F565.2. — Fear test: fighting with a. and horrible spirits H1423.

Ambassador from dogs to Zeus A2232.8; from Turkey misunderstands Christian ceremonies J1825. — Disguise as foreign a. K1839.7; queen makes lowly man a. Q56.3.

Amber originates in poplar trees A2755.3.1. — Island of a. F731.5.

Ambergris made from bitumen eaten by fish F826.2.

Ambiguous oath K1513; oracle M305; questions trick dupe K493.

Ambition as ever-increasing paradox answer H1075. — Prudence in a. J510ff.; overweening a. punished *L420ff.

Ambitions. — Father's a. transferred to child at conception T597.

Ambrosia A153; pond F713.1. — Resuscitation by a. E102.2.

Ambush revealed by bird's movements J53. — Attacking animal killed by another in a. N335.6.1; murder from a. K914; transformation to escape a. D642.4.

Ambushed enemy deceived into declaring himself K607; trickster killed by intended victim K1641.

Amen. —Stones say "A." V229.2.10.

American. — Origin of A. Indian tribes A1611.1.

Ammunition saved till enemy uses his K2378.4.

Amonites as magicians D1711.10.6.

Amorous, see also **Love;** intrigue observed and exposed K1271. — Trans-

formation for repulsing a. advances D661.1; woman restrains a. king J816.4.

Amour of bishop preached about by truth-telling peasant J1211.1.

Amours of king with great men's wives teach him secrets J155.2.

Amphibia. — King of a. B245; magic a. B177; origin of a. A2160ff.

Amphibian vehicle D1533. — Devil as a. G303.3.3.7; helpful a. B493ff.; marriage to person in a. form B645ff.; reincarnation as a. E615; soul in form of a. E736; witch as a. G211.6.

Amphibious monster G346.3. — Why tortoise is a. A2214.5.

Amputated. — Root restores a. hands, feet D1518.2.

Amulet against attack D1381.16; brings love T11.4.7; enlarged to become cloak D489.2; of leaves for menses C146.1; preserves chastity D1387.1; rendered efficacious by charm D1577.2; renders invulnerable D1344.3. — Identification by a. H96; magic stone as a. D931.0.4; magic a. D1070ff, D1273ff, D1392.1.

Amyous defeated in boxing match K13.

Ananias Z71.1.5.

Añan's. — Stealing A.s bait H1151.17.

Anatomy, fatal disregard of J1910ff.

Ancestor of gods A111.3; worship V1.3. — Creator as a. of heaven and earth A75; culture from tribes' a. A1405; giant ox a. of all animals A1791; magic knowledge from mythical a. D1810.11; quest for news of a. H1252.1.1; quest to other world for a. H1252.1.

Ancestors claimed to want hero rewarded K362.11. — Ancient and modern a. (from Troy and Nuremberg) J1357; barber killed: king's a. need him in heaven K964; bribed judge's a. J1192.3; dwarfs are a. of mortals F451.5.3; game with bones of a. P203; gods as a. of mankind A188.2; robber innocent: follows traditions of his a. J1179.4.

Ancestress. — Prophecy: woman as a. of David and Messiah M363.2.1.

Ancestry boasted of by lowly J954. — Tracing a. brings recognition H11.1.4.

Anchor catching in submarine monastery N786; falls on fairies F285; floats on water F1047; stolen by fairies F365.2; of wood would hold if only large enough J2212.3.

Anchors. — Needles and a. as fox's excuse J1391.8.

Anchorite, see also **Hermit;** consumes tree D2082.2; falsely accused of murder K2116.2.1; immune to magician's powers V228.2; prophesies at childbirth M301.5.1; saved by dove T331.5; tempted by money V475.5. — Beast-like a. F526.4; body of a. rises from river E379.2; lover disguised as a. K1826.3; scorned lover becomes a. T75.5; treacherous a. K2285.2; vow concerning dead a. M151.5.1; woman wagers that she can seduce a. T337.

Anchorite's curse M411.14.2; son hero L111.6. — Conception after a. blessing T514.1; dove flies out of a. mouth V345.

Anchorites under temptation *T330ff. — Is town too full of a.? H607.4.

Anchovies. — "Spoiled" a. K344.1.2.

Ancient and modern ancestors J1357. — Animal characteristics from change in a. animal A2210ff.; treasure buried in a. settlements N511.1.2; wild huntsmen in a. costume E501.8.4.

Androcles and the Lion B381.

Andromeda B11.11.

Angel *V230; assigns task H927.2; assists childbirth T584.0.4; of the bush A419.1.1; causes earthquake D2148.1; confers power of self-transformation D630.2.1; as creator A17; of Death's sword F833.11; of the deserts A419.2.1; for each animal B1.1; of earth A400.2; forbids armies to fight F1097.1; gives soul information E759.2; guards treasure N583; of hell A302; helpers in religious tests H1573.0.1; helps find lost pin N211.3; helps perform task H983; holds mass in church V49.2; holds nose when handsome sinner passes V119.3; of lightning A285.0.1; of love compels falling in love T10.2; of mountains A418.1; names child T596.1; rescues abandoned child R131.16; reveals relics V140.1; suckles children T611.5.3; takes form of certain person K1811.4.2; takes mortal to heaven F63.2; of thunder A284.0.1; warns of Christ's danger V211.2.3.0.1; works, prays as lesson to monk H605. —Ability to see a. of God D1825.3.4.1; captive protected by a. R85; cloud-a. A283.1; contest between man and a. H1598.1; cure by a. D2161.5.5; devil becomes white a. G303.8.1.2.1; disguise as a. K1828; disguise as a. of death K1828.1; girl's face resembles an a. D1865.3; locality sanctified against pestilence by a. as result of prayer and fasting D2162.3; magic from A. of Death D1725.1; magic object from a. D812.10; man transformed to a. D44.1; marriage of mortal and a. T111.6; mortal deceives a. of death R185; otherworld journey with a. F7; seduction by alleged orders from a. K1315.1.2.1; suitors as corpse, a., and devil K1218.4; tabu for a. to remain on earth too long C761.4.3; wind-a. A282.0.2; wisdom from a. J158.

Angels *V230ff.; accompany sun's chariot A724.1.2; appear where saint is born V222.0.2; arrange course of heavenly bodies A703; battle Leviathan and Behemoth A1082.7; change size D631.4.2; of the day A1171.3; of death cannot bring soul to heaven E754.2.2.1; defend road to heaven V511.1.2; feed exposed child S353.2; as God's messengers A165.2.3; oppose man's creation A1217.1; in otherworld F167.13; as rescuers R168; of Satan G303.10.18; set over clouds, winds, rains A1130.1; separate souls for heaven, hell E755.0.2. — Creation of a. A52ff.; demons partly like a. G302.4.1; figtree stays with a.: rewarded A2711.7; god dealing with a. A195.1; humility of a. J902; journey with speed of a. D2122.4; magic invisibility of a. D1981.6; magic knowledge of a. D1810.0.6; man created by a. A1291.1; man's strength equals a. D1830.1; planets supervised by a. A780.1; rebel a. A54; riddle about a. visiting Abraham H828; sight of a. over heads of the good D1825.3.2; souls of pious as a. E754.7; stars supervised by a.

A769.3; time of creation of a. A52.2ff.; wings of a. protect earth A1128.1; worship of a. V1.2.4.

Anger aroused so master may win fight J1682; bargain K172, F613.3; as cure for sickness F950.2; of God A102.17; is sin J153.2. — Animal bursts from a. F981.1.1; army faces enemy rather than a. of their king J216.1; when in a. say the alphabet J571.1; avoiding punishing in a. J571.4; "control your a." J21.2.6; dwarfs in a. F451.6.8; explanation of a. from hermit J153.2; extraordinary nature phenomena at saint's a. F960.4; extraordinary physical reaction to a. *F1041.16; hero's contortions in a. A526.6; incurring animal's a. H1156; king quick to a. P12.13; king struck in a., life saved N656; minister in a. leaves king H1385.12; ogre's a. at killing his livestock G614; pretended a. K1772; quest for the a. of God H1376.3.1; quest: learning what a. is H1376.3; sign of a. (nudity) Z181, (red garment) Z141.1; strong man bites, powders brass in a. F639.10; test of valor: rousing servant's a. H1561.4.

Angleworm B491.4.2.

Animal aids abandoned child(ren) S352; army B268; behavior as evil omen D1812.5.1.12; behavior teaches man what to avoid J134; betrays thief K427; -birth slander K2115; bride B600ff.; brothers-in-law B314; buried alive to cure disease D2161.4.6; burned to cure disease D2161.4.7; cannot change his nature J512; captor appeased by being fed captive's family K614; characteristics A2200—A2599; comes to life E3; as creator A13ff.; as creator's companion A33; cries misunderstood J1811; as culture hero A522; by day, man by night D621.1; -descent slander K2115.1; disguises as human being K1822; indicates election of ruler H171; escapes by shamming as another K521.7; escapes by slipping out of skin F1088.4; executed for crime B275.1; faithful B301ff.; fight as suitor contest H331.15; foot on human being F551.1; ghosts *E520ff.; helpful B300ff.; hides sun behind body, causes eclipse A737.6; husband C36ff.; horns bloom, bear man as fruit A1263.5; in human form recognized H48; killed from within K952; kills ogre G512.9; king B240ff.; kingdom (community) *B220ff.; languages B215ff.; languages learned *B165ff., *B217ff.; learns to fear men J17; magically paralyzed D2072.0.2ff.; with unusual members B15; as messenger *B291ff.; mistaken for something else J1760ff.; nurse B535; offspring from marriage to animal B632; ogres *G350ff.; overawed K1710ff.; paramour B610ff.; parliament B230ff.; performs spinning task H1092.1; punishes broken promise M205.1; raises future hero L111.7; recognizes his returned master first H173.1; reincarnated as god E657; reincarnated as man E656; reports master wealthy and wins girl K1917.3; rescuer B540ff.; retains other animal's powers E780.2; reveals substitution of false bride *K1911.3.1; saved from pit B301; sent to go by itself J1881.2; serving only certain man H172; sinks into earth F949.1; skin grows on man's back Q551.2; statue F855.3; substituted for child served at meal K512.2.1; substituted for human sacrifice A1545.2; suckles strong hero

F611.2.1; suitor B620ff.; swallowed F911; swallows man (not fatally) F911.3; thought to be a person J1762ff.; transformed to god D43.1; transformed to object D420ff.; transformed to person D300ff.; warfare B260ff.; wedding B280ff.; wounds self to blame other animal for eating young K2153.1. — Abduction by a. R13; adventure from following a. to cave N773; adventures from pursuing a. N774.3; animal characteristics: change in ancient a. A2210ff.; ascent from lower world on a. F101.6; attacking a. killed by another in ambush N335.6.1; bringing a. heads H1154.0.1; bringing the devil an unknown a. K216.2; capture by hiding in artificial a. *K754; child born with a. head T551.3; child promised to a. S215; conception from eating a. T511.5; cooked a. comes to life E168; creation of a. life A1700—A2199; criminal confesses because of misunderstood a. cries N275.1; cure by transferring disease to a. *D2161.4.1; curse by a. M411.19; dead a. comes to life E3; death as a. Z111.3.1; unexpected death at hands of an a. N335; deity takes form of a. to visit mortals K1811.5; demon as a. G303.3.2; demons on a. feet F401.3.0.1; descent to lower world on a. F98; detection through aid of a. J1145; the devil in a. form G303.3.3ff.; divination from a. activity D1812.5.0.8; dragon as compound a. B11.2.1ff.; earth from body of slain a. A831.6; entrance to woman's room in hollow artificial a. K1341; fairy in form of an a. F234.1; fairy as giant a. F234.1.0.1; faithful a. B301ff.; familiar spirit in a. form F403.2.2.1; fettered monster as ferocious a. A1072.2; flesh of a. reveals guilt D1318.7.1; foolish imitation by a. J2413; fools and the unknown a. J1736; free a. saves captured friend F642; ghost a. guards treasure E291.2.2; ghost transformed into a. E453; giant as a. F531.1.8; gift or sale to a. J1850ff.; god in a. form *A132; gods with a. features A131; the great a. *X1201; helpful a. B300ff., (acquisition) B310ff., (reward) B320ff., (death) B330ff.; helpful a. aids fugitives R243; hero follows a. into lower world F102.1; hero son of a. A511.1.8; human and a. offspring from marriage to animal B633; illusory a. shapes on hilltops K1886.6; injury to a. kills witch G275.12; journey to underground a. kingdom *F127; killing a. in refuge tabu C841.0.3; killing an a. revenged Q211.6; lame a. magically cured D2161.3.7.1; life bound up with that of a. E765.2; looking at certain a. tabu C316; magic adhesion to a. *D2171.3ff.; magic a. proof against burning D1841.3.1; magic a. proof against drowning D1841.6.1; magic a. proof against hound D1841.7; magic a. proof against weapons D1841.5.2; magic image of a. relieves from plague D1586.1; magic object teaches a. languages *D1301; magic object found on grave of slain helpful a. D843.3; magic power from christening an a. D1766.4; magic powers from baptising an a. *D1766.3; magic skin of a. D1025; magic strength from helpful a. D1834; magic treasure a. killed D876; man by day: a. by night D621.1.1; man disguised as a. sent among enemy K2358; man disguises as a. K1823; man transformed to a., kept

as pet by heroine T33; mankind from human-a. mating A1221.6; marriage of person to a. *B600ff.; mountain-man in a. shape F460.1.1; mountains from primeval a. A961; mysterious a. punishes penitent Q554.5; offending a. wife tabu C35; ogre captured while transformed to a. G514.4; one a. mistaken for another J1750ff.; origin of a. sacrifice A1545.3; origin of a. worship A1546.7; person with a. face F511.1.3; person returns to original a. form when tabu is broken C963.1; person has small a. within his body F529.4; person thought to be a. J1765; person transformed to a. refuses human food D686.1; pestilence in a. form F493.0.1; poisoned food fed to a. instead of to intended victim K527.1; prophesying through knowledge of a. languages M302.1; pursuing certain a. forbidden C812; pursuit of a. leads to ogre's house G402.1; quest to a. realm H1289.1; quest assigned because of hero's knowledge of a. languages H1214; quest for remarkable a. H1331; quest for unknown a. H1383; recognition by overheard conversation with a. H13.1; recognition of person transformed to a. H62; reincarnation as a. *E610ff.; reincarnation: a. to man E656; resuscitation by passing helpful a. over corpse E79.1; revealing help of a. tabu C427; revealing knowledge of a. languages forbidden C425; revenant in a. form *E423ff.; riddles on a. qualities H842; runner captures two of every a. F681.8; sacrifice to a. V11.7; secret remedy revealed by departing a. N452.2; secrets overheard from a. conversation *N451; seduction disguise as a. K1328; separable soul kept in a. E715; sickness transferred to a. D2064.3; simultaneous birth of a. and child T589.7.1; small a. overcomes large L315; soul in a. form E730ff.; spirit in a form F401.3; spirit protects each a. species F419.3; automatic statue of a. D1620.2; stolen a. returns to owner K423.0.1; task: capturing pair of every wild a. in the land H1154.9; task: selling an a. and keeping him H1152; test: guessing unknown a. H522ff.; theft by trickster's trained a. K366; thief disguised as a. K311.6; transformation to act as helpful a. D659.4; transformation to a. (devil) D102, (god) D101, (man) D100ff., (object) D440ff., (another animal) D410ff., (for breaking tabu) C962, (to seduce woman) *D658.1; transformation by helpful a. D684; transformation by magic a. D684.0.1; transformation: fern to a. D441.4.1. transformation for nourishing a. D518; troll in a. form F455.2.8, G304.1.1ff.; true bride in a. form reveals false K1911.3.1.1; ungrateful a. returned to captivity J1172.3; wife flees a. husband R227.1; wish for a. husband realized C26; witch in a. form G211ff.; witch burned by burning bewitched a. G275.3.1; witch rides unusual a. G241.1ff.; woman gives birth to a. T554; wounding a. without killing it tabu C841.0.2; youngest a. overcomes adversary L72.

Animal's characteristics acquired by eating it D1793.1; extraordinary death F981; extraordinary growth F983; extraordinary protection F984; size changed at will D631.2. — Attention drawn by helpful a. theft of food from wedding table: recognition follows H151.2; earth rests

on a. back A844; eating courageous a. heart makes courageous D1358.1; eating ferocious a. heart makes person cruel D1357; magic a. heart renders invisible D1361.29; soul leaves man's body and enters a. E725.1.

Animals B (entire chapter); abused to cause person's death D2061.2.2.7; advise men B560ff.; in the ark A1853.1, A2031.2, A2145.2, A2214.3, A2232.4; attacked under illusion that they are men K1883.2; as attendants of gods A165; avenge injury Q597; blessed for good services at crucifixion A2221.2; borrowed by fairies F391.1; build road A2233.1; buried with the dead V67.5; called magically D2074.1; carry extraordinary burden F982; carry men B550ff.; change color F985; climb on one another's backs and cry out: frighten robbers K335.1.4; compete as messengers to call father of newborn child H483; created by magic D2178.4; cursed M414.8; cursed by saint M411.8.4; die for desecrating holy place Q558.14.1; duped into fighting each other K1082; eaten by fairies become whole again *F243.3.1; enticed over precipice K891.5.1; exchange duties J512.7; escape when forbidden basket is opened C915.2; as extraordinary companions F601.7; fear men J17; follow wild huntsman *E501.4ff.; friendly B300ff.; gigantic B870ff.; give power of inducing love D1903; glowing B19.4; gnaw on moon A755.4.3; of the gods A155ff.; as gods' messengers A165.2.1; grateful *B350ff.; grateful and ungrateful men W154.8; headless B15.1.1; help hero on quest H1233.6; help man in contest K2; help men at task H982; help in military victory K2351; helpful B300—B349; helpless in sea-voyage together J1711.1; in human form retain animal ways D682.3.1; with human traits B200ff.; hybrid B1114; journey together B296; in legal relations B270ff.; magic B100ff.; magically shriek, frighten enemy D2091.12; magically stricken dead D2089.3; miraculously multiplied D2106.1.2; mistaken for ghosts, killed J1782.4; mythical *B0ff.; nourish men B530ff.; oracular *B150ff.; with jeweled ornaments F826.1; in otherworld *F167.1; in otherworld pass in and out of church and become human beings *F171.5; overcome man's adversary by strategy B524.2; preying on one another teach death's universality J52.1; produced when forbidden drum is beaten C916.2; give prophecy of future greatness M312.0.2; prophetic *B140ff.; pull up trees F621.1; pursued in wild hunt E501.5.5; ransom themselves B278; rejoice at Christ's birth B251.1; religious B250ff.; retort concerning their dangers J1420ff.; reveal how to become saint V229.25; as sacrifice V12.4; sacrificed so that dead have food on way to otherworld E433.3; save person's life B520ff.; speak to one another at Christmas B251.1.2; speaking B210ff.; steal back magic D882.1; stolen from saint miraculously replaced V224.3; swallow animals F911.2; thought to be devils J1785; transformed to stones D471.8; treacherous K2295; bear treasure *B100ff.; treated as if human J1850—J1899; truth-telling B130ff.; unjust decision against man J1172.3.2; war between wild and domestic B262; wisdom-giving *B160ff.; wise B120ff. — Abode of dead a. E480.1; absurd sympathy

for a. or objects J1870ff.; absurdities concerning birth of a. J1533ff.; assignment of edible a. A1422; bargains between men and a. M244; bridge to otherworld guarded by a. *F152.0.1; captured a. avenge themselves Q385; capturing a. (task) H1154; catching wild a. as suitor task H336.2; chain tale: a. killing each other in man's field provide meat Z43.6; covenant of friendship between a. M246.1; creation of a. A1700ff.; cruelty to a. S481; cruelty to a. punished Q285.1; curses on a. M471; deception into killing own a. K940ff.; descent of man from a. A1224; devil's a. G303.25.15; the devil's a. and God's *A1751; devil's a. devour God's A2286.2.1; devil and God create a. *A63.4; division of the a. (riddle) H841; domestic a. fight as owners compete H1588.2; dupe's a. destroyed or maimed K1440ff.; entrance to otherworld guarded by a. F150.2; extraordinary occurrences concerning a. F980ff.; fairies' a. F241; fanciful traits of a. *B700ff.; father rescues son stolen by a. R153.3.2; festival of a. B299.7; fighting a. seen in otherworld F171.4; food kept for a. tabu C248; fool makes shoes for a. J1873.1; foolish attempt of second man to overhear secrets from a. *N471; former friendship between domestic and wild a. A2493.0.1; formerly a. talked A1101.2.3; game a. magically made overwary D2085; giant's enormous a. F531.4.11 giants' a. F531.6.7.1.1; giants' a. help him in fight F531.6.16.2; god of a. A440ff.; goddess protects a. from hunters A189.12; healing by a. B510ff.; helpful a. lost in wager W2.4; hero's extraordinary a. A524.1; hidden a. attack owner of house K1161; images of a. ridden (driven) D1631; magic invulnerability of a. D1840.2; kindness to a. rewarded Q51; kinds of helpful a. B400ff.; king of a. B240ff.; magic control over a. D2156ff.; magic dominance over a. D2197; magic knowledge of a. language D1815.2; magic object gives power over a. D1440ff.; magic power from a. B500ff.; magic sight as gift of grateful a. D1821.11; man rules all a. H1421.1.1; men and a. readjust span of life A1321; origin of domesticated a. A1443; pairs of a. in ark *A1021.1; parts of slain a. as token of slaying H105; pestilence sent upon a. D2094; princess brought to laughter by small a. H341.2; punishment of lazy a. A2233.1; punishment: being eaten by a. Q415; miraculous punishment through a. Q557; quest for dangerous a. H1360ff.; quest for devastating a. H1362; quest over path guarded by dangerous a. H1236.2; rakshasa eats domestic a. at night G369.1.3; recognition by overheard conversation with a. H13ff.; rescue from ogre by helpful a. G552; resuscitation by a. E122; resuscitation of a. devouring each other E32.2; sacrifice of a. to dragon B11.10.0.1; sale of worthless a. K130ff.; secret remedy overheard in conversation of a. N452; services of helpful a. B500ff.; short pregnancy in a. T573.0.1; small a. dupe larger into trap L315.15; souls of a. E730.1; strong hero sent for wild a. F615.2; strong man kills a. with own hands F628.1; sun, moon carried by a. A728.4; sun's a. A732; tabu to eat live a. C221.5; tabu to kill sacred a. C92.1; talkative a. incense master J2362; taming wild a.

H1155 tasks contrary to the nature of a. H1024; theft of fire by a. A1415.2; topographical features caused by a. A903; troll's a. G304.3.2; unique survivor from destruction of a. Z356.1; what a. are to be eaten by man A1422.0.2; why a. serve man A2513; why a. sources of food A1422.0.1; why certain caste is kind to a. A1599.13; wisdom acquired from a. *J130ff.; witch brings death, disease to a. G265.4; witch causes a. to behave unnaturally G265.6; witch causes a. to die G267; witch transforms her lovers into a. G263.1.

Animation of body by soul E726; of jar beneath banyan tree A199.1; of statues by water or wind F855.2.

Ankles of exposed child pierced S333; tied to lay ghost E442.1. — Deluge reaches giant's a. F531.2.1.3.

Annihilating army single-handed (task) H1135.

Anniversaries, royal P13.7.

Announcement of own death by dead E545.3; of death of Pan F442.1; of prohibition by mysterious voice C601; of time for sunrise and sunset by bird B122.4. — Wraith as a. of death E723.6.

Annoyance. — How can people be freed from a.? H1292.19; when will animal be freed from a.? H1292.9.

Annual resuscitation of a god E155.2.

Annulment of witch's spells by drawing her blood D1741.2.1.

Anointing with honey protection against ghosts E439.10; of kings P13.5.1; for magic invulnerability D1846.1. — Quest for a. oil H1265.

Another. — Animal characteristics: obtaining qualities of a. A2240ff.; betrothed girl can never marry a. T65.1.1; devil enters body of a. G303.18; fairy in likeness of a. F234.2.4; punishment: carrying corpse of murdered man until a. can be induced to take it Q511.2; reincarnation in a. human form E605; sacrifice of child to save a. life S260.1.4; shrew tamed by setting a. shrew against her T251.2.1; transformation: one animal to a. D410ff.; transformation to likeness of a. person *D40ff.

Answer to cry mandatory C681; to all foreigner's questions: "I don't understand" J1802.1; rewarded with gold ring Q91.4; to three questions in rhyme secures devil's help G303.22.3. — Animal characteristics: punishment for discourteous a. to God (saint) A2231.1ff.; child born in a. to prayer T548.1; cobold avenges uncivil a. F481.1; finding a. to certain question (test) H508; plant punished for ungracious a. to holy person A2721.3; princess gives right a., monkey, wrong H343.2; princess's a. to all questions is "No" K1331; quest: a. to certain question H1388; quest for riddle a. H1278; ridiculous a. at end of each tale Z13; soft a. turneth away wrath J817; tabu: uncivil a. to holy (or supernatural) being C94.1; unwelcome a. given by man hidden behind image K1971.8; wall of snow around hut in a. to prayer D2143.6.2.

Answers to devil's riddle permit escape H543; in foreign language C495.2.2; found in other world to questions propounded on the way

H1292, (riddles) H544, (to questions) given magic object D1311ff., (coconut shell) D1311.9, (mirror) D1311.2, (sun) D1311.6.3. — Baffling malice with ready a. J1251; deaf men and their a. X111; king and peasant vie in riddling questions and a. H561.6; lady a. queen so straightforwardly she gets light punishment J751.1.1; magic object gives a. for fugitive *D1611ff.; prearranged a. bring comic results C495.2, J1741.3, X111.9; quest to morning star for a. to questions H1282; quibbling a. J1252; riddling a. H583ff.; oracular images occupied by spirits or priests who give the a. K1972; woman who asked for news from home gets many impossible a. J2349.4.

Answering call when asleep tabu C811.3; fool's questions next day J571.7; only "yes" and "no" J1255; questions only when on throne J1189.1; questions just like woman settles her ownership J1153.2. — Hero not a. questions until dressed P644; man a. all questions F645.1; single speech a. many questions H501.2.

Ant bites as punishment Q453.1; bites tongue, voice made smooth F556.1.2; carries load as heavy as himself A2251.1; collects incense and myrrh for Christ A2221.4; and lazy cricket (grasshopper) J711.1; grateful for preventing destruction of nest B365.2.1; helpful B481; keeps stored grain in sun J711.5; keeps house with animals J512.7.1; language B215.6.1; neither man, beast nor bird (riddle) H862; oracular B154.2; pinching frog causes accidents N381.1; thieving K366.3; thrown from heaven: hence narrow waist A2214.2. — Beetle makes immoderate request, a. modest: inverse awards A2232.3; child taken to defecate over a. hole K1461.2; creation of a. A2011; devil as a. G303.3.3.8; dupe persuaded to sit on a. hole K1023.3; enmity of bear and a. A2494.8.2; enmity of elephant and a. A2493.11.3; fairy as a. F234.1.16.3; friendship between a. and pheasant A2493.29; giant a. B873.4; grasshopper builds no house for winter; a. strikes him blind A2233.4; man becomes a. D182.2; man hears a. leave nest fifty miles away F641.2; man transformed as a. N453; little a. finds a penny (cumulative tale) Z32.3; reward to a. for industry Q86.1; man rides on a. F535.2.5; speaking a. B211.4.1; spider hands box to a. and refuses to take it back A2243.1; spirit in a. form F401.3.4.2; transformation: a. to person D382.2; transformation: man to a. D182.2; transformation: monkey to a. D411.5.3; transformation to a. to gnaw bow-strings of enemy D651.4; wedding of a. B285.1; why a. collects resin A2453.1; why a. has small waist A2355.1.2; why a. lives in ant-hill A2432.1.

Ants ask God for wings: wind blows them away A2232.9; burrow into elephants' brains B524.1.8; carry silk thread to prisoner R121.4; overcome serpent L315.14. — Creation of man from a. A1224.7; dupe persuaded to pick up biting a. K1023.2; giant man-eating a. B16.6.1; gold-digging a. B756; helpful a. sort grains H1091.1; how a. can secure longer life H1292.11; king of a. B246.1; kingdom of a. B224.1; man kills nest of a. J96; nest of a. thrown on ogre K621.1; war

between elephants and a. B263.2; why a. carry large bundles A2451.1; why a. fall upon every man A2479.7; why a. don't live on hare's back A2584.2; why a. are lords of the bush A2433.5.5; why black a. are everywhere A2434.1.4; why small a. live in houses, driver ants in bush A2433.2.1.1; why white a. are a pest A2522.3.

Ant-bear eats insects A2435.3.8.

Ant-hill. — Boy lives in a. F562.5; digging alleged treasure from a. K1125, K1388.1; man becomes a. D287.1; rainbow from a. A791.8; transformation to a. C961.5; why ant lives in a. A2432.1.

Antaeus invincible in wrestling K12.3.

Anteater created A1896; deceives jaguar K1721.2.

Anteater's proboscis, origin of A2355.3.1.

Antediluvians. — Wisdom from a. J166.2.

Antelope becomes goat D411.4.2; hostile to other animals A2494.1; sends leopard for fire, eats game K345.4; transformed (to another animal) D411.4, (to nut) D421.2.1, (to dog) D411.4.1. — Fool tries to shoot dead a. until it will come to him J1909.2; friendship between a., woodpecker and tortoise A2493.32; helpful a. B443.2; killing a. tabu C841.8.1; many-eyed a. B15.4.1; mythical a. B19.8.

Antelope's. — Origin of a. long neck A2351.4.3; why a. antlers reach backward A2326.3.3.

Antelopes. — King of a. B241.3.13.

Anthony crosses river on cape D1520.6. — Fish come to hear A. of Padua preach B251.2.7.1.

Antichrist a one-eyed monster A1075; uproots trees F621.2.1.

Antichrist's coming prophesied M363.1.1; flat body F525.4. — Signs before A. birth A1075.1.

Anticipatory whipping J2175.1.

Antidote. — Magic a. for poison *D1515; moly as a. to spells and enchantments D1385.2.

Antigone buried alive as punishment for disobedience Q456.0.3. — Funeral rites forbidden A. V62.1.

Antimony D1331.3.3.

Antipathies, see also **Dislike, Enmity;** of giants F531.6.11; of trolls G304.2.4.

Antique. — Spirits dressed in a. clothes F401.1.

Antler. — Deer with giant a. B15.3.3.

Antlers. — How stag got long a. A2326.3.2; magic transportation on a. D1520.32; stag with golden a. and silver feet B101.4.1; stag proud of a. L461; suitor contest: splitting a. H331.8; why antelope's a. reach backward A2326.3.3; why deer has a. A2326.1.1.1.

Anus. — Dupe puts hand up animal's a. K1036.1; golden a. F521.3.3.2; monster swallows people through a. F917; resuscitation by pricking a. E29.3.

Anuses. — People without a. F529.2.

Anvil driven into ground by strong man F614.1; salvager to be king H1574.3.1; to which one sticks D1413.10; swims river (lie) X1741.4. — Bewitched child struck on a. G271.9; dispute of hammer, a. J461.6; hill from a. A963.6; magic a. *D1202, D2143.1.6; shower of fire from magic a. D1566.1.5; shower of gems from magic a. D1469.3.

Anxiety, see also **Worry;** of dwarfs to speak F451.2.0.4; prevents resuscitation E186.1.

Ape, see also **Monkey;** creation of A1862; plucks feathers from heron who has carried him across water W154.5.1.3; pretends to louse heron, but plucks out his feathers K874.1; throws away nut because of its bitter rind J369.2; tricked into jumping on to stakes K891.2; tries to flee with favorite child: neglected child saves himself L146.1. — Ass tries to jump on the roof like a. J2413.2; dispute of elephant, a. J461.8; fight between a. and tortoise B264.5; flying a. B49.2; fox spoils food rather than divide with the a. W152.1; helpful a. B441.1.1; man transformed to a. D118.1; man-a. B29.9; person with a. face F511.1.3.1; why a. has red back A2411.1.5.1.1.

Apes. — Army of a. B268.1; liar rewarded by the a. J815.1; raven killed by a. who will not receive his teachings J1064.1.

Aper K836.

Apertures of animals' bodies closed up F998.3.

Aphrodisiac given naked woman in stream K1395. — Magic a. D1355.

Aphrodite. — Plants from tread of A. A2621.2.

Aphrodite's team of sparrows (doves) A136.2.1.

Apia (bird) is flat-chested A2353.1.

Apostacy. — Punishment of Jew for a. Q232.2.

Apostles of Christ V292.

Apparent injustice over greater wrong J225; and real values J230ff.

Apparitions, see also **Ghosts.** — Owner frightened from goods by a. of the dead K335.0.5; punishment: meeting frightful a. Q552.11.

Appeal of dying lawyer X315.

Appearance of angel V231; of brownie F482.1; and disappearance of garment in reply to command D2188.1.1; of devil G303.3ff.; of dwarf F451.2; of fairies F230ff.; of Fortuna N111.2; of giant F531.1ff.; of the gods A120ff.; of mermaid B81.9; of mountain-men F460.1; of object when tabu is broken C917; of revenant E420ff.; of spirits F401; of trolls F455.2, G304.1; of wild huntsmen E501.7ff.; of witches G210ff. —Causes of animal a. A2400—A2499; choice between worth and a. J260ff.; circumstances of the devil's a. G303.6; disguise by changing bodily a. K1821; friends identical in a. F577; hero (heroine) of unpromising a. L112; magic a. D2188.1; magic change to different a. *D52; person changes a. at will *D631.1.1; personal a. of various peoples A1660ff.; professions according to bodily a. A1650.3.2; time of a. of wild hunt E501.11ff.; vows concerning personal a. M120ff.

Appearances deceive U110ff.; kept up to deceive suitors as to girls' undesirability K1984.

Appearing before king unsummoned tabu C563.5. — Banished devil a. on earth A106.2.1.1; demons a. at stated times G302.6.1; house a. overnight to shelter priest V229.21; person a. many places at once D2031.18.

Appeasing enemies with women's breasts K774.1; giants by feeding them G582; ogre by calling him uncle Q41.1.

Appetite magically diminished D1927. — Curse: a. of twelve men M416.1; prospective bride shams small a. K1984.2; two monks renew their a. J1606; strong hero's enormous a. F612.1; unnaturally large a. cured by saint V221.10.

Applauding music when told W116.6.

Apple as chastity index *H434.1; as chastity test *H411.14; divided and eaten as love charm D1905.2; extraordinary *F813.1ff.; followed to otherworld F159.3; slays Cain F839.3.1; test (worthiness for friendship) H1558.0.1.1, (innocence) H256, (obedience of sons) H1557.1, (suitor) H316, (unknown father) H481.1; thrown in race with bride *H331.5.1.1; tree grateful for being shaken D1658.1.5; trees bear after saint's blessing D2157.3.1. — Bride test: thrifty peeling of a. H381.2.1; conception from eating a. T511.1.1; disenchantment by eating a. D764.4; fatal a.-throwing game K864; first man born from a. A1253.1.2; golden a. as prize in beauty contest H1596.1; golden a. thrown to remind merman's wife not to forget to return to him C713.4; infant indicates his unknown father by handing him an a. H481.1; love letter hidden in a. K1872.3; magic a. *D981.1, (as fairy gift) F343.15; magic a. tree D950.10, F162.3.4; man becomes a. D211.5; murder with poisoned a. S111.4; pomegranate and a. tree dispute J466.1; pursuit of rolling golden a. H1226.3; quest for marvelous a. H1333.3.1; recognition by unique ability to break iron a. with first stone cast H31.6; resuscitation by magic a. E106; resuscitation by removal of poisoned a. E21.1; skillful marksman shoots a. from man's head F661.3; soul in golden a. E711.8; soul hidden in a. in salmon E713.1; statue of infant Jesus takes a. V128.1; suitor test: a. thrown indicates princess's choice H316; tabu: touching a. C621.2.1; test of innocence: a. and gold offered H256; throwing a. to test sex H1578.1.4.1; transformation: man to a. tree D215.5.

Apples at Christmas F971.5.2; immovable D1654.2; impaled on stiff hair F555.8; transformed to grain D451.3.1; transformed to pig bristles D451.3.4; of youth D1338.3.1. — Ash tree bears a. F971.4.1; bridge of a. F842.1.3; demon formed from charmed a. F402.5.1; fugitives sustain selves on a. R257; magic a. cause horns to grow on person D1375.1.1.1; magic a. under sea F162.3.4.1; recovery of magic object by use of magic a. D881.1; souls as golden a. E745.5.1; stealing magic healing a. H1151.20; task: stealing golden a. H1151.1; test of girl masking as

man: nuts and a. offered H1578.1.5; three golden a. as identification H91.3.

Appraisal. — Trickster's a. sells worthless glass as diamond K451.4.

Appraiser of horse a one-eyed man X122.

Apprentice receives magic D829.1. — Devil promises to help mistreated a. G303.22.12; hungry a. attracts master's attention by telling lies on him J1341.5; magician's a. D1711.0.1.

Approach. — Brass (copper) statue at city gates blows on trumpet at stranger's a. *D1317.9.1; escape by falsely reporting a. of rescuers K545; fairy prevents mortal's a. F395; ghostly warner of wild hunt's a. E501.6; too familiar a. to danger J655.

Appurtenances. — All a. demanded on buyer J1293.5.

Apricot. — Transformation by eating a. D551.1.2.

Apron. — Devil drops stones from a. A977.3.1; hero formed from mother's a. A511.1.4.2.

Aquatic. — Hero kills a. animal F628.1.4.

Aquila, origin of A779.2.

Arabia. — Gold appears in A. at Christ's birth N529.1.

Arabians as liars X661.

Arachne transformed to spider A2091.1.

Arbitrator. — Don't be a. without being asked J21.45; tree appealed to as a. D1311.4.1.

Arch. — Sea waters a. over people F931.9.1; stream forms a. over otherworld isle F162.2.9.

Archangels drive Satan from heaven G303.8.1.2; as porters of heaven A661.0.1.3. — When a. created A52.2.4.

Archbishop. — Fool asks a. about his family J1747; man magically made to believe himself a. D2031.5.

Arched. — Why cat has a. back A2356.2.3; river a. over saint's body like a vault F932.2.

Archer. — Magic statue of a. D1620.1.5; mighty a. F638.

Archer's skill in shooting eggs F661.4.1; skill as suitor test H326.1.2.

Architect kills pupil surpassing him W181.2.1. — Hawk as sky palace a. J2060.3; king kills a. after completion of great building, so that he may never again build one so great W181.2; thief enters treasury through passage made by him as a. of the building K315.1.

Argo, origin of A779.3.

Argonauts H1332.1.

Argument. — No a. good without witness K1655.1; princess offered to man who can defeat her in a. H507.1.1; princess skillful in a. J1111.1; queen banished for defeating king in a. S416; trickster steals during a. K341.27.

Argus has eyes all over body F512.2.2, D1961.

Ariadne abandoned on an island S145; rescues lover R162.

Ariadne-thread given as a clue out of the labyrinth R121.5.

Ariel. — Archangel A. as porter of heaven A661.0.1.3.

Arion B551.1.

Aristotle and Phyllis K1215; rises from sick bed to battle for country P711.7.

Aristotle's. — Cause of A. wife's death K987.

Ark as God's home A151.10.1; suspended in air F1083.0.1.2; of the temple V112.0.1. — Animals in the a. (flies) A2031.2, (griffin) A2232.4, (mouse) A1853.1, (snake) A2145.2, (unicorn) A2214.3; deluge: escape in a. A1021; the devil and the a. *G303.23ff., K485, C12.5.1; dove returns to a. in obedience to Noah A2221.7; the giant on the a. F531.5.9; helpful animal stops leak in Noah's a. *B527.2; magpie refuses to get into a., sits outside jabbering A2542.1.1; raven does not return to a.: black color as punishment A2234.1.1; those excluded from Noah's a. build another A1021.0.1.

Arm broken by Christ's image J1823.1.2; to fall off (curse) M431.4; grows from giving alms F1095; shortened for breaking tabu C946. — Birth from an a. T541.6; companion's a. allowed to be cut off so as to prevent detection K407.2; compulsion to bend a. D2069.2; earth rests on God's a. A849.2; giant's a. pulled off G512.6.1; god's marvelous a. A123.5.2; man carries his head under his a. F511.0.4; monster's a. token of dog's innocence H105.3; new a. from another's arm bone F668.5; new moon with old moon in her a. a sign of storm D1812.5.1.5.1; ogre's long a. thrust down chimney G369.5; pressing hundreds beneath a. H599.4; return from dead to punish theft of golden a. from grave E235.4.1; magic sight by looking under a. D1821.3.1; substituted a. E782.3.1; sun at night lowers a. A722.5; thin a. indicates desire for human flesh G95; wife sacrificing a. for husband's safety T211.1.3; wild huntsman carrying skull under a. E501.7.4; witch withers a. G269.11.2.

Arms, see also **Weapons;** cut off as punishment Q451.1.5; of fairy F231.1; restored E782.3. — Bringing a. to capital tabu after sunset C752.1.1; cutting off a. for sleeveless sweater J2131.3.1.1; falling in love at seeing woman's a. T16.1; fighting with opponent's a. P643; giant peculiar as to a. F531.1.6.7; giving a. in pledge tabu C855.6; god with many a. A123.5; identification by coat of a. H126; keeping the measure by stretching out the a. J2036; learning feats of a. from woman in bed T453.1; magic causes a. to fall from shoulders D1403.3; magic flaming a. D1645.8; magic drink restores a. D1518.1; man with luminous a. F574.2; men with seven a. F526.5; mutilation: cutting off a. S161; no ransom of captured without a. P557.1; oath taken on a. M113; person unusual as to his a. F516; spirits with heads under a. F401.4; test of sex of man masking as girl: a. placed among baskets H1578.2; woman instructs in art of a. P461.4.

Arm-pit as hiding place F1034.4. — Fairies' hole in a. F232.1.1; familiar

spirit acquired by carrying egg under left a. F403.2.1.1; god born from mother's a. A112.7.2; vagina in a. F547.5.7.

Arm-pits. — Lightning from hero's a. A526.9; man vulnerable only in a. N476.2, Z311.4.

Arm-ring transformed to serpent D444.7. — Recognition through a. H94.6.

Arm-tassel compels woman to follow ogre D1427.2.

Armadillo as creator's companion A33.4.1; with silver plate over forehead B119.3. — Creation of a. A1897; giant a. B871.2.9; horned a. B15.3.4.2; sacred a. B811.7.

Armageddon A1080ff.

Armed vagina F547.1.1. — Combat with one-a. opponent P557.4.4.1; devil is a. G303.9.6.0.1; man must enter spirit world a. E480.3; one-a. hero L112.10; poorly-a. hero overcomes well armed L311.2.

Armless deity A128.3; people F516.1; revenant E422.1.2.

Armor ordered thin in front and thick in back J673; rattles as owner dies E761.7.1.0. — Air-tight a. F824.1; child born with complete a. T552.5; disenchantment by ripping a. D712.8; dwarf's magic a. D838.7; extraordinary a. F824; hero buried in a. V61.3.0.1; husband in a. establishes mastery T251.2.2; husband traps wife and paramour with magic a. K1563; magic a. *D1101, (protects from attack) D1381.10; quest for a. from a grave mound H1392; warrior buries oversized a. to prove prowess K1969.2; widow in a. routs would-be ravisher T320.2.1.

Army P551; of animals B268ff.; appears like forest K1872.1; of cannibal monsters G11.16; destroys giant F531.6.12.6.1; drowned by unnoticed tide N339.7; extraordinary F873; faces enemy rather than anger of king J216.1; of the gods A165.7; of half-animals, half-men B20.1; intoxicated and overcome K871.1; leaders in single combat for victory H217.1; origin of A1596; saved from ambush by observation of birds' movements J53; of spirits, ghosts F403.2.3.7; stopped by saint's curse D2091.13; of strong men F628.2.4. — Animals from Pharaoh's drowned a. A1715.1; arrow indicates attacking a. D1314.1.7; birds from Pharaoh's drowned a. A1901; creation of sandpiper: Pharaoh's cook calls drowned a. to dinner A1944.1; enchanted a. tabu C549.2; fairy a. F252.3; fairy a. on Hallowe'en F255.4; groom has to fight bride's a. H332.4; helpful bees (hornets) sting opposing a. B524.2.1; hero fights a. alone F614.10; magic a. of snakes, frogs D2091.2.1; magic oath stops invading a. D1400.1.11.1; magic object summons a. for rescue D1421.5; making broth for a. H1022.5.1; phantom a. attacked K1883.1; phantom a. created out of puffballs and withered leaves F585.1; river rises to prevent a. from crossing F932.8.2; saint drives away a. with cloud V229.7.1; soldiers of magic a. resuscitated E155.1.2; sleeping a. *E502; task: annihilating a. single-handed H1135; task: clothing an a. from one hank of flax H1022.2; task: feeding a. from one measure of meal H1022.5; task: making ladder which whole a. cannot set up H1147; transformed

soldiers of fairy a. disenchanted when overcome F383.5; treasure hidden by retreating a. N511.1.7; Virgin Mary's shift as banner causes blindness to opposing a. D1331.2.3; witch's a. of dragons, lions, bears G225.5.

Armies like seeds and peppercorns J1625; miraculously separated F1097; separated by magic illusion D2031.8.

Aroma of God A139.7.

Around. — Riding three times a. the hill to free captive confined within R112.2; tabu: looking a. C332; walking a. by magic (circumambulation) *D1791.

Arrested farmer maligns sons H581.4; men tell who they are H581ff. -- Silence wagerers a. as thieves J2511.2.

Arrival. — Accidental a. in lower world *F102; rejoicing at a. of rich man in heaven E758.

Arrogance comes with wealth J1085.2; repaid L430ff.; toward deity tabu C53.2. — Peacock given ugly feet so as to prevent too great a. A2232.7; world-fire from a. A1031.5.

Arrow accidentally grazes woman's breast N331.1.2; accidentally makes prize shot N621.1; accidentally slays man in church M381; as boomerang F661.11; extraordinary *F831; falls at death E761.7.1.2; kills one-eyed giant G511.1; made to appear crooked D2031.9; magic *D1092; as man's message shows lion how terrible man himself must be J32; shoots sky rope F51.0.1; shot to heaven returns bloody F1066; shot into leg of sun's horse A732.2.1; splits khijur leaves A2741.5. — Ascent to upper world on a. F65.1; ascent to upper world on a. chain *F53; dragon swallows a. (thunderbolt) intended for hero B529.2; eagle killed with a. made with own feather U161; god with a. of flames A137.14.1.1; island created by shooting a. A955.2; lucky shot with a.: foot and ear of deer N621; luring man by securing his a. K1399.4; magic a. flight D1526.1; mighty feats with a. F638; murder by burning a. K955.3; one a.-shot kills many tigers F679.5.3; pursuit of magic a. leads to adventures H1226.2; resuscitation by shooting a. E61; resuscitation by striking with a. E11.2; riddle about a. H751; shooting a. through iron H1562.13; shooting a. to win race deceptively K11.8; shooting game: blind man's a. aimed K333.1, K863; soul in a. E711.13; spring from sacred tree shot by a. A941.7.2; Virgin Mary intercepts an a. in battle D2163.3; woman wins a. contest F610.0.1.1.

Arrows darken sky J1453; of fire F831.2, (as punishment) Q552.13.0.1; from magician's fingers D2091.14; invisible D1655.1.1; substituted *K1617; turn aside for king H71.10.7. — Chain of a. transformed to bridge D469.3; Cupid with a. of lead and gold A475.0.1; god's a. A157.2; numskulls try to kill mosquitoes with bows and a. J2131.0.1; origin of bows and a. A1459.1.1; people choose bows and a. instead of guns and horses A1614.4.3; precocious hero demands bows and a. F611.3.3.0.1; shooting rope of a. F661.7.3; splintering a. with sword

F667.2; stars from a. shot at sky A763.1; victim's a. made harmless K818.3; wind returns a. shot against Christians F963.2; wounds from poisoned a. D2161.4.14.1.1.

Arsenic. — Devil chased by a. fumes G303.16.14.2.

Arson. — Judgments concerning a. J1175; thieving innkeepers guilty of a. J1149.9.

Art. — Fantastic beasts, birds, etc. in a. B5; origin of decorative a. A1465; possessing an a. admits one to king's hall P14.7; wanting to learn a. of love T4.

Arts taught to man by angel A1460.1. — God of the a. A465; god of many a. A450.1; culture hero teaches a. and crafts A541; origin of literary a. A1464.

Artemis goddess (of hunting) A452.1, (of chastity) A476; as leader of wild hunt E501.1.8.2. — Flesh of A. eaten as quail or bear V30.1.1.

Arteries severed instead of feeling pulse K1017.

Arthur and Excalibur D813.1.1, D878.1.

Articles, see also **Objects.** — Household a. act at command D1601.9; magic a. made during mass D1766.5.2; magic household a. answer for fugitive D1611.9; recovered magic a. dropped by rescuing animals into the sea D882.2.

Artificial heavens F792; paradise and hell to punish and reward F705; whale made as strategem K922. — Capture by hiding in a. animal *K754; child of a. impregnation abandoned S312.4; flight on a. wings *F1021.1; oracular a. head *D1311.7.1; recognition by a. hands H57.5.

Artificers, dwarfs as F451.3.4.1.

Artillery. — Sound of a. simulated to overawe enemy K2368.1.

Artisan blinded to prevent duplication S165.7.

Artisans P440ff.

Artisan-god A451.

Artist hoodwinks king: cuckold can't see picture J1492; loses results of labor in moment of procrastination J1071.1; punished for foul portrayal of Jesus Q222.3. — Why a. painted too few birds J1491.

Aryan. — Baptismal water vanishes before A. bishop V325.

Ascending. — Dragon king a. to sky H1292.14; god a. to heaven A171.0.2; hero a. to heaven A566.2; male sun-god while a., female while setting A227.1.

Ascent of mankind from under the earth A1232; to sky on cloud *F61.1; to stars A761; to upper world on arrow chain *F53.

Ascetic aids quest H1233.3.1; carries woman in his hair F1034.2.1; imitates Brahmin, goes to hell J2415.5; kills son born after seduction T338.1; plows field, it turns to gold D2102.2.1; sees scorpions as gold D1825.8; as villain K2285.1. — Austerities of a. sacred C94.9; birds mock a. B787; elephants look after a. in jungle B530.2; disguise as a. K1826.2; domestic vs. a. life H659.21; hospitality to a. rewarded Q45.3; lovely a. (disguised girl) wins rich woman's love K1322.1; magic

object from a. D812.14; magic power through a. practices D1733.3; rich woman accuses a. of adultery K2113.2; villain disguised as a. or nun K2285.

Ascetics beg alms of own mother N735.1. — Chastity methods of a. T302; women disguised as a. K521.9.

Ascetic's. — Seven rooms in a. house F771.11.

Asceticism *V462ff.; rewarded Q39.1.

Aschenputtel L52, L55.1, L131.

Ash pole appears at death E767.1; stakes driven through slain S139.2.2.7. —Sacred a. V1.7.1.2; snake avoids white a. B765.18.1; transformation: a. to hazel D451.1.2; white a. stick protects against snakes D1447.3.

Ash-tree bears apples F971.4.1; becomes hazel D451.1.1; late at distribution of qualities at creation: therefore buds last A2725.1, A2771.1. — Magic a. *D950.6; man transformed to a. D215.3.

Ashen. — Driving horses over a. yoke tabu C833.4.

Ashes become gold D475.1.1.1; blown into face of scoffer Q554.3; of corpse put through sieve S139.2.2.8; of dead dog speak E521.2.1; of dead thrown on water to prevent return E431.9; dissolve animals F981.5; as eye remedy K1011.2; falling form path K321.1; form trail R267; of hero revive E174.1; as hero's abode L131.1; on moon's face A751.5.2; sold as gold K121; transformed into animals D441.6.1; transformed into insects, snakes protect hero K2351.2.2. — Blowing a. in animals' faces K621.2; burning houses to sell a. K941.3; burning and scattering a. (punishment) Q414.3; detection by strewing a. J1146; dupe burns house because trickster reports high price paid for a. K941.2; falling to a. for breaking tabu C927.2; ghost detected by strewing a. *E436.1; heart's a. cast into river F932.7.1; hot a. poured by gods on kingdom Q552.13.0.3; magic a. *D931.1.2; magic glance reduces tree to a. D2082.1; man created from a. A1268; man transformed to a. D286; milky way as a. A778.8; money turns to a. D475.2.3, (devil's) G303.21.1; mosquitoes from a. of bad woman A2034.3; mustard-seed reduces man to a. D1402.16; ogre's a. cast on stream cause rapids to stop G655; person magically reduced to a. D2061.1.1, (hunter by heroine's chastity) *D2061.2.5; punishment: eating a. Q478.5; resuscitation from a. E42; resuscitation of cremated man by blowing on the a. E66.1; resuscitation through a. thrown on funeral pyre E132; serpent's gaze reduces man to a. B765.14.1; sham miracle: rupees turn to a. K1975.2; sugar transformed to a. D476.2.4; sun throws hot a. on moon's face A751.5.2.1; thief learns location of dupe's food supply by strewing a. *K321; trail of a. R135.0.6; transformation by throwing a. D575.1; wind raised by throwing traitor's a. on lake D2142.1.4.1; women throw a. in eyes of attacking soldiers K2356.

Ashore. — Crab comes a.: killed by fox J512.1; giant mermaid cast a. B81.13.13.

Asinus vulgi J1041.2.

Asking costs nothing J1338; questions (counseled against) J21.6, (forbidden) C410ff., (rewarded) Q85. — Effects of wild hunt remedied by a. the huntsmen E501.19.2ff.

Asleep, see also **Sleep, Sleeping.** — Answering call when a. tabu C811.3; boy learns lesson while a. in saint's lap V223.4.1; castle in which everyone is a. F771.4.4; cuckold feigns to be a. K1501.2; culture hero a. in mountain *A571; death respite until victim a. K551.27; "don't fall a. in strange place" J21.41; falling a. on rock which shoots upwards N314; hero a. while sweetheart marries another T92.4.1; importunate lover put a. in street Q473.4; lover a. at rendezvous D1972; undesired suitor killed a. Q411.2.1; victim killed while a. K834; when one is a. the soul is wandering E721.1ff.; witch recognized by seeing wasp enter her mouth while a. *G251.1.

Asmodeus F402.2.1.

Aspen cursed for serving as cross A2721.2.1.1. — All trees except a. refuse to make Christ's cross Z352; devil throws sand at a.: hence rough bark A2734.1, A2751.2.1; why a. leaves tremble A2762.1.

Ass associates with lion, disdains own family W165.2; beheaded (first thing king meets) J1169.4; betrays deity's secret: hence ugly bray A2239.3; brays on hearing conch shell J2211.4; brays to warn of thieves J2413.1.1; tries to caress master J2413.1; who carried divine image thinks people bow before him J953.4; claims to have killed cow, frightens tiger K1715.10; consulted about the loan J1552.1; has cross on shoulders from being struck by Baalam A2239.6; deprived of his saddle (punishment) J1862; determines road to be taken B151.1.1.2; envies horse in fine trappings J212.1; falls into water and catches fish in his ear N626; follows after lion and is punished J952.2; avoids food eaten by animals before being slaughtered J12; foolish to kick against the pricks J833; -god A132.3.3; gold-producing *B103.1.1; good living but not dead (riddle) H841.1; thought to be hare J1754; without a heart K402.3; helpful B402; is not at home when man wants to borrow him J1552.1.1; with human intelligence B22.2; indifferent to enemy's approach U151; insults dying lion W121.2.1; is jealous of the horse until he learns better L452; tries to jump on the roof J2413.2; knows where to find hidden wind B133.0.1.1; laughing J1169.5; in lion's skin unmasked when he raises his voice J951.1; loaded and commanded to go home J1881.2.1; tries in vain to play lyre J512.4; with magic wisdom B121.4; gets progressively worse masters N255.2; as mayor J1882.2; who has worked with ox thinks himself equal to ox J952.4; in the potter's shop J973; predicts weather B141.3; punished for stealing mouthful of grass U11.1; refuses to drink after it has enough J133.2; as sacrifice V12.4.8; with silver nose hunts hares (lie) X961.32; speaking B211.1.3.1; as tollkeeper B292.13; thought to be devil J1785.3; transformed into horse D412.6; transformed to person D332.1; turns on his driver who would save him from falling over

the precipice J683.1; insists upon payment of tithes B259.1; "of twenty older than man of seventy" J1352.2; carries usurer's body to the gallows B151.1.1.2.1; worship V1.8.10. — Baalam's a. V237, (advises that angel is barring way) B151.1.1.2.2, (perceives angel) B733.1; boar refuses to fight with lowly a. J411.1; body of man, hoofs of a. B22; breeding fine horses from an a. J1909.4; buyer returns a. which has associated with lazy companions J451.1; person calls another an a. J1352; camel and a. together captured because of ass's singing J2137.6; camel with a. on his back dances J2133.1; St. Christopher and the a. J1269.9; how much the a. cost J1601; death respite for teaching a. to speak K551.11; devil rides away on an a. G303.7.2; what is difference between you and an a. (counterquestion) H571.1; enmity of hyena and a. A2494.3.1; fairies steal a. F365.1; ferocious animal frightened by a. braying K2324.1; numskull cannot find a. he is sitting on J2022; fool thanks God that he was not sitting on the a. when it was stolen J2561; fox leads a. to lion's den but is himself eaten *K1632; friendship between wolf and a. A2493.15; frogs reprove a. for lamenting when he falls into morass J2211.1; guests call each other ox, a.: given appropriate food J1563.4; hard-hearted horse allows a. to be overburdened W155.1; king's capriciousness censured: the a. in the stream J1675.3; the lazy a. loaded with sponges J1612; lion as king makes a. his lieutenant J421.1; lost a. offered as reward to the finder J2085.1; marriage to person in a. form B641.4; miller, his son, and the a. (trying to please everyone) J1041.2; mourning dead a.: cumulative tale Z32.5; numskull knocks figure of Jesus from the a. J1823.1.4; old lady reminded of a. by priest's singing X436; peasant ashamed of being thrown off by a. J411.4; pseudo-magic money-dropping a. K249.3; teaching an a. to read H1024.4, *K491; red pepper for the slow a. (man tries it on himself) X11; revenant as a. E423.1.4; rider relieves the a. of his burden J1874.1; man scolds his a. and frightens robber away N612.1; shepherd taken to be a. J1765.1; "stick fast": fool seizes a. J2489.9; strong man lifts a. F624.1; the tailless and earless a. J2373; thief claims to have been transformed into a. K403; monster three-legged a. B15.7.2; tiger frightened off by threatening with a. K547.8; tiger mistaken for a. J1758.3; transformation to a. Q551.3.2.6; man transformed to a. D132.1, (by putting on bridle) D535, (plays lyre) *D693; truth-telling a. B133.0.1; wager: will jackal howl or a. bray first? N92; wedding of a. B281.7; why a. does not have cloven hoof A2376.1.1; why a. has cross on back A2356.2.7; why a. smells his own excrements A2495.2; why a. is stupid A2537.2; why dung of a. is triangular A2385.1; wild a. envies tame ass until he sees his burdens L451.2; why a. has long ears A2325.3.

Ass's behavior predicts the weather B141.3; charter in his hoof J1608; jawbone supplies water D1472.1.24.2; magic jawbone kills D1402.3.4. — Deduction: horse drinks a. milk J1661.1.5; person with a. ears F511.2.2;

girl bewitched into thinking lover has a. head G269.22; magic a. head *D1011.0.2, (fulfills wishes) D1470.1.7; man's body, a. head B22.1; pumpkin thought to be an a. egg J1772.1; too much a. flesh eaten (foolish diagnosis) J2412.4; vampire with a. ears E251.4.2.

Asses. — The burden of two a. J1352.1; Egyptians fond of a. A1689.12; lies about a. X1242.0.1; lions despise what a. admire V149.1.

Assailant. — Girl slays brother's a. P253.4.

Assailants. — Man pardons his a. W11.5.1.1.

Assassin. — King frees would-be a. P15.5; moon warns of a. F961.3.3; sun warns of a. F961.1.4; suspected a. given murder opportunity H1556.3.

Assassination. — Father orders son's a. S11.3.7; king takes measures against a. J634.

Assassinator's friend asks to die with him P319.2.

Assaulting. — Animals punished for a. women A2239.5.

Assembly of fairies at milestone F217.2; of gods A167; or group transformed to animals D103. — Don't uncover weapon in a. J21.2.4; tabus concerning entry into a. C853.

Assignation. — Lovers' a. by symbolic messages Z175.2; maid substitutes for mistress at a. H1556.4.3.

Assigners of tasks H920ff.

Assignment of bride to another T141; of crafts and professions by creator A1440.1; of edible animals A1422; of food to animal A2435.1; of quest H1210ff.; of superhuman task to determine true husband of woman J1176.5; of tasks H900ff., (to suitors) H335.0.2.

Assistance, see **Aid, Help.**

Assistant. — Thief's numskull a. prevents theft J2136.5.4.

Associates, choice of *J400ff.

Association of dwarfs with mortals F451.5.8; with fools J1710ff.; of equals and of unequals J410ff.; of great and lowly J412; with those of another faith punished Q431.18.

Assumption by divine beings of their own shape in sleep D796; of human forms by demons in order to deceive F402.1.4; of various shapes by wandering soul E721.5.

Assumptions. — Logical absurdity based upon certain false a. J2210ff.

Astonishment of God that I sit on horse and king on ass H797.2. — Dumbness magically cured by a. D2025.4; expressing a. at marvel (forbidden) *C491, (causes transformation) D512.

Astray. — Fairies lead travelers a. F369.7; importunate lovers led a. K1218; people led a. (by mermaid) B81.3, (by mists) K1886.2, (by spirit) F402.1.1, (by Will o' the Wisp) F491.1.

Astride. — Exposure a. wood in river S141.3; giant a. a church-roof F531.3.3.

Astrolabe, divination by D1311.6.0.1.

Astrologer P481; -magician D1712.0.1. — Devil as a. G303.3.1.22;

disguise as a. K1825.8; magic object from a. D818; man deriding faith in stars becomes a. N186; sham a. K1964; treacherous a. K2299.1.
Astrology M302.4.1. — Origin of a. A1487.1.1.
Astronomer shoots down falling star J2275.1. — Farmer surpasses a. in weather prediction L144.2.
Astronomers P429.1.
Astronomy. — Absurd theories in a. J2270ff.; origin of a. A1487.1.
Asunder. — Corpse drawn a. S139.2.2.6; life token: ring springs a. E761.5.3.
Atalanta's race *H331.5.1.1, *R231.
Atheists V323.
Athena chooses olive tree J241.1. — Why raven sacrifices to A. J821.1.
Atlantis A692.
Atlas supports earth on shoulders A842.
Atonement V315.
Attack on hare (crayfish) J2612; by hypocrite who pretends friendship K2010ff.; on intruders by ogre G475ff.; on soldier by dwarfs F451.5.2.11; on saints by Satan G303.9.6.2. — Amulet against a. D1381.16; animal's means of a. A2463; animals warn against a. B521.3; girl aids brother against a. P253.4; magic a. against enemy D2091; magic object protects from a. D1381ff.; retreat in return for cessation of a. M263; wandering ghost makes a. E261.
Attacker. — Escape by making a. believe there are many defenders K548; moon interferes between a. and person attacked A737.5; witch impervious if she looks at a. G221.4.
Attacking. — Advice on not a. hastily J21.2.1; bears a. men A2524.3; demons a. men G302.9.1; fish a. anything they find A2524.4; foolishness of a. real allies J683; hospitality repaid by a. enemy Q45.5; "kill man a. you" J21.52.6; vow on a. enemy M161.1; wise man considers whom he is a. J612.
Attar river in otherworld F162.2.5.
Attempts (vain) to circumvent theft of fire A1415.4; to escape fulfillment of prophecy M370ff.; of fettered monster to reach sword A1074.2; to kill hero *H1510ff.; of devil to vivify creations A1217.
Attendance of dwarfs at weddings F451.5.1.7; of human midwife on fairies F372.1; at mass outweighs evil deeds V44. — Reward for a. on holy man Q38.
Attendant. — Animal as constant a. of man B575; dead arises when shroud bursts and pursues a. E261.2; hero's faithful a. A515.4.
Attendants around God's throne A152.4; disenchanted D799.3; of the gods A165; of silver king F576. — Giants' a. F531.6.16; wife's a. chase wrong man, miss lover K1549.6.
Attention attracted (king's in clever ways) J1675.1, (recognition follows) H151ff., (by telling lies) J1341.5, (by trickery) *K477, (by magic object) D1420ff., (by magic) *D2074ff., (of sweetheart) T56, (of men by

women) A1373; distracted (by sight of beloved) T26, (by repeating strange action till it becomes commonplace) J1075.1, (from misgovernment by beginning war) K2381; to warnings J1050ff. — Attracting girl's a. by breaking her head J2461.9; cleverly attracting king's a. J1675.1; enchanted person attracts a. of rescuer D794; gambler's a. distracted by women N8; ogre attracts a. by whistling G653.

Attractiveness to men tested H1596.0.1.

Attributes. — Recognition by physical a. H50ff.; sun's a. A738.

Auction in hell draws Jews from heaven X611. — Owner bids up goods at a. K465.

Auctioneer praises worthless cow till owner buys her back J2087.

Audacious water bolder than continent husband T315.2.1.

Audhumla (cow) B19.2.1, B715.

Audible. — Giant a. to man only when resting on elbow F531.2.10; ghost a. only to person summoning him E389.2.

Audience of one hired to hear bad singer X145.1; secured with the pope by rudeness K477.1. — Escape by pleading for larger a. K579.8; using lamb to get a. J1653.

Augean stable H1102.

Auger, magic D1187.1.

Augurer, see **Divination, Oracle.**

Auk. — Darkness from a. swallowing sun A721.2.1; giant a. B872.4.

Auks. — Stones become a. D565.9.

Aunt P294; marries nephew T421. — Cruel a. S72.

Aunt's. — God Vishnu torments a. lover K1578.

Aurora Borealis as bridge to otherworld F152.1.8. — Origin of a. A795; souls of dead as a. E742.3.

Ausgelohnt F451.5.10.9.

Auspicious days N127. — Delaying birth until a. day T589.8; wager: it is a. day N53.

Austerities. — Magic object acquired by religious a. D855.2; reward for a. of hermit Q34; vow to destroy kingdom by a. M193.

Authenticity. — Deity attests a. of sacred writings A1996; testing a. of relics V140.4.

Author, see also **Writer;** believes his book stupid, fools praise it J1714.4.

Automata. — City of wooden a. D1628; God makes a. and vivifies them A141.1; magic a. *D1620ff.

Automatic oar D1523.2.1; object *D1600ff.; service in otherworld F183.1. —Alleged a. object K119.1; constructing a. peacock H326.1.1.

Automaton. — Jewish a. will not work on Saturday V71.1.

Automobile, see also **Car.** — Ghost rides in a. E332.3.3.

Autumn is richest (riddle) H636.1. — Goddess of a. leaves A430.1.2; sitting on sepulchral mounds tabu in a. C755.5; why days shorten in a. A1156.

Avalon as abode of gods A151; as happy otherworld where dead are healed *E481.4.1; journey to *F111.

Avarice punished *Q272.

Avaricious man given gift of benevolence by fairies F343.4; man transformed to ant A2011.2.

Ave on the tongue V254.3. — Flower with A. on leaves E631.0.2.1.

Aves. — Efficacy of saying A. V254ff.; Virgin Mary refuses to help wife against her rival who has always said her A. T285.

Avenging bride's former fiancé H335.1.1; father's brother P293.5; murder (bride's father's as suitor task) H335.1, (faithful animal at grave) B301.2, (magic horse) B184.1.7, (warning by God's voice) M348; by nearest blood relation P525.3; scorned love (by fairy) F302.3.3; self by feigning dullness J1675.7; uncivil answer (by cobold) F481.1. — Animal a. injury B857; blood-brethren a. each other P312.2; brothers a. each other P251.3.1; external soul a. murder E710.2; faithful servant a. master P361.6; foster brothers a. each other P273.1.1; friends a. each other P310.2; girl in man's clothes a. father K1837.4; god a. self on giant A162.5; prophecy on a. own death M322; quest a. king H1228.1; return from dead for a. E234.3; sister a. brother's death P253.5; son a. father P233.6; tournament a. king P561.2; woman a. scorned love T71.2.

Aversion of Evil Eye D2071.1ff.; of fairy spell by turning coat F385.1; of woman to marriage T311.

Avis J1154.1.

Avoidance of devil's power G303.16ff.; of evil spirits at childbirth T582.1; of fatigue by magic D2032; of men by young sparrows J13; of others' power J640ff.; of places which have been fatal to others J644; of all pronouns in tale Z15; of prophecy fulfillment M391.1; of punishment J1180ff.; of religious ceremonies by witches G285; of things harmful by nature J656; of shrewish wife T251.1; of wild hunt E501.17.5ff.

Awake. — Driving insane by keeping a. S191; "he who lies a. gains" J21.41.3.

Awakening of dead after three days E489.1; of fearless hero by cold water H1441; in morning by magic ring D1317.5.2; of sleeper forbidden since soul is absent E721.1.1; of sleepers prevented by hand-of-glory D1575.1. — Friar a. girl for seduction K1354.3.1.

Away. — Guardian enticed a. K629.2; impregnation from far a. husband T539.5; ogre vulnerable only if face turned a. Z315.

Awkward servant J2665.

Awl, magic *D1187.

Axe becomes golden D475.1.17; dropped in water: modest choice Q3.1; in stump removed by finger F614.2.3; thrown at one animal misses, kills another N337.3; turns into tiger D1594.5. — Boot mistaken for a. sheath J1772.11; breaking iron with wooden a. H1116.2; cat in wood-

pile prevents a. from cutting D2186; cutting rocks with brass a. H1116.1; extraordinary a. F837; finger becomes a. handle D457.9; two giants with one a. G151; god with a. A137.1.1; identification by a. H131; iron a. becomes silver D475.3.4; magic a. *D1206; man invulnerable from a. D1841.5.3; milk transferred from another's cow by a. handle D2083.3.1; murder by a. S139.4; origin of the a. A1446.2; quest for a. which sticks in beam outside a tower H1338; man searches for a. which he carries on shoulders J2025.1; sight of wild hunt causes one to stick a. or knife in food E501.18.9; soul in a. E711.14; squaring lumber without blunting a. H1199.13; teeth like a. heads F531.2.12; tooth becomes a. head D457.8; tree cut down with a. for which it has furnished a handle U162.

Axes ground on rolling boulders X1012.1; thrown away J2171.4. — Animal killed by a. left in tree K897.2; father ties a. to fool abandoned daughter S338.

Axeman, skillful F666ff.; (lie) X986.

Axle. — Carrying a wagon a. which has broken a wheel (task) H1183; crooked a. accused H659.18.1.

Ay ay. — Buying eggs and "a." H1185.1.

Ayikha bush. — Why a. is firmly rooted A2774.1.

Baalam as magician D1711.1.3. — Ass has cross on shoulders after struck by B. A2239.6.

Baalam's ass B151.1.1.2.2, B733.1, V237; family as magicians D1711.11.1.

Baarlam and Josaphat M351.

Babe. See **Baby.**

Babes in the wood S300ff.

Babel, tower of *C771.1, D2004.9.1, F772.1.

Baboon as shepherd for man B292.1.1. — Color of b. A2411.1.5.2; creation of b. A1863; enmity between b. and fox A2494.9.1; where b. got tail A2378.1.1; why b. has bare place on back A2317.10; why b. has crooked tail A2378.9.2; why b. walks on all-fours A2441.1.2.

Baboons abduct boy R13.1.1. — Birhors eat b. A1422.2.

Baby, see also **Child, Infant;** drags mill-stone F64.3.2.2; finds mother, goes to her for suckling H495.1; giants' size F531.2.14; ordered killed for pulling father's beard S327.2; son hurled into battle to punish mother Q469.11; swallowed by tigress, comes out F914.3. — Dead mother returns to care for neglected b. *E323.1.2; fairy-mortal b. with long hair, beard F305.3; house-spirit as b. F480.4; man kills giant's b. F531.5.14; maternity test: producing b. within year H494; nature of a b. misunderstood J1911; newborn b. reveals secret N468; ogre abducts newborn b. G442.1; revenant as woman carrying b. E425.1.4; saintly b. holds arms in form of cross V229.2.1; stolen sheep dressed as b. in cradle K466.2; transformation: man to b. at will D55.2.5; why eagle cries like a b.: tortured baby became eagle A2426.2.15.

Baby's cry imitated to distract owner K341.7.0.1.

Babies exchanged P313.1. — Devil appears to girl who prays over b. she has killed G303.6.2.7; stone substituted for newly-born b. K2115.2.1; why b. die easily A1326; why b. have soft spots in head A2875.

Babyhood. — Friendship starts at b. P313.1.

Babylon, stallions of H572.

Babylonians don't keep oaths M108.1. — Why B. are roundheaded A1663.1.

Bacchic. — Refusal to take part in B. rites C57.2; woman performing B. rites C312.2.4.

Bacchus A481; personifies wine Z139.3.1.

Bachall, magic *D1277. — Christ leaves b. V211.2.2; saint transfers disease to his bell (b.) D2161.4.2.2; saint's b. defaces idol V356.3; saint's b. used in cursing D2175.2; swearing by saint's b. M116.1.

Bachalls. — Friends exchange b. P311.0.1; saints exchange b. P311.7.

Bachlach, disguise as K2357.14.

Back. — Alligator's rough b. A2356.2.11; birth through b. T541.15; bringing b. person from the dead F81.1; breaking witch's b. H1562.8; brown man with white b. F527.4; carrying child on one's b. into house tabu C875; counting hairs in pig's b. H1118; devil carries away a lord on his b. G303.9.5.2; disenchantment of girl by carrying her on b. D732.1; dupe rides trickster's b., captured K726; earth rests on animal's b. A844; eyes in b. of head F512.4; fairy's b. rough F232.1.2; fearless hero awakened by eels down his b. H1441.1; flight carrying another on b. F242; fool given the truth on his b. J551.2; giant carries man on b. F531.5.1.1.2; ghost carries coffin on b. E592.2; ghost rides on man's b. *E262; huckauf jumps on man's b. *F472; image cut into man's b. by flaying, salting S114.2; loathly bridegroom carried on b. in basket by wife T216; looking b. forbidden C331; marvelous sensitiveness: blister on b. from lying in rose leaves F647.9; murder by breaking b. S116.3; mutilation: skin cut from b. S166; ogre jumps on one's b. and sticks there G311; ogre tricked into carrying his prisoners home in bag on his own b. G561; one eye in b. of head F512.1.3; origin and nature of animal's b. A2356ff.; person without b. F525.6; plea for stabbing in chest, not b. W45.1; punishment: animal skin grows on man's b. Q551.2; punishment: thong of leather cut from b. Q451.8; slave bathing mistress's b. in stream pushes her into crocodile hole K831.1; reincarnation of b. into hoe handle E649.3.1; straw on horse's b. restrains him D1442.2; trickster pretends lameness and is taken on woman's b.: violates her K1382; why camel's b. humped A2356.2.13; witch begs man to scratch her b.: kills him *G269.1; wife carries mutilated husband on her b. so that he may beg T215.1.

Backs. — Animals climb on one another's b. and cry out: frighten robbers K335.1.4; fairies have hollow b. F232.1; images at church turn b. D1639.3; wild huntsman makes people carry him on their b. *E501.15.3.

Backbone for horse made from stick X1721.1; of ogre's mother broken G512.7.

Backwards. — Why antelope's antlers reach b. A2326.3.3; bells rung b. P651.3; devil notes people looking b. in church G303.24.1.7.2; devil works b. G303.13.2; devil's knees are b. G303.4.5.6; dwarf's feet twisted b. F451.2.2.1; hero can turn feet, knees b. A526.8; invisibility by reciting formula b. D1985.2; knees b. F517.1.5; mutilation: turning feet b. S162.5; numskull rides b. J2024; power of prophecy by crawling b. around grave D1812.2.1; reading Bible b. reveals witch G275.2; resuscitation with head on b. E34.1; riding b. on donkey as punishment Q473.5.2; runner runs b. F681.7; spirits' fingers, toes point b. F441.4.4; walking b. around church gives witching power G224.8; walking b. to leave false trail K534.3; walking b. to obey oath K2312.2; wild huntsmen with heads on b. E501.7.3.

Backwoods couple found "living in darkness", cut window J1738.6.

Bacon changed to iron D476.3.2. — Fish promised in return for b. K231.11; numskull drags b. on string J2461.1.1; skating with b. to grease huge griddle X1031.4.1; "Take yourself to hell with the b." K419.4; turnips called b. J1511.2.

Bad character shown by the eyes H1550.1; dream as evil omen D1812.5.1.2; luck put into a sack N112.1; man (i.e. devil) *G303ff.; omens D1812.5.1ff.; rearing causes son to bite father's nose off Q586; ruler, bad subject U210ff. — Associating with b. friend fatal J429.2; black stars seen over heads of the b. D1825.3.2; boy behind the tree complains of b. food K1971.3; breaking b. news to a king J1675.2; crickets as b. omens B147.3.2.1; "don't keep b. company" J21.25; father drives away b. son P233.2.1; father in vineyard doing good and b. (pruning vines) H583.2; good and b. in all books J174; good and b. culture heroes *A525; good, b. fairies battle F277.0.3; the house is burned down — that is too b. Z51.1; peacock a b. king J242.4; persistent b. luck N250ff.; persons bring b. luck N134.1; revenant with b. breath E422.1.5; revolt of b. gods against good *A106.1; no b. tidings given king P14.9; why certain animals b. B792.

Badger transformed to person D315.3. — Helpful b. B433.2; man becomes b. D124.4.

Badgers slain in violation of pledge K2023. — Capturing b. H1154.10.

Bag, see also **Sack;** conjuring *D1274.1; laid by fence-hole for hares X1114; of lies threat to tell queen's adultery K1271.1.1; magic *D1193; in the moon A751.9.2; with rice for the road K444.3; of tricks J1662; of winds C322.1; wishing D1470.1.27. — Burial of cut-up body in b. E431.18; cake b. full of cobras K444.2; captor's b. filled with animals or objects while captives escape K526; child born in b. T561.3; clothes b. cut in two with sword F667.3; deception into entering b. K711; detection of theft by finding b. repairer J1141.5; eating contest: hole in b. K81.1; evil eye covered with b. D2071.0.1.1; ghost as b. E426.1; giving

away the old water b. in which the money is hid J2093.1; hiding in b. in order to be carried K1892.1; looking into b. forbidden C322; ogre carries victim in b. G441; ogre tricked into carrying his prisoners home in b. G561; pseudo-magic wealth-providing b. K111.3; quest for b. of truths H1376.4; rain from emptying b. D2143.1.8; reincarnation as b. of water E636.1; resuscitation by magic b. E64.14; sacred hosts fill b. in coffin V35.2; spirit in b. as helper F403.2.2.4; stabbing b. of blood *K1875; taking prisoner's place in a b. K842; thief hides in money b. K307.1; transformation to be put in food b. D657.1; wife carried up tree to the sky in b. in husband's teeth J2133.5.1.

Bags. — Negligent priests buried under b. filled with words omitted from service V5.2; new b. for old K266.

Bagpipe as devil's bellows G303.10.14. — Death respite while playing b. K551.3.5; fairies teach b. playing F262.2; playing b. frightens robber K335.1.5.

Bailing out pond with thimble H1113.1; out stream J1967.

Bait. — Getting b. from trap by luring in another animal K1115.1; human eyes as fish b. S165.6; stealing Añan's b. H1151.17; tiger gives man food for dear b. K361.3; unique fish b. Z312.4.

Bakali. — Quest for b. flower H1333.5.3.

Baker P442; substitutes for imprisoned princess R83. — Cuckoo a transformed b. A1993.1; dwarf as b. F451.3.4.5; giant as b. F531.3.7; lover disguised as b. woman K1214.1.1; witch as b. G246.

Baker's. — King called b. son J816.2; owl is b. daughter who objected to dough given Jesus A1958.0.1.

Baking without fire D2158.1.5.2. — Dwarfs b. F455.3.5; fairies b. bread F271.10; fugitive king disguised and set to b. K521.4.1.2; how husband knows wife b. J1713.1; lie: remarkable b. X1031.4; mother is b. the bread we ate last week H583.4.2.

Balance. — His faith into the b. V512.1; ordeal by b. H226; religious exercises weighed in b. V4.1.

Balcony. — Chickens thrown from b. J2173.5.

Bald cow H1331.3.1; daughter as accursed H659.18.1; man aims at a fly J2102.3; man and the cynic J1442.9; man finds comb J1061.2; man tries to sell hair-restorer J1062.2.1. — Origin of b. heads H1315.2; swallowed person becomes b. F921; why certain animals are b. A2317.

Balder's death K863.

Baldness from breaking tabu C949.2; magically cured D2161.3.4. — Magic helmet prevents b. D1389.8; wife exposes second wife's b. T257.2.1.

Balky. — Trading b. horse K134.6.

Ball falling into water puts person into ogre's power G423; of fire haunts murderer E530.1.2; game in lower world E494; of human brains F839.5; thrown indicates princess's choice H316.3. — Animal killed by forcing b. into throat K951.5; Apple (or b.) containing man's soul

can be split only by man's own sword D1651.10; conception from putting b. into bosom T532.6; counselor killed in own treacherous b. game K1626.2; dead persons play b. E577.1; devil as b. of fire G303.3.4.2.1; devil as a black b. G303.3.4.2; disenchantment by crystal b. D771.12; dropped b. leads to adventures when recovery is attempted N777; fiends play b. with soul E752.1.2; head used as b. S139.2.2.4.1; heroine's three-fold flight from b. R221; lucky cast of b.: kills dog through mouth N623.2; magic b. *D1256, (of thread) *D1184.1, (of hair) D991.3; magic b. of string to which one sticks D1413.18; marvelous b. player F697; origin of b. game A1495.1; power of chaste woman: making b. of water H413.2; prince sees heroine at b. and is enamored N711.6; pursuit of rolling b. of yarn H1226.4; reincarnation as b. E637; seduction by seeking lost b. K1349.9; soul in golden b. E711.9; test of sex of girl masking as man: b. thrown into lap H1578.1.4; tabu: letting b. fall into water *C41.2; tabu: staying too long at b. C761.3; throwing b. to princess as suitor test H331.16; thunder as gods play b. A1142.6; witch-b. kills G262.4.

Balls. — Mines found where b. fall N533.5; sun and moon as b. of feathers A738.1.1.

Balm. — Giant has wound-healing b. F531.6.5.3; magic b. *D1244; thirteen rivers of b. in otherworld F162.2.7.

Balsam rivers in otherworld F162.2.5. — Bath of b. F872.7; water becomes b. D478.8; witch kills b. plant G265.9.1.

Bamboo goddess A435.1; to be returned exactly as it is K196.3; stalks as life token E761.3.1; transformed to person D431.10. — All seeds in b. cut by hero A1425.1; alleged oracular b. cup K114.4; butterfly becomes b. D424.1; contest: bringing grain from closed b. K69.1; iron in b. in deceptive contest K44.1; magic b. tree D950.15; origin of b. A2681.6; soul in b. E711.2.6; why b. has nodes A2756.

Ban on trolls F455.9; on tournaments rescinded P561.1. — Person under religious b. cannot rest in grave E412.

Banana large as elephant's tooth F813.6.1; leaf becomes fish D441.5.2. — Fool eats wrong part of b. J1732.2; meat transformed to b. D457.5.2; origin of b. A2687.5; speaking b. tree D1612.1.2; touching b. tabu C621.2.2; why b. bears fruit from crown of tree A2771.4.

Bananas distract pursuing fairies F381.2.1; hide when stone is thrown D1641.16; ripen from bottom up E761.3.1.1; magic b. *D981.13; monkey cheats fox of b. K171.9.

Band, see also **Bracelet.** — Iron b. forged round a man's waist Q522.5.

Bands. — Iron b. around heart to keep it from breaking F875.

Bandage. — Identification by b. H118.

Bandicoot as children's nurse B535.0.2. — Helpful b. B437.1.1; man transformed to b. D117.3.1.

Bangle, magic *D1075.

Bangles. — Man exchanges b. for son M101.3.2.

Banished minister found indispensible and recalled P111; wife or maiden S411; wind A1122.3; youth becomes king L111.1.1. — Actors b. along with vagabonds P471.1; bad luck b. N250.4; brother b. S73.2; fairies b. from fairyland F252.4; fairy mistress insists wife be b. F302.5.4; man b. into moon for theft A751.1.4; misunderstood wife b. by husband S411.1; mother b. to stables by king S21.4; nobleman b. by king coveting his castle P12.8; poets b. P427.7.9; rain-god and wind-god b. by sun-god A287.0.1; revenants b. E437; revolting devil b. to hell A106.2.1; son b. by father S11.5, S322.1.5.1; wife b. S411; youngest son b. for telling king truth J551.6.

Banishment for breaking tabu C955; caused by dream of future greatness L425; as punishment Q431; tests suitor's sincerity H314.2. — Inverted shoes indicate b. Z174.1; magic b. D2099.2.

Bank. — Murder revealed to thieves climbing into b. N615; trickster gets money from b. by raising alarm K484.1.

Banks. — Dwarfs live in high b. of seashore F451.4.1.8; separation by being on different b. of stream N315.

Banker's ability to recognize honest merchant J1661.1.9.

Bankrupt father sells his daughters in marriage to animals S221.1.

Banner. — Large b. gives away jackal king J951.5; magic b. gives victory D1400.1.16; Virgin Mary's shift as b. causes blindness to opposing army D1331.2.3.

Banners appear like flock of birds K1872.5.

Banquet of the dead E499.1. — Drunken enemies slaughtered in b. hall K871.2; enemies invited to b. and killed K811.1f.; magic b. D1030.2; magic healing b. D1500.1.30.

Banquets of the gods A153.3.

Banshees as prophets M301.6.1.

Banyan leaves become gold D475.1.3.1; tree on moon A751.6.1. — How b. got its milk A2791.3; jar beneath b. tree animated A199.1; offending spirit of b. tree C43.1; origin of b. tree A2681.10; why b. roots hang down A2791.13.

Baptism, see also **Christening;** *V81; of animal gives magic powers *D1766.3; of children lays ghost E443.6; by druids P427.1.3; of heathen V332; as magic cure D2161.4.9; rescues man from devil G303.16.6; of saint by angel V241.4. — Heretical b. V322; king demands b. of guests P337.1; phenomena accompany b. of wonder child V229.2.4; resuscitation for b. E176; transformation by b. D587; water miraculously produced for b. D925.1.0.1.

Baptismal water (as magic object) *D1242.1.1, (vanishes before Aryan bishop) V325. — Man enabled to read b. service by washing in holy water K1819.4.1; ring as b. token H82.4.

Baptized wine J1312.3. — Disenchantment of monster child when b. D741.2; stone on which saint b. D931.0.3; why magpie hybrid: not b. during flood A2382.1.

Baptizer. — Magic power from b. D1722.1.

Bar. — Devil strikes man dead with iron b. G303.20.3; ogre killed with own iron b. G519.2.

Barber P446; alone praises usurer X511; becomes king L113.8; clever J1115.3; cured by telling secret D2161.4.19.1; discovers secret physical peculiarity N465; ghostly E571; hired to cut king's throat sees warning on the bottom of the basin J21.1; killed: king's ancestors need services in heaven K964; kills child: blames thin skin J1166.1; leaves inexpensive village for high wages in city J342.1; makes demands while wielding razor J625; as matchmaker T53.5; passes for a Brahmin K1827.0.2; rescues abandoned boy R131.8.8; shaves wife's beard (lie) X1727.1; skillful F665; suggests task H919.1.1; tries to become trader J513.2; unskillful J1484. — Before b. great incline head and give blood and money H581.1; customer agrees to demands of b. while razor is at his throat J625; disguise as b. K1825.3; one-eyed b. sees thread stretching to sea F642.6; thief disguised as b. K311.13; treacherous b. K2253.

Barber's contest in shaving H504.2; and jackal's common garden K171.8.

Barbers. — Jokes about b. X252.

Bard P427.7.5; rescues child R131.19; vows against making requests M164.

Bare, see **Bald, Barren.**

Barefoot. — Neither b. nor shod H1055; salamander enters b. person B784.1.8.

Bargain in anger F613.3, K172; is deceptive *K100ff.; is foolish J2080ff.; is lucky *N421. — Dead return to fulfill b. E342; devil made sick of his b. K262.1; drinking only after a b. K236.2; family carried away to fairyland as part of b. F327; immortality gained from b. with death D1851.2; love-compelling man sickens of b. K837; payment precluded by terms of the b. K220ff.; priest dies from deceptive b. F1041.1.3.4; touching head as sign of accepting b. P675.

Bargains and promises *M200ff. — Chain tale: progressively worse b. Z41.5; trickster undertakes impossible b. and collects his part M291.

Bargaining sends family off to fairyland F327. — Lover b. with husband K1581.10.

Bark of plant A2751ff. — Animals from b. thrown on ground A1714.2; disguise in birch b. K1821.9.1; land made from b. D476.1.4; magic b. D952; tanning shoes with b. from saint's tree Q551.6.2.1; why tinsa tree has no b. at bottom of trunk A2751.2.3.

Bark-cloth for chiefs alone C564.4; origin of A1453.5.

Barking. — Dogs' b. causes forgetfulness D2004.10; dog driven away from other animals because of b. A2494.4.0.1; dog b. to dog in moon K1735; how dog's b. began A2425.1; man's b. D2063.6; why dog b. at thief A2426.1.5.

Barley plant droops if prince is in trouble D1310.4.3; in wounds as false remedy K1016. — Magic b. D965.15, D973.2; origin of b. A2685.4; wheat becomes b. D451.2.2.

Barmecide feast P327.

Barn. — Birds magically confined to roofless b. D2072.0.2.2.1; burial in b. as punishment Q491.1.2; cleaning manure-filled b. H1102.2; destructive bird killed, b. found full of gold B103.7.1; fairies dance in b. F261.3.5; feathering b. H1104.1.1.

Barnacle goose B712.

Barrel of ale fairy gift F348.9; filled miraculously with penitent's tears F1051.1. — Building b. around a bunghole W152.14.1; casting into water in b. as punishment Q467.1; descending sea in glass b. J52.2; devil as rolling b. G303.3.4.5; fatal game: rolling down hill on b. K866; forbidden b. C624; fox and noisy but empty b. J262.1; king in glass b. to study fishes P15.6; look! look! she cries from the b. W136.1; man can stand on b. rolling down hill F679.4; man in b. grabs wolf by the tail and is drawn out of danger X1133.3; magic b. D1171.9, (supplies drink) D1472.1.18; naked lover as devil in sooty b. K1555.2; thief in oil b. K312; wind raised by putting cat under b. D2142.1.5.

Barrels. — Lie: b. of tears shed over lying X909.1.1.

Barren hillside turns to wheat at Christ's presence V211.1.8.3; trees as punishment for Fall of Man A2721.8; wife banished S411.3; wife conceives in time to prevent husband's leaving N681.2; wife exposed by husband S62.3; wife gives husband handmaid T282; wife makes child by magic K1924; woman assigns quest for dusty cloth H1377.4; woman pretends to bear child K1923.3. — Land made magically b. *D2081; dragon's shriek makes land b. *B11.12.2; magic chain renders orchard b. D1563.2.1; magic song makes b. land fruitful D1563.1.2; refusal to accept alms from b. woman V436; river b. of fish D2085.1; second wife taken because first b. T145.2.

Barrenness induced by magic T591; magically cured D2161.3.11; removed (by blood) D1347.2, (by charms) D1501.1, (by eating or drinking) D1925.1, (by prayer) D1925.3, (by sacrifice of child) S271; as result of fright F1041.17.1.

Barrier to otherworld (river of fire) *F142, (water) *F141.

Barrow as home (of dwarf) F451.4.1.9, (of troll) F455.1.1. — Magic object from b. D838.5.

Barrows. — Dead live in b. E481.3.1.

Bashful dwarfs F451.5.19; suitor wooes oak T69.4.

Basil, the pot of T85.3.

Basilisk B12ff.

Basin, magic *D1171.12; to which one sticks *D1413.7. — Tale of the b. *K1217; warning on the bottom of the b. J21.1.

Basket of things becomes iron D479.5; tied to wolf's tail and filled with stones K1021.2. — Air-castle: b. of glassware to be sold J2061.1.1; air-riding b. D1118.1; bride in b. C169.1; coin left in b. borrowed to measure money betrays secret wealth N478; dropped b. leads to adventures N777; dupe enters trickster's b. and is killed K814; escape from

deluge in b. A1029.5; escape by leaving pursuers in b. K676; exposure of child in b. S141; future hero found in b. L111.2.1; god with b. A137.4; hair tied to b. causes dupe's death K1021.1.1; insect asks to be put in loosely-woven b. K581.6; light kept in b. A1411.1; looking into b. forbidden C327; magic b. *D1171.11; magic b. (box) furnishes livestock D1477.4; magic b. (box) furnishes slaves D1476.3; man drawn up into female apartments in b. *K1343.1; monkey instead of girl in floating b. K1625; ogre carries victim in b. G441; one b. of wit better than carloads J1662.1; paramour pretends to be returning winnowing b. K1517.11; prince finds girl floating on water in b. N711.5; sky b. F51.2; soul hidden in fish b. E712.6; thief enters city in b. K312.2; trick exchange: b. of stones for bread K149.1; trickster's b. for tiger partner K2033; trickster hides in b. K1892.1.2; Vergil in the b. K1211; victim suspended in b. over filth and thrown in Q474; victim tricked into entering b. K714.4; weapons concealed in food b. K929.11; wife has husband carried off in b. K1514.6; woman dupe puts thief in food b. K359.3.

Baskets. — Animals escape when forbidden b. opened: origin of animals C915.2; capture by hiding in food b. K758; lies about b. X1756; origin of b. A1446.5.5, A2828; resuscitation by magic b. E64.20; sunlight carried into windowless house in b. J2123.

Basket-makers. — Why some men are good b. A1650.3.1.

Bastard, see also **Illegitimacy;** hero L111.5, Z255. — The cynic and the b. stone-thrower J1442.7; deduction: the king is a b. J1661.1.2; prophecy: princess to marry b. M369.2.1.2; slander: prince is b. K2128.

Bastards, tabus of C575.

Bat created A1895; diver, and thornbush shipwrecked A2275.5.3; falls due to sun's extreme heat: hence peculiar feet and nose A2214.6; giant B31.4; helpful B449.3; lifts stone before rescue H1562.2.2; makes sun smile, ends eclipse A1046.1; rescues man from height B542.1.2; sleeps in day: curse for being asleep when devil tempted man to eat forbidden fruit A2236.3; in war of birds and quadrupeds B261.1. — Eight-eyed b. B15.4.1.4; friendship of b. and owl A2493.2; soul in form of b. E731.7; witch as b. G211.2.10; woman reborn as b. E692.1; why b. is bald A2317.8; why b. flies by night A2491.1; why b. sleeps by day A2491.1.1.

Bat's body made larger A2301.4.

Bats in house a ghost sign E436.3; keep fireflies B788. — Eternal b. B19.9; why b. cry as they fly A2426.1.6.

Bath of blood as cure for leprosy F955.1; of blood of beloved to cure love-sick empress T82; in blood of king as cure for mange D1502.5.1; extraordinary F872ff.; in magic milk rejuvenates D1338.4; in milk of white, hornless cows as antidote for poison D1515.3. —Acid b. for unwelcome lover K1227.4.1; blood b. causes woman to be carried off

by a bird N335.2; boiling water poured on master in b. K1462.1; bride's garments stolen in b. K1911.1.8; cynic at b. J1442.2; escape by pretended b. K551.4.7; good b. (cat to mouse) J1422; helpful mare cools boiling b. for master B526.2; king in the b. D2012.1; lover put off till after girl's b. K1227.1; muddy b. for blemished king J815.3; only person in b. J753.1; poisoned b. accidentally used N332.1.1; tabu: going into b. on return from serpent kingdom C711; victim killed in b. K831; weekly b. taker comforted by yearly taker J882.3; wounds healed by marrow b. F959.3.3.

Baths. — Fool at b. believes he's someone else J2012.6; public b. as adulteress's tryst K1587.

Bathhouse of fairies F265.1.

Bather's. — Abduction by stealing b. clothes R32; bird carries off b. garments N352.2.

Bathing in boiling water as suitor test H328.5; in common place tabu J21.33; fairy F265; in fairyland lake tabu F378.2; forbidden C721; girl visited by devils G303.10.4.2; hair in buffalo milk makes it unusually long D1337.1.3.1; infants in milk T601; pool reserved for royalty P92; in waters compulsory C663; witch G245. — Abortion by long b. T572.2.6; blindness cured by b. F952.7; compulsion: b. in certain waters daily C663; conception from b. T523; dead person b. E599.13; death respite for b. K551.4.4; disenchantment by b. (in milk) D766.4, (in water) D766.1; enemy surprised while b. R4.1; escape by b. guard in boiling water K629.1; eyes restored by b. in spring F952.7; fairies b. in enemy's blood F259.2; falling in love with b. person T16; lover first sees beloved b. N716; magic cure by b. D2161.4.14; magic results from b. *D1788; men tricked into b. in "disease-water" K1077; ogress b. in pool becomes beautiful G264.0.1; punishment of b. people in hell remitted Q578; races dark-skinned from b. after white men A1614.2; resuscitation by b. E80.1; ritual b. V96; seduction (or wooing) by stealing clothes of b. girl K1335, R32; sight of mermaid b. makes man immortal B81.13.3; slave b. mistress's back in stream pushes her into crocodile hole K831.1; speaking while b. tabu C401.6; spirit in hell endlessly b. people Q501.9; substitute products used in b. rich man: his substitute pay J1511.2.1; suitor b. in boiling water H1023.24; sun b. in stream of fire A722.5.1; tabu: b. without straining stream afterwards C 721.3; tabus concerning b. fairy child F378.6; transformation by b. D562; tree maidens b. at midnight F441.2.1.4; women meet when b. P611.

Bathroom in minaret J2237. — Attempt to suffocate king in b. P16.3.1.1; suffocating in b. S113.2.2.

Batting. — Sham dead detected by b. eyes H248.5.

Battle P551, see also **Army;** captives sold as slaves P173.3; carnage personified Z132.0.1; at end of world A1080ff.; of fairies and the gods F277; of giants, dwarfs F535.5.1.1; of the gods at world's end

A1081; of islands F748; between lice of Strassburg and of Hungary X651; noise precipitates birth T581.6; rage *F873.0.1, N349.2; reactions of warriors F1041.16.6; as suitor contest H331.2.1. — Adultery to aid husband in b. T455.2.1; angel as helper in b. V232; baby son hurled into b. to punish mother Q469.11; cairn marks b. site A989.4 capture on field of b. R5; certain person to fight particular b. M369.3; cohabiting with woman after b. C664.0.1; dead buried after b. V69.1; dead king carried into b. P12.5.0.1; defeat in b. at world's end A1084; demons b.: hills torn up A964.3; devil as helper in b. G303.22.14; devil interrupts mass by pretended b. G303.9.9.2; escape from b. by flying in air R324.1; extraordinary nature phenomena during b. F960.3; fairy aids mortal in b. *F349.2; fairy offers man change of form and feature for aid in b. F343.11; fairies b. F277.0.3; faithful animal killed in b. B335.5; father kills son in b. rage N349.2; furious b. *F1084; god helps mortal in b. A185.1; gods intervene in b. A172; good king never retreats in b. P12.5; hero aids followers in b. A581.2; hero sleeping during first of b. K2378.5; king in disguise flees b. K1812.10; king pretends going to make peace: really b. K1774; land changes from b. between gods A901.1; leaving b. while lord alive cowardly W34.3; lost memory recovered in b. N645; magic defense in b. *D2163; men go mad in b. F1041.8.6; messenger sent is only b. survivor N693; mock b. scares off enemy K2368.2; prayer before b. brings victory V52.3; prophecy: death in b. M341.2.18; prophecy: loss of b. M356.1.1; rather death in b. than in bed M161.6; recurrent b. A162.1.0.1; relics carried into b. V144.1; scolding contest introduction to b. H507.5; spirits hover in air over b. F418; substitute in b. K1845; suitor contest: bride offered to the one distinguishing himself most in b. H331.2.1; tabu: going to b. without being clothed in silk C878.2.1; transformation to another form to persuade men to go to b. D659.9; Virgin Mary intercepts an arrow in b. D2163.3; vow to become Christian if b. won M177.1.1; waves reverberate at preparation for b. F931.4.1; warrior refuses to delay b. W33.2; wild hunt appears in old b. field E501.12.6.1; witch in b. G275.10.

Battles. — King loses b. for plundering church Q556.6; oath concerning b. for Jesus M177.1.2.

Battle-axe D1097, F837.

Battle-pen P552.1.

Battle-shouting A1341.1.

Battlefield. — Birds hover over b. F989.14; ghostly voice heard on b. E401.0.1; soldier's ghost haunts b. E334.5.

Battling. — Hero b. under lake F691.0.1; rival lovers b. T92.7; woman b. demons for husband's soul E756.5.

Baucis and Philemon Q1.1.

Bauerntochter, die kluge H561.1.

Bavarian language X652.

Bawds, see also **Prostitutes;** T452.

Bay leaves protect against witches G272.2.4.

Baying dogs in wild hunt E501.4.1.10, E501.13.4. — Hounds' b. indicates nature of quarry F679.5.2.

Bazaar, advice on going to H588.18.

Bazaars, fairy frequents F234.2.8.

Beach. — Child born on b. T581.9; mermaid is washed up on b. B81.13.2; why turtle lays eggs on b. A2433.6.1.2.

Beacon, origin of warning A1599.1.

Beads break ice jam D1549.11; cling together E761.4.8; sorted as task H1091. — Besiegers scatter b. in protecting K2367; flowers become b. D451.4.0.1; magic b. *D1071.1; man becomes b. D263.4; witch's knees b. G229.4.4.

Beak, see also **Bill.** — Bird with b. of iron B15.7.13.1; bird with fiery b. B15.7.13; crow's b. and tail alternately stick to tarred bridge Z39.3; disenchantment from bird when queen milks own milk into bird's b. D759.2; hawk hard to hold by b. H659.2.1; man with bird's b. F514.2; monster's b. as slaying proof H105.5.3; origin of bird's b. A2343; why bird's b. is colored A2343.2; why kingfisher's b. is long A2343.1.5; why starling's b. is split A2343.3.1; why woodpecker has sharp b. A2343.3.2.

Beam across door protects from witch B272.7.1; breaks at giant's glance F531.3.14. — Falling b. in cave kills travelers K1172; quest for axe which sticks in b. outside a tower H1338; strong man carries huge b. F631.6; trying to get a b. through a door crosswise in otherworld *F171.6.3; trying to stretch the b. J1964.1.

Beams of light tie sun to earth A733.4. — Beard projected over b. of hall F545.1.2; builder's throw away b. from the scaffolding J2171.3; two b. of fire shoot from devil's eyes G303.4.1.2.3.

Bean split from laughing sewed together F662.3; straw and coal F1025.1. — Hospitable fire of b. merchant sought H581.2; magic b. *D983.1; why b. has black stripes A2741.1, A2793.1.

Beans. — All b. cooked, fill room J1813.9; black b., white soup J1291.1; I boil those which come and go (b. rising and falling in water) H583.6; coins thought to be red b. J1772.3; eating b. forbidden C224.1; the meal of b. X754; origin of b. A2686.6; task: sorting b. H1091.

Bean-goose E423.3.11.

Bear abducts girl, makes her his wife B601.1.1, R13.1.6; asks boy to stay with her cubs B299.4; becomes goose D411.10; bites the seemingly dead horse's tail K1047; boasts of having eaten horses J2351.4; builds house of wood: fox of ice J741.1; could formerly lift mountain B746; thought to be dog J1753; fears man, who falls out of tree on him J17.1; fishes through ice with tail A2216.1, K1021; frightened by sneezing K2354.2; frightens off robbers K335.1.9; -god A132.5; as grandfather (bluff) K12.2; hard to hold by claws H659.2.1; heplful B435.4; husks millet for man B571.4; in human form B651.7; keeps human wife captive

in cave R45.3.1; killed from ambush K914.1; as king of animals B240.1; knows if person looks at his track K1813.0.1; learns how to catch crabs with his hairy claws J102; mistaken for log J1761.9; mistaken for man, strangled J1762.8; paramour *B611.1; plays games with heroine H1537.1; on haywagon thought to be the preacher J1762.2; put off guard by listening for hunters K832.4; put to sleep by rubbing, killed K836; riding horse lets paws fall on horse's flanks J2187; says he is boy's father, asks food B635.1.3; serves saint B256.6; sold as watch-dog K133.2; substituted for woman in box: kills villain K1674; summoned by magic D2074.1.1.3; as suitor B621.1; throws hens to the fox K1022.3; and trainer K1728; transformed to bow D421.6.1; transformed to man D313.3. — Alleged gold-dropping b. K1252.1; bird-b. B44; blood of b. venomous B776.5.5; bridling a ferocious b. (task) H1154.3.2; coward boasts of frightening b. K1953.1; creation of b. A1836; culture hero's pubic hair thought to be b. hair J1772.4; devastating b. killed B16.2.5; devil as b. G303.3.3.8; eaten meat of b. lover causes unborn son to have b. characteristics B635.1.1; enmity of b. and ant A2494.8.2; enmity of tiger and b. A2494.10.3; escape from b. takes from summer to winter X1133.2; first parents b. all children they wish A1277.2; flesh of Artemis eaten as b. V30.1.1; food of b. A2435.3.3; fool releases b. while master is away J2191; fox persuades b. to lie in hay, sets it afire K1075; frightened b. falls out of tree at cat's shriek K2324; giantess kills monstrous b. F531.3.12.3; ghost in form of b. sneezes E552; ghost of b. E522.2; godless man attacks b. as saint J1762.2.1; why b. has hump on back A2356.2.6; joke on man chased into camp by b. X584.1; why b. lives where he does A2433.3.17; lion, b., and wolf resuscitate master B515; log becomes b. D441.3.2; magic b. B182.2; magic hair of b. D1023.1; man accidentally killed by b. trying to chase away flies N333.2; man-b. B29.7; man and b. in hay-rick B855; man crawls inside b., cuts way out K952.2.1; man disguised as b. K1823.4; man, lion, and b. in pit J685.1; man sets dogs on b. who rescued him W154.25; man transformed to b. D113.2; marriage to b. B601.1; mother ape burns b. L315.4; one b. child escapes death, ancestor of all A1006.8; origin of the Great B. (Ursa Major) A771; ox-demon transformed to b. D412.2.5; why grizzly b. is peaceable A2531.2; reincarnation as b. E612.8; revenant as b. E423.2.1; robber disguised as b. K311.6.1; she-b. as false bride K1911.1.6; soul as b. E731.8; speaking b. B211.2.3; strong man kills b. F628.1.1.4; tame b. rings church bells X412; tiger, jackal, and b. each learn to fear man J17.1; troll has b. in stable G304.3.2.3; how b. lost tail A2216.1, A2378.2.4; why b. has short tail A2378.4.2; strong man son of b. who has stolen his mother F611.1.1; what the b. whispered in his ear J1488; witch in form of b. G211.2.1; witch transforms man to b. G263.1.1; woman in b. form D743; woman reveals husband's whereabouts to b. T244.1.

Bear's den A2432.6; enemies A2494.8; food C25; foster child B635.1.2; son B635.1. — Escape by dressing in b. skin K521.1.2; hare causes pursuing b. death K929.13; helper in b. skin aids escape K649.7.2; man threatens to cleave b. skull with penis K1755.1; quest for b. milk H1361.2; tricksters eat b. food K361.2; woman rescued from b. cave R111.1.13.1.

Bears devour the wicked Q415.6; as giants' dogs F531.4.11.1; as God's messengers A165.2.1.1.4. — Deceptive game: b. sway in tree K855.1; female b. have no breasts: young suck paws B725; grizzly b. A2367.2.1, A2524.1; lies about b. X1221; strong man captures b. F615.2.4; trolls afraid of b. G304.2.4.2; why b. attack men A2524.3; why b. do not have breasts A2353.4; why b. hibernate A2481.1; why b. have short, crooked legs A2371.2.4; why grizzly b. have three stripes on inside of stomach A2367.2.1.

Beard of dwarfs F451.2.3ff.; as path to heaven F57.3; shaved as punishment Q497; on she-goat does not make a male U112. — Baby killed for pulling b. S327.2; barber shaves wife's b. (lie) X1727.1; catching fish in b. F634.1; child born with b. T551.13.2; custom of wearing b. A1597; dead body incorruptible (b. and fingernails continue to grow) E182; devil's b. G303.4.1.3; devil fastened to hell's door by b. G303.17.3.2; disguise by dying b. K1821.1; disguise by shaving off b. K521.2.1; dwarf caught by b. F451.6.1; fairy-mortal baby's b. F305.3; giant with long b. F531.1.6.4; how goat got his b. A2322.4; god with red b. A125.2; god with white b. A137.18; had a good b. (only word of praise) X511; grain to grow without b. J2072.2; green b. F545.1.1.1; why hair is gray before b. H771; helper's b. and eyebrows cut N810.2; how much is king's b. worth? (riddle) H712; Jesus's long red b. V211.2.1.2.1; a long b. and sanctity J1463; magic strength of b. D1831.2; magic b. D991.1; maid given b. T321.1; man suddenly acquires long gray b. on scaffold F1044; monster's b. proves visit H105.4.1; numskull's b. cut off (does not know himself) J2012.1; ogre's b. caught fast K1111.1; origin of b. A1315.3; pulling b. as insult P672; quest for three hairs from devil's b. H1273.2; philosopher spits in king's b. J1566.1; remarkable b. F545.1; singeing b. to avoid assassination J634.1; transformation: grass to b. D451.5.4; vow to kill anyone touching b. M166.3; wife persuaded to cut hair from husband's b. K1085; witch with b. G219.2.

Beards. — Dwarfs' b. in three strands F451.2.3.1.1; first men without b. A1597.1; fur made from b. of conquered kings P672.1; lies about b. X1727; only brave may wear b. P642; youths wear false b. K1821.4.

Bearded woman F545.1.5; woman ghost laid by shaving E451.7. — Gray-b. fairy F233.10; tabu: b. man (going dirty to bed) C891.2, (abusing women or children) C867.1.0.1, (laughing when shaken) C461, (refusing combat) C835.1.1, (refusing request) G871.0.1, (sleeping at sunrise) C735.1.1; tabus for b. men C565ff.

Beardless hero Z257; man F545.1.0.1; villain K2275.
Bearer. — King will kill b. of bad tidings J1675.2.
Bearers of God's Throne A152.7.
Bearing. — Budding and b. of plant A2771ff.; dead wife b. children for husband E322.1; flower from grave b. letters E631.0.2; magic object b. person aloft *D1532ff.; miraculous blossoming and b. of fruit F971; woman transformed to animal b. animal T554.0.1.
Bearskin F821.1.3.1; creator clothed in A18.4.
Beast forced to bring back stolen child D2156.3; furnishes omens B147.1; -giant B871ff.; invokes saint's protection B251.4.1; -men B20ff.; paramour B611ff.; as suitor B621; wedding B281. — Abduction by wild b. R13.1; adventures from seeking domestic b. N774.2; beauty and the b. D735.1; domestic b. transformed to person D330ff.; exposed child carried off by wild b. S355; feeding ravenous b. to satisfaction (task) H1123; ghost of wild b. E522; guardian b. overcome by mirrors K335.1.7; killing ferocious b. H1161; man transformed to wild b. D110ff.; marriage to b. in human form B651; marriage to b. by day and man by night *B640.1; marriage to person in b. form B641; marriage of person to b. B601ff.; mother kills son thinking him a wild b. N325.3; playing game with ferocious b. H1537; separation of twins through being carried off by b. N312; wild b. transformed to person D310ff.; witch as wild b. G211.2.
Beasts and fishes exchange places: fatal to both V136.2; guard castle F771.5.1; helpful B400—B449; hostile B17.1; with magic wisdom B121ff.; in otherworld F167.1.1. — King of b. B241ff.; man given dominion over b. A1421.1; mythical b. B10ff.; passing among b. as fear test H1408.
Beast-man. — Stone becomes b. D432.1.2.
Beaten, see also **Pounded.** — Allowing self to be b. as bride test H386.1; changeling b. F321.1.4.6; husband b. by paramour K1514.4.1; importunate lover b. K1218.8; king in disguise b. by own men K1812.0.1; numskull b. J2131.1; priest b. to death J1786.4; returning husband b. by servants K1514.4; person b. (by magic club) D1401.1, (by magic whip) D1401.3, (by whips for breaking tabu) C982; Peter b. at inn K1132; lazy wife is b. by husband W111.3.4; wife b. for refusal to bring warm water T254.6.1; wild huntsman has his horse b. E501.15.2; will work when b. J1545.1; witch bound and b. G275.7.
Beating arouses sham sick man K1676; bewitched object G271.4.5; brings about recognition H182; to death as punishment Q422.0.1; the devil G303.16.19.19; gift bearers W154.20; own foot J1867.1; wife before food purchased so she will cook it right J2175.1.1; wife daily M134. — Creator b. his wife A32.3.2; creation of animals as punishment for b. forbidden drum *A1731; daily b. of transformed dogs D691; disenchantment by b. D712.5; father b. son with shoes H36.1.1; friends agree to b. wives K1394; ghost b. man with whip E261.5; ghost laid by b.

body E446.3.1; husband b. wife in paramour's place K1569.4; incognito prince, receives b. for his courtesy and realizes his folly J18; resuscitation by b. *E11; the soldier receives a b. promised the boy K187; thanks long-dreaded b. is over J2568; thunder-spirit b. his children A1142.5.1.2; torture by b. S186; wife b. husband daily T251.8; wisdom acquired from b. J18.

Beatings. — Daily b. as punishment Q458.1.

Beatrice, Sister K1841.1.

Beatus prayer for condemned souls V51.4.

Beautification by magic *D1860ff., *D1337. — Miraculous b. upon conversion to Christianity V331.3.

Beautiful fairy woman exhibits self F397; giantess F531.1.0.1.1; goddess A125.4; mantle F821.4; land of dead *E481.4; princess's look kills F574.1.3; wife as enemy J2462.3; witch G229.5; woman in disguise K1821.7; woman married to hideous man T268. — Death from sight of b. woman F1041.1.6; disguised flayer tightens skin to look b. K1941.1; fairy as b. woman F234.2.5; fairy-mortal child b. F305.2; fairies give b. clothes F343.5; flame indicates presence of b. woman F1061.1; fool wins b. woman L161.2; heroine in menial disguise discovered in her b. clothes H151.6; hideous person magically makes self seem b. D2031.4; hideous youth becomes b. D682.4.2; madness from seeing b. woman *F1041.8.1; magic object makes b. *D1337ff.; mermaid half-b., half-monstrous B81.9.3; ogre eats b. girl G13.2; otherworld people ever young, ever b. F167.9; ogress bathing in pool becomes b. G264.0.1; planting b. garden H1199.1; quest for the most b. bouquet H1302; quest for the most b. of women H1301; quest for b. girl H1214.1; quest for most b. ring H1319.3; rakshasa in form of b. wench G369.1.5; serpent's b. wife J155.1.1; trickster exacts b. wife from curious K443.6.1; useful preferred to b. J242, J245; visitors to island become b. F129.4.3; what is most b.? (riddle) H641; which most b.? luck or ill-luck? N141.3; wooing the strong and b. bride T58.

Beauty and the beast D735.1; contest H1596.1, (between goddesses) A163, (between peacock and crane) J242.5, (between swallows and crows) J242.6; contest dependent on first greeter K176.1; contest won by deception K98; doctor K1013, J1062.1; of giant F531.1.0.1; of various peoples A1664. — Animal tamed by maiden's b. B771.1; apparent b. of least importance J264; cause of animal's b. A2401; fainting from seeing a b. T24.2.3; fairy queen's b. temporarily destroyed by intercourse with mortal F304.2; geese tell of b. of their mistress and bring about recognition H151.12; goodness preferred to b. J244; god of b. A462; choice: loss of b. or speech J213; hero's irresistible b. spot A526.3; hero spared for his b. F1088.1; magic object gives b. D1337ff.; prophecy: b. for girl M312.4; remarkable b. F575; seduction by sham b. test K1339.4; sinful b. converted V229.12; sleeping b. D1960.3; waiting many years to see a b. T24.7; wife granted b. wish, elopes J2075.4;

woman's b. lights up the dark F574.1; woman's b. reported to king causes quest T11.1.1.

Beaver borrows muskrat's tail and never gives it back A2241.10; and muskrat exchange tails A2247.6; and porcupine trick each other K896.1; sacrifices scrotum to save life *J351.1. — Color of b. A2411.1.4.2; dwelling of b. A2432.3; why b. lives along rivers A2433.3.12; where b. got tail A2378.1.6; why b. has flat tail A2378.7.1; why b. splashes his tail in water and dives when attacked A2462.2.

Becalmed. — Witch aids b. boat G283.1.2.2.

Bed changes size D631.3.7, D1620.3.2; fatal to all his ancestors J1474; heating in hell for certain person Q561.1; of totem-tree tabu C848. — Advice from woman in b. T453; beggar buys right to sleep before girl's door, at foot of b., in b. K1361; bride and groom conducted to b. T137.2; capture in trap b. K735.4; cuckold husband hides under b. K1514.4.2.1; death cheated by moving b. *K557; death at head or foot of b. forecasts progress of sickness D1825.3.1; disenchantment by admission to woman's b. D734, D759.7, K1361.1; disguised man takes wife's place in b. K521.4.1.4; "don't sit on b. without touching it first" J21.34.2; dupe sleeps on "king's b.": falls into well K1078; dwarfs plan to dig underground b. for Rhine F451.5.22; entrance into girl's b. by trick *K1340ff.; equal share of chief's b. J2526; extraordinary b. F787, F846; friar's trousers on adulteress's b. K1526; ghost in b. with living E472; ghost leaves body mark on b. E568.1; giant's enormous b. F531.4.10; girl takes impostor's place in marriage b. K1611.3; goddess's b. of snakes A155.6; going to b. with Odin (task) H1199.11; going to b. for sorrow F1041.9.1; guest forces host into his b: host killed K1611.2; guest keeps calling for more b. clothes J1563.1; gullible husband under the b. K1532; Judith kills Holofernes in b. K872; king buys spendthrift's b. J1081.1; knife in b. as protection against witches G272.3; knife left in innocent person's b. K2155.1.1; learning a trade in b. W111.5.9; leper laid in queen's b. K2112.2; literal penance: not to lie in b. (sleeps on eider down) J1161.5; lover's gift regained on refusal to leave b. K1581.8; lovers in b. only kissing H1556.4.1; magic causes b. wetting D1379.4; magic b. *D1154.1; magic b. and pillows as chastity test H411.10; magic restlessness in b. D2063.2; maidservant given to lover's companion as b. partner T484; make the b. but do not make it (task) H1068; man carried off on b. escapes R219.1; man pinned in b. by weapon caught in quilt N386.2; man will not move in b. when water drops in his eyes W111.1.3; murderer strangles companion in b. K951.0.2; ogress killed in bridal b. G519.1.3; old maid in b. X752; owner tells thieves to come back later, not yet in b. J1392.2.1; paramour hidden in b. K1521.4; Procrustes makes men fit his b. G313; recognition by describing unique b. H16.4; robber stabs at clothes in b., misses victim K437.1; sham figures of wife, paramour in b. K525.1.1; servant lays skin of dead dog in the b. of

his mistress and master K2134; sleeping on feather b. tabu C735.2.7; sleeping in saint's b. forbidden C93.1; stealing sheet from b. under person (task) H1151.3; substituted object left in b. K525.1; substitutes in b. (forgotten wife for false bride) D1978.4, D2006.1.4, (goat for disgusted wife) K1223.1, (old woman for girl) K1317.2.1, (strong servant for husband of strong bride) K1844.1, (wife for mistress) K1843.2; talking b. reveals king's identity N617; to whom princess turns in b. H315; vow not to go to b. with wife until enemy killed M152; hero wakened from magic sleep by wife who has purchased place in his b. from false bride *D1978.4; wraith goes to b. at home, real body away E723.4.1.

Beds exchanged with ogre's children K1611; in otherworld F166.8. — Glowing b. of dead E487; object set between b. of couple T353; trickster exchanges b., gets food K499.8.

Bed-legs. — Magic b. *D1154.1.1; speaking b. overheard N454.1.

Bed-ticks H1129.2, H1129.7.

Bedbug. — Reincarnation as b. E616.5; terrapin from b. eggs J1772.1.1; why b. is flat A2305.2; woman reborn as b. to annoy husband E693.2.

Bedbugs, lies about X1291.

Bedclothes. — Ghost pulls b. from sleeper E279.3; spirits pull off person's b. F470.1.

Bedcover of chastity T351.1; stolen J2672. — Ear used as b. F542.2.

Bedding. — Feast of "b. and handspreading" T162; prince feels hair on b. F647.9.1.

Bedside. — Death at b. of dying sweetheart T81.1.

Bedstead warns of danger of snake D1317.11. — Legs of b. talk D1610.17.1; magic b. legs kill dangerous animals D1402.17; magic b. protects D1380.12; magic transportation on flying b. D1520.17.1.

Bee fetches balm from heaven to restore hero's speech B514.2; as God's spy A33.3.1; helpful B481.3; as matchmaker B582.2.4; as messenger from heaven to earth B291.4.1; rests on water lily which closes over it at night and kills it J2137.3; sting damages king's son; swarm destroyed J1179.14; transformed to person D382.1; vitalizes tiger D1594.3; as witch's familiar G225.1: — Charm calls down b. swarm D1441.2; creation of b. A2012; dungbeetle thought to be b. J1751; great b. (lie) X1282.1; the hunt for the lost b. (lie) X1861; marriage to b. in human form B653.1; origin of color of b. A2411.3.1; Pleiades as b. swarm A773.6; recognition of disguised princess by b. lighting on her H162; reincarnation as b. E616.1; sleeper's soul leaves body as b. E721.1.2.4; speaking b. B211.4.2; why b. is sacred A2541.1; separable soul in b. E715.3.1; soul in form of b. E734.2; man transformed to b. D182.1; victim asked to catch b. nest: gets clubbed K815.19; Wash B. Day J1743.3; why b. is blind A2332.6.9; witch as b. G211.5.2.

Bee's. — Dupe strikes b. nest: bitten K1023.5; fools see b. nest reflected in water: try to carry off the well J1791.9; man escapes from b. nest

on bear's tail X1133.4; shape of b. body A2300.1; why b. sting not fatal to man A2346.2.

Bees born from carcass of ox B713.1; and bugs can't eat same food J1565.2; build church of wax to contain consecrated host B259.4; caught in sack which is opened at home J2131.2.1; drop honey into woman's mouth F561.6; feed infants B531.1; leave honey on infant's lips B147.3.1.2; mistaken for Jutlanders J1762.5; in otherworld F167.1.3.1; sting honey-thieves Q597.3; thrown into redoubt drive out enemies K2351.2. — Charm calls down swarm of b. D1441.2; creation of honey-b.: transformed man A2012.0.1; first b. in Ireland A2012.2; garden with golden, silver b. F818.1; god sends stinging b. to punish men A2012.3; helpful b. sting opposing army B524.2.1; honey as excrement of b. A2385.3; king of b. B246.3; lies about b. X1282; riddle about b. and honey in lion's carcass H804; saint sends b. against enemy B524.2.1.1; sound of swarming b. disguised as children's singing K1023.4; why b. eat their own children A2435.5.1.1; why b. die after they sting A2346.1, A2232.2; why b. may not get honey from red clover A2435.5.1, A2231.3.2.

Bee-hive changes to wasps (sham miracle) K1975.1; hoax K1023; in troublemaker's bed K2138. — Consecrated host put into b. C55.3; honey from royal b. H1332.7; thief in b. K335.1.6.3; who gets the b. J1451; witch rides on b. G241.4.4.

Beef. — Task: furnish b. neither male nor female H1074.

Beer becomes wine D477.3; brewed in egg-shell F451.5.17.1; foams (life token) E761.6.4; let run in cellar J2176; magically kept from brewing *D2084.1; returned for bread, neither paid for K233.4. — Drinking b. without touching pot H1046.3; leek in b. poison protection D1383.5; magic b. *D1045; sign of cross protects b. D1766.6.4; stingy innkeeper cured of serving weak b. J1341.7; well of b. D925.0.2.

Beetle as creator A13.3.2; created A2021; cursed for betraying Holy Family: now has eyes always on ground A2231.7.1.1. — Enmity between hen, b., and duck A2494.13.10.2; hum of b. A2426.3.1, A2231.11; over-hasty b. X1862; sacredness of b. A2021.1; soul as b. E734.6; why b. creeps on ground A2441.3.1; A2232.3; witch as b. G211.5.3; witch recognized by seeing b. enter mouth while asleep *G251.1.

Beetles mistaken for food, eaten J1761.7; in wounds as false remedy K1016. — Why b. live in manure A2433.5.4.

Before. — Dwarfs in land 1000 years b. mortals F451.1.4; escaping b. enemy can strike J641; foolish demands b. death J2174; make peace b. rather than after war J156.1; people in otherworld hitch horses both b. and behind wagon F171.6.4; prophecy: death b. certain age M341.1.3; eating b. certain time forbidden C231; doing things b. certain time forbidden C756; three blasts on horn b. sunrise to rescue prisoner from mound R112.1; wine wished b., during, and after meal J1343.2; witch powerless when person speaks b. she does G273.2.

Befouling. — Maidens b. selves to escape rape T327.4.

Begetting by earbox J1919.7. — Disguised queen b. child with husband K1812.8.3; fairy b. son with human queen K1844.4; pseudo-magic charm for b. child K115.1.4; guest b. child with host's daughter P32.5.1.

Beggar asks goldsmith for goldplate J1338; with small bag surpasses the one with the large L251; buys right to sleep before the girl's door K1361; claims to be emperor's brother J1337; on cross in place of Christ L435.4; in disguise spits at queen Q471.2; disguised as gentleman *K455.3; gets little no matter how long he begs N264; refused hospitality escapes from fire N177; frightens lawyer into giving by telling him of lawyers in hell X312; with horse, wife, or dog considered rich by poorer beggar U65; laid in queen's bed K2112.2; overlooks money N351.2; refused payment for standing in tank all night K231.14; returns to his mother child stolen by fairies F321.4; rewarded for poem P163; served coals for food K492.1; transforms wedding party into wolves T155; treacherous K2291; ubiquitous K1982. — Ascetic's life as b. V462.9; Christ disguised as b. V211.2.1.2; defeated king as b. L410.4; devil as b. G303.3.1.23; father-in-law disguised as b. *K1817.1, H384.1; enigmas concerning b. H594; forgotten wife recalled as she gives b. food D2006.1.10; help from b. N826, N 825.3.1; infertile rajah marries b. T121.8.1; king becomes b. L419.2; magician as b. frees prisoners D2031.4.3; poverty as diseased b. Z133.1; princess sent to b. in trunk N712.1; persistent b. invited upstairs J1331; protean b. D611; reward for sharing food with b. Q42.1.2; saint gives little to b. J225.6; "save it for the b." C490.1.1; seduction by posing as b. K1315.10; suitor as b. tests bride H384.1.1; sultan as b. tests friends H1558.7.1; thief disguised as b. K311.17; wife substitutes calf for b. husband abuses K1846; witch poses as b. K764.

Beggar's curse M411.2; ghost laid by pig E451.6. — Blind b. money stolen from stick K333.4; burning b. clothes yields gold K245; confederate in b. disguise aids escape K649.7.1; dead b. stick will not stay until back in b. service D1651.5; treasure in b. hat N524; man as b. bride K1911.4.

Beggars P160ff. — Ghost laid by giving b. money E451.5.1; gods disguised as b. K1811.1; jokes on b. X530ff.; newly rich enjoy giving to b. U130.1; repartee concerning b. J1330ff.; trickster gets coins from blind b. K1081.1.1.

Beggaring. — Man b. self by charity V432.

Begging ghost E599.4; man to scratch witch's back *G269.1; before stone statues H1553.1; from wife's new husband L432; from wife's suitors K1568. — Ascetics b. from own mother N735.1; dead b. food E541.5; origin of b. A1599.15; relative b. from one he's formerly abused L432; vow to answer b. M172.1.

Beginning formulas Z10.1; of social relationships A1470ff. — Date

with b. like its end, its top like its bottom (1691) H707.1; warrior b. combat may desist P557.4.2.

Begun. — Thing b. must be kept up all day J2073.1.

Beheaded criminal calls "Ave" V254.7.1; man carries his head under arm F511.0.4; man swims F1041.14; man's head laid at feet to prevent return E431.7; man's head replaced crooked F511.0.6; sailor swims F1041.14.1; simpleton's head replaced backwards J27. — Ass b. J1169.4; drunken man thinks he is b. J2311.10; eyes of b. person gouged out S165.1; head of b. witch mends if rubbed with salt G223; king b. in bed by wife K873.1; man to be b. for watching fight J21.51; man asks to be b. in water tank, ducks K558.2; witch b. G275.7.1.

Beheading, see also **Decapitation;** bargain M221; for breaking tabu C929.3; giant to escape prison R211.8; giants one by one K912; as punishment Q421; witch as task H1191.1. — Chief b. sentinel who does not recognize him F1041.16.9; murder by b. S133; St. Cecilia lives after b. D1840.1.3.

Behemoth: mythical gigantic animal B18. — Animals changed through fear of B. A2294; angels battle B. A1082.7.

Behind me night and before me day (formula for girl fleeing) R255. — Bought b. the village J1169.2; cooking what is b. you J2485; the devil creates devils by casting water b. himself G303.1.4.1; murder from b. K959.4; people in otherworld hitch horses both before and b. wagon F171.6.4.

Beholding woman fatal G264.1. — Man b. angels V230.1.

Bel surrounded by the priests like king and nobles (riddle) H825.

Belches. — Lakes originate from b. A920.1.5.1, D921.2.

Belching. — Sham magician b. fire K1963.4.

Belfagor T251.1.1.

Belfruit. — Woman becomes b. D211.3.

Belief in approach of husband secures confession from adulteress *K1572; in Christianity tested H1573.1; in own greatness induced in pupil by magician as test of gratitude H1565.1. — Erroneous b. as to own identity J2013; never believe what is beyond b. J21.13; prophet never secures b. M301.0.1.

Beliefs, religious V300ff.

Believing. — Father kills self b. that son is dead N344; liar b. own lie X902; lover kills self b. mistress dead N 343; two persons b. each other deaf X111.3.

Bell breaks and priest's patron whistles at mass X442; on magic dog dispells grief D1359.3.1.3; rings to indicate location of well D1314.4.1; to be rung when child is born T583.3; sounds at saint's approach V222.6; from underwater monastery F725.6. — Angel brings b. as drinking utensil for child T611.7; animals ring b. and demand justice B271.3; cow wears church b. X1235.1.1; dead hear saint's b. E545.14; devil exorcised with b. G303.16.14.4; disenchantment by ringing b. D789.10;

fox rings the b. K1114; ghost laid by burying church b., clapper separately E459.6; ghostly b. E533; hiding from ghosts under church b. E434.1; homage to saint's b. C94.8; little b. says "he's here" J1812.3; magic coin fills b. with money D1452.5; magic b. *D1213; magic healing b. D1500.1; mother ties b. on child, cat cuts it off, etc. Z39.6; raising sunken church b. C401.4; ringing b. tabu C756.0.1; ringing b. to announce chess win: fire alarm disregarded J2199.1; ringing of church b. causes devil to lose his power G303.16.12; ringing church b. as fear test H1412.1; ringing of church b. by nun tabu C94.7; saint transfers disease to his b. D2161.4.2.2; saint's b. heard, never found K1887.3.1; spring from water in saint's b. F933.1.1; stolen b. refuses to sound D1602.8.1; sunken b. sounds *F993; supernatural wife summoned by b. T111.0.2; swearing by saint's b. M116.2; tabu: looking under certain b. too soon C326; tree grows through saint's b. F979.6; water poured from saint's b. produces fountain D1567.3.

Bells hung at every corner of ship P651.1; on horse's mane P651.2; ring at saint's birth F960.1.4; rung backward as alarm P651.3. — Church b. *V115ff.; dress of gold, silver, and diamond b. F821.3; dwarfs dislike church b. *F451.5.9.3; enemies flee as church b. ring D1400.1.9.1; origin of church b. A1466; saints curse by ringing b. M411.8.1; saints exchange b. P311.7.1; tame bear rings church b. X412; wild hunt heralded by ringing of b. E501.13.1.4.

Bell-ringing the sweetest sound H635.1.

Bellerophon H918.

Belling the cat J671.1.

Bellowing of bull heard over entire land B741.4; of cow defeats army B741.3.

Bellows. — Bagpipe is devil's b. G303.10.14; beast with human head, shape of smith's b. B96; origin of b. A1447.1; strong man carries b. F624.10.

Belly, see also **Stomach;** and the members J461.1, A1391. — Animal with men in its b. playing cards F911.3.3; animals hide boy in their b. B529.1; man builds boat and sails about in giant's b. F911.5.1; escape under ram's b. *K603; flood from b. A1013; fool thinks b. is speaking to him: stabs himself J1817; needle in elk's b. L391; origin and nature of animal's b. A2354ff.; ogre kills self when he sees crumbs lying on his b. G523; ogres who have no b. G366.1; person with enormous b. F529.6; rescue from swallower's b. F913; thumbling in animal's b. persuades latter to go to his father's house K565; true bride lives in b. of fish K1911.2.2.1; wee cock: "Get into my b." K547.1; why salmon has purple b. A2412.4.2.1; why women have marks on b. A1310.4.

Bellies. — Landlords have biggest b. J1289.17.

Beloved. — Man scorned by his b. T75; quest for unknown b. H1381.2.1.1; what is the most b. (riddle) H647ff.

Below. — Confinement b. earth M372.1; creator from b. A25; emergence

of gods from b. A115.5; girl seduced b. ground K1344.1; vehicle travels above and b. ground *D1533.2ff.

Belt transformed to bridge D454.3.3. — Child unwittingly promised: "What your wife has under her b." S242.1; fairy has b. F236.3; fairy's magic destroying b. F302.5.5; giant with gigantic chain as b. F531.4.2; magic b. *D1057, K525.8.1; power of dwarf in his b. F451.3.1; stealing b. from queen (task) H1151.5; tightening b. to counteract hunger F1076; wild huntsman has b. E501.8.5.

Beltane festival A1535.5, V70.1.1.

Benares. — Penance until spires of B. reduced, rebuilt Q521.7; pilgrimage to B. V533.

Bench, see also **Chair, Seat;** to which person sticks D1413.5. — Bride b. T136.4.1; magic b. *D1151.1.

Bender of pines G314. — Remarkable b. X947.

Bending bow as test D1651.1, H31.2, H331.4.2; the tree K1112. — Bird escapes hunter b. his bow J641.1; reeds b. before wind save themselves J832; stake miraculously b. F1093; tree b. to certain person D1648.1.

Benediction. — Merman's wife not to stay till church b. *C713.1; punishment for not giving b. Q223.13.2.

Benefactor falsely accused of theft W154.13. — Reincarnated b. helped E601.2.

Benevolence of witches G220.0.1. — Devil's b. to impious people G303.22.5; fairies give avaricious man gift of b. F343.4.

Bent. — Why buffalo's horns are b. A2236.3.4; murder by springing b. tree S135, H1522.1; return from lower world by being slung by b. tree F101.2.

Beowulf fights dragon B11.11; found in boat L111.2.1.

Bequeathing of animal characteristics to man B592; of helpful animal to hero B312.3; soul to devil M211.3. — Father b. four symbolic pots to sons J99.2.

Berry picker identified by scent F652.1. — Blowing on b. disenchants D778.1; conception from eating b. T511.1.2; magic b. D981.10; magic tree from b. D951.1.

Berries. — Bringing b. in winter H1023.3; hero returning with b. sent back for tree H1241.1.1; magic b. cause horns to grow on person D1375.1.1.10; man too lazy to pick b. W111.1.6; origin of b. A2687.3; quest for b. from tree guarded by giants H1333.3.3; why wren eats no b. A2435.4.11.1.

Berserk F610.3. — Curse by b. giant M411.10.

Berserks banished after defeat Q431.14.

Bertha F475.1.

Besieged city set afire by birds K2351.1; women's dearest possession J1545.4.1. — Enemy chief vows to marry b. city's princess M146.7; enemy induced to give up b. city K2365.

Besiegers crushed by treasure cast on them K2353.

Besieging. — Only one way of b. city Z316.
Besom. — Extraordinary b. (broom) F857.
Best. — Each likes his own children b. T681; "it is for the b." W25.2; quest for b. cap H1319.2; quest for b. meat H1305.1; truth the b. policy J751.1; what are b. and worst stones? (riddle) H659.3; what is b.? (riddle) H648ff.; what do you like b. J171.2.2.
Bestiality T465; punished Q253.1.
Bestowed. — Gifts b. on living by ghosts E373; immortality b. D1851.
Bestriding. — Giant b. mountain F531.3.5.1; giant goddess b. entire land A133.2.
Betel. — Extortion of b. leaf addict W193.1; origin of b. A2691.5.
Betel-nut grows on person as punishment Q551.1.1; as weapon F839.6. — Magic b. D985.5, D1524.11.
Bethlehem. — Star of B. D1314.13.1.
Betrayal of brothers' hiding-place by fool J2668; of clandestine visit of princess to hero by token H81.2; of devil by his goat hoofs G303.4.5.4.1; by dwarfs F451.6.11; of each other by thieves K307; of fox by peasant's pointing K2315; of fugitive by magic objects *D1612ff.; of hero by extraordinary companions F601.3; of husband to father-in-law K2213.7; of husband's secret by his wife K2213.2ff.; into ogre's power G410ff.; of parents' misdeeds by children J125; of person's rank by habitual conversation H38ff.; of secret by magic speaking reed *D1316.5; of self by fugitive compelled by magic object D1612.2; of self to enemies by talkative animal J2351; of thief by clever animal K427; of thief by breaking of stick with money in it H251.3.4.
Betraying. — Animal cursed for b. holy fugitive A2231.7.1; captain not b. king's secret P361.7; changeling deceived into b. his age F321.1.1; child b. own illegitimacy T644; lover b. woman K2232.1; mortal b. dwarfs' secrets F451.5.1.6.1; plant cursed for b. holy fugitive A2721.4.
Betrothal, see also **Engagement;** of children T69.2; of young man to statue T376. — Punishment for breaking b. Q252, Q416.0.1.
Betrothed, see also **Fiancée.** — Hero returns rescued princess to her b. R111.4.
Better things at home K1952.2. — Let me catch you b. game K553.1; maid behind statue of Virgin advises the mistress to give servants b. food K1971.3.1; making b. from good (hedging field) H583.2.3.
Betting, see also **Gambling;** contest between two kings N1.3. — Advice against b. J21.8.1.
Between two thieves (dying like Christ) X313. — Boy sleeps b. couple to safeguard virtue T352; cross b. shoulders as sign of royalty H71.5; magic sight by looking b. dog's ears D1821.3.4; path b. monsters (Scylla and Charybdis) G333; pig carrying scissors, comb, and razors b. ears H1154.1.
Bewailing a calamity that has not occurred J2198. — Weeping man turned into owl: still b. A2261.5.

Beware of following an interested adviser J758; of man (precept of the lion to his sons) J22.1.

Bewitched fairies F254.3; objects G265.8. — Cows b. by dwarfs to give no milk *F451.3.3.5; people b. by dwarfs F451.3.3.5.1; witch burned by burning b. animal G275.3.1.

Bewitcher. — Killing queen's b. H346.1.

Bewitching, see also **Witches;** *D2070ff.

Bhuiya yoke cow and bullock together A1689.1.

Bible V136; exorcises witch G271.2.5; nullifies fairy power F382.4; texts as magic spells D1273.3; under doorstep detects thieves D1817.0.1.5. — Devil cheated of his victim by boy having a b. under his arm K218.2; devil unable to read b., loses bargain K211.1; ghost laid by b. E443.8; gold in b. H261; reading b. backwards reveals witch G275.2; riddles based on the b. or legend H810ff.; weighing witch against b. H234.

Biblical figure as magician K1711.1; heroes as wise men J191.2; worthy as giant F531.0.1; worthy as prophet M301.7. — Levity about b. passages J1262.4.

Bier. — Enchanted person on b. D5.2; physician forced to carry patient's b. P424.3.1; remarkable b. F788; thieves carry abducted woman on b. K419.8.

Bifrost F152.

Big, see also **Great, Large;** ears F542.2; trees' small fruit A2771.9. — Choice: b. piece of cake with my curse or small piece with my blessing J229.3; frog tries in vain to be b. as ox J955.1; giant with eyes as b. as cauldrons F531.1.1.2.1.

Bigger. — Magic animal grows b. B195; thief hoping for b. booty, loses smaller K421.1.

Bija. — Why b. tree often struck by lightning A2791.12.

Bill (bird's beak), see also **Beak.** — Crane will not weep at crucifixion: must suffer thirst in August and break b. A2231.2.1; crossbill's b. from aiding Christ at crucifixion A2221.2.4.2; crow must wash his b. in order to eat with other birds Z41.2; disenchantment from bird by cutting off b. D711.3; the hawk frightened at the snipe's b. J2616; hornbill borrows tomtit's b. A2241.9.

Bill (reckoning) of sale written on sandal F1015.3. — The other man to pay the b. K455.4; b.-paying hat sold K111.2.

Billygoats. — Three B. Gruff K553.2.

Bilskilnir. — Five hundred forty rooms in B. F781.2.1.

Bin. — Filling grain-b. through bottom hole H1023.2.3.

Binding, see also **Bound;** by magic *D1411ff., D2072ff.; together sand and string Q512.2; waves of the sea (task) H1137. — Fairies b. man to ground F361.2.3; man b., marrying fairy F302.4.4; transformation by b. with string around neck D585; vow: not b. hair till enemy is conquered M122; witch's hair has power of b. G221.1.1.

Bindweed, origin of A2655.

Birch. — Disguise in b. bark K1821.9.1; magic b. tree D950.12; magic b. twig D953.2; origin of b. trees A2681.4; revenant with hat of b. E422.4.1; why b. is cursed A2776.1; why b. has white bark A2751.4.1.

Bird advises man to treat his lazy children as she does her young Z24.1.2; avenges caged mate Z52; -bear B44; betrays hiding-place of the Virgin B131.6; boasts of capturing the rabbit J2173.3; brings flower F982.4; call enables trickster to escape K648; calls as evil omen D1812.5.1.12.2; cares for blinded master B536.1; carries food from deserted child to starving parents S361; carries a grain of sand from a mountain, etc. (measure of eternity) H701.1; carries off magic horn D861.7.1; carries off magic ring D865.1; carries man across water B551.2; carries person to upper world *F62.1; carries off persons R13.3; carries off ring (lovers become separated) N352; catches fishes by imitating friend K756.3; with changing color B731.13; characteristics from flying contests A2254; as child's nurse; has new clothes made: flies away without paying K233.1; coloring as reward for obedience to deity A2221.6.1; controls off-springs' sex, appearance F987.1; council assigns coats to different birds B238.2; council assigns place and work to all B238.1; as creator A13.2; as creator's companion A33.2; as culture hero A522.2; deity A132.6; determines road to be taken B151.2; as devil's messenger G303.10.17; as domestic servant B292.2.2; feathers sink as hero dies E761.7.7; without feathers on tree without leaves (riddle) H764; feeds young to threatening fox K1788; with fiery beak B15.7.13; flies into large animal's ear and kills him L315.1; flies with man to safety B542.1; as god's ancestor A111.3.3; with gold head, silver wings B15.7.3, B101.1; grateful for being saved from serpent B364.4; grateful for release B375.3; grateful for rescue of its young B365.0.1; as guardian of primordial fire A1414.6; in the hand J321.1; has red spot on tail as reward for moving woman's organ A2229.6; heals man B511.5; helper on quest H1233.6.2; calls out the hours F989.3; of ill-omen B147.2.2; indicates election of king H171.2; indifferent to pain Z49.3; having injured man avoids reconciliation J15; with iron beak B15.7.13.1; kills snake attacking master's family B524.1.6; language B215.1; as magician B191.6; as messenger B291.1; gives milk B735; must bring orphan to king H901.0.2; nests on top of one in morning, of another in evening (riddle) H725.1; as ogre G353; overcareful about food killed by eagle J2183.3; overpowered by stepping on his shadow D2072.0.4; from paradise B39.1; paramour B614; pecks hole in sky-roof F56.2; plays timpan B297.1.1; pleads with bow for life F836.5; plucks another bird's feathers out K2382.1; prevents mother from killing babe B524.4; of prey catching quarry a good omen D1812.5.2.4; protruding from king's stomach J1842.3; puffs up until it dies J955.1.2; punished by being thrown into air K581.4; as reincarnated girl resumes original form E696.1; rejuvenates person B594.1; rescues man from sea B541.3; rests on person's shoulders B575.2; running before sun bears golden letters

B7.3; as sacrifice V12.4.11; scouts sent out from ark A1021.2; sent daily to tell of hero's condition (life token) E761.7.6; as shadow of god A195.3; gives shelter with wings B538.1; shows way by singing B151.2.0.3; with silver wings B101.1.1; sold as messenger K131.2; steals island B172.11; stepmother feeds young thorns S31.3; substituted for stone in throwing contest K18.3; as suitor B623ff.; without tail K402.2; with tail of fire B15.7.14; tears out feathers in grief F1041.21.6.2; sheds tears B736.1; tears restore sight D1505.5.1; thinks he must support sky J2273.1; trained to cling to trapped paramour K1574.1; transformed to animal D413; transformed to person D350ff.; is transformed youngest brother N733.4; of truth B131; shows way by dropping feathers every seven steps *B151.2.0.1; warns against adultery, killed J551.1.1; wedding B282ff.; whistling leads searcher B157.1; with magic wisdom B122ff. — Adventures from pursuing b. N792, N774; alleged oracular b. skin sold K114.2; angel in shape of b. V231.1; animal criticized by b.: nest destroyed B275.4; aquatic b. carries man across water B551.2; origin and nature of b. beak A2343ff.; book-satchel becomes b. D444.5; breath of b. withers B777; building a lodge of b. feathers in one night (task) H1104.1; cannibal b. as ogre G355; capture by hiding in artificial b. K754.3; capturing b. H1154.7; captured b. bargains for freedom M244.2; child follows b. and loses its mother N313; clever b. J1118; color of b. A2411.2ff.; conception from eating b. T511.5.4; counting feathers in b. (task) H1118; cow sold to b. J1852.1; origin of b. crests A2321ff.; cries of b. *A2426.2ff.; dead father returns as b. E327.5; daughter promised to monster as bride to secure b. she has asked for S228; dead wife returns in form of b. E322.4; deaf man with b. in tree X111.8; destructive b. killed, barn found full of gold B103.7.1; devil as b. G303.3.3.3ff.; disenchantment from b. (when queen milks own milk into bird's beak) D759.2, (by cutting off bill) D711.3; disguise as b. tender K1816.5.1; drink this wine which a b. took to nest (riddle) H806; magic b. dung D1026.1; dupe strikes at b. on child's head and kills child K946; dwarf with b. feet F451.2.2.2; nature of b. eggs A2391ff.; enmity between b. and lizard: latter muddies water A2494.16.4; magic b. entrails D1015.3.1; escape from lower world on b. F101.6.1; evil eye sets b. on fire D2061.2.1.1; red eye of b. cooks meat F989.2; fairy as b. *F234.1.15; fairies with b. feet *F231.2.1; man can transplant feather from one b. to another F668.3; origin of b. feathers *A2313ff.; forgotten fiancée remembered by b. D2006.1.7; fox persuades b. to show him how she acts in a storm K827.1; friendship between b. and crab A2493.27; ghost of b. E524; girl as b. visits lover D641.1.1; god rides b. A136.1.4; goldmaking b. B103.1.5; golden b. B102.1ff.; golden b. stolen from fairies F359.2; hearing b. cry good omen D1812.5.2.5; hills from flopping of primeval b. A961.1; identification by feather taken from hero transformed to b. H78.2; identification by hair dropped by b. H75.2; immortal b. B37; jealous husband kills b. which wife falsely says she has been listening to Q587; magic

jewel carried off by b. D865; killing murderous b. H1161.1; king refuses to quarrel with b. J411.9.1; lazy woman sees how b. pecks hole in stone J1011; little b. as large bird's mate J1293.1; magic b. liver D859.4.2, D1015.4.1; lover as b. visits mistress D641.1; magic b. *B172ff.; magic b. head D1011.0.1, (produces treasure) B113.2; magic b. heart D859.4.1, *D1015.1.1; magic b. nest *D1292; magic horn carried off by b. D861.7.1; magic leaves turn white b. black D1337.2.1; magic object pointed out by b. D849.2; making many kinds of food from one small b. (task) H1022.6; man transformed to b. D150ff., G263.1.5; man waits for b. shot eight days ago F638.3; mankind from featherless b. sent from sky A1231.1; marksman shoots b. through eye F661.5.2; marriage to b. B601, (in human form) B652; marriage to person in b. form B642; mother b. searches for root entangling young D839.1; mouse, b., and sausage keep house together J512.7; murder discovered through knowledge of b. languages N271.4; the oldest b. A1904; one b. escapes as hunter bends his bow: other remains and is shot J641.1; prediction by b. that girl will have dead husband M353; princess catches rajah's golden b. N713.1; procuring b. out of season H1024.6; prophecy: b. to become king M369.4.1; prophetic b. B143ff.; pursuit of b. leads to ogre's house G402.1; quest for b. of truth H1331.1.1; quest for lost b. H1386.3; quest for marvelous b. H1331.1, (caused by sight of one of its feathers) H1213; quest for princess caused by sight of one of her hairs dropped by b. H1213.1; reincarnation as b. *E613ff.; reincarnation: boy to b. to boy E610.1.1; resuscitation by b. flying over dead E79.1.1; revenant as b. E423.3ff.; secret overheard by masking as b. G661.2; separable soul in b. E715.1; hero sewed up in animal hide so as to be carried to height by b. K1861.1; shepherd transformed to b. still calls sheep *A2261.1; sick queen under red satin carried off by b. N335.2.1; sky measured by b. A702.6; soul in form of b. E732ff.; soul leaves body as b. E722.1.4; speaking b. B211.3, (tells where treasure is buried) N537; speech magically recovered when certain b. is caught D2025.2; stealing eggs from under b. H1151.12; storm because of b. singing D2141.0.6; tabu to eat b. C221.1.2; tabu to kill sacred b. C92.1.6; tame b. and wild b. L451.1; tardy b. alone succeeds at b. convention L147.1; tears on sight of b. H14.1; theft of fire by b. A1415.2.1; thieving b. K366.2; fool thinks b. reflected in water is gold J1791.10; three teachings of b. *K604; three-headed b. B15.1.2.2.1; transformation to b. C962.2; treasure carried by b. to nest N527; treasure-producing b. killed B192.3; treasure-producing parts of b. B113ff.; twelve-legged b. B15.6.3.3.2; voices from eggs plot against b. mother J646.2; water b. takes dupe to sea K1042; well throws up b. bones F933.8; wind a b. dwelling in mountain-hole A1122.2; witch as domestic b. G211.3; witch as wild b. G211.4; woman bears b. T554.10; woman transformed into b. D11.2, Q551.3.2.2; years seem moments while man listens to song of b. D2011.1.

Bird's breath withers B777. — Chain tale: b. pea stuck Z41.6; eaten b.

head teaches animal languages *D1301.4; river in b. ears D915.2.1; spirit in b. form F401.3.7; trickster hides in tree, eats b. food K1971.1.1; talisman found in b. stomach N527.2; why b. head is large A2320.5.

Birds beat waters with wings to welcome saint B251.2.5; build canoe for master B572.2; call at canonical hours B252.2; captured by imitating their song K756.1; of Cirencester K2351.1; cling to sky in flood A2211.7; cursed M414.8.4; of different habits unfriendly J416.1; discuss the trap J655.1; drip blood at Judgment Day B259.5; drop quill for man's pen B159.1; drop stones on enemy D2163.5.1; get drunk A1427.0.1; exchange eggs A2247.4; enticed into bag K711.0.1; take back their feathers from ungrateful wolf Q597.2; fight, cause accidents Z49.6.1; fill sea with dirt, end flood A1028.2; set fire to besieged city K2351.1; flee from cuckoo J645.1; fly away with net K687; forced from nest by mother J65; frighten enemy's horses K2351.5.1; of the gods A155.3; hatched from broken eggs repaired by skillful tailor have red line around necks F662.1.1; hover over battlefield F989.14; indicate building site for church V111.3.1; indicate where town to be built B155.2.3; lament saint's departure B251.2.9; lift greyhound into air F982.1.1; lighting on heads cause men to kill one another K1082.3; made of iron in hell A671.2.11; magically called D2074.1.3; magically confined to roofless barn D2072.0.2.2.1; as messengers of the gods A165.2.2; mock ascetic B787; in net fly away with it K581.4.1; not to sing around goddess' home C481.1; furnish omens B147.2; in otherworld F167.1.2; in otherworld sing religious songs B251.3; perch on cow's ears B853; perch on saint B256.1.1; point out road to hero B563.2; of prey A2494.13.10.6; promised feast, led into trap K730.5; who aspire to blackbird's coat punished A2232.6; nest in saint's hand B256.1; save man from hunger by pitching themselves into his fire B531.5; as scouts B563.6; seeking richer lands are nearly all killed J513.1; serve saint B256.5.1; singing ceases at revelation B251.8.1; in snare fly out endlessly Z11.2; spit fire B742.2; swallow each other (lie) X1204.2; take part at saint's funeral B251.2.12; talk taught man K1068.1; tear ogre to pieces G512.9.2; throw their feathers to hero, he flies off B540.1; warn of enemy's approach B521.6; weep when man cuts self B303.1. — Abandoned person in woods comforted by b. S465; adventure from pursuing thieving b. N774.1; Alexander carried by two b. with meat held in front of them B552.1; allowing b. to nest in one's hair Q541.5; ambush betrayed by movement of b. J53; army of b. B268.5; banners appear like flock of b. K1872.5; boy eating raw b. G36.2.1; why certain b. may not drink out of river A2435.1.1; cow with two bags: one-legged and twelve-legged b. in them B15.7.9.1; creation of b. A1900ff.; cumulative tale: carpenter releases caught b. Z49.7; devastating b. B33; dwarfs resentful that mortals shoot at b. F451.4.4.1; earth supported on b. legs A844.10; eating food b. have pecked at forbidden C245; election of king of b. B236.1; extraordinary swarms of b. F989.16; fight between one-legged,

twelve-legged b. H619.5; fairy minstrel's b. sing accompaniment F262.3.2; fairies become b. D624.2; flight of b. A2442.1; food of b. A2435.4ff.; fool gives gifts to b. J1851.2; formerly b. talked A1101.2.3; fruit transformed to b. D441.2.1; giant b. B872ff.; god cheats b. of tamarind K499.6; grain trail eaten by b. R135.1; grains sorted by helpful b. H1091.2; haunts of b. A2433.4ff.; helpful b. *B450ff.; helpful b. demand food B322.2; how b. began to lay eggs A2486.4; hunting b. forbidden C841.2; island of b. F743.1; king of b. B242ff.; king brought to sense of duty by feigned conversation of b. J816.1; kingdom of b. B222; lies about b. X1250; magic b. cause hosts to sleep by shaking wings B172.9; magic b. chained together B172.7; magic b. die when owner is killed B192.0.1; magic b. keep falling off perch D1649.1.2; magic spell causes b. to roost D1442.6.2; man looking at b. pulled into pool K832.6; markings on b. *A2412.2ff.; men with beaks of b. F514.2; mythical b. B30ff.; nests of b. A2431ff.; numskull tries to shake b. from tree J1909.3; omens from flight of b. D1812.5.0.2; parliament of b. *B232; resuscitation by cutting off b. heads E29.5; silver, gold, and diamond b. B731.5; souls await Judgment as b. E751.2; tabu: b. feeding on hero's land C566.2; tabu: listening to fluttering of b. after sunset C885.1; tabu: swimming with b. C858; thorns planted to kill b. when they light K959.5; trees with green b. hanging by claws F811.9; unusual migration of b. as Doomsday sign A1002.2.4, A1091.4; war of b. and quadrupeds B261; war between b. and reptiles B263.4; war between groups of b. B263.5; warning b. B143.1ff.; why artist painted too few b. J1491; why b. do not live in societies A2492.2; why b. are everywhere A2434.1.1; wonderful b. guarded by monster G375.

Bird-beast B40ff.

Bird-heart. — Magic b. eaten unwittingly D859.4.1.

Bird-liver. — Magic b. eaten unwittingly D859.4.2.

Bird-men B50ff.

Birhors eat monkey, baboon flesh A1422.2.

Birnam wood comes to Dunsinane K1872.1.

Birnli will nit fallen Z41.

Birth of child with chain around neck: sign of royalty H71.7; of child as cannibal G33; delayed by magic T574; of fated child retarded M376.4; of gods A112; of magic object with hero *D857; of moon from first couple A745.1; prevented until mother confesses slander Q559.5.1; rites confer royalty P37; of saint predicted by miracles V222.0.1; same day as conception T573.1; of strong man F611.1; of sun from first couple A715; trees *T589.3. — Absurdities concerning b. of animals J1533ff.; all sins since the b. of Christ J1743.1; conception and b. *T500ff.; culture hero incarnated through b. from virgin A511.1.3; culture hero speaks before b. A511.1.2; curse given at b. of child M412.1; curse: monstrous b. M437; origin of customs con-

nected with b. A1560ff.; diseases cured at holy man's b. D2161.6.3; extraordinary nature phenomena at b. of holy person F960.1; fairy predicts b. of child *F315; fairy presides at child's b. F312; false bride takes true bride's place at b. of child *K1911.1.2; fate decided before b. N121; giant immortal so long as he touches land of his b. D1854; god swallows his pregnant wife to prevent b. of son M376; king of fishes prophesies hero's b. B144.1; lovers mated before b. T22.1; mentioning land of person's b. forbidden C442; miraculous b. *T540ff.; monstrous b. (as punishment for girl's pride) *T550ff.; mother assists at b. (riddling answer) H583.4.1; hero has lain motionless since b. F583; offspring of fairy and mortal has long hair and beard at b. F305.3; old woman prophesies at child's b. M301.2.2; woman who has prevented b. of children casts no shadow Q552.9; preventing b. of enemies J622; prophecy: death at child's b. M341.1.7; prophecy: hero's b. at certain time, place M311.0.2; prophecies about b. M369.7; twins quarrel before b. A511.1.2.1; release from curse with b. of child M421; roads appear at hero's b. *F1099.2.1; simultaneous b. of predestined lovers T22.4; soul forgets everything at b. E705; soul received at b. E726.1; star indicates b. of holy person F961.2.1; new star for each b. E741.1.1.1; shooting star signifies a b. E741.1.2; supernatural b. of culture hero A511; tabu imposed at b. C901.2; no time, no b., no death in otherworld F172; b.-control punished *Q251; trees grow to honor hero's b. F979.11; weeping at child's b. P617; woman pretends has given b. to aid fugitive K522.1.1.

Births. — Monstrous b. from incest A1337.0.7; royal b. occur in special place P10.1.

Birth-rate. — Determination of relation between b. and death-rate A1322.

Birthday. — Pious die on their b. F1099.7.

Birthmark. — Dead man's hand touches b. and thus removes it E542.2; recognition by b. H51.1.

Birthmarks T563. — Test: guessing princess's b. *H525.

Birthright. — Father transfers b. from oldest son P233.11; older brother has b. P251.7; younger brother given elder's b. L41.

Biscayans put medicine into rice J2134.2.1.

Bishop absurdly given military mission J1536; disguised as priest K1826.5.1; exchanges places with prisoner W16; fond of lawsuits J552.2.1; forced to ordain ignorant priest U41; foretells saint's birth M364.7.3; and prince J1289.2; refuses to eat small fish as he did when abbot J703.2; struck for breaking the peace J1823.2; wishes all monks castrated X457.1. — Deaf b. and drunken priest X111.13; father wants grandchild to be b.: allows seduction K1398; four-footed b. J2283; girl falsely accuses b. K2111.6; ghosts attack b. who has suspended pious priest E243; greedy b. dies at peasant's death D1715.2; incognito prin-

cess travels as b. K1812.8.2; man magically made to believe himself b., archbishop, and pope D2031.5; nose of falsely accusing b. bitten off Q451.5.3; oil bursts forth as saint made b. V222.5; paralysis for scorning b. Q573.2; plowing as test for b. H1573.2.3; priest catches b. in incontinence J1211.1.1; princess disguised as b. to flee man T323.1; sham b. K1961.4; treacherous b. K2281.

Bishop's. — Bad associates cause b. death J45.2; numskull thinks the b. snoring is his death rattle J1833; peasant preaches about b. amour J1211.1; reptile leaps into unjust b. throat V229.2.11.1; symbolic interpretation of points on a b. hat H608.1.

Bison as child's nurse B535.0.1.1. — Creation of b. A1878; devastating b. B16.2.9; helpful b. B411.4.1.

Bitch eats wheat dough: origin of noblemen A165.6.1. — Ghosts cannot near spayed b. E439.6; woman transformed to b. *D141.1; weeping b. K1351.

Bitches transformed to women D341.1. — Magic b. B182.1.2; magic b. enchanted by fairy music B182.1.7; women transformed to b. B297.2.1.

Bite causes series of accidents Z49.6.2; of wild huntsman's dogs drives other dogs mad E501.15.6.3. — Amorous b. T467; charms as antidote for b. of snake D1515.1.1; cure for snake b. F959.5; death from b. of stone lion (prophecy fulfilled) M341.2.10; serpent's b. produces treasure B103.6.1; snake b. for broken tabu C992; snake b. test H1517; snake sucks poison from b. D2161.4.10.2.2; spider b. cured by Virgin Mary D2161.5.2.5.

Biting fingers to see if one is dreaming F1041.13; the foot K543; off corpse's finger for ring leads to cannibalism accusation N342.6; off of parent's nose by son on gallows Q586; off own tongue K825.3; off victim's tongue K825.1.1; metal in anger pulverizes it F639.10; relative instead of kissing K2021.2; on stone as toothache remedy K1015.1. — Chain tale: b. grain in half Z49.8; contest in b. a stone K63; corpse b. off woman's nose E259.1; dog alternately b. and caressing hares K2031; indentions on plants from b. A2732; magic air journey from b. an ear D2135.2; metaphor on b. the ear J2489.3; nut falls and prevents snake from b. man N652; paramour b. off mistress's nose S172.1; resuscitation by b. victim's bone E29.1; riddle on b. the ear H588.15; serpent b. a file J552.3; severed head b. earth F1096.3; sleeping in shoes to avoid b. insects J2102.1.

Bitten. — Animal characteristics: members b. off A2216ff.; god's head b. off A179.4; husband lets self be b. to death to save wife T211.1.2; punishment: being b. by animal Q453; woman b. by own watchdog K1651.

Bitter water drunk as chastity test H411.4.1; water grateful for being praised D1658.1.3. — Ape throws away nut because of b. hull J369.2; dupe induced to eat b. fruit K1043; impious man's head turns well

water b. F933.4; sweet and b. fountain in otherworld garden F162.1.2.1; when sweet fails, try b. J1088; why tree has b. fruit A2771.8.

Bittern. — Creation of b. A1965; song of b. A2426.2.3, A2261.1.

Bitumen. — Ambergris made from b. eaten by fish F826.2.

Black beans, white soup J1291.1; berserk F610.3.2; birds B172.10; dog good omen D1812.5.2.10; dogs in wild hunt E501.4.1.5; Donald (name for devil) G303.2.4; dummy indicates banishment Z174.1.1; giant F531.1.7.3; god A123.7.2; is guard against Evil Eye D2071.1.4; horse in wild hunt E501.4.2.2; as magic color D1293.4; man becomes white D57.2; man *F527.5; man changes color by prayer V52.11; nipples reveal virginity loss T494; as raven, red as blood, white as snow Z65.1, T11.6; sheep turn white F985.1; spots on moon A751.9.1; as symbolic color Z143; tribe because woman put on fire A1614.8; and white horses chasing each other (riddle) H722.2; witch *G219.7. — Why b. bears are better eating than grizzly bears A2511.1; body turns b. from anger F1041.16.8; body turns lake b. F934.5; demons as b. birds F401.3.7.2; devil called "the b. one" G303.2.2; devil dressed in b. G303.5.1; devil has b. horses G303.7.1.1, G303.7.3.1, G303.17.2.9; devil as b. wench G303.3.1.12.3; devil's face b. G303.4.1.7.1; dwarf wears b. F451.2.7.9; why tip of ermine's tail is b. A2378.8.4; excommunication makes host turn b. V84.2; fairies b. F233.9; Fortuna half white, half b. N111.2.3; Frederick the Great drives dwarfs across B. Sea F451.9.1.13; ghost b. E422.2.4; the gray and the b. hairs J83; "have a b. look" J2489.7; hero in disguise of b. knight rescues lady R169.1; idol turns b. at unchaste woman H411.9.1; magic leaves turn white bird b. D1337.2.1; mirror becomes b. (life token) E761.4.3; negro so b. that he makes whole garden somber F573; numskull tries to wash b. hen white J1909.6; objects on one side of palisade in otherworld garden b., on other side white F162.1.2.3; pasturing b. sheep until they become white Q521.4; picture turns b. (life token) E761.4.2; planet in b. chariot pursues sun, moon A735.2; pot calls the kettle b. J1063; why raven is b. A2411.2.1.5, A2218.1; raven does not return to ark: b. color as punishment A2234.1.1; revenant b. E422.2.4; rivers of b. water in hell A671.2.2.4; silver object turns b. (life token) E761.4.5; soul as b. entity E722.1.2; soul as b. or white spirit over coffin E722.1.1; spirit as b. dog F401.3.3; spirit as small b. man F403.2.2.6; transformation to b. man D57.4; trolls b. F455.2.3; troops of b., white, and red soldiers F873.1; washing b. wool white H1023.6; white field, b. seed (riddle H741; white sheep comes to upper world, b. to lower F67; white woman bears b. child T562; why the b. clothes J1304; why center of eye is b. A1319.7; why ebony is b. A2751.4.2; why ebony tree has b. wood A2772.4; why sky is b. A702.8; why tip of weasel's tail is b. A2378.8.3; wild huntsmen dressed in b. E501.8.1; wild huntsman with b. fur cap and white staff E501.8.6; witch rides on b. cat G241.1.4.1.

Blackbeetle reproduces inside person B784.1.5.

Blackberries. — Why b. red when green J1291.1.1.

Blackbird avenges wife's capture K481.1; to be caught alive yearly C684.1; as creator A13.2.1; orders ants to burrow into elephant's brains B524.1.8. — Capturing b. yearly H1154.7.2; color of b. A2411.2.1.9; creation of b. A1924; devil in form of b. G303.3.3.3.3; giant b. B31.6.1; how the b. received its name A2571.1; man becomes b. D151.7.

Blackbird's wedding B282.11. — Birds who aspire to b. coat punished A2232.6.

Blackbirds destroy crops B33.1.3. — Quest for fat of water b. H1331.1.5; saint's bell rung against b. D1385.12.1.

Blackening. — Woman b. face as disguise K1821.7.1.

Blackmail of adulteress by lover K1582; of careless watchers K443.3. — Money acquired by b. K443; threat to tell of amorous intrigue used as b. K1271.1.

Blacksmith, see also **Smith;** chants Dante J981. — God as b. A142.0.1; origin of b. work A1447.2.

Blacksmith's and horse-trader's dreams J1622.

Blackthorn branch under cloak H527.

Blade of grass transformed to horse D451.5.1. — Witch in form of b. of straw G212.1.

Blades in food kill ogre G519.4; to wound and detect wife's lover K1565.

Blame for theft fastened on dupe K401. — Misfortune with oneself to b. the hardest U160; shifting b. to another J1166.

Blamed. — Devil always b. G303.9.3.4; devil b. by monk who takes what does not belong to him G303.25.10; evidence of crime left so that dupe is b. K2155; image b. for unwelcome answer given from behind image K1971.8; image b. by suppliant for misfortunes V123; object foolishly b. J1891.

Blaming supernatural wife forbidden C31.4.

Blandishments. — Resisting b. of leader's fiancée W34.1.

Blanket. — Child divides b. for cruel father's old age J121; embroidering b. in one day (task) H1093; ghost pulls b. off sleeper E544.2; resuscitation by magic b. E64.11; short b. must be patched J1179.3.

Blason populaire X681.

Blasphemer paralyzed except for tongue saying "Ave" V254.3.1; stricken dead Q558.4. —Knight fights b. J1164; man who has received sacrament overcomes b. V34.3; Satan as b. G303.9.8.11.

Blasphemer's. — Blood flows from b. mouth Q551.6.5.1.

Blasphemy prevents church bell's raising V115.1.3.2; punished Q221.3. — Dumbness punishment for b. Q451.3.4; phantom driver wanders for b. E512.

Blazing. — Devil disappears amid b. fire in river G303.17.2.4; god with b. eye A124.1; witch's b. eyes G213.4.

Bleaching. — Devil's grandmother b. (snow) *G303.11.4.2; fairies b. linen F271.4.1.

Bleating of goat frightens animals assembled for fight K2323.2. — Calf's b. as accusation J1895.

Bleeding animal exorcises witch G271.4.4; bone F991.2; from breaking tabu C949.4; heavens F961.0.6; image D1624; lance F991.1; rock F809.4; trees A2766, E631.0.4, F811.20; wood as Doomsday sign A1002.2.2, A1091.2; wounds do not deter hero H1507. — Absence of b. reveals witch G229.4.3, G259.3; corpse b. when murderer touches it D1318.5.2; cure by fall which causes b. N644; mouth b. as death omen J2311.1.2; murder by b. K923; opening own veins and b. to death Q427; stone b. before being skinned (task) H1023.10.1; stone b. before church plundered D1317.12.1.

Blemish tabu on king C563.2. — Foster parents fined for b. on child P270.1; reproach of b. punished Q284; secret b. revealed N465.0.1.

Blemished children born of monstrous parent T550.5. — Muddy bath for b. king J815.3.

Blessed plants A2777. — Animals b. for good services at crucifixion A2221.2ff.; animal b. for helping holy fugitive *A2221.5; animal b. for honoring infant Jesus *A2221.1; iron b. by saint incapable of wounding D1674; land of the b. F701.2; liquor b. by saint causes magic sleep D1364.7.1; paradise of the b. F111.4; plant b. for pious act A2711ff.; water b. by saint as love-philtre D1355.2.1; whomsoever demons curse is b. M493; why certain plants and trees are b. A2777.

Blessing not worth a penny J1261.4. — Barrenness removed by saint's b. D1925.4; brother secures b. due another K1988; child's b. fills countries with what they are famous for M393.1; curse magically changed to b. D2175.5; dead saint gives b. E367.2; devil's power avoided by b. G303.16.2.3; ghost laid by b. grave E443.1; disenchantment by b. D781.1; disguise as older brother to obtain b. K1839.11; fairy wounded by mortal is healed only by obtaining mortal's b. D2161.4.10.2.1; god b. mortal A182.3.3; god changes curse to b. M425; not b. mountains gives mountain-men power F460.4.6; big piece of cake with curse or small piece with b. J229.3, L222; saint's b. to descend from generation to generation M321.1; saint's b. renders man skillful F660.2; saint's b. makes stone oracular D1311.16.0.1; saint causes b. by druids D2076; transformation to obtain b. D659.5.

Blessings as hospitality reward Q45.1.1; as reward Q195. — Prince forfeits b. if he fails to claim throne P38.

Blest, Islands of the *A692.

Blighted garden magically restored D2195.

Blind ancestress guides hero to heaven A566.2; comforted by soul's inner eyes J893.1; and deaf cure each other by blows N642.1; dupe K333.1; fiancée betrays self K1984.5; giant F531.1.1.3, G121; girl marries lame man T125.2; god A128.1; lame, and deaf as witnesses in court X141; leading blind falls into pit J2133.9; man carries lame man N886; man who feels young wolf recognizes his savage nature

J33; man's exchange with devil G303.25.16.1; man's extraordinary perception F655; man's magic sight D1820.1.1; man's robber detected J1149.5; man carrying lame man treasure guardians N577; man recovers treasure by deceiving thief K1667.1; man sees unborn rats F642.3.3; man as soothsayer D1712.2; man steals from neighbor K306.4; man and the bull X123; man's arrow aimed (Balder's death) K863, (slain game stolen) K333.1; men duped into fighting K1681; men accidentally hurt each other N388; men's conclusions about elephant J1761.10; poet unintentionally kills friend N337.1; poets P427.7.3; promise M223; thief killed by rope slipping on withered date tree K436; town X1503.2; villain K2273.1; wife, deaf husband happy T202; wives bear children in pool T581.2.2; wildboar in wild hunt E501.4.3.2. — Behavior of the b. U170; devil b. G303.4.1.2.7; flower visible only to b. F814.5; Fortuna b. N111.2.1; how b. men get about J2387; hunchback leads b. man N886.1; husband says that good food will make him b. K1971.1; infant born b. drowns self T585.3; king goes b. from overweeping F1041.3; lake bursts forth where b. king plucks rushes A920.1.12; man fishes up two b. women from a well F1065; man stricken b. as punishment Q559.2; men originally b. A1316.3.3; princess rescued by b. man restores his sight R161.2; prophecy: unborn child to be b. M355; rescuer impersonates captive and deceives b. guardian while captive escapes R121.2; saint cures b. hyenas B384; sham b. man throws suspicion on real b. K2165; theft from b. person K333; thief robs b. miser: gives tenth to charity K2096.2; trading b. horse K134.5; trickster gets coins from b. beggars K1081.1.1; why bee is b. A2332.6.9; why certain animals are b. A2332.6; why leech is b. A2332.6.8; wind is b. A1129.3; witch renders b. G263.4.5.

Blinded ogre G511; slave's revenge K1465; trickster directed by trees *D1313.4. — Abandoned queen b. S438; artisan b. to prevent duplication S165.7; bird cares for b. master B536.1; greedy man magically b. J514.3; man b. trying to heal girl N395.

Blindfolded emperor traveling to paradise J2326.3. — Drinkers cheat b. bartender K233.2; husband b. by adulteress K1516.5; man washes clothes b. F1017.

Blinding with dust, then robbing K2356.1; the guard *K621; by magic D2062.2; by needles in eyes S165.3; opponent to win race K11.7; as punishment Q451.7ff.; a witch (task) H1191. — Capture by b. K783; choice between emasculation or b. J229.12; man b. brother S73.3; mother b. son S12.4; murder by b. K957; son b. father S21.2.

Blindman's Buff. — Bear plays B. H1537.1.

Blindness in animals A2332.6ff.; cured by killing snake D2161.4.10.5; magically cured D2161.3.1; miraculously cured F952; from sight of holy person D2062.2.2. — Angel of b. A478.6; fairies cause b. F362.1; how to cure snake of b.? H1292.4.2; husband feigns b. and avenges himself on his wife and her paramour K1553; magic object causes b.

D1331.2ff.; magic object causes both supernatural sight and b. D1331.3; magic object cures b. *D1505ff.; magic b. as punishment remitted Q571; origin of b. A1339.1; saint cures b. V221.12; sight of wild hunt causes b. E501.18.7; vulture cures b. B511.5.1; water-spirits cause b. F420.5.2.11.

Blindworm has no eyes A2332.6.1, (borrowed by nightingale) A2241.5. — Adder harmful to holy person transformed to b. *A2145.5.

Blink. — Why men b. A1316.2.

Blister on back from lying in rose leaves F647.9.

Block dressed as child, saves child from death K525.1.3.

Blocked. — Road b. by spirit F402.1.2.

Blocksberg (witch's sabbath) G243.

Blood of animal considered venomous B776.5; of certain animal said to be sweet A2236.1, K961.0.1; bath causes women to be carried off by bird N335.2; bath as leprosy cure F955.1; -brotherhood P312; and brains (escape by shamming death) K473, K522.1; of brother and sister refuses to mingle F1075; catches fire F964.3.2; of scourged Christ on certain spiders A2221.2.3; covenant M201.1; from cross on robin redbreast A2221.2.2; of dragon B11.2.13; on end of each hair F555.6; as evil omen D1812.5.1.1.1ff.; flowing from Jesus' image converts V331.1.1; flows from desecrated building Q222.0.2; flows from blasphemer's mouth Q551.6.5.1; indicates guilt or innocence *D1318.5ff.; as life token *E761.1ff.; as magic drink *D1041; as sacrifice V12.1; shed in battle pollutes D1563.2.2.1; smeared on innocent person brings accusation of murder K2155.1; stops flowing from wound E761.1.13; streams from angry warrior's head F1041.16.6.1; in spittle as test of subjection H252.2; sucking chafer B16.6.2; transformed to another object D457.1; transformed to animal D447.3; turns black D492.2; from wizard becomes red grain of cedar A2731.3. — Adhesion of b. (test of paternity) H486.1; all living things from Jesus' spattered b. A1724.3; animal's b. venomous B776.5ff.; bath of b. F872.3; bath of b. of beloved to cure love-sick empress T82; bath in b. of king as cure for mange D1502.5.1; betrothal by lovers' drinking each other's b. *T61.1; birds drip b. at Judgment Day B259.5; birth from b. T541.1; brother about to drink b. of seemingly guilty sister P253.1; brownie murders, catches b. in cap F363.2; carrying murdered man's b. (ordeal) H227; child sacrificed to provide b. for cure of friend S268; child's b. makes earth red A1277.3; Christian child killed to furnish b. for Jewish rite V361; church stone sheds b. Q222.0.1; cock's b. substituted for sacrificial human's K525.9; conception from b. T534; cry of b. of Abel A1344.1; curse: hero not to stand sight of b. M438.2; deception by sham b. *K1875; deep streams of b. flow during battle F1084.1; disease caused by menstrual b. A1337.0.4; disenchantment by drawing b. D712.4; disenchantment by drinking b. D712.4.1; "don't shed women's b." J21.2.5; dragon's b. B11.2.13; drawing witch's b. annuls her spells D1741.2; drawing b. renders witch powerless G273.6; drinking b. teaches animal languages

D1301.2; dwarfs have b. F451.3.5.4; earth created from b. of gods' victim A831.8; earth reddened with b. of human sacrifice A1241.4; enemy tricked into first spilling b. K2358; executioner substitutes animal's b. for victim's K512.1.1; fairies bathing in enemy's b. F259.2; flaming spear must be cooled in noxious b. D1645.8.1.1; flood from b. A1012.3; ghost as b. E422.1.11.5; ghost summoned by pouring b. of sacrifices into trench E382; girl's b. examined to see if she is pregnant T579.2; god with body of b. A123.1.6; gods have no b. A1399.2; ground defiled by menstrual b. C144; ground dries up when first woman's b. drips on it A856.2; hero to drink dying monster's b. M257; horse shall wade in b. at Armageddon A1080.1; horse weeps tears of b. B301.4.2; human b. accidentally tasted brings desire for human flesh G36.2; human b. makes leaky tanks waterproof S261.0.1; husband nourishes starving wife with his own flesh and b. T215.3; insect fries human b. to eat A2435.5.2; insects from b. of slain animal A2001.1; lake of b. F713.6; magic b. (human) *D1003, (of animal) *D1016, (healing) *D1500.1.7.3; magic lost with b. D1741.2; magic object stanches b. D1504ff.; magic power from shedding b. D1766.2.3; magic rod turns waters to b. D1549.9; maidens befoul selves with b. T327.4; man created from b. A1263.1; man created from game animal's b. A1263.1.2; man dies from drop of killed hound's b. Q582.4; man made from animal's b. A1241.4.1; man sweats b. and absorbs hair into head on exertion of strength F1041.10; man's b. made of water A1260.1.5; man sweats b. F1041.10; mandrake from b. of person hanged on gallows A2611.5; milk becomes b. D457.2, D476.2.3.1; moon turns to b. F961.3.1; ocean made from b. A922; ogre says he smells human b. G532; ogre sucks victim's finger and drinks all his b. G332.1; ogre with monstrous b. G367; origin of b. A1319.6; origin of serpent's b. A2367.3.1; pact with devil signed in b. M201.1.2, (sealed in b.) M218.1; person with remarkable b. F554; Pisācas drink b. and eat human flesh G312.1; plant from b. of slain person E631.0.3; quest to hell for b. of sorceress H1277; rain of b. F962.4; rain produced by spitting b. toward sky D2143.1.4; rakshasa can be defeated by hero who has rakshasi b. in veins G369.1.2; rakshasa's mistress lying in pool of b. G369.1.7; red as b., white as snow Z65.1; red sky from b. A1147.1; resuscitation by b. *E113; river of b. F715.2.1, (in hell) A671.2.2; river from b. of sick mortals F162.2.13; rose from b. of slain of War of Roses A2656.2; rue from drops of Christ's b. A2611.7; saint's tears of b. V229.2.6.1; secret escapes with man's b. N481; seed mixed with b. as love charm D1355.3.1; serpent sucks man's b. B16.5.1.2.1; snake from b. of slain monster A2145.1; soul (life) in b. E714.1; ghost bursts into spray of b. H175.5; springs from innocent king's b. A941.5.8; streams of b. magically drawn down on foe D2091.3; stars as moon's b. A764.2; streams of battle b. F1084.1; substitute specimen in b. test K1858.2; sun b. color F961.1.8; shower of b. F962.4; sun, moon animated by human b. sacrifice A714.8;

sun, moon vivified with b. A717.1; sun's children turn into b. in daytime A736.5.2; tabu: marriage with person whose b. one has drunk C165; tears of b. F541.9; tears of b. as evil omen D1812.5.1.1.1; tears of b. from excessive grief F1041.21.1; tears of b. as sign of royalty H71.8; tests for noble b. H1574.1; toad sucks b. B766.3; transformation by applying b. D595; treasure found by sprinkling ground with b. of white cock D2101.1; tree from innocent man's b. E631.0.5; trees grow from b. F979.12; using b. tabu C893; vampire sucks b. E251.3.3; waters transformed to b. F930.4; well of b. F718.8; unwitting adultery with wife of b.-brother N766; why gods accept only b. A153.6; why leech feeds on human b. A2435.6.3; wife drinks b. of slain husband P214; witch feeds animal familiar with her own b. G225.0.1; witch sucks b. G262.1.

Blood-clot. — Birth from b. T541.1.1; man created from b. A1263.1.

Blood-oranges, origin of A2687.1.

Blood-test for inheritance J1176.3.

Bloodhounds decapitate victim B17.1.2.1.

Bloodstain ineradicable E422.1.11.5.1.

Bloodthirsty animal by trickery admitted to fold: kills peaceful animals K828ff; revenants E250ff.

Bloody key as sign of disobedience C913; knife F1066.1. — Arrow shot to heaven returns b. F1066; cows made to give b. milk D2083.2.1; object becomes b. (life token) E761.1ff.; transformation: objects become b. D474.

Bloody Cap murders travelers F363.2.

Blooming staff *F971.1, H331.3; staff as chastity index H432.4. — Animal horns b. bear man as fruit A1263.5; flower b. when touched D2195.1; flowers b. in winter F971.5; garden b. in winter H352; marriage dependent on cut branch b. M261.1.1; sexual promise dependent on garden's b. in winter M261.1; tree b. nightly F811.13; tree b. out of season D2145.2.2.2.

Blossom, see also **Flower;** *D975.

Blossoms, singing F979.21.

Blossoming staff *F971.1. — Miraculous b. and bearing of fruit F971; trees magically b. D2157.3.

Blotches on face punish satirist Q265.2.1. — Magic poem raises facial b. D1403.1; successful suitor to be without b. H312.1.

Blow on the ears J2494, K2376; at end of year (labor contract) F613.1; recalls memory of mother's milk Z61.4; from spirit causes paralysis E265.1.1; of staff brings water from rock *D1567.6. — Accepting b. in face to show patience H1553.4; first b. must kill C742.1; giant's b. makes cleft in rock F531.6.6.4; not flinching under b. (test) H1561.3; insane man accidentally cured by b. on head N642; mountain opens at b. of divining rod D1552.1; second b. resuscitates *E11.1; seven at

a b. (boast) K1951.1; value of a b. J1193.2; villain killed by b. intended for victim Q581.2; vow not to give more than one b. M166.1.

Blows aimed at others strike donors D2184.1; shared K187. — Chapel endowed with b. for friar X454; dog receives b. K2171; giant b. to prevent approach of ship F531.3.1.4; Peter receives the b. twice K1132; three b. for every one given J2213.2.

Blower slows down princess in race H331.5.1.1.1; turns mill F622. — Lie: remarkable b. X935.

Blowing contest won by deception K26; the house in Z81; magic into ears D1721.3; mountain away by magic D2152.3; serpent B743. — Devil b. skin off man G303.18.3; disenchantment by b. on victim D778; elf-knight produces love-longing by b. on horn F301.2.1; ghosts b. smithy into air E279.7; lion b. life into cubs B751.4; person b. poison on another is himself poisoned K1613.1; resuscitation by b. trumpet E55.3; resuscitation of cremated man by b. on the ashes E66.1; transformation by b. D588; wild huntsman b. horn E501.15.1; wind raised by b. into tobacco pipe D2142.1.6.1; witch keeps winds from b. G283.2.

Blubber. — Tabu to eat b. C221.3.4.

Blue beard F545.1.1; dogs and cats B731.6.2; -eyed horse H1331.4.1; fortunate in love matters T3.1; lights follow witches G229.7; man F527.3; ox: lie X1237.2; red, yellow horses in fairyland F241.1.1.3; snow X1653.2; as symbolic color Z144.1; teeth F544.3.3; tooth identifies man H79.8. — Devil dressed in b. clothes G303.5.4; fairies in b. clothes F236.1.2; half-red, half-b. man F527.6; magic b. ribbon D1078.1; magic b. stone D1382.12; one eye brown, other b. F541.6.1; transformation: stone to b. man D432.1.1; water-spirits dressed in b. F420.1.6.6.5; why sea is b. A1119.1; why sky is b. A702.4.

Bluebeard S62.1.

Bluebell as model for church bell A1466.1.

Bluebirds. — Why b. are everywhere A2434.1.2.

"**Bluecap**" mining spirit F456.2.

Bluejay as culture hero A522.2.1. — Flight of b. A2442.2.4.

Bluffing frightens owner away from goods K335.0.4. — Deception through b. *K1700—K1799.

Blunt — Chopping down large tree with b. instrument (task) H1115.

Blushing. — Women b. in presence of male statue F647.4.

Bo-tree, sacred V1.7.1.4.

Boar as confederate of adulterous wife B598.1; with golden bristles B101.2.1; guards holy man's swine B256.6.1; licks holy man's wounds B256.6.3; makes music for holy man B256.6.2; with nine tusks in each jaw B15.7.8; refuses to fight with lowly ass J411.1; sings song B211.1.4.1; in spider's web F989.18; in wild hunt E501.4.3; wins duel with tiger K97.1. — Capturing, binding b. (task) H1154.3.3; cuckold's knife cannot carve head of b. H425.1; dupe tricked into measuring b. with poisoned bristles K898; earth made of mud shaken off primeval b. A822; enmity

of tiger and b. A2494.10.2; fairy in form of wild b. F234.1.3; falcon and heron eaten by wild b. recovered alive from his body X1723.2; ferocious b. fed and put to sleep by rubbing K836; giant b. B871.1.2; giant devastating b. B16.1.4.1; great wild b. X1233.1.2; helpful b. B414.1; hero accidentally wounded by wild b. N337.2; lion and wild b. make peace J218.1; magic b. B184.3.1; magic b. slain F98.1.8; man rides b. F989.4; man transformed to b. D114.3.2; origin of wild b. A1871.1; prophecy: hunters will encounter b. M397; quest for marvelous b. H1331.2; reincarnation as wild b. E611.3.1; self-luminous artificial b. D1645.7; singing b. B214.1.2; slaying thieving b. H335.3.3; venomous b. B776.4.2; vow to kill wild b. alone at night M155.1; why tiger does not attack wild b. A2257.1; wild b. hunted by man, once faithless wife A1422.3; wild b. as ogre G352.2; wild b. obeys saint D2156.4; yoking together lion and wild b. (task) H1149.1.

Boars. — Army of b. B268.12; king of b. B241.2.12.

Boar's bristles remarkably long X1233.1.1. — Cobold from b. testicle F481.0.1.1; earth supported on b. tusk A844.9; inexhaustible b. flesh D1652.1.9.1.1; obtaining wild b. lard H1154.11; wild b. haunt tabu C619.2.

Boards from forest endure forever F812.7. — Coffin-making b. announce death D1322.1.2.

Boast of bird about capturing the rabbit J2173.3; forces warriors to face enemy H945.1. — Foolish b. of ancestry by lowly J954; freedom abridged till b. confirmed Q433.12; king overhears girl's b. as to what she should do as queen N455.4; king's b. about wife brings about death T295; overheard b. about hidden money brings about robbery N455.1; pardon given if hero produces the lady about whom he has made b. M55; poor boy's b. concerning fate made good N234; quest assigned because of hero's b. H1215; tasks assigned because of b. H915.1; tasks imposed because of wife's foolish b. H916.1.

Boasts. — Foolish b. bring trouble J2353.1; ogre overawed by hero's b. about marvelous relatives K1718.

Boaster hurls back flung stone H1562.5; of victory over a weaker person reprimanded J978.

Boastfulness W117.

Boasting after danger over J2626; coward J2631, K1837.1, K1951.4; fly-killer K1951.1; forbidden *C450ff.; at home safe J552.6; numskull in unimportant post J2331; of sexual prowess P665; of supernatural wife forbidden *C31.5; woman casts ring into sea L412.1. — Sham warrior intimidates soldiers with his b. K1951.3; son to be killed for b. S327.1; tasks assigned because of mother's foolish b. H914.

Boat, see also **Ship;** F624.7; drawn by swans B558.1; expected to grow into ship J2212.7; journey to otherworld F157; to land of dead *E481.2.2; to lower world F93.0.1; lured to land, wrecked in vengeance K815.12; made invisible D1982.5; race as suitor test H331.5.4; stopped

by magic D2072.0.3; of the sun A723; gets tired J1884; towed by dog B541.4.1; transforms self at will of master D632. — Angel carries b. to water V232.2.0.1; child abandoned in b. rescued R131.15; crocodile as b. R245.1; cut-throat terrorizes b. passengers N695; dead drag b. to strand E543; dead placed on b. V61.1; deity departs in b. A192.2.2; disembarking from b. from other world C524; dupe makes b. of mud J2171.1.3; embarkation in leaky b. Q466; escape from deluge in b. A1021; escape by rowing b. stern foremost K534.4; exposure in b. *S141; exposure in b. as sin test H263.1; extraordinary b. *F841ff.; fairy b. F242.2; fairy harper in bronze b. F262.3.1.3; father abandoning children in b. S141.2; fools make b. go over precipice J2129.1; future hero found in b. L111.2.1; giantess almost sinks b. F531.2.13; giant's stone b. F531.4.8; girl enticed into b., abducted R12.4; girl with treasure in b. N572.3; hedgehog and crab jump from b. after turtle J2133.11; hero arrives in b. A513.2; hole in b. to let water out J2119.4; journey to otherworld in crystal b. F157.1; leaf as b. D1524.8; looking at certain b. forbidden C315.1; luminous b. of witches G222.2; magic b. *D1121ff.; magic b. to fairyland F213.1; magic b. keeps thief at sea Q559.10; magic sod as b. D1524.7; magic stone serves as b. D1524.3; making b. from splinters of a spindle and shuttle (task) H1022.7; man builds b. and sails about in giant's belly F911.5.1; man transformed to b. D255; man's long legs steady b. F517.0.2.1; many-oared b. mistaken for animal J1772.14; marking place on b. J1922.1; mermaid asks b. blocking her dwelling be moved B81.13.1; mouse sails in b. of bread-crust *B295.1; ogre tars hero's b. J2171.1.2; quenching burning b. J2162.3; rapid b.-builder F671.1; river-god stops b. for sacrifice S263.4; rowing contest in sawed b. K14; rowing in b. which is tied up J2164.2; sailing in leaky b. without sinking D2121.13; saint changes course of b. in answer to prayer T321.6; seduction by enticing aboard b. to inspect wares K1332; self-sacrifice to save b. S264.1.2; selling soul for b. sailing in sky M211.6; shell transformed to b. D452.2.1; skillful tailor sews together scattered planks of capsizing b. F662.2; strong man breaks b. F614.4; strong man as rower: rows one side of b. against many people at other F614.4.1; strong man tears b. apart with hands F639.6; tabu: disembarking from b. C524; tabu: grumbling at narrowness of certain b. C881.1; tabu: pointing b. towards god's island C51.9; vow to recover loose b. or go to hell Q221.4.2; winged serpent as b. (passengers within) F911.3.2.

Boats, see also **Ships;** of skin unsuccessful C841.0.1. — Bridge of b. F842.2.3.1; ghost sets b. adrift E299.5; holes bored in enemies' b. prevent pursuit K636; lies about b. with light draft X1781.

Boat-building. — Origin of b. A1445.1; shortsightedness in b. J2171.1.

Boatman ignorant of bookman's work J251.1. — Transformation to b. D23.1.

Body, see also **Corpse;** dismembered so soul cannot return E721.1.2.3.1; of dwarf F451.2.1ff.; of fairy F232ff.; of living corpse E422.1ff.; magi-

cally saved from corruption after death D2167; thrown in lake turns water black F934.5. — Animal with b. of horse, legs of hound B14.2; animal guards master's dead b. F576.4; animals distribute parts of man's b. in accordance with prophecy F989.10; animals from different parts of b. of slain giant *A1724; animal gives part of b. as talisman *B501; animals from transformed parts of b. A1724; child born without b. T550.7; child removed from b. of dead mother T584.2; concealment in another's b. *F1034ff.; cynic asks b. be exposed J1442.4.1; dead b. incorruptible E182; dead b. not to be moved E411.0.3.1; debate of b. and soul E727; devil enters b. of another G303.18; devil can touch b., not soul G303.25.18; exchanging parts of own b. for food M225.1; fairy women take b. of dead hero to fairyland F323; flood from b. fluids A1012; food from b. of slain food-goddess A1420.1; ghost carries man with half a b. E261.1.3; ghost carries own dead b. E592.1; gods born from various parts of creator's b. A112.3; headless b. sings D1615.8; headless b. vital E783.6; insects from b. of slain monster *A2001; interred b. of saint performs miracles K1685; lover's b. kept embalmed for years by grieving mistress T85.4; lucky marks on b. N135.4; magic b. of water *D910ff.; magic passes from b. to b. D1751; magic object speaks from inside person's b. *D1619.2; man made from creator's b. A1211ff.; man's b. of clay A1260.1.5; minerals from b. of dead culture hero A978.1; mountains from part of deity's b. A962.1; one animal jumps through b. of another F916; origin of animal's b. A2300ff.; origin of fire: found in person's own b. A1414.2; own b. as stake N2.1; parts of b. as hiding place F1034.3ff.; parts of human b. furnish treasure D1454; person enters animal's b. X1723.3; person with flat b. F525.4; person with mouths all over b. F513.0.2; person with transparent b. F529.5; plants from b. of slain person or animal A2611ff.; power of mind over b. U240ff.; relation of b. to soul E727; saint's b. remains unspoiled in earth V229.2.8; scalding mush scatters on heroine's naked b. H1503; self-returning b. D1602.12.1; soul cannot enter heaven till b. buried E750.0.1; soul in form of heavenly b. E741; soul kept in special part of b. E714ff.; soul leaves b. at death E722ff.; soul leaves or enters the b. E720ff.; soul as replica of b. E747.1; soul of witch leaves b. *G229.1; speaking from swallower's b. F915; taking a stick from the b. (task) H1021.7; two wives each claim part of husband's b. T145.4; universe from b. of slain giant A642; universe from parts of creator's b. A614; wife refuses to give up husband's dead b. T211.4.2.1; witch carries her children in her own b. G229.2; witch's b. injured while witch is away G275.14; woman's b. used as still F891.1.

Body's. — River rises to prevent b. passage across F932.8.1.

Bodies of victims in front of ogre's house G691. — Animal with one head, two b., six legs B15.7.11; artificial heavenly b. F793; cannibals cut off parts of children's b. G86; demons without b. G302.4.3; devil appears to girl who prays over pit where she has thrown the b. of her babies G303.6.2.7; extraordinary behavior of heavenly b. F961;

extraordinary b. of water F710ff.; giants with shaggy hair on b. F531.1.6.3; goddess with three b. A123.1.7; magic object controls heavenly b. D1546; rakshasas have power of extending b. eighty miles G369.1.1; sun, moon as divine b. of gods A718.2; two persons with b. joined F523.

Body-dirt. — Animals from b. of deity A1725.2; girl's b. golden F521.3.3.1.

Bodily members as advisers D1312.1. — Animal pressed: hence b. marks A2213.2; arrangement of man's b. attributes A1310ff.; curse: b. injury M431; fanciful b. members of animal *B720ff.; lie: persons with remarkable b. parts X916; magic b. members *D990ff., (animal) *D1010ff.; magic object restores b. members D1518; professions according to b. appearance A1650.3.2; recognition by b. marks or physical attributes H50ff.; vital b. members E780ff.

Bog becomes flowery mead D479.1. — Saint's journey over b. D2125.0.2.

Bogey imitates mother, kills child K2011.1.2.

Boil transferred to a post D2161.4.2.1; on youth for keeping a secret F1041.9.2.1.

Boils. — Magic object cures b. D1502.8.

Boiled. — Numskull feeds hens hot water so they will lay b. eggs J1901.2; pig can be b. only after true stories H251.3.11; suit for chickens produced from b. eggs J1191.2; hatching b. eggs (task) H1023.1; unchaste woman's skin b. away H411.11.1.

Boiling blood as life token E761.1.5; to death in pitch or oil S112.1; horse's heart releases curse M429.2; liquid as life token E761.6.3; lover's hair fetches him D1355.3.5; oil doesn't harm compassionate woman Q151.12; in oil as punishment Q414.1; pot seen as threat, broken J1813.10; of river from magic trousers D1549.3.3; those which come and go (beans rising and falling in water) H583.6; water for master's bath K1462.1; water meant for hero, used on man preparing it K1626.3; water to wash in J2465.4.1. — Bath of b. oil F872.2; bathing in b. water H328.5; bathing in b. water without cooling it H1023.24; beautification by b. and resuscitation *D1865.2; cool and b. fountain in otherworld garden F162.1.2.2; escape by bathing guard in b. water K629.1; escape from b. oil R215.2; man proof against b. water D1841.2; murder by b. victim's gloves D2061.2.2.5.1; oath on b. oil H412.4.2; ogress falls into b. spring G519.1.4; ordeal by b. water H221.4; rejuvenation by b. D1885; resuscitation by b. *E15.1; ring makes b. water cold D1566.2.5; river b. F932.7; saint unhurt by b. water D1841.2.1; water b. when angry warrior immersed F1041.16.6.6; water not b. until fish returned to well V134.3; witch drinks b. oil G525.1; witch keeps water from b. D2137.1; witches b. wizardry cauldron G249.5.

Boldness of the blind U170ff.; of dogs K2524.6; punished Q333.

Bole. — Swine shaking tree b. H1199.6.

Bolster. — Waiting for thief to return b. J2214.3.2.

Bolt from heaven kills animal F981.4.

Bolts. — Three b. left on hell by Christ V211.7.3.
Bombax. — Why b. tree has thorns A2752.1.
Bon mot. — King rewards scullion for b. Q91.2.
Bonbons. — Inexhaustible vase of b. D1652.5.5.
Bond woman girded with rope P171.2. — Debt with worthless b. repudiated K231.5.
Bonds cannot be loosed save by man who fettered them D1651.9. — Abandonment in b. S148.
Bondmaid. — Man weds his b. T121.6.
Bondo women not to wear clothes C181.6.
Bone of man jumps from fire E15.0.1; transformed to dog D447.8; transformed to other object D457.12; transforms self to person D437.1; in wolf's throat removed from crane W154.3. — Accidental death from flying splinter of b. N335.4; alleged resuscitating b. sold K113.1; animal grateful for removal of b. lodged in its throat B382; animal with head of b. B15.1.3, cannibal crunching human b. says noise is only eating of peas G87; captive sticks out b. instead of finger to cannibal G82.1.1; conception from smelling b. dust T532.1.4.1; death from fish b. in throat N339.12, F363.1; giant with enormous b. weapon F531.4.5.3; gnawed b. as weapon F839.1; human b. in demon's stomach becomes boy E149.1; magic b. (of animal) *D1013, (human) *D1007; magic object heals broken b. D1518.4; man created from animal b. A1263.7; prophecy: death by means of b. M341.2.14; resuscitation by biting victim's b. E29.1; return from dead to punish theft of b. from grave E235.4.3; swallowed b. causes woman to appear dead N694.1; swelling b. as forgiveness sign F991.2.1; vivification by hitting with b. D1594.0.2; witch b. G224.11, D1442.8.
Bones of dead collected and buried E607.1; of dead thrown into river E607.1.1; of birds constantly thrown up from well F933.8; wrapped in holy sheepskin revive E174. — Animal born from b. B716; animal characteristics: b. A2367.1ff.; bird with magic b. and feathers *B172.4; breaking b. of eaten animal forbidden C221.3.2; bringing quantity of mosquito b. H1022.9; climbers temporarily remove b. F1054; devil leaves sinner's body, only b. remain G303.18.0.1; disenchantment by assembling b. D717; dwarfs from giant's b., blood F451.1.1.1; earth created from b. of gods' victim A831.8; fish b. mistaken for peas J1772.6; in fish division dupe gets b. K171.6; game with ancestor's b. P203; ghost takes b. from grave E593.4; ghost's b. brought home from foreign soil E459.2; goddess scatters pubic hairs on fish: why he has so many b. A2211.15; heroes born from swallowed b. A511.1.4.3; house of b. F163.3.2.2; house-spirit without b. F480.5; insects from b. of slain animal A2001.1; jinns without arm b. F499.3.1; king's b. sent back so people will know of their freedom M14; ladder of b. up slippery mountain F848.3; lost husband's b. found among cannibals G691.4; man's b. made of stone A1260.1.5; mankind from b. of dead brought from underworld A1232.1; modest choice of parting gift: b. instead

of meat L222.2; mountains from b. of slain giant A961.5; mosquitoes from b. of slain demon A2034.2; person reduced to pile of b. D2061.1.1.1; pillars of dead chief's b. A151.4.4; planting b. to produee young J1932.4.2; prophecy: miraculous removal of saint's b. M364.8; puppies' b. as evidence woman ate own child K2116.1.1.1.1; rejuvenation by burning and throwing b. into tub of milk D1886.1; relic b. jump away from flame V140.4; resuscitation by rubbing b. on ground E29.2; saint's b. for lack of worship remove themselves from church V143; sex tabu broken: child born without b. C101; singing b. reveal the crime *E632ff.; son recovers father's b. R154.2.2; sorcerers use marrow of corpses' b. D1278.2; stepmother feeds children fish b. S31.4; strong man breaks man's b. F614.6.1; tabu to lie on ancestors' b. C541.4; tabu: touching b. of murdered person C541.3; talking b. advise hero E366.3; vessel of human b. F881.2; vision of dry b. V515.1.5; when devil leaves dead sinner's body, only b. remain G303.18.0.1; why animal b. sacrificed A1545.6; woman exchanges a horse for a sack of b. J2099.1.

Bone-powder changed into cheese D476.1.10.

Boneless man turned over to produce seasons A1152; person F529.7. — Swallowed person becomes b. F921.1.

Bonga, see also **Fairies;** F201, F365.4; girl as flame F234.3.2; house full of animals F221.2; lends dishes to mortals F343.6; lives in tree F216.2; made village headman F347.1; mistress F302.0.1; pegged to ground, placed under stone F386.3; returns stolen goods for man F302.3.1.1.

Bonga's namesake first daughter F302.5.1.1.

Bonito. — Origin of b. A2122.

Bonnet. — Ghost with pulled-down b. E422.4.2.

Boo. — Tale-teller yells "b." Z13.1.

Book brought back from fairyland F379.2.1; dropped in water by saint not wet F930.1; of fate N115; magically preserved D2167.2; by marvelous memoried man D1910.0.1. — Account b. of dead E481.8.1; alleged idol to pay for b. K1971.13; angel dictates b. V246.0.2; author of b. against heretic honored by Virgin Mary and angels V327; carrying saint's b. insures victory D1381.25; cow swallows b.: cause of maniplies in stomach A2219.2; devil exorcised with b. G303.16.14.4; divination from sacred b. D1311.14; extraordinary b. F883.1; fools praise b. so author finds it stupid J1714.4; ghost steals b. from priest E593.2; illiterate's sham weeping over b. K1795; magic b. *D1266, (conjured away by throwing it on stream) D2176.4, (furnishes wealth) D1469.6, (removes itself) D1641.11.1; man believes himself wise because he owns b. J2238; mountain men give children a b. F460.4.2.4; murder with poisoned b. S111.5; oath taken on sacred b. M114.1; otter recovers lost b. from water B548.3; prophecy from b. M302.8; reading from b. makes fallen tree stand D1571.3; sacred b. does not burn D1841.3.3; spring breaks forth where animal delivers b. left behind by saint A941.5.4; unique ability to read magic b. H31.7.2; value of b. depends on appreciation of it J1061.5.

Books in church read without man's tongue F1055; sorrow for owner, fall from shelf F994.1. — Curse makes b. illegible D2089.5; devils two b. for noting sins G303.24.1.9; divine inspiration of sacred b. D1811.2.1; good, bad in all b. J174; magic dew destroys b. D1599.6; many b. do not make a scholar U111; origin of medical b. A1487.2; origin of worship from holy b. A1546.5; recognition through b. H134; sacred b. received from Buddha in person V212.1; saint curses hidden b. M411.8.5; sanctity of b. tested in fire H221.1.3, (in water) H222.4; sham wise man burns up b. K1956.8; sorcerer and b. in mountain F721.2.3; Sibylline b. J166.1; wisdom from b. J166; witches' power from b. G224.3; youth tricks mother by carrying many b. U111.1.

Book-satchel transformed to bird D444.5.

Bookholder. — Deer's horns as saint's b. B256.3.

Bookkeeper. — Cheating b. excused: gave money to poor V416.1.

Boomerang. — Arrow as b. F661.11; saint causes missiles to b. D1093.1.

Boon granted, son released from prison R123. — Any b. desired J1593; ingeniously worded b. asked of God K2371.3; reward: any b. that may be asked Q115.

Boorish. — Fairy's b. clothes F236.5.

Boot mistaken for axe-sheath J1772.11.

Boots sent by telegraph J1935.1. — Catching fish in b. while wading X1112; detection for theft of bull escaped by putting b. on the bull *K412; judge's bad-luck b. N136; large supply of b. for journey H1231; lie: remarkable b. X1021.1; magic b. *D1065.1ff.; magic b. render invisible D1361.38; Puss in B. B582.1.1; shoemaker's apprentice greases b. as he would grease a fowl J1631; seven-league b. D1521.1; taking off undesired lover's b. K1227.4; thief undetected cuts soles off b. F676.2; trickster cheats pair of b. from two cobblers K233.3; water enters into giant's b. from above F531.3.1.1.

Booty. — Clever thief, having seen his victim in a disgraceful position, may keep b. J1211.2; dupe loses b. through singing J2351.3; effects of wild hunt remedied by asking to partake in b. of hunt E501.19.4; king gets first choice of b. P13.9.1; lion divides the b. J811.1.1; thief hoping for bigger b., loses smaller K421.1; wolf as commander orders all b. divided, but keeps his own U37.

Boring as animal's occupation A2456; hot irons through ears Q469.9; way out of prison R221.2. — Flood from animal's b. into ground A1016.1.

Border. — Inn at b. of otherworld F147.4; wood at b. of otherworld F143.

Born, see also **Birth.** — Beings b. in hell A671.6; child b. too soon J1276; children b. on same night betrothed T61.5; divination as to which son to be b. first D1812.5.0.17; earth b. of chaos A801; eldest god b. in front, younger at back A161.5; friends b. at same moment P311.4; hero b. three times A511.1.7; prophecy: child to be b. M311.0.3; vow

to marry one b. under same circumstances M146.2; what not yet b., given life? H832.

Borrowed bread (that we ate last week) H583.4.2; feathers *K1041; horse deceptively wins tournament K28. — Comb b. by fairy from Christian maid to comb hair of changeling bride F322.1.1; dwarfs return b. goods F451.5.10.4; eyes b. by animal *E781.3; money b. from fairies F358; object b. for a day retained K2314.1; stomach b. by animal E787; witness claims the b. coat: discredited J1151.2.

Borrower's absurdities J1531; and lender's (practical retorts) J1550ff.

Borrowing friend's money, coat to teach lesson J21.38; money from fairy F342.2; from mortals by dwarfs F451.5.10.3; from mortals by fairies F391; from peasant by mountain-men F460.4.5. — Animal characteristics: b. and not returning A2241ff.; chain b. brings huge amount on little credit K455.10; girl b. from fairies, abducted F324.1; lover's gift regained: b. from the husband and returning to the wife K1581.3; spirits b. from mortals F417.1; trolls' b. F455.6.2.

Bosom. — Conception from putting ball into b. T532.6; giant carries man in his b. F531.5.1.1; mother's b. (softest) H652.2.

Both? K1354.1, K437.

Bottle becomes gold D475.1.14; hidden in thigh F1034.3.2. — Alleged inexhaustible b. sold K117; burying b. prevents witch's urinating G271.4.7; coin noisy in empty b. J262.2; complaint about the empty b. K455.6; creator distributes b. A1440.1; death enclosed in a b. Z111.1; deception into b. (vessel) K717; demon enclosed in b. *D2177.1, (released) R181; filling water-b. with spout downward H1023.2.2; ghost corked up in b. E464; jinn escapes b. to kill captor J339.17; magic b. *D1171.8, (supplies drink) D1472.1.17; opening b. tabu C625; saint throws ink b. at devil D2176.3.3.3; soul hidden in water b. E712.7; spirit as fly going into b. F401.3.4; spirit in b. as helper F403.2.2.4; stopped b. as protection against witches G272.10; ten serving-women carried in b. D55.2.4; test of strength: breaking heavy b. over a loaf of rye bread H1562.3; thief hides in b. K439.11.

Bottlefly finds stolen woman in sky B543.1.

Bottom. — Earth brought up from b. of primeval water A811, A812; quest for the b. of the sea H1371.2.

Bottomless lakes (pools) H713.2; tub magically holds water D2199.1. — Filling b. water tube H1023.2.4; filling leaky vessel with water from a b. jar Q512.1.

Bough does not burn F979.5. — Fire bends b. to shape of crozier F964.1; magic b. *D954.

Boughs. — Tree grateful for having b. trimmed D1658.1.5.1; twelve cypresses with thirty b. each (riddle) H721.3.

Bought, see also **Buying;** game used to prove hunting prowess K1968.1. — Admission to woman's room b. T45; child b. to serve as sacrifice to demon S273; chest containing hidden paramour b. by trickster as sham-magician K1574; good counsels b. *J163.4; dream of treasure b. N531.3;

eyes b. back and replaced *E781.2; flower (enchanted girl) b. from her mother by prince T52.1; place in husband's bed b. by forgotten fiancée D2006.1.4; woman's hair b. by devil G303.25.13.

Boulder. — Ogress pegged to b. G514.5.1; strong man lifts mighty b. F624.2.

Bound, see also **Binding.** — Devil b. with chain A1070ff., G303.8.4.1; life b. up with light *E765.1; pestilence spirit b. by magic F493.3.2; thief b. as family god K439.8; vow against being b. M166.2; witch b. and beaten G275.7.

Boundary. — Dead returns to replace b. marks he has removed E345.1.

Boundaries, god of A414; of the otherworld F140ff.; spirit of F494.2. — Elephant draws plow to mark empire's b. B599.3; origin of b. A997; origin of erection of monuments to mark b. A1599.2.

Bouquet. — Flower b. leads to brothers' recognition H16.3; love through seeing b. T11.4.3.1; quest for b. of all flowers (bee-hive) H1377.2; quest for the most beautiful b. H1302.

Bovine, see also **Cow.** — Transformation: b. animal to person D314.1; transformation: man to b. animal D114.1.

Bow, see also **Arrow;** brings luck to king D1812.5.2.9. — Aesop with the unbent b. J553.1; Amazons cut off left breast of daughters so that they can handle b. F565.1.1; baby hands disguised father a b. H481.1.1; bear becomes b. D421.6.1; bending b. of woman's absent husband (suitor contest) H331.4.2; child born with magic b. T552.5.2; conception from god's b. T532.9; death by rebounding b. N335.3; divine twins make b. A527.1.1; extraordinary b. F836; girl makes enormous b. F624.9; god with b. of fire A137.14.1; god's b. A157.6; magic b. *D1091; magic musical b. D1233.1; magic transportation on musical b. D1520.33; one bird escapes as hunter bends his b. J641.1; prince born with gold b. H71.7.2; rainbow as b. of thunder god A791.1; recognition by unique ability to bend b. H31.2; witch eats b. G269.6.

Bows. — Numskulls try to kill mosquitoes with b. and arrows J2131.0.1; origin of b. A1459.1.1; peoples choose b. and arrows or guns and horses A1614.3; precocious hero demands b. F611.3.3.0.1.

Bow-string. — Remarkable b. F836.0.1; wolf tries to eat b. J514.2.

Bow-strings. — Mice gnaw enemies' b. and prevent pursuit K632; transformation to ant to gnaw b. of enemy D651.4.

Bowed. — Why certain fish have b. backs A2356.2.4; why sheep walk with b. heads A2221.9.

Bowel. — Auguries from b. movements D1812.5.0.8.1.

Bower. — Captivity in b. R41.2.2; crystal b. for fairy's mistress D2185.1; crystal b. in otherworld F165.3.5.1; shining b. for fée F224.

Bowing. — Cloud b. to female mountain A969.2; crucifix b. as sign of favor D1622.1; image b. to indicate favor D1622.2; king selected by elephant's b. to him H171.1; magic object b. D1648; tree b. before prince H71.10.1.

Bowl mistaken for helmet J1772.5; transformed D454.6.1. — Devil as

round b. G303.3.4.8; magic b. *D1172.2, (restores strength) D1519.1.1; sun a golden b. with peacock on rim A724.2; washing in magic b. produces immunity from old age D1349.2.2.

Bowling. — Dead persons b. E577.3.

Box connection of poor to rich man J1561.6; on the ears J2494, K2376; opened by right person D1651.12; swallowed by dragon leads to underground kingdom F721.3.2; transformed to carriage D454.1.1. — Attempt to keep wife chaste by carrying her in b. *T382; bear substituted for woman in floating b. K1674; children abandoned in potter's b. S152; compressible magic b. D491.2.1; descent into ocean in glass b. F1022.1; disease brought to man in b. A1337.0.1.1; escape from deluge in b. A1029.5; ghost prevents removal of b. from abbey E299.2; heroine in b. which is bought by prince K1342.1; husband carries off b. containing hidden paramour K1555; impostor demands b. K1944; impostors carry hero in b. K1942; light kept in b. A1411.1; looking into b. forbidden *C321; magic basket (b.) furnishes livestock D1477.4; magic basket (b.) furnishes slaves D1476.3; magic b. *D1174; (furnishes money) D1452; moon kept in b. A754, A755.1; ogre trapped in b. G514.1; pope tests women's obedience: not to look into b. H1557.4; prince first sees heroine as she comes forth from hiding-b. N712; purchase of b. without knowledge of its contents N91; river contained in b. D915.3; soul hidden in b. E712.4; spider hands b. to ant and refuses to take it back: hence ants carry huge loads A2243.1; sun a bowl in crystal b. A724.2; sun kept in b. A721; touching magic b. tabu C533; treasure b. filled with trash: owners quarrel K2131.4; trick into entering b. K714.2; trickster hides in b. to be carried K1892.1.1.

Boxes ordered placed in temple by captive general cause relaxed vigilance and permit his escape K536.

Boxing-match: fatal boxer defeated K13.

Boy borrows python's hands and feet A2241.8; corps P551.5; as helper N832; hero Z251; kills his animal father B631.0.2; lives on ox F562.1; and the mantle H411.7; overhears witches, gets their magic D838.9; persuades father not to plow up crop, saves own life J92; resuscitated by lie H252.4.1; says "I know", gets into difficulties; now says "I don't know" J21.52.7; shot from cannon X1852; slays ogre G512.8.3; twitted with illegitimacy seeks mother H1381.2.2.2.1. — Adulteress disguised as b. elopes K1593; angels help b. prince V232.1.1; animals hide b. in their belly B529.1; bone in demon's stomach becomes a b. E149.1; chain tale: b. changes self to nut Z43.5; clever b. *J1113; delivery b. frightened, gives up chickens K335.0.9; devil enters the body of dead b. G303.18.1; hero's exploits as a b. Z231; ogre as small b. G376; persecuted b. hidden in mare's belly K551.3.6.2; reincarnation: b. to bird to b. E610.1.1; seven-year-old b. begets child T579.3.1; small b. overcomes gorilla L311.5; spirits teach b. how to sing F403.2.3.3; substitution of low-caste b. for promised child H38.2.5; supernatural mother to return if b. born M272;

taking b. to enemy's tent as fear test H1418; tasks assigned because of foolish boast of b. H915; water-spirits take mistreated b. F420.5.2.2.2; woman seduces b. by feigning illness K1393.

Boy's golden body royalty sign H71.2.1. — Oath taken on b. head H252.4.

Boys as hostages P533.1.1. — Disenchantment by drinking milk of queen who has borne two b. D764.1; little b. help hero win girl T66.2; living b. transformed into plants A2617.1; ogress invites b. to live with her G414; resurrected b. return to heaven E755.0.1.

Bracelet gift from river goddess N815.0.2.1. — Magic b. *D1074; magic wishing b. D1470.1.39; recognition by b. H95.

Bracelets, extraordinary F827.6.

Braggart. — Drowning punishment of b. Q552.19.0.1.

Brahma as creator A1.4; cursed by other gods: has no temples A162.4; takes men to Siva F12.3; -world A697.1. — Reward: birth in B.-world V526.

Brahmin forced to pay cow's burial fee K499.5; gives servant polluted fish K344.1.1; in love with washerwoman T91.7.1; may marry from any caste T131.9; punished for killing animal Q231; in rags treated as beggar; steals to feed guests W11.4.1; takes shape of prince K1952.0.1; teaches king wisdom J179.1; ungrateful to goose rescuer W154.12.2; unwittingly kills calf N361.1; wins discussion on religion V351.1.1. — Absurdity of turning king into B. J1293.3; ascetic imitates B. J2415.5; barber passes for a B. K1827.0.2; chain tale: why B. worships himself Z42.3; curse of B. M411.14.3; fate takes form of pupil of B. K1811.4.1; honest B. spared by tiger Q151.10; king can't execute B.; brings about his suicide J1181.0.1; penance: inviting B. to dinner Q527; stupid B. J1705.2; treacherous B. K2284.2; wells as B. women H1292.1.1.

Brahmins. — Almsgiving to B. C94.1.2.

Braiding. — Dwarf b. hair for sleeping maids F451.5.1.13; transformation by b. hair D577.

Brain of forgetfulness D1365.11; transformed to serpent D447.10. — Clouds from Ymir's b. A1133.1; magic animal b. D1011.7; magic b. *D997.2; magic b. assures heaven for man who dies upon it D1588.1; magic dog b. cures D1502.8.1; removable b. F557.1.

Brains as snakebite cure D1515.4.6. — Ball of human b. kills enemy N623.3; compassionate executioner: substituted b. K512.2.0.1; eating own b. K1025.1; enemies' b. used as balls S139.2.2.4.2; human b. as ball weapon F839.5; insects from b. of slain animal A2001.1; pottle of b. as metaphor for clever girl J163.2.1; sham blood and b. K473, K522.1.

Brain-fever bird's cry A2426.2.16.

Bramble chosen king of trees P11.0.2.1. — Devil has not been seen since he created b. G303.17.3.4; lake rises from b. bush F934.2; ogress reincarnated as b. bush E631.4.

Brambles heaped to halt enemy K2369.12. — Forced dancer in b. N55.1.

Branch dries up water in river D1542.3.3; leaps from hand to hand D1641.6; of tree transformed to animal D441.3. — Ambitious b. chosen king of trees J956; bringing b. of tree guarded by ghosts (task) H1151.10; doing penance till green leaves grow on dry b. Q521.1; dry b. on innocent man's grave blossoms E631.0.5.1; magic b. *D954, (musical) *D1615.2; magic b. produces rice harvest D1563.1.6; man kills son thinking that he is cutting a b. N325.1; tree b. transformed to palace D451.1.0.1; youth asks for b. of tree H611.

Branches of tree guarded by dragon H1333.6; turn upward to avoid idolators F979.20; of world-tree H619.3. — Capture between b. K742; numskull sticks his head in the b. of a tree J2131.5.3; tree b. prove journey H84.1; tree with musical b. F811.6; tree with silver b. D1461.0.2; tree with twelve b. (riddle) H721.1; twining b. grow from graves of lovers E631.0.1.

Branching tree as roadway for souls E750.2.3.

Brand. — Life bound up with burning b. E765.1.2; strong hero engendered from burning b. F611.1.10.

Branding person makes him one's slave for life P171; as punishment Q472; of sacred animals H55.2. — Ghost b. drunkard E279.5; recognition through b. H55.

Brandy. — Acquisition of b. A1427.1; making a knot of spilled b. (task) H1021.4; sea people give ogre b. G525.

Brass, see **Brazen;** apple F813.1.4; clothes F821.1.2; seeds pave city F761.5.3; serpent as snakebite antidote D1515.4.5; statue at city gates blows on trumpet *D1317.9.1. — Acquisition of b. A1432.3; city of b. F761.2; ship b. within, steel without F841.1.6; tree with b. leaves F811.2.1.1.

Brave. — Only b. wear beards P642; sham b. man K1953; why lion is b. A2524.5.

Bravery W32; as tribal characteristic A1676. — Deed of b. required before feast W213.1; money received from ghosts as reward for b. E373.1; origin of b. A1381.

Bravest know to wait J572.1.

Bray. — Ass betrays deity's secret: hence his ugly b. A2239.3.

Braying of ghost donkey E402.2.2. — Ferocious animal frightened by ass b. K2324.1.

Brazen, see **Brass;** tower F772.2.1. — Earthen and b. pots in river J425.1; magic b. dog B182.1.8; oracular b. lion D1311.7.2.

Brazier of the gods A142.1.

Bread accidently dropped from tree on bear's nose kills bear N331.2; baked with onions for undesired guest J1563.3; becomes cake D476.4; dropped in mud: messenger returns for more K343.1.1; of fairies F243.1; made from mud D476.1.1; made by a sick woman (deduction) J1661.1.3; made from tree leaf D476.1.2; stolen by saint restored V412.1; transformed to another object D454.2, D471.1; transformed to serpents D444.4;

tree springs from crumb D454.2.2. — Badly baked b. for father-in-law S54.1; beer returned for b., neither payed for K233.4; beggar wants b., not you J1332; baking b. we ate last week H583.4.2; bleeding b. F991.3.1; consecrated b. *D1031.1.1; cutting both ends of b. loaf brings devil G303.6.2.13; deceptive bargain: as much b. as he wants to eat K173; devil makes amends for stolen b. G303.9.3.1.1; devils disappear when priest blesses b. G303.16.2.3.3; devil eats unblessed b. V31.5; dream b. K444; dwarf bakes b. F451.3.4.5; dwarfs dislike b. baked without salt F451.3.7.2; dwarfs emigrate because mortals put caraway seeds into b. F451.9.1.1; fairies give mortals fairy b. F343.19; fairies baking b. F271.10; fatal b. J1824; identification by ring baked in b. H94.2; lazy wife throws b. out of window W111.3.3; lies about b. X1811; literal host: b. and salt J2476; long-staying guest given black b. J21.9.1; magic b. *D1031.1, (inexhaustible) D1652.1.1, (furnishes treasure) D1465.1; "may your b. turn to stones" M411.2; misusing b. forbidden C535; murder by feeding with b. full of pins K951.2; murder with poisoned b. S111.1, K951.3; not to step on sacred b. C55.1; not to wipe children with b. C851.1.1; ordeal with b. and cheese H232; peasants fed white b. demand rye b. U135.3.2; pig becomes b. D422.3.1; quarrel over b. eaten by invisible man K1883.6; quest for the best of b. H1305; rejected b. resought J1923; respite from death gained by tale of the preparation of b. K555.1.2; riddle: always eat b. with honey H588.11; rubies baked in b. J1655.2; scraping b. tray as bride test H381.2.2; task: eat b. but bring it back whole H1071; task: eating mountain of b. H1141.1; test of strength: breaking a heavy glass bottle over a loaf of rye b. H1562.3; transformation by eating b. D551.4; two loaves of b. as parting gift N782; why he did not eat the b. J1345; wild hunt avoided by holding b. E501.17.5.6; witches bake b. G246; witches lack b. and salt G229.3; wolf who wanted to make b. Z49.5.2; woman gets b. by prayer D1766.1.8.

Bread crumb. — Abandoned children find way back by b. clue R135ff.

Bread crust. — Mouse makes boat of b. *B295.1.

Breadfruit. — Origin of b. tree A2681.11; resuscitation by b. wood image E53.2; tabu to eat b. C224.3.

Breadmaking as bride test H383.1.

Breaker of iron (strong man) F625. — Lie: remarkable b. X946.

Breakfast. — Enigmatic request for chickens for b. H599.6; evil eye before b. causes death D2071.0.3; farmer's b. for help: glass of water and lantern W152.12.1; groom invited to wedding b. with bride T137.3.

Breaking of bargains M205; girl's head to attract her attention J2461.9; of glass occurs by threes D1273.1.1.2; heavy glass bottle over loaf of rye bread as test of strength H1562.3; of goddess into five parts causes river's five branches A934.11.3; mirror as evil omen D1812.5.1.3; of object as life token E761.5ff.; of promises M205; huge rock to pieces (task) H1116; of stick with money in it betrays thief H251.3.4; twig

forbidden C513; upon a wheel Q423. — Banishment for b. water pots Q431.16; cannibal b. wind as attack G93; continued b. wind D2063.5; devil causes noise of b. wind G303.6.2.15.1; disenchantment by b. lamp D789.2; disenchantment by b. tabu D789.4; disenchantment from flower by b. stalk D711.4; disenchantment from leaf by b. it from tree D711.5; dwarf b. wind so hard canoe collapses F451.3.13.3; earth from egg b. A814.9; girl summons fairy lover by b. tabu *F301.1.1; origin of rocks from b. of God's sieve A971; punishment for b. betrothal Q252; trained deer b. leg by drinking wine thereafter abstains J133.3; transformation by b. tabu D510ff.; witch b. limbs G269.12; witch causes b. wind in public G269.21.1.

Breast, see also **Bosom, Pap.** — Amazons cut off left b. of daughters F565.1.1; conception from fruit thrown against b. T532.3; giant with lips hanging onto b. F531.1.4.2; ghostly horse puts hoofs on b. of sleeper E281.2; headless person with eyes and mouth on b. F511.0.1.1; husband becomes cannibal from eating wife's b. G36.1; maid cuts off b. to heal man's serpent wound D1515.4.1; milk suddenly appears in woman's dry b. T592; mother's b. (is softest) H652.2, (is sweetest) H633.3; ogress with one b. G369.6; origin and nature of animal's b. A2353ff.; person with ears on b. F511.2.1; person with mouth in b. F513.0.4; princess wins wrestling match with suitor by revealing her b. H331.6.1.1; punishment: burial alive up to b. Q456.1; remarkable b. F546; robin steals fire, has b. scorched A2218.5; severed b. regrows when woman bears child E788; snake sucks from woman's b. A2435.6.2.1; turf laid on b. of dead to prevent return E431.6.

Breasts. — Date palm's fruit like old woman's b. A2791.11; elephant loses its b. A2353.3; female bears have no b. A2353.4, B725; giantess (fairy, mountain-wife) throws her b. over her shoulder *F531.1.5.1, *F232.2, *F460.1.2, *G123; loom of woman's b. F856.1; magic b. of woman D1009.3; maiden sends to her lecherous lover her b. which he has admired T327.1; mermaid has large b. B81.9.2; origin of women's b. A1313.4; punishment: snake sucks woman's b. Q452; punishment: woman's b. cut off Q451.9; recognition in bed by large b. H79.6; recognition of son by gushing up of milk in mother's b. H175.1; sun, moon from b. of mother earth A715.4; vision of seals sucking chieftain's b. V515.2.1; wife offers starving husband milk from her b. T215.2; witch sucks blood from b. G262.1.2; woman's b. dry up as punishment C942.4; woman suspended by b. Q451.9.1; women's b. on foreheads A1313.4.1.

Breastplate, magic *D1101.3, D1079.3.

Breath in the cold thought to be tobacco smoke J1801; of dragon kills man B11.2.11.2; of dragon renders hideous D1337.2.2; of magic horse blows off or sucks in those he pursues B184.1.5; slows down princess in race F622.1, H331.5.1.1.1. — Anchorite's b. consumes tree D2082.2; angry warrior's b. heats adversary F1041.16.6.8; bad b. magically cured D2161.3.9; bad b. reveals disguised snake's identity K1822.3; birds

wither everything with their b. B33.1.1; cat sucks sleeping child's b. B766.2; catching a man's b. (task) H1023.13; cauldron warmed by b. of nine maidens F686.1; complaint about bad b. K2135; foul b. from breaking tabu C985.3; ghost searches for b. E599.1; ghost sucks people's b. E251.3.4; inducing bad b. to escape man's lust T320.4.1; magic b. *D1005; man created from b. A1262.1; man's bad b. proves wife's fidelity T221; man's b. made from wind A1260.1.5; men live by gods' b. A1394; revenant with bad b. E422.1.5; soul in the b. E714.6; thumbling in danger of being sucked in by man's b. F535.1.1.4; wishes repeated in one b. granted D1761.0.2.1.

Breathing on enemy causes death D2061.2.9; magically lights lamp D1933; nine days under water F691; on sacred fire forbidden C51.1.3; tree X1116. — Animal b. fire *B742; creator's b. causes the winds A1121; doctor cures heart: patient stops b. X372.1; horse in wild hunt b. fire *E501.4.2.4; resuscitation by b. on corpse E66; sponge in corpse's mouth causes illusory b. K1885.1; tide caused by b. of sea monster A913.2.

Breeches, see also **Trousers.** — Jumping into the b. J2161.1; magic b. *D1055; rascals pull off judge's b. and leave him exposed K1285; thieving contest: first steals eggs from under bird, second meantime steals first's b. K305.1; why Russians wear their shirts outside their b. A1683.1.

Breviary. — Priest uses cook-book for b. V467.

Brewing ale from milk H1021.10; beer by means of magic song D1045.0.1; in eggshell F451.5.17.1, F481.4; magically prevented *D2084.1. — Introduction of b. A1426.3.1.

Briars. — A fleeing fox loses an eye in the b. J2182.

Briar-patch punishment for rabbit K581.2.

Bribed boy sings wrong song *K1631; executioner releases culprit K513; guards let prisoner escape R211.9; judge J1192ff., (punished) Q265.1; witness nonplussed: wrong question asked J1157. — Animal b. for help B325; death's messengers b. Z111.6.1; demons b. with food G582.1; priest b. to betray confessional V468; witch b. for secrets G275.5.1.

Bribery of courtiers by smith to protect wife T257.9. — Escape by b. K626; murder induced by b. K986; priest refuses small b. J1263.2.3; upright judge refuses b. W35.2; wisdom lost by b. J186.

Brick. — King works at b. building P15.7; magic b. *D935.4.

Bricks transformed to gold D475.1.7. — Gold hidden in b. N518; palace of gold, silver b. F771.1.1.2.

Bricklayer P455.

Bridal, see also **Bride, Marriage, Wedding;** couple seized by tiger for religious failure Q557.7; party will not pass over bridge for fear of water-demon G424. — Bad omen for two b. processions to meet D1812.5.1 8; dangers to husband in b. chamber T172ff.; husband driven from b. chamber T171; ogress killed in b. bed G519.1.3; throwing fruits on b. couple A1555.1.1.

Bride, see also **Marriage, Wedding;** abducted by fake carpenters K1825.7; accidentally kills husband N331.1.3; in basket C169.1; enchanted by witch loses organs D2062.4.1; fetched by groom after wedding T137.5; given away T135.7; has maid sleep in husband's bed to conceal pregnancy *K1843.1; helps suitor perform his tasks H335.0.1; like moon Z62.2; magically provided D1595; offered to correct guesser H511; offered to man who can defeat her in repartee H507.1; offered to man who can find answer to question H508.2; offered to man who can out-riddle her *H551; purchased T52; resuscitates hero E121.1.3.1; saves self from ravisher T320.3; stealing K1371; substitutes picture, escapes groom K525.1.2; tests *H360—H399; whose kissing annoys husband says she did not know it was he J1485; wounded accidentally on way home T152. — Abducted b. hidden in fairyland F322.4; casting sheep's eyes at the b. J2462.2; changeling b. F322.1; choosing b. by horoscope T54; choosing smallest possible b. J229.10; covenant to get friend a b. M246.3; devil tries to get man to kill his b. G303.9.4.3; divided b. (Solomonic judgment) J1171.2; dividing the winnings: half of the b. demanded M241.1; eagle seeks king's b. D647.2; faithful servant accompanies b. to new home T133.1; false b. unable to finish true one's weaving H35.3.1; false death message to secure another's b. K1864.1; favorite performs task to win b. for king K1848.2; foolish b. J2463; foster brother steals b. K1371.1.2; ghost substituting for b. E363.1.1; hero wakened from magic sleep by wife who has purchased place in his bed from false b. *D1978.4; ignorant b. castrates groom J1919.5.1; keeping questionable b. for fear of worse J229.9; king mourns disappeared b. F1041.9.1.2; king's son woos father's b.: both killed K1094; leaving earthly b. for service of Virgin T376.1; magic arrow shot to determine where to seek b. D1314.1.3; man drowns b. S62.2; murderous b. T173; ogress's daughter as b. H305; ornaments b. wore in former birth H1371.4; otherworld journey to get b. F87; oversensitive b. K2052; quest for b. *H1381.3.1; quest for b. for king H1381.3.1, T11.1.1; quest for the most beautiful b. *H1301.1; quest for b. richest and poorest H1311.2; real wife thwarts husband's acquiring b. J1112.1.1; recognition of maidservant substitute b. by her habitual conversation H38.2.3; runaway horse carries b. to her lover N721; rescue of b. from mysterious perils by hidden faithful servant R169.4.1; smallest woman best b. J1442.13; substituted b. *D1911ff.; substituting false b. for father K1094.1; suitors put to severe tests by prospective b. or father-in-law *H310—359; thief disguised as b. K311.16.2; thieves abduct b. from palace K315.3; umbrellas welcome b. A1555.3.

Bride's instinctive expertness in love J64. — Disguised man takes b. place: leaves goat for bridegroom K1836.3; giant b. equipment F531.1.13; testing b. chastity H452.

Bride-race. — Loser in b. must die H331.5.0.1.

Bridebench. — Gifts on b. T136.4.1.

Bridegroom T137.3ff.; abducted by giantess R10.4.1; alone plucks flowers

from bride's grave H31.12.1; attacked in bride's apartments K778.4; bribes thief to leave wedding J1392.5; buys widow cloth for bride Z140.4; castrated by ignorant bride J1919.5.1; chosen from pictures T131.1.2.2; dies from joy F1041.1.5.1; driven from bridal chamber by magic T171; killed by lightning on wedding night N339.4; to meet disaster on elephant M340.4; and men come for bride T133.5; murdered while bride asleep K873.2; permits visit to lover H1552.1; prisoner in giantess' room R41.4; propounds riddles H540.5; slain on way to bride T153; substitutes bedmate to overhear her secret K1844.3; like sun Z62.2. — Betrothal token to parents of b. T61.4.4; cowardly b. W121.7; dangers to b. in bridal chamber T172; disguise a b. to enter girl's room K1349.1.4; false b. K1915; foolish b. follows instructions literally J2462; god as b. A137.12; ignorance of b. on wedding night J1744.1; literal b. drowns bride J2489.11; loathly b. D733; man gets b. drunk, enjoys bride K1371.5; numskull b. unwittingly detects thieves N611.3; oath to marry daughters only into family with b. for each M149.5; princess brings ill luck to b. K443.12; quest for unknown b. H1381.7; robber b. K1916; shirt for father of b. H383.2.3; substitute b. K1915, (to save husband from poison maiden) H1844.2; swine b. disenchanted D733.2; thief disguised as bride robs b. K311.16.2; thief disguised as b. K311.8.3; trickster masking as b. K1354.3.2; witch breaks leg of b. G269.12.1; woman engages false b. for daughter K1624.

Bridge-building contest K48; connecting earth, heaven A657.1; -crossing as righteousness test H1573.6.1; cut from under sinner, he falls into hell Q417.3; of the Gods A986; of heaven A661.0.5; to land of dead *E481.1.2.1; made by magic *D1258.1; to otherworld *F152; tests souls H210.1; of untouchable tree's wood M172.2. — Animals as b. across stream B555; animals build b. B299.8; bargain with devil evaded by driving dog over b. first S241.1; belt becomes b. D454.3.3; blind man crosses a narrow b. which his guide is afraid to attempt U171; bridal party will not pass over b. for fear of water-demon G424; building a b. of cattle K1441; building enormous b. (task) H1131; crossing stream on an ashen b. (by use of staff) H586.6; the crow on the tarred b. Z39.3; deaf man on the b. X111.5; devil builds b. G303.9.1.1, H1131.2; devil builds b. minus one stone G303.14.2; do not cross a b. without dismounting from your horse J21.7; dragon guards b. to otherworld B11.6.6; dragon makes b. across steam for holy man B549.2; dream of treasure on the b. N531.1; dupes lured onto tree-trunk b.; fall to death K983.2; extraordinary b. *F842ff.; fugitives cut support of b. R235; ghost frightens people off b. E272.3; stubborn goats meet each other on a b. W167.1; ghosts gathered on a b. E496; long tongue cut out and used to b. a stream F544.2.2.1; magic b. *D1258; maiden at b. to hell A672.2; monkeys construct b. across the ocean B846; ogre attacks intruders on b. G475.2; perilous trap b. *F842.2.1; rainbow as gods' b. A791.3; recognition by overheard conversation with b. H13.2.1; secrets

overheard from b. N451.1; self-folding b. prevents pursuit D1642.1; smoke becomes b. D469.2; soul-b. A661.0.5.1; soul crosses on scythe blade as b. E721.6; stone b. appears for fugitives, disappears for pursuers R246.1; tabu: crossing sacred b. C93.4; wand becomes b. D451.6.1.1; if witch grabs horse's tail on b. man is safe from her G273.4.1.

Bridges, lies about X1817.

Bridle goes with horse when horse is brought P621. — Bewitching with magic b. G241.2.1.1; disenchantment by taking off b. *D722; fortune from informing foreign king of use of saddle and b. N411.3; horse losing b. tabu C884.2; loosing b. in selling man transformed to horse tabu C837; lost ass, saddle and b. offered as reward to the finder J2085.1; magic b. *D1209.1; transformation to horse by putting on b. *D535.

Bridling a wild animal (task) H1154.3.

Bright, see also **Gleaming, Glowing, Luminous, Shining;** eyes as sign of royalty H71.6; star indicates birth of holy person F961.2.1. — Devil wears a b. green coat G303.5.2.3; dwarf king has b. torch F451.7.4; extraordinarily b. sword F833.3; saint's hand made b. V222.1.2.

Brightest stars are sun's children A764.3. — What is b.? (riddle) H651ff.

Brigit, festival of V70.6.

Brimstone. — Water becomes b. D478.13.

Brine becomes wine D477.2.

Bringing back person from the dead F81.1; documents from distant city in one day H1107; as many horses as there are days in the year (task) H1117; an ogre to court H1172; water from distant fountain more quickly than a witch H1109.1.

Bristles. — Boar's b. poisoned K898; boar's b. remarkably long X1233.1.1; hog with silver b. H355.2.

Broad and narrow road in otherworld F171.2; path to hell F95.2. — Breast b. and made of metal F546.1; extraordinarily b. spear F834.2; giantess more b. than tall F531.2.5.1; remarkably b. men F532.

Broken leg saves man from fatal fight N178.1; objects restored by saint V229.10; vessel leads to adventure N783. — Boat b. by strong man as rower F614.4; cup given by fairy not to be b. F348.2; death from b. heart F1041.1.1; devil has b. foot G303.4.5.2; earth made from b. ground A824; emeralds from b. vase A978.3; enemy's sword b. by magic wand D1414.1; fixing the two pieces of a b. sword (task) H1023.8; identification through b. ring H94.5; identification by b. weapon H101; lover's gift regained: the b. article K1581.1; mending a b. jug (task) H1023.9; money from the b. statue J1853.1.1; mountain-men leave b. implement for man to mend F460.4.3; object miraculously b. F1098.0.1; promise to dying man b. M256; punishment for b. oaths M101; recognition by b. tooth H57.1; sewing together a b. mill-stone (task) H1023.7; skillful tailor sews up b. eggs F662.1.

Bronze boat F841.1.2; fairy boat F242.2.2; fortress in otherworld F163.5.1;

man (Talos) F521.3.1; palisade around otherworld F148.4; pillars in otherworld F169.1.1; sail F841.2.5.

Brooch. — Lost b. found in fish N211.1.5; magic b. D1072.3; raths marked out with b. A1435.2.1.

Brood. — Dove disregards experience and loses b. J16; dove's pride in her large b. linked with fear for their loss U81.1.

Brook, see also **Stream;** spirit F424.1. — Gathering all stones from b. (task) H1124.

Broom across door protects from witch G272.7.2; strikes sky, raises it A625.2.3; transformed into porcupine drives away ravisher B524.5. — Extraordinary b. F857; golden b. F857.1; lion's tail as b. H1151.11; magic b. D1209.8; origin of b. A1446.5.1; sweeping with a stick instead of a b. J1822; wife with b. frightens devil K212.1; worn-out b. at head of wild hunt E501.10.2.

Brooms. — Devil summoned by spitting on castaway b. G303.16.19.2.

Broom-corn. — Why b. is covered with blood-red spots A2751.4.5.

Broomstick. — St. Peter's wife meets him with a b. T251.3; witch flies through air on b. G242.1.

Broth, see also **Soup.** — Making b. for army H1022.5.1; saint cheated of b. without butter K499.2.1.

Brothel. — Adulteress's tryst in b.: scares off husband K1514.13; bull-keeper accused of maintaining a b. J2521.1; king's daughter put into b. to catch thief K425; saint accused of evil in entering b. N347.2.

Brother accused of impregnating sister K2121.1; aids task H981; causes brother's death by sending him to robbers K991.1; chosen rather than husband or son P253.3; Dead (ogre) pursues G323; in disguise aids quests H1233.2.2; eats brother G73.2, S73.1.2; flogs unchaste sister to death Q458.2.1; kills brother in duelling game K867; kills sister's husband J482.1.2; rescues brother from ogre G551.4; rescues sister(s) R156; secures blessing due another K1988; and sister arrange marriage of their unborn children M146.4; -sister incest M365.3, *T415; -sister marriage Q520.3, (of first parents' children) A1552.3; of the gods A164.1; throws away what he catches and what he does not catch he carries with him H583.3; transforms self to deer, seeks sister D647.1; wins sister's suitor test H310.2. — Angry b. mistakenly kills sister's husband N342.5; beggar claims to be emperor's b. J1337; blood of b. and sister will not mingle *F1075; burial of living man with dead blood b. S123.2.1; cruel b. S73; culture hero fights with his elder b. A525.1; culture hero's blood b. A515.3; disguise as older b. to obtain blessing K1839.11; dying man assigns bride to his b. T141.1; earth from murder of first b. and sister A831.4; eldest b. as hero Z221; escape by substituting b. K527.2; enigmatic counsels of a b. H596.1; false boasting of having killed foster b. K1766.1; foolish b. prays, acquires clever brother's property V52.12; foster b. steals bride K1371.1.2; ghost reminds b. of will E236.4.2; girl flees incestuous b. R224; girl getting child by b. D45.4;

girl seduced by b. becomes cannibal G37; god issue of b.-sister marriage P3; helpful animal foster b. B311.1; his b. cannot pray either J2352.1; husband, wife disguised as b. and sister K1839.14; impoverished youngest b. seeks work from elders L432.4; incestuous b. burned to charcoal D1865.2.1; insects from b.-sister incest A2006; is that you or your b.? J2234; king slays b. and brother's son S11.3.5; lecherous b. T415.1; lost b. recognized by modeling palace H16.1; lover kills his rival b. T92.5; man tricked into being sworn b. K2384; man's anger at eating with b. F1041.16.10; mild b. triumphs over warlike L353; money to good b., poison to bad D1663.6; moon, sun are sister and b. A736.1.1ff., A736.1.4.2; moon as sun's younger b. A745.3; prophecy: youngest b. to rule M312.2.2; punishment for killing foster b. Q211.9.2; queen in love with own b. K2213.3.4; quest for lost b. H1385.8; rescue from ogre by b. G551.1; resuscitation by b. E125.3; sham death to stab b. K911.2; sister and b. *P253; sister treacherous to b. K2212.0.1; treacherous b. *K2211; vow not to fight with b. M166.4; white b., black sister (riddle) H722.1; woman deceived into sacrificing honor for release of b. K1353; younger, preferred b. substituted by mother for elder K1855; youngest b. alone succeeds on quest H1242; youngest b. helps elder L31; youngest b. shares wealth with older ones W11.14.

Brother's consent for sister's marriage needed T131.1.1. — Clever younger b. property choice J242.8; dead b. return E226, (friendly) E326; madness over b. death F1041.8.10; nipple from b. caress J1833.1.1; troll's life in his b. forehead E714.3.1.

Brothers *P251; as creators A15.2; deceive sister swimming to her lover T83.1; die at sight of brother they sold into captivity N384.13; eat their sister G73.1; flee being sacrificed S272.1; as heroes *Z210ff.; identical in appearance F577.2; killing each other over paternity slander K1092; pose as princes K1952.3; rescue abandoned sister S357; rescue brothers R155; settle quarrel J552.5; and sisters do not marry A1552.1; having extraordinary skill *F660.1, (rescue princess) R166; and sisters *P250ff. — Accidental meeting of b. N733; berserk b. F610.3.3.1; combat of unknown b. brings about recognition H151.10; cruel b. forced to beg from abused sister L432.1; culture heroes are b. A515.1ff.; curse: all b. to be killed by single man M441.1.1; disenchantment by sewing shirts for enchanted b. D753.1; dream reveals death of b. D1813.1.4; elder b. impose task H934.4; enemy b. unite against common enemy J624.3; extraordinary companions are b. F601.5; flower bouquet brings recognition of b. H163; fool betrays his b. J2668; four b. construct a woman — whose is she? Z16.1; gifts from the b. J1283; hundred b. seek hundred sisters as wives T69.1; king's b. as joy, woe H1378.2; king's foster b. banished Q431.2.3; magic fish talk so that ogre thinks hero has many b. with him D1613.1; magic object stolen by b. D861.3; maiden will not give her troth to two b. successively T65.1; moon is wife to twelve sun b. A753.1.4.2; orphan b. as heroes L111.4.3; seven b. and one sister

Z71.5.1; seven b. marry seven sisters Z71.5.8; sun b. each work for one month, play for eleven A739.3; sun and moon as b. A736.3; tasks assigned at suggestion of jealous b. H912; three b. contest in wishing H507.3.1; three b. take turns using mule J1914.2; three hunchback b. drowned K2322; two b. at ogre's home G401.1; undesired combat between sworn b. N731.2.2; weak son condemned to be servant of b. M438.5; witch estranges b. G269.7.

Brother-in-law *P263; made king's inferior by holding his sword K1292; seduces sister-in-law T425. — Magic object received from animal b. B505.1; murder of b. punished Q211.9.1; suitor in contest with b. H332.2; treacherous b. K2211.1; wisdom from b. J177.

Brothers-in-law. — Helpful animal b. *B314.

Brows. — Giant three spans between b. F531.2.2.

Browbeaten husband shown by cock how to rule his wife T252.2.

Brown horse in wild hunt E501.4.2.3; man with white back F527.4; patches on soil where marvelous cow lay A989.1; as symbolic color Z146. — Dwarf wears b. F451.2.7.8; one eye b., other blue F541.6.1; fairies b. F233.8; mermaid's b. skin B81.9.5.2.

Brownie murders travelers for their blood F363.2.

Brownies F482.

Bruidhen as otherworld F135. — Smith as lord of b. P447.3.

Brunhilde T173.1.

Brush transformed to mountain D454.7. — Diving match won by deception: breathing under b. K16.1; man in moon burns b. as punishment for doing so on Sunday A751.1.1.

Brushwood at a distance mistaken for a ship K1886.4.

Bubble. — Devil created out of a b. G303.1.3.2; transformation: doe to b. of water (enchanted woman) D421.2.2; water b. becomes person D439.3.

Bucket dropped in well leads to adventures N777.2. — Children in moon with yoke and b. A751.7; drawing b. of well water without rope H1023.20; magic b. *D1171.10; ordeal by stone from b. H233; wolf in one b. and fox in the other K651.

Buckets. — Inexhaustible b. as source of lakes A920.1.1.

Buckeye as repository for fire A1414.7.1.

Buckwheat. — Why b. produces twice a year A2793.9.

Buds A2771ff. — Extraordinary tree b. F811.17; mankind emerges from b. on trees A1236.1; trees bear first b. to commemorate reign of primitive hero A2771.5.

Buddha V212. — Casting of image of B. delayed until a maniac's mite is thrown into the furnace V125; ceremony of the proclamation of a B. V88; journey to B. F12.4; punishment for doubting religion of B. Q225.3; saint's relics assume form of B. D457.16.1; slander: B. killed woman K2155.2.

Buddhist otherworlds A697.

Buddhists slaves of Taoists V355.

Buffalo as animals' king B240.7; eating up turban J1192.1.1; magically called D2074.1.1; helps tiger quench fire: white mark left on buffalo's neck where tiger held on while being ducked in water A2211.12; as king of animals B240.7; refuses tiger's dinner invitation J425.2; sucks up hero, releases him F914.2. — Bathing hair in b. milk D1337.1.3.1; boy as housekeeper for b. herd N832.1; blind man mistakes woman for b. X124.1; bride as reward for b. killing T68.2; cannibal devours b. raw H46.1; creation of b. A1878; custom of eating b. flesh A1515.1; deity rides b. A136.1.6; devastating b. G357; duel of b. and tiger B264.3; fools try to use b. tongue as knife J1971; flying b. B43.1; friendship of tiger and b. A2493.3; giant b. B871.1.1.3; helpful b. B411.4; horse sewed in skin of b. F984.1; how b. got hair under chin A2322.1; Indra sends down b. whose milk offered to saints B184.2.3.3; man becomes b. D112.5; man catches b. by rope and is dragged to death J2132.1; man transformed to b. D114.1.4; marriage to b. in human form B651.2; origin of b. A1878.1; origin of hide of b. *A2311.6, A2247.1; overcoming savage b. H1161.2; porcupine and b. K952.1; punishment: reincarnation as b. Q560.1.1; reincarnation as b. E611.2.4; sacred b. B811.3.1; sale of dead b. by making him seem alive K136; skinning b. alive X983; speaking b. B211.1.5.2; sun sits on back of b. A722.8; tabu to slaughter b. in temple C935.5; trickster puts on b. skull J2131.5.1; transformation to b. so as to eat grass D655.1; why horns of b. are bent A2326.3.4; why tiger eats b. A2435.3.9.4; wild b. herd used by trickster to steal K335.0.13.

Buffalo's eyes turn into protecting dogs D699.1; fate in bamboo growing from head N119.2.

Buffaloes emerge from earth, first man holding tail A1714.3.1; fail to come at god's leavetaking: now killed by tigers A2231.12; give hero horns to summon them B501.1; grateful for being cleaned B395.1; grateful for care of their calves B395; sacrificed for ghosts E433.4.1; save hero from tiger B524.1.5.1; tramp hero's enemies to death B524.1.5. — Blood of b. vitalizes tiger D1594.4; bringing much mud without b. H1129.1.1; cheese from white b. milk H1361.6; creator of b. A84.1; fighting b. as task H1165; gate takes twelve b. to open F776.1.1; god's b. A155.7; goddess of b. A441.1.1; thief serves king lost b. J1289.15; quest for devastating b. H1362.1; riding b. H1155.5; transformation to milk b. D659.13; treasure appears on horns of b. N549.1; wind drives b. for god A199.4.

Buffoon. — Disguise as b. K1818.3.1; reward for generosity to king's b. Q42.5.

Bugle. — Alleged resuscitating b. K1138.

Bugs, bees can't eat each other's food J1565.2. — Creation of b. A2052; dog-eating b. J1531.2.1; why b. smell bad A2416.6.

Builder. — Careful b. outside when storm comes is killed: careless b. saved N174; devil (giant) as a b. G303.9.1ff., F531.6.6.

Builders throw away beams from the scaffolding until it all falls down J2171.3. — Fairies as b. F271.2.

Building causeway as suitor test H359.1; enormous bridge (task) H1131; castle (task) H1133, (in one night) H1104; falls because of breaking tabu C931; home one wattle at a time J67.1; too large a structure forbidden C771; nests learned by bird A2431.1; sinks into earth F941; site determined (by halting of animal) B155.1ff., (by magic arrow) D1314.1.2, D1314.1.4, (by magic staff) D1314.2.5; village in one night H1104.2. — Acquisition of b. craft A1445; animals b. palace for man B572.1; devil builds b. G303.9.1.13; dwarfs b. tower F451.3.4.1.1; enchanted b. D6; escape from deluge on floating b. A1021.0.6; fairies b. for mortal F346.2; friendly ghost haunts b. E338; ghost laid inside b. E437.6; ghost-like b. E531; god b. temple A141.2; great b. X1033; magic b. provides treasure D1457; magic discovery of place for b. D1816.6; magic object produces b. D1483; man becomes b. D268; man learns b. from wasp A1445.2.2; man sells soul to devil in return for devil's b. house M211.2; magic lyre charms stones into their places in b. D1565.2; omen at laying foundation of b. D1812.5.2.8; prophecy: child to build religious b. M311.2; strong man pulls down b. F627; treasure hidden in b. N517.

Buildings bewitched G265.8.5; in otherworld F163. — Dwarfs destroy b. F451.5.2.5; extraordinary b. F770ff.; giants by night move b. built by men in day F531.6.6.1; ghosts haunt b. E280ff.; lie: remarkable b. X1030ff.; magic b. and parts *D1130ff.; religious b. *V110ff.

Built. — Castle (hell) b. by devil G303.8.3.2; devil destroys by night what is b. by day G303.14.1; devil in each stone of church b. with ill-gotten wealth G303.8.4.2; fires b. by dead persons E578; palace b. by mountain-spirits F460.4.2.1; road b. by devil for farmer in one day G303.9.2.2; soul wanders and demands that a temple be b. for him E419.1.

Bulbul. — Chain of killings: from b. to boy **Z49.13.**

Bull, see also **Steer;** in the china shop J973; determines road to be taken B151.1.2; draws one hundred carts for master's wager B587.3; -god A132.9; with human hands, feet B15.6.4; lows musically B297.0.1; with man's head B23.2; melts away after evil spirit has issued from him F981.2; mistaken for horse J1759.4; Nandia, provides warrior's equipment D2107.1; paramour *B611.4; recognizes princess H162.3; refuses to fight goat J371.1; survives plague F989.6; with three cranes A137.7; transformed to person D333.1; worship V1.8.1.1. — Arrow shot at b. returns F831.4; beating calves to punish b. J1863.1; bewitched man believes dead b. chasing him G269.24; blind man and the b. X123; brazen-footed, firebreathing b. B19.1; bellow of b. heard over entire land B741.4; deceptive division of shared b. K171.7.1; devastating b. B16.1.5.3; devil as white b. G303.3.3.1.4; divinity reincarnated as b. E611.2.1; earth supported by b. A844.2ff.; enmity between dog and b. A2494.4.8; escape by riding on sacred b. K551.6.1; fairy in form of cow (b.) F234.1.1; frogs fear defeated b. J613.2; fugitive b.-calf returns,

defeats father L111.1.2; ghost as fiery b. E421.3.4; giant b. B871.1.1.2; gnats apologise for lighting on horn of b. J953.10; god rides a b. A136.1.3; heifers impregnated by supernatural b. T539.4; helpful b. B411.1; hornless b. B15.3.0.1.1; jackal makes lion suspicious of b. K2131.2; killing fierce b. H1161.2.2; lifting b. over fence J2199.3; magic b. B184.2ff.; making a b. bear a calf (task) H1024.1.1; man transformed to b. D133.2; marriage to god in b. form *B641.3; milking a b. (task) H1024.1; mouse torments b. who cannot catch him L315.2; prophetic dream induced by eating meat of b. D1812.3.3.6; punishment: riding through streets on b. Q473.1; "Rain" as ogre in b. form G372; raven on horns thinks he has led b. J953.10.1; sacred b. B811.3.2; soul as b. E731.13; stealing two horns of savage b. (task) H1151.7; sun as black b. A728.3; taming the b. by cutting off his horns J2107; winged b. B43.

Bull's bellow B741.4; eye transformed to hornets D457.11.1; magic legs D1012.1.1; tail exterminates army D1400.1.21; urination thought to be bleeding J1818.1. — Dragging to death by b. horns Q416.2.2; magic supplies from b. belly D1470.2.6; palace from b. legs D1483.1.

Bulls. —Fight of lions and b. J1022; sick man offers deity more b. than he owns K231.3.5; shadows of b. given to imaginary owner J1551.7.

Bullet. — Magic b. D1096.3; silver b. injures devil G303.16.19.14; silver b. protects against giants D1385.4.

Bullets cannot hit devil G303.4.8.11; ineffective on serpent B765.17. — Dupe wastes b., then seized K724; sheet protects army from b. D2163.9; witch catches, sends back b. G229.4.2; witch's familiars impervious to b. G225.0.4; witch throws b. back G265.8.3.1.2.

Bullfight as suitor contest H331.15.2; as task H1165. — Why man picked as b. judge W35.1.

Bullfinch's wedding B282.7.

Bullfrogs can not swim: never in water X1643.1.

Bullock mistakes cotton pods for own fat J1772.8; struck on hindquarters to kill it J1906.1. — Cow and b. yoked together A1689.1; deceptive b. wins swallowing contest K82.4; frog abuses b. J952.5; helpful b. B411.5; lion divides slain b. Q3.2; magic b. wins master's fight K1.1.1; master's horse exchanged for vicious b. K1456; old b. left to die W155.1.1; reincarnation as b. E611.2.1.1; speaking b. B211.1.5.3; wager on b. defeating elephant N77.

Bullocks. — Lie: two b. go where one cannot X1743.2.

Bulrushes. — Moses in the b. L111.2.1; trickster joins b. in a dance J1883.

Bumblebee, see also **Bee.** — Helpful b. B481.3.1; man becomes b. D182.1.1.

Bumblebees crossbreeding with mosquitoes X1280.1.1.

Bundle of wood magically acts as riding-horse D1523.3. — Bringing b. of faggots without rope H1023.19; dead person sails over sound on b. of straw E581.7; devil as b. G303.3.4.10; fairy as b. of rags F234.3.3; large b. identifies chief H41.10; making sails for a ship from one b. of

linen H1022.3; quarreling sons and b. of twigs J1021; writing tablets become b. D454.11.

Bundles. — Why ants carry large b. A2451.1.

Bunghole. — Building barrel around a b. W152.14.1; looking into b. of fairy barrel tabu F348.9.

Bungholes. — Eating b. X1761.2.

Bungling barber P446.1; fool J2650—J2699; host J2425.

Bunkhouse. — Lie: great b. X1033.

Burbot, color of A2411.4.3, A2218.

Burden of two asses J1352.1. — Animals carry extraordinary b. F982; ghost carries b. E592; relieving the beast of b. J1874.

Burdens. — Animal useful for bearing b. A2515; largest b. laid on smallest asses U12.

Bureaucrats debate who shall put out fire J2532.

Burial, see also **Burying;** alive *S123, (as punishment) *Q456, (of aged mother) S21.1, (to banish plague) S266; in certain ground assures heaven E754.3; in church wall cheats devil of soul K219.4; mounds as fairy dwellings F211.0.1; in old grave to deceive angel J2212.2; places as homes of dwarfs F451.4.1.9; service for fairy queen F268.1; service read into hat to prevent dead walking E431.1; among underworld folk F268. — Angel directs saint's b. V241.1.1; animal determines b. place of saint B155.3; arrow shot to determine b. place D1314.1.5; aversion to b. in foreign soil P711.8; cairn marks b. place A988; cow's b. fee K499.5; the cynic's b. J1442.4; dead grateful for b. E341.1.1; dead head grateful for b. E783.8; dead returns on b. day E586.1; dead returns third day after b. E586.2; disgraceful b. as punishment Q491.1; escape by dire prophecy on b. K575; escape by shammed b. K522.5; ghost enforces b. wishes E419.8; ghost haunts b. spot E334.2; ghosts prevent b. of corpse E273.1; ghost returns to demand proper b. E235.2; leek under tongue b. protection D1389.12; magic as reward for b. D812.4.2; origin of b. A1591; saint directs own b. E545.15; saint's b. place unharmed by sea F931.3; singing at b. P617; special b. exorcises witch G271.7; spirit disturbs b. vault F473.6.9; spring breaks forth to commemorate place of heroes' b. A941.4.1; usurer refused b. Q273.2.

Buried ghost E231.4; object found by magic D1816.4; treasure N511ff. — Animal b. alive to cure disease D2161.4.6; blind man recovers b. treasure K1667.1.1; bones of dead collected and b. E607.1; captive b. alive freed after struggles with jackal R212.1.2; corpse begs sinner not be b. on top of it E545.9; dog b. alive to prevent ghosts from walking E431.8; earth rejects b. body E411.0.6; everyone b. in saint's soil to go to heaven M364.11; fool has himself b. because he stinks J2193; ghost laid when leg is b. E441.1; ghost returns because not properly b. E235.2.2; gospels b. with saint V136.1; lights show where saint b. V222.1.4; live person b. by mistake J1834; lovers b. in same grave T86; man b. alive escapes tomb when it is robbed R212.1.1; man b. in sea F931.3.1; moon b.

in pit A754.1; mountain from b. giant A969.1; no one b. in saint's church shall go to hell Q174.1.1.2; ogre persuaded to go into hole: b. alive G512.4; persons b. with dead king P16.4; promise to be b. with wife if she dies first M254; raising a b. treasure (task) H1181; soul cannot enter heaven till body b. E750.0.1; storm from calling up spirits to help find b. treasure D2141.0.2; swindler b. on dungheap Q491.1.1; tail b. K1021.1; test of wife's ability to keep secret: the b. sheep's head H472.1; wheel b. in doorstep to prevent deviltry D1385.10; Virgin Mary has dissolute monk b. in consecrated ground V255.

Burlesque of church services K1961.1.2.1, (in witch's sabbath) G243.

Burned clothes restored by saint V229.10.1. — Clothes b. by magic D2089.8; clothes b. to rid them of insects J2102.6; colored face after being b. F1082.1; corpse b. to prevent return E431.13; country b. up by magic sphere D1408.1; coyote b. when hay is set afire: hence yellow patch behind his ears A2218.4; criminal's house b. down Q486.1; desecrated church b. through saint's power Q222.5.5; dupe persuaded to be b. in order to go to heaven K843; enemy lured into house, b. up K811.4; fairies' palace cannot be b. F222.1.1; fires b. in streets to ward off witches G272.4; giantess with b. arms F531.1.6.7.3; hair b., victim dies D2061.2.2.4.1; harlot b. as punishment Q243.1.1; heretic b. in bed by insane man V321; house b. down (to deliver man imprisoned in it) R121.3, (to rid it of insects) J2102.4, (when trickster reports high price paid for ashes) K941.2; how was town b.? J2062.3; invulnerability by being b. D1846.1; ogre b. to death G512.3; onlooker b. by woman's beauty F574.1.1; paramour b. in barrel of tow K1554.1; person b. up by magic object D1402.0.1; priests b.: dying woman wished cauterization J1511.18; ravisher's grave and body miraculously b. Q414.0.4.1; rescue from being b. R117; sky prevents earth being b. A651.1.1.1; souls in hell alternately b., drowned Q562.2; tree in which eagle has his nest b. by fox L315.3; uxorious king b. to death N339.5; victim b. (in building) K745, (in his own house) K812; victim b. up under dry-leaves covering K1010.1; witch b. by furrows G273.5.1; witch causes person to be b. G269.14; wizard b. as saint saved H1573.3.4; world b. as fire poured on A1031.4.1; world would be b. up if all sun brothers work together A739.3.

Burner. — Charcoal b. drives fairies off with fire F389.1.

Burning animal husband C36.1; animal in straw to release curse M429.3; bodies vomit F1099.5; caterpillars C841.3; cut hair to prevent witchcraft D2176.5; to death *S112ff.; to death after bringing devil's fire Q582.2; down house for seduction access K1349.7; dupe who gets into grass to learn new dance K1055; food test H1511.2; house quelled by stone cast F679.6; land after sowing seed J2460.1; by magic D2144.4; magically evaded *D1841.3; to make wife beautiful K1013.2.1; object forces witch to reveal self G257.1; oil thrown on ogre G572.1; pillar reaching heaven F774.2; as punishment for breaking tabu C927; river F715.6; saja wood tabu C514; stones F809.6.1; thatch protection against

witch G272.17; wasp nest J2102.5. — Animal characteristics from b. *A2218ff.; animal saves man from death by b. *B526; cat leaps through man, b. him to ashes B16.1.1.2; changeling returns child when threatened with b. F321.1.4.5; changeling told house b., leaves F321.1.4.9; color of flame indicates what is b. F1061.2; cure by b. grain where man has died D2161.4.8; deceptive game: b. each other K851; devil exorcised by b. wood G303.16.14.2.1; disenchantment by b. magic hair D771.1; enemies' feet magically b. D2091.10; evil spirit exorcised by b. fish D2176.3.1; fairy's look b. mortal F363.4; fakir's imperviousness to b. H1576.2; fire b. up whole tree at once H1129.5; flood from b. hot liquid A1016.2; fool tries to purify cotton by b. it J1974; ghost laid by b. body *E446.2; ghost laid by b. hair E446.2.1; giant rescues woman from b. at stake R151.2; girl beautified by b. D1865.2.1; house b. for no reason F473.2.4; husband rescues wife from b. N658, R151.2; jackal's b. tail K581.5; kingdom b. at night H1292.20; life bound up with b. brand E765.1.2; literal fool b. down house J2516.3.4; magic object b. animals D1445.6; magic object protects against b. D1382ff.; magic results from b. D1787; man b. to death, too lazy to put out fire W111.1.1.1; miraculous b. as punishment Q551.9.1; murder by b. *K955ff, N657; ogre killed by b. soul G512.5; ogre tricked into b. his throat K1033; old man b. self with gunpowder, burns self worse with hot water N255.6; ordeal by b. H221ff.; punishment: b. alive Q414; quenching the b. boat J2162.3; rabbit b. self when stealing ember A2218.7; release from curse by b. vomit M429.1; sham wise man b. down own house K1956.8; son rescues mother from b. at stake R154.1.1; son tries b. up mother S112.7; secret learned by b. hand N482.1; soul of sleeper prevented from returning by b. the body E721.1.2.3; sparrow carries b. straw to desecrated church Q222.5.5; strong hero engendered from a b. brand F611.1.10; unconsumed b. bush F979.5.1; victim kills swallower from within by b. F912.1; whose duty to put out fire? meanwhile town b. up J2183.6.1; witch burned by b. bewitched animal G275.3.1; witch exorcised by b. stick G271.1.

Burns. — Charm for b. D1503.3.1; magic cure of b. D2161.2.3; man in moon b. brush as punishment for doing so on Sunday A751.1.1; tempted man b. himself to avoid temptation T333.5.

Burr-woman G311.

Burrow of mole A2491.3; of rat into enemy city K2351.8. — Why crabs b. in sand A2433.6.3.2; why hyena stays in b. A2433.3.4.

Bursting buttons from violent emotion F1041.6; of frog when he swells to be big as ox J955.1; of ogre who tries to drink pond dry G522; of stone as sign of unjust judgment *D1318.1.1; of sword in son's hand when he is about to kill his father *D1317.6.1; of troll when sun shines on him G304.2.5; of vessels reveal disobedience D1318.12.1. — Dead arises at b. of shroud and pursues attendant E261.2; miraculous spring b. forth for holy person F933.1; object b. as life token E761.5ff.; origin

of culture hero from b. stone A511.1.4.1; river b. from well in pursuit A934.7; serpent b. asunder F981.1.

Burying, see also **Burial;** bewitched animal alive G271.4.10; dupe's hair to catch him K1021.1; the mole as punishment K581.3. — Deity b. mortal A185.4; disenchantment by b. victim and sowing grain over him D719.1; ghost laid by b. church bell, clapper separately E459.6; money received for b. sham-dead person K482; ogre suitor b. woman's murdered lover K912.3; promise on b. father in homeland M258.3; ravens teach Adam b. of dead A2223.7.

Bus. — Ghost rides b. E581.4.

Bush by day, woman by night D621.2.1; loses clothes in shipwreck: hence catches passerby's clothes A2741.4; mistaken for elephant J1771.4. — Angel of the b. A419.1.1; god speaks from b. A182.3.0.1; lake rises from bramble b. F934.2; magic b. D964; self-burning b. D1672.2; spurge-laurel is devil's b. G303.10.11; unconsumed burning b. F979.5.1; why ants are lords of the b. A2433.5.5; why b. holds on to passerby A2792.1, A2275.5.3; why hare lives in b. A2433.3.3.

Bushes. — Eavesdropping wife hidden in b. killed unwittingly by husband N322.2; future hero found in b. L111.2.1; hero an abortion thrown into the b. T572.2.3.

Bush-buck, red color of A2411.1.6.3, A2219.1.

Bush-cat, cry of A2426.1.1.

Bush-rat bites off tortoise's tail A2216.4.

Bushel. — The level b. K223; wind raised by putting cat under b. D2142.1.5.

Bushmen, origin of A1611.3.1.

Bushy. — Why animal has b. tail A2378.6.

Business relations of dwarfs and mortals F451.5.10ff. — Animals in b. relations B294ff.; hero made b. partner of rich man Q111.1; lucky b. ventures *N410—N439; modest b. plans best L250ff.; not in his line of b. J1354; paramour pretends to be coming on b. K1517.10; thanks for being out of b. J2569; worldly-minded learn to pray by thinking of their usual b. V51.2.

Bustard hatches but two eggs A2486.2, A2284.2.

Busy. — "Cease being king if too b. to hear me" J1284.2; executioner kept b. until rescue comes K555; peasant always b. A1655.1; pretending to be b. K1773.

Butcher *P448. — Prophecy: son will be killer; parents make him a b. M306.2; queen is placed in kitchen and abused by b. Q482.2; sheep killed by b., who, they are persuaded, will spare them J2137.5; treacherous b. K2249.4.1.

Butcher's. — Heads of b. family demanded by buyer J1293.5.

Butchers. — Jokes on b. X230ff.; oxen decide not to kill b. since inexpert killers might replace them J215.2.

Butter becomes bloody D474.5; made from nettles D476.1.5; magically

kept from coming D2084.2; transferred from another by magic D2083.4; weighed with the bread K478. — Boy with hat of b. X914; charms to make b. come D1573; clarified b. recognized as leavings F647.11; curse: milk will not turn to b. M471.1.1; deceptive b. loan J1556.1; fairy prevents b. coming F369.6; filling cracks with b. J1871; fool squeezes sixteen pounds of b. from dog J1919.3; giants like b. F531.5.13; man made of b.: it melts A1226.1; meat disguised as b. during Lent K498; mountain-man has stack of b. before his door F460.2.4; mud sold as b. K144.3; parson smears his hand with b. X417; pot deceptively sold as b. K144.2; saint makes b. D1573.1; stingy man only looks at b., doesn't eat it W152.5; water becomes b. D478.11; woman created from b. A1275.5.

Butterby Church Z61.3.

Buttercask stolen by playing godfather K372; thought to be a dead man J1783.1.

Butterfly transformed to bamboo D424.1. — Creation of b. A2041; dress becomes b. D444.10.1; friendship between moose and b. A2493.28; man becomes b. D186.1; monkey jumps into water after a b. J2133.10; reincarnation as b. E616.2; soul in form of b. E734.1; wasp twits b. with coming from ugly crysalis J312.1; wedding of b. B285.6.

Butterflies. — Origin of marks of b. A2412.3.2; thieving b. K366.7; transformed b. are rainbow's origin A791.9; why b. haunt urine A2433.5.6.

Butting. — Deceptive game: b. one another like rams K868.

Buttocks. — Bare b. as mock sunrise K1886.3.2; goddess with one and a half b. A123.8; magic b. D1006; ogre cutting off own b. G528; origin of animal's b. A2362; stinging of b. as cough cure N643.

Buttons burst as consequence of violent emotion F1041.6.

Buyer and deaf seller X111.11. — Attempt to cheat the b. J2083.

Buying, see also **Bought;** forbidden C781; off masked thief K152; same article several times K258.2. — Dwarfs b. peas for more than they are worth F451.5.10.5; drunk man tries b. island X812; ignorant youth b. medical degree K1955.8.1; numskulls b. things in common: paying full price J2037; wife b. husband T296.

Buzzard hatched by hawk ejected for fouling nest Q432.1; steals coyote's eyes K333.3; transformed to door flap D423.4. — Food of b. A2435.4.5; origin of crest of b. A2321.7; why b. is bald A2317.3; witch as b. G211.4.5.

Buzzards. — Lassoed b. rescue man from hole B547.2.1.

Cabbage. — Carrying wolf, goat, and c. across stream H506.3; the great c. (lie) X1423.1; transformation by eating c. D551.2.1.

Cabbages, meat fed to J1856.1.

Cabinet-maker P444.

Cackling geese spread alarm B521.3.2; of guinea hen A2426.2.13.

Cadaver arm trick renders insane N384.0.1.1.

Caesar's scorn of his wife's advice leads to disaster J155.3.

Caesarean childbirth a custom T584.3.

Cage, see also **Prison.** — Adulteress confined in a c. Q433.1.1; enormous c. F899.3; ogre trapped in c. G514.1; soul in bird c. E711.15; thief hidden in c. K312.1.

Cages. — Captivity in c. R41.7.

Cain drinks Abel's blood in dream D1812.3.3.7; slain with apple F839.3.1; slays Abel with camel bone F839.3; stole ducks from Eden A2426.4.1.1. — Animals refuse to devour C. B591.0.1; Formorians descended from C. A1659.1.1; giants as descendants of C. F531.6.1.9; mark of C. Q556.2; pygmies as descendants of C. F535.0.1.

Cairn marks battle site A989.4; marks burial A988. —Battle-c. P554.

Cake bag full of cobras K444.2; becomes bloody D474.3; vendor robbed on way to fair K475.3. — Alphabet written on c. learned by eating it D1819.4.2; bleeding c. F991.3; bread becomes c. D476.4; eating c. in famine if there is no bread J2227; enemy cured by poisoned c. F959.6.1; identification by ring baked in c. H94.1; magic c. *D1031.2ff.; magic c. restores speech D1507.5; magic rolling c. D1313.1.2; man worships a c. which from time to time he eats V1.10.1; planted c. grows cakes F1005.1; pseudo-magic c. tree K112.3; pursuit of rolling c. leads to quest *H1226ff.; single c. for Lent made large *K2311; tiger-shaped c. fulfills death prophecy M341.2.10.1; why c. not eaten during Lent V73.6.3; wolf bringing c. from the window-sill beaten K1022.4.

Cakes. — Alfred and the c. K521.4.1.2; charging thirty c. for cooking twenty-five K255.1; coins mistaken for c. J1772.3.1; guest of stingy host brings along c. to eat J1575; how he knew she was baking c. J1713.1; poisoned c. intended for husband eaten by thieves N659.1; pupil eats c. given as alms to master W125.4; rhymes about c. wife has stolen K435.1; throwing c. into uncles' faces H35.5; tree of c. D2106.3, F811.1.10; wall of c. separates enemies D2163.6.2.

Calabash. — Animals escape from forbidden c. C915.2.1; child born carrying c. T552.3; goddess with c. in moon A751.8.3; life bound up with c. E765.3.2; looking into c. tabu C324.1; magic c. *D965.2; man transformed to c. D221; origin of sea from overturned c. A924.1; recognition by c. H133; soul in c. E711.2.1; universe created from c. A617.2.

Calabashes magically broken D2099.4. — Flood from broken water c. A1016.4.

Calamity, see also **Catastrophe, Disaster.** — Bewailing a c. that has not occurred J2198; crow's maxim on flying away from c. J171.3.1; devil's presence presages c. G303.15.1; ghost light indicates impending c. E530.1.5; ghost as c. omen E575; wraith as c. omen E723.8.

Calamities at hero's birth T583.2; of the world A1000ff.

Calculation of changeling's age by the age of the forest F321.1.1.5; of time and the seasons A1485. — Interrupted c. J2035; riddles of difficult c. H680—H719.

Calendar, Russian A1689.7.

Calf all one color belongs to devil G303.10.9; asks for respite until he

grows up K553.0.2; mistaken for colt J1759.4.1; pitying draft ox is taken to slaughter L456; as sacrifice V12.4.4.2; -sheep B14.3; transformed to person D333.2; weeps B736.6. — Brahmin unwittingly kills c. N361.1; devil as c. G303.3.3.1.4; did the c. eat the man? J1815; eating c. forbidden C221.1.1.2; forgotten fiancée reawakens husband's memory by serving as milkmaid and talking to c. *D2006.1.2; ghost of c. E521.4; ghost as c. E423.1.8.1; god assumes form of c. D133.4.1; golden (silver) c. B102.5ff.; golden c. entered by Satan G303.18.4; golden c. moves D1639.5; hatching out a c. from a cheese J1902.2; helpful c. B411.3; Holy Ghost has just had a c. X435.4; image of golden c. vivified D445.3; islands from transformed cow and c. A955.5; line drawn by saint's bachall separates c. from its mother D1574; magic c. B184.2.5; magic knowledge of unborn c. D1819.8; making a bull bear a c. (task) H1024.1.1; man named "C." frees veal thief K579.7; man transformed to c. D133.4; origin of c. sacrifice A1545.3.2; parson made to believe that he will bear a c. J2321.1; prophecy: death from c. M341.2.22; punishment for flaying live c. Q211.6.1; quest for golden c. H1331.3.3; reincarnation as c. E611.2.3; riddle about golden c. H832; saint gives c. to wolf W10.2; slain c. alive next day *E155.5.1; speaking c. B211.1.5.5; swift when only a c. J2212.5; tabu to kill sacred c. C92.1.2; transformation to c. Q551.3.2.8; why is cow beaten by c.? H1292.16; wife substitutes c. for beggar husband abuses K1846; wolf substitutes for c. D2156.8; worship of golden c. V1.11.1.

Calf's bleating as accusation of stealing J1895; head to death's head D465, (punishment) Q551.3.3. — Cow punished for c. misdeeds J1863; getting the c. head out of the pot J2113; person with c. head F511.0.9.2; tail in ground betrays c. killing K1686; water on the c. back J1903.1.

Calves kept from cows to commemorate death V65.1; kept from cows during fast P623.0.7. — Beating c. to punish bull J1863.1; fairies admit c. to cows F366.1.2; fairies ride c. F366.1.3; four c. to one cow at birth T586.4.1; men must have been c., fond of milk J2214.6; "why dost thou frighten the silly c.?" K1784.2.

Calf-shed. — Future heroine found in c. L111.2.1.1.

Calf-statues, origin of A1546.0.3.

Call: Dord fían R187.1; for help from distance D1827.2. — Magic object comes at owner's c. D1649.2; treasure found when obeying c. of nature N534.6.

Called. — Animals c. together by magic object D1441; devil becomes powerless when c. by name G303.16.19.9; devil's castle c. hell G303.8.3.2; king's sons c. kings P30.1; girl not to eat before being c. by father C231.1; man c. for help by animal B383; mortals c. to by fairies F276.

Calling on devil makes him come *G303.6.1.2. — Fairy c. victim only once F363.5; ghost c. E402.1.1.1; ghosts summoned by c. E386.3; sham c. to helpers frightens off robbers K548.3; tabu: c. (on ogre or destructive animal) C20ff., (on God) C94.4, (on spirit or devil) *C10ff., (on

supernatural wife) C31.6; wind raised by c. on devil D2142.1.3; wood-spirit c. in woods F441.6.4.

Calm when wind-spirit sleeps A1128.2. — Making weather c. H335.6; quiet c. brings man fortune Q6.1.

Calming of whirlpool D2151.4.

Calumniated princess's corpse fails to rot H251.3.14; wife reunited with husband N741.3.1; woman intercedes for accusers W11.5.9.1. — Feigning sleep with c. hero H1556.5.

Calumniators try to make friendly kings fight K1084.4.

Calypso, isle of F131.1.

Camel as animals' king B240.11; and ass together captured because of ass's singing J2137.6; bone slays Abel F839.3; and donkey trade undeserved compliments J867; determines road to be taken B151.1.5; determines road to be taken B151.1.5; helpful B405; induced to offer self as sacrifice K962; and jackal exchange food J512.11; killed by lion in game K869.3; lures wolf, crushes him K839.5; mistaken for religious holiday J1738.7; tries in vain to dance J512.3, J2133.1; wishes long neck J2072.5. — Creation of c. A1873; goat eats while c. talks H334.2; jackal puts head in anus of sham-dead c. K1036.1.1; man overloads, starves c. W155.1.2; mice overcome c. L315.10; one-eyed c. (deduction) J1661.1.1; men at first frightened at c. take him into their service U131.2; speaking c. B211.1.6; tabu: touching resting c. C537.1; treacherous c. K2295.5; why ears of c. are such A2325.4, A2325.7, A2232.1; why neck of c. bends upwards A2351.1; winged c. B47.

Camel's tail cut off, turns to grass R231.2. — Jackal demands c. tongue K255.4; rat imagines self c. owner J953.17; why c. back humped A2356.2.13; wolf puts head in c. mouth J2131.5.5.

Camels fall from sky into girl's eyes F615.3.1.2. — Copulation of c. A2496.3; giant roasts c. G171; lie: tying up c. in sheet X942.1; loading ferocious c. H1154.3.5; man, c. rise into air F1083.2; thank God that c. have no wings J2564.

Camouflage K1872ff.

Camp. — Disguise to enter c. K2357; enormous army c. F873.2; transformation to gain enemy's c. D641.2.

Campfires. — Pursuit by following c. R272.

Camping. — Leaping a c. place tabu C876; warrior reveals c. place J2366.

Camphor, island of F732.3; tree of F811.1.5.

Camrōsh B35.

Can, magic D1171.5.

Canaanites go nude A1683.4; have curly hair A1661.3; have red eyes A1666.1.

Canal dug by saint on tree D2121.14. — Bluff: digging c. instead of bringing water in skin K1741.3.1; "where did dirt go when c. dug?" J1309.3.

Canary. — Color of c. A2411.2.1.14; why eggs of c. are yellow A2219.1, A2391.1.

Cancer from ghost's slap E234.1, E542.1.4.1. — Magic cure for c. D1502.10.

Candle becomes stone D471.9; burning quickly as holiness test H257.1; of human fat K437.2; kept at right so as to tell one's right hand in dark J1735.1; light protection against ghost E434.9; light used to examine sun dial J1943; put in the stove to dry J2122; stuck with pins as love charm J1355.3.6. — Animal with c. mistaken for ghost J1782.5; adulteress sends husband out for c. K1521.4.1; burned c. causes death D2061.2.2.6; cat and c. J1908.1; chaste woman can blow out c. with one puff and relight with another H413.1; devil exorcised with c. G303.16.14.4; each drop of innocent blood turns to c. D1318.5.3; ever-burning c. D1652.11; let me live as long as this c. lasts *K551.9; life bound up with c. E765.1.1; magic c. *D1162.2ff.; minister swallows c. to outwit devil G303.12.5.4; miser dies rather than buy c. W153.11; pope's c. lights itself H41.3; resuscitation by c. E64.6; sailor offers saint c. as large as mast K231.3.1; soul as c. E742.1; substitute for c. repaid with substitute for money J1551.5; trespass betrayed by dripping c. C916.1.

Candles. — Creation of bee to provide wax for c. in church A2012.1; deer with c. atop antlers B253.6; disenchantment by maidens walking with lighted c. in procession D759.6; holy c. V133; thief places c. on crabs K335.0.5.1.

Candle-moth. — Monkey transformed to c. D411.5.2.

Candlemas, festival of V70.6.

Candlestick, jewelled F789.2.1.

Cane as evidence of robbery N614. — Giant c. for strong man F612.3.1; thrown c. becomes child T549.2.

Canes. — Origin of c.: from whip in ground A2825.

Canidae, creation of A1830ff.

Canine animal transformed to person D313ff. — Man transformed to c. animal D113ff.

Canis B331.2.

Canister. — Heart breaks at third drink from silver c. F1041.1.1.1.

Cannibal *G10ff.; bird G353.1; bird as ogre G355; gods A153.8; killed by wife's relatives G551.5; nature of woman recognized when she devours dead buffalo raw H46.1; offers wealth for life G683; ogre G312. — Cutting toenails of c. woman G519.1.2; husband rescues wife from c. R151.3; normal man transformed to c. D91; person becomes c. G30ff.; quest to land of c. giants H1289.3.1; sun as a c. A711.2; witch's familiar a c. G225.0.7.

Cannibals G0—G99; persuaded to take snuff and killed K827.2. — Culprit eaten by c. Q429.1; ghormuhas: c. half-horse, half-man B15.7.5; lost husband's bones found among c. G691.4.

Cannibalism *G10—G99, (accidental) X21, (occasional) G50—G79, (regular) G10—G49; out of vogue C227.1; of Pisācas G312; punished

Q215. — False accusation of c.: biting off corpse's finger to get ring N342.6; threatened c. frightens off robbers H335.1.10.

Cannon. — Boy shot from c. X1852; nobody can move c.: guard quits J1849.4; treasure buried in c. barrel N511.1.8.

Canoe hauled over dead man's body causes return from dead E607.3; island D1524.4; of sand J2171.1.3.1; transformed into coconut tree A2615.3; transformed into rock D454.10.2. — Birds build c. B572.2; clam swallows c. party F911.4.1.1; cocoanut c. F841.1.4.1; compressible c. D631.3.1; enormous c. F841.3.3; fairies build c. F271.2.3; god as c. builder A451.2.1; hibiscus blossom becomes c. D451.4.2; magic c. *D1122; man becomes c. D255.1; merman lays hands on side of c. B82.7; phantom c. E535.3.1; stone c. D1524.3.1; women in c. tabu C181.10.

Canoes formerly self-propelling A1346.2.4.

Canoe-bailer transformed to person D434.3.

Canonical hours V48. — Birds call at c. hours B252.2.

Canons compared to stew J81.3.

Canopy. — Wedding c. over bride and groom T135.14.

Canopies in otherworld F166.9.

Canute vainly forbids tide to rise L414.

Canvas. — Ship wrapped with feather-beds and c. F1031.

Cap of invisibility F455.5.3, K1349.10; o' Rushes K521.4.3, K1815, R221. — Ghost of man buried without c. E412.3.1; ghost in red c. E422.4.6; huldra-woman's c. F460.1.4.3; magic c. *D1067.2; permission to pick up c. gives entrance to heaven K2371.1.1; quest for best c. H1319.2; trolls' c. of invisibility F455.5.3; wild huntsman with black fur c. E501.8.6.

Caps of dwarfs F451.2.7.1, F451.2.7.6, F451.3.3.8; of mountain-men F460.1.4.1ff. — Devils' c. from man's nail parings G303.25.5.1; fairies with red c. F236.3.2; substituted c. cause ogre to kill his own children *K1611.

Capaneus. — Zeus smites C. while he is climbing a ladder L472.

Cape, see also **Cloak, Mantle.** — Magic transportation by c. D1520.6.

Capital punishment Q410ff. — Bringing arms to c. after sunset tabu C752.1.1; leaving c. ninth night tabu C751.6; parishoner glad to get back c. J1583; wager: fortune made from c. or from working at vocation N66.

Capon and the hen J1269.6.

Capriciousness of luck *N170ff. — King's c. censured: ass in stream J1675.3.

Captain buried with his crew V67.4.1; hangs own son for violating order M13.2; will not betray king's secret P361.7. — Mermaid asks c. to move boat B81.13.1.

Captive freed for having kept word Q54.2; king's children made slaves P173; in ogre's house helps hero G535; sends token of safety H85; released because of ability to recite story J1185, V151.1; spirits of dead H972.1. — Animal rescues c. *B544; former c. recognizes chieftain

H173.2; god protects tormented c. A185.2.2; magic object enables c. to escape D1395ff.; man's love for c. wife rewarded Q56.1; mountain-men chain c. peasant F460.4.4.2; rescue of c. *R110—R199; woman c. in elephant's ear H1151.18.

Captive's. — Cannibal cuts c. finger to test fatness G82.1; magic as c. ransom D859.8; recognition of c. voice brings about rescue from ogre G556.

Captives and fugitives R (entire chapter); re-blinded if they cross stepping-stones without stumbling H1575.1; as slaves P173. — Journey to disenchant c. H1385.0.1; mortals c. in fairyland *F375.

Captivity *R0—R99; preferred to death J217. — Animal grateful for ransom from c. B366; crab sings about his c. B214.1.8.1; daw fleeing from c. caught by thread around foot N255.5; death preferred to c. J227.1; fettered monster's c. A1074; ogre in animal form lures victim into c. G403; transformation to escape from c. D642.1; ungrateful animal returned to c. J1172.3; wild man released from c. aids hero G671.

Captor beguiled *K500—K699; contributes to captive's ransom W11.5.8; persuaded into illusory punishment K580ff. — Escape by overawing c. *K540ff.; joining c. out of gratitude R71; magic object helps overawe c. D1613; princess rescued from c. R111.1; punishment which proves fatal to c. K582; rescue by daughter of c. R162.

Capture of animals A2465ff., as task H1154ff.; of castle by feigning death K2362; by deception K700—K799; by magic object *D1430ff.; of moon J2271.4; by ogre G420ff.; of town by boy-hero F611.3.2.6; of two of every animal F681.8. — Numskull brings about his own c. J2136; selling soul to escape c. M211.7.

Captured animals avenge themselves Q385; fairy's promises for her release F341.2.1; queen commits suicide P26. — Demon sees image in mirror, thinks he is c. J1795.1; dwarfs promise to emigrate if c. dwarfs are released F451.9.1.5; fairy c. F387; fairy c. by mortal escapes F329.4.3; father rescues son c. by enemy R153.3.1; hero c. by man he has rescued N763; maiden c. by mermaid B81.4; mermaid c. B81.13.11; ogre c. G514ff.; person aids ogre and is c. G411; soul of sleeper c. in animal form E721.1.2.1; souls c. on leaving corpse E752.1.3; sultan's daughter in love with c. knight T91.6.4.1.

Car, see also **Automobile, Carriage.** — Fairy c. F242.1; man before whom riderless c. stops chosen king H171.4.

Caraway. — Dwarfs dislike c. seed in food F451.3.7.1, F451.9.1.1.

Carbuncle, incandescent D1645.1.

Carcass. — Animal born from c. B713; animal caught in c. J2136.6; bees born from c. of ox B913.1; capture by hiding in animal c. K751.1; haunted house where horse c. drops down chimney H1411.1.1.

Carcasses. — Eating one hundred c. as suitor test H331.17.

Card. — Ghost scares c. players E293.2; magic c. *D1267; magic object stolen in c. game D861.6; magic wishing c. D1470.1.48; picking up c.

fallen to ground forbidden C525; soul won from devil in c. game E756.2; spirit summoned by writing on c. D2074.2.4.

Cards. — Dead persons play c. E577.2; devil appears when c. are played G303.6.1.5; devil plays c. N4; Krishna plays c. with wives A164.3.1; men in animal's belly playing c. F911.3.3; parson plays c. N5, N71; playing c. with devil in church (fear test) H1421; power of winning at c. N221; sermon begun with illustration from c. N71; symbolic interpretation of playing c. H603; trickster cheats clerks at c. J1115.1; weighted order c. J1382.2.

Cardinal. — Color symbolism of c. points Z140.2.1; treacherous c. K2282.

Cardinal's decision on monks' sounding matins J1179.13; luxury J1263.4.1.

Care against future tyranny J643; of children *T600—T699; of favorites by deity A185; in selecting the creature to carry one J657. — Crown brings too much c. J347.2; inscription on home of riddle-solver: "I have no c." H562; will take c. of the thirst J1322.1.

Carelessness causes thief's capture J2136.5. — Husband made to believe that yarn has changed to tow through his c. J2325.

Caressed. — Hares (sheep) treacherously c. by dog K2031, K2061.3.

Caresses. — Son disenchants animal father by enduring his c. without fear D735.4.2.

Caretaker. — Sun as c. of the poor A739.8.

Caribou becomes person D314.1.2. — Creation of c. A1876.1; how c. got antlers A2326.1.2, A2247; looking at c. tabu C316.2; man becomes c. D114.1.6; why c. migrated A2482.2; why c. has no teeth A2345.7.3; why c. has small eyes A2332.3.3.

Carnage. — Battle c. personified Z132.0.1.

Carnal. — No c. sin in otherworld F167.10.

Carnation transformed to person D431.1.2. — Hero's power to transform girl to c. brings about recognition H151.7; man (woman) transformed to c. D212.1.

Carnivora, creation of A1810—A1839.

Carols. — Knockers sing c. at Christmas time F456.2.3.2.

Carp. — Man transformed to c. D171.

Carp's wedding B283.2.

Carpe diem (advice from fool) J2197.

Carpenter P456; blames the nails J1891.2; of the gods A143; makes magic horse D853.1; races wooden horse D1719.1.4. — Animals as c. B572; cumulative tale: c. releases caught birds Z49.7; disguise as c. K521.2.5, K1816.11, K2357.12; ingenious c. F675; remarkable c. X994; magic c. constructs expandable bed D1620.3.2.

Carpenters. — God of c. A451.2; men disguised as c. abduct bride K1825.7; why c. are everywhere: flood scatters them A1445.2.1.

Carpentry. — Origin of c. A1445.2; shortsightedness in c. J2171.

Carpet. — Countryman's avoidance of c. J1742.5.1; extraordinary c. F783; half a c. to keep father warm in old age J121; incendiary c. of

giants' cave set afire K812.1.1; magic c. *D1155; magic c. takes hero to girl's room K1346.1; magic shuttle makes c. D1485.1; paramour rolled into c. K1521.7; quest for most beautiful c. H1319.3.

Carriage as swift as thought D1521.4. — Animal characteristics: c. A2440ff.; animal drives c. B295; box transformed to c. D454.1.1; devil disappears into c. drawn by four black horses G303.17.2.9; devil's c. drawn by white horses G303.7.3.4; extraordinary c. F861; fairy hangs onto c. F366.5; forgotten fiancée magically stops wedding c. of new bride D2006.1.5; ghost on c. ride E332.3.2; magic c. *D1111f.; man throws c. with horses, driver on haystack F624.3.1; pumpkin transformed to c. D451.3.3; woman has worn out c. load of shoes with walking F1015.1.2.

Carried. — All that can be c. as wages K1732; burden c. by ghost E592; castle in air c. by eagles F771.2.1.2; church c. across a stream by giants F531.3.6; curse: to be c. off by evil spirit M432; dead wife c. with man E322.5; death feigned in order to be c. K1861; dupe c. aloft and dropped *K1041; exposed child c. off by wild beast S355; extraordinary burden c. by animals F982ff.; fée c. off by mortal F304.6; giant c. to eagle's nest F531.6.17.3; giant load c. by strong man F631ff.; giant so large he cannot be c. by horse F531.2.7; girl c. off because of broken tabu C951; head c. under arm F511.0.4; hero c. by bird to mistress's chamber B582.2.1; hero c. over water by magic salmon *B175.1; king always c. by slaves P14.5; man c. in giant's pocket F531.1.5.1; men c. by animals B550ff.; lover c. on mistress's shoulders: no footprints K1549.3; mortal c. by dwarf F451.3.8.1; owner c. with magic object thrown ahead D1526; paramour c. off in box K1555; people c. away to fairyland *F320ff.; person c. off by wild hunt E501.18.4; person c. off to otherworld for breaking tabu C954; person c. to or from upper world by bird *F62; souls c. to heaven by doves E754.2.1; stolen goods c. to dupe's house so that he is accused K401.2; ten serving women c. in bottle D55.2.4; thorn stick c. by devil G303.4.8.5; Thumbling c. up chimney by steam of food F535.1.1.2; trees c. by giants F531.3.10; trickster hides in bag to be c. K1892.1; ungrateful ape plucks feathers from heron who has c. him across water W154.5.1.3; victim c. in bag by ogre G441; wild huntsman c. on people's backs *E501.15.3; witch c. off by devil G275.1.

Carrier. — Lie: remarkable c. X942; river c. throws passenger off to drown S131.1.

Carrion as vulture's food A2435.4.5.1.

Carrying child on back tabu C875; corpse of murdered man (punishment) Q511; each other and shortening the way (telling tales and amusing) H586.3; ever-increasing burden up mountain H1114.2; off huge quantity of money (task) H1127; hundreds of sheep across stream one at a time (task) H1111; large load identifies chief H41.10; many water jugs as

suitor test H331.10; mountain on head H1146; murdered man's blood (ordeal) H227; person to remedy instead of opposite J2214.8; water in a sieve (task) H1023.2. — Angel c. mortal V232.2; animal c. man across water B551ff.; animal characteristics from contest in c. A2251; dead try c. off living E266; devil c. off people G303.9.5; disenchantment of girl by c. her on back D732.1; fish c. man shakes him off when struck M205.1.1.1; flight c. friend on back R242; familiar spirit acquired by c. egg under left arm-pit F403.2.1.1; giant c. prodigious burden F531.3.13; god c. siblings on back A137.4.1; impostors tricked into c. hero in box K1942; king c. off subject's wife P15.2.1; king to be succeeded by person c. his body P17.12; man marries fairy c. him off F302.3.1.3; ogre tricked into c. his prisoners home in bag G561; revenant as woman c. baby E425.1.4; reward for c. Christ across a stream Q25; servant c. master, drops him in stream J2133.5.1.1; servants c. master to search for dog J2163.2; tabu: unseemly acts while c. divine image C56; trial by ordeal subverted by c. magic object D1394.1; trickster c. girl across stream, leaves old woman K1339.7; trolls c. off people F455.6.6; vow against c. a woman M142.

Cart, see also **Carriage, Wagon;** as back legs for crippled pig X1202.1. — Devil in c. G303.7.4; extraordinary c. F861ff.; flying c. F861.2.1; ghost rides in c. E272.1; magic c. D1112; phantom c. driver E512; strong hero lifts c. F624.3.

Carts to shade roof J1879.1. — Man draws sixty c. of wood X953.1.

Cartridge. — Magic c. kills D1402.7.4.

Cartwheel. — Cauterizing sick c. J2412.7; devil helps man place c. G303.22.4.

Carving boar's head impossible for cuckold H425.1. — Magic c. knife *D1173; origin of wood c. A1465.5; recognition by c. H35.4f.; wise c. of the fowl H601.

Case. — Sun kept in a c. A721.0.3.

Cash payers favored J1382ff.

Cashel, vision concerning V515.1.3.2.

Cask. — Devil to fill c. full of money K219.3; escape from deluge in c. A1021.0.2; exposure in c. *S141; ghost as rolling c. E426.2; magic c. D1171.9; odor of the wine c. J34; punishment in spiked c. Q463; resuscitation by assembling members and leaving in c. for nine days E37; sea issues from marvelous c. F711.1; treasure buried in c. N511.1.8; treasure found in c. N525; water sold as wine in partitioned c. K476.3.

Casks. — Chaste wife tricks suitors into c. K1218.1.1; thieves hidden in oil c. K312.

Casket with Good Luck in it given to men by Zeus N113.1; lid furnishes money D1452.3. — Children in c. floating down river H157.

Caskets, three H511.1, L211, D1658.3.2.

Cassandra destined never to be believed M301.0.1.

Cassawary. — Man becomes c. D169.4; tabu to eat c. C221.1.2.1.

Cast. — Divine child c. out at birth A112.11; disposal of c.-off wife S430ff.; evil spirit c. out of person E728.1; hills from stones c. by giants A963.5; lucky c. of weapon N623; ogre's ashes c. on stream cause rapids to stop G655; no shadow c. by ghosts E421.2; c.-forth wife must sit at horseblock of palace Q482.4.

Caste of supernatural husband C32.2.3; tabus C551. — Falling in love with different c. T91.7.2; god enamored of low c. woman T91.3.3.1; princess cannot marry into low c. P41; quarrel of dog and cat over which has higher c. A2281.1.2; untouchables are certain c. whose touch is considered a pollution C551; woman curses her c. M464; why certain c. is kind to animals A1599.13.

Castes. — Origin of c. A1651; tabu to eat with certain c. C246.

Casting animal's eyes K1442; in graveyard tabu after sunset C752.1.5; lots as truth test H245. — Devil creates devils by c. water behind himself G303.1.4.1.

Castle, see also **Palace;** disenchanted D705.1, D789.8; in magic box D1174.1; magically made smaller D491.5; magically transported D2136.2; in lower world F80.1.1; sinks into earth F941.1. — Building c. (task) H1133, (in one night) H1104, (suspended between heaven and earth) H1036; building wax replica of c. H1133.6; captivity in c. R41.1; capture of c. (by feigning death) K2362, (by pretending to surrender and entering) K777; destruction of iron c. H1562.12; devil builds himself a c. and calls it hell G303.8.3.2; devil prophesying in enchanted c. H1411.3; disenchantments concerning c. D759.4, D759.5; dragons live beneath c. B11.3.4; dwarfs in underground c. F451.4.1.2; dwarfs move mortal's c. F451.5.1.12; drawfs' gold c. F451.4.3.6; fairy c. F222; friendly ghost haunts c. E338.1; eagles carry c. in air F982.1; enchanted c. D6; extraordinary c. *F771ff.; ghost at c. every seven years E585.2; ghosts haunt c. E282; giant lives in c. in air G162; giant ogres possess c. G111; hedgehog builds c. B191.5; key to enchanted c. D791.4; king angry at hero entering c. without permission P14.11; king banishes nobleman whose c. he wants P12.8; magic object found in magic c. D846; maiden found in magic c. N711.2; objects found in deserted c. where hero is served by unseen hands H1239.2; outcast's c. like king's H153; owner disguised as monk enters own captured c. K2357.0.2; quest for c. of jewels H1343; troll's c. G304.3.1; wild hunt appears at c. E501.12.8; woman in c. gives guest directions H1232.3.

Castles. — Dog between two c. J2183.1; giants live in ruined c. F531.6.3.1.

Castor and Pollux A116.

Castrated. — Bishop wishes all monks were c. X457.1; friar accused of rape c. K2111.3; joker asks to be c. N334.3; Virgin saves life of c. man V256.4.

Castration bargain (wife sent) K241; by magic D2062.4.2; as mutilation S176.1; of paramour by husband K1558.1; as punishment Q451.10.1; of self by beaver to save own life J351.1; to test wife H492.3; through

ignorance J1919.5. — Choice between c. or blinding J229.12; husband prepares for c. of crucifix K1558; making the dupe strong by c. K1012.1.

Cat aids confession of debt J1141.1.11; alleged to fish for master K341.11.1; as beast of ill-omen B147.1.2.2; beaten for not working W111.3.2; and candle J1908.1; carries person B557.7; carrying lantern K264.2; castle F771.4.2; causes enmity between animals K2131.1; ceases catching rats as soon as he is given home in monastery U271; chooses rat meat at feast U135.1; commanded to pray so as not to slay man: why he purrs A2236.8; crawls to steeple and tries to fly J2133.3; crossing path ghost sign E436.2; curses woman eating fish cat has caught Q281.3; and devil G303.3.3.1.2, G303.10.1, J1785.5; of divine origin: is praying when it purrs A1811.3; drives away, doesn't eat, rats J766.1; fails to be beguiled into releasing mouse K561.1.1; garbles message from man to tiger A2281.1.1; grows large as cow F983.3; to guard cheese J2103.1; guards imprisoned beauty T50.1.4; hangs on wall pretending to be dead K2061.9; harms dead and dying B766.1ff.; invites hens to a feast and kills them K815.4; as judge between sparrow and hare K815.7; kills attacking rat B524.1.3; leaves house when report is made of death of one of his companions *B342; lures foxes with music K815.15; made to mew, distract owner K341.7.2; makes truce with mice, then eats them K815.13; offers to act as doctor for cock and hen K2061.7; as ogre sucks blood G351.2; omits teaching tiger all he knows A2581; and parrot cheat each other at dinner J1565.3; as sacrifice V12.4.2; scratches out bear's tongue (lie) X1211.1; as servant B292.6ff.; shrieks and the frightened bear falls out of the tree K2324; skin sold as mink K261.1; steals sausage from table but dog receives blows K2171; sucks sleeping child's breath B766.2; as thumbling's horse F535.1.1.6; trained for gambling N7; transformed to person D342; transformed to maiden runs after mouse J1908.2; transformed to other animal D412.1ff., A1945.1; unjustly accuses, eats cock U31.1; in warehouse J1175.1; and witches D1766.4, G211.1.7, G224.11.12, G241.1.4, G225.3, G243.2.2, *G252, G262.1.1, G262.3.2; witness to betrothal punishes violator M205.1.2; in wood-pile prevents axe from cutting D2186. — Abduction by c. R13.2.3; animal thought to be a giant c. J1756; association of rat (mouse) with c. ceases as soon as mutual danger has passed J426; belling the c. J671.1; boy to see whether there is fire in the house feels of c. W111.2.5; creation of c. A1811; why c. eats first A2545.2; dead c. better than crown to crow J242.7; devastating c. B16.1ff.; fat c. Z33.2; food of c. A2435.3.2; fortune to go in direction c. jumps K2.1; ghost of c. E521.3; giant c. B871.1.6; giant ogre as c. G126.1; giant tricked into becoming mouse and eaten by c. K722; helpful c. *B422, (borrows measure for his master's money) K1954.1, (wins wife for master) B582.1.1, (helps steal back magic stolen object) *D882.1.1; horse used by mortal under fairy spell changes to gray c. F234.4.1; humans with c. characteristics B29.4ff., F511.2.2.1 (ears),

F512.1.4 (eyes), F514.3 (snout); hare escapes galloping c. K562.2; hostile c. B17.1.5; how c. was domesticated A2513.2; husband reincarnated as c. H1385.4.1; killing c. tabu C841.11; lifting a certain c. (task) H1149.2; is the big c. still living? K1728; why c. keeps chimney-corner A2433.3.1.1, A2223.1; magic c. B181.1ff.; magic object received from c. woman D825.1; man transformed to c. D142; man reincarnated as c. E611.5; mouse created by Lucifer, c. by Michael to destroy mouse A1751.1; mouse transformed to c. D411.6.2; moving dead c. tabu C537.3; poor boy said by helpful c. to be dispossessed prince K1952.1; revenant as c. E423.1.2; getting rid of c. J2101; sacred c. B811.4; sea-c. B73; singing c. B214.1.3; speaking c. B211.1.8; stolen meat and weighed c. J1611; tabu: resurrecting c. for trifling purpose C96.1; talking to c. obtains serving for student J1341.10; truth-telling c. B135; turnips called bacon: c. called rabbit J1511.2; tying c. to horse's tail K2383; Whittington's c. N411.1; why c. hides its excreta A2385.4, A2495.1; why c. keeps chimney-corner A2433.3.1.1; why mouse does not defend self against c. A2462.3.

Cat's bodily characteristics A2325.6 (jagged ears), A2326.2.1 (lack of horns), A2356.2.3 (arched back), A2365.2.0.1 (penis), A2441.1.10 (walk); curse causes woman to bear cats M437.1; enemies A2281.1ff., A2494.1ff.; friendships A2493.9ff., A2493.18; marriage B281.9ff., B282.4.2, B601.12; only trick J1662; paw cut off (woman's hand missing) D702.1.1; supernatural qualities B121.3 (magic wisdom), D1032.2 (magic flesh), D1840.2.1 (invulnerable), D2071.1.2 (averting Evil Eye), D2142.1.5 (raises wind), E731.2 (as soul), G283.2.1 (prevents wind), N542.2 (locates treasure); tail mistaken for worm J1759.5. — Curse: god to live c. life M414.13.1; deity with c. head A131.3.1; giant as black c. son *F531.6.1.3; lighting the c. tail J2101.1; milk overheated to break c. taste for it K499.4; ogre with c. head, tail G369.4; origin of c. skin A2311.2.

Cats crossing one's path sign of ghosts E436.2; infest haunted house H1411.2; unite against wolf J1025.2. — Army of c. B268.11; country without c. F708.1; dance of c. B293.1; fear test: night watch with magic c. H1411.2ff.; four c. carry coffin F982.2; king of c. B241.2.3; lies about c. X1211; magic fishhook catches c. D1444.3; how mice can rid themselves of c. H1292.10; mouse teaches her child to fear quiet c. J132; rats cause c. to be killed K2172; saint kills king of c. F981.7; scratching c. in hell A671.2.13; slain c. hung up and covered with grain (penance) Q523.6; tiger-cubs mistaken for jungle c. J1758.6.

Cataclysm. — Leviathan produces c. by striking earth with tail B16.4.1.1; vow binding unless c. occurs M117.

Cataclysms. — Succession of creations and c. A632.

Catapult-hurled stones thrown back at enemy F636.4.2.

Cataract. — King's death spear cast into c. P16.5.

Cataracts, origin of A935.

Catarrh. — Wife cures c. F950.2.1.

Catastrophe, see also **Calamity, Disaster.** — Escape by announcing c. K686; mermaid as omen of c. B81.13.7; world c. A1000ff., M357.

Catch tales X903, Z13. — Great c. of fish X1150.1.

Catcher. — Hero as marvelous c. F698.1; lie: remarkable c. X944.

Catching, see also **Caught;** animal devil G303.9.9.7; the devil G303.16.19.18; a noise (task) H1023.12; huge fish without nets or tackle (task) H1154.4; wild animals as suitor task H336.2. — Bird of prey c. quarry a good omen D1812.5.2.4; dwarf driven away by maid c. and kissing him F451.5.19.1; first man c. woman in snare A1275.10; resuscitation by c. in snare E23; transformation to fish by c. in fish-trap D533.

Caterpillar. — Burning c. tabu C841.3; god with body of c. A123.1.5; helpful c. B484.1; man becomes c. D192.1; marriage to person in c. form B643.3; why hairy c. is venomous A2532.2.

Caterpillars. — Why c. climb trees A2479.6.

Catfish transformed from children carry marks of knife holder A2261.3.1; transformed from woman carries woman's tatoo marks A2261.3. — Giant c. B874.7; man becomes c. D177; origin of c. A2127.

Cattle bewitched G265.6.2; formerly ate rice and pulse A1101.2.2; killed as punishment Q595.2; let loose so as to distract owner's attention K341.7.1; magically disappear D2087.3; as men's masters A1101.2.1; produced by magic D2178.2; and sheep of the sun (riddle) A732.1; step on lobster, flatten it A2213.2.4; of the sun A155.1; thief struck by lightning Q552.1.8.1; tied so tightly they strangle K1447. — Building bridge of c. K1441; enmity of c. and snails A2494.12.3.1; fairy c. F241.2ff., F356; fairy gives man horses, c., etc. F343.9; fairies steal c. F365.6; faithful c. at master's death B301.6ff.; first c. in Ireland A1877.1; forbidden direction while tending c. C614.1.0.1; ghost stampedes stolen c. E234.2; ghostly reenactment of c.-driving sounds E337.1.4; giant cane holds fifty c. F612.3.1; giant eats a thousand c. F531.3.4.1; herd of c. put into magic cup D491.1.1; herd of c. transformed to wolves D412.2.1; horse takes c. out to pasture X1241.2.1; hostile c. B17.1.3; huldra c. F460.2.9; huldra as c. traders F460.4.2.5; innocent boy hanged for c. theft N347.3; killing more c. than necessary tabu C766.1; man-eating c. B16.1.5; merman demands c. as offering B82.2; monk brings back all stolen c. possible J2499.4; murrain upon c. as punishment Q552.3.7; pasturing witch's c., her daughters H1199.12.2; people choose c. A1614.4.3; quest for marvelous c. H1331.3; sacred c. of sun god B811.3.3; saint's bell keeps c. from straying D1446.1; servant must keep horns and hide of his c. that are slain P622; stealing c. which are guarded by a marvelous dog (task) H1151.8; thirsty c. fight over well B266.1; trolls ride on c. F455.3.3.3; two-footed c. demanded: silly pundits sent J1717; when cow calls calf, all c. graze B852; washing black c. white (task) H1023.6; why flies sit on eyes of c. A2494.14.3; witch rides on c. G241.1.6.

Caught, see also **Catching.** — Animal c. by magic object D1444; animal's habits when c. A2466ff.; dwarf c. by beard in cleft of tree F451.6.1; ogre c. in noose and killed G514.3; speech magically recovered when certain bird is c. D2025.2; sun c. in snare A728; transformation to be c. D646.

Caul. — Child born with serpent in c. T551.8; exposure of child with c. S325.0.1.1; murder by showing man his c. D2061.2.7; waves break c. of abandoned child N655; worm from c. born with child B714.

Cauldron of greed W151.0.1; magically sticks to wall D2171.4.2; of regeneration E607.5; on water-monster's head K2314.2.1. — Bluff: huge c. called hero's kitchen-pot K1718.3; gigantic c. F881.1.1; magic c. *D1171.2, (in otherworld) F166.4.2, (received from lake spirit) D813.1.2, (reveals guilt) D1318.13; theft of c. detected J1661.1.10; witches boil wizardry c. G249.5.

Cauldrons. — Giant with eyes as big as c. F531.1.1.2.1; origin of c. A1439.4.

Cauliflower, children said to come from T589.6.5.

Caulker, pope disguised as K1816.2.

Causeway. — Building c. as suitor test H359.1; building c. as task H1129.6; fairies build c. F271.2.2; underwater c. to otherworld F842.2.4.

Cauterized. — Priests burned: dying woman asks to be c. J1511.18; sick cartwheel c. J2412.7.

Caution, wisdom of J580ff.

Cavalcade, fairy F241.1.0.1.

Cavalry of dogs B268.2. — Mice and hogs let loose put elephant c. to flight K2351.3; runaway c. hero K1951.2.

Cave call K607.1; entrance to lower world F92.6, A671.0.3; opens to hide fugitives D1552.5; as refuge R315; as repository of fire A1414.7.3; of winds A1122. — Abandonment in c. S146.2; adventure from following animal to c. N773; animal rescues from c. B549.4; beam in c. kills travelers K1172; captivity in c. R45.3; covering of giants' c. set afire K812.1.1; deer lures victim into demon's c. K714.7; dwarf c. F451.4.1.1, F451.4.3.1, F451.6.14; escape from deluge in c. A1024; extraordinary c. F757; gods' home in c. A151.1.2; hunter discovers girl being reared in c. N724; magic deer reveals c. entrance D1552.9; magic in giant's c. D845.1; ogress keeps princesses in c. G334.1; origin of c.-digging A1435.0.1; ogre kept in c. G514.2.1; princess rescued from giant's c. R111.2.3; river issuing from c. controlled by race of Amazons D915.5; rock at c. entrance falls D2153.2; spending night in c. as penance Q524.1; statue in c. entrance frightens giantess K1726; sun and moon from c. A713; sun hides in c. A734.1; travelers taken from c., eaten G94.1; treasure in underground c. N512.

Caves. — Chiefs buried in hidden c. V61.8.1; giants enchanted in c. F531.6.13.1; giants live in c. F531.6.2.1; habitable c. in otherworld

F164; huts replace c. as dwellings A1435.3; mankind emerges from c. A1232.3; rocks enter c. F1006.4; spirits live in c. F402.6.4.1.

Cecilia. — St. C. lives after beheading D1840.1.3.

Cecrops F526.6.

Cedar. — Blood from wizard becomes red grain of c. A2731.3; magic c. tree D950.18; origin of c. tree A2681.13; iron created to punish pride of c. A978.2.

Cedars. — Temple c. bear fruit F811.7.2.1.

Ceiling. — Chamber with crystal c. (in otherworld dwellings) F165.3.1.1, (in dwarf cave) F451.4.3.3.

Celebrations of dwarf weddings and christenings F451.6.3.2; of marriage T130ff. — Deer lost through premature c. J2173.4; prisoners released in c. of victory P14.1; religious c. *V0—V99.

Celestial, see **Heavenly.**

Celestial spheres, see **Heavens.**

Celibacy and chastity *T300—T399; and continence *T310ff.; at the altar J1264.2. — Origin of c. A1556.2; peoples practicing c. F566.

Cellar. — Familiar in magician's c. G225.0.5; fool lets wine run in the c. J2176; penance: being locked in c. and key thrown into water Q544; treasure in c. of ruined house N511.1.6; wine c. entered by removing lock K317.2; wolf overeats in c. K1022.1.

Celtic fairy mistress dominant F302.6.1. — Pagan C. otherworld like Christian paradise A694.1.

Celts, origin of A1611.5.4.

Cemetery, see also **Graveyard.** — Cannibals live at c. G18.1; dead move when c. is moved E419.4; light moving toward c. as sign of death D1322.2; looking over c. walls tabu C334; parson thinks he hears devil in c. cracking nuts X424; sleeping in c. tabu C735.2.5; shooting man to start c. X1663.2.

Cenn Cruaich, festival of V70.8.

Cenotaph. — Woman thinking lover dead erects c. and mourns before it T85.1.

Censer. — Aaron's c. J1446; sulphur in the c. J1582.2.

Censure. — Miracle saves saint from unjust c. V229.2.11.

Census. — Taking c. tabu C897.2.

Centaur B21; befriends abandoned man R143; rescues man from jungle B547.3. — Blood of c. as love philtre D1355.2.2.1; ghost as c. E423.6; man transformed to c. D199.1.

Center. — Determination of world c. A1181; mountain at c. of earth A875.1.1; person (giant, wood-spirit) with one eye in c. of forehead *F441.4.1, F512.1.1, F531.1.1.1; what is c. of earth? (riddle) H681.3.

Centipede kills ogre B524.1.10; magically enlarged D2038.1; plays with pearl B109.2. — Devastating c. B16.6.5; helpful c. B491.4.1; magic c. aids captive D1395.9; man becomes c. D192.2; poisoned sting of c. brings death to world A1335.13.

Centurion wants to be killed rather than converted Q151.8.

Century. — Bird carries a grain of sand from a mountain each c. (measure of eternity) H701.1; treasure reveals itself each c. N541.2.

Cerberus *A673, B15.7.1. — Quest for C. in hell H1271; sop to C. B325.1.

Cereal thrown on floor in anger F1041.16.10. — Magic c. D1033.

Cereals, origin of A2685ff.

Ceremonial continence T310.1; friendship P311.6.

Ceremony of the proclamation of a Buddha V88; of sacrifice V18. — Betrothal c. T61.4; eating during c. C231.5; evil spirit exorcised by religious c. D2176.3.2; fairies disappear when c. of church is used F382; magic results produced by religious c. *D1766; other religious c. as magic cure D2161.4.9.1; parody of church c. at witch's sabbath G243.2; prayer as c. V58; repeating the c. J2498; wedding c. T135; witch's power from altering religious c. G224.5.

Ceremonies used at unearthing of treasure N554. — God ordains c. A176; misunderstanding of church c. causes inappropriate action J1823; religious c. *V0—V99; witches avoid religious c. G285.

Certain. — Fairies visible only at c. times F235.2; ghost finds rest when c. thing happens E451; ghosts walk at c. times E587; invulnerability from c. things D1841; otherworld dwellings open only at c. times F165.2.

Certificate. — Cat loses dog's c. A2281.1.

Cesspool. — Paramour falls in c. K1517.4.1.

Chafer. — Blood-sucking c. B16.6.2; fierce black c. B16.6.2.1.

Chaff sky-rope F51.1.4. — Making a rope of c. (task) H1021.2.

Chagrin. — Death from c. because man cannot answer question F1041.1.3.10; laughter from c. F1041.11.1.

Chain, see also **Series;** around neck tests truth H251.3.6; of arrows transformed to bridge D469.3; of borrowings bring huge amount K455.10; of punishments Q401; tales Z20. — Ascent to upper world on arrow c. *F53; breaking of c. in anger F1041.16.3.1; child born with c. around neck H71.7; disenchantment by putting c. around neck D723.1; dragon keeps maiden tied with golden c. B11.10.1; devil bound with huge c. G303.8.4.1; drop of honey causes c. of accidents N381; extraordinary c. F863; filing away c. with teeth R121.10; forging of c. for fettered monster A1071.2; giant with gigantic c. as belt F531.4.2; gold c. as otherworld support F169.6; hind with gold c. on neck B105.1; iron c. hangs from heaven F51.1.6; magic c. (ornament) *D1078, (iron) D1251, (renders orchard barren) D1563.2.1; magic c. protects D1381.19, D1388.0.3; magic power in c. lost when it is stolen D1561.2.3; origin of mountain c. A965; quest for animal with golden c. H1332.4; recognition of twins by golden c. under their skin H61.1; thieves stretch c. across road and evade pursuers K413; tying sun with stone c. H1023.23.

Chains. — Castle suspended on four c. F771.2.1.1; disenchantment by putting c. around neck D723.1; fettered monster's weakened c. renewed

by supernatural power A1074.7; fiery c. in hell A671.2.4.7; ghost sounds c. E402.1.4, E565; mountain-men put peasant in c. F460.4.4.2; noise of c. leads to buried ghost E231.4; quest for the finest of c. H1303; souls in c. in hell E755.2.2; transformation by removing c. from neck D536; wild hunt heralded by rattle of c. E501.13.1.2.

Chained. — Animals c. in couples B845.2; girl c. to wall by giant R111.2.3.1; magic birds c. in couples B172.7; pregnant queen c. to king T579.7; prisoners c. R51.2; soldiers c. together to prevent flight P551.2.

Chair moves toward pope A171.6; over fiery pit as figure of precariousness of life J85; rocked by spirit F473.2.1. — Death glued to c. Z111.2.2; devil's c. in hell made from thrown-away nail parings G303.25.5; extraordinary c. F786; ghostly c. E539.4.1; heaven entered by sitting in St. Peter's c. K2371.1.4; heavenly music caused by columns under Lord's c. A661.0.2.1; horse's forehead as golden c. F874.2; magic c. *D1151.2; man lured into mechanical c., killed K984; person killed by spike magically made to appear on c. D2061.2.6; recognizing sweetheart's sedan c. H324.1; ring prevents person from rising from c. D1413.2; salt prevents witch's rising from c. G254.2; self-rocking c. D1601.28; weeding garden from rocking c. W111.5.13; witch cannot rise from c. with four-leaf clover under it G254.

Chairs in heaven A661.0.3, H619.1, V515.1.1, Z71.1.2. — Origin of peoples according to choice of c. A1614.4.2; witches rock empty c. G249.11.

Chalice used in guilt test H233.1. — Magic c. D1171.6.4; priest throws c. at owl J1261.2.7.

Chalk marks identify mistress H58.1; transformed into oil tins D454.13.

Challenge to battle P556; at otherworld entrance F150.3; to revenant to combat E461.1. — Hero's c. to warriors in his land C566.5.

Challenger. — Customs concerning c. to combat P557.4.4; small child beats giant c. F611.3.2.5.

Chamber with crystal ceiling in otherworld F165.3.1.1. — Forbidden c. *C611; suitor test: entering princess's c. *H344; underground treasure c. F721.4.

Chamber-pot, magic *D1171.13.

Chameleon duped by elephant K1042.1; plays xylophone B297.1.2; saves hero's life: may change color A2223.8. — Creation of c. A2148.1; enmity of c. and lizard A2494.16.2; movement of c. A2441.4.4; why c. can change his color A2411.5.6.1.

Champion test H1568; vindication by H218.0.1. — King's c. enforces respect P14.15; valor as bird hovering over c. Z124.1.

Champions of gods A145. — Queen pours liquor for c. P29.3.

"Champion's portion" of meat P632.2.1.

Chance and fate N (entire chapter).

Chandelier of crystals in dwarf home F451.4.3.4.

Changes of bodily appearance so as to escape K521.2; in bodily form at fall of man A1310.1; in color of blood (life token) E761.1.6; of color not to be attempted J511; in the earth A850ff.; of form impossible for devil G303.3.6. — Attempted c. of animal nature absurd J1908; magic c. in man himself *D50ff.; magic object effects c. in persons D1300—D1379; magic object works physical c. D1330ff.; reincarnation with c. of sex E605.1; simulated c. of sex to baffle Evil Eye D2071.1.3; yearly c. in hyena's sex B754.1.1.

Changeableness W175.

Changed message K1851; remarks K1775. — Adulterous love c. into chaste one T372; angel c. into the devil G303.1.1.3; animals' dwelling-place c. A2433.1.2; animal's color c. F985; clothes not to be c. till a certain time M125; horse used by mortal under fairy spell c. to gray cat F234.4.1; person's disposition c. by magic object D1350ff.; person's size c. by magic object D1377; sea's place c. F931.1; size c. at will D631; transformation: material of object c. D470ff.; voice c. by work of silversmith F556.2.

Changeling *F321.1ff., F451.5.2.3. — Eagle prefers own offspring to c. J497; mother casts out c. P231.6.

Changelings, trolls as F455.6.7.

Changing of luck or fate N130ff.; places or caps in bed K1611. — Cow with c. colors B731.4; disguise by c. bodily appearance K1821; princess c. clothes with maid to flee man T323.1.1; punishment for c. faith Q232; rejuvenation by c. skin D1889.6; transformation by c. clothes D537; wives c. clothes with imprisoned husbands R152.3.

Channel. — Underground c. to otherworld F153.1.

Channels. — Lies about underground c. X1545; origin of sea c. A920.2.

Chanticleer believes that his crowing makes the sun rise J2272.1.

Chanting of saint kills animal D1445.3; of spell over shadow D2061.2.2.2. — Future poet c. in womb T575.1.4; heavenly bodies c. God's praise F961.0.4; Satan c. God's praises G303.9.8.9.

Chaos. — Earth born of c. A801; evil spirits born in c. G302.1.2; first deity grows out of primeval c. A115.1; creator comes out of c. A22; primeval c. *A605.

Chapel endowed with blows for friar X454; in otherworld F163.2; remarkable F773. — Stones in c. from transformed salmon A977.5.2.

Chaplain administers sacrament and saves woman's soul from devil G303.16.5.1. — Treacherous c. K2284.1.

Character of kings P12ff. — Tests of c. H1550—H1569; traits of c. W (entire chapter).

Characters. — Mysterious c. on fire rock F809.6.2.

Charcoal burner P458, (drives fairies off with fire) F389.1, (treacherous) K2262; sack magically multiplies D2106.2. — Expensive wood burned to make c. J2094; origin of c. making A1452; raised treasure turns into

c. N558; transformation: handkerchief with three knots to clod, potsherd, and c. D454.3.2.1.

Chargers. — Faggots become c. D441.3.1.

Chariot of fire A13.6.3.1; of the gods A156.5; horses spring at one unentitled to throne H71.10.4; invisible D1982.3; of light carries souls to heaven E754.5; magically collects flowers D1601.33; of the sun A724; tilts under false royalty H41.9.1; wheels throw up wall R5.1. — Angel guides c. V232.5.1; crossing water in c. D2125.3; dead persons draw c. E583; deceptive grant: land c. travels K185.7.3; divination from c. wheels' sound K1812.5.0.12; driving c. over displeasing person Q227.3; entering c. tabu after certain food C756.4; escape to sky in magic c. R323.2; fairy c. F242.1; fairy c. pulled by pole through horse F241.1.6; god drives c. over waves A171.0.1; god rides in c. A171.1.1; god's c. goes through air A136.3; god's c. bears bodies to heaven E722.2.10.1; goddess's c. drawn by one-footed horse A136.2.2; heavenly c. takes couple to sky A761.2; journey to upper world in c. F66.1; magic c. *D1114; moon c. A757.1; planet in black c. pursues sun, moon A735.2; pregnant woman crushed beneath c. S116.2; race won by deception: c. disabled K11.4; saint's resurrection where c. breaks down M364.4.1; stealing c. from king H1151.13.3; swans harnessed to c. B558.2; tabu to proceed after c. mishap C833.7; winged c. F861.2; winged serpents pull c. B558.7.

Chariot's. — Turning c. left side tabu C643.

Chariots join in keen F994.2. — Stars melt iron c. F961.2.6.

Charioteer faithful to death P361.1.3; killed instead of saint N338.1; of the sun *A724.1; taunts master, arouses him J1682.

Charioteers. — Hero refuses to slay c. W11.5.12.

Charitable man's death postponed Q151.1.

Charity *V400—V449; rewarded by birth of child T584.4. — Admittance to heaven for single act of c. Q172.2; devil frustrated by c. G303.16.19.11; double return for c.: savings given away J2489.6; heaven entered by demanding back the c. gift K2371.1.2; hypocrisy concerning c. K2096; intemperance in c. J562; trickster takes goods given in c. to his family K461; what is the greatest? c. H659.7.3.

Charm, see also **Spell;** against theft of children by fairies F321.2; around neck transforms D585.1; causes horns to grow on person D1375.1.3; dries (life token) E761.4.6; makes root bitter D479.3; to win cases in law court D1406.1; written in blood has magic power D1273.0.1. — Alleged c., fly, escapes: damages claimed K251.3; ghost summoned by c. E386.2; impregnation by use of c. T527; magic c. (formula) *D1273ff., (fetish) *D1274, (medicine) *D1241, (ghoulish) *D1278, (writings) *D1266.1; ogress seduces with c. G264.3; ogre's c. stolen G613; rain c. sold to aid eloping couple D2143.1.10; witches c. causes paralysis D2072.2.1; witch's c. opposite of Christian *G224.1; word c. gives witch power G224.12.

Charms cause witch to reveal self G257. — Dead mother called up from grave to give her son c. E323.3; finger cut because of absorption in the c. of beloved T26.1; origin of c. for pregnant women A1562.1; pseudo-magic healing c. sold K115.
Charming. — Fairies c. prince into sleep F302.3.4.5; wife c. husband back R152.4.
Charnel. — Fetching skulls from c. house (fear test) H1435.
Charon A672.1. — Fee of C. A672.1.1, E489.3, P613.
Charter. — Ass's c. in his hoof J1608.
Charybdis and Scylla G333.
Chasing devil away G303.16.11.3; mutilated man into forest S143.3; night by day A1172.3; ogres away by fire G581. — Fairies c. man who dares them F361.17.8; fairies c. overseer F361.3.2; ghost c. pedestrian E272.4; priest c. devil away G303.16.14.1; wife's attendants c. lover K1549.6.
Chasms mark leaps of giants A972.5.2.
Chaste sleeping together T350ff.; woman deceives gallant with a substitute in bed K1223.4; woman has magic power *D1714.1; woman promises herself to her lover when the rocks leave the coast *M261; woman refers lover to her husband for permission K1231; woman surprised in adultery K2063; maiden at prayer vanishes from would-be ravisher's embrace D1714.1.1; wife tricks importunate lovers K1218. — Girl with c. mother chosen as wife J482.3; wild animal will not harm c. woman B771.0.1.
Chastity *T300—T399; tests *H400—H459; wager *N15. — Adulteress makes pretense of c. K2051.4; cut-off finger proves wife's c. K1512.1; demon has to serve girl whom he cannot persuade to break vow of c. G303.16.19.5; magic object preserves c. *D1387ff.; message of c.: uncooked meat left behind T386; sword of c. T351; promise to sleep in c. with woman broken J1174.2.1; transformation to preserve c. D664; wife's heavy c. belt T373.
Chastizing. — Son c. father for scorning mother P233.9.
Chasuble. — Hairs on saint's c. release souls from hell Q174.1.1.1; sinners going to heaven numbered by hairs in saint's c. M364.3.1; white c. becomes red D454.3.1.1.
Chasubles. — Maidens unharmed by fire in c. D1841.3.2.4.
Chateaux. — Devil as builder of c. G303.9.1.5.
Chattering dwarfs F451.3.13.2; squirrel in the earth-tree A878.3.3.
Cheap price country J342.1.1. — King and c. slippers J829.1.
Cheated. — Devil c. (at card playing) N4.0.1, (in race) K11.0.1, (of his promised soul) *K210ff., (by dismissing mass early) G303.16.16; farmer who trades horses with the devil is c. G303.25.12; numskull talks and allows himself to be c. J2355; scornfull mistress c. by scorned lover posing as rich man L431.2.
Cheater cheated *J1510ff.; discovered by fishing in the street J1149.2; as hero L114.4; put out of countenance by raising alarm J1216. — Virgin pardons repentant c. V261.2.

Cheaters *K300—K499; examined apart J1141.3; sell each other valueless articles K148; visited by god in animal form Q554.6. — Trickster masks as doctor and punishes his c. K1825.1.3.

Cheating by illusory transformation of animals D612.1; as suitor test H331.13. — Clever girl c. robber K434; deer's antlers reward for not c. A2326.1.1.1; dupe's casual words used in c. K1155; fairies revenge for c. F361.13; foolish attempt at c. buyer J2083; ghost slaps c. son: cancer grows E234.1; magic object acquired by c. K830ff.; man c. god in dice A189.3; rogues c. each other J1516; thief c. other thieves K307.2; two cheats c. one another K421.3; Virgin Mary reveals c. V252.1.

Check. — Leaving c. on coffin K231.13.

Cheek bitten K2021.1, (as death warning) D1812.0.1.1. — Devils leave hermit who turns other c. when struck G303.16.15; mutilation: c. cut off S166.2; ointment cures left c., not right D1663.2; remarkable c. F545.3.

Cheeks like blood as suitor test H312.5; stuffed with food operated on for swellings X372.4.1. — Giant's peculiar c. F531.1.6.8; husband disapproves of wife painting c. Q331.2.1.3; mouth full of food: c. cut open for abscess J1842.2; vain woman's c. burned Q331.2.1.2.

Cheese from buffalo milk H1361.6; -covered dung sold as cheese K143.1; smeared on crab lures giant K827.5; transformed to stone D471.4; thrown down to find way home J1881.1.1. — Bone-powder changed into c. D476.1.10; cat to guard c. J2103.1; diving for c. J1791.3; getting a sword to lift the c. J2173.2; grindstone's picture mistaken for c. J2685; magic c. *D1036.1; numskull tries to hatch out a calf from a c. J1902.2; one c. sent after another J1881.1.2; ordeal by bread and c. H232; raven with c. in mouth K334.1; sowing c. to bring forth a cow J1932.2; thrifty cutting of c. (bride test) H381.2; trickster squeezes a c. K62.

Cheeses concealed from saint turned to stone Q552.16.1.2. — Rolling c. to scare off Indians K548.1; stones are transformed c. A977.5.1.

Cherry tree has lotus flowers F811.7.2.3. — Healing with c. tree J2412.5; magic c. *D981.4; magic c. tree *D950.4.

Cherries. — Father shares c. with sons J1341.9.

Chess game as test H509.3. — Gods play c. A163.1.1; invention of c. A1468.1; king playing c. when important news arrives P14.3; monkey plays c. B298.1; origin of c. (cumulative tale) Z21.1; parrot advises queen playing c. B565; skill at c. F679.8; unique ability to play c. H31.10.

Chessboard made from slain enemy S139.2.2.4.3. — Divination with c. D1311.23.

Chest, see also **Box;** of murdered child becomes moon A1277.3. — Animal in the c. K1515; cuckolded man shuts wife's paramour in c. and lies on the c. with the latter's wife K1566; dying woman lures paramour into c.: asks for it to be buried K1555.0.1; entrance into woman's room by hiding in c. K1342; exposure in floating c. S141, S331; girl catches thief in c. K434.3; husband takes off c. containing paramour K1555.0.2; lover hidden in c. with feathers K1517.4; magic c. *D1174; man hiding in c.

catches thief K751.2; money exacted from watchers who permit c. to be stolen K443.3.1; moon from c. of sacrificed youth A741.2; murder by slamming down c. lid S121; paramour hidden in c. K1521.2, (frightens off robbers) K335.1.6.1, (and carried off) K675.1, (priest) K1218.1.4; queen lures husband into c. K2213.15; seduction by having maiden placed in floating c. K1333; sham-magician buys c. containing hidden paramour K1574; soldier asks to be stabbed in c. J216.4; supposed c. of gold induces children to care for aged father P236.2; thrall cursed to sit on c. M455.3; treasure buried in c. N511.1.8; treasure found in c. N525; unjust banker deceived into delivering c. of money K1667; victim tricked into entering c. K714.2.

Chests. — Worthless c. as security for credit K455.9.

Chestnut. — Magic c. *D985.2, (as food) *D1035.1.

Chewed. — Magic charm of c. flesh D1273.0.3.

Chewer. — Lie: remarkable c. X933.

Chewing of spruce gum by Indians A1681.1. — Devil c. up church papers G303.24.5; goat pretends to be c. rock K1723; magic results from c. D1799.5.

Chicken, see also **Cock, Hen;** feet of spirits *F401.3.5; as laborer B292.9.2; picks out attacker's eyes B524.8. — Arrows rubbed with c. fatal D1402.7.5.1; blindness cured by c. dung F952.6; creation of c. A1988; enmity of civet cat and c. A2494.1.8; enmity of fox and c. A2494.9.2; helpful c. B469.5.1; husband in the c. house K1514.1; hypocrite will not share in stolen c.; only takes gravy K2095.2; magic c. B171; magic c. thigh D1013.1; magic warmth of c. wing D1481.1; man transformed to c. D166.1; peasant's share is the c. J1562.2; priest's guest and eaten c. K2137; speaking c. B211.3.2.1.

Chickens. — Automatic hen and c. of gold D1620.2.2; educated c. tell of woman's adultery K1271.1.3; enigmatic request for c. for breakfast H599.6; enmity between birds of prey and c. A2494.13.10.6; fool kills c. by throwing them off a balcony J2173.5; fox is promised c.: is driven off by dogs K235.1; guarding c. from the fox by weighting them down in water J2125; mother kills c. (cuts off heads of the well) H583.4.3; old woman gives c. to devils G303.25.6; stolen c. turn to stone D471.8.1; strong hero asks that c. stop scratching F615.3.1.1; teaching c. to talk J1882.1; thieves' funeral for c. K375; trickster buys c., says priest will pay K455.4.1; why wildcats eat c. A2435.3.15.

Chief asks another for yam cutting (daughter) H611.3; of dead frightens visitors H1401.1; recognized by large bundle H41.10. — Creator appoints a c. for each class of things A1187; first man made world's c. A1285.1; high-spitting as test of a c. H41.2; men buried with dead c. V67.4; storm heralds newborn c. F960.1.1.3; unknown prince chosen c. of children in play *P35.

Chief's. — Tabu not to eat c. food C241.2; warriors surrender after c. death R75.2.

Chiefs buried in hidden caves V61.8.1. — Tabus of c. C564ff.

Chieftain recognized by swineherd H173.1. — Deceptive land grant to wounded c. K185.7.3.

Chieftainess fans mist off river A937; preparing food tabu C564.8; of too high rank to be wooed P281.1.

Chieftainship as reward Q112.1.

Child, see also **Baby, Infant;** adopted by rich man in order to get rid of him K2015; born as cannibal G33; born with objects indicating fate N121.1; borne off by tiger, which is caught by griffin, which is killed by lioness, who rears child with her whelps N215; in cradle guesses devil's riddle H543.2; cursed by father cannot rest in grave E412.4; of deity visits earth F31; of demon king marries mortal F402.2.3; develops from man's urine T512.2.1; feeds snake from milk-bottle B391.1; follows bird and loses its mother N313; forced to cry till magic given D835; found on deserted island A1234.3; as foundation sacrifice smiles and wins freedom S261.1; as helper N827; killed by one left to care for it K1461; of moon and mortal A753.1.5; and mountain people F460.4.1.2.1, F460.4.2.4; mystically recognizes mother H175.2; plays with magic object *D861.10; as prophet M301.20; recognizes relative's flesh when it is served to be eaten G61.1; as result of prayer Q192, T548.1; reveals murder N271.6; sacrifice S260.1.1, S268; saved from death by dressed-up block K525.1.3; sick from witchcraft struck on anvil G271.9; -stealing demon G442; threatened with ogre actually abducted *C25.1; throws down a kid (lie) X1856.1; throws millwheels from one town to another (lie) X1856.2; in womb gives guest directions H1232.5. — Abandoned c. joins parents in game: recognition follows H151.9; adult becomes c. D55.2.5; animal rescues c. B549.3 (dog), B522.4 (eagle); animals with human c. as slave B292.0.1; beautiful c. F575.3; cast-off wife and c. exposed in boat S431.1; compassionate executioner: substitute c. K512.2.2; cooked c. revived by saint E121.4.1; criminal detected by having c. hand knife to him H211; crocodile goes after second c. J2173.6; crying c. ceases only to gather strength W182; devil as c. G303.3.1.16; devil c. born with horns G303.4.1.6.2; disguise as c. K1839.12; distress over imagined troubles of unborn c. J2063; "don't adopt a c." J21.27; dragon hears cry of c. B11.12.6; dupe cares for c. while robbed K345.3; dwarf makes return of c. dependent upon guessing of riddle F451.5.15.2; dying c. assigns task H937; earth from c. (children) A831.5, A831.3; exposed or abandoned c. rescued R131ff.; fairy c. kept by mortals F329.4.1; fairy gives mortals a c. F343.13; fairies adopt human c. F311; fairies help forgotten c., strangle another J2415.4; false bride makes c. demand mother's clothes K1911.1.8.1; false bride takes true bride's place when c. is born *K1911.1.2; father of illegitimate c. must walk in front of cross J1515.1; father's ghost rebukes c. E327.4; fool kills c. J1842.2, J2465.3f., J2661.1, K946; fool thinks he has given birth to a c. by letting wind J2321.2; friendly return of dead c. E324; ghost of murdered c. E225;

ghost of unknown c. passes over parents H175.5; giving a c. a name tabu C437; god punishes man by killing his c. A1335.15; healing power of saint as c. V221.0.3; heart of unborn c. renders person invisible D1361.8; hill as adopted c. A969.6; human c. of sky-mother longs for earth father D2006.2.1; impostor claims to be father of c. of princess K1936; innocence of c. tested H256.1; journey to hell to circumcise c. F81.3; light-giving c. H1396; like parent, like c. U121; lovers' c. sent with token H82.3.1; magic object received from c. D828; magic object for service to c. D817.1ff.; magic placates crying c. D883; man as God behind the tree forces the girl to admit having illegitimate c. K1971.5.1; magic calabash cooks and cares for c. D1601.1; magic sight given to abandoned c. D1821.6; offending supernatural c. (tabu) C33; people eating c. become supernatural G55; pious c. able to carry water in sieve H1023.2.0.2; posing as relative to kill c. K2011; prophecy on killer of c. M306.5; protection from devil by holding three-year old c. through the night G303.16.19.6; rakshasa eats c. G369.1.4; reincarnation as c. E605.7f.; reincarnation of murdered c. as bird *E613.0.1; retort from underfed c. J1341ff.; revenant as c. E425.3; sham physician predicts sex of the unborn c. K1955.3; small c. beats giant F611.3.2.5; Solomon's judgment: the divided c. J1171.1; soul as c. E747; stolen c. found in hollow tree R311.3; stolen c. rescued by animal nurse B543.3; tabu to carry c. on one's back C875; touch of c. resuscitates E149.3; transformation to c. to be adopted D646.2; transformation: salmon to c. D376; transformed mother called by her c. D792; transformed mother suckles c. D688; trolls size of twelve-year-old c. F455.2.1; ugly husband placates wife, says he wants handsome c. J1541.3; unborn c. affected by broken tabu C993; unknown parent of c. sought H1381.2ff.; victorious youngest c. *L0—L99; why can't c. talk? H1292.15; wisdom of c. decides lawsuit J123; wolf defends master's c. against serpent B524.1.4; wolf waits in vain for nurse to throw away c. J2066.5; woman seeks unknown father of her c. H1381.2.1.

Children abducted R10.3; ask too difficult questions J2370.1; born during husband's long absence J2342.2; in casket floated down river H157; devoured by ogress come from fire F913.2; disenchanted after long period are aged D799.1; of the East J192.1; envious of money given by deceased father to bishop have vision V415; prefer father they know to real father they do not yet know J325; flee from father who turns cannibal G31; not left alone when asleep A1579.1; lured into ogre's house G412; play hog-killing N334.1; of polygamous marriage A1576; punished for parents' offenses Q402; refused food leave home R228; rescue parents R154; sold or promised S210ff.; of the sun A736.5; transformed into horsemen D98; unwittingly promised (sold) S240ff.; wander into ogre's house G401; and wild hunt E501.2.7, E501.5.4, E501.18.1.3.1. — Abandoned c. identified by rice H49.1; abandoned or murdered c. *S300—S399; abusing c. tabu C867.1; animals care for c. B535ff.; beggar's many c. P161; betrothal of c. T61.5; blood of c. as cure for leprosy

D1502.4.2.1; boasting of c. forbidden C452; burning c. to give them fawn's spots K1013.2.2; care of c. *T600—T699; catfish transformed from c. carry mark of children's knife holder A2261.3.1; close resemblance of two c. F1072; criminal's wife and c. sold into slavery Q437.1; cruel c. S20ff.; cure by putting c. on roof D2161.4.11; curse: c. will be sick M460.1; dead mother returns to aid persecuted c. *E323.2; dead wife returns and bears c. for husband E322.1; death of c. for breaking tabu C920.1; death of c. as punishment Q553.4f., Q559.9; deception by substitution of c. K1847; deceptive agreement to kill c. K944; demons strangle c. G302.9.4; devil's c. G303.11.2.2; dishonor to c. for breaking tabu C930.1; dog and hog dispute over their c. J243.1; dragon devours c. B11.10.3; dumbness as punishment for hiding c. Q451.3.1; dwarfs and c. F451.3.5.3, F451.3.5.5, F451.5.2.3, F451.5.21; dying woman's wraith visits c. E723.4.4; each likes his own c. best T681; encounter with clever c. dissuades man from visit J31; enemy's c. H1397.2 (quest), K930ff. (murder); fairies and human c. F310ff., F321, F326; father unwilling but mother willing to sell c. H491.1; father mutilates c. S11.1; first couple bring in c., clothe them A1277.4; first parents bear all c. they wish A1277.2; first parents c. of god A1271.3; folly of father's giving all property to c. before his death P236.1; friends and their c. P310.4, (become enemies) P312.4.2; giants' c. F531.6.8.6; innocent woman accused of killing her new-born c. K2116.1.11; legitimacy of c. tested by dipping them in river H222.1; living c. buried with dead mother S123.3; magic power of c. D1717ff.; male c. killed by Amazons F565.1.2; man betrayed into eating own c. K940.1; man transformed to woman has c. D695; as many c. as holes in a sieve (formula) Z75; many c. at a birth T586.1; monkeys from c. hidden by Eve when God visited her A1861.1; mortal saves fairy's c. F337.1; mother who devours her c. when they grow up (riddle) H734; mountain with c. F755.5; mountain men give c. a book F460.4.2.4; murder of c. punished Q211.4; murderer's c. become dwarfs F451.1.2; ogre kills noisy c. G478; ogre steals c. G305; origin of c. (explanations to c.) T589.6; origin of relation of mother and c. A1575; parents and c. *P230ff.; playing with c. helps great man J25; poisonous toad sits on food of undutiful c. Q557.1; prophecies about birth of c. M311.0.3, M369.7; punishment for refusal to have c. *Q251; rank among c. P632.3; reduced number of c. as punishment Q553.3.7; repartee concerning parentage of c. J1270ff.; rescue of c. from ogre by brother G551.3; return from dead to demand stolen c. E236.2; river formed where seven c. place stones A934.2; shark-ogre eats c. G308.5; shortsightedness in dealing with c. J2175ff.; song of c. incriminates thief K435; stars as c. of sun, moon A764.1, A764.3; stolen mother returns from fairyland each Sunday to minister to her c. *F322.3; substituted c. K1920ff.; suckling c. rock mother in cradle (lie) X1856; sun, moon and darkness as god's three c. A700.8; treacherous c. K2214; true bride's c. thrown away at birth K1911.2.3; two c. in moon A751.7; unbaptized c. (as fairies) F251.3, (in wild hunt) *E501.2.7, (pursued by

fairies) F360.1, (pursued in wild hunt) *E501.5.4, (reincarnated as birds) E613.0.2; underworld people from c. which Eve hid from God *F251.4; undutiful c. P236; ungrateful c. punished *Q281.1; unknown prince chosen chief of c. in play *P35; unnatural c. eat parent G71; unnatural parents eat c. G72ff.; various c. of Eve *A1650.1; wagers on unborn c. N16; walling up as punishment for murder of c. Q455.1; water-spirit drags c. into river F420.5.2.1.5; why bees eat their own c. A2435.5.5; why c. learn to walk late A1321.1; why prince plays with c. J1661.1.7; wisdom learned from c. J120ff.; witch carries her c. in her own body G229.2; witch steals c. *G261; woman with three hundred sixty-five c. L435.2.1.

Children's — Cannibals cut off parts of c. bodies G86; mutilation of c. bodies for identification H56.2; power of flying from eating c. hearts D2135.1.

Childbed. — Intercourse with woman in c. S185.2.

Childbirth, see also **Birth** T580ff.; bell sounded falsely: not heeded in need J2199.1.2; magically delayed T574. — Banishment till rose grows from table for preventing c. Q431.4; charms make c. easy D1501.2; despite c. pain women become pregnant H659.13.1; dead father helps daughter in c. E327.2; fairy aid to queen in c. F312.3; goddess of c. A477; husband abandons wife in c. S143.4; husband looking at supernatural wife in c. forbidden C31.1.4; letter alleged to aid c. K115.1.1; origin of c. A1351; painful c. as punishment Q553.3.6; sacrifice at c. V17.9; tabu connected with c. C150ff.; tabus following c. C154; tree bows to help Virgin Mary in c. D1648.1.2.1; Virgin Mary helps abbess in secret c. T401.1.

Childless couple adopt hero N825.1; couple promise devil a child S223; woman lost while fugitive woman burdened with child is saved N185; woman reborn as fish E694.4; woman rescues boy R169.9. — Prophecy: child to be born to c. M311.0.3.1; seduction by giving c. man's wife medicine K1315.2.4; unlucky to look at c. person T591.2.

Childlessness, curse of M444.

Chili plant causes dumb man to speak F954.4. — Enemy blinded with c. powder K783.1; jealous woman reborn as c. E692.4; rattlesnake harmful because earth worm feeds him c. pepper A2211.11; soul in c. plant E711.2.3.

Chimera B14.1.

Chimney. — Why cat keeps c. corner A2223.1, A2433.3.1.1; corpse drops piecemeal down c. H1411.1; devil descends c., spoils pudding C12.5.5; devil goes up c. in smoke G303.17.2.1; fairies descend c. F275; intruder captured in c. K732; intruding wolf falls down c. and kills himself J2133.7, K891.1; looking up c. tabu C337; magic object found in c. D847; ogre's arm thrust down c. G369.5; paramour hidden in c. K1521.1; theft through c. K316; Thumbling carried up c. by steam of food F535.1.1.2; witch steals child with hand through c. G261.1; witches come, go by c. G249.3.

Chimpanzee, see also **Monkey;** leads lost hunter home B563.1.2. — Enmity of c. and man A2494.12.9; origin of body hair of c. A2322.6; why c. has large teeth A2345.9; why c. lives in forest A2433.2.1.2; why c. lives with men A2433.2.4.1.

Chin. — How buffalo got hair under c. A2322.1; mutilation: c. cut off S166.2; woman so old her c. reaches her knee F571.3.1.

China first land in world A802. — Bull in the c. shop J973.

Chips from tree return to their places as cut D1602.2.2; of wood become animal D441.10. — Magic feather (song) causes c. from tree to return as fast as cut D1565.1; recognition by unique manner of carving c. H35.4; remarkable thrower of c. makes forest F636.2.

Chipmunk. — Lies about c. X1224; stripes of c. A2217.2, A2413.2.

Chirping. — Annoyance of swallows' c. less than sandpipers' J215.1.4.

Chisel. — Creator with hammer and c. in hands A18.5; why magpie's tail like c. A2378.7.2.

Chittagongs formerly braver A1676.1.

Choice, see also **Choosing, Chosen;** of kings P11; between life or heaven V311.3; of dangerous road tests valor H1561.9; of magic object from worthless D859.5; of weapons alternates P557.4.3. — Animal or object indicates c. of ruler H171; apple thrown indicates princess's c. H316; criminal allowed c. of method of execution P511; first at combat field gets c. of weapons P557.4.1; girl to wed man of her c. T131.0.1.1; girl must marry father's c. T131.1.2.1; grateful objects help in c. of caskets D1658.3.2; Hobson's c.: take what is offered or get nothing J201; modest c. best L210ff.; origin of death from unwise c. A1335.3; princess's unrestricted c. of husband T131.0.1; starved lover given c. of lady or food K1218.1.3.1; tribes from c. Sun offers A1610.5.

Choices *J200—J499; by chance N125. — Little gain, big loss in c. J340ff.; origin of tribes from c. made A1614.4.

Choir imitates apologizing minister J2498.1. — Angel c. responds to saint V234.1.3; mermaid sings in c. B81.3.2.

Choked. — Departing husband c. by deserted wife K951.0.1; lord who robs poor widow of her cow c. on first mouthful Q552.6; scoffer c. to death by mysterious stranger who blows ashes into his face Q554.3; woman's undutiful son c. by serpent Q557.2.

Choking lawyer with smoke Q469.5. — Death by c. for breaking tabu C922.1; murder by c. K951ff.

Cholera. — God of c. A478.3; man mistaken for c. J1786.3; origin of c. A1337.2.

Choosing, see also **Choice;** correctly from three caskets H511.1; flowers as test of sex of girl masking as man H1578.1.3; princess from others identically clad H324; tree on which to hang K558.

Choosy. — Too c. princess married to idiot J2183.5.

Chopping. — Deceptive contest in c. K44; marvelous sensitiveness: fracture from hearing man c. wood F647.8.1; task: c. down large tree with blunt implements H1115.

Chopsticks. — Seven pairs of c. H1199.16; younger twin unthinkingly hands c. to elder H255.

Choral singing accompanies saint V222.3.

Chosen, see also **Choice, Choosing;** people V317. — All three gifts c. by trickster J1202; brother c. rather than husband or son P253.3; early death c. rather than long life without lady M366; remaining transformed to mule c. rather than living with shrewish wife T251.1.3; remaining in Purgatory c. rather than returning to shrewish wife T251.1.2; unpromising magic object c. *L215.

Christ (Jesus) *V211; accused of trying to fool the people J1823.1.1; appears to St. Martin after charity V411.8; carries water in cloak F866.7.2.1; causes animal characteristics A2287ff.; changes stones to peas D452.1.6.1; creates fire in hell from his blood A671.0.2.1; in desert overcomes devil by fasting V73.0.1; in disguise as leper Q25.1; grants immortality to Nephites D1856.2; has too many debts J2477; kills man plotting murder J225.4; magically ages one of the magi D1897; as matchmaker T53.2; not having married, knew nothing about suffering T251.0.2; puts knots in wood A2738; prophesies people will live "till coming of Patrick" M300.1, M363.1.2; releases soul from hell E754.1.6. — Actor does not want to be C. J2495.3; all living things from splattered blood of C. A1724.3; all sins since the birth of C. J1743.1; animals blessed for honoring infant C. *A2221.1; animals lick C. child B251.10; animals worship infant C. B251.1.1; beggar on cross in place of C. L435.4; crossbill's bill from aiding C. A2221.2.4.2; devil appears as C. G303.3.2.1; devil tries to pass for C. K1992; dialogue between C. and souls in hell E755.2.8; dog created as watch-dog for C. A1831; dying like C. — between two thieves X313; five wounds of C. Z71.3.2; hot springs arise where C. bathed feet A942.1; image of C. wounds nun V122.1; indentions on rocks from footprints of C. A972.1.1; infant C. shown to nun D1766.1.2; Jews crucifying C. punished in Cornish mines F456.1.1.1; like C. on Palm Sunday J1265.1; leopards guide C. to Egypt B563.5; likeness of C. criticized V124; man behind the crucifix says "Good Evening" to drunk man who thinks C. is speaking to him K1971.7; numskull knocks figure of C. from ass J1823; oath concerning battles for C. M177.1.2; owl is baker's daughter who objected to dough being given C. A1958.0.1; in Passion Play C. says, "I am thirsty": thief on left speaks up, "I too" J2041.1; pilgrimage to roads C. walked V531.1; pike helps C. cross stream: made king of fishes A2223.4; plant blessed for help at birth of C. A2711.1; plant cursed for disservice to C. A2721.1; punishment for foul portrayal of C. Q222.3; punishment for opposition to C. at crucifixion *Q221.2; return from dead to prophesy coming of C. E367.3; riddle about C. in thirtieth year H826; spider steals thread from C. A2231.6; springs rise where C. bathed his feet A942.1; seven whistlers are souls of Jews who crucified C. A1715.3; shoemaker cursed for spitting at C. P453.1; standing up for C. as friendless J1738.5; statue of infant C. takes apple V128.1; swallows torment C. on cross A2231.2.2;

three whom C. raised from dead Z71.1.11; tree protects C. from rain: is green all year A2711.4.

Christ's coat of mercy protects Pilate from punishment D1381.4.1; forty-days' fast V73.6.1; height as magic measurement D1273.4; image has broken his arm J1823.1.2; image wounds nun V122.1; letter protects *D1381.24.1. — Animals rejoice at C. birth B251.1; animals speak at C. nativity B211.0.1; all locks opened at C. nativity D2088.0.1; appearance of C. body to prove transformation of host V33.1.1; blood from C. wounds restores sight D1505.8.1; children speak in wombs at C. birth T575.1.5; death at news of C. crucifixion F1041.1.3.9; dead prophesy C. coming E367.3; devil exorcised at C. nativity G303.16.19.10; diseases cured at C. birth D2161.6.1; eight miracles of C. body Z71.16.1.3; fetters loosed on C. nativity D1395.8; giant whale cast ashore on C. nativity B874.3.2; gold appears in Arabia at C. birth N529.1; hero born at C. nativity T589.7.2; indentions on plants from C. biting them at crucifixion A2721.2.2; Jews rubbed C. body with garlic A1662.1; markings on animals as recollections of C. life and sufferings A2221.3; Romans hate C. poverty V385; rue from drops of C. blood A2611.7; swallows lift C. crown of thorns from his brow A2221.2.4; spring flows at C. command F933.1.2; tree for C. crucifixion A2632.2; treasure found at C. nativity N541.4; wells break forth at C. birth A941.5.0.2; wild huntsman released from wandering by mould from C. grave *E501.17.7.1; woman taught that it is better to pray before C. image than before a saint's V51.4.

Christened. — Oath not to be c. until Christian battles fought M177.1.2.

Christening, see also **Baptism;** V87. — Animal c. B299.10; dwarfs celebrate c. feasts of their own F451.6.3.2; dwarfs invisibly attend c. feasts of mortals F451.5.1.7; magic power from c. an animal D1766.4; troll bluffed away from c. K1736; witches c. cat G243.2.2; wolf kept at door until c. is finished K551.8.

Christian burial service for fairy F268.1; fairy F243.0.1, F389.2; frees poor from sacrifice K1603; king demands baptism of guests P337.1; laws profitless J1825.1; paradise A694; paradise and pagan otherworld F160.03; traditions cencerning Jews *V360ff. — Devil can't approach C. girl G303.16.19.12; druid's spells kill C. king D1402.13; druids kill C. king F402.1.11.1; fairy borrows comb from C. maid to comb hair of changeling bride F322.1.1; fairies disappear before name or ceremony of C. church F382; magic spells mixed with C. prayers *D1273.0.2; oath literally obeyed: to tell no C. K2312.1; origin of C. worship A1546.3; prophecy that youth shall abandon his religion and become C. M351; runes protect against curse of dead C. D1385.20; vow to become a C. M177.1; what is best religion, C. or Mohammedan? H659.5.1; witch's charm opposite of C. *G224.1.

Christians crushed in cave R315.2; and giants F531.5.8; prohibited from whistling in dark lest the devil appear G303.16.18.1. — Arrows shot against C. blown back F963.2; coffins of C. V61.6; foul disease for per-

secuting C. Q570.1; Jew thinks C. have merciful God J1263.3; mountain-men make sausage of C. F460.4.4.4.

Christianity. — Belief in C. tested H1573.1; conversion to C. V331; dead convert to C. E367.4; dwarfs and C. F451.5.9ff.; dwarfs emigrate because C. offends them F451.9.1.6; fairy demands lover deny C. F302.8; fairy professes C. F251.8; first Irish convert to C. A1546.3.1; giants converted to C. F531.5.8.3; giants hostile to C. F531.5.8.1; pagan punished for conversion to C. Q232.1; power of C. tested H1573.3; setting house on fire rather than accept C. V328; trolls and C. F455.7.

Christmas *V72. — Animals speak to one another on C. B251.1.2; apples at C. F971.5.2; cows kneel on C. Eve B251.1.2.3; devil in woods to gather nuts on C. Eve G303.8.13.3; fernseed gathering on C. Eve C401.5; flowers blooming at C. F971.5.3; giants and men fraternize at C. F531.5.1.2; knockers' C. Eve mass in mines F456.1.2.3.1; man attacked on C. night by dancing ghosts E261.3; Schlaraffenland lies three miles beyond C. X1712; treasure reveals itself only on C. midnight N541.1; trolls steal fish at C. F455.6.3.1; trolls visit people C. Eve F455.6.5.1; twelve days (gifts) of C. Z21.2.1; water to wine on C. D477.1.1, M211.1.1; wild hunt appears between C. and Twelfth Night E501.11.2.2.

Christopher and the ass J1269.9; and Christ child Q25.

Church built by usurer's money collapses Q273.4; built where giants throw stones F531.3.2.1; desecrator cannot rest in grave E412.5; dignitaries *P120ff.; in otherworld F163.2; produced by magic D1134.1; as refuge R325; services burlesqued in witch's sabbath G243; services of the dead *E492; sinks underground F941.2; spared in flood because of prayers D2143.2.1; stones sheds blood Q222.0.1; supernaturally moved at night D2192.1; which refused to bury saint burned Q552.13.2.2. — Angel abides in c. V242.2; angel holds mass in c. V49.2; angel tells where to build c. V246.1; angels build c. V232.10; animal burns neglected c. B596; animals in otherworld pass in and out of c. and become human beings *F171.5; burial in c. wall cheats devil K219.4; Butterby C.: no c. at all Z61.3; cleaning the c. by moving it J2104.1; contest in jumping from the c. tower K1.7.2; criminal in c. mistakes service as accusation N275.5; curse for plundering c. Q556.6; cursed c. clock runs incorrectly H252.6; dead arise when one plays organ for first time in c. E419.5; devil in c. G303.8.4, G303.24ff.; devil in each stone of c. built with ill-gotten wealth G303.8.4.2; devil may be escaped by going to c. daily G303.16.13; devil disguised as man goes to c. to confess K1987; devil makes mischief on c. G303.24.4 (destroys steeple), G303.24.1.7.1 (disturbs worshippers), G303.9.9.18 (moves seats), A977.2.2 (throws stones); destruction, rebuilding of c. prophesied M364.10; discontinuing use of a c. forbidden C51.1.6; dog lets devil into c. to steal A2229.2; dwarfs hold c. services F451.6.3.6; dwarfs live in a c. F451.4.2.4; dwarf seeks to enter c. F451.5.9.5; fairies disappear when some name or ceremony of Christian C. is used F382; friendly ghost haunts c. E338.2; ghost effects return of stolen c. plate E236.7; ghost rebukes those withholding c. money

E415.2; ghosts haunt c. E283; giants carry a c. across a stream F531.3.6; guarded maiden first seen by hero in c. T381.1; heat prevents c. theft D1389.2.1; images at c. turn backs as mark of disfavor D1639.3; lightning strikes excommunicated person who enters c. V84.1; lime used in building c. as cure D1500.1.10.6; magic arrow indicates place to build c. D1314.1.4; magic c. D1134.1; magic stone protects c. from oppression D1389.1; man becomes c. D268.0.1; man whose death prophesied takes refuge in c. M381; man promises to build c. if he is saved at sea M266; mermaid sings divinely in c. B81.13.6; merman's wife not to stay till c. benediction *C713.1; misunderstanding of c. customs or ceremonies cause inappropriate action J1823; mountain gives stones for c. D1552.7; mountain men throw person over c. roof F460.4.4.3; mountains and hills from stones thrown by giant at c. A963.5; moving c. tower J2328; numskulls buy c. in common J2037.1; parody of c. ceremony at witch's sabbath G243.2; prophecy: saint to found c. M364.1.1; punishment for desecrating c. Q222.5; books in c. read without man's tongue F1055; person to live as long as c. stands E765.3.1; playing cards with devil in c. H1421; prince sees maiden at c. and is enamored N711.4; punishment for scoffing at c. teachings *Q225; neglect to attend c. punished Q223.5; radiance fills c. when saint dies V222.1.1; remarkable c. F773; repartee based on c. or clergy J1260ff.; robber or dog in c. thought to be a ghost J1782.1; speechless vigil in c. (test) H1451; spending night in c. H1412; stealing from c. punished by hanging Q411.11.2; stone bleeds before c. plundered D1317.12.1; symbolism of c. and image H619.2; thief reveals self in c. J1141.15; threat to build c. in hell K1781; turf from c. roof gives clairvoyance D1323.7; vision concerning state of Irish c. V515.1.3.1; walking backward around c. gives witch power G224.8; wedding ceremony in c. T135.9; white mare thought to be c. J1761.2; his wife the c. J1264.1; wild huntsman wanders for disturbing c. service E501.3.8; witch marks c. steeple G241.3.3.

Churches *V111. — Devil as builder of c. G303.9.1.6; giants throw stones after c. F531.3.2.1; half of Irish c. to be named for Ciaran M364.9.

Church bells *V115ff., ring selves at holy person's death V222.6.1, rout enemy D1400.1.9.1, speak D1610.15.1, cannot be raised because silence is broken V115.1.3.1, rung as protection against storm D2141.1.1. — Dwarfs dislike c. F451.5.9.3; ghost laid by burying c., clapper separately E459.6; hiding from ghosts under c. E434.1; mermaid prevents raising of sunken c. B81.13.10; origin of c. A1466; trolls cannot endure c. G304.2.4.1; what c. say V115.4.

Churchdoor. — Recognition by overheard conversation with c. H13.2.4.

Churchman. — Disguise as c. K1826; seduction by posing as c. K1315.6; sham c. K1961ff.

Churchmen in wild hunt E501.2.5. — Animal c. B252; treacherous c. K2280ff.; wild hunt powerless against c. E501.17.1.2.

Churchyard ghosts E273, (friendly) E333. — Dancing in c. forbidden

C51.1.5; magic c. mould *D1278.1; tabu to dig in c. C93.3; wild hunt appears in c. E501.12.2.
Churl. — Disguise as c. K2357.14; transformation into c. D29.1.
Churn. — Breaking spell on bewitched c. G271.4.11; coin in c. releases curse M429.6; fairies bathing in c. F361.17.5; fox struck with c.-dash: hence white tail A2215.5; salt in c. protects against witches G272.16.1.
Churning. — Dwarfs c. F451.3.4.7; fairies c. F271.7; origin of c. A1439.5.1; origin of c. stick A2823.
Ciaran. — Irish churches to be named for C. M364.9.
Cicada. — Man transformed to c. D183.1.
Cicadas ordered to sing God's praises D2156.7.
Ciconiiformes. — Creation of c. A1960ff.; transformation to c. D155ff.
Cicuta. — Transformation by eating c. D551.2.2.
Cider as man's enemy J1319.1.
Cigar, magic D1261.
Cimmerians, voyage to land of F129.3.
Cinderella L102; male L101.
Cinderella's three-fold flight from ball R221.
Cinders. — Man created from c. A1268.
Cinnamon, origin of A2686.8.
Circe transforms lovers into animals G263.1.0.1.
Circle. — Devil cheated by having priest draw a sacred c. about the intended victim K218.1; dwarfs cannot harm mortal with c. drawn around him F451.3.2.3; magic c. *D1272; magic c. keeps devil out G303.16.19.15; sitting in c. of feasts P338; saints' land surrounded by fiery c. A661.0.10; warriors fight in c. P552.1.
Circles. — Sun, moon as animated wooden c. A714.8.
Circular house rotating on cock's claw F771.2.6.1.
Circuit. — Earth scattered on c. of four directions on primeval water A814.6.
Circuitous path quickest J2119.2.2.
Circumambulations. — Magic power by c. *D1791; repeated c. with prayer V58.3.
Circumcised. — Child born c. T585.9; first man created c. A1281.5.
Circumcision V82. — Dust on c. wound A1567.1; journey to hell for c. of child F81.3; magic c. blood D1003.2; mother suckles all babies at c. H495.3; neglect of c. punished Q223.11; origin of c. A1567.
Cirencester, sparrows of K2351.1.
Cistern. — Cleaning enormous c. in one day (task) H1097.2.
City built by magic D2178.1; buried in sand F948.5; burned with all inhabitants S112.0.1; of demons F402.3; founded on spot (where cow lies down) B115.2, (where arrow falls) D1314.1.2; of gods A151.5; hurled down precipice in punishment Q552.22; infested by jinns, deserted G307.4; of king opposing saint burned Q552.13.2.1; person ignorant of farm J1731; populated by wooden automata D1628; saved from disaster

as reward Q152; sinks in sea F944; without provisions but with much money starves J712.1; of women F112.2. — Bringing documents from distant c. in one day (task) H1107; building c. as task H1133.5; conqueror spares c. W11.5.5; countryman misunderstands c. comforts J1742.5; covenant: c. not to be taken from inhabitants without their consent M293; curse on c. M475; defeated surrender their c. R75.1; deity to restore c. A185.8; dragon encircles c. B11.2.8.1; earth swallows heretical c. Q552.2.3.2.2; enduring insults to enter c. gate H1553.3; fairy gains entrance to locked c. D2088.1; faithless widow offers c. to husband's killer T231.3.1; god of c. A412; illusory c. separates companions K1886.5; inhabitants of c. transformed to fish D692; magic object protects a c. D1380.0.1; man ordered to number fools in c. J1443; monkeys decide not to build c. J648.1; old man contented till forbidden to leave c. H1557.3; only one way of besieging c. Z316; philosopher saves c. from destruction J1289.10; pious man renders c. invulnerable D1846.5.2; reward: being saved from destruction of c. Q150.1.1; righteous save sinful c. from destruction M294; ruler delivers c. to enemy K2369.3; sage curses c. M411.24; sinful c. burnt as punishment Q486.1.1; strong man carries off c. gates F631.2; truth leaves c. because there is no place left for her Z121.1; voice from heaven curses c. Q556.0.2.; wild hunt appears over c. E501.12.9.

Cities, extraordinary *F760ff.; of refuge P518, R345; submarine F725.2. — Jokes concerning c. X680; origin of c. A995; remarkable c. X1560; three c. in heaven A661.1.2.

Civet. — Enmity of c. and chicken A2494.1.8; hare tricks c. into being eaten by lion K813.2.

Civilization personified Z136.

Clad, see **Clothed.**

Claim. — Devil asserts c. to soul offered in jest G303.6.1.3; false c. to powers of a god forbidden C51.6; impostors' c. of reward earned by hero K1932; property c. based on lie X905.3; thief shows up owner's unjust c. J1213; thief's successful c. that stolen goods are his own K405; why a mother has prior c. on her children A1575.1.

Clairvoyance given by magic object *D1323ff., D1331.1; from prayer D1323.18.

Clam swallows canoe party F911.4.1.1; test H1521. — Giant c. B874.6; great c. fights hero's pursuer B523.3.

Clams. — Giant c. in otherworld F167.1.4.1.

Clam-shell lures man into sea G308.7. — Animal preserves fire for abandoned children in a c. S352.1; creation of universe from c. A617.

Clan gods A415, M119.2.

Clans. — Marriage within c. sanctioned T131.5.1.

Clandestine lover recognized (by tokens) H81ff., (by paint marks) H58, (by scratches) H58.2; paramour *T475; visit of princess to hero betrayed by token H81.2.

Clapper. — Ghost laid by burying churchbell, c. separately E459.6.
Clapping hands when dangling from tree fatal J2133.13. — Magic from c. hands D1799.2.
Clarifying. — Nut c. waters F930.8.
Clarinet. — Gun mistaken for c. J1772.10; magic c. *D1223.
Clashing rocks D1553, H1525; swords herald wild hunt E501.13.1.3.
Class tabu C550—C599. — Transformation to person of different social c. D20ff.
Classes. — Humor of social c. X200—X599; origin of different c., social and professional A1650ff.; stupid c. J1705.
Claw. — Circular house rotating on cock's c. F771.2.6.1; transformation by putting on c. of helpful animal D532.
Claws caught in tree cleft K1111; on dragon's feet B11.2.4.2. — Animal characteristics: c. and hoofs A2376; bear hard to hold by c. H659.2.1; bear learns how to catch crabs with his hairy c. J102; child born with c. T551.9; devil has c. G303.4.4; devil puts c. through girl's hands G303.10.4.5; giant with nails like c. F531.1.6.1; how crab got its c. A2376.4; lion suitor allows his c. to be cut J642.1; men with iron c. cannibals G88.1; monster's c. as slaying proof H105.5.3; person with c. on feet F517.1.4; priest separates girl from devil's c. G303.16.14.1.1; trees with green birds hanging by c. F811.9.
Clay dropped from sky forms hill A963.9; model causes king to recognize lost brother H16.1. — Boat of c. J2171.1.3.2; carrying water in a leaky vessel by repairing it with c. H1023.2.1.1; consecrated c. as remedy D1500.1.6.2.1; covering with c. to escape K521.3.1; hardened c. is hard to mold J21.52.3; magic c. D935.2; man made from c. A1241.4.1; man's body of c. A1260.1.5; origin of c. A998; tribes from creator's c. models A1610.6.
Clean. — Food denied until hands c.: impossible task K278; salt to keep people c. A1372.10; seduction access by waiting for c. clothes K1349.6.
Cleanest girl to be eaten K619.1.1.
Cleaning Augean stable H1102; child by removing intestines K1461.1; church by moving it J2104.1; dagger on robe's inside A1599.7; enormous cistern in one day (task) H1097.2; horse with boiling water K1443; houses with cow-dung C536. — Four places c. soul Z71.2.4; magic power from c. D1799.1; rancher unrecognizable after c. up W115.3; reward for c. loathsome person Q41.2.
Cleanliness. — Lice as c. test H1585.
Cleansing fountain in heaven A661.0.4.
Clearing land (axe broken) K1421, (as task) H1129.6; out manure by digging hole K1424; out the room (throwing out the furniture) J2465.5. — Fairies c. land F271.5; god c. plains A181.1; strong man c. plain F614.9.
Cleaving boulder frightens witch K547.13; horse and rider in two F628.2.10.
Cleft. — Cure by passing patient under c. of tree D2161.4.5; dwarf caught

by beard in c. of tree E451.6.1; female overpowered when caught in tree c. K1384; giant's blow makes c. in rock F531.6.6.4; magic imprisonment in c. tree Q435; mankind from c. rock A1245.3.

Clement V duped into abdicating K2282.1.

Clergy *P426. — Curse of c. causes death D2061.2.4.2; giants exorcised by c. F531.5.8.2; repartee based on church or c. J1260ff.

Cleric, see also **Monk, Priest;** goes with saint whom his cow follows B159.3; as helper N846; as riddle-solver H561.8; robbing grave K335.0.8; as saint's successor D1812.5.0.7.2; son realizes mother's incest H582.2.1; tempted by devil G303.9.4.4; tempts self with women Q537.2. — Angel in form of c. V231.4; animal leads c. to holy place B563.4.1; dead saint exonerates c. E376.1; fly buzzes when c. returns B251.2.4; fly, wren, fox live with c. B256.10; imprisoned c. answers saint's prayer D2074.2.5.1; transformation into c. D25.2.

Clerics exempted from military service P551.3; fast for revelation P623.0.1.1; fishing F986.1; mistaken for fairies F234.2.4.1; sail in skin boats C841.0.1; saved from drowning F1088.3.1. — Debtor c. punished Q499.5; devil's book for sins of c. G303.24.1.9; fairies hate c. F399.3; horses travel unguided between c. B151.1.1.0.1; mutinous c. expelled P226.2; whale helps voyaging c. land B256.12.

Clerical virtues and vices V460ff. — Neglect of c. duties punished Q223.13; repartee concerning c. abuses J1263ff.

Clerk who enters tavern arrested with others for murder N347.1; mistranslates order, gets pie K362.8.

Clever daughter-in-law defeats wealthy J185.1; Elsa J2063; peasant girl asked riddles by king H561.1; person deceives robbers, summons help K432; persons and acts J1100—J1699; person's defeat pleases inferior J885; queen P20.1; remark wins jester's pardon by prince J1181.3; retorts J1250—J1649; sister saves brother's wife P253.8; wife in disguise wins husband H461.1; youngest daughter L61. — Encounter with c. children J31; foolish person becomes c. J1116; husband's c. remark discomfits adulterers K1569.8; king and c. youth H561.4; quest for c. woman H1381.3.3; sham magician exposed by c. girl K1963.1; stupid fear c. J423; stupid youngest son becomes c. L21; sun as moon's c. brother A736.3.2.

Cleverness *J1100—J1699; as bride test H388; rewarded Q91; as suitor test H327. — Falsely accused minister reinstates himself by his c. K2101; king pleased with thieves' c. J1198.1; strength preferred to c. J246; tests of c. *H500—H899; tasks performed by c. H961.

Client, the lawyer's mad *K1655.

Cliff from lover's leap A968.2; ogre thrown to his children G519.3. — Abandonment on c. Q466.2, S147.1; child falls from c.; uninjured N653; child's falling over c. to punish mother Q559.9; climbing extraordinary c. H1199.14; demons live in white c. F402.6.4; dwarfs live in a c. F451.4.2.1; extraordinary c. F808; fatal game: throwing from c. K854;

fright into falling down a c. J2611; murder by pushing off c. K929.9; murderess forced to leap from c. Q417.1; magic c. D932.1; ogre kicks victims over c. G321; owl saves man from plunging over c. B521.5; rejuvenation by jumping over c. D1889.11; stretching c. D482.4; throwing moon over c. J2271.3; victim pushed off c. as he looks for tree K832.5; witch dwells on c. G231.

Cliffs. — Origin of c. A968; trolls live in c. F455.1.2.

Climate, see also **Weather;** same at home and abroad J2274.3. — Lies about c. X1660.

Climax of horrors Z41.10.

Climber. — Marvelous c. F684.1; stealing from tree c. K341.4.1.

Climbers. — Tree c. temporarily remove bones F1054.

Climbing into air on magic rope D1582; down as he climbed up J2244; extraordinary cliff H1199.14; glass mountain (task) H1114; the mast (bluff) K1762; match won by deception K15; red hot rod (punishment) Q469.2; on roof prohibited women C181.4. — Attempt at c. to heaven L421.1; disenchantment by c. D753.4; dupe c. rope for food injured K1034; hero c. up girl's sari killed N339.11; souls c. pillars to heaven E754.6; tribe c. down from sky to earth A1631.2; wolves c. on top of one another to tree J2133.6.

Clinging. — Beings born in hell c. to walls A671.6; journey to otherworld by c. magically to an object *F155; magic object c. to guilty person *H251.3.8.

Clink. — Payment with c. of money J1172.2.

Clitoris. — Extraordinary c. F547.4; origin of c. A1313.2.1.

Cloak, see also **Mantle;** dipped in water as false proof of storm K1894; fits all sizes D1692; from fur of all animals F821.1.3.2; given to a stone to keep it warm J1873.2; transformed to other object D454.3.4. — Abduction by giving soporific and rolling up in a c. R22.1; amulet becomes c. D489.2; carrying coals in c. without harm H221.1.1; devil in a black c. G303.5.1.1; devil in fold of knight's c. G303.8.9.1; devil steals knight's c. G303.9.9.3; fairy gives magic c. F343.5.1; identification by feather c. H111.2; magic c. *D1053; magic c. makes person old D1341.2; putting head under saint's c. reveals rewards in heaven D1329.1; transformation by donning c. D537.2; thief steals c. left as surety K346.5; thief borrows c. to carry food, steals it K351.2; "what is under my c.?" H526.

Clock as reward for passing curiosity test H1554.2; stops at owner's death E766.1; ticking thought to be gnawing of mice J1789.2. — Cursed church c. runs incorrectly H252.6; magic c. flies D1651.14.

Clod. — Murder by putting c. in person's windpipe K951.4; transformation: handkerchief with three knots to c., potsherd, and charcoal D454.3.2.1.

Clods from horse's hoofs appear like birds K1872.5.1.

Clog. — Dog proud of his c. J953.1.

Cloister haunted by ghost E284. — Devil seduces monk from c.

G303.3.1.12.4; friendly ghost haunts c. E338.3; girl to be king's bride kept in c. T381.0.1; warrior retires to c. Q520.6.

Closed. — Dwarf cave c. by iron doors F451.4.3.1; magic journey with c. eyes D2121.2.

Closing the door tight with iron nails K1417. — Images with opening and c. eyes D1632; miraculous opening and c. of magic object *D1550ff.; opening and c. tree to give saint passage F979.2; waters magically dividing and c. *D1551ff.

Closet. — Lazy servant looks into dark c. to see if it is yet light W111.2.1; skeleton in the c. V115.

Clot of blood, birth from T541.1.1.

Cloth on back protects against being eaten H119.1; becomes bloody (life token) E761.1.8; causes magic sleep D1364.13; as chastity index H431; for chiefs alone C564.4; large or small at will D631.3.6; as long as river H1149.8; sold to statue J1853.1; transforms D572.3; working as bride test H383.2. — Animals from transformed c. A1714.1; boy born in c. wrapping T581.11; covering with white c. disenchants D777.1; dwarfs spin, weave c. F455.3.4; earth from couple dancing on c. A825; eating food without untying c. H506.7; fairies work on c. F271.4; goddess's c. spread on ground: spring flows A941.5.6; guessing nature of devil's c. H523.2; how much c. would it take to make God's coat? J1291.3.1; identification by c. H110ff.; ignorant priest forces rolls of c. instead of bread down a dying man's throat J1738.1; imaginary coler of c. J1551.8; king orders piece of c. shown after his death J912.1; lover's gift regained: piece of c. as gift K1581.5; magic c. *D1051; origin of bark-c. A1453.5; origin of designs on c. A1465.3.2; origin of raffia c. A1453.7; quest for dusty c. H1377.4; quest for marvelous c. H1355; rat and serpent imprisoned together in a sevenfold c. covering K1182; resuscitation by wet c. over corpse E80.2; stingy woman's c. stolen K341.13; thief advises c. be left out overnight: steals it K343.2.2; thief throws needle containing stolen c. K341.13.1; thievish tailor sews the stolen piece of c. on the outside of his coat X221; tying c. between legs tabu C181.5; washing black c. white H1023.6; weaving c. from two threads (task) H1022.1; widow c. J2301.2.

Cloths, altar V135.

Cloth-making, origin of A1453.

Clothed. — Coming neither naked nor c. H1054; naked person made to believe that he is c. J2312ff.; nude woman c. in own hair F555.3.1; ogre c. in rock G371.1; parents c. from palm-tree A1420.5.

Clothes, see also **Garments;** auctioned in hell attract Jews X611; burn when owner dies E767.2; burned magically D2089.8; burned to rid them of insects J2102.6; changed so as to escape K521.4; confer invulnerability D1845.2; carry owner over water D1524.2; from magic nut D1470.1.6; magically clinge to body D2171.6; hung on sunbeam *F1011.1; of knight who kneels in mud before host as it passes miraculously kept

clean V34.4; producing tree K118.1; put into nutshells F1053; thrown into the cooking food J1561.1. — Abduction by stealing c. R32; beggar's c. burned, yield gold K245; boy with c. of paper X1853; bride test: wearing deceased wife's c. H363.1; bringing c. soonest in bride contest H375.2; burial in c. of one's murderer V68.3; capture by using enemy's c. K761; correct wearing of c. as suitor test H312.6; creator paints c. on models of men A1453.6; dead grateful for c. E341.4; devil hides in c. of running people G303.6.2.1.2; disguise in killed enemy's c. K2357.7; disguise by wearing other person's c. K1810.1; disguise of woman in man's c. *K1837; diving for c. K1051.2; dupe fights bear, c. stolen K1252.1; dupe's c. stolen K343.5; emperor's new c. *K445; escape by arranging captor's c. so as to delay him K634; exchange of c. between master, servant K527.3; extraordinary c. F821ff., (in otherworld) F166.3; fairy leaves when he is given c. F381.3; fairies give beautiful c. F343.5; fool in new c. does not know himself J2012.4; giant's c. F531.4.7; heroine in menial disguise discovered in her beautiful c. H151.6; king changes c. with thief K346.1.1; magic c. *D1050ff.; magic object furnishes c. D1473; magic power from donning magician's c. D1721.0.1; magic sight by turning c. inside out D1821.9; man gulled into giving up his c. K330.1; man to be judged by his own qualities, not his c. J1072; man's c. identify werwolf H64.2; miser wants to enter heaven in gold-filled c. W153.15; no c. needed for Day of Judgment J1511.7; paramour steals husband's c. K1549.1; polluted c. J2184; princess changing c. with maid T323.1.1; profaning hallowed c. and vessels forbidden C93.2; recognition by exact fitting of c. H36; respite from death until c. are changed K551.4.1; respite from wooer while he brings c. all night K1227.3; serpent's bite produces ornaments and c. B108.6; sewing c. onto skin H1505; saint restores burned c. V229.10.1; shame for nakedness appears to first woman (leaves for c.) H1383.1; spirits dressed in antique c. F401.1; stealing c. from ghosts (fear test) H1431; touching certain c. tabu C545; transformation by changing c. D537; tribe wears c. like dogs A1683.2; thief in owner's c. K311.8.4; trickster permitted to try on c. K351; vow not to change c. till a certain time M125; washing enormous number of c. (task) H1096; wearing all his c. J1289.5; welcome to the c. J1561.3; what were the c. of Adam and Eve? H812; why the black c. J1304; wives change c. with husbands in prison R152.3; woman sells favors for beautiful c. T455.3; wooing by stealing c. of bathing girl H1335.

Clothing bewitched G265.8.2; of brownie F482.2; as chastity index H431; with embroidery as tokens H86.2; of gods A158; the servant J2491; transformed to other object D454.3.1; tabu to Bondo women C181.6; of wild huntsmen E501.8ff. — Deity c. his father, the sky A625.2.4; devil is in green c. with hat G303.5.2.1; disenchantment by covering with deliverer's c. D789.1; extraordinary c. and ornaments F820ff.; first couple c. children A1277.4; food does not spoil saint's c. F1091; fore-

thought in provision for c. J730ff.; girl hides lover under c. K1892.2; god c. self with lightning A179.7; identification by c. H110ff.; lie: remarkable c. X1021; magic c. furnishes treasure D1455; murder by abuse of victim's c. D2061.2.2.5; otherworld c. never wears out F166.3.1; plants from c. of deity A2625; poisoned c. test H1516; return from dead to demand c. stolen from grave *E236.1; selling used c. forbidden C782.1; stealing witch's beautiful c. H1151.23; spirit slashes c. F473.6.2; swallowed person bereft of c. F922; tabus concerning c. C878.

Cloud bears dying man's message D1715.3; bows to female mountain A969.2; folk visit earth F33; gives crops rain or drops it in ocean J88; god A283; magically made to cover sun D2147.1; marks Nativity site V211.1.3; obstructs view of man promised all he can see Q552.15; obstructs vision in deceptive land grant K185.12; symbol of misfortune Z156. — Ascent to sky on c. *F61.1; black c. blown upon enemy D2091.11; cannibal recognized by c. of dust raised H46; dead's c. house E481.8.4; fairy disappears in form of c. F234.3.1; fool seeks the ears of grain in the direction of the c. toward which he has sowed them J1922.2.1; god in c. A137.11; magic c. *D901; magic journey in c. D2121.7; marking the place under the c. J1922.2; prisoner carried off in c. R122.2; saint drives away army with c. V229.7.1; soul as c. E744.2; soul borne away on c. E722.2.1; throwing contest: golden club on the c. K18.2; trickster threatens to throw weight into c. K1746; troll in form of c. G304.1.2.1.

Clouds above and below earth A873; beaten for not watering crops X1642; as props of the sky A702.7. — Absurd theories about c. J2277; animals drop from c. A1795; bird wants sunshine, worm c. U148.1; colored c. as evil omens D1812.5.1.11; divination from c. D1812.5.0.10; extraordinary behavior of c. F967; extraordinary c. F795; god with c. as shields A137.14.3; mad warriors fly up into c. F1041.8.7; magic control of c. D2147; origin of c. A705.1, A1133; origin of Magellanic C. A778.0.1; origin of thunder c. A1142.4; stars are trees growing on c. A769.1.

Cloudland. — Gods live in c. A151.1.4; tabu to sleep before seven days in c. C735.2.1.1.

Clove, origin of A2663.

Cloven hoof (of cow) A2376.1, (of dragon) B11.2.4.2.

Clover (four-leaf) brings good luck D1561.1.5; gives clairvoyance D1323.14; makes fairies visible F235.4.6. — Magic c. *D965.7; witch unable to rise from chair with c. under it G254.

Club strike kills ogre G512.8.1. — Devil has c. foot G303.4.5.8; extraordinary c. F835; giant's huge c. F531.4.4; god with c. A137.2; magic c. *D1094, (gives victory) D1400.1.7.1; magic transportation by c. D1520.27.1; thief-catcher caught by own c. K1605; throwing contest: golden c. on the cloud K18.2.

Coach. — Devil in c. drawn by headless horses G303.7.3.3; hay on shaft urges c. horses on J1671; phantom c. E535.1.

Coal of fire offered in innocence test H256.1; jumps, gurgles in bin E539.5; transformed to person D439.2. — Bean, straw, and c. go journeying F1025.1; lazy girl on live c. W111.1.1.5; magic c. *D931.1; ordeal by burning c. H221.1; origin of c. A1431; wild huntsman's dog when seized becomes black c. E501.15.6.7; woman puts live c. in lover's cloth K1581.5.1.

Coals transformed to gold D475.1.1. — Beggar served c. for food K492.1; devil picks up live c. G303.4.8.12; eyes of live c. F541.1.3; fairies give c. that turn to gold F342.1; murder by live c. in garments S112.4; sack of c. as fairy gift F343.20; saint invulnerable to glowing c. D1841.3.2.2; saint's breath kindles c. D1566.1.4.1; swallowing hot c. because husband unfaithful T81.8.

Coat. — Boy in church calls out that rich man has taken his c. to hell with him X435.5; compassionate executioner: bloody c. K512.1; Christ's c. of mercy protects Pilate from punishment D1381.4.1.; devil wears a bright green c. G303.5.2.3; fairy spell averted by turning c. F385.1; foul-smelling skin-c. to repel lover T323.2; frightened robber leaves his c. behind K335.1.0.1; harlot weeps to think that she has left impoverished lover his c. W151.1; identification by c. of arms H126; light c. fits in palm F821.2.1; magic c. protects against attack D1381.4; the marked c. in the wife's room K1543; saint exchanges c. with beggar V411.2; thief tricked into robbing himself by changing the place of his c. K439.3; thievish tailor cuts a piece of his own c. X221.1; witness who claims borrowed c. discredited J1151.2; wooden c. F821.1.4.

Coats. — Bird council assigns c. to different birds B238.2; dwarfs wear red c. F451.2.7.5; servants would not have left the c. J1179.5.

Cobbler, see also **Shoemaker;** gives shoes to poor boy, rewarded later Q42.9; reforms shrewish queen T251.2.4. — Disguise as c. K1816.10; the minstrel repays the c. J1632; monkey imitates c. J2413.4.3.

Cobblers. — Jokes about c. X240ff.; trickster cheats boots from two c. K233.3.

Cobold avenges uncivil answer F481.1; made to surrender booty F480.3.1.

Cobra carries person B557.8; grateful for milk B391.1.1; grateful for ulcer cure B388; grateful for thorn removal N647; writes letter on prince's tongue B165.1.3. — Back scratching stick changed into c. A1335.14; conception from hiss of c. T532.10; earth rests on head of c. A84.4.8; enmity between c. and viper A2494.16.3; friendship between crab and c. A2493.19; light from shield of c. A1412.1; man falling into well kills c. N624; prophecy: death from c. M341.2.21.1; resuscitation by removing c. flesh E21.1.1; starting fire near abode of c. H1156.1.

Cobras in boxes as punishment gift Q415.3.1. — Cake bag full of c. K444.2.

Cobwebs as medication X252.1.

Cock advises of coming enemy B122.7; as ambassador of god A165.2.2.1; believes his crowing makes sun rise J2272.1; calls the dawn B755; carries

god to upper world F62.3; crows, "Christus natus est" B251.1.2.1; crows at church and the sexton awakes and begins to sing X451; and dog enemies A2494.4.11; with elixir to lighten people B739.1; with enormous ears F989.19; feigns death to overhear hens H1556.1.1; -god A132.6.3; hears inaudible voice of dying man B733.2.1; of hell A673.2; and hen build pyre B599.1; killed by his captors in spite of his plea of usefulness to man U33; with horns on feet, knob on head (riddle) H746; and others gain possession of house K1161; persuaded to crow with closed eyes K721; persuaded to cut off crest and spurs K1065; persuades fox to talk and release him K561.1; under pot crows for guilt H235; prefers single corn to peck of pearls J1061.1; shows browbeaten husband how to rule his wife T252.2; to sing for fox, asks dog to listen K579.8; as suitor B623.5; in Valhalla awakens the gods A661.1.0.4. — Alliance of c. and seafowl B267.4; cat offers to act as doctor for c. and hen K2061.7; cat unjustly accuses, eats c. U31.1; chain tale: c. strikes out hen's eye Z43.2; continent husband reproved by seeing c. and hens T315.2.2; dead c. rises, crows, and spatters scoffers so that they become leprous Q552.8; death of the c. Z31.2.1.1; demons' c.-feet G302.4.5.1; devil disappears when c. crows G303.17.1.1; devil flees when c. is made to crow G303.16.19.4; devil in form of c. G303.3.3.3.5; "each c. crows in his own barnyard" J552.6; eaten grain and c. as damages K251.1; egg becomes crowing c. F989.20; fox confesses to c., then eats him K2027; fox persuades c. to come down and talk to him, kills him K815.1; friendship between c. and dog A2493.16; ghost of c. E402.2.1, E524.2; ghost demands body: given c. E459.1; golden c. in earth-tree A878.3.6; golden c. warns of danger D1317.15; golden c. warns against attack B143.1.5; helpful c. B469.5; Indra carried by c. B552.3; lion comforted for his fear of the c. J881.2; magic c. carries great loads in ear B171.1.0.1; magic from christening c. D1766.4.1; magic power from sacrificing (christening) a c. D1766.2.2; man transformed to c. D166.1.1; mythical c. B30.2; one c. takes glory of another's valor J972; origin of c. sacrifice A1545.3.3; originally c. had horns A2326.2.3; person simulates c. crow K1886.3.1; prophecy on c. fight D1814.1.1; quest for jeweled c. H1331.1.3.1; roasted c. comes to life and crows E168.1; sacrificing of c. is at last carried out K231.3.3; silver c. crows D1620.2.2.1; series: white c., red c., black c. Z65.2; sheep, duck, and c. in peril on sea voyage J1711.1; speaking c. B211.3.2; thread made to appear as a large log carried by a c. D2031.2; treacherous c. K2295.3; treasure found by sprinkling ground with blood of white c. D2101.1; treasure to be found by man who ploughs with c. and harrows with hen N543.2; village founded where c. crows B155.2.1; wedding of c. and hen B282.22; wee c. overawes beasts K547.1; why c. scratches for food A2435.4.8.1; why c. crows to greet sunrise A2489.1.1; why c. crows on roof with neck stretched out A2426.2.18.1; why c. does not speak A2422.10; why c. lives in town A2433.4.2, A2250.1; why c. is vain and selfish A2527.1; why c.

wakes man in morning A2489.1; why elephant flees when c. crows A2531.3.1; witch as c. G211.3.1.1; woman crowing like c. K1691.2.

Cock's advice proves disastrous to himself K1633; blood substituted for sacrificial human K525.9; crowing interpreted J1811.4; cry "cock-a-doodle-do" A2426.2.18; escape from fox K561.1; food A2435.4.8; second mate lets stepchildren starve J134.1; whiskers (cumulative tale) Z41.3. — Basilisk hatched from c. egg B12.1; circular house rotating on c. claw F771.2.6.1; cobold hatched from c. egg F481.0.1.1; devil has c. feet G303.4.5.9; dragon from c. egg B11.1.1; lions fear c. crowing J2614.3; nut falls on c. head *Z41.4; origin of c. red crest A2321.10; preserving the c. freedom J1892; river contained under c. wings *D915.2; why c. comb becomes white A2321.10.1.

Cocks who crow about mistress's adultery killed J551.1; kept from intercourse have tender meat B754.5. — Mouse teaches her child to fear quiet cats but not noisy c. J132; why c. crow A2421.6.

Cockaygne, land of X1503.

Cockcrow. — Between midnight and c. best time for unearthing treasure N555.1; disenchantment at c. D791.1.7; ghost (fairy, witch, dwarf) laid at c. *E452, E587.3; stone moves at c. D1641.2.3; witch's familiar disappears at c. G225.0.6.

Cockfight as suitor contest H331.15.1.

Cockle. — Marriage of mountain and c. shell T126.2.

Cockroach. — Creation of c. A2061; enmity of fowl and c. A2494.13.3; magic whistle vitalizes c. D1594.6; wedding of mouse and c. B281.2.2; wedding of c. and rat B285.8, B281.11.1.

Cockscomb plant used to kill sun A1156; whitens D492.1. — Devil avoids c. flowers G303.16.14.5; man becomes c. plant D213.1; reincarnation as c. E631.1.4.

Coconut canoe F841.1.4.1; shoots restore sight D1505.18.1; transformed to philosopher's stone D451.3.2; tree from head of slain monster A2611.3; tree is tall A2778.1. — Canoe transformed into c. tree A2615.3; creation of woman from c. A1253.2.1; fish struck by c.: hence flat tail A2213.5.2; magic c. (as food) *D1035.2; magic c. shell *D985.1; magic c. water restores sight D1505.5.5; origin of c. A1423.3, A2681.5.1; soul in c. E711.2.5; springs from c. shell F718.12.

Coconuts. — Light and dark skinned peoples made from light and dark c. A1614.3; monkeys attack by throwing c. B762; people who live on c. F561.3; why c. absent from certain island J2031.3.

Cocoon's. — Making large shawl from one c. silk H1022.4.3.

Codfish, markings on A2412.4.3.

Coffee. — Dead husband asks for c. E321.3; magic c. pot *D1171.1.1; origin of c. A2691.1.

Coffer. — Adulteress throws c. out window to distract husband K1514.15; wrecked man saved on c. of jewels becomes rich N226.

Coffin buried upright V61.3; bursts, dead arises E261.2.1; carried through hole in wall to prevent return of dead E431.4; cover transformed to person D434.4; with iron band prevents tiger ghost's return E431.20; lands at burial site D1314.12; moves itself D1641.13; what one buys who does not want it or use it H878. — Bursting c. of one sold to devil E411.9; corpse in c. refuses to be moved in wagon D1654.9; corpse makes room in c. for friend E477; devil removes disciple's body from c. M219.2.5; dowry in c. E228; extraordinary c. F852ff.; fairies borrow tools to make c. F391.3; four cats carry c. F982.2; ghost carries c. on back E592.2; glass c. F852.1; hinge of c. as remedy D1500.1.15.2; king's c. sunk into river P16.9; leaving money on c. K231.13; magician carries woman in glass c. *D2185; pole for c. rests appears at death E767.1; sacred hosts in c. V35.2; soul as black or white spirit over c. E722.1.1; spectral c. E538.1; tiger enticed into c. K714.2.2; tools announce death D1322.1; victim tricked into entering c. K714.2; wraith selects c. lumber E723.7.5.

Coffins. — Christians' c. V61.6; reward for providing c. for poor Q42.2; spirit disturbs c. F473.6.9.

Cohabitation, see also **Sex, Sexual intercourse;** of hero with sleeping girl and leaving of identification token with her H81.1; of living person and ghost E474; brings change of luck N131.1; among lunatics X541; with first woman met C664.0.1. — Moon's c. with man A753.1.3; moon's c. with woman A753.1.2.

Coil, magic D1282.

Coin in churn releases curse M429.6; left in money scales betrays secret wealth N478; multiplies self D2100.2; placed in mouth of dead to prevent return E431.11. — Chapperbands c. false money A1689.8; contest: c. first attracting fly wins K92.1; devil holds molten c. in mouth G303.4.8.2; as dwarfs emigrate each deposits a c. into kettle for mortals F451.9.4; fish with c. in mouth B105.4.1.; little c. noisy in bottle J262.2; magic c. *D1288; perspiration-covered c. believed weeping J1875.4; philosopher forgets to put c. in mouth before death (Charon's fee) E489.3; putting c. in dead person's mouth P613; short weight c. for charity K2096.1; "you must pay in better c. than is your wont" K1228.

Coins concealed in jar J1655.3; mistaken for cakes J1772.3.1; thought to be red beans J1772.3. — Crushing c. in fingers F614.12; deceptive bargain: the ogre and the copper c. K183; dividing four c. among three persons J1241.2; fool leaves c. lying on roadside J1836; murder by slipping c. into meat K929.5; origin of gold c. A1433.1; silver c. from pumpkin A1433.2.1; stones transformed to gold c. D475.2.1; trickster gets c. from blind beggars K1081.1.1; what workman does with four c. he earns H585.1.

Coition, see also **Sexual Intercourse;** as illness cure *F950.4, J1149.4.

Cold personified Z139.4; produced by magic D2144.1; test (attempt to freeze hero to death) H1512; water magically warmed D2144.3.1; in

winter A1135.1; before theft of fire impedes speech: explanation of difficulty of certain languages A1616.1. — Alternate heat, c. in hell A671.3.3; breaking window to let c. out J1819.2; contest in enduring c. H1541; contest of heat and c. D2144.2; do not discard clothing till c. weather is over J731; dog swallowing up the c. K135.1.1; flight so high that eyelids drop from c. F1021.2.2; giants in region of c. F531.6.2.6; god sends c. to prevent stones from growing A975.1; land of c. F704; lies about c. weather X1620; magic control of c. D2144ff.; magic object protects against c. D1382ff.; man in c. consoles himself thinking of rich man in hell J883.2; marvelous withstander of c. F685ff.; origin of illness from c. A1337.8; origin of c.: sun turns upward A1135.1.1; porcupine as controller of c. D2144.1.1; primeval c. A605.2; punishments by c. in hell Q567; revenant with c. (hands) E422.1.3, (lips) E422.1.4; sleeping naked in c. as test H1504; taking c. in effigy J1628; why toad lives in c. place A2433.6.7.

Coldest. — Which is c. season? J1664.1.

Coldness in hell A671.3.1; of otherworld F169.7. — Scorned woman complains of man's c. T71.2.1.

Coleoptera, creation of A2020ff.

Colic, demon of F493.1.2.

Collar. — Crow causes serpent to try to swallow stolen c. and thus be accused of theft K401.2.1; deception into putting on a c. K713.2; ghost steals c. of priest E593.1; magic c. *D1068; magic c. indicates falsehood by squeezing throat, truth by falling to ground D1316.8; magic hunting c. D1068.1, (insures death of game) D1449.2; sheep with fiery c. B19.4.3; strong man attacked with millstone puts it on as c. F615.3.1.

Collecting as animal's occupation A2453; debt in hell through help of dwarf F451.5.1.14; enormous amount of material H1149.4; for impossible bargain M291.

Collier P415; and fuller cannot live together U143.

Color of dragon B11.2.2ff.; of fairy F233; of fairy's (clothes) F236.1, (cows) F241.2.1, (horses) F241.1.1; of flame indicates what is burning F1061.2; of ghostly dog E423.1.1.1; of giant F531.1.7; formulas Z65; magically changed D492; of revenant E422.2ff.; of plants A2772ff.; symbolism *Z140; transformed D682.4; worn signifies rank P632.4. — Animal's c. as reward for piety Q149.1; animals change c. F985; attempt to change one's c. foolish J511; barber paid to change c. of woman's face burns her with acid J1161.6; blood changes c. (life token) E761.1.6; chameleon saves hero's life: may change c. A2223.8; change in person's c. D57; city of extraordinary c. F741; creator establishes twelve winds, each a different c. A1129.1; custom of differentiating social classes by c. of dress introduced A1650.2; dress c. of sun, moon, and stars F821.1.5; each world corresponds to different c. A659.4; earth's c. from slain child's blood A1277.3; eyes remarkable as to c. F541.6; fanciful c. of animal B731; handkerchief c. of sun, moon, and stars F822.1; imagined

c. of cloth J1551.8; islands of extraordinary c. F741; magic c. *D1293f.; man cursed with c. of the dead Q556.4; origin of c. of animal *A2411ff., *A2219.1; origin of c. of animal's (back) A2356.3, (eyes) A2332.5ff., (legs) A2371.4f., (tail) A2378.8ff., A2286.2.4, (tongue) A2344.3f.; origin of bird's c. A2221.6.1; origin of sea's c. A925.2; person changes c. F1082; person of unusual c. F527; praying man's c. changed V52.11; river given c. D1658.1.6; rock of extraordinary c. F807; sea changes c. F931.7; skin changes c. because of broken tabu C985; skin c. A1614.6; stone's c. indicates guilt or innocence H233; tree of extraordinary c. F811.3; turning c. from emotion F1041.11.2; why chameleon changes c. A2411.5.6.1.

Colors of otherworld F178. — Cup of three hundred c. F866.1; origin of c. at sunrise and sunset A797; rainbow's three c. A791.4.

Colored traitor K2260ff. — Artificially c. horses B731.2.2; many-c. god A123.7.1; multi-c. hair F555.5; ogres' blood many c. G367.1; origin of c. races A1614; why bird's beak is c. A2343.2.

Colt, see also **Foal, Horse;** mistaken for devil, addressed J1785.4.1. — Real mother of c. will swim to it J1171.4; reductio ad absurdum: the decision about the c. J1191.1; starving c. fierce with hunger J2214.10; treasure found if one goes with one-night old c. on to one-night old ice N542.1; untrained c. result of master's neglect J143; wolf thought to be a c. J1752.

Colter. — Heating plow's c. to release curse M429.4.

Column, see also **Pillar;** to upper world F58. — Fool thankful that God has built a palace without a c. J2565; four-sided c. in otherworld F169.1.3; man transformed to a marble c. D231.2; wild hunt disappears in c. of fire E501.16.4.

Columns under lord's chair cause music A661.0.2.1. — Fiery c. in hell A671.2.4.11; four c. around otherworld fire F165.7.1; huge rock c. combat each other, form landmarks A901.2.

Comb drips blood (life token) E761.1.7; transformed to mountain D454.7.1. — Adventure from returning for c. N773.2; baldheaded man finds the c. J1001.2; escape by sending for forgotten c. K629.1.1; fairy borrows c. from Christian maid for changeling bride F322.1.1; girl borrows c. from fairy F324.1; golden c. F827.5; harrow as hero's c. K1718.4; magic c. *D1072.1; magic pig carrying scissors, c., and razors between its ears H1154.1; man transformed to c. D263.3; murder with poisoned c. S111.3; picking up c. tabu C543; quest for c. H1347; resuscitation by removal of poisoned c. E21.3; why cock's c. becomes white A2321.1.0.1; why crab's legs like teeth of c. A2376.5; woman goes back for c., robbed K346.3.

Combs, iron S187.2.

Combed. — Children's hair c. by fairies F313; dead's hair c. V68.2; gold and silver c. from hair D1454.1; sleeping maid's hair c. by dwarf F451.5.1.13; woman's hair c. by devil G303.9.5.5.

Combing hair of fairies (task) H1192; hair forbidden C723f. — Devil c.

witches makes sparks fly G222.1; fatal c. of victim's hair K875; horse's magic strength from hair c. D1835.2; magic sleep by c. hero's hair D1962.3.1.

Combat, see also **Contest, Fighting;** between god of light and dragon of ocean A162.2. — Army leaders in single c. H217.1; customs concerning single c. P557.4; disenchantment by c. D763.2; eagerness for c. W212; huge columns c. each other, form earth's features A901.2; refusing c. forbidden C835; revenant challenged to c. E461.1; single c. between gods A162.7; single c. to prove valor H1501.2; tabu: going to (leaving) certain place without c. C866f.; transformation c. D615; undesired c. between sworn brothers N731.2.2; unwitting c. (of brothers) H151.10, N733.1, (of father and son) *N731.2, (between sons of friends) H767; trial by c. H218; wild hunt in c. E501.17ff.; wit c. H507.

Combats. — God of single c. A485.3.

Combatants become sworn brethren P311.1. — The two c. without hands or feet or words (bull and buffalo) H861.

Combustible. — Why wood c. A2782.

Comedian, equanimity of W25.

Comet. — God in form of c. A124.5; impregnation by c. T525.2.

Comets, origin of A786.

Comfort. — Words of Christian c. cause devil to vanish G303.16.4.

Comforted. — Abandoned person in woods c. by prophet and birds S465; devotee of Virgin c. at death V267; repentant sinner c. by angel V235.2.

Coming. — Butter magically kept from c. D2084.2; riddle about girl's c. and flood H583.10.

Command, see also **Order;** to use only one phrase J2516.3.3; would become permanent J1521.3. — Magic results produced by c. *D1765, D2102.2; one c. as test of wife's obedience H473.2.

Commands. — Enigmatic c. to girl H580.1.

Commandments. — Twenty c. better than ten J2213.5.1.

Commemoration of death V65. — Lakes burst forth in c. of hero A920.1.4, A934.3; spring as c. of hero's experiences A941.3.2, A941.4.1.

Commemorative religious meal A1549.1; trees F979.11.

Commended. — Demons powerless over souls c. to God before sleep E754.1.1.1; poor miller c. by priest X212.1; wife c. to devil guarded till man's return C12.4.

Commerce, origin of A1471.

Commiserated. — Robbers c. J1392.2.

Common citizen saves country's honor P711.3; man transformed into exalted personage D22; names for dwarfs F451.8.1. — Friendship between prince and c. man P311.8; king mingles with c. people J914; must drink from the c. cup J1467; prince refuses to play with c. children J411.3; recognition through c. knowledge H10ff.; uniting against c. enemy J624, J145.

Commonplace. — Time renders all things c. J1075.

Communication with god fatal C52.1; of lovers T41; by pouring milk into stream K1549.5.

Communion, see also **Eucharist, Excommunication, Sacrament;** feast to placate dead A1541.1.2; table dust breaks spell G271.2.6. — At c. witches spit out wine over shoulders G285.1; misunderstandings of c. J1824.1; woman eating before c. can't swallow wafer V39.9.

Compact, see also **Bargain, Contract.** — Luck in gambling from c. with devil N6.1.

Companion, see also **Ally, Comrade;** tries foolishly to imitate good luck J2415. — Coming neither with nor without a c. H1061; horse as witch's c. G225.2; impostors abandon c. and usurp place K1931; incognito king rewards c. strangers K1812.13; labor contract: as much money as my c. (strong man) can carry F613.2.1; magic wisdom possessed by extraordinary c. D1719.4; talkative man betrays his c. J2352; thief accuses c. of their mutual theft K401.0.1.

Companions arrive as hero is about to be killed N699.3. — All children born same day as prince are his c. P32.1; animals as creator's c. A33; creator's c. A30ff.; divinity's c. A195; extraordinary c. *F601ff.; fool objects to fools as c. J1715; hero with animal c. Z235; skillful c. create woman: to whom does she belong? *H621; origin of devil and his c. G303.1ff.; riddling remarks of traveling c. interpreted by girl at end of journey H586ff.

Company. — Curse: lack of good c. M443.1; "don't keep bad c." J21.25; eating in c. tabu C285; educated men as choice c. J146.

Companies. — Heaven's inhabitants divided into c. A661.1.1.

Comparison, riddles of H660ff.

Compassionate executioner K512; woman unharmed by boiling oil Q151.12; youngest daughter L54.

Compelling, see also **Forcing;** innocent man to write treasonable letter K2156; person by magic book to do evil D1678. — Magic object c. person (to dance) *D1415ff., (to follow) D1427f.; woman drives away the hungry, c. the filled to eat H583.4.4.

Compensation, scc also **Pay, Payment.** — Reincarnation as c. E694.

Competition in friendship between prisoner and jailor P315.1; between student and master P342.

Competitors. — Misinforming guest c. about country's water, wood supply H1239.4.

Complacency, wife's H474, *N11.

Complaint about bad breath K2135; of dissatisfied rivers against the sea W128.3; of snake to Zeus that people step on him J623.1.

Complexion. — Disguise by dyeing c. K1821.5.

Compliments tabu C499.2. — Donkey, camel trade c. J867.

Compound. — Dragon as c. animal B11.2.1ff.; person with c. body F526.

Compressible objects *D491ff., D631.3ff.

Compulsion. — Image under c. V123.1; magic c. to make journey D2121.15.

Compulsions, unique *C650—C699.

Comrade, see also **Companion;** slain, believed to be enemy K1883.5. — Devil cheated of his promised soul when the victim sells his to a c. K219.2; jumping into the river after their c. J1832; loyal friends won't fight disgraced c. W34.2.

Comrades. — Bonds can be loosed only by c. of man who tied them D1651.9.1.

Concealed wife awaits favorable moment to come forward N741.1. — Fugitive c. by opening tree D1393.1; ghost c. with dwarfs F451.5.4.1; magic power to see c. things D1825.4; person c. in another's body *F1034ff.; pregnancy c. by having maid sleep in husband's bed *K1843.1; weapons c. in basket kill opener K929.11.

Concealing boys' identity by scolding K649.3. — Clever c. of jewels J1655; fairies' c. mist F278.2.

Conceived. — Christ c. on same day crucified V211.0.2; last born twin c. first T587.3; magically c. children to marry M146.3; where were you when your mother c.? J1291.4.

Conception and birth *T500—T599. — Belief in Immaculate C. V312; evil enters body with c. A1384.2; father's ambitions transferred to child at c. T597; immaculate c. of hero A511.1.3.3; magic c. of hero Z216; prophecy: hero's c. at certain time M311.0.2.1; woman talks to her child before its c. T575.2.

Concern. — Whose c. it is J1353.

Concert by hogs J1675.5.

Concessions. — Wisdom of c. to power J811ff.

Conch. — Ass brays on hearing c. shell J2211.4; child born in c. shell T561.1; ghost sounds c. shell E402.1.3.1; man issues from c. shell D621.6; magic c. shell furnishes money D1452.4.

Concoction. — Magic c. causes evil eye D2071.0.2.

Concubinage *T450ff.

Concubine, see also **Courtesan, Prostitute.** — Devil's c. haunts E411.2.2; father's counsel on c. H588.10; friar steals from c. K1839.5; jealous c. plots against real wife's children S322.3.2; priest's c. cannot rest in grave *E411.2.1; priest's c. unable to rise from stone Q551.2.7; punishment for taking c. Q243.3; treacherous c. *K2222.

Condemnation because of death without confession V22. — Hasty c. or killing *N340ff.

Condemned friend tests friendship H1558.13; man revealed as king's son N731.4; soul as black E722.1.2; soul recovered E754.1ff. — Beatus prayer for c. souls V51.4; devil as advocate of falsely c. man G303.22.11; queen intervenes for c. courtiers P21; rich man who does not repent until ready to die c. by devil Q271.2; substituting self for one c. K528.2; woman who saved his life c. to death by suitor W154.14.

Condemner. — Punishment escaped by discomfiting c. J1182.

Conduct of bridal couple before ceremony T134. — Decisiveness of c. J1040ff.; man refuses to follow friend in wicked c. P318; origin of code of c. between husband and wife A1571; taking a pattern (picture) of c. J2471; wise and unwise c. J200—J1099.

Conductor of the dead A311. — Devil shepherd's c. to hell to collect debt from nobleman F451.5.1.14.

Coney. — Squirrel borrows tail of c. A2241.7; stripes of c. A2413.6; why c. lives among rocks A2433.3.5.

Confederate persuades captor to throw away trickster K649.12. — Escape by help of c. K640ff.; ghost as man's c. E379.4; lie corroborated by a c., who poses as a newly-arrived stranger K455.7; theft by c. K365.

Conferred, see also **Bestowed.** — Invisibility c. on person D1983.

Confessed. — Ghost laid when crime has been c. E451.1; recognition when parents come to son to be c. H151.3.

Confession of all treachery wins bride H331.11; discredited by declaring it all a dream J1155; made easy for peasant J1263.7; obtained by a ruse *J1141; of sins *V20ff.; without giving up sin punished V25.2. — Complacent judge disregards the c. P521; death respite until c. K551.1.1; devil is made impotent by c. G303.16.9; after c. of sins fox is immediately ready to steal again K2055; ghost causes murderer's c. E231.5; husband as God behind tree forces c. of adultery from wife *K1971.5; of misdeeds by ghost E376; pretending not to hear in c. X441.1; reward for c. of sins Z36.1; seduction by priest during c. K1339.6; weather changes on deed's c. D2140.3.

Confessional. — Neglect to hear c. punished Q223.4; punishment for betraying c. Q224; priest induced to betray secrets of c.: money then exacted from him for silence K443.8, V468.

Confessor duped into being go-between for adulteress and lover K1584; and penitent exchange confidences V29.7. — Ghost laid by c. E443.2.3; live c. better than dead martyr J1261.9; man without c. like body without head V20.1.1; ruler wants lying c. J1263.6; search for c. V29.1.

Confidence. — Excess of c. punished Q330ff.; pretended exchange of c. about one thing that can kill K975.1; wealth gained by seeming to be in king's c. K1782.

Confinement to keep child in ignorance of life J147; of girl during menses C141; of girl at puberty C131; in tower to avoid fulfillment of prophecy M372; of wicked son on island Q433.9.

Confines. — Quest to c. of hell for blood of sorceress H1277.

Confirmed. — Dwarfs listen to singing by c. children F451.5.21.

Confiscating conspirators' estates K487; goods after failure to consummate relations with princess P616. — Mortals c. dwarfs' property F451.5.10.7.

Conflagration, see also **Fire.** — General c. as punishment C984.6.

Conflict of good and evil creators *A50ff. — Flood from c. of gods A1015.1; revenants in c. E460ff.; weak overcomes strong in c. L310ff.

Conflicts of the gods A162; between religions *V350ff. — Forethought in c. with others J610—J679.
Confounding. — Poet c. student J1684.
Confucius, sacrifices to V11.4.
Confusion caused to aid escape K649.9; of tongues *A1333. — Hero causes c. in enemy camp K2369.10.
Congenital helpful animal *B311.
Congregation. — Church and c. sink to bottom of sea F941.2.2; the devil accuses c. of sins G303.24.1.
Conjugal, see **Marital.**
Conjurer, see also **Magician;** P483; brands sacred animals H55.2; must leave before sunrise C752.2.2; restores lost wife R133.2. — Man wishing to be c. fears devil's help C12.1.1; reincarnation as c. E605.9.
Conjuring bag *D1274.1; away evil spirits in name of deity *D1766.7.1.1; away quest obstacles H1237. — Power of prophecy from c. D1812.2.2; rejuvenation by c. D1889.10.
Conquered. — Animal helpful after being c. B315; enemies c. by magic object D1400.1ff.; magic object vomited by c. monster D826.1; quarrelsome wife c. by silent husband T256.1; tribute required of c. foreigners T531.1.1.
Conquering gambler N1.2. — All-c. spear F834.4.
Conqueror returns defeated man's family W11.5.4; rewarded by revenant E465. — Chaste woman resists c. T325; warriors enter service of c. R74.
Conquest. — Prophecies concerning c. M369.5.
Conscience as judge's tribunal W35.2.
Conscientiousness W37.
Consecrated bread as magic object *D1031.1.1; healing ring D1500.1.15.1; host put into beehive C55.3; objects cure D1500.1.10; wine *D1046.1, (used to discover treasure) N533.4. — Animals refrain from spoiling c. food B259.4.1; bathing in c. water D2161.4.14.2; man kept alive by c. sword E163; princess sick because toad has swallowed her c. wafer *C55, D2064.1, V34.2; shepherd's c. staff keeps cow from straying D1446.3; surrendering life for c. land V463.1.
Consecration of ignorant priest J1263.1.2; price J1263.2.1.
Consent of brother for sister's marriage needed T131.1.1; of spear to combat F834.7. — Relative's c. to marriage necessary T131.1.
Conservative but absurd ways kept U139.2.1.
Consider the end: counsel J21.1.
Consolation in misfortune J850—K899. — Husband's c.: seeing greater shrew than wife T251.9.
Consoling message from the dead E361.2. — God c. mortal A182.3.1; philosopher c. woman J152.4.
Consort. — Promise to have but one c. M262.

Consorting with princess without sleeping (test) H347; with woman tabu C193. — Punishment for c. with lower class Q243.5.
Conspiracy. — Magic detection of c. D1817.0.4.
Conspirators frighten boastful coward K1951.4. — Accusing c. to confiscate their estates K487.
Constancy as bride test H387. — Wife's c. resuscitates husband T212.1.
Constant hunger caused by magic object D1373ff.; replacement of fighters E155.1.1.
Constantine's vision of the Cross V515.1.4.
Constantinople. — Virgin Mary destroys army beseiging C. V268.3.
Constellations bewailing death F961.2.5.1; origin of A766.
Consummation of marriage J1306; *T160ff.; of marriage to own mother N681.3.1.
Consumption demon F493.1.1.
Contact. — Conception from casual c. with man T531; disenchantment by physical c. D782; magic results from c. with water D1788.1; magic results from c. with earth *D1778; tabu: c. (with the dead) C541ff., (with the supernatural) *C0—C99, (with things belonging to a king) C501, (with women at childbirth) C153.
Contagiousness of bad company J451; of yawns J1448.
Container. — Extraordinary c. for fluids F866.7; rain from c. in sky A1131.4; relics kept in c. so as to prevent pestilence J762.1.
Contemplation. — Comfort in the c. of impossible pleasure J864; transformation by c. D584.
Contempt. — Hand cut off for c. of court Q451.1.2.
Contentiousness W188; punished Q300ff.
Contentment of old man till forbidden to leave city H1557.3; with what you have J346.
Contest arranged by Virgin Mary A1372.7; in beauty H1596, (between goddesses) A163, (between peacock and crane) J242.5, (between swallow and crow) J242.6; of dogs H1588; between god of fire and god of rain A975.2.1; in generosity H1552.2; of heat and cold D2144.2; in hunting H1592; in laziness W111.1; in magic D1719.1; between rose and amaranth J242.1; between runner swift as thought and one swift as sight F681.3.1; in shooting H1591; over souls E756; in stealing K305; between sun, moon A736.11; of wisdom and wealth J185; won by deception *K0—K99. — Animal characteristics result of c. A2250ff., (between God and devil) A2286.2; animal haunt established by c. A2433.1.1; animal king chosen as result of a c. *B236.0.1; animal wins c. for man B587; animal characteristics from c. in watching A2256; betting c. between two kings N1.3; boasting scares opponent from c. K1766; bride c. H375; deceiver in swinging c. killed *K1618; decision made by c. H217; devils and angels c. for man's soul E756.1; disenchantment by magic c. D785; disenchantment by overcoming person in c. D716; giant in c. with man F531.5.11; giants, dwarfs in c. F451.10.2; king chosen by c. P11.2.1;

magic animal used in c. B195; moon-god loses c. to mortal A182.3.6; mountain from ancient c. A964; mowing c. with household spirit F488.2; rock-casting c. D1731.3; strong woman wins arrow c. F610.0.1.1; transformation c. between magicians D615.1; useful wins c. over beautiful J242.

Contests in endurance H1540ff.; in lying X905; in riddling H548. — Witch makes man enter dangerous c. G292.

Contestant who circles stones wins J2119.2.2.

Contesting. — Flaying alive as punishment for c. with a god Q457.1; rivals c. for girl T92.11.

Continence *T310ff.; vow until enemy killed M152.

Continent. — Islands originally a c. A955.11.

Continually falling in love T10.4. — Firewood c. swept away from swimming man H1129.5.1; journey to upper world by keeping thoughts c. on heaven *F64.

Continuing magic acts *D2172ff., (hurting selves) D2184, (sneezing) D1372, (what one starts in morning) D2172.2. — Man c. work after night joined by devil G303.22.9; princess hangs up weapons of dead lover as c. reminder T85.2; wisdom from c. reminder of foolishness in the past J167.

Continuous fighting F1084.0.3; winter destroys the race A1040ff.; action started by breaking tabu C916; prayer sustains man through frightful vigil V52.2. — Fool locked in dark room made to believe that it is c. night. J2332.

Contortions in anger A526.6, F1041.16.5.

Contraband gold discovered K447.

Contract, see also **Bargain;** with the devil destroyed M218; in blood M201.1. — Journey to hell to recover devil's c. F81.2, H1273.1; strong man makes labor c. F613ff.

Contracts P525.

Contraction of person into smaller space D55.2ff. — Serpent's dilation and c. B91.5.1.

Contradictions. — Chains involving c. or extremes Z23; tales with c. Z19.2.

Contrary. — Life in land of dead c. to ours E489.2; magic object works in c. fashions D1663; objects behaving c. to their nature F473.2; tasks c. to laws of nature H1020ff.

Contrasts found in otherworld garden *F162.1.2. — Peasant and wife c. to king and queen P411.1.1; two brothers as c. P251.5.4.

Control. — Fairies have c. over mortal's destines F312.2; magic c. (of the elements) *D2140ff., (of fires) *D2158ff., (of seasons) *D2145ff., (of waters) *D2151ff.; magic object has c. D1300—D1599, (over disease) *D1500ff., (over the elements) *D1540ff., (over fire) D1566ff., (over person's will) D1379.1f.; moon under deity's direct c. A759.6; witches have c. over weather G283; youth trusts self to horse over which he has no c. J657.1.

Controller. — Man as c. of sun's rising and setting A725; porcupine as c. of cold D2144.1.1.

Conundrum. — Recognition by answer to c. H19.2.

Convent, see also **Nun;** guest put to needle-threading test H509.1. — Disguised prostitutes take wife to "c." K1592; man acts as statue of saint in order to enter c. K1842.1; man disguised as gardener enters c. and seduces nuns K1323; seducers in disguise enter c. K1321.4.

Convention of long-nosed people X133; of trees F979.13.

Conversation between clouds F967.3; between the dead E545.1; with dead E545.7; of fire-spirits F497.1; of lovers T42. — Animals' c. reveals how to become saint V229.25; fox holds c. with his members J2351.1; forgotten fiancée reawakens husband's memory by c. of magic doves D2006.1.3; king brought to sense of duty by feigned c. of birds J816.1; rank betrayed by habitual c. H38ff.; recognition by overheard c. with animals or objects H13ff.; secrets overheard from animal c. *N451; slave recognized by his c. H38.3; treasure information from overheard c. N534.4; thieves deceived by prearranged c. J1517.

Conversations, formulistic Z18.

Conversing. — Soul c. with dead E721.8.

Conversion by dead E367.4; of fairy wife into woman F302.5.2.1; of Jew by Virgin Mary V266; of King to Hinduism absurd J1536.2; from one religion to another V330ff. — Miraculous beautification upon c. to Christianity V331.3; saint to succeed in c. M364.3.

Convert. — First c. to Christianity A1546.3.1.

Converts. — Reward for securing c. Q23.

Conveyances, magic *D1110ff. — Fairies' c. F242; ghost-like c. E535.

Cook as helper N842. — Devil as c. G303.3.1.13; lie: remarkable c. X1005; poor man wants high office: made c. L427; thief disguised as c. K311.12.1; treacherous c. K2254.

Cook-book. — Priest uses c. for breviary V467.

Cooked animal comes to life E168; child revived by saint E121.4.1; cock crows E524.2.1; human flesh speaks out G64. — Animals already c. for eating X1208.1; beating wife so food will be c. right J2175.1.1; cannibals advised to be absent while hero is being c. K619.1; flesh of stolen animal cannot be c. D1318.7.1.1, Q212.4; gods like c. food A153.7; hills flat where gods c. A972.5.5; magic fruits c. D866.1; meat c. by bird's red eye F989.2; numskulls sow c. grain J1932.1; people c. in kettle by devil G303.25.4; planting c. food K496; quest for best-c. dish H1305.2; sowing c. grain *H1023.1.1; tiger formerly c. its food A2435.1.2; unsuccessful imitation of being c. without harm J2411.6.1; why food is c. A1518.

Cooking as bride test H383.4; food on hot breasts F546.5; griddle cakes as bride test H383.1.2; by magic calabash D1601.1; interrupted G475.1; processes misunderstood J1813; rice with fire far away J1191.7; rice without fire H506.9; spit recovered from sea H1132.1.6; what is behind you J2485; without fire D2158.5.2. — Corpses used as c. fuel S139.2.2.5;

escape by pretended c. K611.2; exorbitant charge for c. K255.1; fairies steal c. F365.7; firelike river used for c. F932.11; foolish thief c. wakens house J2136.5.5; glutton eats all meal while c. it W125.2; leaven tabu for c. C888; lie: remarkable c. X1031.3; literal fool c. wrong amounts J2461.1.4.1; magic c. pot obeys only master *D1651.3; magic porridge-pot keeps c. C916.3; miser doesn't want wife c. too much W153.2.1; origin of c. A1455; recognition by unique c. H352; servants touch c. pot J1563.5.2; sun c. for saint D2149.3; sun's rays c. saint's meat V222.13; tiger lives on self-c. food F989.22.2; woman c. for paramour K1549.8.

Cookstove, witch as G212.2.

Cooled. — Scout sees whether earth has c. after fire A1039.1.

Cooling ears by breaking vessel on head J2469.4; off sick by hanging in well J2412.6. — Sun c. off at night A722.5.2.

Cooperation. — Creation of a person by c. of skillful men F1023; man created by c. of the gods A1218.

Cooperative birth T589.1.

Copper apple F813.1.3; castle F771.1.3; -colored house F165.8; horseman indicates road *D1313.3; statue at city gates blows on trumpet at stranger's approach *D1317.9.1; transformed to gold D475.1.9; tree F811.1.3. — Acquisition of c. A1432.4; bow of gold, silver, and c. F836.1; golden boat with c. rudder F841.1.8; magic c. *D1252.2; pygmies dressed in c. F535.3.1; two c. vessels are steaming over fire under earth A857.1; water becomes c. D478.9.

Copperhead guides rattlesnake to prey B765.13.

Copulation, see also **Sexual Intercourse;** of animals A2496; of devil as queen with horses G303.3.1.12.5. — Sham-death for c. with divine maidens K1325.0.1; universe from c. of objects A615.2.

Coraciiformes, creation of A1950ff.

Coral. — Goddess as c. reef A139.8.2; man becomes c. D237; why c. is soft A2872.

Cord. — Penance: wearing friar's c. on bare skin Q522.7; umbilical c. tabu C531.1.

Cordelia H592.1, M21.

Cordon. — Monk's c. saving him from hell J1261.8.

Corduroy. — Wagon run over c. bridge to simulate artillery K2368.1.1.

Cormorant's color A2411.2.5.1; tongue pulled out by putting louse on it *K825.1.

Corn from body of slain person *A2611.1; carried away grain at a time Z11.1; comes up with black ears after mud flood Q552.14.2; grows so fast it pulls up own roots X1532.1; roots in hair F1099.4; transformed to person D431.8. — Deceptive grain division: the c. and the chaff K171.2; devil gives Eve two grains of c. G303.9.4.1; dwarf groans while carrying ear of c. F451.3.9.1; fairies snip c. from stalks F369.5.1; god of c. A433.1; inexhaustible c. D1652.1.3.2; lazy man: "Is c. shelled?" W111.5.10.1; lies about c. X1455; magic c. *D965.8; magic c. turns to

gold D2102.5; making ale from single grain of c. H1022.6.1; man from ears of c. A1255.2; mule carrying c. escapes while one carrying gold is robbed L453; so hot c. pops X1633.1; soul of c. E701.5; why c. does not yield in the middle A2793.10; witch's spells blight c. G269.7; woman threshing c. in moon A751.8.2.

Cornelia shows children as her jewels T256.

Corners. — Spider transformed for greediness: now occupies dark c. A2261.2.

Cornish. — Jews' ghosts punished in C. mines F456.1.1.1.

Cornucopia, god with A137.5.

Coroner. — Ghosts disappear for c. E599.2.

Corps sans âme F963.4.

Corpse, see also **Body, Ghost;** bleeds when murderer touches it D1318.5.2; burns of own accord F964.3.3; cannot be moved D1654.9.1; to be cut in two: feigned death revealed J1545.8; drops piecemeal down chimney H1411.1; exclaims over miracle E545.10; with his feet cut off X422; handed around K2151; leaps up as saint passes E597; lost, live person buried J1834; magically saved from corruption D2167; set up to frighten people K2321; spits out Host V39.7; thrown among robbers frightens them from treasure K335.1.2.1; transformed to serpent D449.2; watched over before burial E752.10.1; of woman dying in childbirth C153.1. — Adulteress's c. drawn through streets Q473.0.2; animal prevents anybody coming near master's c. B301.1.2; animals eat c. of holy man, die B275.3; arm of husband's c. catches wife, drowns her N339.14; curse: c. to be cut in three M453; dead grateful for treatment of c. E341.1.1; demon's c. turns to worm H47; demon enters c. E121.6.1; devil (beats wicked man's c.) Q491.3, (follows lawyer's c.) G303.25.8. (hidden in c.) G303.8.15; drowned c. found by magic D1816.4.1; eyes, ears, fingers of c. substituted for those of demanded victim K512.2.0.3; flames issue from mouth of c. E421.3.7; ghost watches own c. E599.3; ghosts (eat c.) E256, (flay c.) E255, (prevent burial of c.) E273.1; gratitude for having c. ransomed *E341.1; grieving man goes to die near wife's c. T211.9.2.1; hand of c. as remedy D1500.1.6.1; head of c. thrown on water to prevent return E431.9.1; indignity to c. S139.2.2, (as punishment) Q491; joke involving girl's c. causes priest's death N384.8; live man thought to be returning c. K2151.1; the living c. *E422; magic object saves c. from corruption *D1585; mare not to draw c. C181.11; marvelous sensitiveness: meat (wine) tastes of c. E647.1; money tied on c. thrown overboard from ship in order to secure burial V64; monk digs up sweetheart's c. T334; mother does for another what the latter cannot do for her (lays out a c.) H583.4; multiplication of saint's c. D2106.1.4; murdered man's c. sticks to murderer Q551.2.4; murderer's c. mutilated Q491.6; only prostitutes can carry the c. of a prostitute X521; opening c.-wrapping tabu C328; penance: lying with every c. Q524.2; praying over c. saves soul from devil K218.7; precautions to keep evil spirits from getting c.

E752.10; pretending to address c. as heir K451.5; punishment: carrying c. of murdered man Q511; resuscitation by (breathing on c.) E66, (licking c.) E17; return from dead to punish indignities to c. or ghost E235ff.; ring to put on finger of c. K362.2; river flows from c. A511.1.1.1; saint's c. sits up in grave E235.8; servant in master's c. K1969.3.1; shooting at father's c. test of paternity H486.2; sitting up with c. H1461; sleeping with c., thinking it alive J1769.2.1; soul wanders till c. decays E722.3.2; souls captured on leaving c. E752.1.3; spirits put c. into river F402.1.8; spouse's c. kept after death T211.4f.; substitute for the c. J1959.2; suitors as c., angel, and devil K1218.4; tabu: leaving c. at shrine C51.1.14; taking down c. of hanged man tabu C541.5; thief disguised as c. K311.1, (detected) J1149.7; thief frightens away c. guards K335.0.7; thing thought to be c. J1783; toads and snakes devour c. of rich man in his grave Q491.4; trickster throws c. in river and accuses princess of murder K1383; two devils extracted from c. G303.1.8; only usurers can carry the c. of the usurer X514; water thrown on c. to prevent return E431.2; witch's c. heavy G259.4; woman substitutes c. in lover's bed K1223.4.

Corpses. — Cat mutilates c. B766.1; escape by prophesying c. will ruin city K575; foes' c. dismembered P555.2; giants keep c. on hand to eat G691.1; hurling-match for c. H1436; monster made from parts of c. G377; room heated by crowded c. F686.2; speaking c. J2311.9; test for demons in c. E431.0.1; vampires eat c. E251.3.1; wives killed: large price for c. K941.1.1.

Correct wearing of clothes as suitor test H312.6. — Ogre's c. guess wins princess G463.

Correcting. — Animal c. examination paper for rescuer B579.3; man blames master for not c. him in youth J142.2; stingy dead woman c. laundress's overcharge W152.3.

Corroborating ghost's appearance E421.5. — Second liar c. first X907.1.

Corroded. — Skin c. by hydra's poison F1041.5.

Corruption of maids in household by faithless menservants P365.1. — Corpse magically saved from c. D2167; loss of c. as reward Q150.2; magic object saves corpse from c. *D1585.

Corset — Murder by lacing c. tight K953.1; resuscitation when strangling c. lace breaks E21.2; tight c. stifles woman to death Q331.2.2.

Cosmic egg *A641.

Cosmogony A600ff.

Cosmology A600ff.

Cost price of stolen coat recovered (nothing) J1397. — Points of view on c. of wine J1315; what the ass c. J1601; sickle bought at great c. given back J2514.

Costliest. — What is c.? (riddle) H638.

Costumes. — Hero wearing so many c. taken for many K1883.9.

Cot, golden D846.1.

Cottage. — Fairies' neat c. F221.4.

Cotton as best flower H659.23; in ears J672.2; at first already spun A1346.2.1; pods mistaken for fat J1772.8; transformed to leaves D451.2.4; transformed to snake D441.8; tree on moon A751.6. — Adventures from running after blown c. N777.1; leaves become c. D451.8.1; magic c.-wool D1299.4; origin of c. plant A2684.3; purifying c. by burning it J1974; quest for c. driven by wind H1355.5; why hares have c. tail A2378.9.3.

Cottonwood cursed for serving as cross A2721.2.1.3.

Couch. — Avoiding sitting on foot of c. H506.6; magic c. *D1154.

Couches for men of high rank P632.1.

Cough as soul re-entering body E721.3.1. — Dead man identified by his c. J1937.1; stinging buttocks as c. cure N643.

Coughing tabus C484.1; universe into being A618.1; up magic object K331.4; thief blinds watchmen D2062.2.6. — Origin of c. A1399.4.

Council of animals assigns place and work to all B238; of gods A167.1.

Councillors, old men preferred as J151.2.

Counsel, see also **Advice, Precept.** — Brothers scorn brother's c. P251.4; listening to mother's c. forbidden C815; return from dead to give c. E366; reward for giving c. Q43; spirit gives c. F403.2.3.6.

Counsels chosen for parting gift L222.1; proved wise by experience *J21ff. — Enigmatic c. of a father H588; good c. bought *J163.4; porter's revenge for wise c. J1511.6; proverbial wisdom: c. J171ff.

Counselor killed in own treacherous game K1626.2. — Angel as c. to mortal V246; court c. P14.15.1; treacherous c. K2298.

Counselors. — King seeks bride only because c. insist T64.

Count (numerical) only waves before you J311.1. — Absurd inability to c. J2030ff.; literal following of c. J2466; man forgets to c. self, dies E791; numskull throws money to frogs so that they can c. it J1851.1.1; so many leaves on the tree and if you don't believe it go c. them H705.2.

Count (personage) in disguise K1812.20. — Impostor impersonates dead c. K1936.

Counted. — One tiger-cub c. many times deceives tiger K933; stones cannot be c. F809.1; swine cannot be c. accurately B184.3.0.5; years not c. before monk entered monastery J181.

Countenance, see also **Face.** — Parson put out of c. X434; clever man puts another out of c. J1210—J1229.

Counteraccusation follows admission of robber's false plea J1162.2.

Countercharm exorcises witch G271.6.

Counterfeit money burned up J1511.10. — Money turns to c. C939.2; prostitute paid with c. K1581.11.

Counterfeiting. — Burning as punishment for c. Q414.0.6.1; ghost foils c. of will E236.4.1.

Countermagic against Evil Eye D2071.1.5.

Counterquestions H571, J1291.

Countersunwise circuit for ill luck D1791.2.

Countertasks *H951. — Payment evaded by setting c. K248.

Countess. — Dwarf follows c. around like dog F451.5.8.1.

Counting fairy gifts tabu F348.6; hairs in pig's back (feathers in bird) H1118; out pay with hole in the hat and hat over a pit K275; possessions forbidden C776; tabus C897; tasks H1118ff.; the waves H1144.2.

Country, see also **Land;** where everything is cheap J342.1.1. — Forbidden c. C617; king returns to rescue native c. R191; magic object devastates c. D1480ff.; magic sight of whole c. at once D1825.2.2; man who saves c. rewarded with princess T68.2; prophecies concerning destiny of c. M356; town mouse and c. mouse J211.2; wolves of his own c. dearer than dogs of another P711.1; why ptarmigan lives in c. A2433.4.3.

Countries. — Why animals live in certain c. A2434.3ff.

Countryman in the great world J1742.

Couple, see also **Pair.** — Boy sleeps between c. to safeguard virtue T352; earth made by first c. dancing A825; earth by sacrifice of children of first c. A831.3; estranged c. each pay for reconciliation K441.4; first c. parents of (moon) A745.1, (sun) A715; primeval human c. A1270ff.; sinless c. H1381.4.; stone from sky kills all but one c. A1009.3; wicked c. to be killed by own child M343.4

Couples placed to establish tribes A1610.2. — All animals created in c. A1704; animals chained in c. B845.2; magic birds chained in c. B172.7.

Couplets. — Recognition by matching c. H12.2.1.

Courage conquers all U243. — Dragon wants to see "c." J2488.1, K722.1; mother kills sons lacking c. P231.4; wine gives c. to face Pope J1318.

Courageous. — Eating c. animal's heart makes c. D1358.1; magic spell makes person c. D1358.2.

Course of wild hunt E501.1.4ff. — Angels arrange c. of heavenly bodies A703.

Court, see also **Law;** keeps the change J1193.2.1; orders bride to consummate marriage T166; in otherworld F177.1. — Bluff in c.: the stone in the purse K1765; bringing an ogre to c. (task) H1172; cleverness in law c. J1130—J1199; contempt of c. punished Q451.1.2; exposed infant reared at strange king's c. S354; expulsion from c. saves counselor's life N178.3; ghosts tried in c. E573; girl in disguise at lover's c. K1816.0.2; hero takes refuge at king's c. R331; jests on unfavorable c. decision J835; magic object helps win in law c. D1406ff.; not leaving God's c. for king's J1269.13; poor girl masks as doctor and is made c. physician K1825.1.2; robbers' secret used in c. against them N455.2.1; swallow killed in c. house by snake laments injustice in house of justice U27; unknown son returns to father's c. N731.1; women disqualified as c. witness A1589.1.

Courtesan, see also **Concubine, Prostitute;** pursued in wild hunt E501.5.1.2; as thief K302.1. — Capture in house of c. K778.3; newborn girl fated to be c. N121.3; priest's c. cannot rest in grave *E411.2.1; queen forced to become c. L410.7.

Courtesans in wild hunt E501.2.4.

Courtesy. — Deed of c. forbidden C740ff.; disguised king taught c. by peasant P15.1.1.

Courtier in love with queen T91.6.1.1; rewarded for resisting princess Q87.2; shields king's love affair J1211.3. — Boor transformed to c. by love T10.1.2; princess loves c. T55.1.1; princess marries c. T121.3.

Courtiers. — Queen intervenes for condemned c. P21; riddle of king and c. H731.

Courting another man disguised as a woman K1321.3. — Boy c. his mother T412.4; silence in c. ugly woman J1074.2; trickster rides dupe c. K1241.1.

Courtship of stork and crane B282.23. — Jokes on c. *X760ff.; origin of customs of c. and marriage A1550ff.

Cousins P295. — Accidental meeting of c. N746.

Couvade T583.1.

Covenant, see also **Bargain, Contract;** with animals B279; between god and mortal A185.9; of friendship A1599.12, P311.5. — Blood c. M201.1; rainbow as c. between creator and man A791.10.

Covering with cloth disenchants D777.1; face instead of putting out lamp W111.2.9. — Disenchantment by c. with deliverer's clothing D789.1; disenchantment by removing (destroying) c. of enchanted person D720ff.; long hair as c. for girl F555.3.3; origin of animal characteristics: body c. A2310ff.; person with unusual c. F521; resuscitation by c. body E134.1; why certain animals are bare of c. A2317.

Coverings. — Soul hidden in a series of c. E713.

Covetous goldsmith P447.8; wish to the enemy J2074.

Covetousness punished Q277. — Wealth refused, c. feared J347.1.

Cow, see also **Calf;** Audhumla B19.2.1; the animal that is good living and dead H841.3; bears man child B631.5; with breeches on reveals witch G257.5; and bullock yoked together A1689.1; with changing colors B731.4; climbs to roof (lie) X1235.4; as creator A13.1.1; determines road to be taken B151.1.2.1; disappears New Year's night D2087.3.1; has foaled: explanation for lover's horse K1549.4; follows saint B159.3; gives marvelous milk for saint B597; gives twelve measures of milk for twelve apostles B251.2.10; god A132.9.1; grants all desires B184.2.1.3; grateful for being milked B394; imprisoned, had eaten men R9.5; with inexhaustible milk D1652.3.1; killed to get all milk at once J1905.6; licks saint's feet B251.2.6.2; licks stone, discovers saint's relics V140.3; lowers ocean by drinking F989.11.1; mistaken for devil addressed J1785.4; as nurse cares for children B535.0.1; partly brown after resuscitation E33.1; punished for calf's misdeeds J1863; puts bread in oven (lie) X1255.5; with red ears B731.4.2; refuses to move in grief for master B301.6.2; refuses to help stepdaughter, killed B335.7; as sacrifice V12.4.4.1; with silver horns B15.3.2.3.1, B101.8, H355.1; springs from rime of universe's creation B715; strikes at flies while boy eats B579.2; supplies saint, disciples with milk D2156.2.1; survives plague F989.6; swallows book: cause of maniplies in stomach A2219.2; taken to roof to

graze J1004.1; with tallow liver B15.7.9, H1331.3.2; thief grabs tiger by mistake N392; touched by arrow becomes pregnant T532.4; transformed to another animal D412.2ff.; with two bags: bird in each B15.7.9.1; with white ears B731.4.1; worship V1.8.1. — Advising buyer c. is thief J2088.2; bald, white-headed c. H1331.3.1; bellowing of c. defeats army B741.3; buying c. in common: each paying full price J2037.2; buying monkey instead of c. J2081.4; color of c. A2411.1.6.4; creation of c. A1877; cross marked on bewitched c. breaks spell G271.2.1.1; curse: c. will give red milk M471.1; deceptive division of shared c. K171.7.1; destructive c. possessed by demons B16.1.5.2; devil as c. G303.3.3.1.4; devil drives c. mad G303.7.8; divided ownership of c. J1905.3; divine c. descends to earth F35.1; dwarf home is beneath c. stable F451.4.1.5; dwarfs request that c. stable be moved F451.4.4.3; enmity of dog and c. A2494.4.10; enmity of hyena and c. A2494.3.4; fairy in form of c. F234.1.1; fairy warns owner that c. is choking F339.1; fish guards c. B576.3.1; fool does not milk c. for month so that she will give plenty for a feast J1005.1; fool interested only in how c. could have got on the pole where he finds c. dung instead of his purse J2382; foolish bargains: horse for c., c. for hog, etc. J2081.1; four calves to one c. at birth T586.4.1; friendship between c. (and tiger, calf and cub) A2493.24, (and lioness) A2493.30.2; giant c. B871.1; ghost rides c. E581.3; gold-dropping c. B103.1.2, (exchanged for common) D871.1.1; gold hoard found by c. N534.2; helpful c. *B411; hornless c. B15.3.0.1, (milk from) J1512.1; indentions on rock from footprints of saint's c. A972.3.1.2; islands from transformed c. and calf A955.5; jester takes c., tells king people have milk U67; magic c. B184.2; magic c. dung *D1026.2; man can't drive c. he refused to share Q589.1.0.1; man kills c. with hand F628.1.2.1; man transformed to c. G263.1.3; mankind born from c. A1224.4; marvelous c. and calf leave patches on soil A989.1; marvelous c. offended, disappears C918.1; milk from the hornless c. J1512.1; milk of hornless single-colored c. renders wife fruitful T591.1.2; milking c. directly into mouth J2173.8; milking unruly c. H1155.2; miraculous increase of milk from c. D2156.2; money exacted from watcher who permits theft of wooden c. supposed to be real K443.4; nectar-yielding c. B19.2; numskull sells c. to bird J1852.1; numskull ties the rope to his leg as the c. grazes on the roof J2132.2; offending sacred c. tabu C94.3.1.1; old woman gives only c. to God; sent back a hundred Q21.1; only crippled c. spared by robbers N178.4; pasturing c. which runs all day H1112.2; pearl-dropping c. B103.1.2.1; pouring water over c. J2465.1.1; prophetic c. B141.5; quest for bald, white-headed c. H1331.3.1; rabbit thought to be c. J1757; recognition by conversing with c. H13.1.3; recognition of own c. in huge herd H163; refusal to eat fifth descendant of stolen c. F647.10; reincarnation as c. E611.2; revenant as c. E423.1.8; rich man seizes poor widow's c. U35; Sabbath-keeping c. B259.2; sacred c. B811.3; sea c. B72; settlement site where c. stops, milk flows by itself

B155.2.2; shepherd's consecrated staff keeps c. from straying D1446.3, singing c. B214.1.1; sowing cheese to bring forth c. J1932.2; speaking c. B211.1.5; spring breaks forth where saint's stolen c. is found A941.5.5; steaks cut from live c. who heals herself by magic D2161.2.1; substituting common c. for magic one K476.8; tabu to eat c. C221.1.1.1; tabu to kill, cook sacred c. C221.1.1.1.3; thieving c. K366.1; tiger eats c. friend J427; "to every c. belongs its calf" P526.1; transformation to c. *D133.1; transformed c. advises daughter D688.1; trickster steals farmer's c. and then sells her to the farmer K258.1; truth-speaking c. B132; tying c. with stones to keep from blowing away J2119.8; vampire milks c. dry E251.3.2; when c. calls calf, all cattle graze B852; white c. comes to be milked for infant saint B251.2.10.1; why c (has cloven hoof) A2376.1, (has so few teats) A2363.1, (is always eating) A2231.1.1; why black c. eats green grass, gives white milk, yellow butter J1291.1.1; why c. has no upper teeth A2345.7.1; why is c. beaten by calf? H1292.16; witch as c. G211.1.3.

Cow's feet provide wealth D1469.7; milk with remarkable tastes D1665.2. — Child with c. head T551.3.4; dog rescues c. teats from fire: origin of his black muzzle A2229.1; huldra with c. tail F460.1.5; milker ties c. tail to himself and bees sting cow J2132.3; origin of c. and buffalo's hides A2311.6; riddle: four hang, four walk, two show the road, one wags behind (c. teats, feet, eyes, tail) H743; trickster evades paying c. burial fee K499.5; prophesying sex of c. offspring H528.1; white c. flesh as magic cure *D1500.1.33.2; why c. body hollow on one side A2356.2.12; witch curdles c. milk D2083.2.2.

Cows in church thought to be ghosts J1782.1.1; come up mountain for herdsman's call F679.1; die of shock at being fed W152.13.1; grateful for hero's housekeeping B396; killed for their hides when large price is reported by trickster K941.1; kneel on Christmas Eve B251.1.2.3; lose milk at king's death B301.6.3; magically made dry D2083.1; magically multiply (reward) Q141; to make curds before milking J1905.5; meek H659.21; speak to one another on Christmas B251.1.2.2; of the sun B19.6.1; white-headed during good king's reign Q153.1. — Army of c. B268.10; bath in milk of white, hornless c. as antidote for poison D1515.3; birds perch on ears of c. B853; calves kept from c. (in commemoration) V65.1, (during fast) P623.0.7; cast-off wife sent to herd c. S437; charm makes c. give plenty of milk D1449.1; color of devil's c. changed while he sleeps so that he does not know them A2286.2.4, K483; devil's c. one-horned: God gives them two A2286.2.3; dwarfs bewitch c. to give no milk *F451.3.3.5; fairies milk c. F271.1; fairies milk mortal's c. dry F366.1; fairies' c. F241.2; grazing c. at night render fairies visible F235.9; grazing c. eat same amount B854; jackal covers up clumsiness in catching c. J873.2; king demands milk from all hornless c.: given poison from wooden K839.4; lies about c. X1235; magic bag sucks milk from c. D1605.2; milk gushes from c. in deity's presence H45.2; milk from

saint's c. forms lake F989.9; quest for demon-owned c. H1364; recognizing milk of stolen c. F647.5.3; roads marked out by supernatural c. A989.2; skillful milker milks c. incessantly F678.1; snake milks c. at night B765.4; spirits tangle up peasant's c. F402.1.3; stolen c. cause war K300.1; why c. have two horns A2326.3.1; why c. ruminate A2472.1, A2231.1.1; witch transforms self to hare so as to suck c. D655.2.

Coward boasts of frightening bear away K1953.1; boasts when there is no danger W121.2; gloats over robber slain by another person W121.2.5; hiding from adversaries J2631. —Boastful c. frightened (by conspirators) K1951.4, (by his wife) K1837.1.

Cowards. — Tailors c. as warriors X223.

Cowardice W121; most shameful H659.12.1. — Men shamed for their c. by woman standing naked before them J87.

Cowardly duelers K2323; fool *J2600—J2649; to leave battle while lord alive W34.2.

Cowbell. — Capture by ringing c. K756.2.2.

Cowboy shoots injured wife J1919.9; stands up for friendless Jesus J1738.5. — Ghost of slain c. E337.1.4.

Cowdung goes on warpath F1025.2.1. — Jewels in c. cakes J1655.1; oath taken on c. M114.5.

Cowherd disappears New Year's night D2087.3.1; as foster father N856.2; hero L113.1.6; looking for cattle thief recognizes him in the lion J561.2; rescues abandoned child R131.3.3.

Cowhide falls, robbers flee K335.1.1.2. — Alleged oracular c. sold K114.1; magic c. D1025.5, (assures heaven for man who dies upon it) D1588.2.

Co-wife cruel to pregnant woman S185.1; transforms other wife D665.3 — Jealous c. kills woman's children S322.3; persecuted sons of c. S471; punishment for murder of c. Q211.10; task assigned at suggestion of jealous c. H911.1, H913.1.2; treacherous c. *K2222; younger son of c. a hero L10.2.

Cowl as saint's ransom burns Q552.18.1.1; in thornbrake symbol of Christ V124.1. — Magic c. *D1067.3.1, (protects from fire) D1382.9; monk who dies without his c. cannot rest in grave E411.7; saint's anger sets c. afire F1041.16; saint's c. (protects fox from hounds) D1447.2.1, (untouched by sea) F930.1.0.1.

Cowrie-shell turns into men D432.2.1.

Cowshed. — Cleaning c. H1102.1; tabu to enter c. during menses C141.2.

Cowslip pulled, girl dies E765.3.4.

Coyote as culture hero A522.1.3; as marplot at creation A61; persuaded to break leg: therefore has thin right leg A2284.5; rescues child R131.7; rides with sun A724.1.0.1; throws eyes in air: they are stolen K333.3; as trickster J1117.2; tries to fly J2133.3.1; wears fox's rattle J2136.1. — Color of c. A2411.1.3.2; creation of c. A1834; enmity of rabbit and c. A2494.6.2; enmity between c. and meadowlark A2494.12.4; why c. has

(long muzzle) A2213.4.1, A2335.4.4, (long teeth) A2345.2, (yellowish eyes) A2332.5.1, (yellow patch behind ears) A2218.4, A2412.1.3.

Coyote's body made larger A2301.3.

Cozening K347.

Crab beats deity's forbidden drum: eyes lift out of body *A2231.10, A2332.4.2; carried by crane, cuts off his head K953.3; carries animals in ear F982.8; as child's nurse B535.0.13; comes ashore: killed by fox J512.1; cuts heron's neck J631; hunts hare (lie) X1344.1; mistaken for tailor J1762.1.2; prefers death to imprisonment J216.3; pulled first living creatures from his side A1211.8; saves from crocodile attack J21.36; saves hero from snake B524.1.12, B549.5; shape of husband D719.2; thought to be the devil J1785.2; thrown to ground: breaks into pieces, hence small size A2214.4; on tiger's tail J1762.3; transformed to man D375; tries to lay eggs in boiling water pot J2415.3; walks backward: learned from his parents U121.1. — Bungling rescuer caught by c. J2675; cheese smeared on c. lures giant K827.5; creation of c. A2171.2; discourteous answer: why c. has eyes behind A2231.1.3, A2332.4.2; dolphin and whale scorn c. as peacemaker J411.6; enmity of c. (and jackal) A2494.5.3, (and spider) A2494.16.5; friendship between c. (and cobra) A2493.19, (and bird) A2493.27; giant c. B876.2.1; god becomes c. D175.1; golden c. B102.8; hedgehog and c. jump from boat after turtle J2133.11; helpful c. B478, B495.1; how c. got its claws A2376.4; magic c. B178.1; man transformed to c. D175; marriage to person in c. form B647.1.1; mother c. blames her children for not walking straight J1663.1; mythical c. B94.1; reincarnation as c. E629.2; singing c. B214.1.8; trickster pinched by c. J2136.4; tricky potter reborn as c. E692.3; what is in the dish: "Poor C." N688; why c. is afraid in dark A2534.1; why c. is cunning A2525.2; why c. has no head A2320.4; why c. lifts eyes out of body or has eye behind A2332.4.2.

Crab's exorbitant lending price to frog K255.2; haunts A2433.6.3; offspring born through chest B754.7.1; wedding B283.1. — Cause of c. walk A2441.4.2; cross on c. back A2412.4.4; origin of dents in c. shell A2312.3; why c. legs like teeth of comb A2376.5.

Crabs take moonlight walks, eaten K772.1. — Bear learns how to catch c. with his hairy claws J102; lies about c. X1344; tabu to eat c. C221.1.3.3; tiger's fear of c. exploited K1715.13; thief places candles on c. K335.0.5.1; why c. burrow in sand A2433.6.3.2; why c. live in water A2433.6.3.1.

Crack. — Dupe caught in c. in ground K1111.2.

Cracks. — Animals hop over c. in ground A2441.1.0.1; filling c. in ground with butter J1871; origin of c. in tortoise's shell A2312.1.1.

Crackling. — Deceptive land purchase: fields c. when burnt to be his K185.9.

Cradle. — Betrothal of children in c. T61.5.1; child in c. guesses devil's riddle H543.2; deliverer in the c. D791.1.3; devil takes an upbaptized child out of the c. and substitutes a wooden log G303.9.9.4; disguise as

child in c. K1839.12; dwarfs exchange children in c. F451.5.2.3; Evil Eye averted by swinging cat over child's c. D2071.1.2; fairy steals child from c. F321; flame illuminates sacred person's c. V200.1; goddess of c. A477.1; hero leaves c. for war T585.7; old man sleeps in c. F571.4; stolen sheep dressed as baby in c. K406.2; suckling children rock mother in c. (lie) X1856; tale of the c. K1345.

Craftiest. — Wolf is the devil's c. enemy G303.25.1.

Crafts acquired A1440ff.

Craftsman, God as A141.

Craftsmen, fairies as F271.0.1.

Craftsmanship bestowed by saint D1926.

Cranberry, magic *D981.10.1.

Crane bridge (fugitives helped across a stream) *R246; as child's nurse B535.0.7.2; minister to lion king B240.4.1; outwits, eats fish J657.3; pecks out spy's eye Q557.5; pecks out tiger's eyes S165.2; pulls bone from wolf's throat: wolf refuses payment W154.3; recognizes princess H188; gets resevoir emptied, eats fish J758.2; as suitor B623.1; tricks fish into being carried, eats them K815.14; tries to catch fish like hawk J2413.7; will not weep at crucifixion: must suffer thirst in August A2231.2.1, A2435.4.2. — Conception from c. dung T511.8.5; courtship of stork and c. B282.23; crab carried by c., cuts off his head K953.3; creation of c. A1968; fox and c. invite each other J1565.1; helpful c. B463.3; man marries c. in human form B652.2; man transformed to c. D162; marriage to c. B602.5; peacock and c. in beauty contest H242.5; reincarnation as c. E613.9.1; skin of c. becomes magic bag D1193.1; soul in c. E715.1.4; tiger, c. quarrel J428; woman bears c. T554.3.

Cranes carry away girl B522.4.1; disregard warnings and are killed J1052; fighting together defeat all J1025.1; of Ibycus N271.3. — Bull with three c. A137.7; stork killed along with c. J451.2; war of pygmies and c. F535.5.1.

Crash, ghostly E402.1.6.

Crater. — Giant cooks on volcano c. G171; skillful bowman shoots c. of Vesuvius open F661.6.

Crawling, see also **Creeping;** on all-fours (neither on horse nor on foot) H1053.6. — Magic power by. c. through ear of magic horse D1733.2; penance: c. on knees (to Rome) Q523.1, (and watering dry staff until it blooms) Q521.1.1; power of prophecy induced by c. backward around grave D1812.2.1.

Crayfish. — Attack on c. J2612; fools ignorant as to what c. is J1736.1; friendship of c. and pike A2493.33; origin of c. A2171.

Crazed. — Person c. by Echo D2065.6.

Creaking limbs held apart by fool J1872; wagon dies J1872.0.1; of wheelbarrow frightens J2615. — Cauterizing wheel to stop c. J2412.7.

Cream protected from witch G272.16.1. — Breaking spell on bewitched c. G271.4.11; fairies' c.-colored horses F241.1.1.4; lie about cow's c. supply

X1235.2.1; sea of c. F711.2.2; water becomes c. D478.11; woman created from c. A1275.5.

Created. — Animals c. by devil and God *A63.4; house c. by magic D1133.1; other devils c. by devil G303.1.4; men c. by God A179.6; rock in sea c. by magic D2153.1; woman c. (from cream) A1275.5, (by skillful companions) *H621.

Creation of animal life A1700—A2199; of devil from God's shadow G303.1.1.1; of devil when God strikes stone with his whip G303.1.1.4; of the earth A800—A899; of the heavenly bodies *A700—A799; of hell A671.0.2; interrupted since God must go to a fire A2286.1; of the moon *A740ff.; of man A1200—A1299; of a person by cooperation of skillful men F1023; of souls E703; of the stars A760ff.; of the sun A710ff.; of the universe A600ff. — All miracles created at c. F900.2; devil has not been seen since c. of bramble G303.17.3.4; hare runs away at c.: almost loses tail A2215.2; waters created on first day of c. A910.1.

Creations. — Trickster's false c. fail him J2186.

Creative. — Self-mutilation with c. purpose S160.1.1.

Creator, see also **God, Lord;** A0—A99; in anger creates man-eaters G312.5; appoints chief for created things A1187; commands ants become men A1224.7; creates (earth) A830ff., (man) A1210ff., (the universe) A610ff.; establishes twelve winds, each a different color A1129.1; lives in sky beneath us A651.2.0.1; opens shop, assigns crafts and professions from it A1440.1; of rivers A930.1; sent for water: meantime animals assume their present forms A1713; separates sun and moon to prevent birth of more stars A736.1.4.3; sent down insects to plant plants A2601. — Creation of animals by c. A1702; supreme god as c. A101.1; topographical features of the earth arranged by c. A902; years seem moments to c. D2011.3.

Creator's breathing causes the winds A1121; voice makes the thunder A1142.1. — Culture hero c. son A512.2; giant as c. servant F531.0.2; hero completes c. work A530.1; man created in c. image A1212; opening of c. eyes causes day A1171.

Creators. — Joint c. A37; male and female c. beget gods A112.2; two c. go by different route to establish features of the earth A902.1.

Creatures. — Magic power to see invisible c. D1825.3; marvelous c. *F200—F699; seeing supernatural c. forbidden C311.1; supernatural c. propound riddles H540.1.

Credential tests H242.

Credit. — Deception into giving false c. K455; false articles used to produce c. K476.2; money borrowed on c. of old beggar disguised as gentleman *K455.3; refusing c. to god forbidden C53; saint gives c. for good deeds to another, rewarded Q42.8; three reasons for refusing c. J1552.2.

Creditor captures Sun, Moon R9.1.2; falsely reported insane when he demands money K242; in former existence confiscates goods in next

Q554.7. — Arresting c. to postpone debt payment K238.2; debtor's wraith seeks c. E723.4.3.

Creditors. — Trickster summons all c. at once, precipitates fight, and escapes payment K234.

Creek. — Magic bark sets c. afire D1408.1.1.

Creepers, origin of A2682.

Creeping, see also **Crawling.** — Magic by c. through a hole *D1795; ordeal by c. under sod H228; penance: c. naked through thorns Q522.3.

Cremated. — Daughter has father c. with husband K2214.1.1; dead wagon c. J1872.0.1; heart c. to lay ghost E441.3; resuscitation of c. man by blowing on the ashes E66.1.

Cremation, origin of A1592.

Crepitation, magic D2079.1.

Crescentia K2112.

Crests. — Origin of bird c. A2321; origin of family c. A1578.1.

Crevasse, origin of A969.8.

Crevice. — Ghost comes through c. E445.1.

Crew. — Captain buried with his c. V67.4.1; sick c. accused as magician K2129.2; witch carried off by devil's c. G275.1.1.

Cricket hears water hiss on hot iron: learns his song *A2272.1.2; lights on king's head H162.2. — Ant and lazy c. J711.1; creation of c. A2063; friendship between frog and c. A2493.20; helpful c. B486.2; man transformed to c. D183.2; owl invites c. to share his nectar: kills him K815.5; soul in form of c. E734.5; wedding of c. B285.2.

Cricket's chirp A2426.3.4, A2272.1.2; wings in fox's excrement betray his plans K2061.10. — Ass tries to get a c. voice J512.8.

Crickets as good omens B147.3.1.1; as bad omens B147.3.2.1.

Cries, see also **Cry.** — Animal c. misunderstood J1811; nature and meaning of animal c. *A2426ff.; origin of animal c. *A2425; three c. allowed maiden about to be murdered K551.3.3; three c. of the world Z71.1.17; three first c. to God A1344.1; why eagle c. like baby A2426.2.15.

Crime inevitably comes to light *N270ff.; less serious if committed for lady P517; personified Z139.2; unwittingly committed M360ff. — Accidental discovery of c. N610ff.; animal tried for c. B272.2; child in mother's womb reveals c. T575.1.1; detection of c. through knowledge tooth D1817.3; evidence of c. left so that dupe is blamed K2155; ghost haunts scene of c. E334.1; ghost laid when c. has been confessed E451.1; innocent man accidentally suspected of c. N347; magic detection of c. *D1817ff.; saints magically detect c. D1817.2; severed finger as sign of c. H57.2.1; statue laughs and reveals c. D1639.4.

Crimes punished *Q210ff. — Small trespasses punished: large c. condoned U11.

Criminal allowed to choose his method of execution P511; confesses because he thinks himself accused N275; detected by having child hand knife to him H211; going to death predicts that his judge shall soon

meet him M341.4; may fight against odds rather than be judicially executed P513; saved from fire at stake by Virgin Mary V252.2.

Criminal's property destroyed Q486; wife and children sold into slavery Q437.1.

Criminals buried at crossroads E431.17. — Virgin Mary comforts repentent c. V275.

Crimson rock F807.1; sheep F933.3; tree F811.3.3.

Cripple healed by distributing knowledge H1292.4.3; marvelously cured F953.

Cripples hurry away from shrine lest they be healed and lose their livelihood X531; of shrine frightened and run away without crutches V113.1. — Origin of c. A1338.1.

Crippled mortals of dwarf ancestry F451.5.3; saint receives horse, chariot V221.0.2.1; villain K2272.

Crippling. — Witch c. G263.4.3.

Critic. — Gift of property silences c. U21.2; king honors poet and c. J811.3.

Croaking of frogs at prince's command H71.10.3.

Crocodile as animals' king B240.15; -boat R245.1; carries burden F982.5; carries man across river B551.3; cheated by old man K499.3; dance A1542.2.1; goes after the second child J2173.6; grants boy death respite K551.22.3; masking as log obeys suggestion that he move upstream K607.2; as ogre G354.2; opens mouth, monkey escapes K561.3; paramour B613.2; in strawstack burned to death K1055.1; swallows watersnake, which kills him J2137.4; tells dog to drink in river without fear: plan detected K2061.8; transports saint B557.4; as wooer B622.2. — Bird with c. head B49.1; crab saves from c. attack J21.36; creation of c. A2146; devastating c. B16.5.2; enmity of c. and (dog) A2494.4.2, (elephant) A2494.11.2; fox outwits c., escapes K543.1; friendship of jackal and c. A2493.11; giant c. B875.2; hero kills c. F628.1.4.1; helpful c. B491.3; magic causes c. to go ashore D1449.5; man transformed to c. D194; marriage to c. B604.3; marriage to person in c. form B645.2; origin of c. worship A1546.7.1; reincarnation as c. E614.3; sham-dead c. quivers flesh H248.2.1; thief as c. K311.6.4; trickster employed to teach c.: eats him K931.1; wer-c. D194.0.1; why c. has (marks of water pot on head) A2320.6, (no tongue) A2344.1.1.2, (half a tongue) A2239.7, A2344.1.1.1, (short tongue) A2344.1.1, (rough skin) A2311.7; witch as c. G211.6.2.

Crocodiles. — Journey to land of c. F127.3; monkey in danger on bridge of c. pretends that king has ordered them counted K579.2; ordeal by c. H224.

Crooked. — Giant with c. nails F531.1.6.1.2; giant with c. nose F531.1.6.6.1; luck determined by c.-necked demigod N125.2; person's c. nose F514.4; why flounder's mouth is c. A2341.1.

Crop burned to rid it of insects J2102.7; division between parrot, cat

J1565.3; spirits F445.1. — Boy saves life by showing father foolishness of plowing up his c. (killing his child) J92; deceptive c. division K171.1; fairy steals c. F365.4; harvesting early for half c. J1932.6; magic c. produces stone F809.3; mortal fosters fairy child to prevent c. destruction M242.1; payment to be made at harvest of first c. (acorns) K221; planting, growing c. overnight H1103.2.2; plow animals determine c. share J1179.11; separable soul in c. of sparrow E715.1.2; why munia wears c. on back of neck A2351.7; witches ruin c. G265.9.

Crops burned as punishment Q595.2; stolen by magic *D2087.1. — Absurd practices connected with c. J1932; black birds destroy c. B33.1.3; dwarfs interfere with mortal's c. F451.5.2.5; extraordinary growth of c. in paradise F815.3; failure of c. during reign of wicked king Q552.3; fairies destroy c. F369.5; fairies promise abundant c. F349.4; gods or goddesses of special c. A433; highest ranking man in land to be sacrificed for good c. S263.1; loss of c. as punishment C934.1; magic control of c. D2157ff.; magic growth of saint's c. D2157.2.1; magic spell destroys c. D1563.2.4; menstrous woman will ruin c. C141.1; nobles ruin peasant's c. U35.2; owl advises where to plant c. B569.2; sacrifice for good c. V17.1; saint's bell starts c. growing D1563.1.4.

Crósan. — Demon (c.) causes disease F402.1.5.

Cross between shoulders as sign of royalty H71.5; on breast F546.3; of Christ made of four kinds of wood V211.4.1; on crab's back A2412.4.4; magically raised in air D2135.0.2.1; protects against ghosts E434.8.1; renders invisible D1361.41. — All trees except aspen refuse to make Christ's c. Z352; angel gives saint a c. V232.7.1; appearance of c. causes conversion V331.1.2; why ass has c. on shoulders A2239.6, A2356.2.7; beggar on c. in place of Christ L435.4; blood from c. on robin redbreast A2221.2.2; Constantine's vision of the c. V515.1.4; deer with c. between horns B253.5; disenchantment by sign of c. D788; dwarfs fear the c. F451.5.9.1; devil's power avoided by the c. G303.16.3; earth supported on wooden c. A843.1; elder tree used in making the c. A2711.2.1; fairies fear c. F382.1; father of illegitimate child must walk in front of c. J1515.1; finding of the c. V211.3; ghost cannot pass c. E434.8; magic c. *D1299.3, (removes itself) D1641.9; magic power of holy c. D1719.6; magic results from sign of the c. *D1766.6; runaway cavalry hero grabs c. from graveyard K1951.2; sign of the c. *V86ff., (intimidates Jews) V342; stone c. (indicates treasure) N535.1, (rises into air) F1083.1; saintly baby holds arms in form of c. V229.2.1; sign of c. breaks witch spell G271.2.1; temple about to be taken over by pagans saved by appearance of a sign of the c. V344; tree cursed for serving as c. A2721.2.1; tree blessed that made the c. A2711.2; troll helpless before sign of c. F455.7.2; vigil with hands in shape of c. V462.4.2; windmill thought to be holy c. J1789.1.

Crosses on certain trees A2751.3.2.

Cross-eyes miraculously straightened F959.2.

Crossing river except at source forbidden C833; river impossible for mortals F141.1.2; river on scythe-blade E721.6; stream impossible for witch (ghost, ogre) *G273.4; water by use of magic object *D1524ff.; water when spirits are offended forbidden *C41.3. — Wearing shoes only when c. river F1015.2.

Crossbill's bill from aiding Christ at crucifixion A2221.2.4.2.

Crossbow to shoot guilty J1141.10; spares bird F836.5. — Loaded c. kills wife opening forbidden chest T254.4.

Crossbreeding. — Lies about c. insects X1280.1.

Crossroads. — Magic power at c. *D1786; parting at c. N772; suicide buried at c. E431.16.3; why dogs leave droppings at c. A2473.1.1.

Crosswise. — Tree-trunks laid c. of the sledge J1964; trying to get a beam through a door c. in otherworld F171.6.3.

Crow, see also **Raven;** accepts owl's hospitality, burns him to death K2026; alighting on a falling tree thinks his weight made it fall J953.11; appropriates sparrow's nest J684.2, K354.1; befriends pigeon, steals from his home K359.4; as bird of ill-omen B147.2.2.1; chooses dead cat over crown J242.7; claiming swan wife J1293.1.1; demands young swan in payment K255.3; drops filth on king L410.3; drops pebbles into water jug so as to be able to drink J101; drops stolen necklace in snake's hole, snake killed K401.2.2; fat remedies king's wounds F959.3.5; hatches cuckoo's egg A2431.2.1.1; kills dove singing to save her brood U31.2; learns owls' secrets, defeats them K2042; as messenger B291.1.2; must wash bill in order to eat with other birds (cumulative tale) Z41.2; on the tarred bridge Z39.3; refuses to marry titmouse B282.22.1; releases deer from snare K642.1; sacrifices self to save king of crows P361.9; searches three worlds for happiness J136; sits on sheep's back W121.2.3; slain as he goes to wash mouth K551.4.6; as suitor B623.4; thinks harvesters are stealing his grain J953.7; tied to jackal's tail J2132.3.1; tries to imitate partridge's walk J512.6; tries to prophesy like raven J951.3. — Alliance of raven and c. B267.3; cawing of c. A2426.2.6; color of c. A2411.2.1.6; creation of c. A1919; creator sends c. to scout for earth nucleus A812.3; cumulative tale: louse eats c. Z33.4.1; demon as c. F401.3.7.1; devil as c. misleads travelers G303.9.9.17; enmity of c. (and owl) A2494.13.1, (and kite) A2494.13.2, (and prairie-dog) A2494.13.5; falcon and c. as joint creators A37.1; friendship between c. and (louse) A2493.23, M246.1.2, (snake) A2493.25f.; frog escapes c. by telling him to sharpen bill K561.1.2; ghost as c. E423.3.8; ghost driven into dead c. E437.3; giantess as c. F531.1.8.4; goose mates with c. B671; helpful c. B451.4; magic fat of c. *D1017.1.1; man transformed to c. D151.4, G263.1.5.1; otherworld "where no c. flies" Z91; person simulates cock c. K1886.3.1; prophetic c. B143.0.8; soul in form of c. E732.2; speaking c. B211.3.9; swan blamed when c. drops filth J429.2; swan outlasts c. in flying L394; tiger flatters c., kills her K815.9; troll as c. G304.1.1.4; warning c. B143.1.1; wedding of c. and titmouse B282.8; where c. got

voice A2421.3; why white c. is dumb A2422.3; why c. eats excrement A2435.4.7.1; why c. cannot enter sparrow's nest A2431.3.6.1; why c. has short tail A2378.4.7; why c. is disliked A2522.5; witch in form of c. G211.4.1.

Crow's house full of wren's eggs H1129.9; maxim on flying away from calamity J171.3.1; nest A2431.3.6ff. — Young c. alertness: man and stone J1122.1.

Crows mow meadow (lie) X1252.1; reveal mare's killing B131.1. — Contest in beauty between swallows and c. J242.6; devils in form of c. G303.3.3.3.2; fox shams death, catches c. K827.4; king of c. B242.2.1; kites, c. quarrel over wounded fox J581.5; lies about c. X1252; owls and c. dispute over day or night vision B299.2.1; queen made to scare c. away Q482.5; war between c. and owls B263.3; what do c. do when they are five years old? (start their sixth year) H865; why c. peck at human flesh A2435.4.7; why elephant flees when cock c. A2531.3.1.

Crowbar. — Wall accuses c. J1966.

Crowded. — Dupe c. into the water K892; dupe c. over precipice K891.5.2.

Crowding together of animals seasonally A2484.

Crowing, see also **Cockcrow;** of cooked cock E524.2.1; of demi-coq in king's body *B171.1.1; of ghost rooster E402.2.1; of resuscitated roasted cock E168.1. — Chanticleer believes that his c. makes sun rise J2272.1; cock's c. at sunrise A2489.1.1; cocks c. about mistress's adultery, killed J551.1; cock c. with closed eyes seized K721; devil disappears at c. of cock G303.16.19.4, G303.17.1.1; imitation of cock c. deceives devil G303.16.19.4.1; woman c. in place of rooster, killed K1691.2.

Crown exposes infidelity of husbands H422.1; fits only true king H36.2.1; from heaven (quest) H1261; of the sun A731.2; of thorns given Joseph V211.1.6. — Christ born from c. V211.0.1; dwarf king wears costly c. F451.2.7.7; extraordinary c. F828; fairy king's c. stolen F355; father wears c. but is no king J1264.3; fool wears c. K1810.1.1; god's c. A156.2; king cannot judge without c. P13.1; king's c. in well F166.4.1; king rejects c.; too many cares J347.2; magic c. D1079.1, (of serpent) *D1011.3.1; man becomes c. D263.5; recovering c. from sea H1132.1.7; serpent's c. teaches animal languages B165.1.2; serpent's life in its gold c. E714.2; snake lays aside his c. to bathe B765.2; taking off c. in penance Q523.9; treasure-producing serpent's c. *B112.

Crowns as reward Q193. — Fairies with gold c. on heads F236.4.

Crowning of kings P13.5.

Crozier from heaven F962.12.1; in sod reveals gold N534.3. — Fire bends bough to c. shape F964.1; magic c. *D1277.1.

Crucifix bows as sign of favor D1622.1; wounds bleed D1624.2. — Devil as c. G303.3.2.1.1; ghost leaves c. E544.1.1; how much is c. worth? H716; husband prepares to castrate c. K1558; living c. chosen J1738.2; man behind c. says "Good Evening" K1971.7; punishment for indignities to c. Q222.2; reward for offering food to c. Q32, Q172.1.

Crucifixion V211.2.3; of captured woman S139.3; as punishment Q462; of self as penance Q522.1. — Animals blessed for good services at C. A2221.2ff.; animal characteristics: punishment for hostility at C. *A2231.2ff.; crossbill's bill from aiding at C. A2221.2.4.2; curse for participation in C. Q556.1; death at news of Christ's c. F1041.1.39; feats on hearing of C. F1041.16.3; gypsy helpful at C. A1674.1; origin of tree for C. of Christ A2632.2; plant cursed for disservice at C. A2721.2; punishment for opposition to Christ at C. *Q221.2; stone rent at C. A979.1.

Cruel king invited to execution, killed K811.3; punishments Q450ff.; relatives S0—S99; sacrifices S200—S299; woman reborn as firefly E692.5. — Kind foster parents chosen rather than c. parents J391; magic object makes person c. D1357; maiden abducted from c. father R10.1.2; phenomena at c. treatment of innocent F960.7.

Cruelty to animals punished Q285.1; conquers monk's lust T317.6; punished Q285; tabu C867. — Enemies won more by kindness than c. J26; Flying Dutchman sails because of c. E511.1.1; sea foolishly accused of c. J1891.3; unnatural c. S (entire chapter); wild huntsman wanders because of c. E501.3.1.

Cruet. — Magic c. D1171.8.1; self-returning c. D1602.13.

Crumbs. Ogre kills self when he sees c. lying on his belly G523.

Crunching. — Cannibal c. human bone G87.

Crushed. — Besiegers c. by falling treasure K2353; Christians c. in cave R315.2; thief c. to death by fragments of own boring N339.15; why mouse c. in crossing road A2239.9.

Crushing coins to powder with fingers F614.12; of house by magic D2099.3; iron walls as baby F611.3.2.3; in rice mill as punishment Q414.3.1. — Murder by c. S116, (in false embrace) K953.4; mutilation by c. S167; strong man c. ribs of embracer F639.9; water-spirit c. boat F420.5.2.7.1.

Crustacean. — Flying c. B48; magic c. B178; mythical c. B94.

Crustaceans, origin of A2171.

Cry, see also **Cries;** of the blood of Abel A1344.1; of giant ox impregnates all fish B741.1. — Animal's c. imitated to distract owner's attention from his goods K341.7; baby's c. imitated to distract owner K341.7.0.1; compulsion to answer c. C681; compulsion to regard hunting c. and follow hounds C681.1; dragon hears child's c. B11.12.6; foolish mother does not understand baby's c. J1911.2; spirits answer war c. F418.1.

Crying child (stops to renew strength) W182, (used to obtain magic) D835; induced by magic D2034. — Abbot's excuse for c. J1478.1; animals c. out frighten robbers K335.1.4.1; child c. because father unknown T646.1; to come laughing and c. at once H1064; fox c. out in sleep H48.1; ghost c. E402.1.1.3; laughing and c. at same time *F1041.11; laughing or c. fruits D1619.3; man c. at friend's death F1041.21.4; stolen animal c. out from thief's stomach Q552.4.1.

Crystal boat F157.1; bower in otherworld F165.3.5.1; ball disenchants D771.12; bower for fairy's mistress D2185.1; bridge F842.1.1; castle F771.1.6; column F774.1.1; tree F811.1.6. — Chamber with c. ceiling in otherworld dwellings F165.3.1.1; fence of metal or c. in otherworld F169.5; house of gold and c. in otherworld *F163.3.1; marble cup becomes c. D475.5; magic c. renders courageous D1358.3; moon lives in c. house A759.4; sun a bowl in c. box A724.2; tree with c. buds F811.17.1; tunnel of c. four miles long F721.1.1; walls of c. in otherworld *F169.2.

Crystals. — Dwarf home has chandelier of c. and gems F451.4.3.4; magic c. automatically heat for cooking D1649.5.

Crystal-gazing D1821.3.7.3, K1965.

Crystalline island F731.2.

Cubs give hero lion's milk H1361.0.1. — Man helps animal's c. B383.

Cuchulinn prophesies women's birth M301.5.2. — Battle rage of C. F1041.16.5; why C. abjured kingship P16.1.3.

Cucking-stool as punishment Q474.

Cuckold loses luck N6.2; recognizes wife's ring in friend's possession H94.0.1; weeps at child's funeral, real father sings U119.1.1. — Artist hoodwinks king: c. can't see picture J1492; hidden c. reveals his presence by rhymes K1556.

Cuckolds, tests for H425.

Cuckolded "as per instructions" J2342.2.2. — Man with unfaithful wife comforted when he sees jealous husband who guards wife carefully c. J882.2; teacher instructs pupil in love, c. K1692.

Cuckoo borrows food from other birds A2241.4; delivers other birds from their cruel king: agree to hatch out cuckoo's young A2229.5. — Birds flee from c. lest he later become a hawk J645.1; creation of c. A1993; why c. had red eyes A2332.5.2; father killed by son returns to life as c. A2275.6; fence built to pen c. J1904.2; why c. flies with difficulty and sings with wings spread A2442.2.2; hearing c. call a good omen D1812.5.2.5; hedging in c. so summer will stay year round J1904.2.1; helpful c. B469.8; man transformed to c. D156; why c. has no nest A2231.2.1, A2431.2.1; numskull climbs tree to help c. J1872.1; procuring c. to sing in winter H1023.3.1.1; reincarnation as c. E613.5; resuscitation by c. E122.1; serf in tree shot as c. K1691.1; woman as c. on tree shot down K1691.

Cuckoo's color A2411.2.6.10; feathers A2241.6, A2313.1; food A2435.4.1; song A2426.2.5; voice A2423.2.2; wedding B282.3.2, B282.19. — Crow hatches c. egg A2431.2.1.1; saint causes c. call D2156.9.

Cuckoos cry when asleep: weasels kill them K815.10.

Cuckoo-clock (bird calls out the hours) F989.3.

Cucumber, enormous F816.1.

Cudgel, magic *D1094, D1401ff.

Cuirass, magic *D1101.2.

Cukasaptati (seventy tales of a parrot) K1591.

Culm-borers help win contest K69.1.

Culprit exposed to sinning condition to repent H1573.7.1. — Magic knowledge of offense of c. D1810.0.12.

Cultivated places become desert F969.5. — Origin of c. plants A2684.

Cultivation, magic D2157.6.

Cultivator, god as A181.2.

Cultivators, Agaria as A1689.10.

Culture. — Acquisition of human c. *A1400—A1499; king prefers primitive to civilized c. J245.2.

Culture hero, see also **Demigods, Hero;** A500—A599; creates useful animals A1703; departs A560ff.; establishes law and order A530ff.; expected to return *A580ff.; nature of A520ff.; origin of A510ff.; removes world-props A1058. — Race of c. with ostrich: ostrich loses beautiful feathers A2252.3; origin of minerals from body of dead c. A978.1.

Cumulative, see also **Chain, Kettenmärchen, Series, Succession:** tales *Z0—Z59; tasks H941.

Cunning. — Barbers' c. P446.2; why crab is c. A2525.2.

Cup or contents has greatest gravity? J2391; as feast token H84.2; full of milk symbolic offering to unwanted saint H607.4; given by fairy not to be broken F348.2; made of single ruby J21.49; to be repaired given to thief K362.3; with two and three handles J2605.1. — Alleged oracular bamboo c. K114.4; angel takes c. from old man J225.3; bridal couple drink from same c. T135.11; extraordinary c. F866; guessing nature of devil's gold c. H523.3; hole in c. avoids intoxication K82.1.2; horse accidentally poisoned instead of master when attempt is made to give hero poisoned c. N332.3; identification by c. H121; identification by ring dropped in c. H94.4; knights drink from huge nine-gallon c. F531.1.4.3; loving-c. at betrothal T61.4.2; magic c. *D1171.6, (of bamboo) N455.10, (tests truth) H251.3.13, (protects) D1380.17, (protects against loss of strength) D1389.3; marble c. becomes crystal D475.5; monk loses temper at c. W185.4, (overturned) H1553.5; new c. protection against witch G272.8; one traveler to another: is this c. valuable or not? H586.7; recognition by c. in sack H151.4; skull used as drinking c. Q491.5; theft of c. from fairies when they offer mortal drink F352.1; trading silver for worthless c. J2096; troll's c. stolen F455.6.4.1; were merely measuring king's c. J1391.7; riddle about value of c., daughter's marital status H586.7.

Cups. — Dove sees painted c. of water and dashes into them J1792.1; earthen c. replaced by golden H262.1; monkeys' magic c. K311.6.2; rainbow from gods' emptying their drinking c. A791.6; recognition by overheard conversation with c. H13.2.5.

Cupbearer abducted from Finns P50.4; of the gods A165.3.

Cupid with arrows of lead and gold A475.0.1. — Venus jealous of C. and Psyche's love W181.6.

Cupidity, punishment for Q551.2.8.1.

Curds. — Animal shows c. as spit K1715.12; cows to make c. before

milking J1905.5; earth sets like c. A826; woman created from sour c. A1275.5; woman sells poisoned c. to man A1335.12.

Cure of diseases by Sacrament V34.1; for leprosy by drinking from opposite lip of horn from that which caused it D1783.2; by physician's imitating of sick man's actions F957; of sick by cutting off heads of the well (chickens) H583.4.3; by threatening patients with death K1955.1; yourself before doctoring others J1062. — Banishment of children as c. for feigned illness S322.4.1; bath of blood of beloved as c. for love-sick empress T82; blood of saint as c. D1500.1.7.3.2; child sacrificed to provide blood for c. of friend S268; coition as illness c. J1149.4; deceptive c. by illusion K1889.2; dipping into cold water as fever c. J2214.9; drunkard refuses c. of fever if it is to take away his thirst J343.1; fairies' white powder c. F344.3; flesh of certain animal (person) alleged to be only c. for disease K961ff.; magic c. for specific diseases D2161.1; marriage to prince as reward for c. H346, T67.2; miraculous c. for leprosy F955; reward for c. *Q94; search for c. for prince H1292.4; seduction by asking for sham c. K1326.1; sham c. by pretended extraction of object from patient's body K1871.2; strenuous c. for madness J1434; wife travels for years seeking c. for husband T215.7.

Cures by transferring disease to dead E595. — Marvelous c. F950ff.

Cured. — Promise to have but one consort if c. M262.

Curfew. — Ghosts walk after c. E587.3.

Curing incurable ulcer H1199.2.2; illness of children kills them J2175.6; with waters of saint's fishpool D1242.1.3; wound by treating object causing it D1782.2. — God disguised as doctor c. mortal K1811.3; price for c. ogre's wound G682; quest for only person c. sickness H1319.1; saint c. blind hyenas B384.

Curiosity *W137; punished *Q341; about secret enables animal to be tied K713.1.4; tests H1554. — Animal trapped through c. as to what the trap is K730.1; child's c. exposes thief K433; quest as punishment for c. H1219.8.

Curious wife: wait and see T258. — Trickster exacts wife from c. people K443.6.1; wild hunt harmful to c. E501.18.1.3.

Curlew. — Why c. has red legs A2371.4.1.

Curling. — Upper lip c. over nostril: lower hanging down to neck F544.1.1.

Curly hair holds nuts F555.9. — Canaanites' c. hair A1661.3; straightening a c. hair (task) H1023.4.

Currants. — Reincarnation of eyes into c. E649.5.

Current. — Magic root floats against c. D1547.1.

Curse by disappointed witch *G269.4; evaded by guessing magic names H517; laid by untold stories C672.1; magically changed to blessing D2175.5; by mermaid B81.13.8; of mother on unborn child S223.2; by ogres G269.4.1; as punishment Q556ff., (for broken promise) M205.2, (remitted) Q576. — Accidental meeting with person involved in over-

coming c. N718; army stopped by saint's c. D2091.13; big piece of cake with my c. or small piece with my blessing J229.3; devil's name used in c. (appears) C12.5; dwarfs emigrate because mortals c. F451.9.1.10; fairy lays c. on child F316; magic results from c. *D1792; mother's c. on son causes eclipse A737.2; punishment for undeserved c. Q265.4; runes protect against c. D1385.20; unique exceptions from c. Z357; witch's c. causes illness G263.4.0.1; why elephant hurts self in grass: mouse's c. A2239.10; why mouse is crushed: elephant's c. A2239.9.

Curses *M400—M499. — Old woman's c. inform abandoned hero of his parentage and future S375.

Cursed church clock never runs correctly H252.6. — Why animal is c. A2231.7, A2542; body c. by soul E727.1.1; Brahma c. by other gods A162.4; child c. by father cannot rest in grave E412.4; dancers rude to holy man c. and must keep dancing till Judgment Day C94.1.1; giant c. F531.6.12.1.2; horse owner c. by clerics B133.4.1; king c. by dwarf-smiths P15.4; presence of c. person brings disaster to land M491; sun c. by moon A736.9; tortoise c. for going under water while ferrying goddess A2231.7.3; tree on which Judas hanged himself c. A2721.5; why certain plants are c. A2721, A2776; will-o-the-wisp is girl c. for gathering plants on Sunday A2817.2.

Cursing contest K91; by magic D2175. — Damnation by c. D2061.2.4.1; death by c. *D2061.2.4.1; drinking holy water facilitates c. V132.3; dwarfs c. forced gifts F451.5.2.13; man c. sun and wind for burning L351.2; man put in moon for c. Q235.1, (God) A751.1.2; masses used along with other magic for c. D1766.5.1; prince penalizes c., although he himself curses W133.1; serfs c. master by mistake J1845; son c. father indirectly P236.3; tabu: sailor c. the wind C41.4; teacher c. disobedient pupils P343; wife c. husband who forces her T288.1.

Curtain. — Contest in lifelike painting (mare and c.) H504.1.2, (grapes and c.) H504.1.3; falling in love when c. pulled aside T29.1; heavenly c. around God's throne A152.5; jewelled c. F789.3.1; skillful marksman throws rushes into a c. F661.7.1.

Curtains in otherworld F166.7. — Looking behind c. tabu C336.

Customs *P600—P699; connected with kings P13; connected with unique compulsion C650.1; of giant ogres G130ff. — Culture hero establishes c. *A545; marriage c. *T130ff.; military c. P557; origin of c. A1500—A1599, (connected with birth) A1500ff., (of courtship and marriage) A1550ff., (of eating) A1510f., (of hunting) A1520ff., (religious) A1540ff., (social) A1530ff.

Cut hand gives away thief's complicity J1149.8; off parts of body restored (by saint) V221.9, (by holy man) V229.10.2. — Animal characteristics: members c. off A2216ff.; burning c. hair to prevent witchcraft D2176.5; cannibals c. off parts of children's bodies G86; captive's finger c. to test fatness G82.1; cat's paw c. off: woman's hand missing D702.1.1; ground c. from under adversary F942.2; identification by c. garment

H117; long tongue c. out and used to bridge a stream F544.2.2.1; moon c. in two by sun A755.4; mortal wins fairies' gratitude by letting them c. his hair and shave him F331.2; naked woman pursued and c. in two by rider E501.5.1.1; primeval woman c. in pieces A642.1.

Cuts. — Barber uses hair to stanch c. X252.2; ground dries up when first woman c. her little finger A856.2.

Cuticle. — Earth from creator's c. A833.

Cut-throat terrorizes boat N695.

Cutting off arm as alibi K407.2.1; off arms for sleeveless sweater J2131.3.1.1; off child's ears: fool takes threat as order J2465.11; clothes bag in two F667.3; devil's fingernails (fear test) H1422; down tree tabu C518; off giant's foot G512.6; hair as punishment Q488; off ogre's head, hands G512.1.2.1; off part of own body J213.3.2; into pieces as punishment Q429.3; at plow: fool cuts bullock's legs J2465.8; off son's head to marry fairy H313.2; steer in two to test sword F611.3.3.1; table reveals witch G257.3; things by magic object D1564; thread by shooting arrow F661.12; certain trees tabu C43.2; tree (branches tabu) C513.1, (with one stroke) H1562.1.1, (as unique ability) H31.5. — Abandoned child thinks father c. wood S338; boy c. down trees bribed to spare one N699.5; bride test (thrifty c. of cheese) H381.2, (c. up fish) H383.5; cat in woodpile prevents axe from c. D2186; deceptively c. off victim's hand K825.4; disenchantment by c. off and reversing bodily members D712.1; disenchantment by c. person in two D711.2; escape by c. fetters K649.11; fortune told by c. sand D1812.3.2; man c. off own head F511.0.4.1; murder by c. S118; ogre c. off own buttocks G528; peasant c. wood as guests arrive P411.2; penis c. down trees F547.3.6; sword c. everything F833.5; suitor task: c. open magic gourd H335.2; threats on c. corpse in two reveal feigned death J1545.8; task: c. firewood from rocks with brass axe (rock struck to splinters by lightning used) H1116.1; trickster c. up partridges with "executioner's" knife K344.1.3; victim kills swallower from within by c. F912.2.

Cuttlefish. — Man transformed to c. D174.

"Cutty Soams" mining spirit F456.3.

Cutworm A446.2, A2182.4.

Cycenus cuts off heads of strangers in order to build temple of heads G315.

Cyclone. — Lie: man rides c. X1004.2.

Cyclops F512.1.1. — Proof of slaying C. H105.5.2.

Cynical philosopher lives in tub J152.1; retorts J1442ff.; retorts concerning honesty J1370ff.

Cypresses. — Twelve c. with thirty boughs each (riddle) H721.3.

Cyrus L111.2.1.

Daddy-long-legs. — Why d. has long legs A2371.2.12; why d. has long life A2578.1.

Daedalus flies on artificial wings *F1021.1; puts thread through coils of snail shell H506.4.

Dagger cleaned on inside of robe A1599.7; indicates ogress dead or alive E761.7.15; in wall above bed falls and kills girl N331.1. — Infallible d. D1653.1.9; magic d. *D1083.1; marriage of girl to a d. T117.1.

Daily beating of men transformed to dogs necessary unless hero himself is to be transformed D691; beatings as punishment Q458.1; course of the sun A726; life of angels V247; life of the gods A150ff.; transformation D621; visit to saint compulsory C687.1. — Dead find no rest since someone d. knocks at grave E419.2; devil may be escaped by going to church d. G303.16.13; ghost visits earth d. E585.3; human being devoured d. G15; injunction: to perform certain act d. C687; magic sword slays man d. D1402.7.1.1; pilav as d. food (father's counsel) H588.2.

Dainty. — Food has taste of any d. desired D1665.

Dainties. — Refusal to eat d. V462.2.2.

Dairy-god A411.3. — Evil magic in d. *D2083; magic d. products *D1036.

Dairies. — God's d. A155.7; origin of d. A1439.5.

Dairyman. — Lie: remarkable d. X1082.2.

Daisies. — Tears of Mary at Annunciation become d. A2612.2.

Dal, wheat, rice dispute superiority T461.5.

Dam builder punished for defying God Q221.4.1. — Devil builds d. G303.9.1.2, H1131.2; spear used to d. stream F834.5.

Damage. — Deceptive d. claims K251.

Dame Berchta F475.1.

Damming. — Flood from d. rivers A1019.2; riddle about d. up outlets H588.9.

Damn. — Ram says "D." on Sabbath B211.1.1.1.1.

Damnation by cursing D2061.2.4.1.

Damned souls E752ff.

Damocles. — Sword of D. F833.2.

Damsel, see also **Maiden;** as wager N2.6.3. — Divine d. converts fairy wife into woman F302.5.2.1; poison d. F582; serpent d. F582.1.

Dance, see also **Ball;** of the dead E493; with the dead E238.1. — Backwards and forwards d. K153; camel tries in vain to d. J512.3; changeling's wild d. F321.1.1.2.1; devil haunts d. halls G303.10.4.0.1; devil punishes girl who loves to d. Q386.1; devils come to a d.-loving maid and play when she bathes G303.10.4.2; dupe lured to supposed d. and killed K816; dupe persuaded to d. on trickster's body K827.3; dupe persuaded to get into grass in order to learn new d. K1055; escape by pretending to d. and thus be untied K571; fisherman fails to make fish d. to his flute J1909.1; freemasons forced to d. till they sweat blood Q388.1; frog causes deer to d. into snare K730.2; god of d. A465.4; goddess of d. A112.1.1.1; magic object compels person to d. *D1415ff.; making ducks d. with closed

eyes K826; making pigs d. (task) H1186; mortal wins fairies' gratitude by joining in their d. F331.1, F331.4; persons magically caused to d. selves to death *D2061.1.2; resuscitation by nine-day d. E63.2; thief plays all night for d. while confederate commits theft K411; trickster joins bulrushes in a d. J1883; trolls' d. F455.6.6.1; wife's d. charms husband back R152.4; witch harnesses man and leads him to d. G269.3; witch rides man to d. G269.3.1.

Dances. — Devil d. on grave G303.9.8.3; origin of religious d. A1542.

Dancer stabs spectator K916. — Disguise as d. K1825.6; lightning as torches of invisible d. A1141.7.1; marvelous d. F699.1.

Dancers cheated: one coin payment K231.2.1; as followers of the devil G303.10.4; of the gods A166; upon whom icicles hang F572; rude to holy man cursed C94.1.1. — Devil appears invisible among d. G303.6.2.1; hoodwinked d. K826.

Dancing in afterworld E489.5; alps F471.1.1.2; animals B293; automata D1627; brownies F482.5.1; in churchyard forbidden C51.1.5; to death in red-hot shoes (punishment) Q414.4; ducks K826; dwarf F451.6.3.4; of enchanted person D794.1; fairies F261; giants F531.6.17.1; girl outwits robbers, brings strong men K551.3.6.1; mare rescues boy K551.3.6.2; men defeat captors K551.3.6.3; mountain-folk F460.3.1; naked in church punished Q222.5.3; night spirits F470.2; pigs G265.6.1.1; punished Q386; self to death D2061.1.2, (to repay devil for clothes) K1227.3.1; on sharp instruments as test H1531.1; shoes to pieces daily F1015.1.1; teacher a thief K374; thief directs robbery K341.21; trolls F455.3.2; at wedding T136.3.1; witches G247. — Breaking legs for prowess in d. K1013.6; celestial nymphs d. F642.5; dead lover d. at sweetheart's wedding E214.1; death respite while d. K551.3.6; deceptive d. lesson K153; devil d. with a maid till she dies G303.10.4.1; dog d. on hind legs G265.6.4.1; dwarfs emigrate because they dislike peasants' d. and loud music F451.9.1.9; earth made by couple d. on cloth A825; escape by d. K571.1; escape from d. captors K606.2; fairies d. with child F321.5; fairies d. with youth till he dies F302.3.4.2; girl fond of d. curses C12.5.3; girl shows herself naked in return for youth's d. hogs *K1358; girl sinks into earth for d. in church Q552.2.3.1; girls d. in heaven A661.4; lives spared as reward for d. Q151.13; long d. as endurance test H1501; magic d. *D2174; magic d. object D1646; man attacked on Christmas night by. d. ghosts E261.3; mortal beats drum for d. fairies F302.6.2.1; origin of d. A1462; origin of particular d. A1542.1; pillars d. to magic guitar D1599.1; pixies' d. contest F302.3.4.2.1; providing d. fairies as suitor task H1177.1; quest for d. apple H1333.3.1.2; quest for d. water H1321.4; religious d. V93; small man d. in spider web F535.2.3; stealing food from d. children K341.17; Saora wave axes, shout while d. A1689.4; victim enticed into d.: captured K772, K826.

Dandy tailored by devil, left naked G303.9.9.11.

Danger averted by dream warning K1810.8.3.2; warning restores speech

F954.5. — Agreeing to demands while in d. J625; animal warns of fatal d. B521; approaching d. too familiarly J655; association of rat with cat ceases as soon as mutual d. has passed J426; boasting after d. is over J2626; choice: plainness with safety or grandeur with d. J212; coward boasts when there is no d. W121.2; disregard of d. to objects (or animals) J2120ff.; dream reveals d. D1813.1.6; escape from d. by deception *K500ff.; foolish disregard of personal d. J2130ff.; horse warns hero of d. *B133.1; inattention to d. J651; lie: hunter in d. X1133; magic object warns of d. *B133.1; man sells child in order to save himself from d. S222; no time for minor fights when life is in d. J371; prediction of d. M340.5; red wards off d. D1381.15; sacrifice to get help in d. V17.3; saint incurs another's d. P319.8; shrewish wife reforms after d. T251.2.5; Thumbling in d. of being sucked in by man's breath F535.1.1.4; voice warns of d. in mine V542; witch places man in d. G292.

Dangers to husband in bridal chamber T172. — Animals retort concerning their d. J1420ff.; brothers deliberately seek d. they have been warned against *Z211; fanciful d. from animals B766; forest of d. F812.3.

Dangerous animals unnamed C433.2; husband T181; penances Q525. — Animal rescues man from d. place B547ff.; curse: undertaking d. quest M446; dupe goes to d. place, killed K991; falsely accused hero sent on d. mission K2102; house filled with d. animals J347.5; quest for d. animals H1360ff.; quest for d. bride H1381.3.1.2.3; quest over path guarded by d. animals H1236.2; questions to the dead are d. E545.5.

Danmar tree. origin of A2681.8.

Dante abuses lowly blacksmith chanting Divine Comedy J981; accused of religious negligence J1261.2.5; puts teasing ruler out of countenance J1224.2; unrewarded while minstrel is J1364.

Dao. — Chain tale: man sharpening d. bitten Z49.6.3.

Darby ram X1243.1.

Dark haired people as magicians D1711.9; traitor K2260ff. — Banished devil appears on earth only on day of d. moon A106.2.1.1; dwarfs fear the d. F451.3.6.5.1; fairies seen as d. shadows F235.7; fool cannot tell his right hand in the d. J1735; hungry parson hunts porridge in d. X431; life token: milk turns d. E761.4.5; seduction theme: God can't see in d. V465.1.2.2; why not to eat in d. A1512; why some nights are d. A1174.2; witches see in d. G249.10.

Darkening. — Bird swarms d. sun, moon F989.16.2; magic spell d. sun D1546.1.2.1; object d. as life token E761.4ff.; sun d. at death of holy person F965.2; tree d. whole world F811.14.1.

Darkness as god's child A700.8; of lower world F80.1.2. — Deity arises from shell of d. A115.6; giants in region of d. F531.6.2.6; god dwells in d. A151.13; gods of d. and of light A107; great d. from awk swallowing sun A721.2.1; island of d. F129.4.5; impenetrable d. F965.3; land of d. F706; magic d. D908; miraculous d. as punishment Q552.20.1; premature

d. F965; primeval d. A605.1; slaying under cover of d. K914.3; sun thrown on fire: period of d., rain A1068.

Darknesses. — Tabu: drinking from river between two d. C263.

Dart, recognition by H125.4.

Dashing. — Dropping and d. to pieces as punishment Q417; miraculous d. to death Q551.10.

Date (fruit). — Blind thief's rope slips on withered d. tree K436; magic d. *D981.9.

Date palm. — Why fruit of d. looks like old woman's breasts A2791.11.

Dates. — Ignorance of d. J1743; riddle of d. H707.

Daughter bears son, father dies E765.4.3; encouraged by dead mother E323.6; insulted by father's offer of new husband K2052.4.3; must be named for fairy F302.5.1.1; promised to animal suitor B620.1; punished by marriage to poor man T69.5; rescues father R154.3; succeeds on quest son failed L152; unwittingly turns parents out of doors N367; as wager N2.6.2; wooed, mother dies E765.4.2. — Accidental meeting of (father and d.) N732, (mother and d.) N736; captive king's d. enslaved P173.1; clever d. solves riddles H561.1.1.1; creator's d. A32.2; dead father helps d. in childbirth E327.2; death vowed if another d. born M184; devil wooes an innkeeper's d. G303.12.1; devil's d. G303.11.5; dwarf promises money and property to mortal father for hand of d. F451.5.18.1; false d. accepted as resurrected child K1926; fascination with ogre's d. G455; father and d. *P234; father rescues d. R153.5; father takes his d. to cannibal to be eaten G75; father will die when d. marries E765.4.1; father's deceptive advice to inhospitable d. J1561.5; formerly I was d., now I am mother (riddle) H807; ghost appears to d. E321.5; giantess d. of giant, maiden F531.5.7.1.2; help from ogre's d. *G530.2; with help of captor's d. prisoners slay many of his soldiers at a banquet K811.1.1; hero's d. bears boy A592.2.1; hero's virgin d. A592.2; impoverished father begs from abused d. L432.2; king promises d. she may choose mate Q115.2; king's d. tabu in marriage C196; magic object from d. D815.6; magic object stolen by d. D861.8.1; man made to believe d. has borne child K1923.2; man palms off elder d. as younger K1911.1.5.1; mother abandons remarkably beautiful d. F575.1.1; mother and d. P232, (as rivals in love) T92.6; mother haunts d. E222.0.1; mother wishes lazy d. may marry devil C12.4.1; mother's ghost tries to tear d. to pieces E222.1; murder of wild huntswoman's d. E501.3.10; numskull praises his d. as being pregnant J2427; ogre's d. (burned in his own oven) G512.3.2.1, (killed with father) G512.0.2; old woman loses willingness to die for d. H1556.4.5.1; parent to die same day as d. E765.4.3.1; prostitute claims to be victim's d. K347.1; quest for vanished d. H1385.2; rescue by captor's d. *R162; sacrifice to find abducted d. V17.5.1; second d. won by saying first dead K1366; seventh d. to be magician N121.4; son of abandoned d. becomes hero S371; tabu to look on d. for twelve years C312.3; toad exchanges ugly d. for lizard's K476.5; treacherous d.

*K2214.1; treasure to be found by man who marries original owner's d. N543.3; trickster's d. a dupe J1111.2; troll's d. after being cooked in kettle recognized by golden fingernail H79.1; victorious youngest d. *L50ff.; vow to marry none but d. of certain man M146.5; witch as d. of fairy, man G203.1; woman substitutes for her d. in dark K1317.5; yam cutting symbol for marriageable d. H611.3; youth in court for kissing prince's d. pleads his love for her J1174.1.

Daughter's good fortune discovered by beggar father N732.2.1; intercession saves father wronging her W11.5.9.2; sickness after father breaks tabu C940.2. — Cup's value compared to d. marital status H586.7; dead father stops d. weeping E327.1; death upon d. marriage M341.1.1.3; father opposed to d. marriage T97; man unwittingly causes d. death N320.1; mermaid ruins her d. seducer B81.13.9; tabu: younger d. marriage before elder C169.2.

Daughters meek H659.21; of men and sons of God F531.6.1.1; sacrificed to avert famine S263.2.2; seducing father T411.2.1. — Choice between foolish son or wise d. J226.3; doctor prescribes sexual intimacy to mother: d. follow treatment K2052.4.1; husband leaves home after fourteen d. born N231; lakes as d. of the gods A920.1.14; mountains as d. of gods A962.9; oath to marry d. only into family with bridegroom for each M149.5; seven d. of Humility J901; sun and moon as skygod's d. A736.4; threat to marry d. to first comers N455.12; vow to marry off d. to first men seen M138.1; witch's cattle her d. H1199.12.2.

Daughter-in-law tabu C173. — Bad relations of mother-in-law and d. P262.1; clever d. J1111.3; cruel d. S54; enigmatic permission to d. H588.0.1; lazy d. learns work W111.3.6; mother-in-law humiliated as cure for malady of d. K1945.1.1; mother-in-law plots death of d. S51.1; sour-faced d. H659.18.1; treacherous d. K2214.2; wise d. defeats wealthy J185.1; woman eats d. G79.2.

David as prophet M301.7.2. — God punishes D. for his pride L415; King D. mingles with common people J914.1; prophecy: woman as ancestress of D. M363.2.1; what says D.? X435.1.

Daw as bird's king B242.1.6; fleeing from captivity caught in trees by thread around foot N255.5; tries to carry off lamb like eagle J2413.3; tries to swallow glowworm sparks J1849.2; waits in vain for the figs to ripen in winter J2066.2.

Daw's food A2435.4.10.

Daws. — Kind words for d. but driving them off K2090.1.

Dawn reflection of roses of paradise A1179.2.1. — Animal calls the d. *B755; at d. sun plays with moon A722.9; animal punished for not heralding d. A2236.5; bird of d. B34; day as son of night and d. A1171.4; fairy house disappears at d. F221.1; ghost laid at d. *E452; god of d. A270ff.; gods flee at approach of d. C311.1.8.1; goddess of d. A270.1; phantom house disappears at d. F771.6; wolf announces d. prematurely to collect debt *K494.

Day controlled by magic D2146.1; husband: night husband T482; as mortals' period A189.17; and night as formula Z73; produced by magic D2146.1.3. — Angels of the d. A1171.3; appointing king by d., slaying him by night P13.6; artist's children by d. and by night J1273; the auspicious d. N127; coming neither by d. nor by night H1057; dead quiescent during d. E452.1; dead returns third d. after burial E586.2; devil builds road for farmer in one d. G303.9.2.2; during d. dwarfs appear in form of toads E451.2.0.5; devil destroys by night what is built by d. G303.14.1; during d. moon stays under earth A753.3.3; dwarfs emigrate because mortals desecrate holy d. F451.9.1.11; dwarfs regard D. of St. John the Divine F451.5.9.4; emperor thinks d. lost when he gives no gifts W11.2.1; ghost invisible during d. E452.2; god's d. one thousand years A199.5; if it is d., give me food: if it is night, let me sleep W111.2.3; inexorable fate: no d. without sorrow N101.1; invulnerability for single d. K1845.1; kingdom well by d. burns at night H1292.20; long d. (if the clock is still striking it must be 50 o'clock) J2466.3; magic control of d. and night D2146; magic power to continue all d. what one starts D2172.2; man can stand all d. on one foot F682; marriage to beast by d. and man by night *B640.1; object borrowed for one d., night, retained K232.2; ointment makes night seem d. D1368.1.1; one d. from happiness to misfortune H685.1; one shape by d.: another by night D621.0.1; one sun-god for night, another for d. A227.2; origin of night and d. A1170ff.; origin of custom of catching fish by d. as well as by night A1457.2; owl as watchman goes to sleep: does not see by d. A2233.3; person dead by d., alive at night E155.4; profaning sacred d. forbidden *C58; prognostications from d. of week and first d. of year D1812.5.0.7.3; promise not to kill on "any d.": night killing K929.3; quest to be accomplished in one d. H1245; riddle of the d. and night H722ff.; sending for beef when neither d. nor night H1074; soldiers of fairy king are trees by d. and men by night F252.3.1; souls at Judgment D. E751; sowing and reaping same d. F971.7; tailor occupies God's throne for d. P441.1; wife in heaven by d., with husband by night E322.3; windows and doors for every d. in year F782.1; woman alive by d., dead at night E155.4.1; work of d. magically overthrown at night *D2192; year and a d. Z72.1.

Day's journey from earth to heaven H682.1.1; journey from one end of the earth to the other H681.1.1. — Sun earns d. wages for his daily work H715.1.

Days. — Bringing as many horses as there are d. in the year H1117; dead awaken after three d. to new life and great wisdom E489.1; diminishing number of sacred d. forbidden C58.1; February's shortage of d. A1161; how many d. have passed since the time of Adam (riddle) H706; magic weakness for five d. each year D1837.1.1; mortal wins fairies' gratitude by naming d. of week F331.3; resuscitation by assembling members and leaving in cask for nine d. E37; speaking during seven d.

of danger forbidden C401.2; why d. lengthen in spring A1155; why d. shorten in autumn A1156; why there are more d. than nights H772; years thought d. *D2011; years are d. in Tusita world A697.2.1.

Day of Judgment, see **Doomsday.**

Daybreak. — Servant who is to call his master at d. looks into dark closet to see if it is yet light W111.2.1; truest dreams at d. D1812.3.3.1.

Daydreamer breaks pots, loses future profits J1493.

Daydreaming toad run over J2061.4.

Daylight renders fairy prince mortal F383.4.1. — Acquisition of d. A1412.3; ogre who cannot endure d. G632; supernaturals tricked into d. exposure K839.6.

Daytime. — Darkness comes in d. in order to save life of maiden about to be executed F965.1; star shines in d. F961.2.3.

Dazzling. — Magic d. shield D1645.5.

Dead E (entire chapter); beggar's stick will not stay until back in beggar's service D1651.5; body becomes god A104.2; cannot rest because of a sin E411; dog transformed to money D422.2.1; fish reveals guilt D1318.2; girl frightens father and lover J2621; heads necessary to drinking C281; king carried into battle P12.5.0.1; leaves transformed to gold D475.1.3; and living go together to gate of heaven E754.2.3; lover's return (friendly) E310ff., (malevolent) E210ff.; made to appear alive K1885; man mistaken for living J1769.2; man not killed by weapons tabu C319.2; man stretches forth hand to honor saint V222.7; man tries to come back to life E162.2; men try to carry kettle from hell to heaven A1433.0.1; mother's breasts nourish baby for two years T611.9; opposes return of living from land of the dead F105; place net across river to prevent living man from returning to earth F93.1.1; quarrel with living, hence own land E481.0.2; relative's return (friendly) E320ff., (malevolent) E220ff.; Rider (Lenore) E215; tree comes to life *E2; man's tooth as cure for toothache D1502.2.1; wife marriage test H363. — Abode of the d. *E480ff.; absurd ideas about the d. J1937; adulteress returns from d. as devastating dragon E263; alleged return with gold from d. J2411.5; animal searches for d. man B546; apparently d. woman revives K426, N694; bird reveals d. rider B131.4; captive spirits of d. H972.1; cat hangs on wall pretending to be d. K2061.9; chief of d. frightens visitors H1401.1; child born to apparently d. mother T581.2.1; child born of d. mother T584.2.1; child speaks from d. mother's womb T575.3; conductor of the d. A311; corpse not entirely d. who has left good property H586.5; curse: hero to remain as d. until curser dies M438.4; dance of the d. E493; death feigned to enter land of d. K1866; descent to lower world of d. *F81; devil in d. man's shape G303.3.1.20; devil enters the body of d. boy G303.18.1; devil in place of d. man in shroud G303.18.2; dinner with the d. E238; escape from land of d. R219.2; failure of crops for mistreating d. Q552.3.0.4; fairies as souls of d. F251.2; falling d. at lover's return T211.7; falling in love with

d. body T16.2; Flying Dutchman has d. men as sailors E511.2.1; food placed out for returning souls of d. E541.1; fool tries to shoot d. antelope until it will come to him J1909.2; footsteps in manure proof d. man walked H264; fortune's wheel turned by d. king in mountain N111.3.1; friendly return from the d. E300—E399; girl marries lover who thought her d. K1839.2; god of the d. A108.1; god of the world of the d. *A310ff.; gods are spirits of d. A117.5; grateful d. man *E341ff.; good d. but not living (riddle) H841.2; intercourse with d. human body T466; island in otherworld garden inhabited half by d. and half by living F162.1.2.5; journey to land of the d. E374; kindness to orphans repaid by d. parents Q47; king raised from d. P19.5; light as souls of d. A1412.2; magic d. fish *D1281; magic d. man's tooth *D1009.2.1; magic knowledge from d. D1810.13; magic received from d. D812.4.1; malevolent return from the d. E200—E299; man forced to eat d. father's heart goes mad G91.1; man at grave pretends to be d. speaking K1974; man returns from d. to protest against priest who had been too easy with him at confession V25.1; man wants to be d. one day J2188; mass said for d.: they arise and say "Amen" V45; mould put on table for the d. E433.1; mountain spirits as souls of d. F460.0.1; origin of feast for the d. A1541.1; owner frightened from goods by apparitions of the d. K335.0.5; path to world of d. F95.0.1; people flee man reported d. J1786.8; person d. during day, alive at night E155.4; person made to believe that he is d. J2311ff.; physician forced to carry d. patient's bier P424.3.1; power of seeing whether d. go to heaven or hell B161.4; prayer for journey to land of d. V52.9; pretending man d. to test saint Q591.1.1; punishments in land of d. Q560.1; rescue by grateful d. man R163; resuscitation by frightening d. E25; return of contract sought from d. man H1273.1.1; return from the d. E0—E199, (to do penance) E411.0.2.1, (to reveal murder) *E231; riddle on house full of d. H831; robbers frightened from goods by the d. K335.1.2; room in hell for the d. A678; sacrifice to the d. V11.6; saint commands return from d. V229.1; servant lays skin of d. dog in bed of his mistress and master K2134; sham d. claim reward for information about their death J2511.1.2; sham d. man deceived into making gesture K607.3; sleeper answers for d. man J2618; soul leaves body to converse with d. E721.8; speaking to the d. tabu C497; stingy d. woman raises her head to correct account of laundress W152.3; summoned d. prophesies M301.14; sun's night journey in land of d. A722.3; contact with the d. forbidden C541; tabu: offending the d. C16; tabu: stripping d. and slain C877; tasks accomplished with help of grateful d. H972; thunder drums of the d. A1142.9.1; trading d. horse K134.7; treasure hidden in pillow under d. man's head N522; tree in hell made of living heads of the d. A671.2.3; two d. men struggle over living man E467.1; unquiet d. sinner taken to priest for absolution E411.0.2; vigil for d. father H1462; voices of d. heard from graveyard E401; voyage to Isle of the D. F129.4.4; ways of disposing of d. V61; why opposum plays d. when

caught A2466.1; witch calls up d., makes them walk on water G299.1; witch revives d. G263.5; woman playing d. to spy on husband killed N384.12.

Dead Sea's origin A920.1.15.

Deadly. — Unique d. weapon Z312.

Deaf and dumb man can see soul taken to happiness or punishment D1821.7; and dumb speak F1041.22; blind, and lame as witnesses in court X141; dumb, blind, and lame man catches hare (lie) X1791. — Blind wife, d. husband happy T202; blind and d. cure each other by blows N642.1; deception by playing d. K1981.

Deafness caused by magic object D1332.1; magically cured D2161.3.5. — Feigning d. to lure enemy K911.5; humor of d. X110ff.; magic object cures d. D1506; trickster cheats by pretending d. K231.15; trickster feigns d. and gets hospitality from miser K1981.1.

Dearer. — Mother love d. than gold (riddle) H662.

Dearest. — Exiled wife's d. possession J1545.4.

Death in battle preferable to bed M161.6; caused by (ascetic devotions) V462.2.3, (broken heart) F1041.1.1, (cannibalism) G91.2, (chagrin) F1041.1.3.10, (cursing) *D2061.2.4, (fire from heaven) Q552.13.1, (fairies) F363, (glance) D2061.2.1, (grief) T211.9.1, (grief over death) F1041.1.2, (intercourse) T182, (excess of women) T99.1, (love) T81, (magic charm) D806.2, (meeting ghost) E265.3, (opposing dogma of Immaculate Conception) V312.2, (saint's breath) D1500.4.2.2, (sleepiness, anger, and greed) H803, (speaking with pestilence) F493.2.1, (spirit) F402.1.11, (sight of Wild Hunt) E501.18.10, (waterspirits) F420.5.2.12; cheated by moving bed *K557; of children as punishment Q553.4; as curse M451; of dwarfs F451.3.5.1; escaped through disguise, shamming, or substitution *K520ff.; exposes hypocrisy K2065; of faithful servant for his master P361.1; of father fated at daughter's marriage E765.4.1; feigned (to be carried) K1861, (to meet paramour) K1538, (to live with mistress) K1538.2, (husband's discovered) J1545.8, (to capture) *K751, (to test debtor friends) H1558.5, (to seduce) *K1325, (to steal) K341.2, (to join lover) K1538.1; forestalls evil fates N121.2; of friends for each other P315; fulfills grief prophecy M340.1; follows loss of magic object D860.0.1; of the gods A192.1; is the hardest (riddle) H637.2; of helpful animal *B330ff.; of hero Z292; on horseback E492; from joy F1041.1.5; kills only those whose time it is to die A487.0.1; through lack of foresight J2137ff.; of little hen (cumulative tale) Z32.2; of loving couple from separation T212; -machine's inventor uses it K1681.1; by magic *D2060ff.; message softened by equivocation K2313; omens (through dream) D1813.1.4, (ghost light) E530.1.6, (ghost) E574, (magically heard noises) D1827.1ff., (overly generous gift) W11.13, (snow on house) D1812.5.1.18, (seeing own wraith) E723.2, (dry river bed) D1812.5.1.16.1, (blood) D1812.5.1.1.4, (foreknowledge of hour) D1812.0.1; order evaded K510ff.; as penalty or punishment *Q411ff., Q582, (for losing footrace)

H1594.0.1, (for broken oath) M101.3, (for broken tabu) *C920ff., (for losing bride-race) H331.5.0.1; personified *Z111ff.; postponed (if substitute can be found) *D1855.2, (by saint) D1855.3; preferred above God and Justice J486; prophesied M341; prophecy fulfilled M370.1; preferred to captivity J227.1; preferred to marriage with unwelcome suitor M149.2; preferred to other evils J227; as rescuer R169.16; sends man back to earth E121.13; sentence escaped by propounding riddle king (judge) cannot solve *H542; of snake encircling world A1082.3.1; of snake only after sunset B752.2; of strong man F615.0.1; from sudden realization N383; suspended until god's return A173.1; thought sleep E175; vegetable C662; of witch G278; as wife's paramour J2349.2. — Accidental d. N330ff.; angel of d. A52.1.1, V233; angels of d. cannot bring soul to heaven E754.2.2.1; animal saves man from d. sentence B522; animal's behavior at d. A2468ff.; announcing d. directly tabu C499.1; beautification by d. and resuscitation D1865; burning witch to d. G275.3.0.1; captivity preferred to d. J217; cat leaves house when report is made of d. of one of his companions *B342; charitable man's d. postponed Q151.1; city inaccessible to d. F767.3; condemnation because of d. without confession V22; conversion to Christianity on pain of d. V331.2; creator's d. A76; cumulative tales involving a d.: animal actors Z31; daughter of king of d. E121.1.3.1; deception by feigned d. *K1860ff.; disappearance or d. of giants F531.6.12; discontented ass longs for d. but changes his mind when he sees skins of dead asses at fair J217.2; disguise as angel of d. K1828.1.1; dog caresses sick sheep: shepherd knows that he hopes for sheep's d. K2061.3; dogs howling indicate d. B733.2; escape from d. or danger by deception *K500ff.; extraordinary d. F901, F1041.1, (of animal) F981ff.; extraordinary phenomena at d. *F960.2; extraordinary three-fold d. F901; evil spirits exorcised by saint's d. D2176.3.3.0.1; fairies dance youth to d. F302.3.4.2; faithfulness to marriage in d. *T211ff.; fanciful behavior of animal at d. B752; flogging to d. as punishment Q458.2; foolish demands before d. J2174; god of d. A487; god of d. replaced in forged letter K1851.1; god's kiss causes painless d. A185.6.1.1; grieving to d. over childrens' fate after death J2063.1; Hercules fights with D. R185; hosts refrain from telling guest of d. in household P323; humiliating d. as punishment Q499.2; husband sends d. message after sleeping with disguised wife K1843.2.1; if he does not live, d. may have him J1513.1; illusion of d. K1884; immortality from bargain with d. D1851.2; inviting only those never touched by d. J1577.1; judge's temper leads to unjust d. sentence W185.5; kernel tries to escape d. J1875.1; kinds of d. produced by magic D2061.1; king grows lean from fear of d. U241; learning what d. is H1376.1; learning fear of d. H1376.2.1, J27; magic object (causes d.) D1402ff., (saves owner from d.) D1392; (disappears at owner's d.) D867, (warns of d.) D1322; magic power of seeing D. at head or foot of bed D1825.3.1; magic power from D. *D1724; magic power to see d. circumstances D1825.5; man

converted to belief in future life on d.-bed V311.1; man longing for d. changes mind when Death appears J217.0.1.1; man promises child in order to save himself from d. S222; man's spirit prophesies own d. E489.4; message of d. K978.1, (fatal to sender) K1612; messenger of d. imprisoned R6; moon's phases caused by watchers' d. A755.2; Moses' staff has eaten after its d. (riddle) H824; murdered boy still sings "Ave" after d. V254.7; mysterious d. as punishment Q558, (remitted) Q574; mysterious voice announces d. of Pan F442.1; no mortal escapes d. E361.3; no time, no birth, no. d. in otherworld F172; nobleman after d. must serve as menial Q482.3; numskull catches buffalo by rope and is dragged to d. J2132.1; numskull laughs at his child's d. J2461.3; numskull thinks the bishop's snoring is his d. rattle J1833; object sought brings quest assigner's d. H1248; ogre gives riddle on pain of d. G681; ogre stoned to d. G512.2; old man and D. C11; one man prays either to keep friend from d. or for both to die E165.1; origin of d. A1335; origin of the d. chant A1543.1; originator of d. first sufferer K1681; otherworld journey after d. F6; persons magically caused to dance selves to d. *D2061.1.2; promises connected with d. M250ff.; prophecy: immunity from certain types of d. M367; quest: learning what fear of d. is H1376.2.1; riddle propounded on pain of d. H541.1; roof taken off above sick man that d. may come E722.2.3; saint sanctifies against d. D2176.0.1; sea ghost predicting d. E271.2; sham physician cures people by threatening them with d. K1955.1; singing at approach of d. J2461.1.2.4; slave recommended as immune to d. J1455; slaying king's son to prevent father's d. H1162.2; soul leaves body at d. E722; souls wander after d. E750.1; staff of life and d. E64.1.1; storm at d. of (wizard) D2141.0.4, (wicked person) D2141.0.5; strong man evades d. F615ff.; suitor task: avenging bride's father's d. before marriage H335.1; suitor's sincerity tested by reporting girl's d. H314.1; sun darkened at d. of holy person F965.2; sun does not rise after d. of hero F965.2.1; sun shines day and night after holy d. F961.1.5.1; supernatural manifestations at d. of pious person Q147; swan saves self by singing d. song N651; sword of Angel of D. F833.11; tasks imposed on pain of d. H901; test of d. H248; test of friendship: to go with one to d. H1558.3; tidal wave marks person's d. place A913.1; time of d. postponed D1855ff.; transformation to escape d. D642.2; two persons informed of each other's d. K2142; uncharitable pope wanders after d. V425; understanding of d. from watching animals at prey J52.1; Virgin Mary prevents (retards) d. so as to save sinner's soul V251; vow not to flee in fear of d. M161; wandering after d. as punishment Q503; wands of life and d. D1663.1; water of life and d. *E82; white rose the symbol of d. Z142.1; why men no longer know time of d. A1593; wicked flatter d. J814.4; wife dies so that husband's d. may be postponed T211.1; wife threatens husband with d. if he will not tell secrets T252.3; wild huntsman wanders (because of unshriven d.) *E501.3.4, (because he wished to continue hunting after d.) E501.3.7;

willingness to die for mate disappears at d. H1556.4.5; wise man humble in d. J912; witch causes animal d. G265.4.1; woman d. of all who behold her G264.1; woman dies on hearing of lover's d. T81.7; wraith announces d. E723.6; wraith tells of d. in family E723.4.5; youth saved from d. sentence R169.6.

Deaths come in threes D1273.1.1.3. — Choice of d. J216; mountain-man's six d. F460.2.12; riddle involving d. of elephant, snake, jackal H803; tragic d. on certain days of week N128.0.1.

Deathbed promise will be kept M251. — King prevented from d. disinheritance J1521.2.1.

Debate of animals as to which is the elder B841; of body and soul E727.1. — Listening to d. J1486; wise man beats heretic in d. K3.4.

Debating. — Escape by d. K622.1; senseless d. about usefulness J466; thief caught while d. theft J2136.5.1.1.

Debt confessed with cat's aid J1141.1.11; "if it is promised" P525.0.1. — Beheading as punishment for d. Q421.0.1; dead returns to repay money d. E351; deception in payment of d. K200ff.; debtor refuses to pay his d. *K231; dwarf conducts shepherd to hell to collect d. from nobleman F451.5.1.14; imaginary d. and payment J1551; lawyer tries to evade d. payment K1623; literal payment of d. (not real) K236; no return from dead until d. paid Q271.3; pretence of taking trip to return penny d. K2054.1; three thousand-year old d. J1384; wife demanded as d. payment T52.8.

Debts. — Christ has too many d. J2477; cutting wood burnt last year (paying old d.) H583.2.4; dead cannot rest until d. paid E415.4; notary invents d., collects them K441.2.1; paying unowed d. to save reputation J221.3; retorts concerning d. J1380ff.

Debtor clerics punished Q499.5; punished *Q271; gives self away J1141.1.3. — Insolvent d. drawn through streets Q473.0.1; man behind the tree threatens his d. K1971.2.

Debtor's corpse flogged Q491.2; wife demanded as payment T52.8; wraith seeks creditor E723.4.3.

Debtors do not forgive J2495.2. — Death feigned to test d. H1558.5.

Decalogue. — Words of d. legible on both sides F883.1.3.

Decapitated. — Ghost laid by d. body *E446.3; hero resuscitates d. princess E149.2; ogre d. G512.1.2.

Decapitation to prevent ghost's return E431.7.2; of princess by ogre G335; of victim by bloodhounds B17.1.2.1. — Beautification by d. and replacement of head *D1865.1; disenchantment by d. D711ff.; resuscitation by d. *E12; transformation by d. D566.4.

Decay. — Fish resist d. for year F986.4; magic d. of persons D2061.1.4; magic preservation from d. D2167ff.; reciting martyrology prevents body's d. V52.14; soul wanders until d. of corpse E722.3.2.

Decayed. — Earth from d. matter on primeval water A814.3.

Decaying. — Punishment: body not d. after death Q559.7.
Deceitful person's brains as cure D1515.4.6. — Why women are d. A1372.5.
Deceived. — Changeling d. into betraying his age F321.1.1; ghost d. E432; ogre d. into self-injury *G520ff.; ogre d. into releasing prisoner G560ff.
Deceiver falls into own trap *K1600—K1699. — To be beaten by d. of husband J1182.1; cynic and d. J1442.10; serpent as d. in paradise B176.1.1.
Deceiving. — Demons assume human form for d. F402.1.4; girls keep up appearances for d. suitors K1984; hireling d. master J1114.1; moon d. sun A753.3.1; prophecy: man d. many women M345.2; queen d. husband as revenge K2213.14; repeated transformations for d. wives D616; vow against d. benefactor M168.1; wife not d. husband for man she loves T211.8.
Deception K (entire chapter); by disguise or illusion K1800—K1899; punished *Q260ff., Q451.11.1; revealed in dream D1819.2. — Boy's d. of uncle and climbing tree X905.4.1; self-d. of the lowly J953.
Deceptive nocturnal noises K1887.2. — Repaying d. loan J1556; why animals are d. A2525; appearances d. U110ff.
Decision of lawsuit by child's wisdom J123; left to first person to arrive M92; made by contest H217. — Clever judicial d. J1170ff.; deity changes d. A196.2.1; senseless judicial d. M1.
Decisiveness of conduct J1040ff.
Decoration of house as wife test H473.5. — Origin of tribal d. A1687; stars hung as d. in heavens A763.2.
Decorative. — Origin of d. art A1465.
Decorators. — Thieves disguised as interior d. K311.7.
Decoy. — Capture by d. G514.7, K750ff.; magic objects as d. for pursuer D672.1; transformation to deer d. D643.2.
Decreasing. — Increasing-d. paradox task H1075.
Decree of gods irrevocable A196.2. — Child exposed to avoid death d. S329.1; favorable d. as reward Q116.
Decrees and judgments *M0—M99.
Deduction. — Extraordinary powers of d. H505.
Deductions, clever J1661.
Deed. — Only good d. unintentional V512.2; promise kept in d., not spirit M205.0.1; reward fitting to d. Q101.
Deeds of brownies F482.5; of the devil G303.9ff.; of dragons B11.6ff.; of evil spirits F402.1; of familiar spirits F403.2.3; of the gods A170ff.; of pygmies F535.5; rewarded *Q10—Q99; of vampires E251.3. — Evil d. of witches G260ff.; fairy minstrel lives among mortals to learn of their heroic d. F393.1; magic results from good d. D1799.6; magic reward for good d. D855.5; one wrong and five hundred good d. J1605; saint gives credit for good d. to another man Q42.8.

Deep. — Angel of the d. A421.0.1; extremely d. water F713.2.1; riddle: how d. is (the sea) H681.4, (the earth) H681.2; why hare's eyes are set d. A2332.4.1; why some fish swim d., others shallow A2238.3, A2444.1; wife shows husband d. water J1545.9.

Deepest. — What is d.? H643; wren goes d. into earth K17.1.1.

Deer aids man J461.4; becomes woman D314.1.3; belled and enclosed J1904.2.2; with candles atop antlers B253.6; captured in bird-net, water flows upstream J1534; as confederate of adulterous wife B598.2; with cross between horns B253.5; foster parent resuscitated E138.1; furnish bier and bear saint's corpse to church B256.3.1; with giant antler B15.3.3; with gold and silver horn B15.3.2; of gold and jewels possessing life D1620.2.3; hitched to wagon B558.4; in human form B651.6; lick saint's tomb daily B251.2.6; lures victim into demon's cave K714.7; lost through premature celebration J2173.4; in net freed by animals B545.1; offers herself instead of captured mate T211.1.4; paramour B611.5; with pearls around neck B105.2; persuaded to butt head into tree *K1058; pursued in wild hunt E501.5.5.2; steps on kitten (cumulative tale) Z49.6; summoned by singing D2074.1.1.2; thief keeps counting pieces J2136.5.3; thought to be man J1762.4; transformed to object D421.5; in Valhalla fills fountain A661.1.0.4. — Air-castle: to sell hide of sleeping d. J2061.3; brother transforms self to d. D647.1; capturing d. from herd watched by giant H1154.2; child of mortal and d. B635.3; color of d. A2411.1.6.5; crow, rat release d. from snare K642.1; destructive d. B16.2.7; devil as d. G303.3.3.2.8; dog's horns stolen by d. A2326.2.2; dragon as modified d. B11.2.1.10; enchanted d. reveals cave entrance D1552.9; enmity between d. (and leopard) A2494.2.4, (and terrapin) A2494.12.7; fairies have herds of d. F241.5; fancifully colored d. B731.7; first d. in Ireland A1875.0.1; friendship between d. (and tiger) A2493.17, (and fish) A2493.5; fruit tree grows from d. shot with fruit pits X1130.2; ghost as d. E423.2.6; girl transformed to d. D114.1.1.1; golden d. B102.5, (entices away guardians) K341.7.3; gold-making d. B103.1.4; helpful d. B443.1; hero licked by d. mother B635.3.1; hero son of d. A511.1.8.1; horns of d. as saint's bookholder B256.3; jackal persuades d. to steal K2037; journey on magic flying d. D1620.2.3.1; killing d. tabu C841.8; king of d. B241.2.10; lie about d. bag X1119.2; magic charm binds d. D1411.4; magic d. B184.4; man becomes d. and marries d. B648; man carried by d. B557.3; man transformed to d. D114.1.1; marriage to d. B601.10, (in human form) B651.5; marriage to man in d. form B641.2.1; marriage to woman in d. form B641.2; obstacle race between d., hare K11.9; origin of d. A1875; rain-withholding d. B192.2; reincarnation as d. E612.5; Satan disguised as d. K1823.5; Satan liberates caught d. G303.9.9.21; soul as d. E731.14; soul in d. E715.4.1; story told about d.: fool starts chase J1849.1.1; three-horned d. B15.3.1.1; trained d. drinks wine till he breaks his leg but thereafter abstains J133.3; transformation to d. (decoy)

D643.2, (which is devoured by dogs) Q415.1.1; treasure-d. B105.2; truth-telling d. B136; white markings on d. A2412.1.1; why d. has antlers A2326.1.1.1; why d. has white mark on nose A2335.2.1; why d. run, stop, and run on again A2461.4; why d. scent people from distance A2475.1; why d. tail tastes like liver A2378.9.4; witch as d. G211.2.4; witches drive herds of d. G249.1; woman begs hero for mercy for d. W133.2; woman flays running d. F664.1.1; woman's scented hair attracts d. T257.5.1; wrestling between porcupine, d. K12.5.

Deer's. — Monkey borrows d. tail A2241.11; Rakshasa in d. head swallows men G369.1.6; resuscitation by wax from d. ear E115.

Deer-heads. — Wild huntsmen with d. E501.7.2.

Defeat in battle P555, (as sign of world's end) A1084; personified Z132.2. — Clever person's d. pleases inferior J885; granary now haunted because of devil's d. G303.15.2; lance foretells owner's d. D1311.17.3; princess offered to man who can d. her in repartee H507.1; transformation to d. enemies D651ff.; trickster pretends d.: enemy attacked at ceremony K2366.1.

Defeated, see also **Conquered;** enemy turns friend P310.5; giant gives daughter to victor G510.1. — Enemy d. by storm D2141.2; enemies d. by magic object D1400.1ff.; ogre d. *G500—G599; witch d. G275ff.

Defeating a certain old woman (task) H1149.3; enemies as suitor task H335.4; or ridding oneself of fairies F380ff. — Disenchantment by d. enchanter in single combat D763.2.

Defecating. — Captor d. on smaller animal K683; child d. over ant hole K1461.2; crow d. on king L410.3; escape by d. ruse K551.16; tabu: d. while carrying divine image C56.1.

Defects. — Magic cure of physical d. *D2161.3; origin of physical d. A1338.

Defendant. — Riddle assigned d. in suit H542.1.

Defendants. — Animals as d. in court B272.

Defence against ghosts and the dead E430ff.; when one needs it most J673. — Animal's means of d. A2461ff.; eunuch's d. J1471; man killed in d. of sweetheart's honor T326.2; robber's d. for stealing from rich J1269.8; self-d. against many ships, men H1199.8; trumpeter's false d. J1465.

Defences. — Forethought in d. against others J670ff.; logically absurd d. J2233.

Defiling. — Fairies d. waters F369.2.

Deflowering. — King d. all twelve year old girls T161.0.1.

Deformed child exposed S325.0.1; child as hero L112.3; villain K2270ff. — Disguise as d. men to secure entertainment K1818.4; father kills d. children S11.3.2; man with d. head slays barbers K974; prophecy: unborn child to be d. M355; sight of d. witches causes man to release wife from spinning duty J51; three d. witches invited to wedding in exchange for

help *M233; three witches d. from much spinning *G201.1; wealthy girl marries d. philosopher T121.5; woman deserts husband for d. lover T232.

Deformity cured by waves of sea F959.2.1; as punishment Q551.8. — Curse of d. M442; magic poem causes d. D1403.1.1; person cured by repairing image that has same d. D2161.4.4; reproach of physical d. punished Q284; witch causes d. G269.11; woman takes on lover's d T24.4.

Defying. — Flying Dutchman sails because of d. storm E511.1.3; seaman d. God shipwrecked Q221.4.

Degraded gods become angels A52.0.2.

Deification as reward Q172.9.

Deity, see also Divinity, God; *A100ff.; abducts person R14; aids quest H1233.5; bestows immortality D1851.5; creates valleys from mountains F756.2.2; creates magic objects D803; cursed M414.13; in disguise tests saint H1573.2.2; forces dwarfs to flee F451.9.1.14; in frightening guises H1401; as ghostly rider E332.3.3.2; gives advice in dream J157.0.1; gives hero great powers L103; gives persecuted child flock of sheep S464; has power of self-transformation D630.4; as helper N817; humbled L410ff.; induces magic sleep D1964.6; makes king, wronged subjects change places Q7; orders islands created A955.0.1; performs tasks H975; rears abandoned child S353.1; rescues child R131.11.4; rewards animal for bringing him water A2221.11; saves person to be sacrificed S255; sends woman to tempt anchorite T332.1; settles disputes between races M4; transformed to jackal D113.4.1. — Animal characteristics established by d. A2286ff.; animals from parts of body of d. or saint A1725; attacking d. tabu C62; child of d. visits earth F31; cure by d. D2161.5.3; curse by disguised d. M411.21; disguise as d. K1828; insect points out d. by settling where he is H162.1; journey to see d. *F12; lightning produced by d. A1141.6; magic power from d. D1726; magic results produced in name of d. D1766.7.1; magic stolen from d. D861.0.1; mortal in guise of d D43; night from d. wrapping self in dark mantle A1174.4; plants from clothing of d. A2625; quest of a d. H1266; quest to see d. H1289.4; recognition of d. H45; sacrifice to d. V11.9; sham d. K1969.4; tabu to look at d. C311.1.8; tabu: neglect of service to d. C57ff.; tasks set by d. H927; topographical features caused by experiences of d. A901; woman rejects d. for human lover T75.0.2.

Deity's name breaks witch's spell G271.2.3. — Bird carries d. daughter A2223.2; moon under d. control A759.6; resuscitation by writing d. name E75.

Deities push sun at solstices A1157; test king H1574.3.0.2.

Delay. — Dying lawyer asks d. X315.1; long d. in punishing nobleman U34.1; magic object causes d. of pursuit *D1611ff.

Delaying birth until auspicious day T589.8. — Lover d. gift K1581.7.1; warrior refuses bribe for d. battle W33.2.

Deliberation, wisdom of J570ff.

Delicate girl lives only on perfume F647.12.
Deliverer in cradle D791.1.3; of curse M411. — Prophecy: child to become nation's d. M311.5.
Deliverer's. — Disenchantment by covering with d. clothing D789.1.
Delivery, see also **Birth, Childbirth;** boy frightened into giving up chickens K335.0.9.
Deluge, see **Flood.**
Demands of pregnant woman C152.2, T571. — Agreeing to d. while in danger J625; excessive d. to prevent marriage H301; impossible d. rebuked J1512; haughty mistress makes extravagant d. of lover L431.1; king's d. on guests P337; prudence in d. J530ff.
Demi-coq *B171ff., K481.
Demigod of underworld A305. — Luck determined by crooked-necked d. N125.2; topographical features caused by experiences of d. A901.
Demigods and culture heroes A500—A599; transform things at will so that they assume present form D683.1.
Demijohn. — Ghost rides d. E581.6.
Democratic. — Prince of d. tastes chosen J412.1.
Demon aids quest H1233.4.4; allowed on earth four times a year A106.2.1.2; becomes animal D102.1; becomes larger D486.1; cats infest castle F771.4.2.1; of consumption F493.1.1; drinks river dry J1791.3.2.1; eats sand in otherworld F171.8; enclosed in bottle *D2177.1, (released) R181; enters person and refuses to leave until wishes have been fulfilled K2385; as familiar spirit F403.2.2.5; frightened by own reflection K1715.1.3; gives self-transformation power D630.1.1; as guardian of treasure N571; guide to otherworld F159.4; lover F471.2.0.1; mistaken for goat J1769.3; -owned cows H1364; steals rescued woman R111.8.1; terrorized by small hero's bluff K1715.7. — Abduction by d. R11.2.2; being eaten by d. as punishment Q415.0.1; cannibal d. G11.15; corpse of d. turns to worm H47; eating food of d. forbidden C242; devastating d. kills and eats people G346.2; fury as d. entering man's heart Z123.1; house haunted by d. H1411.4; impregnation by d. T539.3; magic cloth pacifies d. D1409.2; magic herb keeps off d. lover D1386.2; magic knowledge of d. language D1815.3; magic power from d. D1721.1.2; magic strength from d. D1835.6; mortal as d. D47.1; nun eating unblessed lettuce eats d. G303.16.2.3.4; placenta becomes a d. T584.6; princess's loathsome disguise to avoid d.-lover T327.6; resuscitation by d. E121.6, (entering corpse) E121.6.1; soul carried off by d. E752.2; thief disguised as d. K311.5; transformation: d. (in human form) to worm D192.0.1; transformation: man to d. (spectre) D95; witches worship d. G243.4; woman gives birth to d. T556.
Demon's members cut off to prove killing H105.5. — Bone in d. stomach becomes a boy E149.1; resuscitation according to d. instructions E181.2.
Demons, see also **Spirits;** F402, *G302; on animal feet F401.3.0.1; assume human form for revenge D651.1.2; battle: hills torn up A964.3; bribe

trickster to leave their skins K1715.9; burn heretics at stake Q414.0.8; carry off king's soul F402.1.5.1; cause fog D1361.1.0.4; change size D631.4.3; guard marvelous garden F818.2; haunt castle F771.4.5; imprisoned by magic D2177.1.1; plague souls in hell E752.1.2.1; powerless over souls commended to God before sleep E754.1.1.1; propose hide and seek game to kill hero K869.2; set world on fire A1031.3; sleep twelve years F564.3.6; spread pestilence F493.4; in stone images exorcised D2176.3.3.1; as watchmen of the gods A165.4.1.—Death from fear of d. F1041.1.11.2; disenchantment by winning contest with d. D785.1; dream d. F471; drunken man left to temple d. K776.2; earth from saint's grave expels d. D1385.1; evil d. possess gamblers N1.0.1; foolish attempt of second man to overhear secrets from d. *N471; four d. in ring aid task H973.2; holy water disperses d. V132.2, D1385.15.1; invulnerability from d. D1841.9; journey to land of d. F124; Lucifer appointed chief for d. A1187; magic bell disperses d. D1385.12; magic left by frightened d. D859.7; magic sinks d. D1400.1.23.1; magic from temple d. D812.5.1; saint wrests soul from d. E756.4; slander: woman possessed of d. K2125; whomsoever d. curse is blessed M493.

Demonic. — Ground swallows d. wasp F949.1.1; madness from d. possession D2065.1.

Den. — Animal lured into lion's d. K714.6; fox sees all tracks going into lion's d. but none coming out J644.1; imprisonment in lion's d. R45.2; man unharmed in d. of animals B848.

Denial. — Devil tempts youth into d. of Virgin G303.9.4.8.

Dentist duped to pull out two teeth for one J2213.7.

Deo volente J151.4.

Departed, see also **Dead;** race A1401. — Girl masks as doctor to find d. lover K1825.1.4; gray hair the symbol of d. usefulness Z155; the Lord has d. (reports numskull on Palm Sunday) J1823.1.3.

Departing animal counsels man J135; house F1063; husband assigns his wife tasks H922. — Castle stands when all else d. F771.10; fairies d. F388; secret remedy revealed by d. animal N452.2; task left by d. husband for wife to accomplish H1187.

Departure of gods A192.2ff.; of wild hunt forced E501.17.8. — Culture hero's d. A560ff.

Dependence on self J1030ff.

Dependent. — Dwarf makes return of child d. upon guessing of riddle F451.5.15.2; life d. on external object or event *E765; one person's life d. on another's E765.5; strength of witches d. on their touching earth G221.2; why limbs d. on body A1391.1.

Deposed. — Gods d. for a time A173; father d. by son P236.4.

Depositors. — Three joint d. may have their money back when all demand it J1161.1.

Deposits. — Unjust banker deceived into delivering d. K1667.

Dervish as helper N844; who stops work shown his mistake J702.1. — Advice from d. J152.2.

Descendant. — Mule as d. of king's war-horse J954.1; refusal to eat fifth d. of stolen cow F647.10.

Descendants. — Curse: d. of nine robbers never to exceed nine M461; curse: d. not to multiply M461.1; curse: d. to be unshapely M442.1; fairies as d. of early race of gods F251.1; man meets his future d. F1099.8; man's d. shall serve brother's P251.5.6; prophecy: preeminence of man's d. M310.1.1; royal d. as reward Q112.0.7; sacrifice so d. may be kings W215.3; tribe d. of one woman survivor A1006.7.

Descending. — Demigods d. from heaven A513.1; god d. from heaven A171.0.3; god awaits spirits d. to hell A317.

Descent of chimney by fairies F275; of first man to earth A1230ff.; to lower world of dead *F81; of man from animals A1224; of star as human being A762; from tree impossible D1413.1. — Animal d. slander K2115.1; extraordinary d. into ocean F1022; shooting stars' d. to earth A788.

Description. — Love from d. T11.1; recognition by d. of object H16.

Desecrated altar bleeds F991.4.1; well overflows F933.6.1.

Desecration of God's name tabu C51.3.1. — Dwarfs emigrate because of d. of holy day F451.9.1.11; punishment for d. of holy places *Q222; transformation of lovers into lion and lioness because of d. of temple Q551.3.1.

Desecrator. — Church d. cannot rest in grave E412.6.

Desert demons' abode G302.5.1. — Abandonment in d. S144; cultivated places become d. F969.5; fire pillar protects in d. D1380.1.1; following luminous tree in d. K1886.1.1; miracles in d. cease F900.3.1; monk goes into d. to avoid women T334.1; origin of d. A957; river at d. travelers' prayer D2151.2.5.1; treachery punished by banishment to d. isle Q431.2.2; wild hunt appears at d. spot E501.12.7.

Deserts. — Angel of the d. A419.2.1.

Deserted city F766ff.; daughter's good fortune discovered by accident N732.2; wife chokes departing husband K951.0.1. — Adopted child d. when own child born T674; maiden disenchanted, d., and refound D795; man d. by fairy mistress F302.2.1, F302.3.4.3; objects found in d. castle H1239.2; poor boy finds treasure in d. city N534.5; unseen hands serve in d. castle H1239.2.

Deserting. — Lover d. woman K2232.1; man d. wife for fairy F302.5.0.1; punishment for d. fairy mistress Q247; soldiers d. to enemy king K2365.3; vow on d. wife on wedding day M149.4.

Designated. — Favorite for election to office d. by Virgin Mary V261; pope d. by sound of bell D1311.12.1.

Designs. — Origin of d. on cloth A1465.3.2.

Desire, see also **Sex;** for adultery punished Q241.1. — Chaste sleeping with girl to signify d. T356; choice between d., duty J233; conception

after reciprocal d. T514; punishment for d. to murder Q211.8; sexual d. induced by magic D1355, D1900; what women most d. (quest) H1388.1.

Desires, see also **Wishes.** — Cow grants all d. B184.2.1.3; sea yields people's d. F931.9.2; telling story to allay woman's d. K2111.0.1.

Despair. — Fool kills himself in d. because a sparrow has taken one grain from his field J2518.1; man in d. digging his own grave finds treasure N545.

Dessert. — Countryman's ignorance of d. J1742.3.1; maid forced to whistle as she brings in d. W152.12.3.

Destination of emigrating dwarfs F451.9.2; of the soul E755ff. — Angels mark saint's d. V238.3.

Destined hero Z254. — Treasure opens itself for d. hero N552.1.

Destiny better than work, show, or speculation N142. — Deity ascertains baby's d. A189.7; fairies control mortal's d. F312.2; fates allot d. A463.1.2; giant as clerk to God of D. N111.5; prophecies concerning country's d. M356; stone of d. H171.5.

Destitute parents abandon children S321.

Destroyed. — Contract with the devil d. M218; criminal's property d. Q486; druid d. by saint's power V229.6.3; dupe's property d. K1400—K1499; fairy queen's beauty temporarily d. by intercourse with mortal F304.2; home of dwarfs is endangered or d. F451.4.4ff.; magic object d. D866; treacherous priests prolong mass while city is d. K2354.

Destroying festivity purchases by mistake J1846. — Disenchantment by d. covering of enchanted person D720ff., (by d. enchanter) D763, (by d. skin) D721.3; dungbeetle keeps d. eagles' eggs L315.7; numskull d. own property J2461.1.8; objects' attempt at d. humanity A1009.2; philosopher stops king from d. city J1289.10; tabu: d. animal skin of enchanted person too soon *C757.1.

Destruction of an alp F471.1.2.2; by devil at night of what is built by day G303.14.1; of enemy's weapons J621; of fish and nets by strong man as fisherman F614.5; of friendship by marriage T201; of hunting party by devil with terrible wind G303.20.2; of mortal's work by dwarfs F451.5.2.5; of obstacles by magic staff D1562.1; of plants by strong man as gardener F614.3; of property as punishment Q595. — Angel of d. A521.5; curse of d. on city Q556.0.2; fitting d. of property as punishment Q585; god of d. A488; hospitality of a citizen saves a city from d. Q152.1; reward: being saved from d. of city Q150.1.1; upon d. of pestilence-spirit plague ceases F493.3.1; transformation by d. of enemy's property D651.3.

Destructive fairy drink F367; magic object tried out on inanimate object K525.8; magic powers *D2050—D2099.

Details. — Fool admits crime but pleads mistakes in d. of accusation J2499.3; quarrel and fight over d. of air-castles J2060.1; witness discredited by inability to tell d. J1154.

Detaining. — Forgotten fiancée reawakens husband's memory by d. lovers through magic D2006.1.1; ghosts d. wandering soul E721.4.

Detected. — Criminal d. by having child hand knife to him H211; devil d. by his hoofs G303.4.5.3.1; devil, d., goes up chimney in smoke G303.17.2.1; ghost d. E436; poison d. by magic object *D1317.0.1; thief d. *K420ff., (by psalter and key) H251.3.2, (by sieve and shears) H251.3.3.

Detection of hypocrisy K2060ff.; of perjury by magic spring H251.3.9; through ruse J1141.11; and wounding of wife's lover by broken glass K1565. — Cleverness in d. of truth J1140ff.; magic d. of crime *D1817ff.; thief escapes d. *K400ff.; transformation to escape d. D671.0.2.

Detective. — Thief believes d. is mind-reader J1141.1.9.

Determination of luck or fate N120ff.; of the months A1160f.; of night and day A1172; of seasons A1150ff.; of span of life A1320ff.; of world center A1181; of world quarters A1182.

Determined. — King's successor d. by questions asked H508.1; reincarnation in form d. at death E602.

Dethronement. — Prophecy: king's d. by grandson M311.1.

Detonation hurls ships out to sea F1078. — Wild hunt heralded by d. E501.13.1.1.

Devas. — Riddle about king of D. H827.

Devastating animals B16, G350.1, *H1362; monster G346, H1471; swine sent by demon B16.1.4. — Adulteress returns from dead as d. dragon E263; bolt from heaven kills d. animal F981.4; fairies as d. animals kill flocks F366.3; fairies exile d. host F349.3; hero overcomes d. animal G510.4; magic object d. country D1408; vow against d. country M168.

Device. — Noblemen quarrel over a d. J552.1.

Devil (Satan) *G303ff. See, in addition to the following, the extensive list of motifs assembled at G303.—Devil and the ark *G303.23f., *K485; betrays self to woman paramour D1386.2.1; broods over woman A1371.4; chases ghost into chapel R325.1; claims debtor when inscription rots K231.12.1; comes to rendezvous instead of lover K1317.10; decides to leave possessed man of his own accord J829.2; drops stones A977.3; exorcised by "Ave" V254.4; finishes stones D2066.1; in form of dragon B11.1.4; gets shadow instead of man F1038.2; gives smith lantern to light way between heaven and hell A2817.1; gives wishing power D1720.1.1; gives witch familiar G225.0.2; and God torment each other A63.4.1; goes to confession V29.8; hidden in cup of liquor B483.0.1; as husband eats corpses G20.1; impersonates woman's maid at toilette Q331.2.1.1; knows how far it is from heaven to earth for he has fallen this distance H682.1.10; prophesies in enchanted castle H1411.3; runs hands through hair, coins fall D1454.1.1.1; says that his deeds are strong even if not fair J246.1; in serpent form tempts first woman (Satan and Eve) A63.6; sows stones A975.1; substitutes himself for new-born child T684; as suitor assigned tasks H335.0.3; as suitor must build bridge,

dam H1131.2; takes man waiting for water to become wine D477.1.1; throws stones A977.2; transformed to animal D102; turns object to stone A977.4; "won't take me" Q333.1. — Allegorical game of witch, d., maiden, church Z178; baker and d. walking together P442.1; banished d. appears at dark of moon A106.2.1.1; bargain with d. *M210; combat between Thundergod and d. A162.3; creation of mouse by d. in ark A1853.1; dead priest saves gambler from d. E341.5; dog lets d. into church to steal: rewarded with dog-skin A2229.2; eavesdropping man in disguise as d. killed unwittingly by daughter's lover N322.1; fasting against the d. P623.0.2; formula-tale saves girl from d. K555.2.1; girl refuses to dance with d. until well dressed K1227.3.1; gnats created by. d. to worry God A2033.0.1; god cheats d. at mowing K42.2.1; god plagues d. with fleas A2032.4; hermit deceived by the d. kills his own father K943; journey to hell to recover contract from d. F81.2; lakes made by d. A920.1.10; liar escapes from d. H1318; magic circle protects from d. D1381.11; magic journey: man carried by d. D2121.5; magic object recovered with help of d. D885; man sells soul to d. *M211; man thought to be d. J1786; marriage ring protects from d. D1385.3; monk leaves monastery after seeing d. there; sees scores of them in world U230.0.1; naked lover as d. in sooty barrel K1555.2; owner frightened away by thief disguised as d. K335.0.12; payment of money to the d. refused, since debtor hears that the d. is now dead K231.4; punishment for yielding to temptation by d. Q233; putting the d. in hell: seduction trick K1363.1; quest to d. for riddle answer H1278; revolting d. banished to hell A106.2.1; Robert the D. kills wet-nurses T614; saint binds d. with her hair D1831.1; soul carried off by d. E752.2; suitors as corpse, angel, and d.K1218.4; tabu: offending d. C45; thief disguised as d. K335.0.12; thief masked as d. bought off by owner K152; three-night watch over grave to guard man from d. H1463; Virgin forbids d. to take robber saying "Aves" V254.8; Virgin Mary rescues man attacked by d. V264; Virgin Mary substitutes for woman whom husband has pledged to d. K1841.3; wheel buried in doorstep to prevent work of d. D1385.10; witch carried off by d. G275.1; witch struggles with d. G299.2; witches dance with d. G247.1; witches in league with d. G226; worship of d. V1.2.2.

Devil's cows one-horned A2286.2.3; footprint A972.2.2; likeness insulted, punishment C45; likeness kills beholder Q338.2. — Ghost of d. concubine E411.2.2; marks on fish from d. fingerprints A2217.3.2; vision of earth in d. snares V513.2.

Devils instead of angels visit woman who has forgotten God in her prosperity Q559.1; tormenting sinners in hell E755.2.7. — Creation of d. A63; foreigners' heads exchanged with d. A1610.1.1; holy men keep d. under control G315; indentions on rocks from footprints of d. A972.2; magic horseshoe keeps off d. D1385.9; man deceives, escapes d. K611.4; saint dispels pagan d. V356.1; seven d. wives attempt resuscitation ritual K113.0.1; youth who had never seen a woman: "the d." T371.

Devotions. — Stream becomes hot in which saint performs his ascetic d. F932.3.

Devoured. — Infant's flesh d. by maddened women N325.2; lover d. by Lamia G262.0.1.1; offspring d. by first parents A1277.1; whoever breaks devil's pact d. M219.4.

Devouring, see also **Cannibals.** — Cat d. flesh of man's legs B16.1.1.3; creator tries d. his son, the culture hero A71; dragon d. children B11.10.3; dogs d. souls in hell A689.8.1; eclipses caused by monster d. sun or moon A737,1; ghosts d. girl E251.3.1.1; giant d. people G11.2.1; mother d. her children when they grow up (ocean and rivers) H734; resuscitation of animals d. each other E32.2.

Devout. — Priest dreams all d. women in hell X438.1.

Dew of blood F962.4.2; in footprints reveals trail R268. — Absence of d. identifies woman-flower H63.1; Adam creates five devils by wetting five fingers with d. G303.1.5; celestial d. transforms D572.7; conception by drinking d. T512.7; cure by washing in d. D2161.4.14.3; filling pot with d. H1129.4; magic d. *D902.2; resuscitation by d. E80.4.1; snake sucks poisonous d. from grass B765.3; origin of d. A1132; sweet d. F962.7.1.

Dextrotsum circuit D1381.25.1, D1791.1.

Diabetes. — Rascals sew man's trousers leg till he thinks that he has d. J2317.1.

Diabolical, see also **Devil;** person never sleeps F564.1.

Diadem, magic D1079.2.

Diagnosis. — Extraordinary d. F956; imitation of d. by observation: ass's flesh J2412.4; patient laughs so at foolish d. that he gets well N641; physician killed for fatal d. P424.3; pretended d. entirely from urinalysis K1955.2.

Dialect. — Criminal confesses because of misunderstanding of d. N275.2; girl possessed by ghost speaks in unknown d. E725.2.

Dialects. — Parable on learning d. J98.

Diamond castle F771.1.5.1; charms serpents D1442.11; kingdom F707.3; in meat carried to eagle's nest N527.1; reveals underground palaces D1551.7.1; -toothed ogre G363.3; tree F811.1.8; works by being pressed D1662.3. — Clusters of d. and emerald grapes F813.2.1; dress of gold, silver, and d. bells F821.3; inscribed d. recalls lover T56.3; magic d. opens tank passage D1551.7; magic d. reveals palace D1557.3; mountain formed of d. F752.3.2; stealing d. from elephant's forehead H1151.6.1; unbreakable d. penetrates iron F826.3; witnesses make image of d. J1154.2; worthless glass sold as d. K142, K451.4.

Diana as leader of wild hunt E501.1.8.

Dice made from graveyard bones N1.2.2; split so saint wins soul E756.4.1. — Charm aids d. game D1407.4; defeating bride at d. H332.1.2.1; game won with loaded d. K92.2; girl plays d. with suitors K1237; magic d.

*D1284; man cheats god at d. A1893; soul in d. E711.12; throwing certain number on d. proves chastity H413.5.

Die. — Broken d. save man at gambling N1.2.1.

Dick Whittington M312.

Dieb, zögernder J2136.5.1.

Diet. — Origin of d. during confinement A1565; people of unusual d. F561ff.

Difference in animal natures overlooked J2211. — Counterquestion: d. between you and cushion H571.1; the d. between poor man and rich (riches) H875.

Different. — Birds of d. habits unfriendly J416.1; dog leader fears defeat because his forces are of d. breeds J1023; king in red: courtiers in d. colors (riddle) H731.3; porridge eaten in d. rooms J2167; transformation to d. (race) D30ff., (sex) *D10ff., (social class) D20ff.

Differentiation of peoples A1600—A1699.

Difficult. — Riddles of d. calculations H680—H719; transformation to reach d. place D641; transformation to escape d. situation D642; treatment of d. guests J1563ff.; why certain languages are d. A1616.1.

Difficulties. — Consider d. of course you are about to undertake J751.

"Dig here!" inscribed on (image with pointing finger) F855.1, (stone over treasure) N535.

Digger, mighty F639.1.

Digging child from ground T545; first wells A1429.3.1; forbidden *C523; magic object D848; a pond quickly (task) H1105; underground bed for Rhine F451.5.22; without hands X1725. — Angel aids d. for water V232.3.1; buried man d. self out X1731.2.1; disenchantment by d. D789.8; dupe dies of exhaustion from d. K1061; dwarfs d. for treasure F451.6.9; fairies d. for treasure F244.5; lakes from d. of primeval ox A920.1.2; man in despair d. his own grave finds treasure N545; murder discovered while d. house N271.7; numskull d. up a well J1933; rivers from d. of primeval ox A934.1; sky window from d. plant in upper world *F56.1; springs' origin: deity's d. A941.5.7; tabu: d. in churchyard C93.3; thieves d. field for gold K2316; treasure found while d. N534.7.

Dilating. — Sea-serpent d. and contracting B91.5.1.

Diminishing number of sacred days forbidden C58.1. — Goods magically d. D2089.7.

Dining. — Lie: great d. quarters X1032; sun, moon and wind d. with thunder, lightning A153.3.2.

Dinner with the dead (Festin de Pierre) E238. — Fairies' yearly d. to haymakers F343.17; prince preparing giant d. K567.1; why d. time comes soon in mountains J2276.1.

Diocletian. — Earthquake in palace of D. V222.9.

Dipping out sea with spoon (task) H1143; rod D1314.2; water without wetting dipper H1046.1. — Legitimacy of children tested by d. them in river H222.1.

Directed. — Blinded trickster d. by trees *D1313.4; fugitive d. but enemy misdirected by (tree) D1393.4, (crane) R246; hero d. on journey by princess J155.1; mortals d. to treasure by dwarfs F451.5.1.9.

Direction of river's flow magically reversed D2151.2.1. — Bird shows d. by singing B151.2.0.3; forbidden d. of travel C614.1ff.; hero in womb indicates d. for mother to take A511.1.2.2; looking in certain d. forbidden C330ff.; magic object obtained by reaching in certain cardinal d. D859.3; reed as d. finder D1313.5.2; saint's girdle causes tree to fall in right d. D1549.2; wild hunt courses in particular d. E501.14.2.

Directions for getting pay given in return for directions for healing J1551.4; on quest given by sun, moon, wind, and stars H1232. — Child promised to devil for d. out of woods when father is lost S226; "don't start from here" (d.) J1648; earth scattered in a circuit or in four d. on primeval water A814.6; formula: cardinal d. Z71.2.1; land of dead in one of the cardinal d. E481.6.

Dirk stuck into thigh in order to keep from sleeping H1482.

Dirt transformed to pepper D452.4.1. — Birds fill sea with d. A1028.2; magic d. protects D1380.9; man from d. mixed with creator's blood A1211.1; man from d. rubbed from creator's body A1211.5; "where did d. go when canal dug?" J1309.3.

Dirtiness punished *Q322.

Dirty boy as hero L112.4. — Numskulls' efforts not to get d. J2163.1; pretending pants are d. to steal them K344.3; riding d. on horse tabu C891.1; too d. to eat K553.6.

Disability. — Fairies' physical d. F254.1; humor of d. *X100—X199.

Disagreeable child surpasses likeable one L155; tasks set hero H931.2; youth favorite of Fortune N173.

Disappearance of devil G303.17; of fairy gift when tabu broken F348.0.1; of fairy house at dawn F221.1; of fairies when some name or ceremony of the Christian Church is used F382; of fairy in form of a cloud F234.3.1; of fish from sea as punishment for woman's having washed a child with a fish F931.2; of giants F531.6.12.1; of helpful animal when tabu is broken C935; of ill-gotten gains Q552.18; of person caused by magic object D1405; of phantom house at dawn F771.6; of supernatural wives T111.0.1; of trees at sunset F811.11; of treasure C401.3, D1555.3, N553.2, N557. — Appearance and d. of garment in reply to command D2188.1.1; extraordinary underground d. F940ff.; fitting d. of property as punishment Q585; magic d. D2095, *D2188; phenomena at d. of wild hunt E501.16ff.

Disappearing lake F934.4; otherworld island F134.2; sword F833.9. — Animal d. into lake F989.13; magic object d. D867; men d. every night D2087.4.

Disappointed lover becomes a wild man in the woods T93.1; lover induces magic sleep D1964.2. — Curse by d. witch *G269.5.

Disappointment with religious order V475.3. — Clerical vows after d. in love V472; prostitution after love d. T450.2.
Disar, worship of V1.2.3.
Disarming of officer by sentry J1526.1. — Escape by d. K630ff.; prevention of hostilities by d. suspect J626; victim lured into d. K818.
Disaster, see also **Calamity, Catastrophe;** because tabu broken C984; from following instructions J2465ff. — Caesar's scorn of his wife's advice leads to d. J155.3; devil appears to warn of impending d. to a house G303.6.2.6; immunity from d. as reward Q150ff.; presence of cursed person brings d. on land M491; wild hunt as omen of d. E501.20.1.
Disasters from fool's lack of forethought J2661.4. — National d. occur at same date N128.1.
Disbelief. — Tabu: d. in religious teachings C61.
Discarding, see **Disposal.**
Disciple stays in cheap-price country T342.1.1. — Body of devil's d. removed from coffin M219.2.5; greedy d. ignores warning, condemned as thief N347.7; judge becomes prophet's first d. J1169.8; master rescues d. R167; master tests d. by river plunge H1561.10.
Disciples. — Dying hero's promise to d. M257.1; wild animals as saint's d. B251.2.7.
Discomfiting. — Husband d. wife K1569.4; punishment escaped by d. condemner J1182; rivals d. each other T92.11.1.
Discomfiture, humor of *X0—X99.
Discomfort. — Magic d. *D2063; magic object protects from d. on journey D1384ff.
Discontent of pine-tree: cause of pine needles A2723.1. — Plant punished for d. A2723ff.
Discouragement. — Absurd extreme of d. J2518.
Discourtesy to God punished A2231.1ff., Q221.1; punished Q327; toward priest tabu C94.1.3. — Animals from men transformed for d. to God (Jesus) *A1715.2.
Discovered. — Devil d. by his hoofs G303.4.5.3.1; heroine in menial disguise d. in her beautiful clothes: recognition follows H151.6; treasure magically d. D2101; secret of strength treacherously d. *K975.
Discovery of abbot's (abbess's) incontinence brings permission to monks (nuns) to do likewise K1274; of devil by God G303.1.2ff.; of gold by saint's bachall *D1314.3; of new wonder before eating C287; of ring thief H1199.9.1; of treasure N530ff.; of treasure brings luck N135.2.1; of wife's adultery by husband K1550.1. — Accidental d. of crime N610ff.; lover's gift regained: accidental d. of identity K1581.4; magic d. of desired place D1816ff.
Discrediting. — Clever d. of testimony *J1151ff.
Discretion J500—J599.
Discussion by symbols H607ff. — Demons at academic d. G302.5.3; repartee based on doctrinal d. J1262ff.

Disdainful. — Devil marries d. girl G303.12.5.2; fleeing wolf d. of dog J953.5; man put in moon for d. sacrifice A751.1.3; speaking to king makes man d. of own family W165.1.

Disease, see also **Illness, Sickness;** healed as reward Q161.2; transferred to object D2161.4.2ff. — Bathing in "d.-water" K1077; cure by transferring d. to animal *D2161.4.1; cures by transferring d. to dead E595; death from d. for breaking tabu C929.2; death, return to life rids d. E598; demon causes d. F402.1.5; devil strikes dead with d. G303.20.4; fairies cause d. F362; foul d. for persecuting Christians Q570.1; god of d. A478; Leviathan's gorge spreads d. B16.4.1; magic control of d. D2162; magic cure for specific d. D2161.1; magic mouse causes d. B183.1.2; magic object controls d. *D1500ff.; origin of d. A1337; particular d. caused by breaking tabu C941; punishment: death from unknown d. Q551.6.0.2; relics of saint cure d. V221.0.1; remedies worse than the d. J2100ff.; sacrifice as protection against d. S276; spirits of d. F493.1; taking clerical vows heals d. V471; why d. created L482.5; woman prays for d. to repel lover T327.2.

Diseases to combat overpopulation P721; cured at particular time D2161.6.

Diseased child exposed S325. — Ascetic prays to become d. V462.5.0.1; queen's illicit passion for d. man T481.2.

Disenchanted. — Cannibal d. by overcoming it G33.1; enchanted heroine recognized when seen temporarily d. H151.6.1; person d. from animal retains tail H643; recognition of d. person by ornaments under his skin H61.2; transformed fairy warriors d. F383.5; transformed person d. upon admission to girl's bed K1361.1.

Disenchanting. — Fairy d. mortal wife F302.3.2.2; hero d. vanished wife R133.1; journey for d. captives H1385.0.1; treasure from d. N591.

Disenchantment D700—D799; for breaking tabu C968; by dwarfs F451.3.3.4; fails D791.3; by faithfulness of others D750ff.; by removing (destroying) covering of enchanted person D720ff.; by rough treatment D710ff.; by submission D730ff.; as task H1199.5; and transformation at will D630ff. — Marriage to prince as reward for his d. T67.1.

Disfavor. — Images at church turn backs as mark of d. D1639.3.

Disfiguration of perjurer by spring H251.3.9; for speaking falsely H244; by witch's kisses G264.2.

Disgorged, see also **Vomited.** — Animal's broken heart d. F981.6.1; swallowed person d. F914, F912.3.

Disgorging. — Cows d. rice K366.1.4; saintly babe d. unclean food V229.2.2.

Disgrace. — Fairies freed of d. by blood bath F259.2; foolish priest pushed into the water wishes he had drowned so that congregation would have been in d. J2185; "shame and d." C929.1.

Disgraceful journey through streets as punishment Q473.

Disguise as girl to avoid execution K514; as man to escape lover K1236;

as pilgrim to enter enemy's camp K2357.2. — Beggar in d. obtains alms three times from same person K1982; brother in d. aids quest H1233.2.2; capture by d. as dead *K751; confederate in d. helps escape K649.7; deception by d. *K1810ff.; deity in d. tests saint H1573.2.2; devil in d. hunts souls E752.1.1; examine strange country in d. J21.43; father feigning death returns in d. and seduces daughter T411.1.2; fairies in d. F237; guest in d. P322.2; herdsman in d. as abbot answers questions H561.2; heroine in menial d. discovered in her beautiful clothes H151.6; king in d. (to observe subjects) P14.19, (to learn subjects' secrets) N467; loathly husband god in d. D733.3; lover in d. abducts beloved K1371.4; man knowing of murder plot against his friend assumes d. and is killed in his place P316.1; princess's loathsome d. to avoid demon-lover T327.6; recognition through imperfect d. H151.6.2; scorned lover in d. as rich man cheats his scornful mistress L431.2; seduction by d. *K1310ff.; theft by d. as master of the house K362.4; thief's d. as woman K419.2; vanquished ruler in d. gets audience with victor J829.3; woman in d. (becomes pope) K1961.2.1, (overcomes enemies) K778.1.

Disguises. — Escape by successive d. K533; hero in successive d. rescues lady R169.1.

Disguised flayer dresses in skin of his victim K1941; hero attacks enemy at feast K913; hero's hair discovered H151.13; husband visits his wife K1813; god chosen as husband T111.1.1; king punished by peasant P15.1; king recognized by habitual speech H38.1; man recognized by dog H173; man steals back magic object D882.4; mistress identified by chalk marks left on back by lover H58.1; trickster beaten by man he is trying to frighten K1682; wife helps husband escape from prison R152.1; wife thwarts husband J1112.1.1. — Bull recognizes d. princess H162.3; capture by hiding in d. objects K753; Christ d. V211.2.1.1; combat of d. friends P314; father-in-law d. as beggar to test bride's kindness H384.1; devil in form of woman introduces men d. as women for seduction of impious nuns G303.3.1.12.1; fool d. as king, killed N338.2; husband tempted by wife d. in fine clothes T224; lover d. in humiliation K1214.1.1; man d. as woman enters princess's room K1343.2; owner frightened away by thief d. as devil K335.0.12; princess d. to flee man T323.1; one lover d. and carried out of house by other K1517.1.1; princess d. as man accused of adultery with queen K2113; recognition of d. princess by bee lighting on her H162; rescuer d. as officer saves prisoner K649.2; stolen animal d. as person so that thief may escape detection K406; trickster d. to escape notice of creditors K237; villain d. as ascetic or nun K2285; voice d. to lure victim G413; wise men d. as peasants J31.1.

Disgust. — Dumbness from d. F1041.19.

Disgusting. — Hero with d. habits L114.5; woman has d. lover T232.

Dish which husband detests and wife keeps serving him T255.5. — Deaf husband orders deaf wife to prepare certain d. X112; magic d. *D1172;

man transformed to d. D251; quest for best-cooked d. H1305.2; reincarnation as d. E633; silver d. becomes wooden D475.3.5; society like a d.: must be mixed J81.1; what is in the d. (poor Crab) N688.

Dishes become jewels D475.4.3; of the same flavor J81. — Bonga lends d. to mortals F343.6; numskull throws the d. out J1831; securing d. locked in vault H1199.15; trolls' d. golden F455.4.2.2.

Dishonesty W157ff.; habit can't be broken U138.

Dishonor. — Death preferred to d. *J227.2; fairies revenge for d. F361.9; seduction by threatening d. K1397.

Disinheriting. — King prevented from d. adopted son J1521.2.1.

Disintegration (man eats himself up or dismembers himself) F1035.

Disliked child surpasses likeable one L155. — Why animal is d. A2522ff.

Dislodge. — Recognition by unique ability to d. sword H31.1.

Dislodged. — Wild huntsman's dog cannot be d. from house it has entered E501.15.6.5.

Dismembered corpse E422.1.10. — Body d. so soul cannot return E721.1.2.3.1; bones of d. person assembled and buried V63; foes' corpses d. P555.2; perjurer d. by lion H251.1.1; slain person d. S139.2; tabu to look at d. woman C312.2.3.

Dismemberment before burial V61.4.2; of self F1035. — Rejuvenation by d. D1884, D1885.1, resuscitation by d. *E14.

Dismissal with a pittance after years of service W154.1; of mass early cheats devil of reward G303.16.16.

Dismounting from horse forbidden *C521; from magic sack tabu C521.1. — Do not cross bridge without d. from your horse J21.7; shortsightedness about d. J2171.6.

Disobedience *W126ff.; forbidden C31.3, C836; to God punished Q221.5, V245.1; of helpful animals injunctions brings disaster B341; punished *Q325. — Adam's d. blamed H1557.2; animal characteristics as punishment for d. A2234ff.; banishment because of d. Q431.3; burial alive as punishment for d. to king Q456.0.3; flogging as punishment for d. to rulers Q458.0.2; permanent sign of d. for breaking tabu *C910ff.; plant punished for d. A2722ff.; transformation for d. D517; vessels burst and reveal d. D1318.12.1.

Disobedient child burned S326.1; children cast forth S326; wife T254. — Dead mother appears and makes d. child eat fatal serpent Q593; teacher curses d. pupils P343.

Displaced. — Proud king d. by angel L411.

Display of murdered man's head before his own house S139.2.1. — Plain people become rulers, put on d. W116.3; woman's vain d. punished Q331.2.1.

Displaying self as punishment Q473.6. — Seduction by d. obscene likeness K1385.

Displeasure. — Transformation to show d. D659.3.

Disposal of cast-off wife S430ff.; of clothing before winter over unwise

J731; of changeling F321.1.4. — Reward for d. of purchased cobold F481.0.1.2.1; treacherous d. of true bride by false K1911.2.

Disposition of animals A2520ff. — Magic object changes person's d. D1350ff.

Dispute at creation of sun A716; won by wise men disguised as peasants J31.1. — Angel settles d. between saints V229.18; pagan in d. with Christian stricken dumb V352; saint's d. with devil G303.16.11.5; settling dowry d. J1678; unjust umpire decides a religious d. K451.1.

Disputes. — Deity settles d. between races M4.

Disregarding advice of your enemy J646; facts J1850—J1999. — Thunder slays those d. him Q552.1.0.2.

Disrespect to God brings death A1335.6.1; punished Q395; for the sacrament J1261.2.

Disrobing woman outwits robber K551.4.3. — Hero attacked by d. female's confederate K832.3; men d. report they have been attacked K1087.0.1; woman d. to attract enemy's attention Q411.4.2.

Dissatisfaction *W128ff.

Dissatisfied fir-tree finds its own needles best A2723.1; workmen exchange work U136.1. — Fairy d. with fairyland leaves to live among mortals F393.0.1.

Dissolute. — Devil in church fills his sack with d. songs G303.24.1.5.

Dissolving. — Ashes d. animals F981.5.

Distaff sticks to hand as punishment Q559.5.

Distance of otherworld F137. — Animal travels extraordinary d. B744; cooking rice, warming man at long d. J1191.7; devil kept at d. by answering his riddles H543.1; fairy mistrel's music heard at d. F262.3.3; false judgment of d. in mountains J2214.12; formula of d. Z92; giant steps prodigious d. F531.3.5; magic journey by making d. vanish D2121.4; ogress extends limbs any d. G365.2; person sees great d. F642.8; riddles of d. H680ff.

Distant. — Bringing documents from d. city in one day (task) H1107; bringing water from d. mountain more quickly than witch (task) H1109.1; fox in swollen river claims to be swimming to d. town J873; magic knowledge of events in d. place D1813ff.; magic power to see d. objects K1825.2; quest to d. sage for advice H1393.

Distilling learned from devil A1456; of sustenance for saint by magic lime tree D1472.1.3.1.

Distorted. — Punishment: face d. Q551.8.7.

Distracting. — Girl d. opponent, lover wins game K92.3; priest sells d. donkey J357.

Distress. — Alleged messenger from relatives in d. given goods J2326.4; don't lean on relatives in d. J21.44; friend helps friend in d. N455.8.

Distribution and differentiation of peoples A1600—A1699; of man's body by animals F989.10; of tribes A1620ff.; of wit by Hermes L301.

Distrusted. — God d. when he can be brought by a man J1261.2.2.

Disturbing of grave punished E235.6. — Devil d. churchgoers G303.24.1.7.1; wild huntsman wanders for d. church service E501.3.8.

Ditch. — Devil digs d. G303.9.1.8; food lures victim into d. K811.5; ghost throws man into d. E542.3; jumping ocean d. F1071.2; king in battle hides in d. P12.5.1; miserly friar stays in d. W153.5; sun will lock moon in deep d. A1066.

Ditches. — Fairies dance in d. F261.3.4.

Divan. — Magic d. D1154.4; speaking, walking d. *D1310.8.

Diver, see also **Diving;** robbed K341.4. — Creation of d. (bird) A1975; nest of d. A2431.3.2, A2238.4; earth d. A812; mighty d. F639.2; lie: remarkable d. X965; why d. (loon) holds legs backward A2215.6, A2371.2.9; why d. always looks at sea A2275.5.3, A2471.4.

Divided blanket J121. — Booty d. by lion J811.1.1; identification by matching parts of d. token H100ff.; money d. into three parts: (1) for the poor, (2) for pilgrims, (3) for himself and family W11.3; spoil d. for animals by hero B392; Solomon's judgment: d. (child) J1171.1, (bride) J1171.2; waters magically d. D1551.

Dividing after God's fashion: little to poor, much to rich U61; all they have by cutting beds and houses in two J2469.3; which favors the divider J1241; the oyster (one shell to each) K452.1; all winnings M241. — Brother clever in d. property J242.8; clever d. J1230—J1249; fox d. dying man's gifts B294.1; magic stick d. waters D1551.6.

Divine, see also **Divinity, Gods;** beings assume their own shape in sleep D796; intervention prevents lover's suicide T75.6; nurse T605; voice points out magic D849.7. — Choice of kings by d. will *P11.1; conception from d. impregnation T518; plants created by direct d. agency A2634; saints have d. visitors V227; sun and moon as d. hero's wedding presents A759.2; test of d. favor H1577; thief threatened with d. punishment J1141.14.

Diviner D1712. — Man becomes d. D1720.2; resuscitated man becomes d. E564; tribal customs established by d. A1501.

Diviners, origin of A1654.2.

Diving for cheese J1791.3; match won by deception K16; for reflected enemy J1791.5; for sheep K1051. — Animal d. into lake and disappearing F989.13; dupe d. for alleged jewels K1051.1; otherworld reached by d. into water (of well or lake) F153; thief persuades owner of goods into d. for treasure K341.4; woman d. for man's reflection J1791.6.0.1.

Divining D1812.5ff.; bones reveal guilt D1318.6; rod locates hidden treasure D1314.2. — Magic object used for d. *D1311; mountain opens at blow of d. rod D1552.1; soothsayer's d. methods D1712.1.

Divinity, see also **Deity, God, Gods;** reincarnated as (bull) E611.2.1.0.1, (cow) E611.2.0.1. — Gods give d. to mortal A189.16; head of d. as protection of land D1380.3; symbols of d. Z184.

Division of the animals (riddle) H841; of goddess's time between upper and lower worlds A316; of power among gods A161.1; of river's flow

D2151.2.1.1; of all winnings (bargain) *M241. — Beginning of d. of labor A1472; deceptive d. of profits K171; devil and his son fight over d. of earth G303.11.2.1; threefold d. of king's day P14.16; wise d. of the fowl H601.

Divorce given wives before battle P557.7. — Origin of d. A1558.

Djun, river animal B877.3.

Doce palabras retorneadas, las Z22.

Doctor, see also **Physician;** accidentally saves rajah N688.1; loses a horse for the sake of the truth J551.3; ridicules Christian belief V382; snake B765.21; unable to cure himself scorned J1062.2; with unusual skill F668. — Asking d. where it hurts J2021.1; cat offers to act as d. for cock and hen K2061.7; dragon fly as snake's d. B765.24.1; farmer surpasses d. in choosing food L144.2; father calls d. son a murderer H581.4; god disguised as d. K1811.3; malicious wife reports that her husband is a famous d. H916.1.1; paramour poses as d. K1517.2; quack d. a hero L113.7; seduction by posing as d. *K1315.2; sham d. *K1955, (kills his patients) K824, (makes king's army ill) K2368.3; though d. is no longer needed fool goes to tell him so J2241; transformation to d. D25.1; why trip to d. futile J2241.2; wolf as sham d. looks at horse's foot K1121.1.

Doctor's expressions misunderstood J1803.2. — Accidental cure by d. ruse N648; establishment of d. fees A1594.1.1.

Doctors. — King questions six d. J171.2; repartee concerning d. and patients J1430ff.; wager: more d. than men of other professions N63.

Doctoring. — Cure yourself before d. others J1062; deception through false d. *K1010ff.

Documents. — Bringing d. from distant city in one day (task) H1107.

Dodging. — Escape by d. K631.1.

Dodici parole della verità, le Z22.

Doe, see also **Deer;** becomes water bubble D421.2.2; furnishes milk (for abandoned child) T611.7, (for man) B292.3. — Fairy as d. F234.1.4.1; helpful d. B443.1; one-eyed d. outwitted by approaching from her blind side K929.2; woman transformed to d. D114.1.1.2.

Does magically give milk D2156.1.

Dog allowed to warm self in house begins to bark U126; alternately bites and caresses hares K2031; as animals' king B240.9; asks raven why he sacrifices to Athene J821.1; sent ahead so as to avoid seeing husband transformed K2371.4; barking to dog in moon K1735; between two castles J2183.1; bewitched G265.6.4; buried alive to prevent ghosts from walking E431.8; buried with enemy S139.2.2.3; buried instead of foster son K525.6.1; burned in jumping contest over fire: enmity between dog and hare A2253.1; caresses sick sheep hoping for sheep's death K2061.3; as child's nurse B535.0.4; chooses between opposing tribes B134.4; in church thought to be a ghost J1782.1; as culture hero A522.1.1; defends master's child B524.1.4.1; dies on mistress's grave B301.1.2; in disguise

to frighten tiger K1810.2; driven away from other animals because of his barking A2494.4.0.1; driven out of dining room claims to be drunk J874; with droppings of gold B103.1.3; drops meat for reflection J1791.4; has eaten 14 pounds of butter but fool squeezes 16 pounds from him J1919.3; exposes host hiding meat J1562.3; with fire in eyes *B15.4.2.1; follows lion but flees at lion's roar J952.3; follows master's corpse into river B301.1.1; follows washerwoman, hopes bundle is meat J2066.6.1; friendly to guest, barks on street K2031.1; frightened into giving up eating men K1721.1; -god A132.8; granted patent of nobility A2546.1; as guardian of treasure B292.8; guards imprisoned beauty T50.1.4; guards master's life and wealth: may eat before other animals A2223.5; guards master's wife's chastity K1591.2; -headed man with horse's mane B25.1.1; will not help build house: must remain out of doors A2233.2; and hog dispute over their children J243.1; with human head B25.2; imitates wolf, wants to kill horse J2413.5; indicates (hidden treasure) *B153, (pregnant woman) B152.1, (road to be taken) B151.1.6; kills would-be murderer B524.7; language *B215.2, leader fears defeat because his forces are of different breeds J1023; lets devil into church to steal: rewarded with dog-skin A2229.2, A2311.1; looks for most powerful master: stays with man A2513.1.1; loses his patent right and seeks it (why dogs look at one another under the tail) A2275.5.5, A2471.1; made king B292.10; with magic (sight) B141.4, (wisdom) **B121ff.; magically paralyzed D2072.0.2.6; in the manger W156; as messenger B291.2.2; mistakes mussel for an egg and cuts his mouth J1772.2; offered as security for debt B579.6; as ogre G351.1; paramour B611.2; Parsley in the soup J2462.1; and pig's plowing contest K41.2; plows for man B292.4.3; prophesies enemy's coming B141.4.1; proud of his clog, thinking it a decoration J953.1; receives the blows when cat steals K2171; refuses to help wolf K231.1.3; replies to man's remarks B210.1; rescues (cow's teats from fire: origin of his black muzzle) A2229.1, (abandoned child) B549.3, (drowning man) B541.4; returns from dead, clears master B134.5; as sacrifice V12.4.1; who has saved child from serpent killed by father who sees his bloody mouth B331.2; saves man from ghost E439.3; scares fox away from cock K815.1.1; to scent the rice J1341.3; sells rotten peas B294.3; as shepherd B292.1.2; so old head is skinless B841.3; as totem B2.1; transformed to object D422.2; tries to bite man rescuing him from well W154.5; tries to catch fate in its own tail N119.1; transformed to person D341; transformed to another animal D412.5ff.; turned into god D43.1.1; turns water to wine B119.1; vomits gold and silver B103.4.3; waits to be hit with meat J2066.6; warns of pursuit B521.3.4; weeps B736.3; as witch's familiar G225.6; as wolf's shoemaker eats up the materials K254.1; worship V1.8.3; as worthless, faithless lover H587.1. — Adulteress compelled to eat with d. Q478.2; alliance of d. and (sheep) B267.2, (wolf) B267.1; antelope transformed to d. D411.4.1; ass tries to caress his master like the d. J2413.1;

automatic statue of d. D1620.2.8; bear thought to be d. J1753; black d. good omen D1812.5.2.10; boat towed by d. B541.4.1; boy gets back d. from man claiming bugs ate it J1531.2.1; boy to see whether it is raining calls d. in and feels of his paws W111.2.4; carrying master to search for d. J2163.2; cat becomes d. D412.1.3; claim that d.-head captured game J1214.1; creator's d. A33.1.1; crocodile tells d. to drink in river without fear K2061.8; daughter unwittingly promised to d. rescuer S247; dead d. set up to trap woman K2152.1; devastating d. B16.1.2; devil in form of d. G303.3.3.11, (kills people) G303.20.6, (chews up church books) G303.24.5; disdain of the wolf for the d. J953.5; disguised man recognized by d. H173; divination from d. howling D1812.5.0.9; devil invoked through black d. G303.6.1.6; dwarf follows countess around like little d. F451.5.8.1; eaten magic d. howls from eater's belly D1619.2.1; why d. eats first A2545.3; enmity between d. (and cat) A2281.1, A2494.1.2, (and leopard) A2494.2.5; escape, leaving d. as substitute K525.6; fairy as d. F234.1.9; fairy kills d. in revenge F361.17.6; fairies give hunter a d. F343.2; faithful d. (to be killed) B842, (killed by overhasty master) B331.2.2, (threatened with death proves worth and is spared) Q151.4; food of d. A2435.3.1, A2545.4; fool dragged by d. tied to him J2132.2.1; foolish d. finds treasure and dies rather than leave it J1061.3; fox feigns to be playing with sheep when d. drives him off K2061.2; friendship between d. and (cock) A2493.16, (elephant) A2493.31, (man) A2493.4; ghost of d. E521.2; giant d. B871.1.7; girl removes d. from lion's claws B848.2; golden d. B102.7; why d. has hairy paws A2375.2.3, A2245; headless d. B15.1.1.1; healing with hair of d. that bit one D2161.4.10.3; helpful d. *B421; hostile d. B17.1.2; house d. blames master for teaching him lazy habits J142.1; how d. (began to bark) A2425.1, (got its tail) A2378.1.7; hungry wolf envies fat d. until he sees marks of his collar L451.3; hunter beats d. which has grown old in his service W154.4.4; hunting d. tested as puppy by gripping hide H1588.1; indentions on rock from paws of King Arthur's d. A972.5.3; injunction to give sample of food to d. before eating C685; island mistaken for d. J1771.5; king escapes giving d. to hostile tribes K234.1; why d. lacks restraint A2526.1; the lawyer's d. steals meat K488; lazy d. wakes only for his meals W111.5.4; leopard and crocodile both sent for the d. K978.1.1; why d. (is always looking) A2471.6, (looks back at person who has beaten him) A2471.6.1; magic d. B182.1, (brain cures) D1502.8.1, (carries owner in his ear) B557.6, (protects) D1380.16, (shrinks) D491.1.3, (shrinks at night) D621.4.1; man kills giant d. F628.1.5; man made to believe that he is a d. barks at people J2013.2; man reincarnated as d. E611.6; man suckled by d. T611.10; man transformed to d. D141; marriage to d. B601.2, (in human form) B651.4; marriage to person in d. form B641.1; master sets serf as watch-d. J1511.12; mitten becomes d. D444.10.2; monster with huge d. tracks F401.3.3.1; mother feeds child to d. S12.2.1; moving dead d. tabu C537.3; murderer detected by actions of murdered

man's d. J1145.1; my d. picked up a string, but did not wish to give it to me unless I gave her bread (cumulative tale) Z41.4.2; origin of d. sacrifice A1545.3.1; part man, part d. B25; peasants persecuted by d.-headed savages B25.1.2; peddler scolds d. who is waiting J1475; place to live given as patent right to d. A2433.1.3; procurer of wildest d. to be king P11.2.2.1; pseudo-magic d. sold K135.1; punishing the d. by feeding him J2108; quarrel of d. and cat over which was higher caste A2281.1.2; quarrel over d. starts feud N387.1; quest for marvelous d. H1331.6; rakshasa eats d. G369.1.4; recognition by overheard conversation with d. H13.1.2; reed pricks d. urinating on it L391.1; remedy for mad d. bite D1515.5; resuscitation by mummified d. E53.1; revenant as d. E423.1.1; robbers frightened by d. B576.1.2; saint controls mad d. V221.4.0.1.1; sexton's d. steals sausage from parson's pocket X411.1; sheep becomes d. at night D621.5; sheep jealous of d. because he does nothing W181.1; sign of cross kills d. D1766.6.5; singing d. B214.1.4; son of d. B635.4.1; soul in form of d. E731.1; speaking d. B221.1.7; spirit as black d. F401.3.3; stag's horns borrowed from d. A2241.1; stealing cattle which are guarded by marvelous d. (task) H1151.8; stolen magic ring stolen back by helpful cat and d. *D882.1.1; going home before d. precedes forbidden C756.1; tabu to eat d. C221.1.1.4; tabu: fire, weapon, d. together C887; tabu: touching hairless d. C537.2; tame d. prefers food basin to fleeing hare J487; testament of the d. who has been given Christian burial J1607; thief tries to feed watch d. and stop his mouth K2062; thieving d. K366.4; tiger thought to be d. J1758.2; too watchful d. killed B332; tortoise and d. partners as thieves B294.7; transformation to d. Q551.3.2.7, (d. to another animal) D412.5ff., (stone to d.) D442.1; transformed man as hostile d. B17.1.2.3; transformed man as d. prophesies coming of enemy B141.4.1; trickster eating own d. K1664; troll rides on d. F455.3.3.1; truth-telling d. *B134, (killed to hide murder) B339.1; two-headed d. B15.1.2.1.4; unwitting bargain with devil evaded by driving d. over bridge first S241.1; venomous d. loosed against saint B776.3.1; village founded where d. barks B155.2.1; waste of time to make a bed for a d. J562; why can't d. bark? H1292.15; why d. is bald A2524.6; why d. barks after thief A2426.1.5; why cat and d. fight A2281.3; why d. follows animal's scent A2512.1; why d. has no horns: stolen by deer A2326.2.2; why d. howls at night A2427.2; why d. lost speech A2422.1; why d. snaps at fly A2479.8; why lion does not attack d. A2464.1; wife forces husband to kill d. B335.1.1; wife's former incarnation as d. E601.1; wild huntsman's d. when seized becomes stick E501.15.6.7; witch in form of d. G211.1.8; witch rides on d. G241.1.3; witch transforms husband into d. G263.1.4; wolf as God's d. A1833.3; wolf proposes abolition of d. guards for sheep K2061.1.1; woman bears d. T554.2; woman in moon with d. A751.8.2; worm becomes d. D418.2.2.

Dog's characteristic haunt A2433.3.2; claws as grains under paws A2376.2; enemies A2494.4ff.; flesh magic *D1032.3; head soup as cure

D1508.4; head used for divination D1311.8.1; licking of man produces forgetfulness D2004.2.1; tail mistaken for gun J1772.12; tail wagging raises wind D2142.1.1. — Adulteress compelled to eat a d. leavings Q478.3; cat loses d. certificate A2281.1; cause of d. walk A2441.1.3; child with d. head T551.3.1; Eve created from d. tail A1224.3; magic d. (bell dispells grief) *D1359.3.1.3, (breath burns dead bodies) D1566.1.6; magic sight by looking between d. ears D1821.3.4; magic stone in d. forehead B722.2; magician, giant, contest over d. tail D1719.1.3; man with d. feet F551.1.3; making d. tail straight H1023.4.1; monster's arm token of d. innocence H105.3; oil in black d. ear brings rain D1542.1.6; origin of d. skin A2311.1; origin of d. service to man A2513.1; quest for wild d. milk H1361.4; why red d. excrement contains hair A2385.2; wolf as d. guest sings J581.1; wolf prefers liberty and hunger to d. servitude with plenty L451; marvelous sensitiveness: meat is d. flesh F647.5.1; woman's organs like d. F547.5.10.

Dogs born of woman D601; break bonds, kill master's attacker B524.1.2.1; with eyes like plates and tea-cups B15.4.3; as fairy gifts F343.2.1; flee from their master because in time of famine he has killed his cattle J2211.3; of gold and silver F855.3.2; handed over as hostages to the wolves by sheep K191; in hell A673.1; howling as bad omen D1812.5.1.12.1; howling indicate death B733.2; in human shape: friends seducing wife H592.4; incited to devour souls in hell A689.3.1; kill attacking cannibal *B524.1.1; kill ogre G512.9.1; large or small at will D631.2.1; listen to wolves' hypocritical words K815.3; in otherworld F167.1.1.1; protect from spirits F405.5.1; pulling on leash (life token) E761.7.5; rescue fleeing master from tree refuge *B524.1.2; by river try to get food in river by drinking the river dry J1791.3.2; scare away fairies F381.9; tear up lion skin but fear living lion W121.2.4; track down law-breakers B578; warn against witch B521.3.1; in wild hunt E501.4.1; of wolf color join the wolves J2137.2. — Behavior of wild huntsman's d. E501.15.6; bones thrown to d. permit escape L222.2; buffalo's eyes turn into protecting d. D699.1; cavalry of d. B268.2; contest of d. H1588; daily beating of men transformed to d. D691; deduction: animal drinks d. milk J1661.1.5.1; dwarfs fear d. F451.3.6.5.2; eating food offered to d. as penance Q523.3; fairy d. F241.6; fire-breathing d. B742.4; ghost visible to d. E421.1.3; ghosts as d. with glowing tongues and eyes E421.3.6; helpful d. purchased B312.4.1; hero's marvelous d. A524.1.1; hostile d. made friendly by having them fight common enemy, the wolf J145; why d. howl, looking at sky A2471.6.2; why d. hunt A2452.1; keeping four d. in herd (task) H1112.1; king of d. B241.2.7; lean d. envy arena-dog his fatness L455; lies about d. X1215; why d. lift their legs A2473.1; why d. look at one another under tail *A2471.1; magic d. B182.1ff.; magician claims he can make d. grey K1677; names of d. literally interpreted J2493; polychromatic d. B731.6.0.1; power of wild hunt evaded by sacrificing to huntsman's d. E501.17.4.3; being eaten by

d. as punishment Q415.1; quest for the smallest of d. H1307; sheep-d. unite to hunt wolf J624.2; snow transformed to d. D449.4; why d. do not speak A2422.1.1; sorceress's toes become d. D447.5; tribe wears clothes like d. A1683.2; war-d. B268.2.1; why d. get stuck in copulation A2496.1; why d. howl when man is dying A2427.2.1; why d. leave droppings at crossroads A2473.1.1; why d. sniff at one another A2471.1.1; why tigers eat d. A2435.3.9.1; wild animals kept as d. *B575.1; witch allows self to be coursed by d. G211.2.7.1; witch overcome by helpful d. of hero G275.2; wolves as God's d. A165.2.1.1.1; wolves of his own country dearer than d. of another P711.1; Zeus has embassy of d. punished for fouling his court A2232.8, Q433.3.

Dogs' barking causes forgetfulness D2004.10; names give warning K649.5.

Dogfish act like dogs X1316.

Dogflesh: "food you've never eaten" J2469.5.1; is magic *D1032.3.

Dog-headed man has mane of horse (cattle) B25.1.1.

Dogmas V310ff.

Dogskin, magic D1025.6, (transforms) D565.7.

"**Doing** as I say, not as I do" J1433.

Doll. — Automatic d. D1620.0.1; forgotten fiancée remembered by means of d. D2006.1.6; magic d. D1268, (answers for fugitive) D1611.11, (freeing from clutches of) T67.3.1, (freeing king from) H1196, (furnishes treasure) D1469.2, (stolen) K331.4; marriage to d. T117.8.

Dolls become fairies D435.1.2.

Dolorous tower F772.2.5.

Dolphin paramour B612.2; and whale scorn crab as peacemaker J411.6. — Helpful d. B473; man transformed to d. D127.5.

Dolphins seek King Solomon's ring A2275.5.4. — Why d. swim up and down A2444.2.

Domestic vs. ascetic life H659.21; beast transformed to person D330ff. — Animal as d. servant B292.2, B574; bride test: d. skill H383; devastating d. animals B16.1; devil as d. beast G303.3.3.1; god of d. animals A441; helpful d. beast B400ff.; helpful d. fowls B469.5; how animals made d. A2513; man transformed to d. beast D130ff.; origin of d. animals A1443; reincarnation as d. animal E611; revenant as d. animal E423.1ff.; war between d. and wild animals B262; witch as d. beast G211.1.

Domination by fairy mistress F302.6.1. — Magic d. over animals D2197.

Dominion over world as reward Q112.0.6. — Man given d. over beasts A1421.1.

Donald. — Black D. (name for devil) G303.2.4.

Donating, see **Giving.**

Donkey, see also **Ass, Mule;** and camel trade undeserved compliments J867; gift to ruler J2415.1.1; and ox not to plow together C886. — Ghost d. E402.2.2; immortal d. B843.2; mythical d. B19.11; ogress as d. G351.5; priest sells distracting d. J357; reincarnation as d. E611.1.2; trickster

accuses woman of lying with d. K2112.2.1; unjust king compared to d. H592.5; woman will not follow d. on safe path: attacked by robbers J133.4.

Donkey's — Child with d. head T551.3.3; jewel found on d. neck N534.8; striking off d. head to punish it J2113.1; why d. penis is large A2365.2.1.3.

Donkeys ask immediate reward from God: eat their own excrements A2232.11; Genoese compared to scattering d. J1021.2; punishment: humiliating ride on d. Q473.5; repartee on d. not smoking J1289.20; why d. urinate when others begin A2495.3.

Donning. — Magic power from d. magician's clothes D1721.0.1; transformation by d. hood D537.1.

Doom. — Saint made judge of d. Q173.

Doomsday (Day of Judgment) A1002; a long way off J1261.7; resurrection E178. — Bird describes D. B143.2; birds drip blood at D. B259.5; bleeding wood as D. sign A1091.2; fifteen signs of D. Z71.16.11.3; moon by day D. sign A1053.1; no clothes needed for D. J1511.7; sinners to be burnt on D. M341.2.7.1; souls at D. E751; sun at night D. sign A1052.2; talking stone at D. A1091.3; unusual migration of birds at D A1091.4.

Door entrance to lower world F91; to fairyland opens once a year F211.1.1; falls on robbers from tree K335.1.1.1; hung backwards as protection against ghosts E439.9; to otherworld F156; transformed to stone D471.2.1. — Church d. opens magically, proves priest's innocence H216.3; closing the d. tight with iron nails K1417; concealed d. leads to woman's room K1349.8; devil cannot enter house with horseshoe over d. *G303.16.17; devil fastened to hell's d. by his beard G303.17.3.2; devil stands in church d. and writes down names on sheep skin G303.24.1.4; entrance to fairyland through d. in knoll F211.1; forbidden d. (all may be entered except one) C611.1; ghost cannot cross new d. sill E434.10; ghost slams d. E402.1.7; golden d. to troll's castle G304.3.1.1; guarding the d. K1413; he who opens palace d. to be king P11.4.1; horse's head nailed over d. F874.1; kicking through d. F639.5; magic charm opens d. *D1557; magic d. *D1146, (holds person fast) D1413.16; monster guards d. of habitable hill F721.2.2; mountain-man has stack of butter before d. F460.2.4; object across d. protects from witches G272.7; opening mouth makes d. open D1782.1.1; palace with d. at each end for sun's journey A151.4.2; passing through d. guarded by hound as fear test H1423.1; pointing at d. causes fall D2069.1.1; recognition by overheard conversation with church d. H13.2.4; servant to close d. at night leaves it open so that he will not have to open it next morning W111.2.2; slamming d. on exit from mountain otherworld *F91.1; snapping d. K736; trying to get a beam through a d. crosswise in otherworld *F171.6.3; wife and paramour rebuked for not shutting d. K1569.2; wind opens locked church d. F963.3; wraith opens, closes d. E723.7.3.

Doors fly open at death E722.2.6; of heaven guarded by rivers of fire A661.0.1.1.1; in otherworld F165.1. — Dog will not help build house:

must remain out of d. A2233.2; dwarf cave closed by iron d. F451.4.3.1; dwarf cave has large square room with little d. F451.4.3.2; extraordinary d. and windows F782ff.; fairy house without d. F221.5; gods of d. A411.1; hair from fox's tail opens all d. D1562.2; locked d. open for ghosts E599.11; many d. in prison R41.5; power to go through closed d. D2121.12; saint passes through closed d. F694; slamming d. grateful for being fastened D1658.1.4; sun at night closes d. A722.4; Valhalla has 540 d. A661.1.0.1; why fowls never shut d. at night A2433.4.6; wild hunt goes through houses when front and back d. are on a line E501.14.6; witches open d. G249.8.

Doorbell. — Wraith rings d. E723.7.2.

Doorflap. — Buzzard becomes d. D423.4.

Doorframe. — Strong man carries off d. F631.2.1.

Doorkeeper of the gods A165.5; of hell A671.1; with one human eye, one cat's eye F512.1.4.

Doorkeepers, automata as D1639.1.

Doorpost rises for holy person F1009.1.

Doorstep. — Bible under d. detects thieves D1817.0.1.5; magic d. D1146.1; wheel buried in d. to prevent deviltry D1385.10.

Doorway. — Breaking down d. instead of dismounting J2171.6; weaver outwits d. tax J1289.13.

Dord fían R187.1.

Dormitory. — Children sleep in village d. T688; village d. A1559.1.

Double bribe to judge J1212.1; dealers K2030ff.; reward successfully claimed K441ff. — Music teacher charges d. to those who have taken music before X351; rascal claims to be only simple not d. fool J1393; wife who saw d. X121.

Double-meaning verse aids theft K232.1.

Doubling. — Dragon d. his demands B11.11.8; king d. reward to knight W11.12.1; servant d. master's boasts J2464.

Dough. — After three weeks the fiancée still has d. under nails H383.1.1; bitch eats wheat d.: origin of noblemen A1656.1; dropping d. thought to be a ghost J1782.2; giant comes to bake too soon and spills d. F531.3.7; serpent kneaded into d. H1407; snake in d. troll child test F455.10.1; sound of fermenting d. J1812.3; wild huntsman's dogs eat d. E501.15.6.6.

Dove disregards experience in nest-building J16; flies out of anchorite's mouth T331.5, V345; helps deity draw wife into net B582.2.5; and magpie's exchange of eggs A2247.4, A2486.3; as messenger B291.1.3; returns to ark in obedience to Noah: receives raven's sheen A2221.7; sees painted cups of water and dashes into them J1792.1; transformed to person D354.1. — Cooing of d. A2426.2.8; creation of d. A1948; crow kills d. singing to save brood U31.2; devil cannot change into a d. G303.3.6.2; dog becomes d. D412.5.1; fairy as d. F234.1.15.2; fox masks as d. J512.10; golden d. F855.3.3; helpful d. B457.1; magpie as

hybrid of d. and raven A2382.1; man transformed to d. D154.1, G263.1.5.2; monogamous life of d. A2497.1; Noah fails to pay d. for bringing back olive branch: hence its mourning A2291; parson is to let a d. fly in church X418; prophetic d. B143.0.6; raven and d. fight over man's soul E756.3; raven imitates d. J2413.9, (punished) A2232.10; reincarnation as d. E613.6; revenant as d. E423.3.1; soul in form of d. E732.1; speaking d. B211.3.5; tabu to eat d. C221.1.2.3; thrush teaches d. to build nest A2271.1; why d. has two eggs A2247.4, A2486.3.

Dove's graceful step A2441.2.2; nest A2271.1, A2431.3.1; pride in her large brood linked with fear for their loss U81.1. — Origin of markings on d. head A2330.7.

Doves in net console selves J869.1; show monk treasure B562.1.3; tear up wolf (lie) X1256.1. — Aphrodite's team of d. A136.2.1; forgotten fiancée reawakens husband's memory by having d. converse D2006.1.3; king of d. B242.2.2, K815.8; lies about d. X1256; maltreated children transformed to d. S365.1; Mohammed lures d. to his ears K1962.1; souls carried to heaven by d. E754.2.1; tame d. close wild ones in trap and thus help common enemies J683.2.

Down. — Corpse buried face d. S139.2.2.3.1, V61.4.1; garments of mountain d. H1054.4; unnecessary choice: to go uphill or d. J463; what is softer than swan d. (riddle) H672; why animals always look d. A2471.9; wife carried with head d. drowns J1916.

Downfall of ascetic V229.20. — Animal characteristics as punishment for planning man's d. A2236ff.

Dowry in coffin E228; given at marriage T52.4. — Combat among sisters for d. H507.4; foolish bride gives away d. J2463.1; monk helps friend get d. K1915.1; monk appropriates d. K361.4; peacock on king's temple as d. C655.1; settling d. dispute J1678; village as part of d. T52.9.

Draft-animal, unusual B558ff.

Dragged. — Bacon d. on string by literal numskull J2461.1.1; boat d. to strand by dead E543; death by being d. behind horse Q416.2, S117; fool d. by tying dog to himself J2132.2.1; mill d. by strong man F631.1; numskull d. J2132; rain from waterskin d. along sky A1131.4.1.

Dragging. — Demon d. victims beneath water G336.1; rivers from god d. his staff A934.4; water-spirit d. children into river F420.5.2.1.5.

Dragon *B11ff.; as creator's companion A36; enticed into pot K722.1; festival A1541.4.2; god A139.3; haunts lake G308.4; king advises hero B560.1; makes bridge across stream for holy man B549.2; mistaken for log, sat upon J1761.8; parts as identification between lovers H105.6; as power of evil B11.9; as power of good B11.8; as rain-spirit B11.7ff.; seen in sky F796; swallows, releases magic box F721.3.2; swallowing arrow intended for hero B529.2; tongue proof H105.1; wants to see courage J2488.1; worship V1.8.8. — Animal languages learned from d. B217.6; bridal chamber invaded by magic d. T172.2; bringing d. leg as suitor test H322.3; conception from d. rays T521.3; drinking horn becomes d.

D444.6; deeds of d. B11.6ff.; why d. dies by means of fire A2468.3; fight with d. *B11.11ff.; fettered monster as d. A1072.4; form of d. B11.2ff.; giant with d. scales for feet F531.1.3.1; girl offers self to d. to save parents S262.4; habitat of d. B11.3ff.; habits of d. B11.4ff.; killing d. before princess sacrificed H335.3.1; magic circle of saliva kills d. D1402.14; magic d. heart *D1015.1.2; magic d. statue D1345.2; magic tree guarded by d. *D950.0.1; marriage to d. B605; marriage of d. girl, orphan boy T118.2; origin of d. B11.1ff.; overcoming d. as task H1174.2; powers of d. B11.5ff.; prophecy: fiery bolt from d. to kill world M357.1; sacrifice of human being to d. *B11.10f.; sight of d. punishes neglect to fast Q223.9.1; snake transformed to d. D418.1.2; supernaturally impregnated woman bears d. T554.1; transformation: d. to stone D429.2.2; tree guarded by d. H1333.6; why d. king can't ascend to sky H1292.14; witch as d. G211.9.1.

Dragon's breath renders hideous D1337.2.3; heart-blood as remedy D1500.1.7.3.3. — Animal languages learned from eating d. heart B217.1.2; creator with d. head A18.1; devil in d. head on a shield G303.8.10; earthquake at d. death F960.2.5.3, Q552.25.1; eating d. heart makes courageous D1358.1.1; invulnerability through bathing in d. blood *D1846.4; men created from sown d. teeth A1265; quest for d. liver, heart H1332.6; sowing d. teeth (task) H1024.5.

Dragons in hell A671.2.5. — Devil as d. G303.3.2.4; king of d. B248; man kills d. with own hands F628.1.3.1; pigs become d. D412.3.5; witch's army of d. G225.5.

Dragon-fighter. — Identity of d. not to be revealed C422.1.

Dragonfly as snake's servant B765.24.

Dragonsblood as love charm D1355.3.8.

Draining land in one night H1097.

Drake and devil carry waters of English Channel G303.9.2.4.

Draught. — Quest for healing d. H1324.2.

Draughts (game). — Fairies steal d. pieces F365.5; falling in love while playing d. T34.2.1.

Drawbridge partially cut, giant falls K924. — Slamming d. to otherworld *F152.2.

Drawing asunder by horses as punishment Q416ff.; witch's blood annuls her spells D1741.2.1. — Disenchantment by d. blood D712.4; transformation when one expresses astonishment at smith d. water in an egg shell D512.1.

Drawn. — Chariot d. by dead persons E583; corpse d. asunder S139.2.2.6; devil in coach d. by headless horses G303.7.3.3; golden wagon d. (by moles) F861.1.1, (by four golden elephants) F861.1.2; man d. to girl when her heart is magically removed and fed to him D1905.1; magic fire d. down on foe D2091.1; person d. (attracted) by magic object D1420ff.; person d. in by magic object D1412ff.; ship d. by loadstone *F806.1.

Dreadnaughts seek dangers they have been warned against Z211.

Dream bread K444; contests K66; demons F471; of fairy kiss J2345; of future greatness causes banishment L425; interpretation answered by another J1527; of marking the treasure X31; reveals sin to saint D1817.2.1; that all parsons are in hell X438; shows events in distant place *D1813.1ff.; of treasure bought N531.3; of treasure on the bridge N531.1; warning against marriage C168; warns emperor of wife's unfaithfulness *D1813.1.1. — Accidental death through dodging blow in d. N336; advice from d. D1814.2; conception through d. F460.4.1.2.1, F611.1.13, T516; consummation of marriage postponed until revelation by d. of future of family T165.1; cure follows d. instructions D2161.4.0.1; deception revealed in d. D1819.2; detection through feigned d. J1147; devil appears in d. G303.6.1.6; disenchantment by obeying d. D753.3; future revealed in d. *D1812.3.3ff.; imagined ownership derived from d. J1551.7; information received through d. D1810.8.2; journey to otherworld as revealed in d. *D1812.3.3ff.; location of fountain revealed in d. D1816.1; love through d. T11.3; magic knowledge of king's d. D1819.7; magic object received from lady in d. D812.8; magic power received in d. *D1731; magic sword received in d. D812.12.1; man discredits his confession by declaring it all a d. J1155; mine discovered through d. N596.1; monkey saves condemned birds through feigned d. K645; quest assigned because of d. H1217, (feigned) H1212.1; quest for girl seen in d. H1381.3.1.2.2; quest for marvels seen in d. H1229.3; quest for things seen in d. H1320.2; realistic d. F1068; recalling someone else's d. H1042; recognition from d. H24; sham wise man interprets girl's d. K1956.6; snake turns to gold in answer to d. N182; souls seen in d. E720.1; tailor's d. of flag made of stolen cloth J1401; treasure discovered through d. N531; trickster explains d. as dead father's demand for gift J2326.2; wisdom (knowledge) from d. *J157.

Dreams. — Blacksmith's and horse-trader's d. J1622; demons fool men in their d. G302.9.6; god of d. A499.5; interpreter of d. D1712.3; magic object induces d. D1584; marvels seen in d. D1731.2; origin of d. A1399.2; prophecy through d. M302.7; symbolic interpretations of d. H617; supernatural persons seen in d. give advice K2035.

Dreamer. — Greedy d. willing to accept nine coins J1473.

Dreaming. — Biting fingers to see if d. F1041.13.

Dregs. — Fraud detected by measuring wine d. J1176.2.

Dress, see also **Clothes;** of dwarf F451.2.7; of fairies F236; so fine it goes through ring H355.6; of mountain-men F460.1.4; of pygmies F535.3; of revenant E422.4; transformed to animal D444.10. — Adulteress forced to wear symbolic d. Q487; bride test: making d. from wasted flax H381.1; conspicuous d. of maid pledged to devil S223.0.2; custom of differentiating social classes by color of d. introduced A1650.2; disguise of man in d. of woman *K1836; disguise of woman in d. of man *K1837;

extraordinary d. F821ff.; lazy wife in soiled d. thinks husband is bringing her a new dress from market W111.3.1; origin of leaf d. A1453.4; over-zealous visitor cannot wait to d. J2517; trail of d. shreds R135.0.4; touching d. tabu C545.3; tribal characteristics: d. A1683; wife's d. symbolic of sexual generosity H492.2.1.

Dresses of giants, giantesses F531.1.11. — Changing d. to take king's place K1810.1.3.

Dressed. — Drunken man d. as a rich lord J2322; girl refuses to dance with devil until well d. K1227.3.1; how the devil is d. G303.5ff.; spirits d. in antique clothes F401.1.

Dressing. — Lover d. as woman K1214; married man helps bridegroom's d. T134.3; monkey d. in dead mistress's gown K1839.3; self-d. image D1623; shortsightedness in d. J2161.

Dressmaker P452.

Drills. — Fire d. (do not function) D2089.10, (invented) A1414.1.1.

Driller. — Lie: remarkable rock d. X991; oil well d. drills for fifty years W37.1.

Drink, see also **Drunk;** of devils G303.25.14; has taste of any liquor desired D1665.1; irresistible H659.20; from magic cup deprives man of legs D1410.6; magically furnished D2105.4; magically supplied D1040.1; poured out to gods V12.9; refused saint disappears Q552.18.2. — Angel tricked by d. into telling woman how to enter heaven K2371.1.6; animals refuse to help dig well: may not d. from river or spring A2233.1.1; ascetic faster increases sufferings by placing food and d. before himself V462.2.1; ass refuses to d. after it has had enough J133.2; brother about to d. blood of seemingly guilty sister P253.1; crocodile tells dog to d. in river without fear K2061.8; crow drops pebbles into water jug so as to be able to d. J101; dwarfs steal d. F451.5.2.2.2; dying monster requests hero to d. his blood M257; falling in love while d. being poured T34.1; food and d. appear and disappear in otherworld D1982.4; food and d. from magic object *D1472ff.; health as reward for d. Q145.1.1; heart breaks at third d. from silver canister F1041.1.1.1; house without food or d. J2483; liking for food and d. J1343; lover refuses d. T24.6; magic d. *D1040ff., (causes arms to fall from shoulders) D1403.3, (gives immortality) D1346.1, (potion) *D1241, *D1242ff.; magic glass supplies d. D1472.1.16; metaphors about d. J2489.1; must d. from the common cup (the sea) J1467; ogre persuaded to d. pond dry bursts G522; one d. leads to drunkenness, condemnation N340.3; parson takes d. of liquor during the sermon X445.1; person lives without food or d. for a year (or more) F1033; Pisācas d. blood and eat human flesh G312; drunkard's wife should have brought him d. J1323; poison magically separated from d. D2168.1; poisoned d. test H1515.2; sword so heavy that hero must take d. of strength before swinging it F833.1; transformation: water to marvelous d. D478.4; trickster gets strong d. deceptively K231.6.2;

truth in d. U180ff.; vampire brought to life by being fed human food and d. E251.2.3; water becomes marvelous d. D478.4; wolf tries to d. well dry to get cheese J1791.3.1.

Drinkable. — Gods provide d. water A1429.3.2.

Drinker. — Animal as mighty d. F989.11; flask imparts magic strength to d. D1335.7; lie: remarkable d. X932; mighty d. F633.

Drinkers cheat blindfolded bartender K233.2. — Devil's stream kills d. G303.16.2.3.5.

Drinking beer without touching pot H1046.3; blood, milk and wine as pledge P312.1; blood teaches animal languages D1301.2; -bout assembly of animals B237; enormous amount (task) H1142; from fairyland well tabu F378.4; festival in memory of dead V65.2; forbidden *C250ff.; ghost E556; from golden vessel disenchants D771.5; hole in pot lets gruel run out J2176.2; holy water facilitates cursing V132.3; the moon J1791.1; only after a bargain K236.2; up river to get all the fish K231.11; as road to heaven J1314. — Absurd ignorance concerning animal's eating and d. J1903; adulteress d. from paramour's skull Q478.1.2; animal warns man against d. B521.1.2; betrothal by lovers' d. each other's blood *T61.1; bride and groom d. from same cup T135.11; clever deductions by d. J1661.2; compulsory d. at feast A1514; conception from d. T512; cure for leprosy by d. from opposite lip of horn from that which caused it D1783.2; death respite while d. K551.2.1; deceptive d. contest H82; devil d. church well dry G303.9.9.14; devil in d. contest G303.9.8.5; disenchantment by (d. blood) D712.4.1, (eating or d.) D764; doctor d. himself after he forbids it J1433; dogs try to get food by d. river dry J1791.3.2; fear test: eating and d. from skulls H1434; giant d. prodigiously F531.3.4; giant god d. lake dry A133.1; hero treacherously slain at d. bout K929.8; Hindu d. from Mohammedan's vessel V383.2; idol d. milk D1633.1; magic results from eating or d. *D1793; man too lazy for d., loses voice W111.1.5; marriage by d. festival T135.6; mutual love through accidental d. of love philtre *T21; no teeth as excuse for not d. J1391.6; ogre sucks victim's finger d. all his blood G332.1; permission for d. water refused W155.5; though old woman believes she is in hell she calls for d. companions J1321.2; rejuvenation by d. D1889.9; respite from death until prisoner has finished d. his glass K551.2; revenants d. E541.4; spirit d. water supply dry G346.4; stones d. D1641.2.5; transformation by d. D555; trickster d. from another's flask K499.9; victim enticed into d. by over-salting food K839.3; witch prevents person from d. D2072.0.5.1.

Drinking-horn found by stumble N223; transformed to dragon D444.6. — Cure for leprosy by drinking from opposite lip of d. D1783.2; death from d. E765.4.5; dwarf forced to swim in d. X142.2; forbidden d. C622; huldra d. F460.2.10; magic d. *D1171.6.3, D1889.9, (as chastity test) H411.4, (supplies wine) D1472.1.24; self-pouring d. D1601.26; theft of d. from fairies F352.

Drinking-tube as chastity index H439.2.

Dripping clothes of drowned person's wraith E723.7.8. — Comb d. blood (life token) E761.1.7; sound of d. water thought to be ghost J1782.2.1.

Driven. — Anvil d. into ground by strong man F614.1; cannibals d. from land G11.18.1; cobold d. away by brewing in eggshell F481.4; creditor d. away K235; devil shows how he can be d. away G303.13.5; devils d. away by cross G303.16.3.1; devil d. from heaven G303.8.1; dwarfs d. out of land by three sevens in 1777 F451.9.1.3; giant d. by girl F531.5.10.1; giants d. away by men F531.6.12.7; hungry hens d. away and geese stuffed H583.4.4; herds d. off by mountain-men F460.4.4.6; herds of deer d. by witches G249.1; horses d. by dead person E582; images of animals d. D1631; ogres d. away by oaths G571; sinner d. from graveyard by other dead E411.0.5; wagon d. by thumbling sitting in horse's ear F535.1.1.1; two he-goats d. by troll G304.3.2.2.

Driver told to put his shoulder to the wheel J1034. — Ass turns on his d. who would save him from falling over a precipice J683.1; why d. ants live in bush A2433.2.1.1.

Driving off birds after kind words K2090.1. — Father d. away bad son P233.2.1.

Droll dwarfs F451.3.10.

Dromedary. — Horse of d. family B710.2.2.

Drop from magic cauldron gives supernatural information D1310.2. — Each d. of innocent blood turns to burning candle D1318.5.3; "fair d." falls on saint V222.1.0.2; tabu: allowing a d. to fall upon altar C51.1.8.

Drops of water become angels A52.0.7. — Collecting all d. of water H1144.1; how many d. in the sea (riddle) H704; humans from creator's d. of wine A1211.6; magic blood d. impersonate fugitive D1611.6; magic d. *D1242.3; two d. of blood indicate two deaths D1812.5.1.1.2; water d. wear stone hollow J67.

Dropped tub unharmed F1081. — Apparently dead woman revives when d. N694.1; axe d. in water: modest choice Q3.1; book d. in water by saint not wet F930.1; clay d. from sky forms hill A963.9; identification by hair d. by bird H75.2; identification by ring d. in wine H94.3ff.; quest for princess caused by sight of one of her hairs d. by bird H1213.1; recovered magic articles d. by rescuing animals into the sea D882.12; rope cut and victim d. *K963.

Dropping and dashing to pieces as punishment Q417; of fox's tail frightens animals K2323.1. — Animal characteristics from d. ancient animal from air A2214; animal d. magic food B531.4; birds d. stones on saint's enemies D2163.5.1; corpse d. piecemeal down chimney H1411.1; death for d. on emperor's coat Q411.15; devil d. stones A977.3; treasure-d. animals B103.1ff.

Droppings. — Why dogs leave d. at crossroads A2473.1.1.

Drosselbart T76.

Drought produced by magic D2143.2; as punishment Q552.3.3; at world's end A1065. — Farmer as fisherman goes hungry in d. J345.2; goddesses

produce d. A189.10; magic d. against enemy D2091.8; magic object causes d. D1542.2; rivers from saint's prayer during d. A934.5; star deity and d. demon fight A255.

Drowned corpse found by magic D1816.4.1; girl reborn as leech to avenge murder E693.1; man's ghost leaves water puddles E544.1.3; person cannot rest in peace E414; woman's hair speaks E545.20.1. — Adulterers tricked on to thirsty mules, d. K1567; animal d. relieving bee stings K1023.4; army d. by unnoticed tide N339.7; besiegers d. by diverting river K2369.5; dream leads to d. body D1810.8.2.2; female rabbit d. in Flood B754.4; foal d. by witch G265.2; giant d. F531.6.12.8; girl d. in well as river's origin A934.10; infant allowed in river, d. J2175.4; king, foster son jumping into sea, d. F1041.16.7; loaf of bread locates d. man D1314.6; lover d. as he swims to see his mistress T83; man has bride d. S62.2; man d. on mountain (lie) X1857; ogre d. G512.11; reincarnation of d. persons as birds E613.0.4; souls of d. in heated kettles in hell *E755.2.1; souls in hell alternately d., burned Q562.2; Virgin restores life to d. man V256.5; wife carried head downwards in water, d. J1916; wife d. while throwing husband's corpse into river N339.14; wraiths of d. appear in dripping clothes E723.7.8; youth d. gazing at own image N339.10.

Drowning escape by drying up waters D2165.2; of girl abducted by fairy N339.9; man rescued by siren B53.1; princess rescued R131.2.1; as punishment Q428, (for breaking tabu) C923, C927.3, (for drowning) Q581.3.1, (for turtle) K581.1; to save treasure J2146.2; self after beset by elves F324.2; self as sacrifice to water-gods to save husband's boat from capsizing T211.1.1; selves to save virginity T326.1; shipboard rivals K527.4; son to test goddess's favor H1577.2; in swamp as punishment Q467.3; test H1538. — Animal d. out of sea-water H842.1; animal grateful for rescue from d. B362; animal saves man from death by d. B527; captors lured into d. selves K656; curse: death by d. M451.2; death by d. while drinking water M341.2.3; devil plans d. of God at time of creation A63.2; druid's spells cause d. D1402.13.2; escape by shammed d. K522.6; fatal game: d. K853; fathers d. rescuing sons R153.3.5; fish saves hero from d. B175.2; fox attempts d. jug, gets drowned J2131.5.7; ghost causes d. E266.1.1; ghost rescues from d. E379.1; girl d. as she swims to lover T83.1; immunity from d. D1841.6; infant born blind d. self T585.3; king's d. in bath follows literal instructions J2516.3.3; lake bursts forth d. evil doer, A920.1.3, A920.1.8; lover rescues lady from d. R161.3; magic boar d. hound pack B184.3.1.1; magic chain protects from d. D1388.0.3; magic object (causes d.) D1402.0.2, (protects from d.) *D1388ff.; man inattentive to d., drowns J651.2; mermaid's singing causes d. B81.11; miraculous d. as punishment Q552.19; monkey tricked into d. self K891.3; murder by d. K958, S131; owl saves man from d. B527.3; parents meet daughter they tried d. N732.3; prophecy: d. in particular stream M341.3.3; punishment by d. Q467; rescuing d. man forbidden C41.1;

river d. victim F932.8.4; scolding d. child instead of helping him J2175.2; self-sacrifice by d. S264.1.2; slaves spare infant from d. K512.0.1; spring miraculously breaking forth and d. wrongdoer F933.6; wager involving d. self N13; water d. girl filling pitcher D1432.1; water saves prophet from d. F930.3; waters d. wrongdoer F930.2; water-spirit allows d. body to come up thrice F420.5.2.1.4; water-spirits save man from d. F420.5.1.10; wife encourages husband's proposed d. J1545.9; wind raised by d. cat. D2142.1.5; woman d. in attempt to push husband into water K1652.

Drug, see also **Medicine;** hidden in enemy's fingernail K873.4; of invulnerability T325.1. — Magic d. renders invulnerable D1344.2; origin of fish d. A2834.

Drugs. — Seduction by use of d. K1339.5; use of d. to usurp lover's place K1317.6.

Drugged. — Burial alive of d. person S123.1; husband d. by wife on way to paramour K1514.17.1; undesired lover d. T322.3.

Druid *P427; aids task H985; assigns tasks H939.1; causes sun to stand still D2146.1.1.1; converted to Christianity V331.0.1; directs fairies F394.1.1; directs king's death F363.1; interprets dream D1812.3.3.0.1; as magician D1711.4; makes self ugly on one side, beautiful on the other D2031.4.1. — Air above grave of converted d. full of angels V238.4; Christ called d. V211.0.5; demons coerced by d. tabus G583; fairy leaves after d. spell F381.6; magic contest between d. and saint D1719.1.1; no sunshine on d. island F961.1.6; resuscitation by d. E121.7.1; saint in conflict with d. V229.6; transformation by d. D683.9; transformation by saint as proof of Christianity before d. H1573.3.3.

Druid's circumambulation D1791.1.1; hedge prevents attack D1381.1; spells cause drowning D1402.13.2; spells kill Christian king D1402.13. — Fairy defeated by d. magic F389.5.

Druids attempt to poison H1515.1; bereave men of senses D2065.3; bless instead of curse D2076; can pass through trees D1932; cause illusions D2031.0.4; cause magic thirst D2063.3.1; come to adore infant Jesus V211.1.7; direct fairies F394.1.1; guard magic spring D927.2.1; have knot magic D1282.1.1; magically detect crime D1817.1; prophesy saint's coming M364.7.1; as prophets M301.3; raise storms D2141.0.8; send spirits to kill Christian F402.1.11.1; teach immortality V311.0.1; as teachers P340.0.1; turn men into dogs D141.0.2; undergo ordeal (by hot iron) H221.2.2, (by water) H222.0.1; use mistletoe D965.4.1. — Demons coerced by geasa of d. G583; fairies are d. F251.12; funeral rites by d. V60.2; images and d. V120.1; magic hymn protects against d. D1385.16.1; magic invisibility of d. D1981.3; monks as converted d. P426.3.2; sacred groves of d. V114.1; saint magically causes d. to bless instead of curse D2076; spirit sent by d. causes death of Christian king F402.1.11.1; tabu: king speaking before his d. speak C402.1; white robes of d. V131.2.

Druidess. — Chant of d. causes drowning Q467.3.1.

Druidic mist D902.1.1. — Bird reveals d. secrets B122.1.2.

Druidism. — Death for disbelief in d. Q558.13.2.

Drum. — Animals produced when forbidden d. is beaten *C916.2; bees in d. fly out, defeat army K2351.2.1; deity's special d. A159.2; demon-skins for d. K1715.9; dupe allowed to guard king's d. (wasp nest) H1023.1; escape from deluge in wooden d. A1021.0.2; foolish thief beats stolen d. J2136.5.7; ghost summoned by d. E384.1; huldra d. F460.2.8; magic d. *D1211; man inside d. believed to make noise J2026; marriage of girl to a d. T117.3; mortal beats d., gets fairy wife F302.6.2.1; ogre imprisons victim in d. G422.1; ogre keeps girl in d. R49.3; origin of d. A2824; sound of d. followed into ghost town F102.2; stealing ogress's d. H1151.24; tabu: heeding persuasive d. C811.1; toad plays d. B297.1.2; woman not to touch husband's d. C181.1.

Drums announce gods' approach A199.7; beaten before bride T133.3. — Beating d. scares off robbers K548.2; island with nightly noise of d. F745; thunder d. of the dead A1142.9.1.

Drummer drums for own wedding W152.10. — Elephant as d. J1882.3.

Drunk, see also **Drink, Intoxicated;** dancers punished Q386.2; elephant sent against enemy K2351.4; enemies slaughtered K871.2; king sentences unjustly J816.3; man calls judge very wise J1289.12; man made to believe that he has been to heaven and hell J2322; man makes king think him rich K1954.2; man thinks he's beheaded J2311.10; man makes sport of another man for being drunk J1063.2; man thinks Christ is speaking to him from behind crucifix K1971.7; murderers reveal crime N271.11; philosopher's foolish wager J1161.9. — Birds get d. A1427.0.1; creator d. A87; devil cheated of his promised soul by making the intended victim d. K219.1; dog driven out of dining room claims to be d. K874; escape by making watchman d. K625.2; man gets bridegroom d., enjoys bride K1371.5; man made d. left to demon's mercy K776.2; ogre made d. and overcome G521; St. Andrew gets d. A1372.10; saint's breath makes men d. D1500.4.2.1; theft by making owner d. K332; thief feigns pursuit by d. husband K314.

Drunkard cannot drown J2282; cured of seeing double J1623; refuses cure of fever if it is to take away his thirst J343.1; rides lion, thinks it a donkey J1758.5; unrepentant J1321. — Disguise as d. K1839.9; ghost brands d. E279.5.

Drunkenness, see also **Intoxication.** — Condemnation of d. after one drink N340.3; hermit chooses d.: other sins follow J485; humor based on d. X800—X899; magic object cures d. D1511; origin of d. A1386; repartee concerning d. J1320ff.

Dry branch on innocent man's grave blossoms as proof of innocence E631.0.5.1; feet tabu over river C833.5; river bed as bad omen D1812.5.1.16; rod blossoms F971.1; spring restored by removal of certain stone F933.2. — Causing d. spring to flow again (task) H1193; cows magically made d. D2083.1; fairy remains d. in rain F259.3; fountain

magically goes d. D1647; lies about d. weather X1640; magic medicine causes streams to go d. D1542.3.1; magic wand keeps outdoor sleeping place d. D1542.4; man magically keeps d. D1841.4ff.; man sells d. snow for salt X1653.3; ogre persuaded to drink pond d. bursts G522; skillful fencer keeps sword d. in rain F667.1; spring goes d. (life token) E761.7.2, (after fratricide) D927.5.

Dryad F441.2.2.

Drying up lake in one night H1097.1; up of rivers D2151.2.3. — Death respite for d. self K551.12; drowning escape by d. up waters D2165.2; earth d. up D2081.1; earth made by d. up of primeval water A827; ground d. up when first woman bleeds on it A856.2; river d. up for day F932.6.1; sun d. out earth A733.5; woman d. hair scares ghost E432.3.

Dryness. — Goddess of d. A431.4.

Dualism of animal creation A1757.

Ducats. — Rich man shakes d. into pope's lap J1263.2.2.

Duck as ogre G353.3; persuades cock to cut off his crest and spurs K1065; recovers key from sea B548.2.2.2; sheep and cock in peril on voyage J1711.1; transformed to person D365; transformed to precious stone D423.3. — Creation of d A1983; enmity between hen, beetle, and d. A2494.13.10.2; friendship of hen and d. A2493.34; ghost as d. E423.3.10; helpful d. B469.4, (wild) B469.4.1; killing golden d. tabu C841.6; man transformed to d. D161.3; wagon drawn by d. F861.4.2; why d. quacks A2426.2.10; reincarnation as d. E613.1; separable soul in d. E715.1.1; why wild d. has red eyes A2332.5.7; witch in form of d. G211.3.2.

Duck's color A2411.2.6.4; feet A2375.2.8; food A2435.4.12; sandals become his feet D444.10.3. — Creation from d. eggs A641.2.

Ducks in pool in church V134.4; recover lost object B548.4. — Frogs were d. stolen from Eden A2426.4.1.1; "how often do you kill d.?" "Only once" J1309.2; if d. can ford river why not man? J1919.2; man shoots ram-rod full of d. X1111; remarkable d. X1261; roast d. fly (by magic) D2191, (lie) X1208.2; treasure becomes d. D449.3; trickster induces d. to dance with closed eyes K826; witches as d. G269.19.

Ducklings take to water instinctively J64.

Duel with bride as suitor test H332.1.1; with father-in-law H332.3; to prove which religion is better V351; as task H1166; won by deception K97. — Animal characteristics from d. A2257; challengers agree to sham d. K1771.4; fatal d.: brother kills brother in game K867; in d. with long poles the ogre is forced into the pigsty K785; sham d. to bring about recognition K1791; sinking into mud in d. F943; song d. H503.1.

Dueler. — One d. fights with God's help, the other with his brother's J1217.1.

Duelers. — Animals as cowardly d. K2323.

Dueling customs P677. — Giant d. over girl F531.5.7.0.2; origin of d. A1341.2.

Dug, see **Digging.**

Duke's — Lover in disguise as d. son K1831.2.2.

Dulled. — Sword cannot be d. D1081.2; sword magically d. D2086.1.

Dullness. — Feigning d. for vengeance J1675.7.

Dumb hero L124; man recovers speech in order to confess V23.2; person brought to speak F954; person's speech restored by gold D1507.8. — Deaf and d. (man can see soul taken to happiness or punishment) D1821.7, (speak) F1041.22; formerly men d., animals talked A1101.2.3; Jews protesting against marriage of Jewess and Christian stricken d. V343; man who cuts off tongue of swallow has d. children Q552.5.1; man eats father's heart, struck d. G91.1.1; pagan disputant with Christian stricken d. V352; person struck d. by Echo D2065.6; saint cures d. person V221.11; saint restores d. man's speech V221.2; sham d. man wins suit K1656; suitor test: bringing d. princess to speak F954.2.1; witch strikes d. G263.4.4.

Dumbness from disgust F1041.19; feigned to escape unwelcome marriage K523.0.1; magically cured D2161.3.6; as punishment (for breaking tabu) C944, (for hiding children) Q451.3.1; for surly speech Q583.2. — Magic d. *D2020ff.

Dummy set up as corpse K2321.2. — Black d. indicates banishment Z174.1.1.

Dumplings. — Sheep's head has eaten d. J1813.8.

Dung, see also **Excrement, Manure;** bursts into flames D1649.4; drops on washing hands D2194; on moon's face A751.5.2; from rich man's mules coveted P151; transformed to other object D457.13. — Blindness cured by chicken d. F952.5; cleaning with cow d. C536; conception from crane's d. T511.8.5; cow drops gold d. B103.1.2; dog alleged to excrete sweet d. K135.1.3; dropping d. on bribed judge's ancestors J1192.3; dupe induced to eat d. K1044; hero's head smeared with d. F531.5.12, P672.3; magic d. of animal *D1026ff.; magic supplies from bull's d. D1470.2.7; opposing witness's pockets filled with d. K1291; oracular pill is really dog's d. K114.3.1; "pick up everything!": fool collects d. J2516.2.1; sale of d. K143; resuscitation from bird d. E64.19; shooting stars are star-d. A788.4; spoiling the rice-field with d. K344.2; why d. of ass is triangular A2385.1; why fly lives on d. heap A2432.9; witch's rosary consists of goat d. G243.2.1.

Dungbeetle eaten J1761.11; helpful B482.2; keeps destroying eagle's eggs L315.7; prefers his dunghill to all other smells U122; thought to be bee J1751. — Friendship between grasshopper and d. A2493.21.

Dungeon. — Captivity in d. R41.3; children born in d. T581.2.3.

Dunghill. — Changeling is left on d. F321.1.4.4; dwarf's d. home F451.4.4.3.1; swindler buried on d. Q491.1.1; wife washes face in d. puddle H473.4.

Dunmow, ham as prize at T252.4.

Dunsinane. — Birnam wood comes to D. K1872.1.

Dupe cutting off part of own body J2131.3.2; gives trickster horses as dead father's demand J2326.2; loses booty through singing J2351.3. —

Blame for theft fastened on d. K401; blind d. deceived in shooting arrow K333.1; culture hero is d. A521; evidence of crime left so that d. is blamed K2155; god as d. A177.1; property of d. destroyed K1400—K1499; trickster rides d. courting K1241.1.

Duped, see also **Tricked.** — Husband d. into taking wife to paramour K1583; priest dies at being d. F1041.1.3.4.

Duplicating feat on journey C833.6.

Durham's. — Bishop of D. fool J1369.4.

Dust from communion table breaks spell G271.2.6; storm blows eyes shut J1158.1; strewn on circumcision wound A1567.1; of Tabernacle as chastity test H411.18. — Another kind of d. if the wolf's tail breaks X1133.3.2; cannibal recognized by cloud of d. raised H46; conception from smelling bone d. T532.1.4.1; food becomes d. D476.2.1; magic d. *D935.3, (kills snake) D1402.27; person turned to d. C927.1; removing d. from adulterous wife's clothes J2301.3; resuscitation from d. E42.1; rope of d. X1757.1; serpent subsists on d. B768.4; skull of suicide must roll in d. until it has saved a life Q503.1; stones become d. D452.1.12; transformation into d. D294; wolf does not mind d. J352.1.

Dusty. — Quest for d. cloth H1377.4.

Dutchman, Flying E511.

Duty. — Choice between desire, d. J233; filial d. rewarded Q65; king brought to sense of d. by philosopher J816.1.1; knight's d. to perform lady's bidding P52.1; when will ferryman be released from his d.? H1292.8; wraith doing person's d. E723.3.

Duties. — Exchange of d. brings disaster J512.7; king's four d. to subjects P12.6.1; lazy servant gets others to perform his d. W111.2.0.1.

Dwarf falls in love with girl seduced by magic K1672; as foster father P271.3; gods A134; hero of superhuman strength F610.2; as human D49.1; king falls into porridge pot X142.1; king laughs at absurdities about him U15.0.1; punishes for breach of tabu C905.1; as underground spirit *F451ff.; waits for ram, lamb escapes K553.2.1. — King cursed by d. smiths P15.4; magic object from d. *D812.12, (for kindness to child) *D817.1.1; marriage of mortal and d. T111.5; quest for bride for d. H1381.3.1.3; treacherous d. K2277.

Dwarf's beard caught fast K1111.1; magic armor D838.7; magic objects D801.1. — Headache from d. cursing M424.

Dwarfs battle giants F535.5.1.1; change size D631.4.1; and giants friendly F531.6.15.3; from Ham's curse A1614.1.1; and human beings F451.5ff.; magically keep ghosts from rising E439.2; in otherworld F167.2; perform tasks H973.3. — Appearance of d. F451.2ff.; cannibal d. G11.1; characteristics of d. F451.3ff.; during the day d. appear in form of toads or other vermin F451.2.0.5; emigration of d. F451.9ff.; fallen angels become d. V236.1; four d. support sky A665.2.1.2; gift of d. turns to gold F451.5.1.4; helpful d. F451.5.1ff.; home of d. F451.4ff.; human midwife for d. *F451.5.5; magic object summons d. D1421.3; magician and queen

as d. D2031.4.2; malevolent d. F451.5.2ff.; names for d. F451.8ff.; origin of d. F451.1ff.; possessions of d. F451.7ff.; pygmies also called d. F535.

Dwarf-deer pastes other animals' eyes shut and pretends that hunters are coming K2382.2.

Dwarfed. — Why certain trees are d. A2721.2.1, A2775.

Dwelling, see also **Home;** of demons F402.6; of fairy F220ff.; of Fortuna N111.1, (on lofty mountain) F132.2; of god A151ff.; of helpful spirit warriors in rocks and hills F450.1.1; of witches G230ff. — Animal characteristics: d. and food A2430ff.; tabu: woman being in one's d. C193.1.

Dwellings. — Characteristics of otherworld d. F165; huts replace caves as d. A1435.3.

Dye blessed by saint D1684. — Husband drops d. on adulteress's dress K1550.1.1; magic d. D1297.

Dyes. — Girl gathers plants for d., is cursed A2817.2; origin of d. A1439.2, A1453.3; saint causes d. to malfunction D2084.3.

Dyeing beard as disguise K1821.1. — Disguise by d. complexion K1821.5; man's presence unlucky during d. N134.1.1.

Dying, see also **Death;** child assigns task H937; culture hero A565; from fright after prophecy M392; lover sends sweetheart his ring T61.4.5.1; man assigns bride to his brother T141.1; man's curse M411.3; miser tells son to extinguish candle as soon as he dies W153.11.1; and reviving (fatal game) K856; woman lures paramour into chest K1555.0.1; woman's wraith visits children E723.4.4. — Birds d. when owner is killed B192.0.1; cock hears inaudible voice of d. man B733.2.1; devil appears to d. man G303.6.2.8; entire household d. same night F1099.1; fairy d. of longing F259.1.3; fox as divider of d. man's gifts B294.1; friends d. shortly after each other P310.6; faithful horse d. with master B301.4.7; fate prohibits man's d. N101.3; father and daughter d. together P234.2; magic power of d. man's words *D1715; man d. of pretended illness Q591.3; man goes to heaven without d. F11.2; newborn child kisses d. mother T585.6; observation of d. people for a year takes a man's thoughts from lust J62; river rises to prevent body's being carried over it against d. man's wish F932.8.1; shooting star signifies that someone is d. *E741.1.1; translation to otherworld without d. F2; treasure buried by d. man N511.1.0.1; visiting friends take everything from house of d. man W151.2; woman falls in love with d. warrior T89.1; warrior d. faces foe P557.6; why dogs howl when man is d. A2427.2.1.

Dynamite. — Knockers tamper with d. F456.1.2.1.3; lie about hog eating d. X1233.2.1.

Dynasty. — God founds royal d. F32.1.

Eagle as bird of ill-omen B147.2.2.5; cares for baby while mother works B535.0.12; carries (off condemned child) B522.4, (off ill-gotten gain) Q557.3, (giant to its nest) F531.6.17.3, (man to safety) B542.1.1, (off youth) R13.3.2; catches newborn gazelle B754.7.2; as creator of man

A13.2.2; -down rope to sky F61.2.2; eats tortoise J657.2; as god's bird A165.1.2; killed with arrow made with his own feather U161; king of birds B242.1.1; as messenger B291.1.9; as ogre G353.2; as omen of victory B147.2.1.2; prefers own offspring to changeling J497; preys on Prometheus's vitals Q501.4; regains throne for king B589.1; released: grateful B375.3.1; renews youth B758; saves man from falling wall B521.2.1; statue gives wealth D1469.13.1; takes revenge on man B299.1.1; tests eaglets by having them gaze at sun B751.3; transformed to person D352.2; with twelve wings, three heads B15.7.16; warns shepherds that wolf is eating sheep and thus imperils own food supply J715.1. — Cat brings suspicion between e. and sow K2131.1; cat from transformed e. A1811.1; chain tale: man shoots e. Z49.10; daw tries to carry off lamb like e. J2413.3; dragon as modified e. B11.2.1.11; falcon defeats e. L315.9; fight between e. and fish B264.2; food of e. A2435.4.4; fox burns tree in which e. has his nest L315.3; giant e. B872.1; giant as e. F531.1.8.3, F531.1.8.7; gorilla transformed to e. D411.9; helpful e. B521.2.1; man transformed to e. D152.2; marriage to e. B602.1; monkey transformed to e. D411.5.1; mother e. casts out changeling, rears bold son P231.6; mother e. distinguishes between stupid, intelligent eaglets B122.5; prophetic e. B143.0.7; reincarnation as e. E613.3.1; return from lower world on e. *F101.3; soul as e. E732.6; tabu to eat e. C221.1.2.4; tortoise carried by e. J657.2; transformation to e. (to carry hero to safety) D659.4.3, (to seek king's bride) D647.2; treacherous e. K2295.2; war between birds and e. B263.5.1; wedding of e. and kite B282.2.1; why e. cries like a baby: tortured baby became eagle A2426.2.15; why e. has long life A2578.2; wise e. B122.0.5, (in earth-tree) A878.3.4; woman pregnant after e. sits on head T532.7.

Eagle's body made smaller A2213.1, A2302.4; flight A2442.2.8; nest as refuge R322. — Why e. back is brown A2356.3.1; diamond in meat carried to e. nest N527.1; dungbeetle keeps destroying e. eggs L315.7; prince grows up in e. nest B535.0.5; recognition through gold found in e. nest H91.1; resuscitation by e. touch E79.3.

Eagles carry castle in air F771.2.1.2, F982.1.

Eagle-owl turns head around A2351.2.

Ear cornucopia B115.1; of stolen animal protrudes from thief's mouth Q552.4; tips transformed to pelts D457.19. — Bird flies into large animal's e. and kills him L315.1; birth through e. T541.14; "bite the e." H588.15, J2489.3; boy asks sister for an eye and e. T415.7; child born with one e. T551.7; conception through e. T517.3; crab carries animals in e. F982.8; disenchantment by water in e. D766.1.3; dog carries owner in his e. B557.6; dwarf groans while carrying e. of corn F451.3.9.1; flesh struck from ravisher's e. F304.4.1; god born from mother's e. A112.7.1; husband concealed in wife's e. F1034.1; judge saves one e. for other litigant J1289.8; magic air journey from biting an e. D2135.2; magic e. of animal *D1011.2; magic power by crawling through e. of

magic horse D1733.2; murder by hot lead poured into e. S112.3; murder by stabbing in e. S115.1; plucking e. of grain forbidden C512; removing pea from e. J1115.2.2; resuscitation by wax from deer's e. E115; ribbon long enough to reach from e. to e. K195; skillful marksman grazes e. of sleeping person F661.9; slave's e. bored P171.1; testing the evidence by experiment: biting the e. off J2376; thumbling drives wagon by sitting in horse's e. F535.1.1.1; transformation by twisting e. D565.4.1; twins born with one e. in other's mouth T587.2.

Ears cut off as punishment Q451.6ff.; not to be cut off twice J1187.2; of demons cut off as proof of killing them H105.5; stopped with wax to avoid Siren's song J672.1. — Animal languages learned by having e. licked by serpent B165.1.1; animals' e. like elephant's until hare bites them off A2216.7; ass's e. on king discovered by barber N465; bird language learned by having e. magically cleansed B217.5; birds perch on e. of cows B853; boring hot irons through e. Q469.9; box on the e. returned K2376; camel asks for horns: punishment, short e. A2232.1; why cat has jagged e. A2325.6; cock with enormous e. F989.19; cooling e. by breaking vessel on head J2469.4; cutting off e., hat falls over eyes, can't see J2721; fairies with unusually large e. F232.3; flies try to drink water from elephant's e. J971; flowers on e. protect against fairies F384.4; giant's e. six hundred feet long F531.2.2.2; herbs in e. as protection D1385.2.1; house with neither eyes nor e. H583.8; literal fool cuts off child's e. J2465.11; magic blown into e. D1721.3; magic sight by looking between dog's e. D1821.3.4; Midas with ass's e. *F511.2.2. N465; mutilation: tearing off e. S168; origin of animals' e. A2325ff.; origin of e. A1316.4; person without e. F511.2.4; person unusual as to his e. *F511.2ff.; power of soothsaying from serpents' licking e. B161.1; reincarnation of e. into mussel shell E649.4; remarkable e. *F542ff.; ripe, unripe e. in allegorical dream D1812.3.3.5.1; river in bird's e. D915.2.1; sound of wild hunt avoided by sticking fingers in e. E501.17.5.8; stopping e. to keep in wisdom J1977; transformation by seizing e. D565.4; vampire with ass's e. E251.4.2; what makes your e. so big? Z18.1; why camel has no e. A2325.7; why serpent has no e. A2325.8; wind caused by flapping of e. of a giant A1125.1.

Earache. — Magic object cures e. D1502.7.

Earbox. — Begetting child by e. J1919.7.

Ear-wax. — Why e. inside the ear A1319.3.

Earl P50.1; imprisoned for hunting in king's forest Q433.10; killed in combat with man he wants killed K1626.1; throws water at messenger F1041.16.11. — Appointment to e. as reward Q113.1.

Earl's daughter given as reward T68.2; daughter rescued from giant R111.2.3.1; son seduces foster brother's sister P273.2.2. — Impostor claims to be e. son K1952.4.

Earlier universe opposite of present A633. — Maids must rise even e. K1636; "rise e." J21.23.

Earlking G305.

Early death with fame preferred J216.5; pupil finds the gold N633. — Prophecy of e. death M341.1.2; riddle on starting work e. H588.12; start journey e. in the day J21.19.

Earnest. — Sham threat: "In e. or in jest?" K1771.1.

Earning. — Animal e. money for master B579.7; man e. as much as he gave away for charity in former life V411.5.1.

Earnings. — Giving all e. to poor as penance Q542.

Earrings tabu to Saora women C181.9. — Live-bird e. F827.1; peasant demands e. as price of silence after seducing priest's wife K1582.1; recognition by e. H94.11; woman promises marriage for e. K2338.

Earth, see also **Ground;** A800—A899; becomes silver D475.3.1; cursed M414.12; disturbances at end of world A1060ff.; Diver A812; at foot of stairs to swallow up man M341.2.25; gives birth to woman A1234.4; as God's footstool A133.2.2; made by cups of earth placed on spider's web A823; magically dried up D2081.1; opens at command F942.3; opens to rescue fugitive R327; punished for disobedience at Fall of Man A2721.8; red from child's blood A1227.3; rejects buried body E411.0.6; as remedy D1500.1.28; from river bed saves soul E754.1.7; rises F969.2, (from water so saint can cross) D2125.0.1; sinks into sea at end of world A1061; speaks D1610.19; spirit F494.3; subsides beneath flood A1019.1; swallowings as punishment Q552.2.3; swallows up impious horsemen Q221.4.3; swallows up overproud man C770.1; swallows, then vomits, children R142; transformed to (animal) D442.2, (gold) D475.1.8; -tree *A878; trembles at Crucifixion V211.2.3.1; under umbrella A653; as virgin mother of Adam A1234.1. — Absurd theories about the e. J2274; animal born from e. B717; animals created from e. A1714.3; Archangels drive Satan from heaven to e. G303.8.1.2; at beginning people start to eat the e. A1420.6; castle at middle point of e. F771.3.4; Cerberus to be brought to e. H1271; creation of e. A610.2; cure by passing through e. at crossroads *D2161.4.3; curse on everybody on e. evaded by person in earth M427; dead person visits e. periodically E585; devil in interior of e. G303.8.5; disenchantment by touching e. D782.2; distance from e. to heaven (riddle) H682.1ff.; fairy gift not to be taken to e. F348.1; ghost lives midway between heaven and e. E481.5; ghost shakes off e. when he rises from grave E410.2; giant with lower lip reaching e. F531.1.4.1.1; giant's stride spans e. F531.3.5.2; god of e. A400ff., J1441; god issues from e. A115.2; god lays foundations of e. A141.4; heathen swallowed by e. H1573.1.1; heaven and e. (connected by navel string) A625.2.1, (from egg) A641.1, (touch each other) A657.2; heaven mother, e. father A625.1; hiding in the e. K515.6; hills from e. wrinkling up feet A969.4; inhabitant of upper world visits e. F30ff.; journey inside the e. F114; king never touches e. P14.5; kissing the mother (e.) first J1652; magic aging by contact with e. after other-world journey D1896; magic e. *D935, (heals wounds) D1503.12, (pro-

tects) D1380.9; magic e.-mould holds person fast D1413.20; magic e.-slip D2091.15; magic results from contact with e. *D1778; magic sight of e. from otherworld D1825.2.1; magic of stones fixed in e. D931.0.2; man becomes pillar of e. D287.2; man from e. reddened with blood of human sacrifice A1241.4; man made from e. A1241, (from four different places) A1241.5; man thanks e. for saving his life but if he had fallen into well he would have blamed Fortune N111.4.1; man with e. in his shoes says he is standing on his own land J1161.3; marriage of e. and sky A702.5, T126.3; marriage of Mother E. and ogre T126.1; marvelous runner can run round the e. in five minutes F681.5; Mother E. *A401; new race made of red e. after world calamity A1006.3; nine days' fall from heaven to e. A658.1; object sinks into e. F948; ocean the son of E. and Heaven A921; planting the e. A2602; riddles about e. (most beautiful) H641.2, (costliest) H638.1, (distances) H681ff., (fattest) H653.1, (parents separating and mixing) H583.4.5, (strongest) H631.3, (weight) H691.2; river connecting e. and upper and lower worlds A657; sea like e. at man's burial F931.3.1; sinking into e. F942; sinking of e. as punishment Q552.2; sinner wanders between heaven and e. E411.0.4; snake created to suck poison from e. A2145.3; soul of the e. E701.1; speaking e. reveals murder D1318.16; strength is renewed with each contact with e. K12.3; strength of witches depends on their touching e. G221.2; tabu: goddess eating on e. C211.3.1; topographical features of the e. A900—A999; wax turned into e. D479.6; why waters do not engulf the e. A915; wild hunt avoided by throwing self to e. E501.17.5.4; wild hunt goes around the entire e. E501.14.5.

Earthenware pots in river J425.1. — Toad swallows e. F911.6.1.

Earth-mother. — World parents, sky-father and e. A625.

Earthquake accompanies holy man V222.9; at death F960.2.5; as giant falls down F531.3.8.5; at hero's return F960.9; kills giant F531.6.12.5; magically caused D2148; as punishment Q552.25; saves fugitive R236.3; spirit F438. — Extraordinary e. F969.4; fool's fear of e. J2634; god with body of e. A123.1.4.

Earthquakes caused by hungry old woman shaking A843; at world's end A1061.1. — Cause of e. A1145; magic object controls e. D1544; why people do not fear e. A1381.1.

Earthworm with light in tail B722.4; thought to be snake J1755. — Enmity of e. and rattlesnake A2494.16.6; origin of e. A2182.3; rattlesnake harmful because e. feeds him chili pepper A2211.11; why e. is red at one end A2411.5.5.

Earthworms killed whenever earth dug A1599.6.

Easiest. — Riddle: what is e.? H659.14.

East. — Castle e. of sun and west of moon F771.3.2; divinity's departure for e. A562; fairies live in e. F219.3; giants live in e. F531.6.2.3; male god invoked in e. A183.1; otherworld in e. F136.1; prayer with face toward e. V58.2; sun travels from west to e. F961.1.2.

Easter V75. — King in anger punishes misdeed on E. day J571.3; putting fish aside for E. J2124; whale helps clerics celebrate E. B256.12.

Eastern. — Most e. castle in world F771.3.3; taprobane at e. end of world A871.0.1.

Eastward. — Star moves e. F961.2.8.

Eaten god V30.1; grain and cock as damages K251.1; heart *Q478.1, (gives one the owner's qualities) *E714.4.1, (produces magic strength) D1335.1.2; object speaks from inside person's body *D1619.2; person resuscitated E32.0.1. — Ambergris made from bitumen e. by fish F826.2; apple divided and e. as love charm D1905.2; bones of e. man advise hero E366.3; breakfast, dinner, and supper e. one immediately after the other W111.2.6; cloth on back guarantees against being e. H119.1; corpses e. by (ghosts) E256, (vampires) E251.3.1; crumb trail e. by birds R135.1; dead souls e. by spirits E752.8; devil e. by wolf G303.17.3.3; earth e. by early people A1420.6; enemies frightened away by making them think they will be e. K1715.4; god killed and e. A192.1.2; hare and man contest: loser to be e. A2256.1; king e. daily E155.6; magic object e. D859.4; magic bird-heart when e. brings man to kingship D1561.1.1; magic nuts e. produce love D1355.12; milk and bread e. with child by snake B765.6; peasants think that the calf has e. man all but feet J1815; person's entrails e. by witch G262.2; priest's guest and e. chickens *K2137; prodigious amount e. by giant F531.3.4ff.; punishment: being e. by animals Q415; resuscitated e. animal *E32; sick stag's provisions e. up by visitors W151.2.1; spirits believe they will be e. K1715.4.1; weak animal (man) makes large one (ogre) believe that he has e. many of the large one's companions K1715.

Eater of magic bird-heart will become rich (king) M312.3; of magic fish to spit up treasure M312.3.1. — Lie: remarkable e. X931; mighty e. F632; notorious e. J1468.

Eaters of stolen food detected J1144. — Voyage to land of Lotus E. *F111.3.

Eating, see also **Devouring, Food;** continually interrupted X12; courageous animal's heart makes courageous D1358.1; in the dark unwise since devil eats from plates A1512; "death vegetable" compulsory C662; of dough by wild huntsman's dogs E501.15.6.6; enormous amount (task) H1141; entire goat without leaving scrap H1141.4; fish intestines next morning when hungry J1606.1; ferocious animals heart makes person cruel D1357.1; food offered to dogs (penance) Q523.3; gluttonously W125; from hands of menstruating woman tabu C143; before hearing of adventure tabu M151; horseflesh punished Q499.6; human flesh, see **Cannibalism;** of human hearts as cure for insomnia D2161.4.13; a hundred onions J2095; magic food looses magic D1741.9; like man impossible to person once an animal H64.4; the moon (task) H1035; one hundred carcasses as suitor test H331.17; one's own newborn child L71; oneself up F1035, G51.1; pomegranate without letting seed fall H326.2;

after satisfied tabu C766; from skulls as fear test H1434; tabu *C200--C299; tabus for pregnant women C152.3; way out of frozen animal X1723.3.1; what is stolen without sin H1151.19. — Abortion by e. T572.2.2; absurd ignorance concerning animal's e. and drinking J1903; advice on e. before going to bazaar H588.18; animal wounds self, blames other one for e. young K2153.1; animals agree against e. umpire M222; animals e. corpse of holy man die B275.3; animals e. saint's body stricken Q558.11; animals' extraordinary e. F989.22; best time for e. H659.17; brother e. brother S73.1.2; caution in e. J585; clever deductions by e. J1661.2; conception from e. *T511ff.; contest in e. iron K63.1; continual e. of certain animals A2478, A2231.1.1; covenant confirmed by e. together M201.2; cumulative tales involving e. of an object Z31.3; custom of e. buffalo flesh A1515.1; customs connected with e. P634.0.1; deceptive e. contest *K81ff.; deceptive e. game: lion kills camel K869.3; demons e. enormously G302.9.7, F402.4; devil never e. in an inn G303.4.8.4; disenchantment by e. D764ff., (enchanter's heart) D763.1; dog e. before other animals A2223.5; dragon e. ox each meal B11.6.7; dragon e. people for rent B11.10.2; dupe e. stones K1043.2; effects of wild hunt remedied by e. part of flesh thrown down by it E501.19.5; fat giant e. self J2119.5; father e. own children K940.1, S11.3.8; forced e. of frightful meal S183; giants keep corpses for e. G691.1; grief prevents e. F1041.21.3; hart e. the earth-tree A878.3.2; hero bluffs demon with e. threat K1715.7; husband becomes cannibal from e. wife's breast G36.1; innocent woman accused of e. her new-born children K2116.1.11; Jewish child burned for e. consecrated Christian bread V363.1; lie: animals e. each other up X1204; madness from over-e. F1041.8.5; magic results from e. or drinking *D1793; magic weakness from e. D1837.5; make-believe e., make-believe work J1511.1; man before dying e. up his money W151.7; man-e. god A135; man e. sweets calls self "B" K602.2; monster e. people G346.2; mortals not e. fairy food F361.15; mother forces child to break e. tabu S12.2.3; mothers e. own children Z215; mountain spirits e. raw food F460.2.14; nun e. unblessed lettuce eats a demon G303.16.2.3.4; origin of e. customs A1510ff.; person e. only tobacco F561.4; pilgrim rebuked for e. too much J1346; poor host closes eyes not to see e. guest P336.3; punishment: e. ashes Q478.5; punishment for splitting head and e. man's brains Q211.7; rakshasa e. domestic animals at night G369.1.3; revenants e. E541; secret meat-e. betrayed N478.1; secret for not e. foreign food overheard N475.2; serpent inside man e. his food G328.1; servant plans to deceive his master by not e. J2064; sham e. K81; shark-ogre e. swimming children G308.5; spirit e. food F473.6.4; spirit e. person F402.1.11.2; strong hero engendered by e. fruit F611.1.8; sun e. up its children A736.1.4.1, A764.1.2; sun e. up stars A1066; tabu: e. from offerings to gods C57.1.3; talker keeps person from e. J1564; thief e. from plate without detection F676.1; transformation by e. *D551ff.; transformation to buffalo for e. grass D655.1; tribal charact-

eristics: e. A1681; trickster e. own dog K1664; victim enticed into e., killed K839.1; vow against e. until secret learned M151.1; wife banished for e. by stealth S411.4; wife e. up husband's earnings T251.10; wisdom from e. fox's heart B163.1.1; wolves e. each other up so that only tails are left X1204.1; woman e. before Communion can't swallow wafer V39.9.

Eavesdropper overhears secret name *N475; unwittingly killed N322.

Ebb-tide goes to great whirlpool A913.3.

Ebony. — Island of e. F732.1; why e. tree is black A2751.4.2; why e. tree has black wood and smoke-colored leaves A2772.4.

Ecclesiastical. — Quest for lost e. rule H1382.3; seven e. orders Z71.5.6.3.

Echidna B29,2.

Echo A497; abducts person D2065.6; answers K1887.1; as dwarfs' voice F451.2.8; of giantess's song F531.3.8.4; invisible A497.1; as wood-spirit F443. — Abduction by E. R11.2.2.1; evil spirits from e. G302.1.2; magic e. answers for fugitive D1611.15; origin of e. A1195.

Eclipse in God's proximity F961.0.2; as punishment Q552.20; of sun at historical event F961.1.9; after Sun, Moon captured R9.1.2. — Continuous world e. A1046; origin of e. of moon A737.0.1; sun hides face in shame: hence e. A737.8.1.

Eclipses as evil omens D1812.5.1.4. — Causes of e. A737.

Economy. — Shortsighted e. J2199.4.

Eddies. — Fairies travel in wind e. F282.1.

Eden. — Frogs were ducks stolen from E. A2426.4.1.1; souls pass through E. E755.1.3.

Edible substance changed to inedible D476.2. — Assignment of e. animals A1422; inedible substances become e. D476.1.

Edification. — Sacrifice at temple e. V12.4.0.1, V17.8.

Edifices. — Religious e. *V100—V199.

Edric as wild hunt leader E501.1.7.3.

Educated men as choice company J146.

Education of hero A511.3. — Foolish attempt at e. of animals J1882; lack of proper e. regretted J142; strange language used to show e. W116.7; wisdom (knowledge) through e. J140ff.

Eel burned by torch, hence red eyes A2218.8; with fiery mane B15.7.12; -god A132.12; as king of fishes B243.1.2; paramour B612.1; transformed (to object) D426.1, (to person) D373. — Creation of e. A2131; fairy as e. F234.1.10; ghost as e. E423.9; giant e. B874.2; god becomes e. D173.1; helpful e. B476; hostile e. attacks hero B17.2.1.2; magic charm hooks e. D1444.1.4; magic e. pursues man R262; magpie tattles about the e. J551.5; man transformed to e. D173; marriage to e. B603.2; mythical e. B64; tabu to eat e. C221.1.3.2; why e. (has no tongue) A2344.2.2, (is slippery) A2306.1.

Eels killed with snakes in pond J2114. — Fearless hero frightened by

being awakened by e. put down his back H1441.1; god of e. A445.2; king of e. B243.2.2; leaves become e. D441.5.1.

Effigy. — Punishment in e. Q596; taking cold in e. J1628.

Egg becomes bloody D474.4, (as sign of disobedience) C913.1; becomes crowing cock F989.20; creature changes size at will D631.4.4; as reward of appropriate saying K444.1; as shinny ball F878; transformed (to house) D469.1.1, (to mist) D469.1, (to person) D439.4. — Basilisk hatched from cock's e. B12.1; birth of human being from e. T542; breaking e. on castle parapet H1149.6; champion does not break e. upon which he sits H1568.1; choice of one e. or none J201.1; conception from eating e. T511.7.2; cosmic e. *A641; creator born from e. A27; deity in shape of e. A114.2.1; dog mistakes mussel for an e. J1772.2; dragon from cock's e. B11.1.1; earth from e. (breaking on primeval water) A814.9, (from bottom of sea recovered by bird) A812.2; enormous e. X1813; familiar spirit acquired by carrying e. under left arm-pit F403.2.1.1; general hatches out e. K1253; goose that laid golden e. D876; god born from e. A114.2; goose e. becomes hen's D479.4; guess what I have in my hand and I will give it to you to make e.-cake with J2712.1; hero born from e. A511.1.9, F611.1.11; horse born of e. B19.3; magic e. *D1024, (furnishes livestock) D1477.3, (furnishes slaves) D1476.2, (produces soldiers) D1475.7; making an invisible knot with an e. (task) H1021.5; man becomes e. D276; man created from e. formed from sea-foam A1261.2; marooned e.-gatherer *K1616.1; marriage with woman coming from e. T111.3; obstinate wife and the third e. T255.4; origin of sky from e. brought from primeval water *A701.1; pale sun restored with e. A721.4; person returns to original e. form when tabu is broken C963.2; pumpkin thought to be an ass's e. J1772.1; quest for vulture's e. figured with golden letters H1332.2; roc's e. B31.1.1; scholar given third e. J1539.2; seven-headed witch defeated by throwing e. at each head G275.4; sewing together broken e. H1023.7.1; shepherdess born of red and blue e. T542.1; soul in e. E711.1; stream changed to e. D476.1.8; three horses from dove's e. on last day A1091.1; wager: to swallow e. in one gulp N75; witch killed as e. G275.4.1; woman lays e. T565; world as e. A655.

Eggs from eggplant X1495; stolen from fairies F359.1. — Absurd ignorance concerning the laying of e. J1901; air-castle: basket of e. to be sold J2061.1.2; animal thief of e. detected when he comes to a spring to drink J1144.2; why animals lay e. as they do A2486ff.; boy punished for stealing bird's e. Q285.1.2.1; buying e. and "ay, ay" H1185.1; cobold likes scrambled e. F481.0.1.3; crab's attempt to lay e. in pot J2415.3; crow's house full of wren's e. H1129.9; crushing e. tabu C544; dividing the e.: one man's hand in pot at time J1241.5; dividing five e. equally between two men and one woman J1249.1; dove and magpie exchange e. A2247.4, A2486.3; dungbeetle keeps destroying eagle's e. L315.7; first thief steals e. from under bird (second meantime steals first's breeches)

K305.1; goose e. bewitched G265.8.4.2; guess how many e.? you have all seven J2712.2; how birds began to lay e. A2486.4; killing hens to get all the e. at once J2129.3; mankind originate from e. A1222; marksman's skill in shooting e. F661.4; nature of bird's e. A2391; numskull sits on e. to finish the hatching J1902.1; potatoes as e. of the earth J1722.1.2; securing e. from atop glass tower H1114.1; sitting on e. without breaking them H962.1, H1568.1; skillful tailor sews up broken e. F662.1f.; snake e. D551.6.3; soul in three separate e. E711.1.1; stealing e. from under bird H1151.12; suit for chickens produced from boiled e. J1191.2; tabu to eat birds' e. C221.3.3; task: hatching boiled e. *H1023.1f.; trickster hides e. in breeches to avoid tax, made to sit K1693; two e. given tailor to eat so as to stop his singing J1341.4; voices from within unhatched e. J646.2; walking on e. H225.2; wise man destroys serpent's e. J622.1; woman lays, hatches e. F569.1.

Eggplant goes on warpath F1025.2.1. — Eggs from e. X1495; magic e. D983.5; reincarnation as e. E631.5.3; riddle about e. garden H583.2.5; speaking e. D1610.3.4.

Eggshell. — Brewing in e. to drive away cobold *F481.4; smith drawing water in an e. D512.1.

Eggshells. — Witches travel in e. G241.4.2.

Egg-white. — Payment of e. K249.2.

Egypt as demons' abode G302.5.2. — Animals from frogs sent as plague to E. A1734; storks become men in E. in winter D624.1; wisdom from E. J192.2.

Egyptian. — Satan slays first-born E. G303.20.9.

Egyptians fond of asses A1689.12; as magicians D1711.10.3. — Bloody waters for E. F930.4.

Ehod mi yodea Z22; saves girl from devil K555.2.1.

Eight-armed giant F531.1.6.7.2; -eyed bat B15.4.1.4; -eyed giant F531.1.1.5.1; -eyed person F512.2.1.2; as formulistic number Z71.16.1; handfuls of food in ceremony C231.5; heavens A651.1.5; paradises A661.2. — Adam's body made of e. things A1260.1.3; death as e.-headed monster Z111.3; flood lasts e. months A1010.2; man's body from e. sources A1260.1.

Eighteen. — Prophecy: death before e. years M341.1.3.2; prophecy of greatness if boy lives to be e. M312.0.3.

Eighty as formulistic number Z71.16.6.

Eighty thousand as formulistic number Z71.16.8.

Eighteen hundred. — Dwarfs emigrate New Year's Eve of 1800 to return New Year's Eve of 1900 F451.9.3.

Eighteen thousand. — Giants live to be 18,000 years old F531.6.4.2.

Einherjar A165.7.

Eisenhammer, gang nach dem K1612.

Eisenhans G671.

Either .... or (sham threat) K1771.2.

Ejaculation guess N688.

Ejectment as punishment Q432.

Eland. — Man transformed to e. D114.1.2.

Elastic. — Man with e. reach F516.4.

Elbow. — Giant must rest on e. to be heard F531.2.10.

Elbows. — Indentions on rock from e. of hero's enemy A972.5.4; women kill with their e. G341.

Elder brother leads to ogre's home G401.1; brother rescues younger R155.2; brother threatens to kill unborn younger S73.1.3; brothers banished for treachery Q431.2.1; brothers impose task H934.4; brothers unwittingly aid youngest N733.3; children to protect younger P250.1. — Animals debate as to which is the e. B841.1; treacherous e. (brother) *K2211, (sister) *K2212; youngest brother helps e. L31; youngest brother rescues his e. brothers R155.1.

Elders. — Animal e. B1; Susanna and the e. J1153.1.

Elder (tree) cursed for serving as cross A2721.2.1.4; twigs reveal witch G257.6. — Tree-spirit in e. F441.2.3.2; why e. bleeds when cut A2766.1; why e. is never struck by lightning A2711.2.1.

Eldest brother as hero Z221; daughter will marry man only if he will marry all her sisters too T131.3; god born in front A161.5.

Election of fairies' king F252.1.1; of fox B239.1; of king in animal parliament B236. — Animal or object indicates e. of ruler H171ff.; bells sound e. of pope D1311.12.1; Virgin Mary designates favorite for e. for office V261; Virgin pardons e. cheater V261.2.

Electric shock scares away treasure diggers N561; storm breaks island F962.1; storm kills a thousand F968.1.

Elements silent, motionless at Nativity V211.1.5. — Death by e. as punishment M101.3.1, Q552.0.1; deity controls e. A197; four e. Z71.2.2; giants control e. F531.6.5.4; god reduces e. to order A175; magic control of e. *D1540ff., *D2140ff.; primary e. of universe A654; swearing by the e. M119.1.

Elephant accidentally poisoned N332.2.1; as animals' king B240.14; called "earth egg" J2671.3; carries person B557.11; cuts own leg to escape theft accusation K407.3; described by blind men J1761.10; determines road to be taken B151.1.4; draws plow to mark empire's boundaries B599.3; as drum beater J1882.3; eats poison man intended for self N627; frightened by moon's reflection J1791.12; as god's messenger A165.2.1.1.3; keeps house with other animals J512.7.1; killed by cutting off trunk K825.2; killed by mouse smearing poison L315.5.1; lets jackal enter stomach F929.1; loses its breasts A2353.3; offers chameleon ride on oiled tail K1042.1; put in pocket to show friends X941.3; rescues stolen girl B543.3.1; selects king's wife H171.1.1; transformed to object D421.3; transformed to person D314.3; -wrestler F617.1. — Abduction by e. R13.1.10; abduction by e.-man R16.5; airgoing e. B45; beautiful girl holding e. in each hand X943.1; bridegroom to meet disaster on e.

M340.4; bush mistaken for e. J1771.4; capture by hiding in artificial e. K754.2; capturing wild e. H1154.3.4; caring for mad e. H1155.4; creation of e. A1887; damages for broken pot: pay for e. K251.5; devastating e. B16.2.6; devil as e. G303.3.3.2.10; dispute of e. and ape J461.7; divine e. descends to earth F35.2; dragon as modified e. B11.2.1.6; drunk e. sent to attack enemy K2351.4; dwarf draws entrails from e. F451.3.4.11; earth rests on tortoise, serpent, and e. A844.6; enmity between e. and thousand-leg A2494.11.1; false boast: e. killed at one blow K1951.1.1; false claim: killed e. with hand K1787; firewood of e. tusks F811.22; fly jeers at king's e. J211.2.1; fool thinks God in e. J2499.5; friendship between e. and (dog) A2493.3.1, (jackal) A2493.11.2, M246.1.1, (monkey) A2493.14ff.; giant e. B871.5; giant uses e. as fish bait F531.3.12.1; god rides flying e. A136.1.5; god's e. A155.5; helpful e. B443.3; hired e. dies, owner wants live one back J1191.4; how can e. eat with tails at both ends? J1903.4; how e. got its tusks A2345.6; jackal cheats animals of mutually-killed e. K171.0.2; king selected by e. bowing to him H171.1; lark causes e. to fall over precipice L315.5; why e. does not live in town A2433.3.15; why e. lives in Nigeria A2434.3.3; magic jewel from e. B103.0.7; man disguised as e. K1823.2; man with e. head B28; man transformed to e. D114.2; marriage to e. B601.5; mice and hogs let loose put e. cavalry to flight K2351.3; mouse destroying e. H1161.3.1; numskull bribed to keep silent in e. sale N613; overcoming e. as task H1161.3; ox-demon transformed to e. D412.2.6; why e. is peaceable A2531.3; princess's husband selected by e. T63; rabbit and e. partners on trading expedition B294.6; reincarnation as e. E612.11; respite given while captive teaches e. to speak K551.11; riddle about deaths of e., snake, and jackal H803; savage e. lulled to sleep by virgin D1964.1; singing e. B214.1.12; sparrow intervenes in e. quarrel J2143.1; special power of chaste woman: raising fallen e. H413.4; stranger accidentally picked up by sacred e. and chosen king N683; strong man throws e. across sea F624.1.1; tame e. not accepted by wild brethren B261.1.1; test of resourcefulness: weighing e. H506.1; why e. has testicles inside A2284.4, A2365.1; tortoise leads e. into trap K730.4; vampire with e. face E251.4.1; wager on bullock defeating e. N77; white e. controls rain D2143.1.13; with rat transformed to white-winged e. D411.2.1; why e. flees when cock crows A2531.3.1; why e. has white marks A2412.1.5; why e. hurts self in grass: mouse's curse A2239.10; why e. lives without a hut A2432.10; why e. sees half-blindly A2332.6.7.

Elephant's enemies A2494.11. — Cause of e. walk A2441.1.7; animals' ears like e. until hare bites them off A2216.7; ascent to heaven by e. tail F75, J2133.5.2; earth rests on e. back A844.7; flies try to drink water from e. ears J971; god with e. face A131.2; jackal in e. belly eats liver, kills him K952.1.1; jackal imprisoned in e. dead body K1022.1.1; jackal in e. carcass K565.2; lie: child throwing e. carcass X943.1.1; man's ears like e. F531.2.12; princess rescued from e. captivity R111.1.12; person with e.

feet F517.1.7; stealing diamond from e. forehead H1151.6.1; stealing of e. tail (tusks) as task H1151.6; tortoise breaks e. back N335.7; why e. penis is large A2365.2.1.2; why mouse crushed in crossing road: e. curse A2239.9; woman captive in e. ear H1151.18.

Elephants B801; bring rain B791; fear swine's grunting J2614.3; have sexual desire only after eating mandrakes B754.2; lean from fairy music F369.8; look after ascetic in jungle B530.2. — Ants burrow into e. brains B524.1.8; captured e. pull together, escape J1024.1; city of e. F769.3; giant roasts e. G171; golden wagon drawn by four golden e. F861.1.2; hero fells maddened e. F628.1.6; journey to Land of E. F127.2; king of e. B241.2.11; land of e. B221.4; punishment: trampling by e. Q416.3; quest to land of e. H1289.1.1; war between e. and ants B263.2; war-e. B268.3.

Elevating. — Ground e. itself for saint V229.13.

Elevator. — Magic e. (stone on which one steps carries one underground) D1539.1.

Eleven as formulistic number Z71.7; portals to otherworld F156.5; rivers spring from well in midst of earth A875.2.

Elf, see also **Elves, Fairies;** knight entices maiden away and kills her F301.5; produces love-longing by blowing on horn F301.2.1; sets tasks for maid F301.4.

Elfland. — Girl from e. must eat earthly food in order to remain C661.

Elf-mound. — Magic bitches from e. B182.1.2; magic swine from e. B184.3.0.1.

Elfshot *D2066.

Elias drives devils from heaven G303.8.1.1; having had father and mother, is not dead (riddle) H814.

Eligius J2411.2.

Elijah passes to heaven alive D1856.1.1.

Elixir. — Cock's e. lightens people B739.1; conception from drinking e. from goat's horns T512.1; magic e. D1242ff., (to procure a child) T548.3.

Elk. — Capturing e. (task) H1154.5; color of e. A2411.1.6.6; creation of e. A1876; man-e. B29.6; needle kills an e. L391; why e. lives in woods A2433.3.13.

Elk's ears provide food D1472.1.24.3. — Magic e. head keeps falling down D1649.1.1.

Elopement R225; with wrong lover T92.4ff. — Fiancée forces e. with another man T157; man takes lover's place in e. K1317.9.

Eloping girl recaptured by parents R355; with king's daughter tabu C567.1; with woman who desires it obligatory C192. — Cave as e. lovers' refuge R315.1; forest as refuge of e. lovers R312.1; hero e. with king's fiancée slain K929.8; maid e. with pretended lover is forced by him to strip T72.1; princess e. with wrong man N318.2; rain charm sold to aid e. couple D2143.1.10; wooing emissary e. T51.1.1.

Eloquence, god of A465.3ff.

Elsa, Clever J2063.

Elusive. — Why game animals are e. A2552.
Elves, see also **Fairies;** *F200—F399; get stones from fairies D2066.1; have half thumb F232.7; have old men's faces F239.5; set country afire C934.3. — Woman beset by e., drowns self F324.2.
Elysium A151.
Emaciation caused by envy Q551.6.6.
Emasculation, see **Castration.**
Embalmed. — Lover's body kept e. for years by grieving mistress T85.4.
Embalming tabu C541.6.
Embarkation in leaky vessel as punishment Q466.
Embassy. — King imprisons another king's e. R3; royal bride conducted by e. to husband's kingdom T133.2; Zeus has e. of dogs imprisoned for fouling his court *Q433.3.
Embers transformed into animal D441.6. — Maidens unharmed by glowing e. D1841.3.2.4.
Embrace. — Disenchantment by enduring animal's e. D735.4; murder by crushing in false e. K953.4.
Embracing at village gate tabu C194.1. — Devil takes place of girl man is e. G303.9.9.16; lover dies from e. beloved T81.5; man e. other feels for gold K2021.3; princess e. teacher on wedding day M261.2.
Embroidering blanket in one day (task) H1093.
Embroidery on clothing as token H86.2. — Origin of e. A1465.2; recognition by e. H35.3.2.
Embryo, see also **Foetus.** — Soul of e. wanders E721.9.
Emerald box by well H1348.1. — City of e. F761.4.1; clusters of diamond and e. grapes F813.2.1.
Emeralds from broken vase A978.3.
Emergence of first man to earth A1230ff.; of stone from primeval water A816.1; of tribe from lower world A1631. — Witches at e. of mankind F203.2.
Emergency. — Ghost aids in e. E363.1.
Emetic. — Eaters of stolen food detected by e. J1144.1.
Emigration of dwarfs F451.9ff.
Emissary. — Kindness of e. saves girl's virginity T324; ruler pardons murdering e. W11.5.2; wooing by e. T51; wooing e. wins lady's love for himself T51.1.
Emissions. — Night e. from lusting bring near death T24.1.1.
Emotion. — Buttons burst as consequence of violent e. F1041.6; turning color from e. F1041.11.2.
Emotions. — Animals with human e. B773; divinity's e. A194.
Emotional reactions bring recognition H14. — Flood to satisfy e. need A1017.
Emperor blindfolded on ass traveling to paradise J2326.3; friendly to everyone W21; punished for murders Q211.0.3; rebukes overzealous servant as being a nuisance J554; thinks day lost when he gives no gifts W11.2.1. — Devil carries off murdering e. R11.2.1.1; dream warns e.

of wife's unfaithfulness *D1813.1.1; execution evaded by wishing to be e. J1181.2; girl flees lecherous e. T320.5; horse indicates election of e. H171.3; imaginary clothes for e. K445; punishment for deceiving e. Q236; servant plays at being e. J955.2.

Emperor's. — Death for dropping on e. coat Q411.15.

Empire personified Z116.1. — Elephant draws plow to mark boundaries of e. B599.3; prophecy of e. for fugitive hero M314.4.

Employed. — Sham-warrior e. at palace K1951.3.1.

Employees. — Tricks on new e. J2347.

Employment. — Don't work yourself out of e. J766; eavesdropping servant realizes misery of his e. N455.11.

Empousa B15.6.2.

Empress sews to show humility J918.

Empty shoe follows wild hunt E501.10.1. — Devil's shoes e. G303.4.5.1.2; noisy things often e. J262; sleeping in e. hut forbidden C735.2.2.

Emptying lake with pail in one day H1143.1. — Rain from e. bag in road D2143.1.8; rainbow from gods' e. their drinking cups A791.6.

Emu. — Why e. has no wings A2284.1, A2377.1.

Enamored. — Girl e. of monster T118; woman e. of unknown knight in tournament loses interest: he is her husband T236.

Enchanted heroine seen temporarily disenchanted H151.6.1; pear tree K1518; person *D5ff.; princess lives with dwarfs F451.5.4.3; snow K236.3. — Children e. by stepmother S31.2; city of e. people F768.2; giants e. in caverns F531.6.13.1; helpful animal an e. person B313; ordeal by e. water H222.3; person e. by witch's salve so as to be ridden by witch G241.2.2; soldiers of e. army tabu C549.2; stepdaughter e. by cruel stepmother on eve of wedding T154; tabu: destroying animal skin of e. person too soon *C757.1; transformation by plucking flowers in e. garden D515; witch has persons she has e. as servants G263.2.

Enchanter. — Disenchantment by destroying e. D763.

Enchantment by witch *G263. — Dwarfs free people from e. F451.3.3.4; magic object keeps off e. D1578; magic salve protects from e. D1385.6; seduction by feigning e. K1315.3.1; silence under punishment breaks power of e. *D1741.3; sleeping off e. period D1973.

Encircling by circumambulation *D1791, V58.3. — Disenchantment by e. D787; dragon e. city B11.2.8.1; seven seas e. world A872.1; snake e. world A1082.3.1; transformation by e. object thrice D563.

Enclosed. — Death e. in a bottle Z111.1; demon e. in bottle *D2177.1; enemy magically e. by walls D2091.16; fairy harper e. in yew tree F386.1.1; recognition by means of ring e. in wound H61.3; series of e. coffins F852.4.

Encounters, accidental H152, *N700—N799; unlucky N553.2.

Encouraging. — Dead mother e. daughter E323.6.

End formulas Z10.2; of the gods A1085; of king's reign P16; of world A1050ff. — Bringing deluge to e. A1028; castle at world's e. F771.3.1;

cock thinks world is coming to an e. Z43.3; "Consider the e." J21.1; date with beginning like e., (1691) H707.1; distance from one e. of earth to other (riddle) H681.1; divinity retires to e. of world A567; quest for the world's e. H1371.1; riddling remarks of traveling companions interpreted by girl at e. of journey H586; strong man's labor contract: blow at e. of year F613.1; wise man before entering a quarrel considers how it will e. J611.

Ending. — Enigmatic e. of tale H620ff.

Endless tales Z11.

Endogamy, origin of A1553.

Endurance contest won by deception K50ff.; of frightful experiences by youngest son in vigil for dead father H1462.1; of hardships with menial husband L113.1.0.1; powers as suitor test H328. — Contests in e. H1540ff.; tests of e. H1500—H1549; test of wife's e. H465; vampires power overcome by e. and prayer E251.1.1.

Endured. — Churchbells not e. by trolls G304.2.4.1; cross made by straps of knapsack not e. by devil G303.16.3.2; daylight not e. by ogre G632.

Enduring and overcoming curses M420ff. — Fame more e. than life L212.3.1.

Endymion given endless sleep M433.

Enema. — Murder by e. punished Q426.1.

Enemy attempts to kill helpful animal B335.3; chief vows to marry besieged city's princess M146.7; cured by poisoned cake F959.6.1; horses captured by lion join forces and become friends J891; invited for marriage, attacked K2013. — Army faces e. rather than the anger of their king J216.1; avoiding power of future e. J645; bringing best friend, worst e. H1065; bringing e. without weapon M234.2; defeated e. turns true friend P310.5; disregard advice of your e. J646; diving for reflected e. J1791.5; generosity toward e. W11.5; head of slain e. tabu C845.1; heart of e. eaten produces magic strength D1335.1.2; helpful animal killed by hero's e. B335; hostile dogs made friendly by having them fight the common e., the wolf J145; incognito king aids e. K1812.12; liquor as man's e. J1319.1; magic attack against e. D2091; magic object taken from e. D838.12; man keeps word to return to e. M202.2; owner frightened away from goods by report of approaching e. K335.0.1; princess in love with father's e. T95.0.1; prophecy: unborn child to kill e. M359.3; saint heals e. V441.1; saint's e. tries to induce his seduction T337.1; singing friendly song to e. K606.0.3; storm raised to defeat e. D2141.2; transformation to animal killing e. D651.1.1; transformation of e. D665; treacherous priests prolong mass to let e. destroy city K2354; tree points way to fugitive but misdirects e. D1393.4; uniting against common e. J624; vow against eating until e. killed M151.4; vow to attack e. or die M161.1; vow concerning fallen e. M166.1; wolf is the devil's craftiest e. G303.25.1.

Enemy's servant as helper N857; sex organs prove slaying H105.7. — Avoid e. revenge J647.1; capture by putting on e. clothes K761; death preferable to e. service M161.5; deceptive entry into e. presence K477.3; destruction of e. weapons J621; disguise in killed e. clothes K2357.7; falsely announcing e. approach as fear test H1405; killed e. son enslaved P173.2; lover disguised in e. clothes K1810.1.2; magic wand breaks e. sword D1414.1; prayer brings e. death V52.8; shooting at e. reflection in water J1791.5.1; taking boy to e. tent H1418; women spread shawls in e. path and entangle them K2352.

Enemies buried alive S123.6; caused to lose sight of each other K1886.2.1; duped into fighting each other K1082.0.1; make peace rather than slay each other *J218; won more by kindness than cruelty J26. — Animal betrays himself to his e. by talking J2351; why certain animals are e. A2494ff.; defeating e. as suitor task H335.4; foolishness of noise-making when e. overhear J581; friends' children become e. P310.4.2; god has e. kill him A179.3; god's e. A189.14; helpful buffaloes tramp hero's e. to death B524.1.5; hero tells e. how he may be killed K975.1.1; horse kills master's attacking e. B524.1.7; illusory e. K1883; magic causes e. to fight among selves *D2091.4; magic illusion protection against e. D2031.6.1ff.; magic object conquers e. D1400.1ff.; magic sack furnishes mannikin who cudgels owner's e. D1401.2; magic writing makes foster brothers e. P273.2.4; monk's e. quarrel and thus save him J581.3; preventing the birth of e. J622; quest for e. H1397; riddle: what are the two fixed .. the two eternal e.? H851; saint's bachall (brings down mountain on heads of e.) D1549.4, (keeps off e.) D1381.12; sham magician identifies e. as all dishonest K1956.10; transformation to defeat e. D651ff.; trolls as humans' e. F455.6.9.

Energy personified Z126.

Engagement, see also **Betrothal;** by trickery K1372. — Ring broken as token of broken e. Z151.

Engendered. — Strong hero marvelously e. F611.1.8.

Engendering, see also **Begetting.** — Pseudo-magic charm for e. offspring K115.1.4.

England must be full of widows J2214.11.

English. — Devil and Drake carry waters of E. Channel G303.9.2.4; why E. more powerful than Hindus A1689.11.1.

Engraved. — God's name e. on sun A733.2.

Engraving upon fire rock F809.6.2; shield with unique pattern H1199.4.

Engulfing. — Waters of heaven e. earth A810.2.1; water-spirits e. boy F420.5.2.2.2; why waters not e. earth A915.

Enigmas, see **Riddles.**

Enigmatic counsels of a father valuable H588; ending of tale H620ff.; happenings in otherworld F171.0.1; prophecy M306; quests H1377; smile (laugh) reveals secret knowledge N456; statements H580ff. — Daughter construes e. sayings H561.1.1.1.

Enjoying. — Disease to prevent man e. himself A1337.0.6, L482.5; woman e. enemy's ravishings T458.

Enjoyment preferred to wealth J484. — Devil advises e. and not thinking of God G303.9.7.2; husband objects to wife's e. of intercourse T257.8.

Enlarged. — Objects e. D480ff.

Enmity, see also **Enemies;** between animals from original quarrel *A2281ff.; between fisherman and dweller on the river U141; between giants F531.6.8.3; between priests and monks (chickens and eggs) X428. — Inherent e. between members of a family P201; liar brings e. between friends K1084.2; magic writings produce e. D1379.3.

Enoch Arden decision J1179.10.

Enormous, see also **Gigantic, Huge.** — Building e. bridge H1131; cleaning e. cistern in one day H1097.2; collecting e. amount of material H1149.4; dragon of e. size B11.2.12; strong hero sent from home because of e. appetite F612.1.

Enough. — Let well e. alone J513.

Enslaved, see also **Slave.** — Choice: free poverty or e. wealth J211; equanimity of the e. W25.1; ruler e. L410.6.

Entangled. — Enemy e. by women's shawls K2352.

Entering body of dead parrot or rajah K1175; fairyland through well F212.1; house after sunset tabu C752.1.3. — Devil e. another's body G303.18; means of e. house or treasury K310ff.; soul e. body E720ff.; suitor test: e. princess's chamber *H344; tabu on e. woman's quarters C182.2; vow against e. house other than own M182; wise man before e. quarrel considers how it will end J611.

Entertained. — Mortal e. by disguised god K1811.0.1; strangers e. by family to whose hitching-ring they happen to tie their horses P328.

Entertainer. — Trickster as e. steals meat K341.19.

Entertaining strangers tabu C745. — Woman e. every traveler H152.1.1.

Entertainment. — Inappropriate e. repaid J1565; king demands e. from guests P337.

Enticing guardian away K629.2. — Fairies e. to fairyland F301ff., F328; fairies e. by stopping ship F302.3.1.2; seduction by e. aboard ship to inspect wares K1332; wolf tries e. goat down from high place K2061.4.

Enticements. — Fatal e. of phantom women F585.1; rival suitors sleep with princess and vie in e. so that she will turn to them H315.

Entrails substituted for meat K476.1. — Boar's e. torn out F981.8; dwarf draws e. from elephant F451.3.4.11; eating his own e. K1025; excreting own e. Q559.11; fettering with own sons' e. Q469.7.1; hero pretends to eat own e. K1721.1; magic e. of animal D1015.3; man's e. visible when he laughs F594; pigeon's e. fetch lover D1355.3.4; punishment: twisting e. from body Q469.7; soul in e. E714.11; why Santals eat e. of hare A1422.1.1; wild huntsmen with e. stringing from open bodies E501.7.5; witch eats person's e. G262.2.

Entrance to dwarf home leads through filthy place F451.4.1.7; to fairy land underground F211.1, F211.2, into girl's (man's) room (bed) by trick *K1340ff.; of house impossible (for devil if horseshoe is over door) *G303.16.17, (for mountain-man before light is put out) F460.2.3; to lower world F91ff.; to otherworld F150ff.; to upper world F50ff. — Capture by closing e. to victim's home K737; castle revolving at night so that e. cannot be found F771.2.6.2; death on e. to marriage chamber M341.1.1.4; dupe lured into hole, e. closed K737.1; dwarf seeks e. to church F451.5.9.5; lions placed in city to prevent e. B847.

Entrapped suitors K1218.1. — Ogre e. in cage G514.1.

Envious jackal makes lion suspicious of his friend the bull K2131.2; man sets out to kill generous one W18. — Accuser e. of harlot J1351.2; children e. of money given by deceased father to bishop V415; covetous and e. J2074; prince e. of hero's wife assigns hero tasks H931.1; wild ass e. of tame ass until he sees his burdens L451.2.

Environment. — Acquisition of livable e. A1410ff.; animal "punished" by being placed in favorite e. K581.

Envoys debate which due greatest honor W161.1. — Mutilation of e. S160.4.

Envy W195; punished Q302. — Death from e. F1041.1.10; no e. in otherworld F172.1.

Ephesus. — Matron of E. K2213.1; seven sleepers of E. D1960.1.

Epic remembered from one hearing F692.1. — Quest for unknown e. H1382.2; return from dead to repeat e. E371.2.

Epicureans as atheists V323.1.

Epidemic. — Eating cure becomes e. J1511.3; owners frightened away from goods by report of deadly e. K335.0.2; saint ends e. *D2162.1ff.

Epilepsy remedy D2161.3.8.1. — Origin of e. A1337.3.

Epiphany. — Wild hunt appears between Christmas and E. E501.11.2.2.

Epistle. — Magic e. assures wearer will utter truth D1316.9.

Epoch. — New sun starts new e. A719.2.

Equal share of chief's bed J2526. — Association of e. and unequal J410ff.; hero seeks his e. H1381.5; marriage with e. or with unequal J414; princess to marry her e. T50.2.1; wife as one's e. J21.31.

Equals. — Friendship possible only between e. P310.8.

Equanimity of comedian when his house is carried off by flood W25.

Equivocal inscriptions at parting of three roads N122.0.1; oath K550.1, K1513, M105; prophecy of immunity M367.1. — Theft by assuming e. name K359.2.

Equivocation. — Cheating through e. K475ff.; deception by e. *K2310ff.

Erbsenprobe H41.1.

Eric fines P535.

Erin. — Prophecy; death between E. and Alba M341.3.2.

Eriu. — King's espousal to E. P11.6.

Ermanrikr sends sons, nephews to death K948.

Ermine. — Color of e. A2411.2.2; man becomes e. D124.2; why tail-tip of e. is black A2218, A2378.8.4.

Erotic scenes on bedroom walls reform continent husband T315.2.2.1.

Errand. — Escape by pretending to perform e. for captor K567; fool's e. J2346; owner sent on e. and goods stolen K343.1; taking year to do e. J2461.4.

Esau as magician D1711.1.2.

Escape by deception *K500—K699; from deluge A1020ff.; from devil by answering his riddles H543; on flying horse B542.2; from lower world by magic F101.4; from one misfortune into worse N255; from prison by use of magic fiddle D1395.1; from sea on fish's back B541.1; to the stars R321; of trickster without paying K233; on tree R311; from undesired lover *T320ff., (by deceptive respite) K1227; from witch G276ff. — Children e. to sky and become thunder A1142.3; disguised wife helps husband e. from prison R152.1; easy e. of weak (small) *L330ff.; flight of maiden to e. marriage T311.1; fettered monster's e. at end of world A1070ff.; knockers prevent trapped miners' e. F456.1.2.1.4; leave a loophole for e. J762; magic circle prevents e. D1417.1; magic object maintains quiet so that fugitive may e. D1393.2; sack from which one cannot e. D1413.9.1; tasks assigned prisoner so that he may e. punishment H924; transformation to e. difficult situation *D642ff.; transformation to old man to e. recognition D1891; troubles e. when forbidden casket is opened C915.1; vain attempts to e. fulfillment of prophecy M370ff.; wife swims to husband, arranges his e. T215.6.

Escapes *R210ff.; by magic *D2165ff. — Accidental e. N660; extraordinary e. *F1088.

Escaped lamb delivers himself to shepherd rather than to slaughter J217.1. — Detection e. by thief *K400ff.; devil's power may be e. G303.16ff.; execution e. by use of special permissions granted the condemned *J1181; witch overcome or e. *G270ff.

Escaping before enemy can strike J641. — Gods tricked into help in e. one's fate K2371.2; prisoners e. by asking leave K475.2; selling oneself and e. K252; victim e. executioner makes substitution K512.2.2.1; witch e. from locked room G288.

Escort. — Devil as girl's e. to dance G303.10.4.4.

Esdras chain: stronger and strongest (cumulative tale) Z41.2.1.

Eskimo, origin of A1611.1.2.

Establishment of animal life A1700—A2199; of human life A1200—A1699; of natural order A1100ff.; of plant life A2600—A2799.

Estate. — Ghost protects his e. E236.6; post falls when owners lose e. E766.3.

Estranged couple pay trickster for reconciliation K441.4. — Brothers e. by witch G269.7.

Eternal bats B19.9; ferryman P413.1; god A102.6; life without eternal

youth as curse M416.2; youth D1883. — First men had e. life A117.1; two e. enemies (riddle) H851.

Eternity. — Seconds in e. (riddle) H701ff.

Ethereal music E402.4.

Etiquette. — Social e. A1537.

Eucharist, see also **Communion, Consecrated bread, Sacrament.** — Jewish child thrown into oven by father for taking e. V363.

Eumenides A486, C433.

Eunuch visits augurer to see whether he is to be a father J1271; says that his ill fortune is no shame J1471. — Widow rejects e. as estate-manager husband K2052.4.2.

Eunuchs, origin of A1313.0.1.

Europe. — Slaughter from wheel rolling over E. M341.2.20.

Europeans know more than natives A1667.1. — Origin of E. A1611.5.

Eustacius pursued by misfortune N251.

Evaded. — Death e. (person enters on the next life without dying) D1856, (by strong man) F615ff.; death order e. K510ff.; direct answer e. J1254; execution e. by using three wishes J1181.1; guardian animals e. B576.1.1; law e. by marriage for a night T156; ogre's power e. G534; task e. by subterfuge H950ff.; wild hunt e. E501.17ff.

Evangelist. — Seduction on promise issue will be fifth E. K1315.1.2.

Evangelium secundum Pergamum J1741.1.

Eve dreams of Cain, Abel D1812.3.3.7; names female animals A2571.0.2. — Adam learns animal languages from E. B217.8; devil appears to E. G303.6.2.11; devil gives E. two grains of corn G303.9.4.1; devil tempts E. A63.6; disobedience of E. blamed H1557.2; monkeys from children hidden by E. when God visited her A1861.1; new E. (mouse in jug) H1554.1; riddles concerning E. H811, H812, H813; Satan's intercourse with E. G303.12.7.1; tears of E. leaving paradise become trees A2612.1; underworld people from children which E. hid from God *F251.4; various children of E. *A1650.1; why E. not made with Adam A1275.8.

Eve's clothes of light F821.7.

Evening. — Four legs in morning, two at midday, and three in e. (riddle) H761; god of e. star A252; monster comes out of hole in e. G346.0.1.

Evenings. — Lower world people drink, dance in e. F108.2.

Events, extraordinary F900—F1099.

Ever-blooming garden in otherworld F162.1.1; -burning lamp D1652.6.

Evergreen. — Why leaves are e. A2765.

Everyman tests friends H1558.3.

Everyone asleep in castle F771.4.4; falls in love with princess T15.1.

Everything to turn to gold (Midas's touch) J2072.1. — First people have e. they wish A1346.2.2; "pick up e.!": fool picks up dung J2516.2.1.

Evidence of crime left so that dupe is blamed K2155. — Cane as e. of robbery N614; cleverness connected with the giving of e. J1150ff.; ghost leaves e. of appearance E544.

Evil ascetic misuses magic V462.13; deeds of witches G260ff.; demons set world on fire A1031.3; effects of meeting wild hunt E501.18ff.; magic in the dairy *D2083; man cast from grave E411.0.7; omens D1812.5.1ff.; predictions concerning journeys M358.1; spirits *F402ff., G0—G699, (born of echo) G302.1.2, (cast out of person) E728.1, (conjured away in name of deity) *D1766.7.1.1, (exorcised) *D2176.3, (hold back river) D2151.2.3.1, (possess person) E728, (prevented from using body) E752.10. — All e. will have an end J171.2.3; why animal is e. A2523; association of good and e. J450ff.; bull melts away after e. spirit has issued from him F981.2; conflict of good and e. creators A50ff.; culture hero spares certain e. spirits A531.1; devil originates from e. man's spittle G303.1.1.2.1; dragon as power of e. B11.9; father makes an e. greater H583.2.1; horse unable to draw e. dead man E411.0.3; huntsmen cannot die until e. righted E501.3.9; Jesus drives e. spirits into hogs: hence short snouts A2287.1ff.; land without e. F111.6; left hand for e. *D996.0.2.1; loss of all e. as reward Q150.2; magic book compels person to do e. D1678; magic journey during which one must not think good or e. D2121.6; magic object protects from e. spirits *D1385ff.; man speaks no e. W24; "may God spare you from e. man or woman" J21.38; north as abode of e. spirits G633; numskull believes self e. spirit J2013.4; opposition of good and e. gods A106; present e. preferred to change for worse J215; prophecy: unborn child to bring e. on land M356.3; putting out of countenance by telling e. stories J1211; revealing hiding place to e. spirits J2367; revolt of E. Angels against God A106.2; room in hell for e. spirits A678; storm from calling on e. spirit D2141.0.1; to be carried off by e. spirit M432; tree of knowledge of good and e. F162.3.5; transformation by e. spirits D683.6; wisdom from e. spirits J176.

Evils, choice between J210ff.

Evil Eye *D2071ff.; sets bird on fire D2061.2.1.1. — Counter magic against E. D2071.1.5; god with E. A128.2.1; islands transformed by E. of one-eyed god A955.5; magic paralysis by E. D2072.1.

Evolution. — Creation of man through e. A1220ff.; creation of universe through e. A620.1.

Ewe's hide grafted to man's head E785.1.1.

Ewes. — Fairies cause e. to have two lambs F339.3.2.

Ewige Jude Q502.1.

Exaggeration. — Humor of lies and e. *X900—X1899, K657.

Exaltation of the lowly L0—L499, (riddle) H797.1. — Spiritual e. from eating human flesh *G13.

Exalted person rescues abandoned child R131.11. — Wish for e. husband realized *N201.

Examination of strange country in disguise J21.43. — Animal corrects e. paper for rescuer B579.3; Christ's disciples did not pass e. J1263.1.4; separate e. of witnesses discredits testimony J1153.

Example. — Animal gives wise e. to man J133ff.; king's e. makes merchant wealthy N415.
Excavated. — Passage e. by fairies F271.2.1.
Excavation. — Sea from earth e. A924.4.
Excelling. — Man e. woman A1376.
Exception. — Dissolute wife only e. to man's happiness J1355.
Exceptions, unique *Z300—Z399.
Excess. — Death from e. of women T99.1.
Excessive demands to prevent marriage H301; use of magic power C762.1, D877.
Exchange, see also **Bargain;** of clothes between master and servant K527.3; of duties brings disaster J512.7; of forms by persons D45ff.; of gold-filled loaf for common N351. — Animal characteristics from e. of qualities *A2247ff.; betrayal through e. of stolen goods K439.1; deceptive e.: useless for magic object K140.1; devil to help gambler in e for one task yearly M214; female slaves as medium of e. P170.0.1.1; helpful animal obtained by e. B312.2; magic object acquired by e. (no trick) *D851, (trick) D831; man and wife e. duties J2431, *K1687; plant characteristics from e. of qualities A2742; pretended e. of confidences as to the one thing that can kill K975.1; theft of fire by trick e. A1415.3.
Exchanges. — Series of trick e. Z47.
Exchanged. — Children e. in cradle by dwarfs F451.5.2.3; children e. by parents K1921; eye e. for wisdom J163.3; eyes e. for food M225; foetus e. from one woman to another T577; immortality e. D1853; magic object e. for worthless D871.1; organs e. with animal E789.1; wives e. T141.2.
Exchanging objects with the devil G303.9.9.10; soul for witch powers G224.4. — Animal languages learned by e. tongues with helpful dragon B217.6; confessor and penitent e. confidences V29.7; dissatisfied workmen e. work U136.1; men e. duties: each cheated J2431.1; men e. jobs: each thinks other's easier K1687; mothers e. children S216; trickster e. beds, gets rival's food K499.8.
Excitement. — Death from e. F1041.1.3.9.
Excommunicated person cannot rest in grave E412.1. — Hog will not accept food from e. men B259.3; tabu to aid e. C95.
Excommunication V84; of animal B275.2; as punishment Q436.
Excrement, see also **Dung, Manure.** — Birth from e. T541.8.1; deceptive e. exchange K1721.2; extraordinary e. F559.3; horse trade involves eating e. K198; magic e. as cure for cancer D1502.10.1; why red dog's e. contains animal hair A2385.2; resuscitation from e. E41; rope of e. J2133.12; why crow eats e. A2435.4.7.1.
Excrements as advisers *D1312.1.1; of animals A2385; cause approaching animals to fall dead D1402.18; eaten by mistake J1772.9; thought to be berries J1772.9.1; transformed to person D437.4. — Animal's treatment of its e. A2495; doll's gold e. D1469.2; donkeys ask immediate reward: eat own e. A2232.11; magic e. *D1002; man finds cat's e. after

he dreams he is rich X31.1; origin of e. A1317; speaking e. D1610.6.4; treasure from e. D1454.5; trickster creates men from his e. J2186; why pigs feed on e. A2435.3.14.1.

Excreting own entrails as heresy punishment Q559.11. — Dog e. sweet dung K135.1.3; power of e. jewels D1561.2.1; worm e. earth A828.1.

Excuse. — Thief makes a lame e. J1391.

Excuses. — Lovers' absurd e. for intrigue K1271.2.

Executed. — Animal e. for crime B275.1; blood of e. man as remedy D1500.1.7.3.1; fox e. for thefts B275.1.2; ghost of unjustly e. man E234.4; innocent man e. because he is right size J2233.1; man whose neck rope fits to be e. P14.18; ravisher e. Q244.0.1; whoever e. one day destined to become king in next birth J1189.3; witch e. for witchcraft G291.

Execution escaped by use of special permissions *J1181; release by marrying woman P512.1. — Altered letter of e. gives princess to hero *K1355; at e. man revealed as king's son N731.4; criminal allowed to choose his method of e. P511; delay in pardon allows deserved e. N394; escape from e. *R215; fat man chosen for e. N178.2; foolish demands before e. J2174; friend saved from e. P319.3; helpful animals quench e. fire *B526.1; husband's letter protecting wife altered to e. order K2117.1; identity established just in time to avert e. N686; king lured by e. invitation, killed K811.3; king sends regrets for e. K2098; long gray beard suddenly acquired on scaffold at e. F1044; loss of eye saves man from e. N178; making a good e. J2233; man carries written order for his own e. *K978; magic manifestation at e. proves innocence H215; magic object saves person from e. *D1391ff.; sham e. fatal to jester N384.7; speech magically recovered on e. stake D2025.1; substitute for e. obtained by trickery K841; wind blowing flag causes prisoner's e. N394.1.

Executioner miraculously blinded and condemned man saved R176; persuaded another victim ordered K511.1. — Compassionate e. K512ff.; sword magically changes to wood when e. is to decapitate innocent person H215.1; trickster calls self e., gets all food K344.1.3.

Exercises, religious J2495, V4.

Exhibiting. — Fairy woman e. self to warriors F397; person e. own nude figure T55.6.

Exhilarating. — Magic fruit e. D1359.3.3.

Exile returns and is successful L111.1; for seven years Z71.5.5. — Brothers follow each other into e. P251.3; prince chooses e. in honor J347.3.

Exiled king teaches ruler wisdom J55; wife's dearest possession J1545.4. —Accidental meeting of seeker of e. prince with prince at meal N745; devastating host e. by fairies F349.3; subject e. for trivial remark U38.

Existence of animals depends on man's e. A2513.0.1. — Vow fulfilled in next e. M107.

Exit. — Slamming door on e. from mountain otherworld *F91.1.

Exits. — How many e. from paradise? H682.3.
Exogamy T131.5; origin of A1553.
Exonerating. — Dead saint e. cleric E376.1.
Exorbitant price demanded, received K255.
Exorciser torments spirit F405.14.
Exorcising devil by "Ave" V254.4; ghosts E443; giants F531.5.8.2; by magic *D2176ff.; Will o' the Wisp F491.3; witches *G271. — Man killed for e. ghost E247; priest e. demon mistaken for demon J1786.4; spirit gives e. powers D1721.1.3.
Expelling demons from saint's grave D1385.1. — Magic object e. animals D1443; magic object e. person from land D1587; mother e. child S12.5; saint e. devil to hell G303.16.11.4; trickster e. owner from his house K354.
Expenses. — Kingdom's e. outweigh gains J342.2.
Expensive living along with high wages J342. — Child every two months too e. J1276.2; is wine e. or cheap? J1315.
Experience. — Counsels proved wise by e. *J21ff.; enigmatic statement made clear by e. H592; plants originate from e. of holy person A2620ff.; riddle expounded from chance e. H565; wisdom (knowledge) acquired from e. J10ff.
Experiences during magic sleep D1976; leading to adventures N770ff. — Identity tested by demanding account of common e. H15; marital e. of the devil G303.12; revealing e. in otherworld forbidden C423.3.
Experiments. — Man created after series of unsuccessful e. A1226.
Experimental. — Decisions based on e. tests J1176.
Explanation of natural phenomena A1200—A2899. — Quest for e. of dream H1217.1; riddles of e. H770ff.
Explanations. — Three e., last true Z64.
Exploits. — King chosen for e. P11.4; tears at recital of own e. H14.2; tokens of e. H84.
Explosion. — Witch causes gun e. G269.16.
Exposed child rescued R131ff. — Amorous intrigue observed and e. K1271; children e. S301; honey-covered victim e. to flies Q464; impostors e. K1935.1; infidelity of husbands e. by crown H422.1; mistress e. naked to her husband Q476; prince in love with girl e. in jungle T91.6.3.1; queen e. in leather in market Q483.1; sham magician e. by clever girl K1963.1; sheep, oxen protect e. child B535.0.10.
Exposure in boat *S141, (as sin test) H263.1; of infant to avoid fulfillment of prophecy M371; of own baby instead of tyrant's P361.4; to sunlight forbidden C842; astride wood in river S141.3; to ridicule when wig snatched off X52.1. — Cruel e. S140ff.; ordeal by e. H236; punishment: unseemly e. Q495.
Expression. — Allusive e. for gods' incest A1599.16; forbidden e. C498.
Expressions. — Commonplace e. scare off wife's suitors J2461.2.2.
Expulsion from court saves counselor's life N178.3; of devil from heaven

G303.8ff.; from fairyland for breaking tabu F378.0.1. — Fairy mistress demands e. of wife F302.5.4.

Extending. — Giant e. across whole island F531.2.1.4; ogress e. limbs any distance G365.2; rakshasas e. bodies far G369.1.1.

Extermination of mice infesting city H1109.4. — Expensive e. of rodents J2103.

External soul *E710ff. — Animals help man overcome monster with e. soul B571.1; escape by alleged possession of e. soul K544; life dependent on e. object or event *E765ff.; secret of e. soul learned by deception K975.2.

Extinct. — Why griffin is e. A2232.4.

Extinguishing, see also **Quenching;** fire by spitting H221.5. — Miraculous rain e. fire *D1391.1.

Extortion W193; by confessor V29.9.

Extraordinary, see also **Unusual;** actions explained H591; behavior of trees and plants F970ff.; bodies of water F710ff.; buildings and furnishings F770ff.; cities F760ff.; clothes in otherworld F166.3; clothing and ornaments F820ff.; companions F601ff.; cures F950ff.; islands *F730ff.; mountains and valleys F750ff.; nature phenomena F960ff.; occurrences F900—F1099, (concerning seas or waters) F930ff., (concerning animals) F980ff.; persons F500—F599; places and things F700—F899; rocks and stones F800ff.; sights in otherworld F171; sky and weather phenomena F790ff.; swallowings F910ff.; trees and plants F810ff.; underground disappearance F940ff.; weapons F830ff. — Asking questions about e. things inadvisable J21.6; brothers acquire e. skill *F660.1; conception from e. intercourse T517; finding e. object as suitor test H355; horse's head for e. use F874; persons with e. powers F600—F699; quest for e. plants H1333; recognition by e. prowess H32; treasure buried in e. topographical formations N511.1.3; witch with e. members G213ff.

Extravagant wife J1701.1. — Haughty mistress makes e. demands of lover: repaid L431.1.

Extremes. — Cumulative tales involving e. Z51. — Foolish e. J2500—J2549.

Eye bursts from voice overstrain F1085; drops prescribed for stomach ache X372.3; juggler J2423; lost waiting for water to become wine D477.1.2; remedy (for blinding) K1011; transformed to other object D457.11; in vulva F547.5.3. — Bird's red e. cooks meat F989.2; birth from an e. T541.7; boy asks sister for an e. and ear T415.7; cat's luminous e. *B721; charm for diseased e. D1505.11; child born with one e. T551.11, Q556.4.1; crane pecks out e. of spy Q557.5; "crookedness in e." from curse D2062.2.1.1; curse: loss of e. M431.1; demon with one e. G369.7; devil inflames saint's e. G303.9.6.2.1; disguise by cutting one e. out D1821.6; fleeing fox loses e. in briars J2182; foolish lover does not know that his mistress lacks e. J1737.1; fork in e. from breaking tabu

C943.1; fortune has one e. N111.2.1.1; giant with one e. blind G511.1; ghost as an e. E422.1.11.1; god with blazing e. A124.1; horse with blue e. H1331.4.1; hot onion to e. J2412.1; husband's one e. covered K1516ff.; islands transformed by evil e. of one-eyed god A955.5; king gives away his only e. W11.16; left e. only vulnerable spot Z311.1; loss of e. (for breaking tabu) C943.2, (saves man from execution) N178; magic e. D993; magic sight by putting ointment into e. D1821.4; magic watchful e. remains awake while other eyes sleep D1961; man condemned to lose his e. allowed to choose the instrument P511.2; man made from creator's e. A1211.4; man so small he can go through e. of needle F535.2.2; nightingale borrows blindworm's e. A2241.5; one e. exchanged for wisdom J163.3; one e. recedes, other protrudes when angry F1041.16.2; one wishes that he may lose an e., so that other will be blind J2074; parson with one e. marries wrong couples X413; persons blown into woman's e. X941.4; pulling out e. so that pain will cease J2412.2; reward for tearing out e. Q42.6; returning e. to one-eyed man J1512.2; saint plucks out e. to avoid marriage T327.3; saint's prayer restores opponent's e. V52.15; skillful marksman shoots animal through e. F661.5ff.; skillful surgeon removes speck from midge's e. F668.2; soul leaves body through e. E722.2.11; sun's all-seeing e. A739.7; three persons with one e. *F512.1.2, *G121.1ff., G612, *K333.2; throbbing of right e. as favorable omen D1812.5.2.1; watch mistaken for the devil's e. J1781.2; water-spirits' one e. F420.1.1.5; why center of e. is black A1319.7; why soldiers with one e. good J1494; wood spirit gigantic with one e. in center of forehead *F441.4.1.

Eyes of animal substituted as proof for children's K512.2.0.2; burst forth for urging saint to marry Q551.8.4; fall out of blasphemer's head Q551.6.5.2; of giant F531.1.1ff.; exchanged for food M225; lost from looking at forbidden well C623.1; magically replaced D2161.3.1.1; successfully replaced *E781ff.; as sacrifice V12.7; size of brass pots F531.2.12; of stone lion become bloody D474.9; the swiftest (riddle) H632.2, H661; treated for the stomach ache J1603; of various peoples A1666; which can see heaven D1820.3; wagered N2.3.3. — Adulteress binding husband's e. K1566.1; animals with unusual e. B15.4ff.; bad character shown by e. H1550.1; beetle cursed for betraying Holy Family: now always has e. on ground A2231.7.1.1; blind comforted by soul's inner e. J893.1; blindness cured by rubbing sand on e. F952.3; bright e. as sign of royalty H71.6; buffalo's e. turn into protecting dogs D699.1; casting sheep's e. at the bride *J2462.2; cock persuaded to crow with closed e. K721; cross-e. miraculously straightened F959.2; devil's e. G303.4.1.2ff.; devil gives horse four e. but God reduces to two A2286.2.2; discourteous answer: why crab has e. behind A2231.1.3; dogs with e. hanging out over mouth in wild hunt E501.4.1.4; dogs with fiery e. in wild hunt E501.4.1.3; dwarf-deer pastes other animals' e. shut and pretends that hunters are coming K2382.2; eating own e.

K1025.2; eel burned by torch: hence red e. A2218.8; fairy's red. e. F233.3.1; fairies made visible through use of magic stone on e. F235.4.3; fright at animal's e. in the dark J2624; genie sleeps with e. open G634; ghosts as dogs with glowing tongues and e. E421.3.6; god with unusual e. A123.3ff.; goddess born from mother's e. A112.7.3; goddess of thousand e. A475.1.1.1; hare instructs his sons to use their e. to advantage J61; headache cure: removing e. K1011.1; headless person with e. on breast F511.0.1.1; hero's different colored e. A526.5.1; hero's e. would pop out if washed B521.1.1; horse originally had e. on feet A2262.1; horse with fiery e. in wild hunt *E501.4.2.5; host, hostess, and cat have but three e. among them J551.4; house lined with human e. F163.3.2.1; house with neither e. nor ears (enigma) H583.8; images open and close e. D1632; lemur looks where forbidden: has big e. A2234.3; magic journey with closed e. D2121.2; maiden sends to her lecherous lover her e. T327.1; mother's e. the brightest (riddle) H651.2; mutilation: putting out e. *S165; necklace of human e. F827.4; numskull puts out his e. J2131.4; opening of creator's e. creates day A1171.1; origin and nature of animals' e. A2332ff.; origin of e. A1316.3; pepper or tobacco thrown into e. of guard *K621; person transformed to animal recognized by his e. H62.1.1; person unusual as to his e. F512ff.; person without e. F512.5; poor host closes e. not to see guest eat P336.3; putting out wife's e. J2462.3; raven plucks out men's e. B17.2.3.1; reincarnation of e. into currants E649.5; remarkable e. F541ff.; scorpion scoops out men's e. B17.2.4.1; seeing without e. X1724; serpent demands human e. for drink S263.3.2; servant cheats master boasting of e. in back of head J1511.9; severed head opens e. E783.4; sham dead detected by batting e. H248.5; skillful marksman shoots both e. of an ogre F661.5.4; sun and moon (placed for e. in the sky) A714.1, (as Rama's e. torn out) A714.7; tempted rabbi tears out e. T333.3.1; toad trades his tail for mole's e. A2247.5; vampire with e. of owls E251.4.3; washing e. to keep awake H1484.1; where owl got his e. A2332.1.5; why caribou has small e. A2332.3.3; why frog's e. bulge out A2332.4.3; why rats don't stick their e. out in the straw J2371.3; why zabi's e. narrow: laughs so hard A2332.3.2; wife puts out one of her e. to show sympathy with her husband T215.4; wife's e. invulnerable to sea water D1841.4.5; wild huntsmen with fiery e. E501.7.6.2; witch with extraordinary e. G213; witches use animals' e. at night G249.10.1; witness claims e. were blown shut J1158.1; woman with bad e. J1169.1; women throw ashes in e. of attacking soldiers so that they are defeated K2356.

Eyeballs transformed to torches D457.11.2. — Sucking snake's e. T611.11.

Eyebrow. — Magic hair in man's e. kills all who see it D1402.2; poisonous e. causes death to beholder F555.7.

Eyebrows so heavy must be on back to see F441.4.5. — Devil has no e. G303.4.1.2.6; hardest to hold wolf by e. H659.2.1; helper's beard and e. cut N810.2.

Eye-hole. — Giant's skull so large that fowl can pass through e. F531.2.3.1.

Eyelashes. — Origin of e. A1315.6; path to sun on sun's e. (rays) F154.

Eyelid. — God with handle through e. A128.2.2; heavy e. F541.7.

Eyelids. — Flight so high that e. drop from cold F1021.2.2; ogre so old that his e. must be propped up G631; old man with hanging e. F571.1.

Eyesight lost by spying on holy cloak D1410.8; regained with stolen eyes E781.1.1. — Humor of bad e. X120ff.; magic object affects e. *D1331ff.; plea to God for riches, issue, restoration of e. K2371.3; youngest wife's son restores e. to rajah's wives L13.1.

Face of angry warrior aflame F1041.16.6.4; chilled for breaking tabu C948.7; of dwarf F451.2.5; must be wiped dry after washing A1599.4; of saint radiant F574.3.1. — Corpse buried f. down S139.2.2.3.1, V61.4.1; demon with black f. G342; devil's f. G303.4.1.7; fish with human f. B83; ghost as f. E422.1.11.2; ghost with glowing f. E421.3.3; ghost strikes man's f. E542.1.4; girl's f. becomes angelic at death D1865.3; giant's f. elbow-length wide F531.2.2.1; god unusual as to f. A123.2ff.; ill-omened f. of king N119.3; luminous f. as sign of royalty H71.6.1; lips on side of f. F544.1.4; magic f. D992.3; man disfigures f. to remove temptation T333.3; man's destiny read in his f. M302.2.2; mask mistaken for f. J1793; naked Indian not cold: "Me all f." J1309.1; origin of animal's f. A2330ff.; person killed by hitting fly on f. *N333.1; person unusual as to his f. F511.1ff.; punishment: f. distorted Q551.8.7; rat persuades cat to wash f. before eating K562; red, black f. after being burned F1082.1; satire causes f. ulcers D1402.15.3; slap turns man's f. around F1041.24; sun hides f. in shame: hence eclipse A737.8.1; sun turns fiery f. upward A1135.1.1; vampire with elephant f. E251.4.1.

Faces. — Elves' f. like old men's F239.5; fire, hail as sun's f. A733.3; Fortuna with two f. N111.2.2; god with many f. A123.2.1; man born at first with two f. A1316.0.1; men with two f. F526.5; spirits allow people with f. to ground to pass F406.3.

Facial features F545; (of goddess reversed) A282.0.1.1. — Animal pressed: hence f. or bodily marks A2213.2ff.; origin of f. features A1316.

Facing. — Prayer f. east V58.2; warrior dies f. foe P557.6.

Facts, absurd disregard of J1850—J1999.

Fading of spirit into air F407.2; of tree (flower) as life token *E761.3.

Fáfnir a dragon from transformed man B11.1.3.

Faggot. — Magic f. D957, (drips to indicate rising tide) D1324.2.

Faggots transformed to chargers D441.3.1. — Bundle of f. held together by snake H1023.19.

Failure in all efforts (as curse) M441, (as punishment) Q553.6; to bless mountains gives mountain-men power F460.4.6; of crops during reign of wicked king Q552.3; of devil when he tries to wall in too large a piece of ground in a night G303.13.3; of false bride when husband tests her K1911.3.3; in resuscitation because of premature disturbance

of members E37.1. — Continual f. to find treasure N550.1; ghosts punish f. to provide for their wants E245; riddle propounded with penalty for f. H541; wild huntsman wanders for f. to keep fast day E501.3.5; wood-spirits cause f. F441.6.1.

Faint. — Deception by pretended f. K1818.6; woman in sham f. revived by beating K1676.1.

Fainting brings recovery of speech F954.3; from fright for lover T24.2.2; away for love T24.2.1; from noise of wooden pestle and mortar F647.8; at sight of goddess F1041.1.6.1. — Pretended f. when husband strikes adulteress with a rose K2051.2.

Fair by night and ugly by day D621.3. — Fairies f. F233.6; fairies hold a f. F258.1; forbidden horse f. C619.3; man on island of F. Women overcome by loving women F112.1; why go all way to f.? vendor robbed en route K475.3.

Fairs. — Animals hold f. B294.4; origin of f. A1535.2.

Fairest thing in the garden J1472. — Love through prophecy that prince shall marry the f. T12; prize to the f. H1596.1; quest for the f. H1301.1.

Fairy assigns quest H1219.4; assigns task H938; becomes monster D49.3; confers invisibility D1983.2; converses with dead E545.8; curses village M411.16; in disguise lends death-bringing horse K985; dwellings F220ff.; enters locked city D2088.1; in foot-race with mortal H1594.1; as helper N815; helps overcome witch G275.8.2; in husband's form visits queen, begets son K1844.4; imposes tabu C901.1.5, C999.1.1.4; -like witch G264.4; loses stronghold through loan K232.2.1; as magician D1711.5; marrying mortal tabu C162.1.1; mist mistaken for enemy smoke K236.9.9; mistress F302ff.; mound G233, P17.0.3, R121.8; music evil omen D1812.5.1.13; offers warrior long life, happiness D1857.2; otherworld confused with land of dead F160.0.2; parent confers transformation power D630.3; as phantom F585.0.1; performs tasks H973.1, H977; as physician P424.4, (abducted to heal mortals) R33; rescues abandoned child R131.12; seen in dream D1731.2.1; stronghold riddle answer H768; suckles child T611.3; will marry king cutting off son's head H313.2; wins kiss in game K786; wounded by mortal D2161.4.10.2.1. — Child divides last loaf with f. Q42.1.1; dreaming of f. kiss J2345; first man marries a f. A1275.9; flood caused by loosing f. horses A1012.2.1; horse used by mortal under f. spell changes to gray cat F234.4.1; impostor kills f., wears its clothes K1911.1.10; king's family from f. prince A1653.2; lake quells f. war A920.1.7.1; magic beautification of f. D1860.0.1; magic contest of druid, f. D1719.1.2; magic object (received from f.) D813ff., (summons f.) D1421.6; magic power from f. *D1723; magic sword protects woman from f. lover in husband's absence D1386.1; mortal fosters f. child to prevent crop destruction M242.1; mysterious housekeeper f. mistress N831.1.1; pagans flee into f. mounds P426.0.1; pig-f. transformed to fish D412.3.1; power of prophecy from f. D1812.1.1; punishment for desertion of f.

mistress Q247; rescue from f. stronghold R112.3; rejuvenation by f. D1882.2; resuscitation by f. E121.8; returning home after marrying f. tabu C644; saint's horse miraculously preserved as proof of power of Christianity before f. H1573.3.2; spring breaks forth where f. horse lies down A941.1.2; tabu to dig in f. ring C523.2; tabu to offend f. C46; transformation by f. D683.7; transformation by offspring of f., mortal D683.7.1; wife chosen instead of f. mistress J414.1; woman abducted by f. R16.3.

Fairy's knowledge of mortals D1813.0.2; magic power D1719.5. — Bathing f. clothes and magic stolen D838.10; bower for f. mistress D2185.1; magic from f. door D1811.1.1.1; magic weakness from f. curse K1837.3; witch as f. daughter G203.1.

Fairies *F200—F399; aid quest H1233.4.1; in animal form lured into own shapes, killed K821; become birds every other year D624.2; blamed for theft K419.10; cause illusions D2031.0.2; cause sound from many directions K1887.3; as coal miners F456.4.1; in goaling match with mortals H1593; converted to Christianity V331.8; create magic tree D950.14.1; get stones from mermaids D2066.1; help forgotten child, strangle imitator J2415.4; and human children F310ff.; live in range of hills F214; and mortals F300—F399; must not eat mortal food C211.3.2; mutilate mortals S160.3; as prophets M301.6; pursued in wild hunt E501.5.2; transformed to animals fight D615.4.1. — Appearance of f. F230ff.; battle of f. and gods F277; behavior of f. F260ff.; bringing f. to court H1177; combing hair of f. (task) H1192; defeating f. F380ff; dolls become f. D435.1.2; fallen angels become f. V236.1; fasting against f. P623.0.3; indentions on rocks from footprints of f. A972.2; lakes created by f. A920.1.7; magic knowledge of f. D1810.0.4; malevolent f. F360ff.; possessions of f. F240ff.; kissing f. forbidden C122; looking at f. forbidden C311.1.2; quest for queen of f. H1381.3.8; race with f. N775; sleeping king abducted by f. N661; tabu: spying on f. C51.4.3; theft from f. F350ff.; vow to marry queen of f. M146.1; witches married to f. G287; worship of f. V1.2.1.

Fairyland *F210ff.; inhabited by women only F112.0.1. — Eating in f. forbidden C211.1; escape to f. R326; escape from f. R218; fairy leaves f. for mortals F393.0.1; fairies carry people away to f. *F320ff.; giant lives in f. F531.6.3.2; hell confused with f. A671.0.4; hero fights f. giant F176.1; magic tree springs from f. berry D951.1; mortal abandoning world for f. *F373; mortal goes to f. and marries fairy F302ff.; musical rock in f. F803; objects brought home from f. F379.2; ogre tyrannizes over f. G464; quests to f. H1286; return from f. F379.1; silence in f. C405; speaking tabu in f. C715.1; staying too long in f. forbidden C712.1; transformation to lure hunters to f. D659.10; transportation to f. B542.2.1; visit to f. F370ff.

Faith put into the balance V512.1. — Absolute f. as clerical virtue V461.7; lack of f. loses magic D1741.4; magic reward for f. D855.4;

punishment for associating with those of another f. Q431.18; punishment for changing f. Q232; reward for f. Q22, Q27; twelve articles of f. Z71.8.1.

Faiths. — Three true f.; God's and his children's J1262.9.

Faithful animal B301ff.; brother P251.1; old dog (to be killed) B842, (proves worth and is spared) Q151.4; falcon killed through misunderstanding B331.1; foster brother P273.1; servant *P361ff. — Girl cursed so no man f. to her M438.3; girl f. to husband despite lover's return T211.7; sister f. to transformed brother P253.2; what is most f.? H659.25; wife's oath to be f. J2301.1.

Faithfulness in marriage *T210ff.; as suitor test H338; to Virgin Mary, even if not to Christ, rewarded V253. — Disenchantment by f. of others D750ff.; parting lovers swear f. T61.2.1; test of f. of husband and wife H492; tests of wife's f. H460ff.

Faithless, see also **Unfaithful;** foster brother P273.2; servants P305. — Dead sweetheart haunts f. lover E211; disguised husband wins f. wife's love K1813.1; ghost of f. lover's victim E334.3; riddle involving ruby, nectar, f. creature H587.1; what is most f.? H659.26; wife in disguise wooed by her f. husband K1814; wife tries to cure f. husband by furnishing fine accommodations for him at poor mistress's J1112.1.

Faithlessness in marriage *T230ff. — Impalement as punishment for f. Q461.1; ring springs asunder when f. of lover is learned *D1318.9.1; woman as pilgrim learns of lover's f. K1837.2.

Fakir aids quest H1233.3.2; brings back abducted wife R165.3; as helper N844.2; prefers jungle life to luxury W34.4; thankful for shrewish wife T251.11. — Disguise as f. K1817.1.1; god in form of f. A182.3.4.1; rich girl marries f. T121.5.2; wife disguised as f. K1814.3.

Fakir's foreknowledge of guests' coming D1812.0.2.3; skill tested by beat H1576.2. — Loosing sandals destroys f. power D1782.3.1.

Fakirs. — Full pot sign city full of f. J1293.4.

Falcon and crow as joint creators A37.1; defeats eagle L315.9; eaten by wild boar recovered alive from his body X921.9; as messenger B291.1.4; not so good as represented J1826; saves master from poisoning B143.1.4; of Sir Federigo N345; transformed to person D352.3. — Cock has never seen a f. roasted J1423; enmity between f. (and fowl) A2494.13.12, (and hen) A2494.13.10.4; faithful f. killed through misunderstanding B331.1; giant f. B872.3; girl becomes f. D152.4; god as f. has tail cut off: hence falcon's short tail A2216.6; helpful f. B455.2; king strangles f. when it kills eagle Q424.1; kings try to save dying f. N836.2; magic f. brings hero water B172.5; retrieving king's f. H1154.7.1; soul as f. seen in dream E732.9; transformation to f. for rescue D643.1.

Falconiform. — Transformation: man to f. D152ff.

Falconiformes. — Creation of f. A1930ff.

Fall from breaking tabu C996. — Cure by f. causing bleeding N644; holy man's f. from horse evil omen D1812.5.14; lark causes elephant's

f. over precipice L315.5; leaves f. from tree as life token E761.7.3; magic needle makes everything f. to pieces D1562.4; man lets one lip f. to stomach F544.1.2; nine days' f. from heaven to earth A658.1; person magically caused to f. D2069.1; saint's image lets golden shoe (ring) f. as sign of favor to suppliant D1622.3; Satan's f. from heaven A106.2.2; things accidentally f. and kill person N331; witch causes f. G269.13; why monkeys do not f. from trees A2576.

Fall of Man. — After f. first parents fed from tree A1420.5; animal characteristics as punishment for planning f. A2236ff.; earth punished for disobedience at f. A2721.8; Lucifer causes f. A63.5; plants as punishment for f. A2631.1.1.

Fallen angels V236; king in disguise helped K1812.18. — Special power of chaste woman: raising f. elephant H413.4.

Falling after attempt to fly with witches G242.7; furniture threatens bridal couple T175.1; into hell Q417.3; into ogre's power G400—G499; in love T10ff.; star shot down by astronomer J2275.1; of trees reveals Savior's will D1311.4.0.2. — Death from f. on own weapon N339.8; dupes f. over precipice K891.5.4; lies about f. X1731; magic help from f. D2166; magic object keeps f. down D1649.1; man f. from tree frightens off tiger N696.1; man f. underground F949.2; object f. on robbers, they flee K335.1.1; origin of f. stars A788; perilous f. gate *F776.2; rising and f. sky F791; saint prevents rocks' f. D2149.4.1; squirrel's markings and immunity from f. as reward A2221.8.

Falls. — Bridge which f. when mounted F842.2.2; building f. because of breaking of tabu C931; dupe persuaded to climb tall tree, f. K1113.1; life token: staff stuck in ground f. E761.2.2; marvelous picture f. from sky in storm F962.12.3; numskull f. J2133; origin of f. A935; payment to be made when last leaf f. K222; person f. into ogre's power *G400ff.

False accusations *K2100—K2199; alarm of robbery causes cheated man to be imprisoned K484.3; beauty doctor K1013; bride *K1911ff.; bridegroom K1915; claim of reward K442; dragon-head proof H105.1.1; judging punished Q265; pride of son ashamed of his peasant father W165; prophet K1962; swearer not allowed to approach altar M101.1; swearing of oath forbidden C94.2; witnesses cannot describe stolen jewel J1154.3. — Devout possessor of f. relics miraculously receives authentic ones V142; dwarfs emigrate because mortals are f. F451.9.1.2; escape by f. plea *K550ff.; hero awakened from magic sleep by wife who has purchased place in his bed from f. bride *D1978.4; repartee concerning f. reform J1400ff.; sale of f. treasure K120ff.; seduction by bearing f. order from husband or father K1354; service under f. name K1831; trickster's f. creations fail him J2186.

Falsehood personified Z131. — Fairy banished for f. F252.4.2; horse refuses to carry f. speaker B133.4; magic lamp indicates f. by lighting D1316.2; red as symbol of f. Z141.3; wager that f. is better than truth N61.

Falsehoods. — Prophecy: person to tell three f. M369.1.
Falsely. — Devil as advocate of f. condemned man G303.22.11; nose of f. accusing bishop bitten off Q451.5.3.
Falsified message A2276, *K1851.
Fame chosen over long life M365.1; is greatest (riddle) H659.7.1. — Early death with f. preferred J216.5, L212.3; future f. prophesied M310.1; goddess of f. A466; wasp seeking f. stings courtiers W116.5.
Familiar. — Acquisition of f. spirit F403.2.1; demon as f. spirit F403.2.2.5; devils f. spirit M219.3; witch's f. spirit G225.
Familiarity takes away fear U131.
Family *P200—P299; carried to fairyland F327; of demons F402.7; of gods A168; of good man rewarded Q191; resuscitated E181.2; of thieves K301.2. — Animal captor appeased by being fed captive's f. K614; beetle cursed for betraying Holy F. on way to Egypt A2231.7.1.1; conqueror returns defeated man's f. W11.5.4; creator's f. A32; devil founds f. G303.12.4; don't injure yourself to insure future of your f. J322; escape by posing as member of murderer's f. or tribe K601; fairy gift not to leave possession of mortal's f. F348.3; fairy f. lives in cottage F221.4; faithless wife kills f. K2213.3.1; fool asks archbishop about his f. J1747; ghost f. visits grave E324.2; groom becomes member of bride's f. T137.4; king breaks promise to care for f. M205.4; man buried at home so may watch f. V61.3.0.3; man disdains own f. after speaking to king W165.1; master of seven liberal arts begs from wagoner who with his one art supports his f. X371; members of dupe's f. killed K1460ff.; moon's f. A745; mutual agreement to sacrifice f. members in famine K231.1.1; not recognizing own f. J2014; origin of king's f. A1653.2; origin of regulations within the f. A1570ff.; prayers of f. comfort prisoner V53; property division within f. A1585; prophecy: f. will die M359.6; quarrels among f. of dead X113; quest for lost f. H1385.9; saint's vision of king's f. V515.2.2; suitor in contest with bride or member of her f. H332; sun-god's f. A220.2; tree supports pious f. F979.19; unknown member of f. immediately and magically recognized H175; wry-mouthed f. X131; youth absent when entire f. wiped out N659.2.
Famine F969.7; prophesied M359.9; as punishment Q552.3.1. — Arrogant advice to f. sufferers J2227; cake and herrings as cure for f. J2227; cannibalism during f. G78.1; children abandoned in f. S321.1; daughters sacrificed to avert f. S263.2.2; goddess causes f. A431.1.3; king fasts during f. years P14.23; man mistaken for F. J1786.3; old people killed in f. S110.1; recognition of abandoned child when parents come to him for relief from f. H152; storing grain against f. J711.4.
Famished wolf asks sheep to bring him water K2061.5.
Famous. — Blessing fills countries with what they are f. for M393.1.
Fan, magic *D1077, (bears person aloft) D1532.10.
Fanaticism, religious V383.

Fanciful traits of animals *B700—B799.
Fang. — Detached snake f. kills B765.19.
Fangs. — Snake and turtle exchange head for f. A2247.2.
Fanning. — Devil f. fire with tail G303.4.6.2; faithless widow f. husband's grave T231.2.
Faraway. — Quest for f. princess H1301.1.2.
Farewell. — Dead returns to say f. E364.
Farm. — Animal as f. laborer B292.9; child unwittingly promised: what is born on your f. S245; city person ignorant of f. J1731; ghost light on f. indicates pending move E530.1.4; grateful fairies do f. work F339.3.1; nisser belong to particular f. F482.3.3; wild huntsman lives in room on f. E501.15.8.
Farmer kills anyone riding his horse L434; seeks laborer ignorant of sex K1327; sleeping through harvest time Q585.3; surpasses astronomer, doctor in weather prediction and food choice L144.2; who trades horses with the devil is cheated G303.25.12; unable to rid himself of brownie F482.3.1.1. — Arrested f. maligns sons H581.4; devil aids f. in reaping contest G303.19.2; devil appears to claim soul offered to devil by f. in jest G303.6.1.3; devil builds road for f. in one day G303.9.2.2; devil hires out to a f. G303.9.3.1; escape disguise as f. K521.2.4; gift of f. to incognito king rewarded K1812.9; misfortune follows f. N271.7.
Farmers. — "Skinning" f. J2472.
Farming left for fishing J345.2. — Dwarfs do f. F451.3.4.3; lies about f. on mountain X1523.2.
Farrowed. — Obtaining fat from swine not f. H1025; quest for pig not f. H1331.2.2.
Farting, see **Breaking wind;** continued D2063.5.
Fast-growing plants X1402. — Horse so f. fly cannot light on him B184.1.1.1; king wants f. answers P14.8.1; saint as baby refuses nurse on f. days V229.2.3.1; "stick f.": fool seizes ass J2489.9; tree with extraordinary f. life cycle F811.13.1.
Fasts. — Origin of religious f. A1541.7; wild huntsman wanders for failure to keep f. E501.3.5.
Fastened. — Continually slamming doors grateful for being f. D1658.1.4; devil dies when he is f. in hell's door by his beard G303.17.3.2; world columns f. by gods with mother's hair A841.0.1.
Fasting P623; on eleventh day abandoned H313.2; the first month J2135.1; invokes angel V235.0.2; as penance Q535.4; in sackcloth and ashes Q523.10; tabu on holidays C634; women tempted D2031.16. — Abortion by f. T572.2.4; animals f. B251.4; ascetic f. V362.2; beautification by f. D1866.3; contest in f. H1545; deceptive bargain: f. together K177; deceptive contest in f. K53; eight unprofitable types of f. Z71.16.1.4; ghost laid by f. E443.7; hermit f. to death for fame E754.4; intemperance in f. J565; lust repressed through f. T317.4; magic power by f. D1733.3.1; magic results from f. *D1766.8; neglect of f. punished

Q223.9; reincarnation by f. E607.4; resuscitation by f. E62.1; reward for f. Q26; saint ends epidemic by f. D2162.1; strength from f. F611.3.0.1; wisdom from f. J179.4.

Fastrada, ring of T85.4.1.

Fat abbot cured by starving K1955.1.1; cat (cumulative tale) Z33.2; of crow prevents burning D1382.2; giant wants to eat self J2119.5; and lean kine in otherworld F171.1; man chosen for execution M178.2; rendered from daughter's corpse Q478.4; troll (wolf) (cumulative tale) Z33.4; woman with beard F545.1.5.2. — Captured person (animal) persuades his captor to wait till he gets f. K553; crow f. remedies F959.3.5; division of f. and lean fowls J1241.4; extremely f. giant F531.2.5; hungry wolf envies f. dog until he sees marks of his collar L451.3; magic f. of animal D1017.1; quest for blackbirds' f. H1331.1.5; resuscitation by animal f. E116; sun a f. woman walking across sky A738.1.2; tabu to eat animal f. C221.3.4.1; witch smears f. on brooms in preparation for flight G242.1.1.

Fatal bed where his ancestors have died J1474; deception *K800—K999; enticements of phantom women F585.1; imitation J2401; kiss from dead E217. — Accidental f. ending of game or joke N334; avoiding places which have been f. to others J644; basilisk's f. glance B12.2; fairy's kiss f. F302.3.4.1.1.

Fate controls gods A196.1; takes form of Brahmin's pupil K1811.4.1. — Chance and f. N (entire chapter); deceiving f. K2371; fairy prophesies lover's f. in battle F302.7; gods tricked into help in escaping one's f. K2371.2; man's f. written on his skull M302.2; nature of luck and f. N100ff.; ways of luck and f. N100—N299.

Fates A463.1. — Three f. prophesy at childbirth M301.12.

Fated hero M361.

Father bequeathes four symbolic pots to sons J99.2; casts daughter forth S322.1; causes death of son innocent of adultery N344.2; confined at time of childbirth T583.1; and daughter *P234; -daughter incest T411, (prophecy) M344.1, (punished) Q242.2; will die when daughter (marries) E765.4.1, (bears son) E765.4.3; feels son in danger D1813.0.3; forced to share cherries J1341.9; -god A103; of gods A111.2; guards girl from suitors T50.1.2; with handsome son and hideous daughter J244.1; hides wealth to keep son from gambling N94; of illegitimate child must walk in front of cross J1515.1; imposes tabu on son C901.1.1; of incestuous children punished Q242.4; kills child S11.3; kills daughter lest she become prostitute T314; kills self believing that son is dead N344; kills son in battle rage N349.2; leaves sons three jewels, all to be used J462.3.1; of Noah's sons J2713; opposed to daughter's marriage T97; orders son's luck-bringing animal destroyed N251.6; prefers daughter P230.1; promises girl to wed man of her choice T131.0.1.1; rebukes son dragging him past threshold J121.2; reinstates abandoned son N731.3; rescues children R153.2; has been to Rome, hence resemblance to

emperor J1274; saves self, forgets children S141.2; and son *P233, (as culture heroes) A515.2, (as love rivals) T92.9, (in mortal combat) *N731.2; takes his daughter to cannibal to be eaten G75; tests H480ff.; throws son in oven H165; tricked into giving away daughter in marriage K1371.2; wants to marry own daughter T411.1; wears a crown but is no king J1264.3; went five years ago to measure depth of earth (died) H681.2.2. — Accidental meeting of f. and daughter N732; Adam and Eve having neither f. nor mother are dead H813; Adam as f. of mankind A1285.1.1; birth from wound or abscess on body of f. T541.2.1; boy kills his animal f. B631.0.2; boy shows f. foolishness of plowing up crop J92; bride's monster f. T172.3; child begs mother name him good f. J1279.1; child cursed by f. cannot rest in grave E412.4; child miraculously suckled by his f. T611.2; children choose f. they know to the real father they do not yet know J325; children flee from f. who turns cannibal G31; cruel f. S11; cruel foster f. S36; dead girl frightens f. and lover J2621; death of f. as punishment Q411.3; deity clothes his f. the sky A625.2.4; dwarf king prevents a f. from shooting his son F451.5.1.16; Elias, having had f. and mother, is not dead H814; enigmatic counsels of a. f. H588; fairy f. abducts child F326; fairy foster f. F311.2; fish was my f., man was my mother H791; fool advises buyer that horse is worth little or his f. would not sell it J2088.1; ghost f. summoned to get sword E387.2.1; god from f.-daughter incest A112.1.1; goddess's f. as cannibal G11.0.1.2; grandfather as foster f. P291.1; hermit kills his own f., supposing him to be the devil K943; hero locked up while f. murdered R54; inconvenience of having a f. J2222; impostor claims to be f. of princess's child K1936; impoverished f. begs from banished daughter L432.2; incapacitated f. magically restored as lost son returns D2161.4.10.4; king helps revenge f. N836.3; king sends message to dead f. H1252.4; in large family f. unwilling but mother willing to sell children H491.1; Lot's wife, having had f. and mother, is not dead like other mortals H815; lots cast to determine f. of illegitimate child N126.2; lovers' meeting: hero in service of lady's f. T31.1; magic object received from f. D815.2; maiden abducted from cruel f. R10.1.2; man accidentally fed bread which his f. has poisoned N332.1; mother lets daughter marry own f. P232.2; mother sends son to find unknown f. H1216; mother's brothers as foster f. P293.1; promise to dying f. leads to adventures M258.1; prophecy: son will tie f. to horse, strike him M312.0.5; quest assigned by f. H1210.1, (as punishment) H1219.3; quest for lost f. H1385.7; quest to see if f. in heaven or hell H1252.1.2; quest for unknown f. H1381.2ff.; slaying son so f. will not die H1162.2; son blinds f. S21.2; son kills f. who returns to life as cuckoo A2275.6; son rescues f. R154.2; son slays f. in self-defense J675.1; stepfather as foster f. P281.1; suitors contest with bride's f. (in shooting) H331.4.1, (race) H331.5.2; suitor is put to severe tests by his prospective bride or her f. H310ff.; supposed chest of gold induces children to care for aged f. P236.2; sword bursts in son's hand when he is about to kill his f.

*D1317.6.1; sword from summoned dead f. E373.2; tasks assigned by jealous f. *H913.2; tiger f. of human child U128.1; transformation through thoughtless wish of f. D521.1; trickster masking as f. advises intercourse K1354.1.1; unexpected meeting of f. and son N731; unwitting f.-daughter incest N365.2; vigil for dead f. H1462; "What does your f. say when you begin to eat?" X434.2; "Where did the f. stay?" X435.2; wife incites sons to war on f. K2213.9; wise words of dying f. J154; youngest son refuses to shoot at corpse of f. H486.2; youth accidentally takes poison intended for f. N332.4.1.

Father's ambitions transferred to child at conception T597; consent to marriage necessary T131.1.2; dream of bloody sons, omen of their murder D1812.5.1.1.3. — Man forced to eat dead f. heart goes mad G91.1; saint bestows f. goods on poor V437; breaking f. first counsel causes breaking all J21.25; dead f. friendly return E327ff.; fight with f. friend as valor test H1561.2.2; grief at hearing of f. death *F1041.21.5; infant eats murdered f. corpse G25; son avenging f. death H1228.2; magic on f. grave D842.2; queen persuades husband to claim her f. kingdom P23.2; son's acts of charity save his f. soul V413; son on gallows bites off his f. nose Q586; suitor task: avenging bride's f. death before marriage H335.1; swearing by f. life M119.8.2; tricksters feign f. death to collect rent K356; unknown son returns to f. court N731.1; vow against eating until f. death explained M151.3; wife chooses f. side in feud P211.

Fathers have eaten sour grapes, children affected U18; wagering over mastery of unborn children's house N16.2. — Child of three f. born with three stripes T563.1; prophecy: boys to be f. of saints M312.6; twin heroes sired by two f. A515.1.1.1.

Father-in-law *P261; angers strong man F631.2.1; gives enigmatic permission H588.0.1; requires suitor visit foreign country H336.1; sued for not dying as predicted W151.5. — Bride's kindness tested: f. disguised as beggar H384.1; cruel f. S52; duel with f. H332.3; feeding f. badly baked bread S54.1; God as f. J1261.1.1; magic object received from f. D815.5; suitors contest with f. in shooting H331.4.1; sun f. A226; treacherous f. K2218.2.

Fatigue. — Charm prevents f. D1384.4; magic avoidance of f. D1924, D2032.

Fatigued, see also **Tired.** — Guards f. by trickster so that they sleep while goods are stolen K331.2.2.

Fatness, humor of X151; repartee concerning J1410ff.

Fattening girl before wedding T132.1; louse *F983.2; pig by underfeeding J1903.3. — Cannibal f. victim *G82ff.; swine magically kept from f. D2089.3.1.

Fattest goat taken from demon H1423.3. — Riddle: what is the f.? H653.

Fault. — Finding f. punished Q312ff.; finding f. with wife J1701.1; husband finding f. nonplussed J1545.3; man admitted into heaven but must not find f. *F13.

Faults. — Devil writes f. of man on goat-skin G303.24.1.2.

Favor with royalty induced by magic D1900.1. — Child sacrificed to gain f. of gods S263.2; divine f. withdrawn as punishment Q553; fox asking f. set on by dogs J871.1; God's f. lost for breaking tabu C937; image indicates f. to suppliant D1622ff.

Favors. — Dividing the winnings: f. from man's own wife M241.2; dwarfs thwart efforts of mortals to get additional f. F451.5.12; sacrifice to obtain deity's f. V17.0.1; woman sells f. for particular purpose *T455ff.

Favorable omens D1812.5.2ff.; prophesies M310ff.; traits of character W0—W99; wind caused (by magic fountain) D1543.1, (by magic stone) D1543.2. — Clever division f. to divider J1241; time f. for unearthing treasure N555.

Favorite performs task to win bride for king K1848.2; youngest daughter L51; youngest son L12. — Deity cares for f. individuals A185; heroes sons of wife not king's f. L111.8; neglected surpasses f. child L146; spurned f. makes rajah laughing-stock K1670.

Fawn, see also **Deer;** with golden lustre B731.7.2; in spite of his fine horns, runs from the dog U127. — Burning children to give them spots of f. K1013.2.2; prophecy: son catching f. will be king M314.1; wild f. sent to disrupt army K2351.7.

Fear, see also **Fright;** of husband for wife makes him leave behind boots he has won T252.4.1; of mountain-folk for thunder F460.2.1; as sickness cure F950.5; tests H1400. — Abortion caused by f. T572.2.5; angel of f. A489.3.1; animal characteristics from great f. A2212ff.; animal learns through experience to f. men J17; death from f. F1041.1.11; devils' f. of St. Isaac G303.25.2; dwarfs' f. of cross F451.5.9.1; extraordinary result of f. F1041.17; fairies' f. of cross F382.1; giants' f. of lightning F531.6.11.1; girl disenchants animal husband by enduring his embraces without f. D735.4.1; good enter otherworld without f. E750.2.1; hero feigns f. when looked at K1777; illness from f. W121.8; king grows lean from f. of death U241; learning of f. H1440ff.; learning f. of Death J27; magic plant banishes f. D1389.13; origin of f. A1382; plaintiff insists that judge shall put some f. into the defendant debtor J2492; prevention of hostility by inspiring f. in enemy J623; quest: learning what f. is H1376.2; tests of f. H1400—H1449; tabu: f. of threatening animals while treasure is being raised N553.5; thief confesses from f. J1141.10.

Fearing. — Animal rewards man for not f. it Q82.2; weak f. strong J425, J613.

Fearless traffic with devils H1420ff. — Men are f.: tiger made to frighten them L482.4.

Fearlessness. — Boasting of f. tabu C455; reward for f. Q82.

Feast of "bedding and handspreading" T162; at beginning of adventures N770.0.1; for those who have not known sorrow N135.3.1. — Animal characteristics: obtaining for f. and not returning A2242; Barmecide f. P327; bride chosen from f. guests H362; calamity from f. of John the

Baptist A1002.1; cat invites hens to a f. and kills them K815.4; charm prepares f. D1472.2.4; coming to f. tabu after sunset C752.1.4; communion f. A1541.1.2; compulsion to invite singer to f. C682; compulsory drinking at f. A1514; consuming f. without discovering a new wonder C287; cup as f. token H84.2; day after F. Day disputes importance with F. Day F976; deed of bravery required before f. W213.1; disguised hero attacks enemy at f. K913; dwarfs f. mortals in their home F451.6.3.1; fairies f. F263; fairy takes revenge for not being invited to f. F361.1.1; feigned wedding f. to deceive cuckold K1527; fool does not milk cow for a month so that she will give plenty for a f. J1905.1; fountain gives wine on f. days F716.1; hideous food at devil's f. G303.25.14.1; how many dead mice go to a f.? (riddle) H881.1; laws made at yearly f. P541.2; leaving f. tabu C282.1; murder by luring to f. S113.2.3; no room left for f. J2178; prophecy on first participant of f. D1812.5.0.7.1; punishment for working on f. day Q559.4; refusing a f. tabu C282; Satan at f. where poor are absent G303.15.4.3; sleeping trickster's f. stolen J2173.1; Tara f. A1535.4; tabu: partaking of certain f. C286; Thyestian f. *G61; tribe not attending f. must send gift P531.1; trickster's interrupted f. revenged J1564.1; wedding f. T136.1; wild hunt appears on f. days E501.11.2.3; wolves have annual (church) f. B253.2.

Feasts P634; to honor certain god A1541.2. — Devils' f. G303.25.17; dwarfs invisibly attend wedding or christening f. of mortals F451.5.17; origin of secular f. A1535; perpetual f. in otherworld F173.3; religious f. A1541, *V70ff.; seven years between f. Z72.3; sitting in circle of f. P338.

Feasting by night tabu C237. — Stingy man's children f. in his absence J1522.2; tabu: f. for week C230.1; tabus on f. visitor C616; witches f. G248; woman, beasts f. on human flesh G11.6.3.

Feat on spear point H1149.5. — Duplicating f. of skill on journey C833.6; performer of greatest f. to be king P11.2.2.1.

Feats. — Father orders illegitimate boy sent to him when he can perform certain f. T645.3; Gargantuan f. F531.3ff.; hero's remarkable f. A526.7; quest to undertake f. of valor H1223; learning foreign f. of arms as suitor task H336.1.

Feather bed tabu C735.2.7; over door: if girl who enters blushes she is not a virgin H412.3; transformed to person D437.3; transformed to tree D457.7; used as mast F841.2.2. — Burning f. containing ogre's life G512.5.1; descent from upper world on magic f. (life ladder) F61.2.1.1; eagle killed with arrow made with his own f. U161; identification by f. cloak H111.2; magic f. *D1021; magic sight by looking through f. D1821.3.10; man can transplant f. from one bird to another F668.3; ogre's life in parrot's f. in man's pocket E715.1.3.1; one f. makes a hard pillow J2213.9; recognition by f. H78; sacred f. V1.10.3; ship wrapped with f. beds and canvas and pitched F1031; soul as f. E745.1; transformation by putting on f. of helpful animal D532.

Feathers. — Bird tears out f. F1041.21.6.2; bird without f. flies on tree without leaves (riddle) H764; bird f. sink in river (life token) E761.7.7; bird plucks out another bird's f. K2382.1; bird shows way by dropping f. every seven steps *B151.2.0.1; birds throw f. to hero who flies off B540.1; borrowed f. *K1041; building a lodge of bird's f. in one night (task) H1104.1; conception from f. falling on woman T536; counting f. in bird (task) H1118; dragon with golden f. B11.2.2.1; dress of f. F821.1.6, (magic) D1069.2; filling twelve bedticks with f. (task) H1129.2; flight by putting on bird f. K1041.1; gods covered with f. A139.9.3; lecherous king glued with f. K1218.1.8; lost soul in raven f. E752.4; magic causes f. to grow on person D1375.6; man can keep together f. in great wind F673; origin of bird's f. A2313; origin of peacock's brilliant f.: made by culture hero to please woman A2411.2.6.7; how ostrich lost beautiful f. A2252.3, A2402.2; peacock's f. ruffled in presence of poison B131.5; people with f. F521.2; quest for remarkable bird caused by sight of one of its f. H1213; quest for three f. of marvelous bird H1331.1.2; quest in hell for three dragon f. H1274; ravens show Adam how to bury dead: are born with white f. A2223.7; snow from f. or clothes of a witch (Frau Holle) A1135.2.1; sun and moon as balls of f. A738.1.1; tar and f. as punishment Q475; thatching roof with f. H1104.1.2; "thief's f. on head" detects crime J1141.1.5; trail of f. blown away R135.1.1; why bird has two beautiful f. in his tail A2378.8.7; why swallow has black f. and only two A2378.8.6; why young ravens have white f. A2313.5.

Features. — Cannibal with extraordinary f. G11.11; changeling has abnormal f. F321.1.2.1; gods with animal f. A131; ogres with monstrous f. G360ff.; person retains animal f. D702.2; person without f. F511.0.1; physical f. of underworld F80.1.

February's shortage of days A1161.

Fecundity, see **Fertility.**

Fed, see also **Feeding.** — Animal familiar f. with witch's own blood G225.0.1; animal lured by being f. K811.0.1; death passes by man who has f. his stepmother Q151.2; girl's heart f. to man draws her to him D1905.1; guests f. before being questioned P324.2; own flesh f. to helpful animal by hero *B322.1; parents f. from palm-tree A1420.5.

Federigo. — The falcon of Sir F. N345.

Fee used up before main question is reached K265. — Charon's f. A672.1.1; husband collects f. from paramour K1569.1; lawyer asks double amount of damages as f. K488; present or retaining f. J1559.1.

Fée carried off by mortal F304.6. — Shining bower for f. F224.

Fee-fi-fo-fum (cannibal exclamation) *G84.

Feebleness. — Giantess's son scorns father's f. P233.3.1.

Feeding, see also **Fed;** army from one measure of meal (task) H1022.5; the child steaming food J2465.3; mother: fool stuffs, kills her J2465.3.2; ravenous beast to satiation (task) H1123; sheep without fattening them H1072; stolen money in flour to animal K366.0.1; visitors dog flesh

J2469.5.1. — Birds f. on hero's land tabu C566.2; disenchantment by f. enchanted animals D745; disenchantment by f. transformed creature D775; dragon f. on treasure B11.6.3; giants appeased by f. them G582; giant's help secured by f. him N812.0.1; goat f. other animals from its body B535.1; man not f. animal rescuer W154.24; mother f. child to dog S12.2.1; murder by f. sharpened pieces of wood K951.6; thief tries f. watch dog and stopping his mouth K2062.

Feet, see also **Foot, Legs;** cut off as punishment Q451.0.1, (for theft) Q451.2.2; of dragon B11.2.4; of dwarf F451.2.2ff.; of giant F531.1.3; magically fixed to pavement D2171.7; seized in supplication P676; of various peoples A1665; wagered N2.3.2.1. — Animals with unusual legs or f. B15.6; beheaded man's head laid at f. to prevent return E431.7; why birds' f. are bare A2317.9; bishop with four f. J2283; clever girl comes sitting on animal but with f. reaching ground H1053.2; cold hands and f. for the dead man J2311.7; corpse with his f. cut off X422; cow's f. provide wealth D1469.7; devil has claws on his f. G303.4.4.2; devil's f. and legs G303.4.5ff.; devil's horse has human f. G303.7.1.2.1; demons' f. G302.4.5; dry f. tabu over river C833.5; earth to rest God's f. on A5.1; enemies' f. magically burned D2091.10.1; explanation of duck's f. A2375.2.8; fairy's f. F231.2; false bride's mutilated f. K1911.3.31; fire to burn hands and f. (curse) M431.3; ghost's f. backwards E422.1.6.1; giant's large f. F531.1.3.6; giants sit on mountain and wash f. in stream below F531.3.9; god with goat f. A131.5; hanging up by f. as punishment Q462.2; hero's f. backwards A526.8; hills from earth wrinkling up f. A969.4; hurting f. to save shoes J2199.4.1, W152.11; island supported on four f. F736.1; "keep f. warm" J21.29; magic animal f. D1029.3; magic salve restores severed f. D1500.1.19.1; magician's f. must touch ground D1719.10.1; man originally without hands and f. A1225.2; mankind begotten by giant's two f. A1221.1; medicine on f. permits man to walk on water D1524.1.1; murder by driving iron through f. S112.2.2; mutilation: (cutting off f.) *S162, (turning f. backward) S162.5; ogre monstrous as to f. G365; origin of hands and f. A1311; origin and nature of animal's f. A2371ff., A2375ff.; person unusual as to his f. F517.1; person with wings on f. F522.1; person without f. F517.1.1; pins stuck in soles of dead man's f. to prevent return E431.12; pricking f. exposes false corpse J1149.7; pygmies with upturned f. F535.4.2; rabbits freeze f. fast to ice at night (lie) X1115.1; raven singes f.: why its wings clap A2218.6; reincarnation of f. into hoe E649.3; remarkable f. F551ff.; revenant with chicken f. *E422.1.6; shoemaker offers to trim peasant's f. to fit shoes K1783; size of f. as bride test H365; sparks come from man's f. F683; spirit with f. turned wrong way F401.9; springs rise where Christ bathed his f. A942.1; stag with golden antlers and silver f. B101.4.1; suitors chosen with f. as only part seen H312.3; tokens on f. identify god H45.4; transportation by putting magic ointment on f. D1520.26; why guinea fowl's f. red: hot oil poured on them A2375.2.10;

wild hunt throws horses' f. on persons who see it E501.18.3; witch with extraordinary f. G216; wood-spirit without f. F441.4.2; yellowing soles of f. death omen J2311.1.5.

Feigned, see also **Sham** and **Illness** (feigned); death leads to exiled lover's death N343.3; death to test wife's faithfulness H466; ignorance of person's identity K1792; madness unmasked by threatening man's child J1149.1; capture by f. death *K751, K2362; death f. in order to be carried K1861; death f. to escape unwelcome marriage K522.0.1; death f. to meet paramour K1538; deception by f. death (sleep) *K1860ff.; detection through f. dream J1147; king brought to sense of duty by f. conversation of birds J816.1; ogre deceived by f. ignorance of hero G526; quest assigned because of f. (illness) H1212, (dream) H1212.1; seduction by f. death *K1325.

Feigning *K2000ff.; death to kill enemy K911. — Capture by f. illness K757; death as punishment for f. sleep Q558.10; adulteress f. unusual sensitiveness K2051; test of fidelity by f. death H1556.1; trickster f. deafness gets hospitality from miser K1981.1; trickster quarrels with owner of goods and frightens owner away by f. death K335.0.3.

Feline, see also **Cat;** animal transformed to person D312. — Creation of f. animals A1810ff.; man transformed to f. animal (wild) D112.

Felled tree raises itself again at night *D1602.2; tree restored by reassembling all cut parts E30.1. — Pleiades from hunters who f. world-tree A733.5.

Felling forest in one night (task) H1095; tree (deceptive bargain) K178, (with one blow) F614.8; wood with sword F1041.16.3.

Felt. — Resuscitation by piece of f. E64.10.

Female, see also **Woman;** creator A15.1; eater of corpses G21; master thief K302; physician P424.5; revenant E425.1ff.; right to land P61; servant forbidden to priest J1539.1; slaves P170.0.1. — Beef neither male nor f. H1074; cloud on male mountain bows to f. mountain A969.2; Eve names f. animals A2571.0.2; ghost in f. dress E422.4.4; ghosts may eat only f. animals E259.2; male and f. (creators) A12.1, (creators beget gods) A112.2, (waters) A918; origin of f. sex organs A1313.2; transformation to f. to seduce D658.3.

Fence. —Cutting f. down instead of fixing it K1432; metal, crystal f. in otherworld F169.5; thief, "Don't throw me over f." K584; thorn f. around food-plants K1038; throwing f. stakes away J2516.8.

Fences. — Suitor climbs eight f. T46.1.

Fenced. — Land purchase: as much as can be f. in a certain time K185.8; riddle: thorns f. with thorns H583.2.5.

Fencer treacherously cuts off opponent's head K832.2; skillful F667ff.; yields to opponent with pestle J676.

Fencing. — Student challenges f. master P342.1.

Fenris Wolf. — Fetter for F. F864.1; gods battle F. A1082.2.1; Odin battles F. A1082.2.

Fermenting dough's sound J1812.3.

Fern transformed to animal D441.4.1. — Magic f. blossom D965.14.

Ferns. — Devil as bunch of f. G303.3.4.3.

Fernseed gathering on Christmas Eve C401.5; magic *D971.3.

Ferocious animal flees victim K547.5; animal frightened by ass braying K2324.1; animals loosed against attackers B17.1.1; sow G351.3. — Bridling f. bear (task) H1154.3.2; dupe substitutes for trickster when f. animal attacks K846; eating f. animal's heart makes person cruel D1357.1; killing f. animal as suitor task H335.3; killing f. beast as task H1161.

Ferocity. — Why wild animals lose their f. A2294, A2531.0.1.

Ferried. — Dwarfs pay for being f. across water F451.5.10.6; emigrating dwarfs are f. across water F451.9.5; fairies f. across stream F213.2.

Ferry. — Charon's fee to f. souls A672.1.1; pushing f. as strength test H1562.10.

Ferryman P413; to lower world F93.0.1.1; on river in lower world (Charon) A672.1, E489.3, P613; setting people over a stream until relieved by another (penance) Q521.5. — Question (on quest): when will a f. be released from his duty? H1292.8.

Fertile. — Charms make soil f. D1563.1.1, D2157.1; giant's fields f., others arid G112.

Fertility test H1572. — In absence of goddess of f. no reproduction of life A431.1.1; god of f. A431; magic object produces f. *D1347ff.

Fertilized. — Earth f. by magic springs D1563.0.1.

Ferule. — Only one f. fits staff Z322; quest for f. to fit staff H1344.

Festin de Pierre *C13.

Festival of animals B299.7; compulsion C684.4. — Beltane f. A1535.5; intercourse during f. tabu C119.1.4; marriage by drinking f. T135.6; marriages made at f. T147; sudden love at f. T34.1; wedding, funeral f. on same day V65.3.

Festivals. — Sacrifice at religious f. V16.

Festivities of dwarfs F451.6.3; of giants F531.6.8.4.

Fetched. — One object f. by another D1428; skull f. from a charnel house H1435.

Fetching, see also **Bringing.** — Devil f. contracted souls M219.2.

Fetish worship V1.10. — Magic f. *D1241, *D1274; resuscitation by f. E53; slave going near f. forbidden C561.1.

Fetters loosed at Christ's Nativity D1395.8; as punishment Q434; of underground monster *A1071. — Angel looses man's f. V232.4; escape by cutting f. K649.11; rescue from prison by saint, who enters and breaks f. R121.6.

Fettered, see also **Chained;** Fenris Wolf F864.1; monster as dragon A1072.4; monster's escape at end of world A1070ff. — Abducted princess f. in giant's room R41.5; deception into allowing oneself to be f. K713; limbs of dead f. to prevent return E431.5; man f. with own sons'

entrails Q469.7.1; mother rescues f. son R153.4.1; princess f. to chair by hair R111.2.3; sea f. F931.8.

Feud within family P201.1; over trifle N387. — Wife chooses father's side in f. P211.

Feudal tribute P533.

Fever personified Z112.1. — Dipping into cold water to cure f. J2214.9; flea and f. exchange night-lodgings J612.1; magic cure for f. D1502.3, D2161.1.2; origin of f. A1337.4; sickle with f. J1959.1.1; wrestling match of f., stone image K12.4.

Fevers, god of A478.4.

Fiachna's incest H582.2.1.

Fian P551.0.1; calls for aid R187.1.

Fiana, origin of A1658.1.

Fiancé. — Avenging bride's former f. H335.1.1; deceived f. may sleep with seducer's wife J1174.21.

Fiancée, see also **Betrothed;** falls in love with another man at betrothal, elopes T157. — Blind f. betrays self K1984.5; forgotten f. D2003ff., (reawakens husband's memory) D2006.1ff., (recalls lover) T56.3; lover returns to find f. married N391; magic stolen by f. D861.5.1; man resists blandishments of leader's f. W34.1; slovenly f. W115.1.

Fictitious. — Fool appointed to f. office boasts of it J2331.2.

Fiddle. — Devil plays f. at wedding G303.9.8.2; dupe wishing to learn to play f. has finger caught in cleft of tree K1111.0.1; magic f. *D1233; man becomes f. D254.1; respite from death while one plays the f. K551.3.1; spirit plays man's f. F473.6.8; wolf-captor scared by f.-playing of captive ram K2327.

Fiddler in hell breaks strings, must return to earth for repair K606.1.3. — Devil abducts f. for hell G303.9.5.8.

Fidelity, see also **Faithfulness.** — Forcing attentions on friend's sweetheart as f. test K2297.1; husband learns of wife's f. N455.6; oft-proved f. T320.1; olive branch insures f. of husband D1355.8; tests of f. H1556; reward for marital f. Q83.1; transformation to test f. D659.8; woman's naiveté proves her f. T221.

Field at borders of otherworld F144; lying across road accursed H659.18.1; magically cultivated D2157.6; -spirits F445; sprouts wheat at Christ's presence V211.1.8.3; turns to gold D2102.2.1. — Addressing f. of reeds J1883.1; carrying plow horse so as not to tramp up f. J2163; damages for the f. devastated by a flock J1179.1; extraordinary f. T885; father makes better from good (hedges his f.) H583.2.3; gathering all stones from f. (task) H1124; plowing the f.: horse and harness destroyed K1411; plowing f. of vipers (task) H1188; spoiling the rice-f. with dung K344.2; uncut f. is already harvested (belongs to spendthrift) H586.4; white f., black seed (riddle) H741; wild hunt appears in a f. E501.12.6.

Fields set afire, men lured to death K812.2. — Giant's f. fertile, others arid G112.

Fiend, see also **Devil.** — Man tempted by f. in woman's shape T332; tribute taken from fairies by f. at stated periods F257.

Fiends play ball with soul E752.1.2.

Fiery, see also **Fire, Luminous;** aspects of hell A671.2.4ff.; columns rise before warrior F1041.16.6.3; dragon B11.12.3; excreta T559.3.1; pillar guides person to church D1314.10; pillar sign of Christ's visit V211.2.1; serpent B19.4.2; sword F833.4; temple F163.2.2. — Beasts with f. eyes B14.4.2; bird with f. beak B15.7.13; demon as f. pillar G302.3.1; devastating serpent with f. breath B16.5.1.1; devil kills man with f. sword G303.20.1; dogs in wild hunt with f. (eyes) E501.4.1.3, (tongues) E501.4.1.2; eel with f. mane B15.7.12; ghost as f. bull E421.3.4; horse with f. eyes in wild hunt *E501.4.2.5; leaping into f. furnace unharmed H1573.1.4; men put to f. test ask pious man to join them K528.3; sun turns f. face upward A1135.1.1; wild huntsmen leave f. tracks E501.7.6.3.

Fifteen as formulistic number Z71.16.11. — No rainbow for f. years A1002.3; prophecy: child shall hang before f. years M341.1.3.1; witch with f. tails G219.8.1.

Fifth of land's production belongs to king P13.9.2. — Man refuses to eat f. descendant of stolen cow F647.10.

Fifty-feet tall giant F531.2.1.2; -two as formulistic number Z71.16.9; -three as formulistic number Z71.16.15; -six as formulistic number Z71.16.16. — Fox had rather meet one hen than f. women J488; giants f. feet tall with footprints six feet long F531.2.1.2; giant cane holds f. cattle F612.3.1; giant with f. heads F531.1.2.2.7; king with f. sons (daughters) T586.2.1; man can hear ant leave nest f. miles away F641.2.

Fig. — Creation of man from f. A1253.1.1; extraordinary f. F813.7; magic f. *D981.5; stolen f. in mouth, cheek lanced W111.5.8; why flower of wild f. unfindable A2791.4.

Figs. — Clever girl refrains from eating f. which would bring on magic sleep J585.1; daw waits in vain for f. to ripen in winter J2066.2; magic cake of f. D1031.2.2; rain of f. J1151.1.3.

Fig-tree is chief priest of trees A2777.1; from which one cannot descent D1413.1.3; as god A435.2; helps cross river F1071.1; stays with angels: rewarded with sap of all other trees A2711.7. — Magic f. D950.8; why f. is evergreen A2711.4, A2765.1; wife hangs self on f.; friends ask for shoot J1442.11.

Fight of animal and houndpack B264.1; brought about by trickster K1082, K1084; of culture hero and elder brother A525.1; with dragon *B11.11ff.; in dream real F1068.2.2; of the gods and giants *A162.1, F531.6.15.1; between husband and lover T243; of lions and bulls J1022; of men transformed to animals D615.4; on old woman's hand X941.2; between one-legged, twelve-legged birds H619.5; with sea-monster G308.1; of revenant with living person E461. — Animal f. as suitor contest H331.15; charm gives victory in f. D1400.1.10; criminal may f. against odds rather than be judicially executed P513; divination from animal f.

D1812.5.0.8; devil is overcome by man in f. G303.9.6.1.1; devil and his son f. over division of earth G303.11.2.1; disenchantment by overcoming enchanted person in f. D716; dwarfs f. with each other F451.6.4; fairies ordered to f. each other F381.12; fairies return woman after f. over her F329.2; faithful servant remains at home to f. for exiled hero P361.2; foolish f. with sun J1968.1; giant's animals help him in f. F531.6.16.2; holes in hills from f. between gods A964.1; lover kills his lady's relatives in f. T95.1; magic causes enemies to f. among selves *D2091.4; men return home just as needed in f. N699.1; numskull thinks extinguishing of lights at church presages f. J1823.3; quarrel and f. over details of air-castles J2060.1; raven and dove f. over man's soul E756.3; refusal to f. relatives P205; revenants f. each other E467; sham f. to frighten away guests J1563.7; transformation to animals to f. D659.2; trickster attempts to bring about f. between friends K1084.3; trickster bribes guards to start f. K341.10; trickster causes owner and another to f. over goods K348; twelve years' f. as suitor test H328.6; unwitting f. of brothers with each other N733.1; warrior's deceptive f. in "single" combat K2319.2; weak overcomes strong in f. L310ff.; wisdom of deliberation in f. J572.

Fights as valor tests H1561.1.

Fighter. — Devil as f. G303.9.6ff.; lie: remarkable f. X972; magic sleep of dragon-f. D1975.

Fighters. — Constant replacement of f. E155.1.1.

Fighting animals seen in otherworld F171.4; with berserks F610.3.4.1; in fairyland tabu F210.1; in the shade best J1453; with spirits as fear test H1423; stars F961.2.6; on stumps of legs after they have been cut off at knee S162.1; though tired vs. losing for rest J356; with witch G275.9. — Animals f. B266, (for their master) B571.3; continuous f. in battle F1084.0.3; "don't watch two people f." J21.50; friends not f. each other H1558.8; house-spirits f. each other F482.7; hero f. army alone F614.10; hero f. in otherworld F176; hero who wanted to sleep before f. killed K959.2.5; hero uses f. animals to contest with demons B524.1.11; king's attention attracted by f. when it cannot be otherwise gained J1675.1.1; magic object acquired by acting as umpire for f. heirs *D832; maiden queen prefers f. to marriage T311.4; mountains' shape from f. each other A964.2; punishment: f. all who pass through forest Q598; spirit f. person F402.1.12; symbolism: not f. alone Z161; tabus concerning f. C835ff.; no time for minor f. when life is in danger J371; woman induces men's f. over her K1086.

Figure. — Exhibiting own nude f. T55.6; hand of vampire severed by cutting off hand of drawn f. E251.1.2; numskull knocks the f. of Jesus from the ass J1823.1.4.

Figures. — Automatic f. of harp D1620.2.5; instrument's ornamental f. climb down and run about as harper plays D1627.1; lovers converse in f. of speech T42.2; sham f. of wife, paramour attacked in bed K525.1.1.

Filial duty rewarded Q65.

Fill. — Tabu to eat one's f. C205.
Filled. — Barrel f. miraculously with penitent's tears F1051.1; compelling the f. to eat (stuffing geese) H583.4.4; devil's sack f. with dissolute songs G303.24.1.5; house f. by growing snail F983.1.
Filling oneself up before the feast J2178; impossible objects as task H1023.2.2ff.; a sack full of lies (task) H1045; twelve bed-ticks with feathers (task) H1129.2; yard with manure (task) H1129.1.
Filth. — Dupe induced to eat f. K1044; entrance to dwarf home leads through f. F451.4.1.7; why flies live amid f. A2433.5.2; victim suspended in basket over f. and thrown in Q474.
Financier P430ff.
Finch. — Creation of f. A1926; man transformed to f. D151.2; wedding of f. B282.3.6, B282.5.
Find, see also **Found.** — Inability to f. object one is carrying J2025; man admitted into heaven but must not f. fault *F13; way to otherworld hard to f. F150.1; what is most difficult to f.? (truth) H659.19.
Finder. — Lost ass, saddle and bridle offered as reward to the f. J2085.1.
Finders. — Treasure f. must not take all of money N553.3.
Finding certain secret forbidden C820ff.; extraordinary object as suitor test H355; princess (suitor test) H322. — Animal f. stolen goods B543.2; king (prince) accidentally f. maiden marries her N711; king marries girl f. lost object N713; love through f. ornament T11.4.6; sham wise man hides horse and is rewarded for f. it K1956.2.
Fine for failing to solve riddle H541.2.1. — Ass envies horse in f. trappings J212.1; dress so f. that it goes in nutshell F821.2; judge tired of bickering pays f. J1179.9; man pays f. for enemy W11.5.7.1; tasks as f. H928.1; wounded king exacts f. from would-be slayers Q211.8.1.
Fines for rape T471.0.1. — King spies to levy f. K2246.1.1; payment of f. P531.
Finery. — Woman in f. in church thinks people are standing to see her J953.8.
Finest. — Quest for the f. of (chains) H1303, (linen) H1306.
Finger cut because of absorption in the charms of beloved *T26.1; -drying contest won by deception K95; transformed to axe handle D457.9. — Blood springs from murderer's f. when he touches victim D1318.5.1; cannibal cuts captive's f. to test fatness G82.1; cannibal gives girl's f. to her sister G86.1; child's f.-ends cut off S161.1.1; conception from eating f. bones T511.6.2; cut-off f. proves wife's chastity K1512.1; feats of strong man's little f. F614.2.3; golden f. as sign of opening forbidden chamber C911; ground dries up when first woman cuts her little f. A856.2; holes in stones caused by piercing by saint's f. A972.3; image with pointing f. F855.1; identification by ring springing off f. H94.7; life token: ring presses f. E761.7.1; magic f. D996.1; magic knowledge from sucking f. of knowledge D1811.1.1; ogre sucks victim's f. and drinks all his blood G332.1; recognition by missing f. H57.2; river from man's

f. F715.1.3; stealing ring from f. (task) H1151.4; test of wife's obedience: f. in hole H473.1; waking from magic sleep by cutting off f. D1978.1.; witch's f. marks stone G221.3.1.

Fingers as false tokens of wife's unfaithfulness K2112.1.1; raised in sign-languages H607; of saint give light or fire F552.1.2. — Adam creates five devils by wetting five f. with dew and shaking them behind him G303.1.5; animals from severed f. of woman *A1724.1; backward-pointing f. F441.4.4; biting f. to see if one is dreaming F1041.13; child nourished by sucking its own f. T611.1; deceptive contest in pulling f. K74; demons' f. cut off as proof of killing them H105.5; escape from wives by making substitute f. K521.4.6; fire from warrior's f. F683.1.1; ghostly f. leave mark E542.1ff.; god's marvelous f. A123.5.2; hands with unusual number of f. F552.1.1; jinns' four f. F499.3.1; ladder of f. F848.2; mutilation: cutting off f. S161.1; person with unusual f. F515.1; sound of wild hunt avoided by sticking f. in ears E501.17.5.8; stretching f. to make ladder D485; tempted man burns off his f. T333.2; ten f. answer to wife's riddle H582.3; troll lights f. G304.2.1.1; unusual f. F552.1.

Fingernail. — Devils' caps from man's f. parings G303.25.5.1; drug hidden in f. K873.4; magic sight by looking at polished f. D1821.3.7.2; man created from f. A1263.2; murder by poisoned f. S111.9; severed f. identifies corpse H57.2.2; troll's daughter after being cooked in kettle recognized by golden f. H79.1.

Fingernails become gold D475.1.21; become jewels D475.4.6; grow after death E182; of slain cyclops H105.5.2. — Bride test: bread-making (dough under f.) H383.1.1; extraordinary f. F552.1.3; fear test: cutting devil's f. H1422; fire carried from heaven in f. A1415.1.1; origin of f. A1311.3; trimming f. tabu C726; unusual f. F515.2.

Fingerprints. — Marks on certain fish from (St. Peter's f.) A2217.3, (devil's f.) A2217.3.2.

Finished. — Dead cannot rest until certain work is f. E415; disenchantment when superhuman task is f. D791.1.2; numskull stays till he has f. J1814; structure to be f. when king's daughter marries H1292.18.

Finishing. — Reincarnation to enable f. work E606.2.

Finland. — Origin of cockroach in F. A2061.1.

Finns as magicians D1711.10.1. — Cupbearer abducted from F. P50.4.

Fir Bolg, origin of A1657.2.

Fir fer P557.4.4.

Fir-tree. — Dissatisfied f. finds its own needles best A2723.1; marriage custom: going round f. T135.10.

Fire, see also **Afire, Fiery;** alarm scares off fairies F381.8; announced metaphorically makes headway J1269.12; becomes woman, runs away D439.6; bell rung foolishly, disregarded when needed J2199.1.1; -breathing spirit F401.7; brings cold in otherworld F169.7.1; burns man who doesn't understand it J834; burns up tree while builder brings another

H1129.5; crackles as wizard passes G229.8; drill invented A1414.1.1; drills malfunction D2089.10; forces ghost away E439.5; giants F531.1.10; from heaven F962.2, (kills) F797, F981.4, (destroys pagan objects) V356.2; issues from cold hearth when man approaches H175.4; keeps lover awake H1484.1; from lake to burn forest M477.1; lake in otherworld F162.6.1; lights self D1601.7; noises misunderstood J1812.4.1; in otherworld F165.7; as one of sun's faces A733.3; from peacock's tail burns enemy army K916.1; -producing troll G304.2.1; as punishment Q552.13; -spewing giantess G125; set to distract attention K341.23; -ship K2364; -spirits F497; stolen by swallowing K382; transformed to gold D475.1.5; unable to consume special wood F812.8; from warrior's fingers F683.1.1; and water mixed to make sacrifice J1952. — Angel from f. A52.1.2, A52.1.5; angel of f. A493.0.1; after world f., life recreated from tree A1006.9; Agaria not afraid of f. A1689.2; animal breathes f. *B742; animal preserves f. for abandoned children in a clam shell S352.1; animal sets f. to neglected church B596; animal scorches self while putting out f. A2218.1.1; animal grateful for rescue from f. B364.2; animal who steals f. scorched: cause of his color A2218.3; arrows of f. F831.2; ball of f. for ghost's head E422.1.1.2; bath of f. F872.5.1; beggar escapes from f. N177; behavior of f. as omen D1812.5.0.3; bird set on f. D2061.2.1.1; bird with tail of f. B15.7.14; birds fly into tower of f. B172.10.1; birds pitch selves into man's f. B531.5; birds set f. to besieged city K2351.1; black tribe because woman put on f. A1614.8; bone-dust becomes f. D457.12.1; book written with f. F883.1.2; building f. in otherworld H619.4; castle of f. F771.1.11; chains of f. F863.2; changeling thrown on f. and thus banished F321.1.4.3; charcoal burner drives fairies off with f. F389.1; chariots of f. A136.3.1, F861.4.4; chimera breathes f. B14.1; Christ creates f. in hell A671.0.2.1; city of f. F763; columns of f. in front of angry warrior F1041.16.6.3; conception from f. T535; creation interrupted since God must go to a f. A2286.1; creation of monkeys: old woman thrown into f. A1861.2; crossing river of f. H1542.1; crown of f. F828.2; curse: f. lit under stepmother M431.6; daughter of f. and frog mate A1221.5; deity's child becomes f. A199.3; demons flee f. F405.12; devil as ball of f. G303.3.4.2.1; devil holds f. in hands G303.4.8.2.1; devil and sinful priest disappear amid blaze of f. in the river G303.17.2.4; devil drives carriage drawn by horses whose nostrils shoot f. G303.7.3.2; devil saves heretic from f. G303.22.13; devoured children come out of f. F913.2; disenchantment by lighting f. D784; disenchantment by throwing into f. D712.2.1; dog is flame of f. by night B182.1.5; doors of f. F782.5; dupe burned trying to put out house f. K812.1; dwarf wants to warm self at f. F451.5.7.1; dwarf's friend's house spared in f. F451.5.1.21; dwarfs warm heath by underground f. F451.5.1.15; elves set country on f. C934.3; enraged man spits f. F1041.16.1; escape by throwing captor's clothes on the f. K634.1; extraordinary behavior of. f. F964; eyes flash f. F541.1.1; fairy breathes f. F239.3; fairies set f. to

buildings F369.1; father accidentally falls in f. and dies N339.8.1; fingers of saint give light or f. F552.1.2; flesh becomes f. D457.17.2, D457.17.7; flood put out world f. A1019.4; fly steals f. from spider: may eat everywhere A2229.4; fool whose house is burning puts wood on the f. J2162.2; following witch's f. into her power G451; fox produces f. by striking tail to ground D2158.1.1; glow worm thought to be a f. J1761.3; god of f. A493, (and god of rain contest) A975.2.1; god becomes f. D285.0.1; god among seven sheaths of f. A137.17; goddess of f. A493.1; goddess with body of f. A124.3; helpful animals quench executing f. *B526.1; holy man passes through f. unharmed V222.8; horse in wild hunt breathes f. *E501.4.2.4; hospitable f. of his father is sought (bean merchant) H581.2; husband sets f. to house and ousts hidden paramour K1554; illusory f. stops men D2031.11; imitation of jumping into f. unscathed: fool burns J2411.6; jumping over f. H1199.10; ladder of f. F848.4; lake of f. in otherworld F162.6.1; land of f. F702; light f. but do not light it (task) H1067; lightning from f. A1141.7; magic drug gives immunity from f. and iron D1344.2.1; magic extinguishing of f. D2158.2; magic f. *D1271; magic f. moccasins D1566.1.2; magic horse goes through f. B184.1.12; magic journey in f. cloud D2121.7.1; magic object (controls f.) D1566ff., (protects against f.) D1382, (provides f.) D1481.2; magic power by jumping into f. D1733; magic stream quenches f. D1382.8; man brings f. at devil's instigation, burns Q582.2; man transformed to f. D285; man with f. moccasins G345; miraculous rain extinguishes f. used at stake *D1391.1; moon as grinder brings f. from sun A741.3; mother throws children into f. S12.2.2; mountain of f. F753; mountains and valleys formed by f. A969.3; ogre chased away by f. G581; ogre made to believe hero has withstood f. K1733; "only light the f." J2516.3.4; ordeal by f. H221; origin of f. A1414; origin of f. worship A1546.6; origin of illness from f. A1337.8; otherworld f. burns out repeatedly F171.6.5; otherworld people unacquainted with f. F167.8; oven heats without f. D1601.6; passing through f. as chastity ordeal H412.4; penance: hanging for a thousand years head downward over a f. of chaff Q522.6; person in magic sleep surrounded by protecting f. *D1967; pillar of f. F774.2.1, (identifies saint) V222.0.1.2; prisoner whirled away in blaze of f. R122.1; prophecy: death by f. M341.2.7; pursuit by f. R271; quest to upper world for f. H1264; recovering object in large f. H1132.2; riddle about animal living in f. H842.2; river of f. as barrier to otherworld *F142; rivers of f. in hell A671.2.2.3; robin steals f., has breast scorched A2218.5; rock produces f. when struck with steel A975.2; saint unharmed by f. D1841.3.2; salamander subsists on f. B768.2; Satan created from hell f. G303.1.3.5; "sea is on f." J1191.1.1, J1293.1.1; setting f. to house to escape undesired lover T320.6; setting sun mistaken for f. J1806; sham magician belches f. K1963.4; shortsighted use of f. J2162; shortsightedness about f. J2183.6; silver in chain increases in f. D1671; soul of f. E701.4; spear of f. F834.1.1; spirits

ascend by f. F407.1.1; starting f. near cobra's abode H1156.1; stepmother falls into f. from fright N384.3; stones of f. F809.6; suitor contest: riding through f. H331.1.5; sun bathes in stream of f. A722.5.1; sun from f. A712.1; sun as f. rekindled every morning A712; sun from f. flung into sky A714.3; sun god's wife pours f. over earth A1031.4.1; sun thrown on f. A1068; sun, moon and stars nourished on f. A700.7; tabu: lighting f. at certain time C751.1; tabu to throw f. into river C851.2; tabu f., weapon and dog together C887; tabu to urinate on f. C99.1.1; "tank of water caught f." J1531.1.1; task: building a f. H1129.5; theft of f. *A1415; thief detected by building straw f. J1143; thieves set f. to village K336.1; threat to throw on f. causes changeling to cry out and betray his nature F321.1.1.6; throne of f. F785.3; touching f. in otherworld tabu C542.2; transformation to steal f. D657.3; tree of f. F811.1.4; tribe born from f. A1268.1; troll stretches neck so long that f. comes from lips G304.2.1.2; two beams of f. shoot from devil's eyes G303.4.1.2.3; unextinguishable f. at end of earth A871.0.2; universe created from f. world A622; valley of f. F756.1; victim pushed into f. K925; vow not to flee from f. M155.3; water becomes f. D478.3; water resembling f. F710.1; wall of f. F744, (about otherworld isle) F148.1; weighing f. H1145.1; who shall put out f.? J2532; why animals lack f. A2436; wild hunt heralded by f. E501.13.7; wild huntsmen surrounded by f. E501.7.6.4; wild huntsmen exhale f. E501.7.6.1; witch as ball of f. G212.5; wolf makes f. as mock sunrise K1886.3; woman asked for f., abducted K762; woman confesses murder: unharmed by execution f. V21.2; world f. A1030ff.; worship of f. V1.6.3.

Fires burnt in streets to ward off witches G272.4; of hell A671.2.4ff.; hissing mistaken for muffins cooking J1812.4. — Dead persons build f. E578; ghosts gather wood for hell f. E755.2.4; hell f. kindled according to sins E755.2.4.1; king hung between two f. Q414.5; magic control of f. *D2158ff.; stars as f. in ghosts' hearths A761.4; tabu to neglect sacred f. C67; twilight reflects f. of hell A1179.1.1; vision of f. of hell V511.2.1; woman must relight magic f. as punishment Q492.

Firearms, magic D1096.

Firebrand, ghost as E421.3.2. — Stone becomes f. D452.1.7.

Fire-breathing animal *B742; spirit F401.7.

Firefly. — Cruel woman reborn as f. E692.5; helpful f. B482.1; man becomes f. D184.1.1.

Fireflies as lantern-carrying mosquitoes J1759.3. — Bats keep f. B788; creation of f. A2094; lies about f. X1287; speech of f. A2426.3.6.

Fire-maiden imprisoned R9.4.

Firemen, drunken X821.

Fireplace. — Curse by stones in f. M418.1; jackal comes to f. for food, burned K1032.1; moving f. instead of putting out fire J2104; paramour hidden in f. K1521.1.

Fire-steel, magic *D1175.2.

Fire-tongs, automatic D1601.24.

Firewood continually swept away from swimming man H1129.5.1; of elephant tusks F811.22. — Collecting f. to last lifetime H1095.1; cutting f. from rocks H1116.1; ghosts seek f. to roast man E257; inexhaustible f. D1652.10.1; magic f. D1298; saint's f. miraculously replaced V224.1.

Fireworks, fear of J2627.

Firmament prevents water of heaven from engulfing earth A810.2.1. — Creation of f. A701.0.1; heavenly lights from f. A790.1; windows in f. shed light A1171.2.

First of animals, fruits belong to priest P426.1.1; at combat gets choice of weapons P557.4.1; creature to be greeted will be transformed D526; man to arrive after king's death to be heir P17.1; to become angry must submit to punishment K172; man and woman A1280; man's good luck foolishly imitated by second J2415; objects picked up bring fortune N222; people have everything A1346.2.2; to say "Good morning" shall have disputed property K176. — Bed-partner to receive payment from f. man she meets in morning T456; why cat eats f. A2545.2; child unwittingly promised: "f. thing you meet" S241; contest in seeing sunrise f. K52; criminal accidentally detected: "that is the f." N611; dead arise when one plays organ for f. time in church E419.5; decision left to f. person to arrive M92; devil to have man if he gets him at f. grasp K235.3; districts named from f. person met in each N125.4; divination from f. person (thing) met D1812.5.0.7; why dog eats f. A2545.3; emergence or descent of f. man to earth A1230ff.; fasting the f. month J2135.1; fool experiments to see how f. man killed himself J2374; hateful or lovely child to be born f.? T548.1; hero returns and marries f. love T102; irrevocable judgment causes judge to suffer f. M11; injunction: to cohabit with f. woman met after battle C664.0.1; injunction: to marry f. woman met C664; king vows to sacrifice f. thing he meets (ass beheaded) J1169.4; long span of life for f. men A1323; man must be killed with f. blow C742.1; origin of f. parents A1271; originator of death f. sufferer K1681; payment to be made at harvest of f. crop (acorns) K221; present for the journey: what you f. see L221.1; prince prefers f. love to princess he later marries J414.2; princess to marry f. man who asks for her T62; prophecy on f. participant of feast D1812.5.0.7.1; prophet's f. disciple J1169.8; sun born of f. couple A715; tabu: arriving home f. when dog accompanies C756.1; tabu: wife eating f. animal caught in trap C221.4.1; threat to marry daughters to f. comers N455.12; vow to marry f. person performing act M138; wager: who can call three tree names f. N51; waters created on f. day of creation A910.1; who shall go f.? train leaves J2183.2; who shall speak f.? J2511; witch powerless when person speaks f. G273.2; would be f. in all things, even knavery J1269.3.

First-born cannot see ghosts E421.1.1.0.1; son given to Church V451. — Satan slays f. Egyptian G303.20.9.

Firstlings. — Tabu to eat f. C229.4.

Fish bears men-children after swallowing man's rinsings B631.3; brings lost object from bottom of sea B548.2; bursts with pride J955.1.1; carries man across water B551.1; carrying man shakes him off when struck M205.1.1.1; catching with nets A1527; caught with another's cries (lie) X1156.1; to climb trees if river burns J1904.4.1; come to hear saint preach B251.2.7.1; cleaned by girl becomes man D370.1; with coat of wool B737; in deluge deride God: are flattened with blow *A2231.9; disappear from sea F931.2; driven into tiger's mouth X1114.2; eat other fish: guilty must swim deep A2238.3; enticed into trap K714.8; follows sound of music B767.1; -god A132.13; grants hero wish to impregnate princess B375.1.1; grateful for being transferred from tank to river B375.1.2; guards cow B576.3.1; hero snaring a being tabu C566.1; jumps into boat of disheartened fisherman N625; lured by kindness and killed K815.14.1; magically summoned D2074.1.2; paramour B612; in parson's sleeve J1604; perform races to welcome saint B251.2.2; in pot appears to be many J1813.5; pricks and defeats monster L315.8; -producing tree F811.5.3; promises to spare man in coming flood B527.1; recovers lost urn from sea B548.2.5; refused saint changed to stone Q552.16.1.1; rescues ship B541.5; returned to water: grateful *B375.1; as sacrifice V12.4.10; struck by coconut: hence flat tail A2213.5.2; swallows man to rescue him B541.1.1; thought to be chewed sugarcane J1761.4; trained to answer call B771.4; transformed (to man) D370ff., (to object) D426; from waterless field D2106.1.1.1; wedding B283; as wooer B625; worship V1.8.11. — Ambergris made from bitumen eaten by f. F826.2; asking the large f. (boy has been given small one) J1341.2; ass falls into water and catches f. in his ear N626; automatic metal f. D1620.2.6; boy born from f. T549.3; boy swallowed by f. escapes when it is cut open K565.1; brahmin's "polluted" f. K344.1.1; why certain f. have bowed backs A2356.2.4; catching f. in boots while wading X1112; catching huge f. without nets or tackle (task) H1154.4; why f. are caught in nets A2465.1; charm prevents f. being caught D1449.4; child half man, half f. T551.5; child promised to devil in exchange for a good catch of f. S227; city's inhabitants transformed to f. D692; origin of color of f. A2411.4; conception from eating f. T511.5.1; coyote calls the largest f. D2074.1.2.1; crane outwits, eats f. J657.3; crane tricks f. into being carried, eats them K815.14; creation of f. A2100—A2139; curse: no f. in river or sea M476.1; curse renders river barren of f. D2085.1; cutting up f. as bride test H383.5; devastating f. carries off daily victim B16.4; devil as f. G303.3.3.5; dividing three f. among two men J1241.3; in dividing f., dupe gets bones K171.6; dividing f. by scripture quoting J1242.2; dragon as modified f. B11.2.1.3; drinking up river to get all f. K231.11; earth originates from f. brought from bottom of sea A811.1; earth rests on bull who rests on f. A844.5; eater of magic f. to spit up treasure M312.3.1; eating small f. now, larger ones later J703.2; extraordinary f. F986; enmity between white f. and pike A2494.15.1; earth

supported by f. A844.3; evil spirit exorcised by burning f. D2176.3.1; fight between eagle and f. B264.2; fisherman fails to make f. dance to his flute J1909.1; food of f. A2435.6ff.; foolish bargain: good f. for worthless shell J2081.2; fox invites f. to live on land J758.3; friendship of deer and f. A2493.5; ghost of f. E523; giant f. B872ff., (lie) X1301; gifts from f. C847.1; god of f. and reptiles A445, A446; God "upward man, downward f." A131.1; goddess scatters pubic hairs on f.: why he has so many bones A2211.15; goose dives for star, thinking it a f. J1791.8; great f. killed by Bhimsen, cut into sixteen pieces A972.7; helpful f. *B470ff.; ice forms while f. leaps F935.2; inexhaustible f. D1652.1.10; killing certain f. tabu C841.9; king observes f. to learn wisdom J52.2; laughing f. reveals unjust judgment *D1318.2.1; leaves turn into f. D1470.2.1.1; life token: blood of f. calls out E761.1.4; little f. in the net kept rather than wait for uncertainty of greater catch J321.2; lost ring found in f. *N211.1; magic catches f. D1444.1; magic dead f. *D1281; magic f. *B175ff., (when eaten brings man to kingship) D1561.1.1.2; magic from f. having eaten magician D1721.2; magic object in f. D849.5; magic object locates f. D1327; magic song received from f. B505.3; magic transportation by skin of f. D1520.5.1; magic wooden f. attracts live f. to fisherman's net D1444.1.2; man catches f. in beard F634.1; man in f. form eaten, reborn D1889.7; man swallowed by f. and later rescued alive (lie) X1723.1.2; man transformed to f. D170ff.; mankind descended from f. A1224.6; markings on f. A2213.2, A2217.3, A2412.4; markings on flying f. A2412.4.5; marks on f. from devil's fingerprints A2217.3.2; marks on certain f. from St. Peter's fingerprints *A2217.3.1; marriage to f. B603, (in human form) B654; marriage to person in f. form B644; master persuaded to buy big f. since small ones creep out of all parts of his body J2334; meat becomes f. D476.3.4; mountains from hacked-up f. drawn from bottom of primeval water A961.2; mythical f. B60ff.; nest in tree for f. J1904.4; oracular f. D925.2; origin of custom of catching f. by day as well as by night A1457.2; origin of f. drug A2834; parable on big f. eating little J133.6; pig becomes f. D412.3.2; pig-fairy transformed to f. D412.3.1; poisoning f. causes storm C41.4; pond supplies both fresh and cooked f. X1546.1; prophetic f. B144; punishment: being eaten by f. Q415.9; punishment: small catch of f. for child-murderers Q553.5; putting the f. aside for Easter in one big pool J2124; recognition by hair in f. H75.3; reincarnation as child within f. E605.7.1; reincarnation as f. E617; reincarnation: man to f. to man E610.1.2; rescue from deluge by f. A1028; riddle: f. was my father, man was my mother H791; saint calls f. from lake D2105.5; saint fills waters with f. D2106.1.1; saint's bachall catches f. D1444.1.1; separable soul in f. E715.2; servant eats f., tells master they're spoiled K344.1.2; silver f. B102.4.1, (with gold fins) B731.12; shores flooded with f. from sea F986.5; soul in form of f. E735; speaking f. B211.5; stranger presented with first f. A1528; stream containing black f. bursts forth F715.3.2; strong man destroys f. and nets F614.5;

swine eating certain f. H1199.7; tabu: giving away gifts received from f. C847.1; tabu to eat f. C221.1.3; tabu to eat f. caught with improper fishhook C221.4.2; tailless f. as devil's hog G303.25.15.1; today's f. catch traded for tomorrow's J321.1.1; transformation to f. (by catching in fish-trap) D533, (to be caught) D646.1; treasure-f. B107; trickster throws f. off the wagon K371.1; trickster's f. burn up J2173.7; trolls steal f. at Christmas F455.6.3.1; unique f. bait Z312.4; ugly f. borrows handsome one's skin K1918.1; victim pounded up with poisoned f. K838; water won't boil until f. returned to holy well V134.3; water-spirit one-eyed f. F420.1.3.2.1; water-spirit gives mortal f. F420.5.1.7.5; why f. attack anything they find A2524.4; why f. come in seasonally A2484.1; why f. face each other in copulation A2496.4; why f. is stupid A2537.1; wisdom from f. B162; wise f. *B124; woman reborn as f. E694.4; woman refuses to look at male f. F647.4.1.

Fish's enemies A2494.15; reasonings about man J2214.5. — Escape from sea on f. back B541.1; origin of f. flat body A2305.1; origin of f. scales A2315; sun and moon from f. belly A713.1; true bride lives in f. belly K1911.2.2.11.

Fishes with men's bodies, razor snouts F711.6. — Angel of f. A445.0.1; beasts and f. exchange places U136.2; bird catches f. by imitating their friend K756.3; coin-producing pumpkin received from f. A1433.2.1; council of f. decide to get rid of men B233.1; creation of particular f. A2110ff.; directing f. to stop at his house J1881.2.3; eaten f. restored by saint D1652.1.10.1; election of king of f. B236.2; how f. got into wine jug J2281; gold-producing gourd from f. A1432.2.1; king descends sea to study f. P15.6; king of f. *B243ff., (eats subjects) K815.17; kingdom of f. B223; little f. escape from the net L331; magic f. talk so that ogre thinks hero has many brothers with him D1613.1; magic meal of f. D1032.1; mermaids like f. in water, like men on land B81.0.1; parent of all f. B60.1; parliament of f. B233; pike helps Christ: made king of f. A2223.4; plenty of f. as reward Q53.2.1; rain of f. J1151.1.3; sea throws out f. at world's end A1063.1; trickster tells lies to f. and causes them to fight K1084.1.

Fishbait. — Human eyes as f. S165.6; unique f. Z312.4.

Fish-beast B70ff.

Fishbone holds back river water D1549.3.5. — Fairies cause f. to choke king F363.1.

Fish-eagle, oracular B154.3.

Fished. — Blind women f. up from a well F1065; island f. up by hero A955.8; men f. for by piercer-of-souls G322.

Fisherman dragged by seal F1088.3.2; fails to make fish dance to his flute J1909.1; fooled by sham-dead trout K522.4.1; as foster father P271.2; of the gods A165.9; as hero L113.1.3; and hunter exchange catches for variety: soon return to original food U136; rears unknown prince H41.5.1; rescues abandoned child R131.4; and his wife *B375.1,

C773.1. — Enmity between f. (and dweller on the river U141); farmer as f. goes hungry in drought J345.2; giant f. G322.1; hospitality of f. to incognito king rewarded K1812.4; magic reward for rescuing f. Q53.2; mermaid caught by f. B81.13.11.1; merman caught by f. B82.6; mighty f. F634; strong man as f.: destroys fish and nets F614.5; tail f. K1021.

Fishermen console themselves J866.1. — Gods as f. A147; jokes on f. X253.

Fishhook made without proper incantations C221.4.2. — Fish recovers lost f. from sea B548.2.3; giant puts elephant on f. F531.3.12.1; infallible f. D1653.2; magic f. D1209.5, *D1257; man becomes f. D258; origin of f. A1457.1; task: recovering lost f. H1132.1.5; trickster gets caught in f. J2136.2.

Fishhooks. — Using stone f. tabu C895.

Fishing in the flax-field J1821; luck lost C933.2; skill as suitor test H326.4; tabu to men on mission C833.9; under sea F931.6. — Accidental success in f. N620ff.; alleged magic f. rod K119.1.1; bear f. through ice with tail A2216.1, K1021; cat f. for master K341.11.1; cheater discovered by f. in the street J1149.2; devil gives luck with f. G303.10.7; extraordinary f. F986; fat man f. from own window X151.2; giant's f. F531.3.12; god of f. A455; lies about f. X1150; origin of f. A1457; owner's attention distracted by man f. in street K341.11; saint's blessing aids f. V229.17; sham prowess in f. K1968; tabu: f. at certain place C182.1; theft from giant by f. through chimney K316.1.

Fish-maiden, marriage to B654.

Fish-men B80ff.

Fishnet. — Creator distributes f. A1440.1; silver f. in otherworld F169.4.

Fishpool. — Saint's curative f. D1242.1.3.

Fishskin, magic *D1025.2.

Fishtail transformed to shark D447.4.

Fishwives. — Talkativeness of Parisian f. X253.1.

Fissure. — Sun at night enters f. between sky and earth A722.7.1.

Fist full of fleas H1129.10. — Person only "f. high" F535.2.7.

Fists. — Devil's thumb the size of two f. G303.4.3.2; gathering wind in f. H1136.2; hero fights with f. alone J246.2.

Fits become epidemic J1511.4. — Witch causes f. G263.4.2.

Fitted. — Punishment f. to crime Q580ff.; reward f. to deed Q101.

Fitting. — Hollow stone f. anyone F809.2; monster f. men to his bed G313; object f. only one thing Z320; recognition by exact f. of clothes H36.

Five devils created by Adam create other devils in same manner G303.1.5; great roads of Ireland discovered at king's birth A994; heavens A651.1.3; as magic number D1273.1.2.1. — Devil has f. claws G303.4.4.1; first f. living creatures from crab A1211.8; formulistic number: f. Z71.3; giant with f. heads F531.1.2.2.3; goddess breaks self into f. parts: hence river's five branches A934.11.3; magic arrow makes f. wounds D1092.0.1; magic weakness for f. days each year D1837.1.1; marriage to f. women.

each with separate duties T145.1; marvelous runner can run round the earth in f. minutes F681.5; universe created in f. periods A601.1; what crows do when they are f. years old (riddle) H865.

Five-cent piece in churn releases curse M429.6.

Fivefold as formulistic number Z71.3.0.1.

Five hundred years' journey to heaven F76.1; years travel across universe A658.2. — Dwarf king Hibich comes to surface every f. years F451.6.12; one wrong and f. good deeds J1605.

Five hundred forty rooms in Bilskilmir F781.2.1.

Flag. — Color of f. on ship as message of good or bad news Z140.1; wind blowing on f. causes prisoner's execution N394.1.

Flags. — Pieces taken from f. serve to identify H103.

Flageolet, magic *D1224.1.

Flagstone. — Child born on f. T581.7; prayer at saint's f. V52.7; saint's f. follows him D1641.2.1.

Flail witness to threshing in heaven H84.3. — Strong man uses stable-roof as f. F614.7.

Flailed. — Dead f. by demons E755.2.6.

Flame of fire to punish Irish A1031.1; freezes Z1623.3; illuminates sacred person's cradle V200.1; issuing from mouth as sign of royalty H41.4; as miraculous index *F1061; settles on charitable person's forehead V411.9. — Bonga as f. F234.3.2; deity departs in f. column A192.2.4; face of angry warrior lights up with f. F1041.16.6.4; hound f. of fire B19.4.4; life bound up with f. *E765.1; man as king's stepping-stone across f.-filled trench P116; oracular f. D1311.5; riddle: the father not yet born, the son already at the top of the house (f. and smoke) H763; tongue becomes f. D457.14.2; tree half green and half in f. in otherworld garden F162.1.2.4.

Flames around God's throne A152.2; issue from corpse's mouth E421.3.7. — Mouth emits f. F544.0.3; rock in f. at hero's death F960.2.3.

Flaming shield unquenchable D1672.1. — Ogre with f. mouth G363.1; otter carries f. wood in mouth B193.

Flapping. — Hills from f. of primeval bird A961.1; wind caused by f. wings A1125.

Flashing eyes F541.1ff. — God with f. eyes A123.3.2; lightning from f. sword A1141.2.

Flask, see also **Bottle;** imparts magic strength to drinker D1335.7. — Looking into f. forbidden C323; trickster drinks from another's f. K499.9.

Flasks. — Non-buoyant f. float F1047.1.

Flat. — Hills f. where gods slept or cooked A972.5.5; man kills ox with f. of hand F628.1.2; origin of animal's f. body A2305ff.; person with f. body F525.4; why animal has f. tail A2378.7; why helldiver has f. stern A2356.2.10.

Flattening. — Strong man f. hill F626.1.

Flatterer's retort to girl J1356.

Flatterers. — Harm of association with f. J455.

Flattering foreman tricked by his master K1637; lies vs. unflattering truths J267.

Flattery causes raven to sing and drop cheese K334.1; of the great J814; punished Q268; unavailing against king of humble lineage J915. — Escape by f. K572; monk avoids f. V461.6.

Flavor. — Dishes of the same f. J81; special f. of forest wood F812.6.

Flax in well leads to adventures N777.3. — Clothing army from one hank of f. H1022.2; fairy boat of f.-stem F242.2.3; key in f. reveals bride's laziness H382.1; magic f. D965.13; making dress from wasted f. as bride test H381.1; making shirt from single f.-seed H1022.4.1; origin of f. A2684.1; recognition by overheard conversation with f. H13.2.6; respite from death gained by tales of the preparation of f. K555.1.1; riddles about f. H885; robber's beard compared to f. K434.1; swimming in the f. field J1821.

Flayed animal resuscitated E171. — Corpse f. by ghosts E255; magic bull to be f. B184.2.3.1; magic mouse to be f. B183.1.1; servant rides through streets on f. ass J1075.1.

Flayer, disguised K1941; skillful F664, (lie) X983.

Flaying alive as punishment Q457ff. — Cutting image into man's back by f. S166.6; disenchantment by f. D721.1; murder by f. S114ff.; punishment for f. live calf Q211.6.1.

Flea and fever exchange night-lodgings J612.1; makes princess speak F954.4.1. — Creation of f. A2032ff.; devil given f. instead of soul K219.7; helpful f. B483.2; louse and f. wish to marry Z31.2; louse invites f. J2137.1; man becomes f. D185.2; picking the louse and the f. J2415.2; reincarnation as f. E616.3; using f. powder K1955.4.

Flea's bite alarms king B521.3.3; wedding B285.5. — Cause of f. movement A2441.3.2; why f. face is red A2330.5.

Fleas. — Assembling many-colored f. H1129.10.1; crayfish from devil's f. shaken off in water A2171.1.1; fist-full of f. H1129.10; fox rids himself of f. K921; god plagues devil with f. A63.4.1; lies about f. X1285.

Fleece. — Quest for golden f. H1332.1; ram with golden f. B101.3, R175.1.

Fleeces. — Witch blowing away f. G283.1.2.5.

Fleeing, see also **Flight;** pancake Z33.1. — Sweetheart mistaken for enemy by f. man N318.1; tame dog prefers food basin to f. hare J487; vow against f. fire, weapon M155.3; west wind exhausted from f. deity A1127.2.

Fleet. — Borrowed f. scares king into giving daughter K1771.9; deceptive emergence of f. K2369.2.1; giant f. of foot F531.1.3.5; hero f. of foot L141.3.

Fleetness, magic D1936.

Flesh of animal A2381; of certain animal alleged to be only cure for disease K961; of certain person alleged cure for disease K961.2; -eating

spirits G312.3; magically does not regrow D2062.3; regrows E784; reveals guilt D1318.7ff.; struck from ravisher's ear F304.4.1; transformed to object D457.17. — Boy born with one side f. and one iron T551.4; buying gallows f. or living f. forbidden C781.1; cannibal returning home smells human f. *G84; charm sung over f. chewed by wizard has magic power D1273.0.3; child born as formless lump of f. T551.1.1; dwarfs originate from maggots in f. of giant F451.1.1; eating f. of certain animal forbidden C221.1; effects of wild hunt remedied by eating part of f. thrown down by it E501.19.5; giants wear skins with f. still on F531.4.7.1.1; girl serves her father with piece of her own f. K492; why f. of animal is good A2511; healing by replacing f. F950.9; hero feeds f. to helpful eagle *B322.1; human f. eaten unwittingly *G61; husband nourishes starving wife with his own f. and blood T215.3; magic f. (of animal) *D1017, (of human) D1008; marvelous sensitiveness: meat is dog's f. F647.5.1; old woman feasts on human f. G11.6.3; one pound of f. offered: tongue demanded K255.4; people who prefer raw f. F561.1; pound of f. contract J1161.2; queen delivered of piece of f.; abandoned, it turns into boy, girl T569.1; resuscitation by laying covered f. on pyre E134; taste of human f. induces cannibalism G36; tearing off f. with hot pincers Q469.9.1; trickster's burnt f. becomes gum on trees A2731.1; transformation by eating f. D551.3; why crows eat human f. A2435.4.7; why tigers eat human f. A2435.3.9.3; wild hunt throws human f. on persons who see it E501.18.2; women, driven mad, devour their infants' f. N325.2.

Flies, see after **Fly.**

Flight, see also **Fleeing, Flying;** of bird with man to safety B542.1; of brothers from home to avoid being sacrificed S272.1; of children from father who turns cannibal G31; of devil (Satan) when cock is made to crow G303.16.19.4; of dwarfs to caves for protection F451.6.14; of dwarfs through air F451.3.3.6; of god in bird plumage A171.2; of image through air D1626; on magic horse B552; of maiden to escape marriage T311.1; of roast ducks (magic) D2191; of witch through air. G242. — Attempted f. to heaven punished L421; fairy aids mortal in f. F349.1; fools frightened at the f. of a quail J2614.2; hero's f. to maiden's room K1346; heroine's three-fold f. from ball R221; looking back during f. tabu C331.3; magic arrow f. D1526.1; magic ball f. D1526.2; magic f. D670; method and position of bird's f. A2442ff.; omens from f. of birds D1812.5.0.2; obstacle f. *D672, (Atalanta type) *R231; parson put to f. during his sermon X411; pretended f. draws victim K929.4; reversed obstacle f. D673; shammed f. deceives enemies K2378.3; transformation f. D671.

Flights R220ff.; extraordinary F1021ff.

Flinching. — Test of valor: not f. under a blow H1561.3.

Flint, magic *D1175.2; origin of A1414.5.

Flippers. — Boy with seal f. F515.4.

Flitting (moving) away from brownie impossible F482.3.1.1. — Ghost f. between two graves E419.9.

Floating island A179.2, F388.2; islands of the gods A955.12; rock F804. — Anchor f. on water F1047; children in casket f. down river H157; illusion palace is f. K1889.6; man f. in river too lazy to drink W111.1.5; monkey instead of girl in f. basket K1625; non-buoyant flasks f. F1047.1; object f. in air F1083.0.1; prince finds princess f. on water in basket: marries her N711.5; quest for princess caused by sight of one of her hairs f. on river *H1213.1; spirit f. in air F411.2.

Flock of geese transformed to stone D423.1.1. — Banners appear like f. of birds K1872.5; giant f. of birds B878.1; lie: thick f. of birds X1119.1; shearing a f. of sheep in one day H1106; treasure animal introduced into family's f. K2131.5; wolf loses interest in the sermon when he sees a f. of sheep U125.

Flocks. — Enigma: f. are rock H594.3; fairies kill f. F366.3; god of f. A441.1.2; prophecy: all f. will perish M359.6; stupid monk recovers stolen f. L141.1.

Flogging to death S122; debtor's corpse Q491.2; for eating kid on Friday Q223.9.2; as punishment Q458ff.; suspects brings confession J1141.1.10. — Father f. child S11.6; parents f. daughters P237; saint f. woman who tempts him T331.6.

Flood *A1010ff.; from breaking tabu D984.3; caused by breaking forth of springs A941.6; of mud injures corn Q552.14.2; prophesied M359.8; as punishment Q552.19.6; scatters carpenters everywhere A1445.2.1. — Animal characteristics obtained during f. *A2291; animals from transformations after f. A1711; birds cling to sky in f.: cause of tail feathers A2211.7; bodies of water remnant of f. A910.4; church spared in f. because of prayers D2143.2.1; dragon causes f. B11.7.1.1; fish promises to spare man in coming f. B527.1; giants in f. F531.0.3, F531.2.1.3, F531.6.12.8.2; human sacrifice stops f. S267; husband in hanging tub to ecape coming f. K1522; magic f. D915.6, D2151.8; magic hat brings f. D1542.1.3; magic stones keep f. in check D1388.2; reeds bend before f. J832; rescue from f. as reward Q150.1; riddle about girl's coming and f. H583.10; serpent causes f. B91.6; son dies before father after f. A1335.7; sun from kernels thrown into f. water A718.3; Virgin saves her image from f. V284; watersprite transformed to f. D283.3.

Flooded. — Sending letter by f. river J1881.1.7.

Flooding. — Magic song drives back f. D1549.8; saint's bachall drives back f. river D1549.3.1.

Floor. — Innkeeper deceived into going under f., robbed K343.0.1; lovers communicate through f. T41.2; person magically sticks to f. D2171.1.3; prison f. with spikes in it R41.3.3; red-hot iron f. protects city F767.2; task: sweep the f. and do not sweep it H1066; waterskin dragged across sky's f. A1142.8.

Floor's. — Riddle: where is f. root? H883.

Floors in dwarf home covered with pine twigs F451.4.3.5. — Silver f. in otherworld F165.3.3.

Flounder. — Why f. is flat-bellied A2231.9, A2354.1.

Flounder's — Origin of f. flat body A2126, A2305.1.2; why f. mouth is crooked A2231.1.2, A2252.4, A2341.1.

Flour pot broken before sold J2061.1.3; sprinkled on girl at betrothal T61.4.3. — Bringing back f. scattered by wind (task) H1136.1; feeding stolen money in f. to animal K366.0.1; lover sifting f. shown to wife K1214.1; man dies after eating bread from f. used for abscess plaster N383.2; pepper mixed into enemy's f. K2351.6.1.1; reincarnation of stomach into f. vat E649.2; sack of f. descends on peasant in punishment Q296.1; wolf puts f. on his paw to disguise himself K1839.1; why Zuñi girls rub f. on their faces A1687.1.

Flow of blood magically stopped D2161.2.2; of cow's milk increased by licking saint's garment D2182; of molten metal at world's end A1069. — Direction of river's f. reversed D2151.2.1.

Flowing. — River ceases f. F932.6; river f. around the world A872; unneeded water stops f. F930.5.

Flower becomes girl at night D621.2.2; blooms when touched D2195.1; bouquet brings brothers' recognition H16.3; entices beautiful woman T56.4; fresh as long as seen only by owner D877.2; friendship oath P311.2; from grave E631.1, (bears letters) E631.0.2f.; on head transforms D596.1; magically produced D2178.9; spirits F447; transformed to person D431.1. — Bird brings foreign f. F982.4; birth from f. T543.2; blindness cured by f. F952.3.2; bread transformed to f. D454.2.1; conception from f. (smelling) T532.1.1.1, (eating) T511.4; daughter promised to monster as bride to secure f. she has asked for S228; disenchantment by f. D771.11, (by breaking stalk) D711.4, (by throwing f.) D712.3.3; fairies care for f. bed F339.2; fairies' revenge for stealing f. F361.2.2; fox brings f. in mouth B584.1; life token: f. fades *E761.3; magic f. *D975ff., (opens dwarf home) F451.4.3.7; magic f. pot bears plants with gold letters on leaves D1469.1; man (woman) transformed to f. D212; marriage to f. T117.6; picking only one f. as sex test H1578.1.6; prince buys f. (enchanted girl) from her mother T52.1; prince plucks from grave of vampire a. f. which later becomes a girl E251.2.2; quest for marvelous f. H1333.5; recognition from conversation with f. woman H13.4; resuscitation by plucking f. incarnation E29.4; soul as f. E745.4; soul in f. E711.2.2; transformation by eating f. D551.2.4; transformation by touching with f. D565.8; treasure buried under f. N511.1.10; which is best f.? (cotton) H659.23; woman transformed to f. recognized H63.1.

Flowers appear as innocent approaches H216.1; become golden D475.1.18; bloom in winter F971.5; cause magic sleep D1364.3; drop on washing hands D2193; on ears protect against fairies F384.4; fall from lips D1454.2.1; fall from saint's mouth V222.11; grow from saints in graves V229.2.7; magically preserved D2167.3; as sacrifice V12.8; scent from

magic laughter D1773.1; spring up when saint strikes ground F971.6; from tears D1454.4.3; thrown to indicate princess's choice H316.2; transformed to other object D451.4; as token H87; from under the feet of Virgin Mary A2621.1; yield wine F979.9. — Blood becomes f. D457.1.3; boy of f. comes to life D435.1.3; conception from f. hidden in breast T532.3.1; devil avoids cockscomb f. G303.16.14.5; eating f. to cover theft K417.1; extraordinary f. F814; girl gathering f. swallowed by earth and taken to the lower world F92.2.1; girl summons fairy lover by plucking f. F301.1.1.2; goddess (god) of f. A434; instruments of torture transformed to lotus f. D454.16; language of f. Z175.1; lie: remarkable f. X1480; making withered f. green H1023.3.2; obtaining f. as suitor test H335.4; origin of f. A2650ff.; plucking fairy f. tabu F378.5; bridegroom alone plucking f. from bride's grave H31.12.1; quest for bouquet of all f. H1377.2; sewing shirt from f. H1021.9.1; snake reincarnated as f. E691.1; tabu: touching (plucking) f. *C515; test of sex of girl masking as man: choosing f. H1578.1.3; trail of f. R135.0.7; transformation by plucking f. in enchanted garden D515; ugly women complain of falling f. K1984.4; why some f. have no scent A2795.1; women transformed into f. A2611.0.4.1.

Fluid, see also **Liquid.** — Magic f. *D1242; person with pink f. in place of blood F554.1; river of extraordinary f. F715.2ff.

Fluids. — Extraordinary container for f. F866.7.

Flute makes more noise than quarrelsome wife J1541.2; player a hero L113.10; player thinks song meant for the prince is sung to him J953.3. — Bride attracted by f. T56.1.1; dolls vivify as f. plays D435.1.2; dupe wishing to play f. puts tongue in split bamboo K1111.0.1.1; fisherman fails to make fish dance to his f. F1909.1; magic f. *D1223.1; recognition through f. playing H35.1.2; reward for f. playing Q95.1; snake mistaken for f. J1761.6; tabu: playing f. C844; transformation by playing f. D523.1.1.

Flutes announce gods' approach A199.7.

Fluttering of birds after sunset C885.1.

Fly buzzes when cleric returns B251.2.4; cannot light on fast horse B184.1.1.1; dying in meat tub is happy that he has eaten to satisfaction J861.3; helps suitor pass test B587.2; jeers at king's elephant J211.2.1; laughs at dog's death A2479.8; steals fire from spider: may eat everywhere A2229.4; turns into girl's nipple J1833.1.1; warns saint against devil in liquor B483.0.1; as witch's familiar G225.1; worries heretic to death Q415.8; and wren, fox live with cleric B256.10. — Aiming at f. has fatal results N333; why f. is bald A2317.2; bald man aims at f. J2102.3; boastful f.-killer: "seven at a blow" K1951.1; chain tale: f. frightens snake Z43.4; chain tale: old lady swallows a f. Z49.14; contest: coin first attracting f. K92.1; contest in lifelike painting: f. on saint's nose H504.1.1; creation of f. A2031; devil as f. G303.3.3.4.4; enmity between spider and f. A2494.14.1; fairy as f. F234.1.16.1; fairy transforms self

to f., allows self to be swallowed by woman and is reborn as fairy F392; how f. got his eyes A2332.1.2; girl to marry man on whom f. lights B152.2; ghost as f. E423.7; giantess as f. F531.1.8.5; grateful f. warns lion B371.2; helpful f. B483.1; how birds began to f. A2442.9; killing the f. on the judge's nose J1193.1; why f. lives amid filth A2239.2, A2433.5.2; magic ability to f. D2135.0.3; man transformed to f. D185.1; marksman shoots left eye of f. at two miles F661.5.3; prince awakened by f. and saved B521.3.3.1; princess lets trickster's f. charm escape K251.3; saint never drives f. from face W10.1; soul in f. E715.3.2; soul as f. E734.7; spider invites f. to rest on her "white curtain" K815.2; spirit as f. going into bottle F401.3.4; tale about f. forgetting her name Z25; thief calls self "F." K359.2.1; transformation to f. to aid weapon selection *D659.14; wedding of f. B285.4; why f. has no voice A2239.2, A2422.5; why f. is hated A2522.7, A2583.1; why f. lives on dung heap A2432.9; witch in form of f. G211.5.1.

Fly's buzz A2239.2, A2426.3.3, B251.2.4; movement A2441.3.3.

Flies on the ark A2031.2; build bridge (lie) X1294.1; on Christ's body rewarded A2221.2.1; try to drink water from elephant's ears J971. — Causing f. to collect around girl's litter K2129.3; charm expels f. D1443.1; charm to dispel f. brings dissatisfaction Q557.8; covering with honey and exposing to f. Q464; cow strikes at f. while boy eats B579.2; don't drive away the f. J215.1; why f. may eat anywhere A2545.1; hero f. with birds' feathers B540.1; king of f. B246.2; standing whole day in July in tower naked exposed to sun and f. K1212; why f. fly around ox's eyes A2479.9; why f. lack tail A2378.2.8; why stinging f. sit on eyes of cattle A2494.14.3; wishing to destroy all f. J2079.2.

Fly-catchers, deities as A132.6.4.

Fly-whisk of life and death E64.1.1.3; magic *D1287.

Flying carts F861.2.1; contest won by deception K25; dragon B11.4.1; Dutchman E511; fish B62; head as ogre G361.2; horse *B41.2, B542.2, D657.2, (wooden) R215.3; island F738; mountain F755.3; squirrel's body made larger A2213.3, A2301.5; tower F772.2.6. — Artificial f. horse D1626.1; bird characteristics from f. contests A2254; devil f. like bird G303.7.9; devil f. away with sentry box G303.9.9.13; dragon f. to nest with human being B11.6.8; dragon f. away with lion B11.6.8.1; escape by f. through air D2165.1; fairy f. off with woman K786; giant f. over water F531.6.17.2.1; ghost's f. head attacks slayer E261.1.1; god f. A171.3; goddess f. in bird's plumage A136.1.8; hero f. away from death K551.24; magic object gives power of f. *D1531; man learns f. F1021.3; power of f. from eating children's hearts D2135.1; resuscitation by bird f. over dead E79.1.1; swan outlasts crow in f. L394; wings cut from f. mountains A1185.

Flying-fish, origin of A2136.

Flyting M401.

Foal, see also **Colt;** born of Loki and stallion T465.2. — Knight protects

f. from storm Q51.1; mare with f. left behind finds road home B151.1.1.1; new f. heavy to carry, peasant doesn't want horse J2212.8; witch drowns f. G265.2.

Foam on beer as life token E761.6.4. — Bringing ocean f. in cloth H1049.1; god discovers the devil in a piece of solid f. G303.1.2.3; origin of f. on waters A1117.

Focus (what he does with his four coins) H585.1.

Foe, see **Enemy.**

Foetus exchanged from one woman to another T577. — Child born from miscarried f. T549.4; plants from f. A2611.0.2.

Fog produced by magic D2143.3. — Demons cause f. D1361.1.0.4; lies about f. X1651; ogre turns into f. G522.1; origin of f. A1134; soul as f. E744.1.

Fold. — Bloodthirsty animal by trickery admitted to f. K828ff.; devil in f. of knight's cloak G303.8.9.1.

Folded. — Tent-house f. and swallowed F923.

Folding. — Magic f. mule D491.1.2; self-f. object D1642.

Followed. — Countess f. around by dwarf F451.5.8.1; fairies f. by hogs F241.3; friend f. into world of dead M253; lawyer's corpse f. by devil G303.25.8; monster shot and f. into lower world F102.1; sound of drum f. into ghost town F102.2; thief f. home J1392.1; wild hunt f. by empty shoe E501.10.1.

Following the devil G303.10ff.; magic object D1427; where you lead J1515; witch's fire into her power G451. — Adventure from f. animal to lower world N773; child f. bird loses its mother N313; disenchantment by f. enchanted woman through lake to underwater castle D759.5; fool f. nose on journey, climbs tree J2461.6; wise man f. fool against his better judgment put to death J1714.1.

Folly, see also **Foolishness;** of father's giving all property to children before his death P236.1; of marrying twice T251.0.1.

Fomorian ogre G100.1.

Fomorians. — Names of F. Z100.1; origin of F. A1659.1; yearly tribute to F. S262.2.1.

Font. — Not to peep at sacred f. C51.1.7.

Food, see also **Eating;** alone keeps off hunger J712ff.; of animal A2435ff.; becomes gold D475.1.16; changed to dust D476.2.1; demanded, supplied must be eaten C288; denied until hands clean: impossible task K278; of devils G303.25.14; disappears because of wastefulness Q585.4; -dropping trees F811.5; given away by saint restored V411.6; given to object J1856; of the gods A153; -goddess A494; which the husband detests and the wife keeps serving him T255.5; for journey to otherworld E433.3; leaves saint's clothing unspoiled F1091; left on magic stone brings good luck thereafter D1561.1.6; left for transformed person D694; magically disappears Q552.3.4; magically dwindles D2089.7.1; magically preserved D2167.1; magically stolen D2087.6; as marriage present H335.5; must be given everyone on journey C675; mysteriously poisoned N332.6; not

offered to fairy F361.1.2; placed out for cobold F481.0.1.3; placed out for returning souls of dead *E541.1; produced by prayer D1766.1.8; refused saint becomes putrid Q552.16; supply fails as punishment C934; tabu broken, blackmail follows K443.13; tabus during pregnancy C152.3; tabus following childbirth C154.1; thrown on floor in anger F1041.1.6.10; transformed D476, (to muck) D472.1; vision tempts fasters D2031.16. — Abundant f. in otherworld F166.11; acquisition of f. supply for human race A1420ff.; adulteress detected by f. K1550.1.2; adventures when wife takes f. to husband N788; all nature composed of f. in vision D1731.2.2; angels supply mortal with f. V232.3; animal bribed with f. *B325.1; animal grateful for f. B391; animal persuaded to be tied by promise of f. K713.1.3; animals eat extraordinary f. F989.22; animals grateful for being given appropriate f. B392.1; animals provide f. for men B531; animals from transformed men according to favorite f. A1715.4; animal's f. affects him unusually X1203; animal husband provides animal f. B600.2; animals refrain from spoiling consecrated f. B259.4.1; animals unsuccessfully try to exchange f. U147; ascetic faster increases his sufferings by placing f. and drink before himself V462.2.1; attention drawn by helpful animal's theft of f. from wedding table H151.2; blades in f. kill ogre G519.4; boy behind the tree tells woman about the bad f. he gets K1971.3; bride test: procuring f. quickest H375.3; burning f. test H1511.2; chieftainess preparing f. tabu C564.8; child exposed with f. supply S334.1; child hides f. from starving parents S20.2; children exchanged for f. E234; children refused f. leave home R228; clothes thrown into the cooking f. J1561.1; companion sent away so as to steal common f. supply K343.3; conception from eating f. T511.7; consolation for misfortune found in f. J861; cooked f. grows F1005; creator of f. items A1420.3; cuckoo borrows f. from other birds A2241.4; curse: lack of f. M443.1; curse: not to taste f. from own table M435; customs connected with f. P634.0.1; dead beg f. from living E541.5; dead grateful for f. E341.2; deception into disastrous attempt to procure f. K1020ff.; deceptive eating contest: inexhaustible f. K81.3; demon of gluttony coaxed from man's throat with bits of f. F406.4; demon of gluttony devours f. in man's throat F402.1.7; demons bribed with f. G582.1; demons eat much f. G302.9.7; devils eat huge amounts of f. G303.3.0.2; dogs by river try to get f. in river by drinking the river dry J1791.3.2; dogflesh: "f. you've never eaten" J2469.5.1; dupe persuaded to steal f.: cannot escape K1022; dupe's f. eaten and then blame fastened on him K401.1; dwarfs particular as to f. F451.3.7; dwarfs steal f. F451.5.2.2.2; earth as f. for first men A1420.6; "eat spiritual f., not material" J1511.16; eating f. offered to dogs as penance Q523.3; eating f. without untying container H506.7; extraordinary f. F851; eyes exchanged for f. M225; failure to put out f. for fairy F361.14; fairy grateful for f. F332.0.1; fairy music causes loss of f. F262.5; fairies borrow f. from mortals F391.2; fairies' f. F243; farmer as f. chooser L144.2; father's counsel: let cheap fish be your daily f. H588.2; fingernail conceals basin

of f. F515.2.1; fisher and hunter exchange catches for variety but soon return to original f. U136; forethought in provision for f. J710ff.; forgetting name of f., thinking it in sand J1924; fox spoils f. rather than divide with ape W152.1; ghost killing person for f. E253; ghost steals f. E593.5; girl from elfland must eat earthly f. in order to remain C661; god blamed for f. scarcity J2215.4.1; god prepares f. for mortal A185.7; guest made to pay for f. K251.2; habitual f. continued when harmful U139.1; helpful animal demands f. B322; horse taught to live without f. J1914; house without f. or drink J2483; human f. fed vampire E251.2.3; hungry ghosts haunt houses seeking f. E281.1; illness feigned to get better f. K2091.1; injurious f. with sweet taste K1889.4; inexhaustible f. *D1652.1ff.; jealous courtiers accuse jackal of stealing lion's f. K2141; kindness unwise when it imperils one's f. supply J715; lie: remarkable f. preferences X1031.6; liking for f. and drink J1343; living on small amount of f. as suitor test H351; living without f. for year F1033; lover refuses f. T24.6; magic basket supplies f. D1472.1.19; magic bird produces unlimited f. B103.0.2; magic f. *D1030ff., (furnishes treasure) D1465ff.; magic weakness from f. D1837.5; maid behind statue of Virgin advises the mistress to give servants better f. K1971.3.1; man created from f. A1266; man had rather be burned alive than to share f. with a guest W152.2; monotony of one f. compared to marriage J81.0.1; mortals refuse to eat fairy f. F361.5; mother refuses children f. S12.6; mountain spirits eat raw f. T460.2.14; murder by over-hot f. S112.5; mutual agreement to divide f. K231.1.2; no work, no f. W111.3.6; offering f. for woman's favors K1353.1; ogre used as f. G519.3; one man's f. is another man's poison U140ff.; origin of f. from body of slain f.-goddess A1420.1; paradise lost because of forbidden f. A1331.1.1; peasant produces f. for all A1655.1; person transformed to animal refuses human f. D686.1; poisoned f. sent to enemy camp K2369.11.1; poisoned f. test H1515; pseudo-magic power to produce f. K1036; pseudo-magic f.-producing object sold K112; punishment: f. fills with maggots Q501.2.2; quest to otherworld for samples of magic animals' f. H1251; repartee about f. J1340; saint causes two youths to be fed best f. V73.3; saint multiplies f. D2106.1.5; saint renders poisoned f. harmless D1840.1.2.1; saint's f. miraculously replaced V224.2; salt sprinkled on fairy f. renders it harmless F384.1.2; salt, water as only f. H588.21; sham death to get f. K1867; sham miracle: cooked f. turns raw K1975.3; shower of f. F962.6; shortsighted fool loses his f. J2173; social rank determined according to portion taken from cauldron of f. H1574.0.1; songs about improvement in f. J1341.11; sons-in-law driven away by reducing f. P265.1; spirit takes f. from cupboard F473.6.3; starved lover chooses f. over lady K1218.1.3.1; stealing f. from dancing children K341.17; stingy f. to visitor repayed J1511.13; stingy man's wife prays for husband's illness, better f. W152.16; strong man serves ogre as punishment for stealing f. F613.4; supplying f. to ungrateful stepmother rewarded Q65.1; tabu: eating f. of certain person C240ff.; tabu to

carry f. at night C751.8; tame dog prefers f. basin to fleeing hare J487; task: making many kinds of f. from one small bird H1022.6; task: preparing the f. "Oh my" H1185; testing strange f. on animal J21.4.2; thumbling carried up chimney by steam of f. F535.1.1.2; to each his appropriate f. J81.2; touching f. of another caste tabu C551.1; transformation to be put in f.-bag D657.1; transformation to receive f. D655; trickster discovers adultery: f. goes to husband instead of paramour K1571; trickster dupes jealous wife, steals f. T257.10; trickster eats f. while dupe is under water K16.2; trickster hides in f. and eats it K371; trickster pollutes f. in order to be given all K344.1; trickster works spell over f., eats it K353; troll's f. F455.4.2, G304.2.2; twelve kinds of f. (cumulative tale) Z22.2; unsuccessful imitation of magic production of f. J2411.3; unwelcome guest tells about the hidden f. J1344; vampire brought to life by being fed human f. and drink E251.2.3; voice warns against poisoned f. D1317.4.1; vow never to refuse f. to any man M158; wasting f. tabu C851.1; wholesome f. for the day of hanging J2174.2; why animals sources of f. A1422.0.1; why f. is cooked A1518; wild huntsman pacified with f. E501.17.6.2; young ass avoids f. eaten by animals before being slaughtered J12.

Foods in otherworld F183. — Ignorance of certain f. J1732.

Fool digs holes at road's edge J95; disguise K1818.3; disguised as king, killed N338.2; fasts on roof, falls off J565.1; given intelligent wife T125.1; given the truth on his back J551.2; as hero Z253; laughs at the absurdities he sees about him U15; not to be punished P523.2.1; passes as wise man by remaining silent N685; as prophet M301.9.1; rescues and wins girl R169.10.1; told to get brain pot; marry clever girl J163.2.1; wears crown K1810.1.1; wins beautiful woman L161.2; amongst wise men pours milk J1149.12. — Bigger f. in midday heat J1552.1.1.1; courtier called f. by pope refuses to correct those who may call pope a f. J1289.3; gift of the f. J1272; husband answers behind the statue when wife wants to know how to f. him K1971.1; if his son were only a f. he would let him study to be a priest X426; king and f. look identical F577.3; lucky f. N680.1; man plays f. as protection J822; only a simple f. J1393; "whose f. are you?" J1369.4; wives wager as to who can best f. her husband K1545.

Fool's brothers substitute goat for body of man he has killed K661.1. — Answer f. questions next day J571.5.

Fools *J1700—J2799, P192; frightening each other J2632; learn to be peaceable J24. — Association of wise men with f. J1714; easier to number wise men than f. J1443; poets and f. allied P427.7.2.1.1; quest for the greatest of f. H1312; same company of f. J1265.3; those most respected are the biggest f. J171.2.4; wisdom from f. J156.

Foolish association of young and old J445ff.; bargains *J2080ff.; but handsome son M93; married couples J1713; person becomes clever J1116. — Christ looks for stick to beat those who ask f. questions X435.3;

hero in disguise of f. knight, then of black knight, rescues lady R169.1; magic object acquired through f. bargain D837; magic object makes person f. D1353; officiousness or f. questions rebuked J1300ff.; princess brought to laughter by f. actions of hero H341.3; successful f. son L115; tasks imposed because of f. boast H914, H915, H916; three f. wishes J2071; types of f. imitation J2410ff.; when with fools, act f. J1714.3; wise and f. J (entire chapter).

Foolishly. — Same wishes used wisely and f. J2073; testimony discredited by inducing witness to talk f. J1151.1.

Foolishness brings man death Q6.1; of making washerman minister J677; of noisemaking when enemies overhear J581; of premature coming out from hiding J582; of surrendering weapons J642. — Wisdom from continual reminder of f. in past J167.

Foot, see also **Feet;** cut off as punishment Q451.2.3. — Biting the f. K543; conception from hand or f. T517.1; cutting off giant's f. G512.6; escape from deluge on f. A1026; father's counsel: find treasure within a f. of the ground H588.7; frost-bitten f. (cumulative tale) Z42; giant with one f. 531.1.3.3; giant's f. holds back river F531.3.1.2.1; grave equals five times length of any person's f. D482.5.1; hanging by one f. Q413.8.1; why hyena has short left hind f. A2284.6; magic f. D995; magic power of seeing Death at head or f. of bed D1825.3.1; magic sight by treading on another's f. *D1821.1; man beats his f. for slipping J1867.1; man who has given all in charity has f. amputated: restored miraculously V411.3; man can stand all day on one f. F682; ogress' f. makes oven blaze G345.1; one f. in Ireland, one in Scotland: sod of both carried K2319.1; person with one f. F517.1.1.1; saint strikes earth with f.: fountain flows forth A941.5.2; sexton behind statue tells old maid praying for a husband to raise her f. to her neck K1971.9; sight of wild hunt causes one to stick axe or knife in f. E501.18.9; stones punished for injuring holy person's f. A975.1.1; task: coming neither on horse nor on f. H1053; vows taken by placing f. on post M119.4; witch prevents putting f. on floor G269.20; wolf too near to horse's f. K1121.

Footbridge. — Razor-sharp sword as f. (lie) X1817.1.

Footless man outruns swift horse (lie) X1796.1; people in otherworld F167.7.

Footprint. — Detection by f. J1146; devil's f. A972.2.2; earth, water or blood in f. E761.1.3.1; indention on rock from angel's f. A972.2.1; magic f. *D1294; transformation by stepping in f. D578.

Footprints of the gods A901; of holy man still visible A972.1.3. — Devil's f. without toes G303.4.5.3.2; dew in f. reveals trail R268; ghost leaves no f. E421.2.1; giant's large f. F531.2.1.2, F531.2.4; lover carried by mistress: no f. K1549.3.

Footrace between giant and mortal F531.5.11.2; contest H1594. — Woman bears twins after f. T581.8.

Footsteps in manure show dead man walked H264. — Ghost's f. heard E402.1.2; waters follow f. D1547.2.

Footstool before divine throne A152.6. — Earth as God's f. A133.2.2; self-righteous tailor in heaven throws God's f. at old woman thief on earth F1037.1, L435.3; tortoise as God's f. A139.2.

Footwashing as reconciliation sign P673. — Water from f. protects against witch G272.13.

Footwear, magic D1065.

Forbidden, see also **Tabu;** chamber *C611; expression C498; to think J1511.8; tree (fruit) *C621. — Animals eat deity's f. fruit: punished A2234.2, A2371.3.1; creation of animals as punishment for beating f. drum *A1731; funeral rites f. V62.1; laughter f. A1372.7; one f. thing C600—C649; paradise lost because of f. fruit A1331.1; practicing one's religion f. S466; shouting from f. place H1199.3; tide f. to rise (Canute) L414; wife f. to ride on the dog immediately does so and is bitten T254.2; wife opens f. chest: killed T254.4.

Force. — Adaptability to overpowering f. J830ff.; animals overcome man's adversary by f. B524.1; marriage by f. T192; recognition by f. of nature H175.

Forced labor causes subjects to drive away ruler P15.8; peace valueless U220ff.; prophecies unfavorable M340.2. — Hero (heroine) f. to change places with impostor K1934; man f. to eat dead father's heart goes mad G91.1; mother not loving children of f. marriage P230.2; person f. by magic pistol to run behind the ball D1526.3; wild hunt f. to depart E501.17.8.

Forcing princess to say, "That is a lie" *H342.1; wife tabu C164. — Husband f. wife cursed T288.1.

Ford. — Forbidden f. C617.1; saint creates f. across river F932.9; washers at f. as disaster omen D1812.5.1.1.6.

Fords, combats at H1561.2.3.

Forecaster. — Mandrake as magic f. D1331.13.1.

Forehanded servant J1614.

Forehead. — Devil with eye in middle of f. G303.4.1.2.1; flame settles on charitable person's f. V411.9; giant with golden hair on f. F531.1.6.5; Good Luck lives in man's f. N113.2; gold star on f. F545.2.1; horse's f. as golden chair F874.2; lump on f. identifies fool F192.7; magic horns grow on person's f. *D992.1; magic mark on f. renders invisible D1361.43; man dies because he has killed a man with the sign of the Cross on his f. V86.1.3; marks on f. royalty sign H71.1; moon shines on God's f. A123.10; person with one eye in center of f. *F512.1.1; putrescence from f. F1041.18; remarkable f. F545.2; vagina in f. F547.5.6; why rail has red f. A2330.8; why sheep may keep wool which grows on his f. A2322.5; troll's life in his brother's f. E714.3.1.

Foreheads. — Women's breasts on f. A1313.4.1.

Foreign. — Abandonment alone on f. coast S114.1; all f. elements expelled

from country P711.6; aversion to burial in f. soil P711.8; disguise as f. ambassador K1839.7; hero buried unknown in f. country V69.2; task: recovering money owed by a f. king H1182.1; theft signal given in f. language K358; tribute of youths regularly sent to f. king S262.2; visit to f. country as suitor task H336.1; words in a f. language thought to be insults J1802.

Foreigner may not act as legal security P524.2; may not bring law suit P523.1. — Questions of f. answered: "I don't understand" J1802.1; son marries f., mother kills self P231.7.

Foreigners. — Heads of f. exchanged with devils' A1610.1.1; social status of f. P191.

Foreknowledge of hour of death D1812.0.1. — Fairies' f. of mortal's coming F256.1; saints have f. of coming of guests D1812.0.2.

Foreseen. — All aspects of a plan must be f. J755.

Foresight: call undertaker with doctor J2516.9. — Death through lack of f. J2137ff.; magic f. D1825.7.

Forest burns as magician opens eyes D2158.1.4; devil the one which fell in the forest when driven from heaven G303.8.13.2; magically springs up between enemies D2163.6.1; magically cleared D1641.4; as refuge of eloping lovers R312.1; from twig F979.8. — Abandoned queen entertains in f.: recognized H155; abandonment in f. S143, (to avoid fulfillment of prophecy) M371.0.1, (as punishment) Q438; army appears like f. K1872.1; birth of child in f. T581.1; changeling calculates his age by the age of the f. F321.1.1.5; deity lives in f. A151.7; deity of particular f. A419.1; dwarfs live in a f. F451.4.2.3; dwarfs protect the f. F451.5.1.17; fairies live in f. F216; felling a f. in one night H1095; felling the whole f. K1741.1; fetish clears f. D1601.22; enemies defeated by setting f. afire K2364.1; feigning sleep in f. with hero H1556.5; forbidden f. C612; goddess of wild f. plants A431.1.2; ground swallows f. F947; hair transformed to f. D457.4.2; imprisonment for hunting in king's f. Q433.10; lion leads lost king from f. *B563.1; magic f. *D941; making garden quickly in unplanted f. H1103.1; serpent demon guards treasure f. G354.1.1; strong man son of f. spirit F611.1.2.1; tabu: hunting in certain part of f. C614.1.0.2; tasks performed by helpful f. spirits H973; wife, child abandoned in f. S441; witch lives in f. G236; woman abducted in f. K1337; woman lured into f., captured K788; woman overcomes enemies singly in f. K778.1.

Forests. — God of f. A435; magic f. and trees D940ff.; giants in wild f. F531.6.2.7; why salt disappeared from f. A1196.

Forester, helpful N856; rescues abandoned child R131.8.5; sent to hell J225.7; as wild huntsman E501.1.4.

Forest-spirits, see **Wood-spirits.**

Foretelling. — Dead f. future E545.17.

Forethought J600—J799; in defenses against others J670ff.; in preven-

tion of others' plans J620ff.; in provision for life J700—J749. — Air-castle shattered by lack of f. J2061.

Forever: a day and a night K2314, Z61.2. — Prosperity f. or for a day? L291.

Forewarned. — Stealing horse when owner f. H1151.2.1.

Forge. — Goldsmith's magic f. D2178.7; salvaging anvil from burning f. H1574.3.1.

Forged credentials win girl K1917.6. — Magic object f. by smith to order D853; sun, moon, and stars f. by smith A700.5.

Forgery. — Credit based on f. K455.8; theft by f. K362.7.

Forget-me-not, origin of A2657.

Forgetfulness of actor speaking in his own person J2041ff.; of fool J2671ff. — Curse of f. *D2004.1; magic f. *D1365ff., *D2000ff., (for breaking tabu) C945, (as punishment) Q551.11; medicines of f. and of remembering D1365.8.1.

Forgetting Charon's fee E489.3; leashes of hounds as bad omen D1812.5.1.21; name he went on trip to find out J2241.1; sweetheart causes loss of invulnerability D1847.1. — Fool f. master's message punished J2044; man f. to count self, dies E791; misfortunes from f. to say "If God wills" N385.1; soul f. everything at birth E705.

Forgiven. — Monk who has left his order f. and miraculously reinstated V475.2; mother guilty of incest with son f. by Pope (Virgin Mary) T412.1; vanquished ruler f. by victor J829.3.

Forgiveness brings about conversion V331.10.1; of father vs. mother H588.19; as religious virtue V441; the reward of successful quest H1244; of sin for acts of charity Q171.1. — Confession brings f. of sin V21; dead return to give f. E365.1; incognito king asks victor's f. K1812.5; punishment for finding fault with God's f. of sin Q312.3; sincere confession miraculously obliterated as sign of f. V21.1; suitor test: to earn f. H348; swelling bone as f. sign F991.2.1.

Forgotten fiancée D2003, (plea recalls lover) T56.3, (reawakens husband's memory) D2006.1ff.; name confused with lost treasure J1805.3; traditions J1445; wind J755.1. — Devils instead of angels visit woman who has f. God in her prosperity Q559.1; fairies help f. child J2415.4; father has f. to strike mother J122; much-repeated instructions f. by fool J2671.2.

Fork. — Man received f. in eye for breaking tabu C943.1.

Forked glen F144.1. — Why animal has f. tail A2378.5; soul f. from body by Satan E722.2.4.

Form of dragon B11.2ff.; of culture hero A526; of familiar spirit F403.2.2; of fettered monster A1072; of soul as it leaves body at death E722.1; of vampire E251.4; of witch G210ff.; of wood-spirit F441.4. — Dead wife returns in f. of bird E322.4; fairy in f. of an animal F234.1; fairy offers man change of f. and feature for aid in battle F343.11; jinn can take any human f. G307.2.1; man assuming lover's f., sleeps with princess

K1915.2; marriage to animal in human f. *B650ff.; marriage to person in animal f. *B640ff.; promise made merely as a matter of f. not binding M206; reincarnation in f. determined at death E602; transformation to husband's (lover's) f. to seduce woman D658.2.

Forms exchanged D45ff.; in which devil appears G303.3ff.

Former. — Animal habit a reminiscence of f. experience A2275ff.; identity tested by demanding that person say again what he said on f. occasion H15.1; maiden prince's wife in f. life N741.5; reincarnation: f. lives remembered *E601; "why f. days better?" J311.2.

Formless gods A120.4. — Child born a f. lump T551.1.1.

Formula for creating universe A611.0.1; for girl fleeing: behind me night, etc. R255; -tale saves girl from devil K555.2.1. — Disenchantment by magic f. D789.6; invisibility by reciting f. backwards D1985.2; magic f. *D1273, (exorcises witch) G271.3; marriage f.: "you are mine and I am yours" T135.1; pseudo-magic f. for gold K111.4; secret f. for opening treasure mountain overheard from robbers N455.3.

Formulas *Z0—Z99; for fairy travel T282.2; for selling one's soul to devil M211.5.

Formulistic numbers Z71ff.

Fornication. — No place secret enough for f. T331.4; sight of holy garment restrains man from f. V131.1.

Forsaken merman C713. — Madness from regret for having f. wife F1041.8.9; woman f. by husband dies in lover's arms T88; woman arousing love to be f. C686.

Fort. — Location of f. determined by magic D1816.3; magic f. D1136; magic object found in f. D849.1; magic thread makes f. fall D1400.1.1.18; tabu to erect f. on holy ground C93.7.

Forts. — Origin of stone f. A1435.2; seven f. of river, iron, mud, cowdung, brick, stone, wood F789.1; tree amidst seven f. F811.23; tree inside seven series of f. H1333.5.0.2.

Forthputting woman T55.

Fortifications. — Magic renders f. useless D1414.0.1; treasure placed in old f. by supernatural beings N511.3.2.

Fortified. — Saint's curse: dwellings cannot be f. Q556.5.

Fortnight. — Lamp lighted every f. A1599.14.

Fortress built on Sunday destroyed by tempest Q552.14.1; demolished by thunder Q552.1.0.1.1; magically revolves D1381.23; in otherworld F163.5; ravaged after saint refused admittance Q595.1. — Magic head causes f. to crumble D1400.1.20.1; magic wheel prevents entrance to f. D1389.4; prophecy: destruction of f. M356.1.4; transformation to gain access to enemy camp (f.) D651.2.

Fortuna N111.

Fortunate youngest son L11. — Blue f. in love matters T3.1; proud animal less f. than humble *L450ff.

Fortune comes to deserving and undeserving N102; to go direction cat

jumps K2.1; and Intellect, Knowledge, Health dispute which is greatest J461.1.2; learned from serpent B161.2; personified Z134; -telling dream induced by sleeping in extraordinary place D1812.3.3.2. — Advice from f.-teller *D1814.1; amasser of largest f. to be king P11.4.2; deserted daughter's good f. discovered by accident N732.2; dwelling of F. on lofty mountain F132.2; fairy seeks f. among mortals F393.3; good gifts of f. *N200ff.; hero makes f. through gambling N1.1; jokes on f.-tellers X461; just king brings good f. upon people P12.6; loss of f. for breaking tabu C930ff.; madness from f. loss F1041.8.11; overweening pride in good f. tabu C770.1; priest uses f. dishonestly made to erect monuments to himself W157.1; profligate wastes entire f. before beginning his own adventures W131.1; quest to F. to seek f. H1281; quest to god for f. H1263; reversal of f. L (entire chapter); salt in saltless land sold for f. N411.4; shoes (shirt) of f. N135.3; tabu to offend goddess of f. C50.1; ways of f. N100—N299; wife retrieves f. lost by husband J1545.6.

Fortunes. — Inequalities of men's f. A1599.8; noblemen being ruined by long lawsuit decide wisely to join their families in marriage and save their f. J552.2.

Forty of man's sons to die at once M341.0.2; sons born same day T586.1.5; -nine gates of wisdom J182.1. — Formulistic number: f. Z71.12; penance: standing in water for f. days Q541.2.

Foster brother rescues another from ogre G551.4.1; brother steals bride K1371.1.2; mother summoned D2074.2.4.1; relatives P270ff. — Children prefer f. mother T675.1; cock as f. father N842.1; cowherd as f. father N856.2; cruel f. relatives S30; curse by f. mother M411.1.2; dog buried instead of f. son K525.6.1; fairy f. father F311.2; fairy f. mother F311.3; false boasting of having killed f. brother K1766.1; forester as f. father N856.1; helpful animal f. brother B311.1; human f. child with animal qualities B635; impostor pushes f. brother into water K1931.1.1; kind f. parents chosen rather than cruel parents J391; king and f. son jump into sea F1041.16.7; king's f. son damaged by bee sting J1179.14; magic object from f. parents *D815.7; peasant as f. father N854.1; punishment: taking snakes as f. children Q594; smith as f. father N855.1; treacherous f. son K2214.3.1; treacherous f. brother K2211.2; Virgin Mary as f. mother V271; wise giant as f. father of hero N812.1.

Fostering. — Mortal f. fairy child M242.1.

Found, see also **Find.** — Devil f. by God G303.1.2ff.; disenchantment by being f. D783; lost object f. by throwing spade at ghost D1816.2.1; magic object f. D840ff.; origin of fire—f. in person's own body A1414.1.2; stolen person f. by animal B543.

Foundation sacrifice S261. — Omen at laying building's f. D1812.5.2.8.

Foundations. — God lays earth's f. A141.4.

Founders, religious V210ff.

Foundling helper N861; hero L111.2. — Man made to believe f. is daughter's child K1923.2.

Fountain Hvergelmis filled by deer A661.1.0.4; as lovers' rendezvous T35.1; produced (by sign of cross) *D1766.6.1, (by prayer) D1766.1.1, (by drop of water) D1567.7. — Cleansing f. in heaven A661.0.4; cool and boiling f. in otherworld garden F162.1.2.2; false bride takes true bride's place at f. K1911.1.3; hero finds maiden at f. N715.1; location of f. revealed in dream K1816.1; magic f. *D925ff., (in otherworld) F162.8; magic object produces f. D1567ff.; many-colored f. where saint strikes earth A941.5.2; quest for the f. of youth H1321.3; reincarnation as f. E635; soul in salmon appears in f. E713.1; sweet and bitter f. in otherworld garden F162.1.2.1; tabu: drinking from certain f. C261; task: bringing water from distant f. more quickly than a witch H1109.1; tears become f. D457.18.1.

Fountains as chastity index H411.11.2.

Four ages of the world A1101; -armed people F516.2.2; calves to one cow at birth T586.4.1; cats carry coffin F982.2; children at a birth T586.1.1; choices J210.1; demons in ring H973.2; earth-nails A841.4; earthly paradises F111.0.1; -eyed jaguar B15.4.1.3; -eyed tiger B14.4.1.2; fires in hell A671.2.4.13; -footed bishop J2283; -footed man F517.1.2.1; -headed animal B15.1.2.3; -headed person F511.0.2.3; heavens A651.1.2; -horned ox B15.3.1.3.1; as magic number D1273.1.2; mountains support sky A665.3.1; persons survive flood A1029.2; rivers of Paradise *F162.2.1; rivers rise in paradise waterworld A871.2; sky-columns A665.2.1; suns mark world's end A1052.3; world-columns A841; world systems A651.0.2. — Adam's body made of f. things A1260.1.3; Adam's name from f. stars A1281.6.1; angel with f. wings V231.3; castle carried through air by f. eagles F771.2.1.2; castle suspended on f. chains F771.2.1.1; club takes f. thousand men to carry it F835.2.2; colors corresponding to the f. world quarters Z140.2; demon allowed on earth f. times a year A106.2.1.2; devil disappears in carriage drawn by f. black horses G303.17.2.9; dividing f. coins among three persons J1241.2; earth with f. quarters A871; earth scattered in a circuit or in f. directions on primeval water A814.6; eye with f. pupils F541.3.3; formulistic number: f. Z71.2; four stars from f. quarters of heavens A1281.6.1; god with f. faces A123.2.1.2; golden wagon drawn by f. golden elephants F861.1.2; habitable hill raised on f. pillars F721.2.1; island supported on f. feet F736.1; keeping f. dogs in herd (task) H1112.1; literal numskull cuts peas into f. parts J2461.1.4; magic f.-leaf clover *D965.7; magic plantain causes f. tails to grow D1375.4.1.1; man made of earth from f. places A1241.5; man made of f. elements A1260.1.1; moon weighs pound, for it has f. quarters H691.1.1; persons (animals) with f. eyes F512.2.1; physician willing to believe in f. persons of Trinity J817.2; tunnel of crystal f. miles long F721.1.1; what f. things are hardest to hold (riddle) H659.2; what goes on f. legs in the morning, two at midday, and three in the evening H761; what he does

with the f. coins he earns H585.1; woman has f. children: sun, moon, fire, water A700.3.

Fourfold. — Formulistic number: f. Z71.2.0.1.

Fourteen as formulistic number Z71.16.10; lucky daughters N231.

Fourth horse must carry all J761.2. — Suitor contest: riding to f. story of tower H331.1.2; sun created on f. day of creation A719.3; unpromising f. son succeeds L111.10.

Fowl makes another animal believe that he has had his leg cut off J2413.4.1, (neck) J2413.4.2; transformed to object D423. — Chain tale: conflict between f. and thistle Z41.3; enmity of f. and (dog) A2494.4.12, (cockroach) A2494.13.3, (falcon) A2494.13.12; giant's skull so large f. can pass through eye-hole F531.2.3.1; king and peasant: the plucked f. H561.6.1; self-cooking f. D1601.25.1; universe from cosmic f. A647; what is the best f. (riddle) H659.4; wise carving of the f. H601.

Fowls eat gold, silver F989.22.1. — Division of the fat and lean f. J1241.4; enmity of owls and f. A2494.13.4.1; god of domestic f. A441.2; ghosts visible to f. E421.1.6; why f. never shut doors at night A2433.4.6.

Fowler asks ransom for goose, loses both J514.6. — Tortoise outwits f., keeps ruby K439.7.1.

Fox as alchemist B121.2; as animals' king B240.8; asking favor set on by dogs J871.1; as beast of ill-omen B147.1.2.1; brings flower in mouth B584.1; burns tree in which eagle has nest L315.3; claims that certain statues are of his ancestors J954.2; in coffer thought to be devil J1785.6; confesses to cock then eats him K2027; as culture hero A522.1.4; deceives lion into entering pit K714.9.1; deceptively sleeps with tiger's wife K1354.2.3; determines road to be taken B151.1.3; destroys boasting bird's nest L462; disguised as scholar K1822.2; distracts goldsmith's attention, steals K341.25; drinks tiger's milk K362.5.1; eating cake gets caught in pot K1022.6; elected mediator to appease angry lion B239.1; executed for thefts B275.1.2; fools crocodile into letting him go K543.1; forgets fables against lion J811.6; frightened in game with titmouse K869.1; holds conversation with his members J2351.1; and crane invite each other J1565.1; eats his fellow-lodger: accuses another animal and demands damages K443.7; with eight-forked tail B15.7.4; fasts as penance B253.3; feigns to be playing with sheep *K2061.2; feigning illness admitted to hen-roost and kills the hens K828.2; finally converses with lion whom he had feared at first U131.1; about to be hanged asks to be allowed to see geese J864.2; in human form betrays identity H48.1; insults caged lion W121.2.2; invites fish to live on land J758.3; jeers at fox-trap J655.2; language B215.3; leads ass to lion's den but is himself eaten *K1632; with lion protector goes hunting alone and is killed J684.1; loses fear of lion J1075.2; masks as dove, loses murder thoughts J512.10; as messenger B291.3.1; and noisy but empty barrel J262.1; outwits wolf, gets lion to kill him K961.1.1; and panther contest in beauty J242.3;

persuaded to talk and release cock from his mouth K561.1; persuades animals to start with the smallest in eating one another K1024; persuades bear to lie in hay, sets fire to it K1075; persuades bird to show him how she acts in a storm K827.1; persuades cock to come down and talk to him K815.1; persuades wolf to eat his own entrails (brains) K1025f.; persuades wolf to lie on the shock in order to be painted K1013.2; prefers to bear weight of his tail rather than give part of it to ape J341.1; pretends to be guarding sky K1251.1.1; pretends work, really sleeps K499.10; produces fire by striking tail to ground D2158.1.1; is promised chickens: driven off by dogs G235.1; had rather meet one hen than fifty women J488; refuses to mediate between lion and lioness J811.2; rescues man from sea B541.2; rids himself of fleas K921; rings the bell K1114; saves man from turtle J1172.4; shams death, catches crows K827.4; sees all tracks going into lion's den but none coming out J644.1; in sheepskin gains admission to the fold and kills sheep K828.1; as shepherd K934; sings formula for trick exchanges Z47.1; and sour grapes J871; spoils his food rather than divide with ape W152.1; stumbles over violin J864.1; in swollen river claims to be swimming to distant town J873; threatens to catch bird, given her young K1788; transformed to person D313.1; transformed to snake D411.8; tries to drown jug, gets drowned J2131.5.7; understands human speech B212.1; weeps B736.4. — Abduction by f. R13.1.11; animals confess sins to one another: f. and wolf forgive each other, punish ass U11.1.1; bear builds house of wood, f. of ice J741.1; birds fight over wounded f., who escapes J581.5; cock singing for f., dog audience kills fox K579.8; color of f. A2411.1.3.1; creation of f. A1832; devastating f. B16.2.1; devil as f. G303.3.3.2.2; does not know whether it is a f. or a hare, but the girl is downstairs J2671.1; dog language understood by f. B215.2.1; enmity between f. and (dog) A2494.4.5, (baboon) A2494.9.1, (chickens) A2494.9.2; fly, wren and f. live with cleric B256.10; flying f. B49.3; friendship of f. and titmouse A2493.10; how f. got his eyes A2332.1.4, A2245; fleeing f. loses an eye in the briars J2182; ghost of f. E522.1; ghost as f. E423.2.3; how f. got white breast A2411.1.3.1.1; grateful f. fetches f. liver as remedy B514.1; gray f. J1457; guarding chickens from f. J2125; helpful f. *B435.1; hungry f. waits in vain for horse's scrotum to fall off J2066.1; jackal rides on f. B557.13; jealous f. betrays wolf to peasant and then appropriates wolf's cave and food W181.4; luring off girl's f. husband K341.29; magic f. heart D1015.1.5; magic hair of f. D1023.2; man transformed to f. D113.3; marriage to f. B601.14; (in human form) *B651.1; monkey cheats f. of bananas K171.9; nine-tailed f. B15.7.7.1; partridge helps f. obtain curds K341.26; peasant betrays f. by pointing K2315; prophetic f. B144; reincarnation as f. E612.4; revenant as f. E423.2.3; sacred f. B811.6; saint's cowl protects f. D1447.2.1; saint's performing f. killed, replaced V224.4; seller of f. skins mixes otter skins with them and thinks to cheat the buyer J2083.3; sheep dupes f. into running to hunter K1178;

singing f. B214.1.6; soul as f. E731.10; speaking f. B211.2.5; tail of f. *A2378.3.4, A2378.6.1, *A2378.8.1f.; tailless f. tries in vain to induce foxes to cut off tails J758.1; tame f. helps dogs J683.3; the third time f. meets lion she has no fear J1075.2; thorn bush blamed by f. for wounding him J656.1; three teachings of the f. *K604; tooth becomes f. D447.6; troll as f. G304.1.1.1; two sheep kill a f. who has licked up the blood they have spilled in a fight J624.1; ungrateful f. hits rescuer W154.5.1; unsatisfied f. W128.2; wedding of f. and hyena B281.1; why f. is sly A2525.3; wisdom from f. B163.1; witch in form of f. G211.2.3.

Fox's boasting overawes lion cubs K1715.14; desire for needles, anchors J1391.8; double dealings with wolf, tiger K2043; elongated shadow makes him proud J953.13; enemies A2494.9; excuse for farmyard visit J1391.5; heart becomes rattle D457.15.1; plan detected by crickets K2061.10; tail drops and frightens animals K2323.1; thieving nature will show itself U129.1. — Bear helps f. mother get berries K461.1; coyote wears f. rattle, caught in brush and injured J2136.1; hair from f. tail opens all doors D1562.2; why f. legs are black A2371.4.2.

Foxes crawl into whale's house, killed K728; crowd into house and are suffocated N339.3; desert their allies, the hares, when they foresee defeat by the eagles J682.1; as giant's lice F531.4.11.2; gnawing on giant's head F531.5.4.2; will meet at furriers J1424; persuade man to plant cooked food K496. — Buying f. "as they run" K196.1; cat lures f. with music K815.15; fire tied to f. tails destroys enemy K2351.1.1; tiger to help f. divide their young K579.5.2; why f. do not live on a certain island A2434.2.2.

Foxglove. — Fairies dance on f. F261.3.2.

Fragile. — Chopping down large tree with f. instrument (task) H1115.

Fragments of gibbet as cure D1500.1.26. — Moon made from shining f. A742; resuscitation from body f. E35.

Fragmentation. — Multiplication of man by f. A1296.

Fragrance, see also **Perfume.** — Clouds with f. F967.2; flower sending f. far H1333.5.0.1; person's remarkable f. F687; pleasant f. in otherworld F169.9; resuscitation by f. E64.8.1; saint's house filled with f. V222.4.

Fragrances. — Evil smells become sweet f. D479.7.

Fragrant. — Air f. at Nativity V211.1.1; air magically made f. D1599.2; magic dog f. B182.1.6.

Franciscan claims cordon will save him from hell J1261.8.

Francolin eats man's grain: man may kill him A2238.2; markings A2232.6, A2412.2.2.

Fraternity initiate dies of fright N384.4.

Fraternizing of giants and men at Christmas F531.5.1.2.

Fratricide S73.1, (punished) Q211.9. — Extraordinary phenomena at f. F960.6; spring dry after f. *D927.5.

Frau Holle *F475.1.

Freak. — Thumbling sold as f. F535.1.1.9.

Frederic Barbarossa *D1960.2, F451.5.1.8; the Great drives dwarfs across Black Sea F451.9.1.13.

Free. — Choice: f. poverty or enslaved wealth J211; differentiation between "f." and "unfree" A1691; dragon fight to f. (lion) B11.11.6, (man) B11.11.5, (princess) B11.11.4; dwarfs f. mortals from enchantment F451.3.3.4; lion sent to kill man so as to f. him from possibility of sinning and sojourn in purgatory J225.2; penance: planting garden and offering f. hospitality to all Q523.5; test of god: when its image is bound it can f. itself H45.3; woman f. from trouble, worry H1195; woman masks as lawyer (judge) to f. her husband K1825.3; woman sacrifices her honor to f. her husband (brother) from prison *T455.2.

Freed. — Captive knight f. for having kept word Q54.2; captives' love rewarded: f. and enriched Q56.2; condemned woman may be f. by marrying a rogue P512; deer in net f. by animals B545.1; hero f. from wedge by magic cranberry D1564.5; husband f. from death by prayers V52.10; one is f. if he can set a task the devil is unable to perform G303.16.19.3; person f. from prison by magic object D1395; slaves f. P178.

Freedom as reward Q121. — Abridgement of f. as punishment Q430ff.; philosopher chooses poverty with f. J211.1; preserving cock's f. J1892; wealth sacrificed for f. J347.

Freemason in league with devil G303.10.6; as wild huntsman E501.1.5.

Freemasons punished Q388. — Jokes on f. X551.

Freezing, see also **Frozen.** — Heavenly fire f. F962.2.4; lies about f. X1623; Mars prevents moon from f. earth A759.7; river f. at saint's command D2151.2.4; river never f. F141.1.3, F715.5; so hot animals f. to death X1633.1; water f. to form mountains A969.5.

Freischütz *D1653.1, D1923.

Frenzied. — Saint cures f. animal V221.4.0.1.

Fresh water in sea F711.4, (origin of) A925.4.

Friar accused of rape, castrated K2111.3; adds missing nose to unborn child K1363.2; awakens girl, follows mother's orders K1354.3.1; disguises as soldier, steals K1839.5; Rush as mischief maker F470.0.1; seduces woman, claims he is administering sacrament K1354.2.2; strangled for attempted seduction Q424.3. — Disappointed lover becomes f. T93.2.1; girl disguised as f. gets into priest's bed K1315.6.3; happy f. becomes unhappier as he receives over more and more money J1085.1; lover disguised as monk or f. meets sweetheart K1826.1.1; miserly f. stays in ditch rather than aid rescuers W153.5; nun tells f. to castrate himself J1919.5.2. sinning f. pardoned after confession V21.4; transformation to f. to instruct D659.6.

Friars exploit false relic K1976.1; unaware of time passing D2011.2. — Devil vexing f. caused to repent by singing "Te sanctum dominum" G303.24.3.

Friday as auspicious day N127.4. — Fasting on "Golden F." V73.5;

fountain gives water on Wednesday and F. F716.1; transformation to werwolf on F. D622.1; why sun shines on F. A1177.

Friend in kitchen learns of friend's distress, helps him N455.8; rescues hero R169.5. — Child sacrificed to provide blood for cure of f. S268; choice of f. over mistress J496; confessor as soul-f. V20.1.2; corpse makes coffin space for f. E477; defeated enemy becomes f. R74.1; deity f. to one mortal A185.6; fight with father's f. as valor test H1561.2.2; giant becomes victor's f. G510.3; hero fights with f. of father and then reveals himself N731.2.1; husband has f. woo wife H492.2; least loved f. proves truest H1558.1.1; lover's f. steals bride K1371.1.3; man eats f. G74; one man prays either to keep f. from death or for both to die E165.1; supper won by trick: the mutual f. K455.1; task: bringing best f., worst enemy H1065; treacherous f. K2297; unfaithful f. P251.1.

Friends P310; identical in appearance F577.1; in life and death M253; offer to die for each other P315; refuse to fight each other H1558.8; who seduce man's wife called dogs in human shape H592.4; in stealing contest H305.2; tested H1558. — Causing f. wife to leave husband K1394; combat of disguised f. P314; dead f. come for dying soul E722.2.9; dupe lured away from f. K725; enemy horses captured by lion join forces and become f. J891; fool f. with birds and beasts P192.5; why God has few f. J1261.1.2; husband asks f. to share his disguised wife K1843.2.3; judicial combat interrupted by f. of loser H218.1; knight saved from devil by f. G303.16.19.8; loyal f. refuse to fight comrade W34.2; magician's f. give magic D1721.0.2; person buried with f. about him V61.3.0.2; priest has no f. until he becomes bishop, then they flock to him U62; resuscitation by f. E127; return from dead to protect f. E379.3; ruler persecutes f., kind to enemies W154.16; scarcity of real f. J401; sun and moon as f. A736.6; trickster attempts to bring f. to fight K1084.3; trickster makes two f. each suspicious of the other's intentions *K2131ff.; two f. exchange forms D45.3; unwitting combat between sons of f. N767; visiting f. take everything from house of dying man W151.2; wolf tries to make f. with lion J411.5; vow not to see f. until quest completed M151.9.

Friendly animals B300—B599; night spirit F475; return from the dead E300—E399. — Emperor f. to everyone W21; giant f. to man F531.5.1; hostile dogs made f. by having them fight common enemy, the wolf J145; land where all creatures f. F111.5; stealing from ogre to help f. king G610.2.

Friendship *P310ff.; between the animals A2493ff.; covenanted A1599.12; pretended to obtain access to girl K2016; of prince and commoner P32. — Avoid enemies' revenge either by making peace and f. or by killing them all J647.1; covenant of f. M246; former f. between domestic and wild animals A2493.0.1; hypocrite pretends f. but attacks K2010ff.; man pretends f. but attacks king to avenge violation of his wife K2010.1; marriage destroys f. T201; singing f. song to enemy K606.0.3; tests of f. H1558; trolls' f. with men F455.6.1; woman destroys men's f. K2131.3.

Fright, see also **Fear;** tests H1400—H1449. — Barrenness as result of f. F1041.17.1; cowardly f. *J2600—J2649; death from f. N384; dying of f. J955.4; forgetfulness from f. D2004.7; pool girl outwits prince in f.-contest J1525; queen dies of f. after prophecy M392.

Frightened soul cannot re-enter body E721.1.2.5; wife shows marks of affection for husband T284. — Boastful coward f. by conspirators K1951.4; cripples at shrine f. and run away without crutches V113.1; devil cheated by being f. K212; devil disappears when f. G303.16.19.17; devil f. by the shrewish wife T251.1.1; fearless hero f. by being awakened with cold water H1441; ghost f. by own reflection K1715.1.2; husband f. by paramour in hog pen K1542; judge f. into decision J1195; lawyer f. into giving when beggar tells him of all the lawyers in hell X312; magic lost by being f. D1741.5; man abed with his wife is f. away by an intruder who steals his clothes K1272; man in tree so f. of lion he drops sword, kills it N331.2.1; ogre (large animal) f. K1710ff.; owner f. from goods by thief *K335ff.; robber f. away by man who scolds his ass N612.1; robbers f. away by numskull's talking to himself N612; treasure-finders f. away N556; wild hunt f. away by scolding F501.17.8.1.

Frightening enemy by transformation D651.2; thing at bridge to land of dead E481.2.1.1. — Chain tale: animal f. another Z43.4; deception by f. *K2320ff.; deity f. child H1401; dwarfs f. mortals F451.5.2.10; escape by f. captors K547; ghost f. people into stream E272.3; ghosts f. people E293; husband's trick f. off wife's lovers K1569.6; plants and animals magically caused to shriek, f. enemy D2091.12; resuscitation by f. dead E25; tale-teller f. listener Z13.1; theft of money from fairies by f. them away from it F351.2.

Frightful meal S183, (as punishment) Q478. — Continuous prayer sustains man through f. vigil V52.2; old robber frees his three sons by relating f. adventures R153.3.3; trolls f. F455.2.6; youngest son alone endures f. experiences in vigil for dead father H1462.1.

Frog abuses bullock J952.5; as beauty-doctor unable to cure his own ugliness J1062.1; carries person B557.14; as child's nurse B535.0.6; eats plowshare (lie) X1342.3; eats rat, baker, horse F911.3.4; escapes crow by telling him to sharpen bill K561.1.2; as host to woman B530.1; language B215.4; leaps after elephant's reflection J1791.5.3; with magic knowledge B126.1; in moon A751.3; outlives tortoise, fish L395; persists in living in puddle on road J652.1; pierces metals, marbles F989.23; recovers keys from sea B548.2.2.1; recovers Sacred Host B548.5; removed from queen's nose N641.2; rescues man from snake kingdom B547.4; returned to spring: grateful B375.2; rises into person's throat, croaks every spring B784.0.1; sits in leaky vessel's hole H1023.2.1.2; swelling up as big as ox J955.1; transformed to person D395; transformed to object D428.1; wants to be shod J512.12; -woman disenchanted by sight of water D789.3.1; -woman betrays self by croaking J1908.3; works in fields for benefactor B292.9.1. — Animal languages learned from f. B165.2; ant

pinching f. causes accident chain N381.1; cheese brings f. from person's mouth B784.2.3; color of f. A2411.5.2; croak of f. A2426.4.1; earth supported by f. A844.4; enmity between f. and snake A2494.16.1; fairy in form of f. F234.1.6; friendship between f. and cricket A2493.20; giant f. B876.1; girl swallows f. spawn B784.1.4; god of fate as f. A463.0.1; great f. eaten by one larger and this in turn by crow X1342.1.1; habitation of f. A2433.6.6; helpful f. *B493; why f. has hunchback A2356.2.1; jumping f. contest K17.4; magic f. B177.2; man in moon a f. which has jumped into person's face and remains there A751.3.1; man transformed to f. D195; mankind from mating of f. and fire-daughter A1221.5; marriage to f. B604.5; marriage to person in f. form B645.1.2; mythical f. B98; origin of f. A2162; rat and f. tie paws together to cross marsh J681.1; reincarnation as f. E615.1; revenant as f. E423.4; singing f. B214.1.7; snake as f. king's mount J352.2; snake promises to do no harm to f. K815.6; snake wants to eat f. friend J426.2; soul in form of f. E736.1; why f. cannot speak A2422.7; speaking f. B211.7.1; how f. lost tail A2231.4, A2242, A2378.2.3; toad receives water from f. K231.8; transformation into f. Q551.3.2.3; why f. croaks in wet weather A2426.4.1.2; why f. is spotty A2412.5.2.1; why f. toothless A2239.8, A2345.7.2; woman bears f. T554.8.

Frog's cries misunderstood J1811.2; view of cattle J1772.13; wedding B284.1. — Death from f. bite F1041.1.11.4; fear of f. drowning J1909.7; why f. eyes bulge out A2332.4.3; why f. skin rough A2311.8.

Frogs cast themselves into oven, eat bread F989.24; caught in frozen ice X1130.3; croak at prince's command H71.10.3; decide not to jump into the well J752.1; demand a live king J643.1; to eat insects, snakes to eat frogs J2102.8; fear defeated bull J613.2; fear increase of sun's power which will dry up all their puddles J613.1; reprove ass for lamenting when he falls into morass J2211.1; want to collect honey J512.15; were ducks stolen from Eden A2426.4.1.1. — Animals from f. sent as Egypt's plague A1734; army of f. D2091.2.1; community of f. B226.2; dance of f. B293.2; fools shoot at f. all night to keep their croaking from disturbing prince J2105; king of f. B245.1; lies about f. X1342; magic plague of f. drawn down on foe D2091.2; money thrown to f. J1851.1; placing f. in a tree (task) H1024.2; war between toads and f. B263.1.

Frost-giants F531.1.9; -god A289.1; and hare contest in enduring cold H1541.1; produced by magic D2143.5. — Magic stone protects against f. D1382.12; old woman in control of f. D2143.5.1; origin of f. A1135.3; wind overcomes f. in contest in enduring cold H1541.2.

Frown as "black look" H588.14, J2489.7.

Frozen, see also **Freezing.** — Eating way out of f. animal X1723.3.1; everything f. when man wears cap straight D2144.1.2; hero drives log into f. ground F611.3.2.1; man f. to saddle X1606.2.1.

Fructifier. — God as f. of mankind A189.15.

Fruit affected by judge's judgment H251.3.10; with any desired taste D1665.3; broken too soon, hero punished D1962.6.1; causes sexual desire D1355.14; as chastity index H434; decays on tree E761.3.2; falls if oath false H252.3; flies from hungry man's reach Q501.2.1; juice turns to blood D474.8; by magic D2105.7; of magic tree exhilarating D1359.3.3; magically grows in winter *D2145.2.2; -picking time of sexual promiscuity T485; pierced with pins as love charm D1355.3.3; produced out of season at saint's request F971.5.1; transformed to animal D441.2; transformed to person D431.4; transformed to other object D451.3; tree grows from deer shot with fruit pits X1130.2; from tree tabu C762.4. — Animals eat deity's forbidden f. A2234.2; birth from f. T543.3; conception from eating a f. T511.1; conception from f. thrown against breast T532.3; covering mango grove with f. overnight H1103.3; creation of man from f. A1253; disenchantment from f. by plucking it D711.6; disenchantment by opening f. *D721.5; diving for reflected f. J1791.11; eater of f. to become king M312.3.2; eating rind first: too full for f. J2178.1; extraordinary f. F810ff.; forbidden f. *C621; fruitless tree bears f. F971.4; girl lives in f. *F562.4; god of f. A433.4; the great f. X1411; inexhaustible f. D1652.1.7; knocking off single f. from tree H1199.18; magic f. *D981ff., (gives supernatural knowledge) D1310.10; magic tree continually in f. D1668; man as f. of blooming animal horns A1263.6; man transformed to f. D211; miraculous blossoming and bearing of f. F971; murder by throwing hot f. into mouth K951.1.3; paradise lost because of forbidden f. A1331.1; prophylactic f. D1500.2.7; quest for extraordinary f. H1333.3; red f. thrown at rail's head: hence red lump on head A2215.4; sickness from drying, shriveling f. plant D2064.8; soul as f. E745.5; strong hero engendered by eating of f. F611.1.8; sun from f. kernels A718.3; tabu to eat certain f. C225; task: bringing f. in winter H1023.3; task: getting f. from top of tall tree without cutting tree H1038; task: turning f. into gold H1023.15; touching f. tabu C621.2; transformation by eating f. D551.1; tree bearing f. three times yearly F811.18; tree bears f., flower, and leaf simultaneously F811.16; tree blooms and grows ripe f. nightly F811.13; tree with extraordinary f. F811.7; tree from otherworld f. F162.3.0.1; tree in perpetual f. F162.3.3; trickster feigns death and eats ripe f. from the tree K1866; trickster in tree advises that tree and f. belong to him K1971.11; trying to get f. from fruitless tree J1944, J2066.3.1; vine bears 926 varieties of f. F815.7.1; wanderers in shade of plane tree blame it for not bearing f. W154.7; why some trees have no f. A2791.7; why big trees have small f. A2771.9; witches shake f. off trees G265.10.1; woman bears f. which can transform self to girl T555.1; wounds healed by eating f. of magic tree D1503.11.

Fruits that laugh or cry D1619.3. — Extraordinary f. *F813ff.; ghosts with f. in hair K335.1.12; jinns share f. of earth F499.3.2; magic f. and vegetables D980ff.; only one man can pluck tree's f. H31.12; origin of f.

A2687ff.; sea bears f. F931.9.2.2; sour f. made sweet by saint F979.1; tree bearing all f. F811.7.1; tree bearing several f. F811.7.1.1; throwing f. on bridal couple A1555.1.1; tree allows only two f. to be taken F979.16; tribes from f. of trees A1610.4; woman cooks the magic f. D866.1; worthless f. sold K147.

Fruitful island F733; tree chosen J241. — Athena chooses olive tree because it is f. J241.1; magic song makes barren land f. D1563.1.2; prophecy: granddaughters f. M301.17.1; sign of the cross makes barren land f. D1563.1.3.

Fruitfulness. — Nature's f. as proof of kingly right H1574.2.

Fruitless tree bears fruit F971.4. — Nature f. after false judgment H243; nature f. after hero's death F960.2.1; trees made f. D2082.0.1; trying to get fruit from f. tree J1944.

Fruitlessness. — Formulas signifying f. Z63.

Frying. — Insect f. human blood A2435.5.2; man-eater f. victims G312.4.

Frying-pan, magic D1472.1.12.1.

Fuel sticks to stingy man's hand Q551.2.8. — Carrying f. as task H1129.11; corpses used as f. S139.2.2.5; fire from extraordinary f. F964.3; grass as f. for burning ogre G512.3.3; inexhaustible f. D1652.10; saint's unusual f. V229.9.

Fugitive returns so family may collect reward T215.5; slave takes refuge in mill house N255.4; slave takes wrong road and is caught N382; transforms self to stone D671.0.1; woman burdened with child saved while childless woman is killed N185. — Animal blessed (cursed) for helping (betraying) holy f. A2221.5, A2231.7.1; empire prophesied for f. M314.4; ground hides f. F942.1.1; lovers as pursuer and f. K1517.1; magic hair stretches after f. D1436; magic object compels f. to betray himself D1612.2ff.; magic object helps f. *D1393ff.; magic objects betray f. *D1612.1ff.; officer accidentally finds f. N618; plant blessed (cursed) for helping (betraying) holy f. A2711.3, A2721.4; reward for protecting f. Q46; river pursues f. F932.1; ruler marries f. noblewoman T121.4; saint hides f. underground K2319.8; saint's spittle protects f. from attack D1381.2; spider-web over hole saves f. B523.1; sun sets early to hide f. F961.1.10.

Fugitives have way revealed by magic D1813.4. — Captives and f. R (entire chapter); clouds protect f. F967.1.

Fulfillment of bargain or promise M202; of warning in dream D1810.8.3.1. — Fairies give f. of wishes F341; ghost laid at f. of vow E451.3; vain attempts to escape f. of prophecy M370ff.

Full moon and thirtieth of the month (girl's enigmatic message) H582.1.1; pot sign that city is filled with fakirs J1293.4. — Fairy returns vessel ever f. F335.1.

Fuller and collier cannot live together J143.

Fulmar, marriage to B602.2.

Fumes. — Devil chased by f. G303.16.14.2.

Fumigations, transformation by D575.
Funeral for the ineligible husband J1191.3; procession of the hen (cumulative tale) Z32.1; rites *V60ff. — Angels attend saint's f. V241.1; animal f. B257; at child's f. real father sings, cuckold weeps U119.1.1; birds take part in saint's f. B251.2.1.2; dead man demands proper f. E235.2.1; dead without proper f. rites cannot rest E412.3; doctor orders patient's f. X372.5; dupe tricked into jumping on f. pyre K891.4; evil mother has fine f., good father poor J225.8; faithless widow betrothed anew at husband's f. T231.1; foresight of f. procession D1825.7.1; ghost light indicates f. route E530.1.7; king must not attend f. P13.8; king on retiring orders f. obsequies given him P16.1.1; man too lazy to turn around to see f. W111.5.11; man at his lady's f. jests with priest on unequal returns from women J1264.8; neighbors insist on fool's f. although he is alive and well J2311.5; origin of f. customs A1547; precautions at f. against revenant E431; resuscitation through ashes thrown on f. pyre E132; return home to one's own f. N681.0.1; riddle about father at f. H583.4.5; thieves' mock f. for stolen chickens K375; wager ends only on f. pyre J2511.1; wife throws herself on husband's f. pyre T211.2; will spend f. money now J1261.5.
Funerals. — Few f. make bad year for priests X427.
Fungus, birth from T543.4.
Fur made of beards of conquered kings P672.1. — Cloak from f. of all animals F821.1.3.2; dress of raw f. F821.1.3; ghosts seen through f. coat sleeve C311.1.1.1; wild huntsman with black f. cap and white staff E501.8.6.
Furnace falls in on disobedient wife T254.5; transformed to garden D469.5. — Child born in f. T561.2; fiery f. does not harm saint D1841.3.2.1; god of the f. A493.2; man leaping into f. unharmed H1573.1.4; unsuccessful attempt to make gold man in f. J2411.1.2.
Furnished. — Money f. by inexhaustible purse D1451ff.; supplies f. by cobolds F481.2.
Furnishings, extraordinary F770ff.
Furniture in otherworld F166. — Falling f. threatens bridal couple T175.1; ghost moves f. E599.6; gold f. in otherworld F166.0.1; magic f. *D1150ff.; tricksters change f., blame it on demons K1838.1.
Furrows burn witch G273.5.1; from giant's step F531.1.3.4.
Fury personified Z123.
Furies A486.
Fuschia belongs to devil: hence ball and red petals A2743.1.
Futility of distant travel J1076; of trying to hide an obvious deed J1082; of trying to teach the stupid J1064; of weather prophecies M398. — Pupil returns from dead to warn master of f. of his studies E368.
Future creator goes to make afterworld A78; husband (wife) met during magic sleep D1976.2; revealed (in dream) *D1812.3.3ff., (by knowledge tooth) D1810.3.1. — Avoiding power of f. enemy J645; care against f.

tyranny J643; don't injure yourself to insure your family's f. J322; dream (prophecy) of f. greatness causes banishment L425; in planning f., profit by the past J752; intermediate f. world *A693; king for year provides for f. J711.3; means of learning the f. M302, (magic) D1812.3; ordaining the f. M (entire chapter); present values preferred to f. J320ff.; prophecy: death through f. husband M341.2.12; provision for the f. J701; tasks assigned to learn f. M302.5; vision of f. V516.

Gabriel (angel) addressed in throwing contest K18.1.2; drives Satan and other devils from heaven to earth G303.8.1.2; made from snow A52.1.3. — Seduction by posing as G. K1315.1.1.

Gadfly. — Io transformed to cow with g. ceaselessly pursuing Q501.6; transformation to g. to enter giant's stomach and kill him K952.2.

Gaelic titles given to devil G303.2.4.

Gaels invade Ireland F211.0.2.1.

Gai bulga F832.1.1; invention of A1459.1.4.

Gain. — Feeding with loss or g. H583.9; choices: little g., big loss *J340ff.; choices: small inconvenience, large g. J350ff.

Gains and losses J330—J369. — Disappearance of ill-gotten g. Q552.18.

Gait of animal A2441ff. — Raven tries to imitate dove: punished with awkward g. A2232.10.

Gaiters, magic D1065.6.

Galatea D435.1.1, F423.1.

Gall. — Giant's g. (restores sight) D1505.19, (resuscitates) E117.

Gall-bladder of animal, magic *D1015.2. —Stag vomits his g. A2211.13.

Gall-stone the worst of stones H659.3.1.

Gallows ghost E274; rope breaks when innocent hanged H215.2. — Buying g. flesh or living flesh forbidden C781.1; devil at g. repudiates his bargain with robber M212.2; executioner must show the hero how to use the g. (hanged) K715; lover rescues lady from g. R161.4; oxen bear dead usurer to g. to be buried N277; red cap for the g. J2174.1; return from dead to punish theft of liver from man on g. E235.4.4; saint sustains man on g. V221.6; son on g. bites his mother's nose off Q586; staying under g. at night as fear test H1415; Virgin Mary supports robber on g. V254.1.1.

Galoshes. — Fortune's g. N135.3; devil visible to one who walks in minister's holy g. G303.6.2.4.

Gam (mythical bird) rescues hero from shipwreck R138.2; throws sand in a stream and makes lake B31.2. — Cup of eggshell of g. F866.5; giant as g. F531.1.8.6.

Gambler reformed by love T10.1.1. — Clever g. J1115.1; dead priest returns to save g. E341.5; devil to help g. in exchange for one task yearly M214; giant g. as ogre G101; magic object helps g. win D1407ff.; saint gives liberally to g. J225.6; skillful g. always wins *F679.7; soul of g. won by saint's dice E756.4.1; wretched life of otherworld g. F171.8.

Gamblers *N1; beat incognito prince K1812.2.2. — If you want to gamble then gamble with experienced g. H588.5.

Gambling, see also **Wager, Winning;** cannibal G11.13. — Bankrupt father sells his daughters to pay g. debt S221.1; despised boy wins g. game L177; god of g. A482; hangman's noose gives luck in g. D1407.2; hero g. with ruler of afterworld E489.6; punishment for g. Q381; quest assigned as payment for g. loss H1219.1; tasks to pay g. loss H942; wagers and g. *N0—N99; youth sells himself to an ogre in settlement of a g. debt S221.2.

Game with ancestor's bones P203; between gods A163.1; rolling down hill in snowball X1130.1; -tales Z19.1. — Abandoned child joins parents in g.: recognition follows H151.9; accidental discharge of gun kills much g. X1124.3; accidental fatal ending of g. or joke N334; animals play g. B298ff.; antelope eats g. while leopard away K345.4; ball g. in lower world E494; bride contest a g. H375; claim that dog-head captured g. J1214.1; coming neither with nor without g. H1056; despised boy wins gambling g. L177; devil plays disc g. G303.9.9.9; dog sight of which renders g. helpless B182.1.3; falling in love while playing g. T34.2; why g. is easy to hunt A2551; fatal deceptive g. K850ff.; helping losing player in g. C882, C746; hoarded g. released A1421; human beings as g. in fairy hunt F368; isolated child kills increasingly larger g. T617.1; killed g. revives and flies away E161; king in disguise sees child's g. which represents lawsuit J123; lies about plentiful g. X1119; magic object locates g. D1327; magic object stolen in card g. D861.6; magic wishing-pipe supplies g. D1472.2.3; man from g. animal's blood A1263.1.2; origin of ball g. A1495.1; origin of customs: division of g. A1525; owner enticed to chase g. while goods are stolen K341.5; playing g. with ferocious beast H1537; playing g. with reassembled dead man H1433; plentiful g. as reward Q141.2; poor g. proves rich L216; princess won at g. of chance R111.1.10; pursuers play fatal g. K619.3; pursuit of g. leads to upper world F59.2; runner catches g. on the run F681.6; seduction while teaching a g. K1315.7.2; soul won from devil in card g. E756.2; suitor test: to defeat bride in g. H332.1.2; tabu to look at g. before it dies C311.1.7; why g. animals are elusive A2552; wild hunt asked for g., gives dead child E501.18.1.3.1; winning first g., then playing for higher stakes K2378.1.

Games. — Dead persons play g. E577; fairies attend g. F267; funeral g. V65.5; hero stupid at g. L141.3; mountain-men play g. F460.3.2; origin of g. A1535.2, (of skill) A1468; religious g. A1549.3; ruler jealous of happiness prohibits g. W181.7.

Game-board, golden F899.2.1; magic D1209.7, D1407.3.

Gander. — Dwarfs accept as gift goose but not g. F451.3.6.4; man becomes g. D161.2.1.

Gang nach dem Eisenhammer K1612.

Ganges. — Bathing in G. V96.1, (no cure for liar) U235.1; ghost's skull

thrown into G. E459.7; Mother G. Z118.3; soul of G. is sandalwood, frog, cow J1511.2.1; vow to bathe in G. M183.2.

Ganymede carried off by eagle R13.3.2.

Garbage. — Lie: extraordinary g. X1031.7.

Garbling. — Cat g. message from man to tiger A2281.1.1.

Garden becomes wilderness F975; in fairyland F219.2; fills with flowers as innocent approaches H216.1; of the gods A151.2; of Hesperides *F111; under water F725.7; wall that cannot be overleapt D1675. — Barber's and jackal's common g. K171.8; blighted g. magically restored D2195.1; contrasting qualities found in otherworld g. *F162.1.2; entering a g. by swimming down a stream that flows into it K2377; extraordinary g. F818; fairest thing in the g. J1472; furnace becomes g. D469.5; girl sleeps in g. to meet lover T36; goat eats in g. and is caught J2136.3; hero finds maiden in (magic) g. N711.3; holy man restores bloom of g. V222.12; magic g. *D961; magic object from g. D849.4.1; maiden found in magic g. N741.5; making g. in three days H1103.1.1; making g. bloom in winter as suitor test H352; moon steals from a g. A753.3.2; negro so black that he makes whole g. somber F573; planting beautiful g. H1199.1; poor soil transformed miraculously into g. D2157.5; pursuing the rabbit who harmed the g. J2103.2; robbers spade up saint's g. V222.16; sexual promise dependent on g. blooming in winter M261.1; stealing from ingenuously guarded g. H1151.10.1; summer and winter g. D1664; sweet and bitter fountain in otherworld g. F162.1.2.1; task: making g. quickly in unplanted forest H1103.1; turtle induced to rob in man's g. K1022.5; unsuccessful magic production of g. J2411.7; water for thieves in king's g. H1471.1; witch haunting king's g. H1191.2.

Garden of Eden. — Frogs were ducks stolen from G. A2426.4.1.1; souls pass through G. E755.1.3.

Garden of the Hesperides. — Magic apple from G. D981.1.1.

Gardener disguise K1816.1; made king by minister decides against him M13.3; who plants vegetable tends it best J1033; rescues abandoned child R131.8.2. — Flower bouquet tied in certain way by g. H16.3; king tests obedience of g. H1557.6; man disguised as g. enters convent and seduces nuns K1323; son of g. to marry princess H317.3; strong man as g. F614.3; treacherous g. K2257.

Gargantuan feats F531.3ff.

Garland thrown to chosen suitor H316.4. — Ring in g. as identification H94.9; snake becomes g. D425.1.3.

Garlands as token H87; unfading D1652.7. — Marriage by exchange of g. T135.5.

Garlic juice dangerous to poisonous animals B776.0.1; protects against evil D1385.2.8; stalk as knighthood arms for servant J955.3. — Christ's body rubbed with g. A1662.1; extraordinary perception of g. F647.1.1; magic g. D983.4; transformation by eating g. D551.2.6; wedding of g. to onion B286.1.

Garment appears and disappears in reply to command D2188.1.1; fits only true king H36.2; hidden in thigh F1034.3.3; produced by prayer D1766.1.3. — Conception after touching g. T532.5.1; flow of cow's milk increased by licking saint's g. D2182; good thing fool did not have g. on or he would have shot himself J2235; identification by g. H111; magic g. *D1052, (prevents burning) D1382.10, (protects from drowning) D1388.0.4; quest for g. of spider's web H1355.1; red g. to show anger of king Z141.1; sign of cross prevents g. from burning V86.1.2; supernatural wife's g. stolen R227.3; tabu: giving back g. to supernatural wife C31.10; tabu: stealing g. from a rock C91.1.

Garments, see also **Clothes;** of mountain down H1054.4. — Magic shears clip g. from air D1601.12.1; magician makes people lift g. to avoid wetting in imaginary river D2031.1; monster borrows wedding g. one by one and wins girl K1918; old rags preferred to new g. L217; upper g. must be removed above chiefs P94; waterwomen powerless without g. F420.4.6.1; woman's g. cut off: does not know herself J2012.2.

Garter. — Giant slings stone with g. F531.3.2.2; magic g. *D1063.

Garuda-bird B56; attracted by bath of blood carries woman off N335.2.

Gascons. — Don't play tricks on G. J652.4.2.

Gate, see also **Door;** of captured town widened for overlord's spear P555.3; around hell A671.5; entrance to lower world F91; of heaven A661.0.1, E754.2.3; opens, closes to let saint through D1552.6; swallows threatening axes F1009.2; to upper world F59.3. — Cave's entrance as g. to hell A671.0.3; embracing at village g. tabu C194.1; enduring insults to enter city g. H1553.3; extraordinary g. F776; hay wagon and the g. J1411; horse's head nailed over g. F874.1; king demands open g. to vassal's castle P50.0.1.1; perilous falling g. *F776.2; standing neither inside nor outside of g. H1052; temple g. magically opens, shuts D1557.4; tomb g. magically enlarged D482.5.2; vision of g. of hell V511.2.2; wicket g. tabu C614.2; wraith slams g. E723.7.4.

Gates. — Cynic and big g. in little town J1442.6; forty-nine g. of wisdom J182.1; strong man carries off city g. F631.2.

Gathering all stones from brook or field (task) H1124. — Ghost g. wood for hell fires E755.2.4; girl g. flowers swallowed by earth and taken to lower world F92.2.1.

Gay. — Fairies' g. clothing F236.6; literal numskull g. at a fire J2461.1.2.

Gazelle as animals' king B240.6; becomes person D314.1.4; helpful B443.4. — Eagle catches newly born g. B754.7.2.

Geasa. — Demons coerced by g. of druids G583.

Geese, see after **Goose.**

Geist im glas K717.

Gem. — Seduction by alleged retrieving of lost g. K1315.2.2.

Gems, see also **Jewels;** shower from magic anvil D1469.3. — Castle paved with gold and g. F771.1.1.1; dwarf home has chandelier of crystals and

g. F451.4.3.4; eater of fruit will drop g. as he laughs M312.3.2; magic g. sent ruler as wisdom test H501.1; quest for marvelous g. H1348.

Genealogy of summer and winter A1154. — Chiefs' g. tabu C564.6.

General gives kings victory credit W11.8. — Dissension aroused in army by casting suspicion on g. K1088; lowly soldier humbles g. L175.1; what is most g. (riddle) H659.10.

Generalization. — Absurd g. from a particular incident J2214.

Generation. — Blessing to descend from g. to g. M321.1; planting for next g. J701.1; spontaneous g.: child found on deserted island A1234.3.

Generations. — Animal g. compared to men's B841.2.1; man lives nine g. F571.8.

Generosity W11; as amend for stinginess Q589.4; rewarded *Q42. — Man lets himself be sold as slave so as to practice g. W11.4; tests of g. H1552.

Generous. — Vow to serve most g. king M167.

Genesis. Captive released because of ability to recite beginning of G. V151.1.

Genie, see also **Jinn;** called by writing his name on papers and burning them *D2074.2.4; in form of smoke G369.2; sleeps with eyes open G634. — Helpful g. N813; magic object received from g. D812.5; magic object summons g. *D1421.1ff.

Genitals, see also **Member, Penis, Vagina;** cut off through ignorance J1919.5. — Birth from contact of severed male g. with ground T541.9; curse: wolf to carry off man's g. M442.2; enemy's g. prove slaying H105.7; feigning loss of g. to dupe husband K1586; horse's g. (provide treasure) D1469.5, (used in combat) F998; husband feigns loss of g. to test wife H467.1; magic g. *D998; man created from hero's g. A1263.6; misplaced g. A1313.3; mutilated g. S176; oath by placing hand on g. M119.7; origin and nature of animal's g. A2365; placing hand on g. as truth test H252.1; remarkable g. F547; tabu: eating animal's g. C221.3.1; tempted man mutilates g. T333.4; toothed g. F547.1; touching of g. as marriage pact T135.2; women not to eat g. of animals *C229.2.

Genoese compared to beaten donkeys J1021.2. — Why G. children strong J1279.4.

Genoveva K2112.

Gentleman unable to eat excrement, loses bargain K198. — Devil as g. (well-dressed) G303.3.1.2, (invites to feast) G303.25.17.1.

Gentlemen. — Devils as g. G303.3.1.17; devil as three g. G303.3.1.11; thieves disguised as g. K311.9.

Gentlewoman P60.

Genuflexion. — Clerics' continual g. V462.4.1.

Geography, lies about X1500.

Germans, origin of A1611.5.3.

Gestrikland people as magicians D1711.10.2.

Ghee. — Alleged g. deceptively exchanged K144; does g. protect the saucer? J2062.2; soul as g. E745.6.

Ghormuhas B15.7.5.

Ghost conceals herself with dwarfs F451.5.4.1; converses with man running from him J1495.1; frightened by own reflection K1715.1.2; of giant F531.6.14; kills man interfering with him E232.3; of murdered child E225; puts bride in tree, takes her place K1911.1.7; -seer's power from coffin hole D1821.3.5.1; transfers boil to a post D2161.4.2.1; of unknown child passes over parents H175.5; warns of wild hunt's approach E501.6. — Devil chases g. into chapel R325.1; disguise as g. K1833; fool is told that his son has given up the g. J2482; hunter's g. as nightmare F471.1.4; knowledge of g. language D1815.1; lost object found by throwing spade at g. D1816.2.1; magic object received from g. D812.4; man playing g. killed N384.10; mother's g. tries to tear daughter to pieces E222.1; owl (g. of nun) in wild hunt E501.4.5; return from dead to punish indignities to corpse or g. E235, running from g. J1495; sound of drum followed into g. town F102.2; tabu: finding name of g. C824; tabu: masking as g. in graveyard C94.5; tiger made to think goat is g. K547.12; wagon refuses to move because g. is sitting in it *D1317.10.

Ghost's strength waxes and wanes with height of fire *D1836.1.

Ghosts, see also **Souls;** carry off other ghost E446.4; deceived, cannot return to grave E141; with fruits in hair frighten thieves K335.1.12; of objects E530ff.; and other revenants *E200—E599; prevent men from raising treasure N576; seen through sleeve of fur coat C311.1.1; of sun's children cause eclipse A734.4. — Animal g. *E520ff.; animal languages learned from g. B217.3; army of g. F403.2.3.7; copper as defense against g. and magic D1385.5.1; disease caused by g. A1337.0.2; fairy reveals treasure of g. F244.3; fearless traffic with g. H1430ff.; gift of tongues received from g. D1815.0.1; invisible g. E421.1; saint's bachall keeps off g. D1385.8; silver bullet as protection against g. D1385.4; stars as fires in hearths of g. A761.4; sleeping on path of g. tabu C735.2.6; tabu: eating in land of g. C211.2.1; tabu: looking at g. C311.1.1; tabu to laugh at g. C462; things thought to be g. J1782; tree guarded by g. H1151.10; wandering soul detained by g. E721.4; why g. remain on earth A666.2.

Ghoulish charm *D1278, (exorcises witch) G271.8; objects E538; wager won N78.

Ghouls G20ff.

Giant *F531ff., *G100—G199; animal (lie) *X1201ff.; animals *B870ff.; assigns task H939.4; birds *B31.1; breaks from tower prison R211.1; can be killed only with own club Z312.2; carpet F783.1; changes to normal size D55.2.3; as clerk to God of Destiny N111.5; as culture hero A523; cursed: neither heaven nor earth to receive him M445; dog F628.1.5; drinks up ocean A928; eats men on New Year's G15.1; falls

through drawbridge K924; in foot-race with mortal H1594.2; gives reward for advice Q111.5; god A133; as gods' orderly A133.3; guards huge otherworld oxen K1784.2; guards otherworld F150.2.1; guards quest path H1236.4; as helper *N812; herdsman G152; heroes Z261; immortal so long as he touches land of his birth D1854; impales self on javelin K897.2.1; killed by rafter cut half through K959.3.1; kills with magic water D1402.24.1; with limbs, organs only on left side F525.5; in love with giantess F531.6.8.1; lured by cheese on crab K827.5; mermaid B81.9.4, (cast ashore) B81.13.13; in moon A751.9.3; ogre guards tree D950.0.1.1; ox ancestor of all animals A1791; responsible for stones A977.1; reveals life span to dwarf who attacks him N484; robber with club G316; shot into upper world by means of magic bow *F65; with sixty daughters and their big wedding X1071; steals magic armor D838.7; swallows man F911.5; thought to be a hill J1769.1; tree F811.14; tricked into becoming mouse K722.—Abduction by g. R11.3; animals from different parts of body of slain g. *A1716.1; appearance of g. F531.1ff.; beheading g. to escape prison R211.8; black cat as servant of g. B292.6; cannibal g. G11.2; capturing deer from herd watched by g. H1154.2; creator's g. servant (makes valley and mountain) A857.2, (puts trees on earth) A857.3; creation from vapor-produced primeval g. A621.1; customs of g. ogres G130ff.; curse by berserk g. M411.10; dwarfs originate from maggots in flesh of g. F451.1.1; escape from g. bird's nest R253; fairy as g. animal F234.1.0.1; fat g. wants to eat self J2119.5; feats of g. F531.3ff.; fight with g. as valor test H1561.6; foot-race between g. and mortal H1594.2; ghost as g. E422.3.2; god as son of a g. A112.4; god transformed to g. with three heads and six arms D42.1; goddess as daughter of g. A112.4.2; hero fights fairyland g. F176.1; hero leaves home with g. equipment F613.2; lakes made by g. A920.1.10; little girl drives out g. L311.4; little man defeats g. in race L312; magic from g. D1727; magic object (acquired by tricking g.) D833, (from g.) *D812.11, (stolen from g.) *D838.6, (summons g.) D1421.4f.; magic serpent heart kills g. D1402.3.1; magician, g. contest over dog's tail D1719.1.3; mountain from buried g. A969.1; mountains from bones of killed g. A961.5; mountains and hills from stones thrown by g. at church A963.4; oversalting food of g. so that he must go outside for water K337; physical characteristics of g. ogres G120ff.; possessions of g. F531.4ff., (ogre) G110ff.; prince pleads with g. not to eat him K567.1; pygmy turns into a g. D55.1.3; rescue by g. R164; rescue of maiden from g. R111.1.4; servant g. gets liquor A1427.0.4; size of g. F531.2ff.; stealing sword from g. H1151.14; strong hero suckled by g. F611.2.5; strong man (kills g.) F628.2.3, (overcomes g.) F639.4, (son of person and g.) F611.1.7; suitor test: lifting strong princess's g. weapon H345.1; sunlight turns g. to stone F531.6.12.2; theft from g. by fishing through chimney K316.1; transformation into g. D28, D55.1.2; ten g. sisters P252.6.1; treasure from defeated g. N538.2; trees pulled up by g. F621.2; universe from

body of slain g. A642; wind caused by flapping of ears of a g. A1125.1; witch's g. sons G206; wrestling with g. warrior H1166.1.

Giant's daughter loves hero T91.1; help secured by feeding him N812.0.1; soul in mole E714.9; tongue proves slaying H105.2.1. — Bringing back g. two heads H1174.1; cup can be crushed only on g. forehead F866.8; earth from g. body A831.2; flood from g. blood A1012.3.1; magic object in g. cave D845.1; man builds boat and sails about in g. belly F911.5.1; mankind begotten by g. two feet A1221.1; mountains from stones dropped from g. clothes A963.1; princess rescued from g. cave R111.2.3; resuscitation by g. gall E117; sea formed from g. spittle D483; skillful marksman shoots meat from g. hands F661.1.

Giants as builders F531.6.6; dance F531.6.17.1; enticed over precipice K891.5.1; as magicians F531.6.5ff.; in otherworld F167.3; uphold castle F771.2.3; cast stones: hence hills A963.5; dissuaded from eating nephews K601.2; and dwarfs F451.10; go through small plant hole X1743.1; guarding fairy princess F300.1; with names of sinister symbolism Z100.1; return if tabu broken C963.4; steal magic object D861.9. — Age of g. F531.6.4ff.; automatic g. fight D1620.3.1; castle guarded by g. F771.5.2; chasms mark leaps of g. A972.5.2; defeated g. imprisoned in lower world Q433.2; demons as g. perishing in the flood G302.1.1; dwarfs came after g. had almost died out F451.1.3; fairies as g. F232.6; fairies guard g. treasure F244.6; fight of the gods and g. *A162.1, (at end of world) A1082.1; heads of g. cut off one by one as they enter house K912; homes of g. F531.6.3; incendiary covering of g. cave set afire K812.1.1; indentions on rocks caused by g. A972.6; journey to land of g. F122; knockers as ghosts of g. F456.1.1.2; luring Thor into power of g. H1173; men at first as large as g. A1301; mutual relations of g. F531.6.8; one eye of three g. stolen G612; origin of g. F531.6.1; quest for berries from tree guarded by g. H1333.3.3; relations of g. with men F531.5ff.; silver bullet protects against g. D1385.4; stones as transformed g. A974.2; thunder made by g. in sky A1142.9; winds as children of g. A1123.

Giantess F531; abducts bridegroom R10.4.1; aids quest H1233.4.2; curses him who hears her M411.9; frightened of statue in cave entrance K1726; gives magic object D812.8.1; as helper N812.2; killed with own gift sword K818.2; throws her breasts over her shoulders *F531.1.5.1. — Beautiful g. F531.1.0.1.1; cloak of g. makes man grow D537.2.1; dwarfs kill g. F451.10.2.1; god becomes g. D12.1; god as lover of g. A164.6, T111.4; god as son of g. A112.4.1; giant in love with g. F531.6.8.1; groom prisoner in room of g. R41.4; head of g. cut off as she looks out K912.1; hero's son by g. scorns father P233.3.1; man-eating g. transformed to stone D429.2.2.1; punishment of g. pure illusion D2031.0.5.

Giantesses. — God as son of nine g. A112.5.

Gibbet. — Fragments of g. as cure D1500.1.26.

Gift to animal or object J1851ff.; of fool to queen (children) J1272; to magic lance C835.2.1; of property silences criticism U21.2; as sign of submission P531.1; wood must be split W111.5.1 — Bride's g. to husband T55.4.1; captor deceived into receiving g. K611.3; clothing g. wards off spirit F405.11; donkey g. to ruler J2415.1.1; dwarfs accept as g. goose but not gander F451.3.6.4; fairy g. worthless when tabu broken F348.0.1; fire as g. from god A144.4; girl doesn't dare receive g. from man T456.1; heaven entered by demanding back the charity g. K2371.1.2; helpful animals as g. B312.1; husband gets paramour's g. to wife K1581.12; lover's g. regained K1357, K1581; magic object a g. *D810ff.; man chosen as best g. by primeval women A1276; man finds treasure he refused as g. N224; modest choice: parting g. L222; power of prophecy a g. D1812.1; stolen ornament presented to owner as g. N347.4; tabu to open g. box prematurely C321.2; trickster chooses his g. J1282.

Gifts, see also **Presents;** from angels V232.7; from dwarfs F451.5.1ff.; from fairies *F340ff.; fall from heaven F962.0.1; as reward Q114; at wedding T136.4. — Animal gives man g. B584; choice among several g. L212; dwarf takes back g. he gave F451.5.2.12; dwarfs curse g. they are forced to give F451.5.2.13; dwarfs demand g. F451.5.2.14; emperor thinks day lost when he gives no g. W11.2.2; enemies reconciled by mutual g. K2373; fairy g. to half-mortal child F305.1; fairy g. stopped in revenge F361.2.4; fairies bestow supernatural g. at birth of child F312.1; fairies give three g. F341.1; fairy offers g. to man to be her paramour F302.3.2; forgetting own share of g. J2048; ghosts bestow g. on living E373; giants' g. to men F531.5.6; giants' magic g. return to original form in hands of men F531.5.6.1; gifts as reward for g. Q114.2; good g. of fortune *N200ff.; grateful objects give helper g. D1658.3.3; helpers' g. aid quest H1239.3; host greets guest with g. P324; hypocrite refuses g. but stretches out hands K2057; king has own g. stolen back P14.12; king won't eat till g. given W11.2.2; man beats people bearing him g. W152.20; man demands ever larger g. W154.26; seven g. of God Z71.5.6.8; tabus connected with fairy g. F348; tabu: giving away g. received from animal C847ff.; wife shames adulterous husband into g. K1271.3.1; wisdom lost by accepting g. J186.

Gigantic, see also **Giant;** cup F866.2; cauldron F881.1.1; flower F814.1; grapes F813.2.2; leaves F811.2.3; nut F813.3.2; possessions of giant F531.4ff.; shield F839.2.1; spirit F401.8; sword F833.8; vessels F881; vine F815.7.2; wood-spirit F441.5.2, (with one eye in center of forehead) *F441.4.1.

Gilded images substituted for solid gold K476.4.1. — Deceptive sale of g. ware K123.

Gingerbread house F771.1.10, (lures child) G412; man Z33.1.

Giraffe keeps house with other animals J512.7.1.

Girded. — Bond woman g. with rope P171.2.

Girdle of climbing vine F829.2. — Conception from putting on another's

g. T532.5; dupe allowed to guard king's g. (snake) K1023.1.1; identification by g. H116; magic g. *D1057.1, (clairvoyant) D1323.17, (prevents disease) D1500.2.6; ogre released in return for magic g. M242.3; woman's g. as source of sin T336.1.

Girdles of sinners in hell alternately hot and cold Q562.1.

Girl, see also **Maid, Maiden;** abducted by fairy F324; beautified by burning D1865.2.1; bewitched so no man faithful to her M438.3; as bird visits lover D641.1.1; brings bad luck to everyone N265.1; cruel to mother slain Q281.1.2; curses to revenge father M411.11; drives giant F531.5.10.1; drowned in well as river's origin A934.10; eats only kola nuts and tobacco F561.5; escapes in male disguise K521.4.1.1; fed boys' flesh to hasten growth G72.3; gathering flowers swallowed up by earth and taken to lower world F92.2.1; goes to fairyland and marries fairy F301.3; as helper N831; killed during day, revived at night E155.4; kills man sleeping with her K872.1; in man's clothes K1837, (wins rich woman's love) K1322.1; magically made hideous D1871; masks as doctor to find departed lover K1825.1.4; in menial disguise at lover's court K1816.0.2; mistaken for stone J1763.2; offers to sacrifice herself to save parents S262.4; reincarnated as river for god to lie in its bed A934.11.1; removes dog from lion's claws B848.2; saved by lion from ravishment B549.1; in service of witch G204; sleeping naked goddess or mortal? H47; sees vision of mother in hell, reforms V511.2.3; sold for new church bell V115.2; transformed to (comb) D263.3, (man) G263.3.2; tricked into man's room (or power) K1330ff.; visits fairy lover F301.7; with tree carried to moon A751.8.5; as wooer T55. — Clever g. J1111, (cheats robber) K434, (refrains from eating figs which would bring on magic sleep) J585.1, (asked riddles by king) H561.1; cranes carry away g. B522.4.1; devil abducts g. G303.9.5.1; devil advises young g. not to go to a castle G303.9.7.1; devil tempts g. G303.9.4.7; devil takes place of g. in man's embrace G303.9.9.16; disenchantment of g. by carrying her on back D732.1; disenchantment of g. only by lover D791.2.1; disguise as g. to avoid execution K514; dream shows where stolen g. hidden D1810.8.2.1; dwarfs adopt g. as sister F451.5.1.2; fairy a small pretty g. F232.4.1; flower by day, g. by night D621.2.2; foolish marriage of old man and young g. J445.2; lazy g. does not know where the spring is W111.5.2; little g. cursed M414.4; little g. drives out giant L311.4; magic sickness because g. has thrown away her consecrated wafer *D2064.1; monkey instead of g. in basket K1625; panther devours g. in tree: chain tale Z39.7; poor g. masks as doctor and is made court physician K1825.1.2; prophecy: wealthy marriage for poor g. M312.1.1; queen passes off g.-child as boy K1923.6; quest for g. (about whom parrots speak) H1214.1, (seen in dream) H1381.3.1.2.2; sham magician exposed by clever g. K1963.1; sham physician makes g. grow up K1955.5; single combat for g. H217.2; suitor finds g. immature: father protests she is already a mother J1279.3; tabus for g. going to

her husband C161; tabu: g. going forth at puberty C131; tabu: letting sun shine on g. before she is thirty years old *C756.2; thief disguised as g. K311.16; transformation: g. to falcon D152.4; treacherous slave-g. K2251.1; vow to kill self and child if g. born M184; will-o-the-wisp is g. cursed for gathering plants on Sunday A2817.2.

Girl's long hair as ladder into tower F848.1; sham threat to evade husband K1771.6; spirit controls wind D2142.0.5. — Tasks assigned because of g. own foolish boast H915.

Girls dancing in heaven A661.4; eat their sister G73; going into wood for nuts N771.2. — Country of little g. F709.2; living g. transformed into plants A2617.1; melons analogous to g. ready for marriage H611.1; seven g. appear as seven parrots D658.3.3; swinging seventy g. H506.5; thirty g. fall in love with same man T27.1; three g. task: go and return together, but after different periods J2033.

Giver. — Directions followed literally to sorrow of g. J2516; magic object voluntarily restored to g. D878.

Giving away forbidden C783; all earnings to poor as penance Q542; half better than lending all J1552.4; thief what he wants K362.10. — Coward g. purse to thief W121.6; planned g. hare to thief anyway J1395; tabu: g. away (idol) C51.8, (gifts received from animal) C847.

Glaciers, revenants banished to E437.1.

Glance. — Beam breaks at giant's g. F531.3.14; bewitching by means of g. *D2071; impregnation through g. T515; man's g. kills F592.

Glass, see also **Crystal, Goblet;** boat for fairy F242.2.1; book F883.1.1; bridge *F842.1.1; car F242.1.4; coffin *F852.1; house F771.1.6.2; island in otherworld F162.0.1.1; ladder to upper world F52.1; mountain *F751; ship F841.1.14; shoes *F823.2; staircase F848.5; tower F772.2.4; tree F811.1.6; to wound and detect wife's lover K1565. — Breakage of g. by threes D1273.1.1.2; breaking g. during wedding T135.15; breaking heavy g. bottle over a loaf of rye bread as test of strength H1562.3; broken g. on witch's back G219.9; castle with g. wall F771.1.6.1; city of g. in heaven A661.1.2; climbing g. mountain D753.4; descent into ocean in g. box F1022.1; ghostly crash of breaking g. E402.1.6; identification by ring dropped in g. of wine H94.4; island of g. F731.5; magic g. *D1171.6.2; magic sight by looking into g. of water D1821.3.7.1; pillars of silver and g. in otherworld *F169.1; quest for G. Princess H1381.3.2; quest for g. of all waters H1377.1; rock becomes g. D452.1.5; sea of g. in otherworld *F162.4; ship of g. in otherworld *F169.3; test: guessing nature of devil's wine g. H523.6; worthless g. sold as diamond K142, K451.4; wounding by trapping with g. S181.

Glasses, see also **Spectacles.** — Filling g. with water that has neither fallen from heaven nor sprung from the earth H1073.

Glassware. — Basket of g. is to be sold (air-castle) J2061.1.1; king breaks g. to prevent others from doing so J2522.

Gleaming, see also **Bright, Glowing, Luminous, Shining;** spear F834.3. — Fairies in g. clothes F236.1.5; giant with large g. eyes F531.1.1.2.
Glen of witchcraft F756.4. — Perilous g. F756.5.2, (on way to otherworld) F151.1.2.
Glens, see also **Valleys.** — Fiery g. in hell A671.2.4.5.
Glittering well F718.9. — Breast broad and made of g. metal F546.1.
Gloom. — No g. in otherworld F172.1.
Glory compared to four things Z71.2.7; sacrificed for virtue J347. — Hand of g. D1162.2.1; men unable to endure God's g. A182.0.1; prophecy of g. for a people M325; robber with "hand of g." killed K437.2.
Glove and the lion L431.1. — Giant carries man in his g. F531.5.1.1; identification by g. H114; magic g. *D1066; man mistakes giant's g. for house F531.5.2; touch of g. causes sleep D1364.29; transformation by striking wolf-skin g. D566.1.
Gloves drip blood (life token) E761.1.7.1; make spear infallible D1653.1.2.1; thrown after ship cause disease D1500.4.5. — Murder by boiling victim's g. D2061.2.2.5.1.
Glowing, see also **Bright, Fiery, Gleaming, Luminous, Shining;** animals *B19.4; beds of dead E487; ghosts E421.3ff.; wheel mistaken for devil J1781.3. — Devil has g. (thumb) G303.4.3.1, (eyes) G303.4.1.2.2.
Glowworm thinks he shines like stars J953.12; thought to be a fire J1761.3. — Trying to swallow g. sparks J1849.2.
Glue. — Flight so high that sun melts g. on artificial wings F1021.2.1; swallows warn other birds against roosting in tree with g. J652.2.
Glued. — Death g. to chair Z111.2.2; lecherous king g. with feathers K1218.1.8.
Gluttony, see also **Greed;** W125. — Demon of g. *F496, (coaxed from throat by food) F406.4, (devours food in throat) F402.1.7.
Gnat as snakebite antidote D1515.4.4; as witch's soul G225.1. — Buzz of g. A2236.1, A2426.3.2; creation of g. A2033; devil in form of g. G303.3.3.4.1; man becomes g. D185.3; why g. has no tongue A2236.1, A2344.2.1.
Gnats apologize for lighting on bull's horn J953.10; created by devil to worry God A2033.0.1; having overcome lion are in turn killed by spider L478; in hell A671.2.7; think they have thrown horse down J953.6. — Devil pesters God with g. A63.4.1; lies about g. X1295.
Gnawed bone as weapon F839.1.
Gnawing. — Animals g. on moon A755.4.3; ant g. bow-strings of enemy D651.4; dragon g. tree roots B11.6.9; mice g. through metal B747.3; rodent g. away ladder to heaven A666.2.
Gnomes as mine-spirits F456.
Goading. — Demons g. man G302.9.9; devil g. oxen with pulled-up tree G303.9.2.1.
Goal. — Keeping g. in hurling match for corpses H1436.
Goaling match between fairies and mortals H1593.

Goat appears to be two when aimed at D2031.15; carries one hundred cartloads of grease (lie) X1244.1; as child's nurse B535.0.3; eats while camel talks K334.2; eats in garden and is caught (long beard, little sense) J2136.3; feeds other animals from its body B535.1; gives coins instead of milk B103.3.1; with gold, silver horn B15.3.2.2; Heidrun B19.7; pretends to be chewing rock and frightens wolf K1723; as sacrifice V12.4.5; singing threat bought off K1767; swallows gold, voids it for master K366.5; thief catches tiger instead J1758.1; transformed to person D334; in Valhalla gives mead A661.1.0.2; who wouldn't go home (cumulative tale) Z39.1; who wouldn't leave hazel bush Z39.1.1. — Antelope becomes g. D411.4.2; how g. got his beard A2322.4; big g. bears three kids yearly B196; bride escapes from foolish husband and leaves g. as substitute in bed K1223.1; bull refuses to fight g. J371.1; creation of g. A1885; demon mistaken for g. to be stolen J1769.3; devil as g. G303.3.3.1.6; devil has g. feet G303.4.5.4; devil writes faults of man on g. skin G303.24.1.2; devil's mother rides a g. G303.11.3.1; dwarfs with g. feet F451.2.2.3; eaten g. bleats from eater's stomach D1619.2.2; eating entire g. without leaving scrap H1141.4; enmity of g. and (bear) A2494.8.1, (leopard) A2494.2.3; fairy in form of g. F234.1.2; fattest g. taken away from demon H1423.3; flower-covered g. escapes jackal K521.8; fool thinks g. mimicking him J1835; fool's brothers substitute g. for the body of man he has killed and thus save him K661.1; friendship between g. and (hog) A2493.22, (leopard) A2493.8, A2493.35; ghost as g. E423.1.9; giant g. B871.1.4, (lie) X1244.3; god with g. feet A131.5; helpful g. B413; hidden g. discovered by his horn protruding above ground J582.1; how g. got horns A2326.1.5; husband transformed to g. must witness wife's adultery K1531; why g. lives with men A2433.3.8; lion makes lame g. lieutenant J421.2; lying g. (cumulative tale) K1151, (punished by being half-shorn) Q488.1; magic g. B184.5, (entrails) D1015.3.2, (tail) D1029.2.2; man transformed to g. D114.4, D134; marvelous sensitiveness: woman smells like a g. F647.5; ogress as g. G351.4; one wild g. steps over another on a cliff J133.1; Pan part g. and part man *F442; parson sings like a g. X436; penniless wooer: "House of my father with 150 lights and g. pen" K1917.4; Peter, acting as God, must run everywhere after a g. L423; prophetic g. B141.1; pseudo-magic g. sold K135.1; quest for marvelous g. H1331.5; reincarnation as g. E611.4; selling a g. and bringing it back along with the money H1152.1; bad smell of g. A2416.1; speaking g. B211.1.2, (saves girl) D674; speaking loin of g. meat D1610.7; tailor always associated with g. X222; how g. lost tail A2216.2, A2378.2.2; telling sex of unborn g. H1576.1; test of resourcefulness: carrying wolf, g., and cabbage across stream H506.3; tiger made to think g. is ghost K547.12; treasure-giving g. B103.0.5; why g. lives with man A2513.4; wise division of g. H601.1; witch as g. G211.1.5; witch rides on g. G241.1.2; witch as she-g. kills men G262.3.1; witch's rosary consists of g. dung G243.2.1; wolf sold as a g. K132; wolf tries to entice

g. down from high place K2061.4; woman bears g. T554.6; Zodiac grows up, the Kid becomes the G. J2212.6.

Goat's liver heals blindness D1505.14.1; milk inexhaustible D1652.3.2; tongue pierced, witch sick G252.2. — Herd's spirit in last g. tail D859.6; man carried on g. horns B557.1; man with g. head B24.2; origin of g. beard A2322.4; origin of g. mane A2322.4.1; pig attempts to imitate g. tricks J2415.6; spinning wool still on g. back H1024.8; treasure from g. entrails B119.2; trembling g. shaking frightens off tiger K547.7; why g. has shaggy legs A2371.2.8; why g. penis as it is A2365.2.0.1.

Goats driven into well to cool off J1959.1; follow fairies F241.4; heads mistaken for human J1762.9; heat oven (lie) X1244.2. — "Collect g. under tree": carcasses piled up J2465.10; fairy leaves g. as price for girl F343.8; lies about g. X1244; pigs become g. D412.3.4; troll lets two g. pass, waiting for biggest K553.2; two stubborn g. meet each other on a bridge and neither will step aside W167.1; troll drives two g. G304.3.2.2; watching g.: kills them when they wander K1451.

"Goat-heads" from curse of Ham A1614.1.2.

Goatherd hero G462.1, L113.1.5; rescues abandoned child R131.3.2.

Goatskin. — As many stars as hairs in g. H702.2.1.

Go-between. — Innocent confessor duped into being g. for adulteress and lover K1584.

Goblet, see also **Glass;** thrown indicates the princess's choice H316.3. — Drunkard stung by g. would have drunk out of glass J1324; magic g. *D1171.6.2, (breaks spells) D1396.1, (cannot be filled) D1652.5.1, (heals wounds) D1503.8, (indicates falsehood by breaking, truth by reassembling) D1316.6; sun's night journey in golden g. A722.1.

Goblin *F470ff. — Devil as g. horse G303.3.3.5.4; ruler disguises as g. K1812.6.

God, see also **Creator, Deity, Lord;** *V201; battles (hound of hell) A1082.2.2, (Leviathan) A1082.4; becomes (crab) D175.1, (eel) D173.1; is best H648.1; bores hole in hell: hence hot weather A1137; to be brought from heaven H1262; in calf form D133.4.1; in cat form D142.2; changes curse to blessing M425; cheats birds of tamarind K499.6; cheats devil at mowing K42.2.1; compared to toolmaker J1262.6; conquers Satan at world's end A1082.5; consults angels A42.1.1; created all miracles F900.2; creates magic objects D803.1; cursed M414.1; of dead needs men subjects A1335.11; and devil fly together over primeval water A810.1; and devil torment each other A63.4.1; disguised as menial K1816.0.1; dislikes offerings beyond one's ability V10.2; of the earth J1441; enamored of mortal T91.3.3; is everywhere: fool thinks in elephant J2499.5; as falcon has tail cut off A2216.6; finds that his statue sells at low price L417; of fire and god of rain contest A975.2.1; as giantess's lover T111.4; gives Jesus' staff to saint V227.1; grants man twenty years' more life K551.22.2; in guise of mortal D42; as helper

N817.0.1; issue of brother-sister marriage P3; as magician D1711.6; makes birds, devil reptiles A1903; as mare seduces stallion D658.3.2; as matchmaker T53.4; names animals on first sabbath A2571.0.3; as an object A139.8ff.; is oldest H659.1.1; orders angel assign tasks H927.2; plagues devil with fleas A2032.4; promises never again to destroy world by water A1113; in the puddle J1262.2; punishes (David for his pride) L415, (man for killing ants) J96, (man by killing his child) A1335.15, (many for one sinner) J225.0.2; recognized by supernatural powers H45.1; reincarnated as (cat) E611.5.1, (dwarf) E651, (monster) E652; releases condemned soul E754.1.5; reposed on leaf J2495.5; to reveal self to legitimate K445.1; revenges murder after thirty years Q211.0.1; sends Adam to earth A1285.1.1; sends cold to prevent stones from growing A975.1; sends death when tired of man A1335.9.1; sends stinging bees to punish men A2012.3; sends woman to poison man A1335.12; of space upholds sky A665.1; speaks in vision V510.1; stabilizes the sky A665.0.1; is strongest H631.2; as surety, the abbot pays J1559.2; swallows his wife and incorporates her into his own being F911.1.1; teaches people to work A1403; throws diver's feet after him: hence his feet reach backward A2215.6; took power of speech from animals B210.3; transformed to (animal) *D101, (boar) D114.3.2.1, (dove) D154.1.0.1, (giant) D42.1, (hawk) D152.1.1, (giantess) D12.1, (shower of gold) D235.1; transforms nature every seven years A1103; as vampire E251.4.4; visits earth F32; in wolf form D113.1.2. — Ability to see angel of G. D1825.3.4.1; absurd reasoning about G. J2215ff.; advice from G. D1814.3; always say "if it pleases G." J151.4; angels and G. V248; animal characteristics (result of contest between G. and devil) A2286.2, (punishment for discourteous answer to G.) A2231.1; animal reincarnated as g. E657; animal transformed to g. D43.1; animals created through opposition of devil to G. A1750ff.; animals praise G. at Christ's Nativity B211.0.1; annual resuscitation of a g. E155.2; bargain with G. M201.0.1; cannibalistic g. G11.0.1; child nourished by sucking thumb of a g. T611.1.1.; condemned soul released by G. E754.1.5; contract between hungry g. and untouchable M242.2; conversation between G. and Adam's corpse E545.22; created beings rebel against G. A106.3; creation of animals by G. A1701; culture hero as g. A510.1; dead man praises G. E576; death by kiss from G. Q147.3; death preferred above G. and justice J486; death respite for steps towards G. K551.14; deceiving G. K2371; demon takes on form of g. to deceive faithful F402.1.4.1; devil advises youth to enjoy himself and not to think of G. G303.9.7.2; devil originates from g. G303.1.1ff.; devil is thrust into hell by G. G303.8.3.1; direct communication with g. fatal to all except special devotees C52.1; disguised g. chosen as husband T111.1.1; disrespectful answer to G. brings death A1335.6.1; eaten g. V30.1; fasting against G. P623.0.1; first parents children of g. A1271.3; flaying alive as punishment for contesting with a g. Q457.1; forgetting G. leads to wealth J556.2; gambling

with a g. N3.1; generosity to g. in disguise rewarded Q42.3; ghost laid by calling on G. E443.5; hard to think of G. when occupied: proved by milk test J94; hearing voice of G. as reward Q144; heathen beats his g. because of misfortune V381; helpful animal sent by g. B319.1; hospitality to disguised g. rewarded Q45.1; how G. distributed professions A1650.3.2; husband as G. behind tree forces his wife to confess adultery *K1971.5; "I don't want G. to help so much!" J1279.2; inhospitality to g. punished Q292.1; ingeniously worded boon asked of G. K2371.3; invisibility conferred by a g. D1983.1; is shepherd known to G? H1292.17; king shown he is less powerful than G. L418; levity toward name of G. J1261.1; loathly husband g. in disguise D733.3. magic knowledge from G. D1810.9; magic object received from g. D811; magic power from g. (goddess) D1726; man behind statue (tree) speaks and pretends to be G. K1971; man so constantly enriched by G. that he cannot give all his goods to the poor U71; man honored above G.: the dead hen J2215.3; man originates from g. who comes to earth A1215; man put in moon for cursing G. A751.1.2; man sets self up as g. L420.0.1; man willing to sacrifice child to G. S263.2.3; men hide so G. will not see sin J1738.8; marriage to g. in bull form *B641.3; marriage of a mortal and a g. T111.1; misfortune from forgetting to say "if G. wills" N385.1; mortal woman seduced by a g. K1301; mountains from primeval journeys of a g. A962.3; omniscience of a g. D1810.0.1; only man without sin can see G. V510.2; origin of feasts in honor of certain g. A1541.2; peasants want a living G. J2495.4; people taught by G. to work C53.1; person carried to upper world by a g. F63; persecution by a g. N250.3; plants from transformed parts of body of g. A2611.0.4; power of prophecy from g. D1812.1.2; power of self-transformation received from a g. D630.2; quest for the anger of G. H1376.3.1; quest to G. for fortune H1263; recognition of man acceptable to G. H192.1; reincarnation: g. reborn as man E605.2; reincarnation: man becomes g. E605.3; resuscitation by a g. E121.1; riddle on goodness not found by G. H853; riddle: what does G. do H797; rivers where g. drags his staff A934.4; Satan asks G. for man G303.9.8.6; Satan prays to G. G303.9.8.8; seduction by posing as a g. *K1315.1; son of G. sees king; their repartee J1675.8; sons of G. and daughters of men F531.6.1.1; servant of G. beaten J2215.2; soul taken away by G. E722.2.10; spring where g. throws his staff or spear A941.3.2; stars rebel against G. A769.2; steadfastness of love for G. tested H1573.5; sun worships G. by night A722.11; sword with G. engraved F833.10; tabu: disbelief in G. C61.1; tabu: uttering name of g. C431; test of a g.: when its image is bound it frees itself H45.3; thief disguised as g. K311.15; thief as family g., bound K439.8; thinking of G. protects against devil G303.16.2.1.1; three spiritual gifts of G. Z71.1.12; thunder from G. beating his weapon A1142.5.1; transformation by g. D683.5; underworld people from children which Eve hid from G. *F251.4; unsuccessful imitation of g.

J2411.1.2; who is greater than G.? H674; why G. lets sinner die in peace, holy man be slain J225.0.1.1; wisdom from G. J164, (as old man) J151.3; witch's charm: without G. and Holy Mary G224.1; women refuse to show G. the way A1372.8.

God's birth A112ff.; curse M411.4.1; mercy vs. man's shortsightedness J2052; name (engraved on sun) A733.2, (nullifies fairy power) F382.3, (used to lay ghost) E451.4.1; omniscience J1617; promise not to destroy world by water A1011.3; spear of fire F834.1.1; spirit aids strong man F610.9; tears become peas A2612.3; urine (makes chilly fiery) D562.2.1, (used to make pig) A1871.0.1; wastefulness J2215.1; word the sweetest sound H635.2. — Charm containing G. name D1273.0.5; clouds as G. shield A1133.4; conception from G. bow T532.9; demon in G. form F402.1.4.1; devil leaves at mention of G. name G303.16.8; devil's animals and G. *A1751, A2286.2.1; dividing after G. fashion U61; earth rests on G. arm A849.2; eclipse in G. proximity F961.0.2; girl protects self from devil with G. name G303.9.4.7.1; greeting in G. name P682.1; heavens chanting G. praise F961.0.4; hero as g. son A512.3; how much cloth would it take to make G. coat J1291.3.1; lightning as G. messenger A1141.5; man marries g. daughter T111.1.2; mountains made with G. hand A962.2; mythical animals surround G. throne B7.2; not leaving G. court for king's J1269.13; numskulls surprised to hear of G. son J1738.3; one dueler fights with G. help: the other with his brother's J1217.1; shepherd in G. service H1199.12.1; soul leaves body after G. kiss E722.2.12; sun, moon's daily tour under G. orders A726.1; tailor occupies G. throne for a day P441.1; thunder as sound of G. gun A1142.5; trees blossom on G. arrival F971.8; wolf as G. dog A1833.3.

Gods A100—A499; built houses, fashioned tools A1402; captured R8; cause disease A1337.0.1; as culture heroes A520.1; in disguise visit mortals *K1811; exchange forms D45.2; furnish substitute for child sacrifice S263.2.1; help those who help themselves J1034; in human guise A1101.1.3; humble man's pride L473; prophesy about hero M301.16; in relation to mortals *A180ff.; teach people all they know A1404; teach how to seek food A1420.2; transform selves D698; tricked into help in escaping one's fate K2371.2. — Battle of fairies and g. F277; battle of the g. at end of world A1081; degraded g. become angels A52.0.2; demi-g. A500—A599; dwarfs make weapons for g. F451.10.4; fairies as g. F251.1.2; bridge of the g. A986; child sacrificed to gain favor of g. S263.2; end of the g. A1085; fairies as descendants of early race of g. F251.1; flood caused by g. A1015; indentions on rocks from imprint of g. A972.1; heathen g. less powerful than Christian V331.1.3; keeping on good terms with hostile g. J821; magic invisibility of g. D1981.1; making of g. A104ff.; man made from spittle of the g. A1211.3.1; man created by cooperation of the g. A1218; man pursued by hatred of the g. M411.4; milky way as the sperma of the g. A778.6; "not-g." A189.0.1; oaths before g. as test of truth H253; pagan g. become

devils G303.1.3.4; personal offenses against g. punished *Q221; punishment for denying pagan g. Q225.2; rainbow from g. emptying their drinking cups A791.6; sacrifice to appease g. S263; sacrifice to g. so ship can continue S263.4.1; sun, moon as divine bodies of g. A718.2; swearing by clan g. M119.2; tabu: eating food of g. C241; tabu: offending the g. *C50ff.; task assigned the g. H902; three g. none may escape Z71.1.10; unacceptable g. as earth's first inhabitants A1205; unnecessary choice of g. J462.1.

Goddess aids quest H1233.5.1; aids task H975.1; arouses heroes' jealousy K1093; assigns task to suitor H335.0.5; breaks self into five parts: origin of river's five branches A934.11.3; cursed M414.2; divides time between upper and lower worlds A316; of earth A400.1; not to eat on earth C212; as fairy F251.1.1; Fortuna N111; gives birth to islands A955.9; as helper N817.0.2; killed for infidelity with mortal Q246.1; in moon A751.8.3, (beating tapa) A751.8.6; not to see mortal husband naked C313.1.1; mounted on drake with snakes A137.9; prevents suicide V10.1; repeatedly transforms self D610.1; standing on head supports earth A842.1; scatters pubic hairs on fish A2211.15; with thousand faces blowing her noses J1261.10; of world of the dead A310.1. — Brown hair sign child descended from g. Z146.1; disguise as g. K1828.2; fainting at sight of g. F1041.1.6.1; hair on ground summons g. D2074.2.2.1; is sleeping naked girl g.? H45.5; land born from g. A954; lifting of throne of g. D1654.17; love of g. for mortal T91.3.2f.; magic knowledge from g. D1810.10; magic object received from g. D811.1; magic power from g. D1726; man not to look at nude g. C312.1.1; man thrown into jail by g. R110.1; mortal's attempt to defile g. punished Q246; origin of feasts in honor of certain g. A1541.2; plants from tread of g. A2621.2; resuscitation by g. E121.1.2; respect to statue, dress of g. C51.1.13; sea creatures as ancestors of g. A111.3.2; sun, moon born of g. impregnated by wind A715.2; tabu: taking food dedicated to g. C51.2.2.1; tasks performed by aid of g. H975.1; transformation by g. D683.5; vow to be servant of g. M177.2.

Goddess's father (as cannibal) G11.0.1.2, (forbidding her marriage) A106.1.1. — Ogre defeated with g. help G537.1; questioning g. veracity punished Q221.7; test of g. favor: throwing away jewels H1577.1.

Goddesses come to earth, produce drought A189.10. — Twin g. A116.2.

Godfather P296.1. — Child promised to devil for acting as g. S224; cohabitation of g. and godmother punished Q242.1; dwarf as g. *F451.5.1.1; mountain-man as g. F460.4.7; playing g. K372; supernatural g. *N811.

Godiva clothed in own hair F555.3.1, H1054.2; riding nude through town not to be looked at C312.1.2.

Godmother P296.2. — Fairy g. F311.1; magic object received from g. D815.3.

Godparent. — Fairies seek human g. F372.2.

Godparents P296. — Dwarfs have mortal g. F451.5.6.
Goggles. — Green g. on cow fed sawdust X1235.3.
Going to certain place compulsory C666. — Task: g. and returning together but at different times J2033.
Goitre cure by striking J2412.8.
Gold in the Bible H261; causes man to become miser G303.9.8.5; demanded of saint disappears Q552.18.1; doors in otherworld F165.1.1; -digging ants B756; -dropping cow B103.1.2, D871.1.1; from fishes' gourd A1432.2.1; furniture, objects in otherworld F166.0.1; hair F555.1, (as sign of royalty) H71.2; hidden in bricks N518; hoard found by cow N534.2; kingdom F707.1; lump appears in Arabia at Christ's birth N529.1; magically produced D2102; magically stolen D2087.5; mast F841.2.1; moon, sun, star F793.1; ox horn H1151.7.1; pale because it is in great danger J1442.3; pieces in (the honey-pot) J1176.3, (the money-scales) N478; robbed from treasury by disguising as corpse K419.7; as sacrifice V12.5; seeds pave city F761.5.1; ship F841.1.10; and silver combed from hair D1454.1.1; sold for trifle J2093.6; staff resuscitates E64.1.1.1; star on forehead F545.2.1; statue of animal F855.3; stolen from witch G279.2.1; in stool as royalty sign H71.11; thrown on shore by siren B53.3; tint as royalty sign H71.6.2; turns to ashes from child's urine J2325.1; turns humble servant into arrogant J1085.2; transformed to animal D442.3; under tongue restores speech *D1507.8; used in medicine D1500.1.31. — Acquisition of g. A1432.2; alleged g.-dropping bear K1252.1; alleged g.-dropping horse sold K111.1; alleged return from dead with g. J2411.5; animal with g. horn B15.3.2; ascetic sees scorpions as g. D1825.8; ass with droppings of g. *B103.1.1; automatic doll spins g. D1620.0.1.1; automatic hen and chickens of g. D1620.2.2; avaricious woman and her g. consumed by fire Q272.4; beetle demands return of g. from God: must hum A2231.11; bird with g. head, silver wings B15.7.3; bow of g., silver, and copper F836.1; bride purchased for her weight in g. T52.3; castles of g. F163.1.4; castle paved with g. and gems F771.1.1.1; city of g. F761.1, (in heaven) A661.1.2; deer of g. and jewels possessing life D1620.2.3; dog vomits g. and silver B103.4.3; dogs of g. and silver F855.3.2; doors of g. in otherworld dwelling F165.1.1; dragon develops from small worm placed on g. B11.1.3.1.1; dress of g., silver, etc. F821.1.5, F821.3; dwarf turns g. into lead F451.3.3.2; dwarf king turns mill which produces g. F451.5.1.5.1; dwarf's g. castle F451.4.3.6; dwarfs possess g. F451.7.1; dwarfs turn peas into g. pieces F451.3.3.1; early pupil finds g. N633; fairies give coals that turn to g. *F342.1; fairies with g. crowns on heads G236.4; first parents originate from g. which is from body of first man A1271.4; fool thinks g. is being destroyed when snails crawl over it J1816; fish with ingot of g. inside it B107.1; "for g." C495.2.2; fortress of g. in otherworld F163.5.1; fowls eat g. F989.22.1; gifts of g. and silver not to be accepted from fairies F348.4; goat swallows g., voids it for master K366.5; god

transformed to shower of g. D235.1; grass covered with g. F817.4; grass turns into g. D451.5.6; guessing nature of devil's g. cup H523.3; hair, skin turn g. color D57.3; hair turns to g. as punishment in forbidden chamber C912; hairless palms from handling g. J1289.16; hidden g. revealed; trickster promises to make it into ornaments K283; house of g. and crystal in otherworld *F163.3.1; island covered with g. F731.1; island with rampart of g. and palisade of silver F731.3; king orders all g. brought to him P14.4; large price offered for g. reveals contraband K447; life bought for g. M234.3; magic flower pot bears plants with g. letters on leaves D1469.1; magic g. *D1252.3, (restores speech) D1507.8; magic stone turns everything to g. D1466.1; magic transportation by g. uniform D1520.7; mermaid gives g. from sea bottom B81.13.4; moon's reflection as g. in water J1791.3.3; mother love dearer than g. H662; mountain of g. F752.1; mule carrying corn escapes while one carrying g. is robbed L453; 999 g. pieces J1473.1; nugget of supposed g. (lead) given to help build church: money then borrowed K476.2.1; objects transformed to g. *D475.1ff.; owner of g. decided by combat H217.3; peacocks of g. F855.3.1; person with g. body F521.3.3; pool paved with g. F717.1; prayer for shower of g. V57.2; quest for g. flower H1333.5.0.3; quest for g. from grave H1392.1; quest for mountain of g. H1359.4; quest for g. mouth-harp H1335.1; raised treasure turns into charcoal but if one takes it along it will turn back into g. N558; recognition through g. found in eagle's nest H91.1; recognition by g. under skin H61.4; reincarnation as g. E645.1; resuscitation by g. E64.15; reward: as much g. as sticks to hair K199.1; rich men's g. sent below by gods L482.1.1; sack of g. retains at will any hand thrust in it D1318.14; saint exchanges coat with beggar: g. sleeves miraculously appear V411.2; saint's bachall discovers g. *D1314.3; serpent with g. under him B106; serpent's life in its g. crown E714.2; ship with g. nails F841.1.7; shipwrecked given g. for death V64.1; snake becomes g. D425.12.1, (in answer to dream) N182; spinning g. (task) H1021.8; spring in otherworld produces g. F166.2; successful suitor must have g. teeth H312.2; supernatural son can produce g. D2102.4; supposed chest of g. induces children to care for aged father P236.2; taking g. in mouth prophesies marriage H41.6; tears of g. D1454.4.1; test of innocence: apple and g. offered H256; test of unknown father: g. on street H485; three quarts of g. as suitor test H312.8; towers of steel, silver, and g. F772.2.2; transformation: putrescence to g. D475.1.12; trickster asks goldsmith what he would pay for lump of g. of certain size (goldsmith cheated) K261; trickster watchman exchanges g. for worthless bag K126; tree does not flourish because g. is hidden under it H1292.2; turning fruit into g. (task) H1023.15; unlucky man given a loaf filled with g. exchanges it for another loaf N351; valley filled with g. at command D2102.2; washer of g. rescues child R131.8.7; whales disgorge g. B583.1; wishing to be turned to g. J2079.1; woodsman and g. axe Q3.1.

Golden age A1101.1, C939.4, M324; animals B102ff.; apple *F813.1.1, (as prize in beauty contest) H1596.1; bed F787.2, F846.2; boat with copper rudder F841.1.8; body as royalty sign H71.2.1; bridge F842.1.4, (to otherworld) F152.1.3; calf H1331.3.3; castle F771.1.1, (in otherworld) F163.1.2; cave F757.1.1; chairs F786.1; clothes F821.1.1; cock in earth-tree A878.3.6; cock warns against attack B143.1.5; cock warns of danger D1317.15; comb F827.5; coffin F852.2; cot D846.1; cup F866.3, (as fairy gift) F343.14; door to troll's castle G304.3.1.1; dove F855.3.3; finger as sign of opening forbidden chamber C911; fish B102.4; flowers F814.4; fruits F813.0.2; game-board F899.2.1; hair F555.1.1; horseshoe F862.1; key F886.1; mansions of gods A151.4.3; moustache F545.1.1.2; nut F813.3.1; oar F841.2.4; pomegranates F813.8.1; reel F867.1; saddle F868.1; shoes F823.1; son can produce gold D2102.4; spinning-wheel F876; stone F805; swing F895; table F784.1; teeth F544.3.1; temple F773.2; tongue F544.2.1; tower F772.2.3; tree F811.1.1; vessel disenchants D771.5; wagon F861.1f.; wood for knife H1359.1. — Animals with g. members B101ff.; bird with g. (feathers) B102.1, (head) B101.1; disenchantment by throwing g. objects D789.5; disenchantment by drinking from g. vessel D771.5; devil's three g. hairs G303.4.1.8.2; disguised hero's g. hair discovered by spying princess H151.13; dragon with g. feathers B11.2.2.1; dwarfs make new g. hair for woman F451.5.1.3; fairies' g. bird F359.2; giant with g. hair on forehead F531.1.6.5; goose that laid the g. egg D876; horse's forehead as g. chair F874.2; magic transportation by g. apple D1520.4; making the beard g. *K1013.1; man becomes g. object D235; Midas' g. touch D565.1; pillar covered with g. flowers H1322.1; quest for animal with g. chain H1332.4; quest for g. (bird) H1331.1.3, (fleece) H1332.1; quest for vulture's egg figured with g. letters H1332.2; recognition by g. hair H75.1; recognition of twins by g. chain under their skin H61.1; return from dead to punish theft of g. arm from grave E235.4.1; saint's image lets g. shoe (ring) fall as sign of favor to suppliant D1622.3; Satan enters G. Calf G303.18.4; Solomon's g. throne F785.1; souls as g. apples E745.5.1; stealing g. apples (task) H1151.1; stealing troll's g. horse (task) H1151.9; sun a g. bowl with peacock on rim A724.2; shooting g. apples into besieged city K2365.2; transformed g. pumpkin J1531.1; tree with g. (fruit) D1461.0.1, (leaves) F811.2.1.2, (top) F162.3.6; troll's daughter after being cooked in kettle recognized by g. fingernail H79.1; value of a g. plow (throne, crown, palace)? (riddle) H713.

Goldfinch, color of A2411.2.1.12; wedding of B282.6.

Goldfish, reincarnation as E617.2.

Goldsmith changes person's voice F556.2; gives money to one addressing him as friend L363; as lover P447.7; robs treasury, makes gold into corpse K419.7; sells thinly plated gold: cheated in return J1511.20; unlucky N256.1. — Beggar asks g. for gold plate J1338; fox distracts attention of g., steals K341.25; magic forge of g. D2178.7; origin of g. work A1447.3; treacherous g. K224.3.

Golem D1635.
Gond are omnivorous A1689.3.
Gong, magic D1213.1, (stolen) D838.11.
Good and bad in all books J174; and bad culture heroes *A525; and bad fairies battle F277.0.3; and bad acts tallied by gods A189.8; "day—a woodchopper" (deaf men converse) X111.10; enter otherworld without fear E750.2.1; gifts of fortune *M200ff.; inclinations enter body at puberty W2; luck personified N113; omens D1812.5.2ff.; shepherd shears his sheep but does not skin them J530.1; spirits F403. — Angels seen over heads of the g. D1825.3.2; animals furnish g. omens A2536, B147.3.1; association of the g. and the evil J450ff.; casket with G. Luck in it given to men by Zeus N113.1.1; conflict of g. and evil creators A50ff.; dragon as power of g. B11.8; fairies make g. wishes for new-born child F312.1.1; father in the vineyard doing g. and bad H583.2; goddess of g. luck (Lakshami) A482.2; hedgehog draws self up at sight of g. man A2479.4; "let king do what seems g." J814.5; magic results from g. deeds D1799.6; magic reward for g. deeds D855.5; man marrying often: always looking for g. wife T251.0.3; man who asks for g. weather given a box full of hornets J2327; magic journey during which one must not think g. or evil D2121.6; magic ring brings g. luck D1561.1.2; nothing happens except for one's g. J21.52.8; one wrong and five hundred g. deeds J1605; opposition of g. and evil gods A106; person who never said "g. morning" cannot rest in grave E411.6; right hand for g. *D996.0.1.1; that is g. (cumulative tale) Z51.1; tree of knowledge of g. and evil F162.3.5; why certain animals g. B792; why some women are g.-looking A1372.6; you are an adulteress and a thief and I am as g. as you are J2666.1.
Goods. — Dead returns to restore stolen g. E352; false offer to return g. in place of payment K231.6; man so constantly enriched by God that he cannot give all his g. to the poor U71; thief trusted to guard g. K346.
Good-for-nothing. — Disguised husband shows wife he is not g. K1813.1.2.
Goodness found on earth by man but not by God H853; of God A102.14; preferred to (beauty) J244, (wealth) J247.
Goose best fowl since it makes cabbage sweet and bed soft H659.4.1; boasts superiority to mushroom: both served at same meal L419.1; brings master princess B582.1.1.1; dives for star, thinking it a fish J1791.8; egg becomes hen's D479.4; envious of peacock W195.1; that laid golden egg D876; mates with crow B671; as messenger B291.1.5; mistaken for a tailor J1762.1; transformed to object D423.1; transformed to person D364; without a leg (deception) K402.1. — Bad women from transformed hog and g. A1371.3; barnacle g. B712; bear becomes g. D411.10; bewitched g. eggs G265.8.4.2; brahmin ungrateful to g. rescuer W154.12.2; captured g. warns tortoise B143.1.6; color of g. A2411.2.6.3; deceptive land purchase: boundary fixed by flight of g. K185.3; devil

as g. G303.3.3.8; disguise as g.-girl K1816.5; dwarfs accept as gift g. but not gander F451.3.6.4; ghost of g. E524.1; golden g. B102.1.3; helpful g. B469.3; lover's gift regained (g. as gift) K1581.7; magic adhesion to g. D2171.3.1; man transformed to g. D161.2; marriage to g. B602.6; origin of crest of g. A2321.1; reincarnation as g. E613.10; rubies as ransom for g. J514.6; why g. quacks A2426.2.9; revenant as g. E423.3.7; speaking g. B211.3.3; spirits with g. feet *F401.3.5; troll as g. G304.1.1.3; witch as g. G211.3.3; witch uses g. wings as oars G241.4.1.

Geese tell of beauty of their mistress and bring about recognition H151.12. — Boat drawn by g. B558.1; cackling g. spread alarm B521.3.2; dwarfs chatter like g. F451.3.13.2.1; flock of g. transformed to stone D423.1.1; fox about to be hanged asks to be allowed to see g. J864.2; king of g. B242.2.9; lean g. substituted for fat K476.6; lies about g. X1258; hawk flies away with g. on a line (lie) X1267.1; man carried through air by g. (lie) X1258.1; nine or ten g. (absurd counting) J2032.

Goosebridge. — "Go to G.": counsel proved wise by experience J21.16.

Gorge. — Leviathan's g. spreads disease B16.4.1.

Gorgon F526.3. — Blood of G. becomes horse D447.3.2; quest for head of G. H1332.3.

Gorilla transformed to eagle D411.9. — Man tracking g. sees animal's strength and refrains J561.1; origin of body hair of g. A2322.6; python becomes g. D418.1.1; small boy overcomes g. L311.5; why g. has large teeth A2345.9; why g. lives in forest A2433.2.1.2.

Goring to death by elephant Q416.3.1.

Gospel-book of saint buried with him V136.1; causes sight-shifting D1331.4.1; keeps cattle from straying D1446.2; hangs unsupported from shoulders F1011.1.1; restores speech D1507.2.

Gossip punished Q393.2. — Tongue cut out as punishment for g. Q451.4.2; woman tests enduring power of g. by having a servant ride through streets on a flayed ass J1075.1.

Gossipers. — King refuses to exile g. J215.1.2.

Gotham, Wise Men of J1700ff.

Gourd. — Birth from g. T543.5; boat from g. F841.1.12; escape from deluge in g. A1021.0.3; gold from fishes' g. A1432.2.1; magic g. *D965.2; magic produces golden g. seed D1463.3; man transformed to g. D221; marriage to g. T117.7; queen bears g. T555.2; rice-grains magically produced by g. D973.1.1; soul in g. E711.2.1; suitor task: cutting open magic g. H335.2; tabu: opening g. where starwife kept C31.1.5.

Gourds with seven rooms F813.5.1. — Origin of g. A2686.7; refuge from flood in g. A1029.4.

Government *P500—P599; of demons F402.2; among dwarfs F451.4.5ff.; of fairies F252. — Origin of g. A1582; repartee based on church g. J1265ff.

Governor, clever J1115.10.1.

Governors. — Enigma on dismissing old g. for new H599.5.

Gown. — Man forgets magic g., killed N339.6.

Gowther kills his wet-nurses T614.

Grace before meat X434.2; said in host's name by neglected guest J1561.7. — Asking g. causes fairy banquet to disappear F382.6; prisoners refuse individual g. R72; saying g. to show food improved J1341.12; vow to ask nobody for g. M165; vow to die rather than accept g. M161.4.

Graces, three A468.

Gradual disenchantment D701; resuscitation E156; transformation D681; weakening of testimony J1151.3.

Grafting of feathers to bald head D2161.3.4.1; of hide to man's head E785.1.1.

Grail, see **Holy Grail.**

Grain as damages for injury to cat B271.2; to grow without beards (short-sighted wish) J2072.2; imprisoned R9.2; shot down with guns J2196; sown in unplowed field K1428; theft disguised by replacing husks K419.6; turns to gold D475.1.6.1; will be cut when farmer attends to it himself J1031. — Abandoned children find way back by clue of g. R135; ant keeps g. harvest dry J711.5; apples become g. D451.3.1; bird carries a g. of sand from a mountain each century (eternity) H701.1; building granary full of g. overnight H1104.5; chain tale: biting g. in half Z49.8; chain tale: parched g. sticks in post Z41.6.1; cobold furnishes inexhaustible g. F481.2.1; conception from eating g. T511.8.4; contest: bringing g. from closed bamboo K69.1; consecrated g. as remedy D1500.1.10.4; country without g. F708.2; crow thinks harvesters are stealing his g. J953.7; cure by burning g. where man has died D2161.4.8; deceptive bargain: as much g. as will go in rope K174.1; deceptive g. division: corn and chaff K171.2; extraordinary g. F815.2; fool kills himself in despair because a sparrow has taken one g. from his field J2518.1; disenchantment by burying victim and sowing g. over him D719.1; eaten g. and cock as damages K251.1; father makes many out of few by sowing g. H583.2.2; fool seeks the ears of g. in the direction of the cloud toward which he has sowed them J1922.2.1; improvident mouse eats g. stored for famine J711.2; inexhaustible g. D1652.1.3; magic strength-giving rice-g. D1335.1.1; making ale from single g. H1022.6.1; numskulls sow cooked g. J1932.1; origin of red g. of cedar A2731.3, A2755.1; origin of shapes of g. A2793.6; plucking ear of g. forbidden C512; preparing large quantity of g. (task) H1122; rushes become g. D451.2.1.1; seven g. sisters A433.2; showers of g. called down D2105.6; slain father returns as cuckoo and tells where to sow g. A2275.6; stealing ogre's g. H1151.25; storing g. against famine J711.4; strong man's labor contract: all g. he can carry F613.2; supplying superhuman amount of g. H1122.1; threshing g.: granary roof used as threshing flail K1422; trail of g. R135.0.2; transformation: (apples to g.) D451.3.1, (g. to gold) D475.1.6.1, (rushes to g.) D451.2.1.1; trickster demands half of g. supply K446.1; using g. to clean child tabu C851.1.2;

wages: successive harvests from one g. Z21.1.1; why g. grows only at top of stalk A2793.5; why owl eats no g. A2435.4.9.1; witch aids winnowing of g. G283.1.2.4; wood becomes g. D476.1.3; wraith binds g. E723.7.6.

Grains munched to keep awake H1483. — As many stars in the heavens as g. of sand H702.1; characteristics of g. A2793; deceptive wage: two g. and land to plant them K256.2; devil gives Eve two g. of corn G303.9.4.1; magic g. D973; magic speed by eating magic g. D2122.1; man knows how many g. in measure F645.2; sorting a large number of g. in one night (task) H1091.

Grain-bin. — Filling g. through bottom hole H1023.2.3.

Grain-measure runs away from husband: chain tale Z39.8.

Gram (parched grain). — Chain tale: g. sticks in post Z41.6.1.

Granary now haunted because of devil's defeat G303.15.2. — Building g. overnight H1104.5.

Grandchildren. — Cruel g. S20; devil's g. G303.11.2.2; grandfather kills g. S42; grandmother causes g. to be whipped K2175; prince in disguise to kill g. K1812.14.

Granddaughters. — King prophesies g. fruitful M301.17.1.

Grandeur. — Choice: plainness with safety or g. with danger J212.

Grandfather P291; as creator A1.2; kills grandchildren S42. — Boy kills g. S25.1; earth is deep for my g. went into it (died) years ago and has not yet returned H681.2.1; hero slays his g. A525.2; quest for lost g. H1385.7.1; smith as king's g. P447.1.

Grandfathers. — God dwells with g. A111.3.1.

Grandmother P292; causes grandchildren to be whipped K2175; to be sacrificed in famine K944, K231.1.1. — Abandoned child cared for by g. S351.1; attempt to seduce one's g. T423; creator's g. A31; cruel g. S41; devil's g. G303.11.4; hawk loses g.: still hovers and seeks her A2275.5.2; help from g. N825.3.3, (ogre's) G530.4; hero's g. A512.1; I killed my g. because she refused to cook a hare (cumulative tale) Z49.1; man betrayed into killing his g. K940.2; orphan hero lives with g. L111.4.1; thief disguised as g. K311.8.5; washing the g. in boiling water K1462; wolf poses as g. and kills child K2011.

Grandparents, cruel S40ff.

Grandson, cruel S25. — Prophecy: king's g. with dethrone him M311.1; prophecy: murder by g. M343.2.

Grapes in lifelike painting contest H504.1.3. — Extraordinary g. F813.2; fox and sour g. J871; magic g. *D981.8; speaking g. D1610.10.1.

Grass not bent by swift runner F681.12; does not grow (on murderer's grave) E631.2, (where innocent hanged) H215.3, (in certain spot since extraordinary event has happened there) F974; fuel for burning ogre G512.3.3; from grave protects against witches G272.18; grows anew nightly F979.18; from hair of slain person A2611.6.1; huts replace caves A1435.3; pleasant couch for poor U65.1; transformed to other object D451.5; transformed to soldiers D431.5.1. — Birds destroy g. B33.1.2;

camel's tail turns to g. R231.2; dead find no rest since g. is pulled on grave E419.3; dead (fairies) walk on g. without bending it E489.9, F255.5, F973.2; extraordinary g. F817; fairy rings on g. F261.1; god of g. A433.5; knots in g. mark underworld path F95.4; magic g. *D965.12, (furnishes treasure) D1463.6, (holds person fast) D1411.3; man becomes g. D223; man can hear g. grow F641.1; man with g. growing from him F529.3; man made from g. A1256.1; moustache becomes g. D457.10; men ate g. A1101.2.2; mowing g.: meadow torn up K1423; origin of g. A2683; pretending to return stolen g. K323; reincarnation as g. E631.2.1; St. Peter creates g. as medicine for snake-bite A2623; sham miracle: may the g. grow up K1975; speaking g. gives advice D1312.3; transformation to buffalo so as to eat g. D655.1; transformation: g. to beard D451.5.4; visit to lower world through hole made by lifting clumps of g. F92.1; walking on blades of g. without bending them F973.2.

Grasshopper thought to be the devil J1785.1. — Ant and lazy g. J711.1, A2233.4; why g. is born blind A2233.4, A2332.6.3; creation of g. A2064; enmity between g. and starling A2494.13.11.1; friendship between g. and dungbeetle A2493.21; shooting g. kills friend J1833.1; soul as g. E734.8; why g. hides in day A2491.5; wedding of g. B285.3.

Grasshoppers. — Lies about g. X1288; sheep transformed to g. D412.7; war of monkeys and g. B263.6.

Grateful animals B350—B399, (and ungrateful man) W154.8; boys help hero win girl T66.2; dead *E341ff.; dragon saves hero B11.6.1.2; fairies F330ff.; objects *D1658ff. — Helper g. for being bought from slavery N801; magic object received from g. person D817; magic sight as gift of g. animals D1821.11.

Gratitude W27. — Conversion out of g. V331.6; dragon helps hero out of g. B11.6.1; joining captor from g. R71; mortal wins fairies' g. by joining in their sport *F331; tests of g. H1565.

Grave which causes women to laugh C181.7; equals five times length of any person's foot D482.5.1; fills with sand when dug for sinner Q552.17; opened to let corpse spit out host V39.7; removes itself D1641.8; rises with tide D2151.1.2.3; sinks so that grave-robbers cannot get out Q552.2.2 transformed to animal D442.2.2. — Angels appear above girl's g. V243.1; blood-brethren watch at g. P312.3; burial in old g. to deceive angel J2212.2; cleric as g. robber K335.0.8; crawling to g. on knees Q523.1.1; dead find no rest (since someone daily knocks at g.) E419.2, (when grass is pulled on g.) E419.3; death feigned to meet paramour: meetings in the g. K1538; deceived ghosts unable to return to g. E141; devil sings on g. G303.9.8.3; dew from saint's g. as cure D1500.1.18.1; earth from saint's g. expels demons D1385.1; escape from g. R212; faithful animal at master's g. dies of hunger B301.1; food on g. tabu C247; ghost family visits g. E324.2; ghost haunts g. E334.2; ghost laid by (blessing g.) E443.1, (piercing g. with stake) E442; ghost shakes

off earth when he rises from g. E410.2; ghost takes bones from g. E593.4; hand from g. gives salvation E373.3; identity of g. revealed by magic king in dream (advises take treasure from his g.) N531.4; light haunts g. E530.1.3; limb broken for stepping on g. C946.1; living, dead fight in g. E461.2; lovers buried in same g. T86; magic g. *D1299.2, (compels person to laugh) D1419.1.1; magic identification of g. D1819.5; magic object from g. D842, (of slain helpful animal) D842.3, (of mother) D842.1; magic reward for g. quest D855.3; man in despair digging own g. finds treasure N545; mistress springs into lover's g. T86.3; nails driven into g. to lay ghost E442.2; numskull lies in an old g. to see the Day of Judgment J2311.6; path from g. to lower world F95.1; plants from g. A2611.0.1; plucking flowers from bride's g. H31.12.1; power of prophecy induced by crawling backward around g. D1812.2.1; priest made sick of his bargain: three words at the g. K262; prince plucks from g. of vampire a flower which later becomes a girl E251.2.2; refuge in g. leads to adventure N778; reincarnation in plant (tree) growing from g. *E631ff.; return from dead (to punish disturber of g.) E235.6, (to punish theft from g.) E235.4, (to demand clothing stolen from g.) *E236.1; rich man falls into sacrificial g. K1603; robbing of g. punished Q212.2; saint moves over in g. for pious man Q147.1; sham revenant takes refuge from robbers in an open g. J2311.3; sinner's g. cursed, rolls M411.14.1; sinners cannot rest in g. *E411ff.; sons meet at father's g. after learning trade M271; soul cannot go far from g. E722.3.1; spending night by g. (fear test) H1416; stars drop on g. F961.2.9; stepson cursed to g. D5.1.1; three-night watch over g. to guard man from devil H1463; tobacco from g. of virgin A2611.2.1; treasure is found when three-legged cat shrieks over a g. N542.2; trolls live in g. F455.1.1; walking around g. raises ghost E386.4; wild huntsman released from wandering by mould from Christ's g. *E501.17.7.1; wild huntsman's dogs cannot pass over g. E501.15.6.4; woman, rival lovers all buried in one g. T86.1.

Graves of giants F531.6.13. — Ghost flits between two g. E419.9; treasure buried in g. N511.1.1.

Gravedigger finds purse on corpse J21.48.

Gravedigging, origin of A1541.1.1.

Gravel rises from lake bottom F934.1.

Grave-mound. — Burial in g. V61.8; king goes himself into g. P16.3.2; quest for armor from g. H1392.

Grave-offerings. — Dead eat g. E541.3; trickster eats g. K1867.2.

Graveyard, see also **Cemetery.** — Angels rise from g. V242.1; casting in g. after sunset tabu C752.1.5; crossing g. without alighting tabu C883; death from fright in g. N384.2; jinns frequent g. F499.3.3; other dead drive sinner from g. E411.0.5; physician hides eyes as he passes g. P424.1; suitors one by one encircled into g. K1218.3; voices of dead heard from g. E401; waiting in the g. for the thief J2214.3.1.

Gravitation, lies about X1741. — Magic control of g. D2149.4; magic object reverses g. D1547.
Gravity. — Cup or contents has greatest g.? J2391; specific g. of river F715.10.
Gray and black hairs: enemies reconciled J83; hair cured by pulling it out so that person is bald J2112f.; hair symbol of departed usefulness Z155. — Devil a little g. old man G303.3.1.5; dwarfs have g. beards F451.2.3.2; dwarfs referred to as g. F451.2.7.3; fairies in g. clothes F236.1.4; fairies ride dapple-g. horses F241.1.1.2; fairy has g. beard F233.10; hair turns g. from terror F1041.9; horse used by mortal under fairy spell changes to g. cat F234.4.1; magic well makes person's hair g. D1341.0.1; magician claims he can make dogs g. K1677; man suddenly acquires long g. beard on scaffold at execution F1044; old g. fox not so good as young red one J1457; revenant g. E422.2.3; saint restores g. hair to black V229.10.3; why men's hair becomes g. A1315.1, J1461; wicked man reforms when his child finds g. hair in his head J761.1.
Grazing cow on roof J1904.1; of shooting star on earth A788.2.
Grease. — Disenchantment by rubbing with magic g. D771.2; ice transformed to g. D476.1.9.
Greased. — Holding shaven and g. tail of bull as chastity ordeal H412.2.
Greasing huge griddle by skating with bacon X1031.4.1; the judge's palms (woman puts butter on his hands) J2475.
Great, see also **Big, Large;** head as ogre G361.2. — Giants have g. age F531.6.4.1; humility of the g. J910ff.; lie: the g. animal *X1201; policy in dealing with the g. J810ff.
Great Bear. — Heavenly chariot takes couple to G. A761.2; Pleiades stars transferred from G. A773.7.
Greater. — Judge awards decision to the g. bribe J1192.1; lowly tries in vain to be g. than he is J955; murderer's penance complete when he kills a g. murderer and prevents a crime Q545; present to go to g. fool (returned to giver) J156.3.
Greatest liar to get his supper free K455.7. — Heroes seek which is g. H1395; quest for the g. of fools H1312; riddle: what is g.? H659.7.
Greatness. — Animal helps man to wealth and g. *B580ff.; dream (prophecy) of future g. F317, L425, M310.1, M311, M312, M371.1.
Grebe, helpful B469.1.
Greece as otherworld F130.1.
Greed, see also **Gluttony;** W151ff. — Animal characteristics as punishment for g. *A2238ff.; punishment for g. Q552.3.5; trickster's g. while hunting causes him to be deserted J2751.
Greedily. — "Don't eat too g." J2541.
Greediness. — Bride test: g. H385; guests accused of g. P334.1; spider transformed for g.: now occupies dark corners A2261.2.
Greedy disciple ignores warning, condemned as thief N347.7; dreamer J1473; god A139.15; gods impoverish rich men L482.1; host J1562ff.;

man magically blinded J514.3; priest reincarnated as insect Q551.5.1.3. — Barbers g. P446.2; "don't be g. in trade" J21.26; one should not be too g. J514; ruby shatters for g. lapidary D1641.14.1.

Greeks. — Origin of G. A1611.5.1; Trojans warned not to attack G. J652.4.1; wisdom from the G. J192.3.

Green beard F545.1.1.1; chapel (cave in green mound) F773.1; city F762.1; -eyed giantess F531.1.1.6; fairy F233.1; giant F531.1.7.1; goggles on cow fed sawdust X1235.3; horse B731.2; knight F527.2; as magic color D1293.2; as otherworld color F178.2; pigeon cheated A2275.4.1; plants sold as matured K147.1; revenant E422.2.2; she-goat B731.1; as symbolic color Z145.1. — Brownie dressed in g. F482.2.1; devil dressed in g. G303.5.2; dwarf clad in g. F451.2.7.2; fairy in g. clothes F236.1.6; fairies dance on g. F261.3.6; magic object received from g.-clad huntsman D823.1; man transformed to g. knight D57.1; person with g. face F511.1.4; place of saint's martyrdom perpetually g. V229.2.5; quest to animals' land for g. stone H1289.1.1; secret remedies learned from g.-clad woman N455.5; serpents play with precious g. stone B11.6.2.2; swallow avoids g. trees for nest A2431.3.5.1; tree half g. and half in flame in otherworld garden F162.1.2.4; trees with g. birds hanging by claws F811.9.

Greenest. — Riddle: what is g.? H646.

Greeting before dawn bad omen D1812.5.1.7.1; "come and share it" taken literally J2499.6; customs P682.1. — First to give g. shall have the disputed property K176; numskulls quarrel over a g. J1712; riddle on never g. anyone H588.12; transformation through g. D526.

Greetings. — Dying hero sends g. to friends P310.3; fool's talking taken as unfavorable g. J2671.2.1; give separate g. to different ages J152.5; literal following of instructions about g. J2461.2.

Gregory on the stone Q541.3.

Grey, see **Gray.**

Greyhound. — Birds lift g. F982.1.1; fairy as g. F234.1.9.2.

Greyhounds drag mill out of water (lie) X1215.12. — Fairies' horses size of g. F241.1.8.1.

Griddle. — Cooking g. cakes as bride test H383.1.2; rubbing nose on g. as punishment Q499.8; tabu to eat g. cakes C229.3.

Grief, see also **Sorrow;** dispelled by magic bell D1359.3.1.3; at queen's death P27. — Animal pines away with g. B773.2; black as symbol of g. Z143.1; boy sickens from g. P231.1; excessive g. at spouse's death T211.9; extraordinary reactions to g. F1041.21; madness for g. F1041.8.2; magic bird's song dispels g. B172.2; Pleiades girls who died of g. A773.3; pulling out hair g. sign P678; prophecy of g. fulfilled by death M340.1; transformation through excessive g. D516.

Grieving to death over fate of children after one's death J2063.1; mortal taken to heaven, identifies son F12.2. — Man dies from g. over mother's death F1041.1.3.8.

Griffin B42; aids quest H1233.4.3; disdains to go on ark: drowned, hence extinct A2232.4; as guardian of treasure N575. — Hostile g. B17.2.2; transportation to fairyland on back of g. B542.21.

Griffins in hell A671.2.10.

Grinder. — Cobold furnishes g. with inexhaustible grain F481.2.1; moon as g. brings fire from sun A741.3.

Grinding. — Giants g. F531.5.10.2; man in disguise g. corn K521.4.1.3; man g. rocks into powder F639.11; mill not g. stolen wheat D1318.15; murder by g. in mill S116.1; punishment: g. up in a mill Q469.3; youths g. in mill of underworldlings F106.

Grindstone. — Magic g. *D1262; origin of g. A1446.5.3; picture of g. mistaken for cheese J2685; sun as g. full of fire A714.5; woman gives birth to g. T569.2.

Grindstones kill enemies N696.2.

Griselda H461.

Grizzly bears. — Why g. have three stripes on inside of stomach A2367.2.1; why g. are pugnacious A2524.1.

Groaning dead E547.1. — Dwarf g. while carrying an ear of corn F451.3.9.1; listening to g. of violated women tabu C885.2.

Groat. — Never wager more than a g. J21.8.

Groom, see also **Bridegroom.** — Treacherous stable-g. K2256.

Grooming unruly mare H1155.1.1.

Ground, see also **Earth, Land;** dries up when first woman cuts self, bleeds on it A856.2; elevates itself for saint V229.13; trembles or rumbles when ghost rises from grave E410.1. — Birth from g. T545; city girl asks whether turnips grow in the g. or on trees J1731.1; clever girl comes sitting on animal but with feet reaching the g. H1053.2; contest: jumping into the g. K17.1; deceptive crop division: above the g., below the g. K171.1; devil tries to wall in too large a piece of g. in a night and fails G303.13.3; dragon lives under the g. B11.3.5; dupe caught in crack in g. K1111.2; dwarfs have homes above the g. F451.4.2; dwarfs live under the g. F451.4.1ff.; earth made from broken g. A824; father's counsel: find treasure within a foot of the g. H588.7; flowers spring up when saint strikes the g. F971.6; fox produces fire by striking tail to g. D2158.1.1; girl seduced from beneath g. K1344.1; ghost travels under g. E591; house neither on g. nor in sky H1077; life token: staff stuck in g. E761.2; magic found on g. D849.8; magic object dug from g. D848; magic song causes plowed g. to become unplowed D1565.3; magician's feet must touch g. D1719.10.1; mankind emerges from g. A1234; saint's bachall cleaves g. D1564.3; strong man drives anvil into g. F614.1; pitcher magically sticks to g. D2171.4.1; tabu: touching g. C520ff., (on return from fairyland) F378.1; tails in g. K404.1; transformation by touching g. D565.0.1; temple rises where g. bursts open A992.3; treasure found by sprinkling g. with blood of white cock D2101.1; treasure in g. N511; vehicle travels above and below g. *D1533.2ff.; wild hunt in air

very close to g. E501.14.1.1; wild hunt throws person to g. E501.18.5; youth will not eat from g. C219.1.

Grouse. — Markings on tail-feathers of ruffled g. A2412.2.1.

Grove. — Covering g. with fruit overnight H1103.3; death excluded from sacred g. Z111.4.

Groves. — Cutting sacred g. forbidden C51.2.2; sacred g. V114.

Growing crop overnight H1103.2.2; mountain F755.4; oil seed on stony ground H1049.2; and ungrowing grass F817.1; rocks F802. — Beard g. through table F545.1.3; garments g. with wearer F821.9; giant g. because of another giant F531.6.8.8; god sends cold to prevent stones' g. A975.1; island g. foot yearly F734; man can hear grass g. F641.1; plant g. to sky F54.2; sham physician controls girl's "g.-up" K1955.5; tree blooming and g. ripe fruit nightly F811.13; tree g. miraculously fast F811.19.

Growth of culture hero A511.4; of members for breaking tabu C946.3; controlled by magic object D1376. — Changeling has abnormal features or g. F321.1.2.1; extraordinary g. of animal F983ff.; girl fed boys' flesh to hasten g. G72.3; gods' food gives supernatural g. A153.2.1; magic quick g. of crops *D2157.2; man's g. controlled by cloak D537.2.1; man's g. and maturity A1360ff.; miraculous g. of tree D2157.4, F811.19; nurture and g. of children *T610ff.; supernatural g. T615.

Growths. — Magic object causes (or removes) temporary g. D1375; temporary bodily g. from magic D2062.5.

Grub's urine waters tree F979.14.

Gruel runs out drinking hole in pot J2176.2.

Grumbling tabu C881.1.

Guarantee. — Cloth g. against being eaten H119.1.

Guard. — Animal as g. B576; black as g. against Evil Eye D2071.1.4; don't set hungry g. over food J215.1.1; escape by blinding g. *K621; escape by deceiving g. K620ff.; escape by putting captor off g. *K611; extraordinary g. for castle F771.5; fidelity of g. tested H1556.0.2; nobody can move cannon, so g. quits J1849.4; theft by giving g. narcotics K332.1; thief as g. for goods K346; transformation to lion in order to be palace g. D659.4.1; victim killed when off g. K839.1.

Guards. — Bribed g. let prisoner escape R211.9; man caught by g.: guard substitutes with his sweetheart K1317.4; putting g. to sleep, then stealing K331.2.1.2; suitor outwits one hundred g. T46.1; thief frightens away corpse g. K335.0.7; trickster bribes g. to start a fight K341.10; wolf proposes abolition of dog g. for sheep K2061.1.1.

Guarded maiden first seen by hero in church T381.1. — Bridge to otherworld g. by animals *F152.0.1; door of habitable hill g. by monster F721.2.2; entrance to other world g. by monsters F150.2; gate of heaven g. by clap of thunder and mysterious sword A661.0.1.1; girl carefully g. from suitors T50.1; magic spring g. *D927.2; magic tree g. by serpent *D950.0.1; quest over path g. by dangerous animals H1236.2; treasure

g. by spirit in hornet form F403.2.3.1; wonderful birds g. by monster G375.

Guardian angel V238; beast overcome by mirrors K335.1.7; sleeps while lovers visit D1965; spirit of land F494.1; of spirit-land F140.1; of treasure *N570ff. — Animal g. of ogress' soul E710.1; bird as g. of primordial fire A1414.6; calabash as g. of girl D1380.2.1; dog as g. of treasure B292.8; fairy g. relaxes, man killed F311.2.1; false g. betrays lovers K2093; magic knowledge from g. spirits D1810.12; means of hoodwinking the g. or owner *K330ff.; offending g. spirits C44; old woman as g. of gods' islands A955.12; soul as g. spirit E748; stones as town's g. F809.8; tree as girl's g. D1380.2.2; theft by presenting false order to g. K362.

Guardians of imprisoned virgin put to sleep while man enters to her D1965. — Beast g. of the four quarters A417.1; golden deer entices away girl's g. K341.7.3; invisible g. N810.1.

Guarding the door (lifted off and carried away) K1413; as task H1199.17; those having pact with devil M219.3. — Dragon g. (bridge to otherworld) B11.6.6, (holy land) B11.6.4, (hermit's food) B11.6.5, (sandalwood tree) B11.6.10; ghost g. treasure E291.2; giants g. fairy princess F300.1; gorilla and chimpanzee punished for not g. possessions at creation A2322.6.

Guavas. — Divine friends eating g. A1129.2.

Guelph-Ghibelline feud starts over dog N387.1.

Guessing correctly wins princess for ogre G463; dwarf suitor's name drives him off F451.5.15.3; dwarf's name rewarded with money *F451.5.15.1; name of supernatural creature gives power over him *C432.1; of secret transaction brings magic recovery of speech D2025.3. — Dwarf makes return of child dependent upon g. of riddle F451.5.15.2; tests in g. H510ff.

Guest kills host, asked to restore life J1955.1; made to pay for food K251.2; stays too long, gets black bread J21.9.1. —Acquisition of g.-houses A1435.1; eating after g. tabu C236; host offers to send his g. a cask of wine which he has praised M206.1; host robs g. K385; hosts refrain from telling g. of death in household P323; priest's g. and eaten chickens *K2137; relation of host and g. P320ff.; supper won by disguising as invited g. K455.2; suspicious g. forces host to be killed in his stead K1611.2; tabu: failure to sleep with g. unaccompanied by husband C119.2; unwelcome g. tells about the hidden food J1344; various foods given each g. J81.2; wife abuses husband in presence of g. T252.7; woman advises husband to kill g. she covets T481.7.

Guests and hosts P320ff.; strike man who tries to interfere in their quarrel J1072.1. — Angel forewarns of g. coming V246.3; foreknowledge of g. coming D1812.0.2ff.; greedy g. impoverish host W151.2.2; man kills all g., hoping some day to kill rival S110.2; miserly wife exposed to g. by her husband W153.3; peasant cutting wood as g. arrive P411.2;

practical retorts: hosts and g. J1560ff.; thieving g. at inn K365.2; treatment of difficult g. J1563ff.

Guesting, origin of A1534.

Guide. — Angel as g. V232.5; deity as g. for mortal A185.10; demon g. to otherworld F159.4; fairy as g. F234.2.7.

Guiding beast N774. — Boat g. self D1523.2.5; child in womb g. mother T575.1.6.

Guilt detected by heartbeat J1142.2.1. — Escape by discussing g. K573.1; magic object reveals g. *D1318ff.; tests of g. or innocence *H210—H239; twelve-legged bird symbolizes g. H619.5.

Guilty confronted become insensate F1041.1.3.10.1; person deceived into confession J1141.1; protests innocence J1141.9. — Brother about to drink blood of seemingly g. sister P253.1; fool believes not g. plea J2045; innocent made to appear g. K2150ff.; lawyer makes g. client doubt own guilt X319.1; magic object picks out g. man D1318.0.1; ship refuses to move with g. man aboard D1318.10.1; who is g. of accident? Z49.11.

Guinea eats man's grain: man may kill him A2238.2. — Cackling of g. A2426.2.13; color of g. A2219.1, A2411.2.6.6; helpful g. B469.6; why g. has red feet A2375.2.10.

Guise. — Deity's messenger can assume any g. A165.2.0.1; hero assumes ugly g. A527.3.1.1.

Guises. — Deity in frightful g. H1401.

Guitar. — Magic g. *D1234; resuscitation by playing g. E55.5.

Gull as bird of ill-omen B147.2.2.2; transformed to person D354.2. — Color of g. A2411.2.5.4; creation of g. A1945; giant g. B872.2; man becomes g. D154.4; nest of g. A2431.3.4.

Gullet seen through mouth F544.0.1.1.

Gullible fools *J2300—J2349.

Gum. — Indians chew spruce g. A1681.1; leaky vessel repaired with g. H1023.2.1.1; origin of g. in myrrh tree A2755.3.2; trickster's burnt flesh becomes g. on trees A2731.1.

Gun bewitched G265.8.3.1; mistaken for clarinet J1772.10; as tobacco pipe K1057. — Accidental discharge of g. kills much game X1124.3; blade of grass transformed to g. D451.5.3; devil's g. G303.25.16.1; lie: remarkable g. X1121; magic g. *D2096.1; man shoots devil with silver g. G303.25.7; numskull looks through g. barrel J2131.4.1; silver in g. releases curse M429.7; stolen g. works only for master D1651.11; thunder as sound of God's g. A1142.5; witch causes g. explosion G269.16.

Guns rendered ineffective by witch D2086.2. — Grain shot down with g. J2196; peoples choose bows and arrows or g. and horses A1614.4.3.

Gunfire. — Sneeze mistaken for g. J1809.1.

Gunpowder. —Captor's g. removed, ashes substituted K633.

Guru. — Man from loincloth of g. A1211.7.

Gust. — Dragon-king transformed to g. of wind D429.2.1; measuring g. of wind H1145.2.

Gustatory. — Extraordinary g. sense F647.1.1.

Gut covering in sky A1122.4.

Guts, web of F847.

Gutting of dead man S139.2.2.2.

Gyges' ring D1361.17.

Gypsy. — Disguise as g. K1817.5; treacherous g. K2261.1; why g. may steal: helpful at crucifixion A1674.1.

Gypsies. — Origin of g. A1611.2; why g. have no churches X1863.

Habit, power of U130ff.

Habits of witches G240ff. — Absurd disregard or ignorance of animal's h. *J1900ff.; characteristic h. of various peoples A1680ff.; causes of animal h. A2400—A2499; dragon's h. B11.4ff.; evil person's h. punished Q320ff.; fanciful h. of animals B750ff.; hero with disgusting h. L114.5; hero (heroine) of unpromising h. L114; house dog blames master for teaching him lazy h. J142.1; slave recognized by his h. H38.3; thieves' nocturnal h. J1394ff.

Habitable caves and mounds in otherworld F164; hill F721.2.

Habitat of animal A2434ff.; of dragon B11.3ff.; of witches G230ff. — Present h. of animals result of ancient quarrel A2282.

Habitations, acquisition of A1435.

Hades, see **Hell.**

Hag guards girl from suitors T50.1.3; runs race, loser to be beheaded M221.1. — Fairy in form of h. F234.2.1; fighting with h. tabu C835.4.1; goddess of war as h. A125.1; king tricked into sleeping with h. K1235; love charm on cheeks of h. D1355.13.1.

Hags guard quest path H1236.3.

Haidas. — Why the H. surpass in certain industries A1673.1.

Hail as bad omen D1812.5.1.15; leaves twelve chief rivers in Ireland A934.6; as one of sun's faces A733.3; produced by magic D2143.4; as punishment Q552.14.5. — Angel created from h. A52.1.5; magic h. *D902.3, (on lake causes treasure to spring from it) D1469.4; origin of h. A1135.4.

Hailstone among worst of stones H659.3.1. — Birth from h. T546.2.

Hailstones. — Extraordinary h. F962.5; triangular h. F794.2.

Hair becomes gold D475.1.10; burned to summon fairies F398; burned, victim dies D2061.2.2.4.1; combed with iron S187.2; of dead combed V68.2; of drowned woman speaks E545.20.1; of dwarfs F451.2.4ff.; from fox's tail opens all doors D1562.2; gives clairvoyance D1323.11; gray before the beard (it is twenty years older) H771; on ground summons goddess D2074.2.2.1; growing on tongue F544.2.3; like raven as suitor test H312.5; plaits cut off to escape lover T327.7; -restorer injures patient K1013.5; rises on end F1041.2; rolled in wax as witch-ball G262.4; rope transfers milk D2083.3.2; tied to basket causes dupe's death

K1021.1.1; transformed to (another object) D457.4, (plants) A2611.6, (animal) D447.1; turns to gold as punishment in forbidden chamber C912; turns gray from terror F1041.7. — Animal with h. of iron pins B15.7.10.2; animals from transformed h. A1724.2; ascetic carries woman in h. F1034.2; ascetic's h. garment V462.5.1; bathing h. in buffalo milk D1337.1.3.1; boiling lover's h. fetches him D1355.35; brownie with red h. F482.1.1; burning cut h. to prevent witchcraft D2176.5; cannibal without h. G11.11.2; child born carrying handful of h. T552.4; child finds gray h. in wicked father's head J761.1; color of h. changes D492.3; combing h. of fairies (task) H1192; coming neither naked nor clad (clothed in own h.) H1054.2; corn grows in man's h. F1099.4; creature with single red h. H1331.7; culture hero's pubic h. thought to be bear h. J1772.4; cure by putting h. in tree hole D2161.4.18; cutting h. to escape captor K538; cutting h. as insult P672.2; cutting h. as punishment Q488; daughter pulls out father's magic life-containing h. K976; demon with red h. G342; devil buys a woman's h. G303.25.13; devil's h. G303.4.1.8; disenchantment by burning magic h. D771.1; disenchantment made permanent by holding to a h. D793.1; disguise by cutting off h. K1821.10; dwarf washes, combs and braids h. for sleeping maids F451.5.1.13; dwarfs make new golden h. for woman F451.5.1.3; dupe's h. tied: attacked K1021.1; escape by returning for h. ribbon K551.4.8; fairy borrows comb from Christian maid to comb h. of changeling bride F322.1.1; fairy-mortal baby's long h. F305.3; fairies comb children's h. F313; fairies tied together by h. F239.1; fairies' long h. F232.4; fairies' yellow h. F233.5; flying nets of h. in battle F1084.0.2; girl fastened by h. to rafter S182; girl's long h. as ladder into tower F848.1; ghost laid by burning h. E446.2.1; ghost turns h. white E542.4; giant with golden h. on forehead F531.1.6.5; giant with long h. F531.1.6.3.1; giant without h. F531.1.6.3.2; giant's h. grown into earth F531.1.6.9; giant's strength in h. F531.1.6.13; giant slings stones with his h. ribbon F531.3.2.2; giant's h. grows into rock G122; giants with shaggy h. on their bodies F531.1.6.3; goddess of the h. A499.2; gods fasten world-columns with mother's h. A841.0.1; grass from h. of slain person A2611.6.1; gray h. cured by pulling it out so that the person is bald J2112; guessing which sister's h. is golden H511.2; healing with h. of dog that bit one D2161.4.10.3; heavenly being's h. as sky-rope F51.1.5; hen put in witch's h. to scratch while maid escapes G276.1; hero's golden h. discovered H151.13; hero's three heads of h. A526.4; house-spirit without h. F480.5; husband cuts off h. of wife's substitute in bed K1512; husband tests wife by sleeping on her h. H476; husband tied to bed by h. K713.1.7; identification by h. H75; Jesus' dark h. V211.2.1.2.1; large red h. as suitor test H312.8; long h. prized by Irish P632.5; love through sight of h. of unknown princess *T11.4.1; magic h. *D991, (of animal) D1023ff., (ball) D991.3, (ornaments) D1072, (produces soldiers) D1475.5, (summons helper) D1421.0.3, (wishing) D1470.1.36; magic sleep by combing h. D1962.3.1;

magic strength resides in h. *D1831; magic weapon cuts h. D1564.7; man absorbing h. into head F1041.10; man covered with h. like animal F521.1; man transformed to h. D292; men are first covered with h. A1281.2; mermaid has wooly h. B81.9.1; mermaid's h. reaches her waist B81.9.1; mortal wins fairies' gratitude by letting them cut his h. and shave him F331.2; mountain of women with fair h. F131.1.1; mouse causes thief's h. to fall out Q557.4; why nit lives at edge of h. A2236.6; nude woman clothed in own h. F555.3.1; origin of gorilla's and chimpanzee's body h. A2322.6; origin of h. A1315, A2322ff.; why no h. on ox's lips A2221.5.1; pearls from h. as sign of royalty H71.3; partial transformation: person with animal h. D682.2; prince feels h. on bedding F647.9.1; pubic h. believed to be lying, pulled out J1842.1; pubic h. mistaken for calf's tail J1772.4.1; pubic h. remarkable F547.6; pulling out h. in grief P678; remarkable h. F555ff.; reward: as much gold as sticks to h.: hair tarred K199.1; rope made of person's h. F843.1; saint binds devil with her h. D1831.1; saint causes gray h. to turn black V229.10.3; seven souls released from hell for every h. of saint's chasuble Q174.1.1.1; not to shave or cut h. until a certain time M121; shield cutting h. F839.2.2; sleeping enemies' h. tied to an object prevents pursuit *K635; sleeping maiden's h. tied to tree K635.1; snakes will not cross h. rope B765.18.2; soul in h. E714.12; splitting a h. with a blunt knife (task) H1023.14; straightening a curly h. (task) H1023.4; strength of witches in h. G221.1; summoning by burning h. D2074.2.2; tabu: cutting h. C722; tearing h. from grief F1041.21.6; thief ties owner's h. while he escapes with goods K338; tiger made to believe porcupine bristle is his enemy's h. K1711.1; transformation by braiding h. D577; Virgin Mary's golden h. V250.2; washing h. on sabbath tabu C631.3; water-spirit controlled by long h. F420.5.2.2.1; water-spirit with long h. F420.1.4.10; wearing h. "not too long or too short" J1161.8; weaving a silk shirt from h. H1021.6; wife binds giant's h.: he is slain G530.1.1; wild huntsman with long h. E501.7.7; witch's h. on horse becomes iron G265.3.1; witch's long h. G219.4; woman with animal h. F521.1.1; woman drying h. scares ghost E432.3; woman not to bind h. till enemy is conquered M122; woman sells h. to feed husband T215.8; woman's scented h. attracts deer: husband jealous T257.5.1; woman tells wife to increase her husband's love by cutting a h. from his beard K1085.

Hairs become jewels D475.4.7. — As many stars as h. (on goat) H702.2.1, (in the head) H702.2; counting h. in pig's back (task) H1118; goddess scatters pubic h. on fish A2211.15; gold (silver) h. as sign of royalty H71.2; gray and black h.: enemies reconciled J83; how many h. are in the head (riddle) H703; origin of pubic h. A1315.5; pulling h. from bewitched animal's tail G271.4.9; putting h. under arm H599.4; quest for man caused by bird dropping his h. H1213.1.1; quest for princess caused by sight of one of her h. dropped by bird H1213.1; quest for three h. from devil's beard H1273.2; sinners in heaven numbered by h. in saint's

chasuble M364.3.1; young wife pulls out his gray h., old wife his black J2112.1.

Hair-ball for bewitching D2070.1.

Haircut as war preparation P552.5.

Hairdressing, magic sleep by D1962.3.

Hairpin, magic *D1072.2.

Hairy anchorite D733.1; ascetics attacked instead of monkeys J2484; star F961.2.2, (at Nativity) V211.1.2.1. — Bear learns how to catch crabs with his h. claws J102; child born h. T551.13; child born with h. mane T585.5.1; devil as h. man G303.3.1.21; disguise as h. man K1821.4.1; fairies' h. bodies F232.5; wood-spirits h. F441.4.5.

Halcyon builds nest on sea-cliff N255.3.

Half done K372; -friend H1558.1; of kingdom as reward Q112; of offspring like fairy, half like mortal F305.2.1; payment for half-milk, half-water J1551.9; price for half a shave J1522.1. — Army of h.-animals, half men B20.1; boy cut in two: each h. becomes a boy T589.2; Fortuna h. white, h. black N111.2.3; giving up h. property: slave cut in two J2469.3.1; ghost with h. a head, carries h. body E261.1.3; god h. mortal, h. immortal A122; lying goat punished by being h. shorn Q488.1; mermaid h.-beautiful, h.-monstrous B81.9.3; money collected by h.-chick K481; only h. a child born to queen eating half a mango T550.6; parson preaches so that h. the congregation weeps and h. laughs X416; person with h. a body F525; resuscitation of wife by husband giving up h. his remaining life *E165; selling his h. of house J2213.6; spirit has h. a head F401.4.1; thief dressed h. white, h. black K311.0.1; tree h. green and h. in flame in otherworld garden F162.1.2.4; vow to get stubborn girl h.-married only M149.6; youth sees h. of two quadrupeds H583.1.1.

Half-wit abandoned S327.3; as prophet M301.9; successful L121.1.

Halibut, color of A2411.4.1.

Hall of glass F165.3.1. — Beard projected over beams of great h. F545.1.2; fairy h. F223; seating arrangements in royal h. A1539.1; smith as lord of hospitality h. P447.3; tree in king's h. F811.4.3.

Hallowed. — Rich man dragged from h. grave E411.0.5.1.

Hallowe'en. — Dead speak on H. E545.6; devil appears on H. G303.6.1.7; fairy appears to mortal each H. F393.2; fairy army among mortals on H. F255.4; fairy cattle graze on H. F241.2.4; fairy steals on H. F365.0.1; fairies emerge on H. F211.1.1.1; festival of H. V70.5; ghost kills on H. E268; ghosts walk on H. E587.2; going abroad tabu on H. C632; names of those to die heard on H. D1827.1.1; origin of H. A1541.3; roads appear on H. F1099.2; speech magically recovered on H. D2025.5; terrifying experience undergone on H. H1423.2; treasure found on H. N541.3; wonders on H. F900.1.1.

Halter. — Transformation to horse by putting on h. D535.

Halting. — Location determined by h. of an animal *B155; tabu: h. or unloading horse C884.1.

Ham (proper name). — Creatures from curse of H. A1614.1; Fomorians descended from H. A1659.1.1.

Ham as prize for husband who rules his wife T252.4. — Rock substituted for h. K476.1.1; stolen and restolen h. K306.1.

Hamelin. — Pied Piper of H. D1427.1.

Hamlet cutting hooks for father's revenge H591.3. — Enigmatic statements of H. H599.2.

Hammer in coffinmaker's shop makes noise to announce a death D1322.1.1; of thunder god A157.7; worship V1.9.3. — Compressible h. D631.3.5; creator with h. and chisel in hands A18.5; dispute of h. and anvil J461.6; first poetry composed in imitation of tones of h. on anvil A1464.1.1; giant h. F612.3.2; giant thinks blow of h. on head is a nut falling F531.5.4; god with h. A137.1; magic h. D1095, *D1209.4; Thor to give his h. in return for Freyja as wife K235.2.

Hammers. — Persons whose heads are stone h. F511.0.3.

Hammock, magic *D1154.3.

Hampers. — Measuring the tower by piling up h. J2133.6.1.

Hamstringing S162.2, (as punishment) Q451.2.0.3.

Hand cut off for breaking tabu C948.6; of glory *D1162.2.1, K437; from grave gives salvation E373.3; from heaven writes on wall F1036; -less people, F167.6, F515.0.1; of sinner sticks out of grave E411.0.1; of slain enemy nailed to castle S139.2.2.1.5; stuck for beating idol Q222.5.6; of vampire severed by cutting off hand of drawn figure E251.1.2; wagered N2.3.2; withers (as punishment) Q559.5.2, (because of broken oath) M101.4. — Bird in h. foolishly given away in hope of greater gain J321.1; cat's paw cut off: woman's h. missing D702.1.1; conception from h. T517.1; corpse's h. as remedy D1500.1.6.1; corpse's h. used as charm by robber K437.2; curse: person's h. to drop off M431.4.1; cut-off h. transformed to plant D457.9.1; cutting off h. for ring R231.1; dead man stretches h. from tomb to honor saint V222.7; devil cuts off h. of woman and suffocates her S113.2.1; dupe puts h. into cleft of tree *K1111; dwarf promises money and property to mortal father for h. of daughter F451.5.18.1; fool cannot tell right h. in dark J1735; ghost as h. E422.1.11.4; ghostly fingers leave mark on man's h. E542.1.1; god makes man's h. rigid A185.2.2; god with one h. A128.4; greedy person gets h. stuck in jar W151.9; hawk carries man's h. F982.3; hog's forefoot cut off; woman's h. missing D702.1.2; identification by magic h. H145; lotus transformed to human h. D451.4.1; lucky right h. N113.2.1; magic h. *D996; magic healing by h. D1503.9, D2161.4.16.1; magic object clings to h. of guilty person H251.3.8; magic restoration of severed h. D2161.3.2; magic sight by looking in hollow of h. D1821.3.9; man kills ox (cow) with flat of h. F628.1.2ff.; why mole has h. like man A2375.2.6;

mountains made with the h. A962.5; mountains made with God's h. A962.2; oath taken on saint's h. M116; paper in h. which none but king can remove D1654.11; person swearing oath places h. in mouth of image H251.1; price "handful of coppers": h. claimed too J1511.17; pygmy stands on man's h. F535.2.6; recognition by hole burned in h. when woman removes glove H56.1; robber with "h. of glory" killed K437; sack holds person who puts h. into it D1318.14, D1413.9; saint's h. made bright by Lord's touch V222.1.2; saint's h. illumines darkness D1478.1; severed h. as identification H106.1; sham-dead person tested by hot lead poured on h. H248.1; silver h. used as if flesh F1002; softest h. placed between head and pillow H652.1; soul (life) in left h. H714.7; substituted h. E782.1.1; tell-tale h.-mark H58; treasure discovered by h. of unborn child N533.3; victim lured into holding out h.: it is cut off K825.4; Virgin restores saint's severed h. V256.3; waiting for man's h. to fall off J2066.9; witch in form of cat has h. cut off *G252; witch steals child with h. through chimney G261.1; what do I hold in my h. (question to numskull) J2712.

Hands in cleft log as punishment Q469.13; cut off as punishment Q451.0.1; restored E782.1; wagered N2.3.2.1; washed before prayer V58.4. — Boy borrows python's h. and feet: hence python lacks them A2241.8; cold h. and feet for the dead man J2311.7; curse: fire to burn h. and feet M431.3; deceptive contest in squeezing h. K73; flowers drop on washing h. D2193; fool hanging by h. claps them, falls J2133.13; friends clasp h. in death P319.5; giants' magic gifts return to original form in h. of men F531.5.6.1; holy man restores cut-off h. V229.10.2; husband's h. tied, woman drowns K1652; invisible h. (aid task) H986, (serve) E482; magic from clapping h. D1799.2; magic restoration of severed h. D2161.3.2; maiden sends to her lecherous lover h. which he has admired T327.1; man originally without h. and feet A1225.2; mason's h. cut off after building finished S161.0.1; men with tails on h. F515.3; merman lays h. on side of canoe B82.7; mutilation: cutting off h. S161; ogre's h. cut off, hung above gate G512.1.2.1; origin of h. and feet A1311; person unusual as to his h. F515ff.; Pilate appears periodically and washes his h. E411.8; remarkable h. F552ff. revenant with ice-cold h. E422.1.3; robbers' h. cut off K912.0.2; recognition by missing h. H57.4; skillful marksman shoots meat from giant's h. F661.1; soldier with both h. gone fights with teeth P461.1; sons wipe h. on lame brother S12.7; sparks from man's h. F683.1; severed h. as suitor tribute H333.2; strong man kills animals with own h. F628.1, F628.2.5; successful suitor must have whitest h. H312.4; tokens on h. identify god H45.4; tribe all use left h. F515.5; unseen h. lave feet F171.7; unseen h. serve hero H1239.2; warming h. across the river J1945; witch with enormous h. G217; wood-spirit without h. F441.4.2.

Handaxe, magic D1524.12.

Handicrafts. — Aptness in h. as suitor test H326.1; god of h. A451.3.

Handiwork. — Strong man's h. causes quest H1213.2; test of skill in h. H504.

Handkerchief as chastity index H431.2; concealed in nut F813.3.4; left to incriminate woman K2112.5.1; in room condemns innocent wife N348; transformed to other object D454.3.2.1; as token H86.4. — Disenchantment by placing h. between horns D777; extraordinary h. F822; identification by h. H113; love through finding h. T11.4.5; magic h. *D1069.1, (healing) D1500.1.35; princess throws h. high in tree: asks hero to get it H933.1; quest for best-worked h. H1306.1; resuscitation by h. E64.21.

Handle. — God with h. through eyelid A128.2.2; gold, silver knife h. F838.2; tree cut down with axe for which it furnished h. U162.

Handles. — The cup with two and three h. J2665.1.

Handmaid. — Beaten h. reveals secret blemish N465.0.1.

Handprint. — Ineradicable h. proves innocence H215.4.

Handsel. — Bringing h., forgetting purchase J2461.5.

Handsome exterior no indication of soul U119.3; but foolish son M93; man F575.2, (made hideous) D1872.1, (substitutes for ugly bridegroom) K1915.3. — Jealous king massacres h. captives T257.6; father with h. son and hideous daughter J244.1; quest for bride as h. as the hero H1301.1.1; ugly man becomes h. D52.2.

Handspreading. — Feast of "bedding and h." T162.

Hanged, see also **Hung;** man thirsty: demands water E422.0.1; man warns youth E366.2. — Bedridden oldster h. instead of guilty young man J2233.1.1; captured women h. S139.3; deception into allowing oneself to be h. K715; gallows breaks when innocent h. H215.2; god of the h. A310.3; grass won't grow where innocent h. H215.3; if you h. me, you will be in trouble J2185.1; innocent boy h. for cattle theft N347.3; innocently h. person saved by saint R165.2; island sinks into sea after innocent man h. H252.5; lightning strikes where man being h. R341.1; man h. by hair S182.1; slave h. P175.1; tabu to take down corpse of h. man C541.5.

Hanging in game or jest accidentally proves fatal N334.2; sentence remitted Q577; for stealing from church Q411.11.2; on a sunbeam *F1011.2; test H1533; by tongue Q451.4.9; up by feet as punishment Q462.2. — Advice on h. yourself "by the stone which I point out" J21.15; at h. witnesses bigger thieves than culprit U119.1.2; cat h. on wall pretends to be dead K2061.9; deceptive game: h. each other K852; devil cheated by pretended h. K215; devils' feast for woman h. herself G303.25.17.3; dogs with eyes h. out over mouth in wild hunt E501.4.1.4; foolish demands before h. J2174; horse h. self D2061.2.8; lower lip h. down to neck F544.1.1; man finds treasure as h. self N545.1; man h. himself under devil's instruction G303.9.4.2.1; men h. down in chain until top man spits on hands J2133.5; men h. selves to punish sickle J1865.1; murder by h. S113.1ff.; obedient husband h. wife J2523.1;

ogre deceived into h. self G524.1; old man with h. eyelids F571.1; penance: h. for a thousand years head downward over a fire of chaff Q522.6; plea for immediate h. so can get back to work J2174.4; prophecies concerning h. M341.1ff.; punishment: h. Q413; thief advises dupe on h. up slaughtered meat K343.2; thief distracts attention by apparently h. himself K341.3; tower h. in air F163.7.1; tree h. from sky A652.2; trees with green birds h. by claws F811.9; usurer charges for rope cut to save him from h. W154.1.1; wife h. self at husband's death T211.3.2; wife h. self on tree: friends ask for shoot J1442.11; wisdom acquired by h. in a tree J162.

Hangman. — Compliments from the h. J1398.

Hangman's noose cures scrofula D1502.2.3.1; noose gives luck in gambling D1407.2. — Bewitched h. rope G265.8.4.1.

Hank. — Task: making many shirts from one h. of flax H1022.2.

Hans my hedgehog C758.1; im Glück J2081.1. — Ring of H. Garvel G303.9.7.3.

Happiness from eating magic pig D1359.3; during last year of life as reward Q145.0.1. — Crow searches for h. J136; deaf and dumb man can see soul taken to h. or punishment D1821.7; distance from h. to misfortune (riddle) H685; god of h. A467; land of h. *F111; money does not always bring h. J1085; otherworld land of h. F173; quest for h. H1376.6; rich man poor in h. J347.4; ruler jealous of h. prohibits games W181.7; work brings h. J21.50.

Happy couple: wife blind, husband deaf T202; otherworld where dead are healed *E481.4.1. — Apparently h. man lets another see misery of his existence U115; apparently h. woman discloses lover's skeleton U115.1; men too h.: life becomes difficult L482; men too h.: hence pain A1346.2.3; soldier dies h. at enemy's rout P461.2.

Harbinger. — King's face as h. of evil N119.3.

Hard. — Cliffs become h. A968.1; punishment for h.-heartedness Q291; way to otherworld h. to find F150.1; why stones became h. A975.

Hardened clay is hard to mold J21.52.3. — Primeval earth h. A856ff.

Harder. — What is h. than stone? (riddle) H673.

Hardest. — What is the h. H637ff.; what four things are h. to hold? H659.2; what is the h. to skin? H659.15.

Hardheadedness. — Animal punished for h. A2239.8.

Hardness of heart D444.1, W155ff. — Coming neither in softness nor in h. H1054.4; faithless widow's h. repels new suitor T231.4.

Hardship. — Enduring h. as a test H1502.

Hardships. — Heathcock prefers home with h. to travel in foreign lands J215.3; heroine endures h. with menial husband L113.1.0.1.

Hardy. — Why certain tree h. A2788; why plum tree so h. A2711.6.

Hare, see also **Rabbit;** as ambassador of the moon K1716; and bride in pot escape tiger K521.11; becomes person D315.5; carries honey-covered

lion, lures animals K767; changes sex B754.1.2; deceptively strangles wolf, fox K713.3; demands equal rights for all animals J975; escapes lion in brushwood K521.10; eats stuck lion K714.9; flatters other animals, bites off their ears K1018; gets cat to gallop, escapes K562.2; with horns B15.3.4.1; and man contest in watching for leaf to fall; man wins, may eat hare A2256.1; with many friends H1558.4; makes horns of wax and poses as horned animal K1991; instructs his sons to use their eyes to advantage J61; in lion's skin gets meat from lioness K362.5; as messenger B291.3.2; outwits pursuing bear, kills her K929.13; and pig in race H625; promises to dance, escapes captors K571.1; pursued in wild hunt E501.5.5.1; raises animal army for hero B524.6; rejoices when sparrow is carried off by hawk J885.1; rides on elephant B557.11.3; runs away at creation: almost loses tail A2215.2; at third remove J1551.6; as sacrifice V12.4.7; sleeps with open eyes as defense A2461.1; told to go home J1881.2, K131.1; and tortoise race: sleeping hare K11.3; transformed to another animal D411.3; transformed to person D315.5; tricks civet into being eaten by lion K813.2; waits in vain for event J2066.8. — Alleged speaking h. K131.1.1; animals' ears like elephant's until h. bites them off A2216.7; ass thought to be h. J1754; attack on the h. J2612; cat acts as judge between sparrow and h. K815.7; charm to catch h. and monkey D1444.2; chasing h. into every trap in a high tree H1024.3; contest in enduring cold: frost and the h. H1541.1; creation of h. A1856; why h. is deceptive A2525.1; demon in form of h. F401.3.6; devil in form of a h. G303.3.3.2.3; dog chasing h., bringing it to master K135.1.2; dwarf rides on a h. F451.6.2.1; enmity between cat and h. A2281, A2494.1.3; why h. has deep-set eyes A2239.1, A2332.4.1; fairy as h. F234.1.12; fox or h.? J2671.1; friendship between h. and parrot A2493.13; giant h. B871.2.8; why h. shakes head A2474.2; helpful h. B437.4; why h. has short pair of legs A2371.2.11; lion leaves sleeping h. to follow the shepherd J321.3; why h. lives in bush A2282, A2433.3.3; man in the moon a h. A751.2; man transformed to h. D117.2; marriage to h. B601.13; moon is h. covered with silver A759.4; more timid than h. J881.1; obstacle race between deer and h. K11.9; plowing contest won by deception: h. exchanged for horse K41.1; reincarnation as h. E612.3; revenant as h. E423.2.2; skillful barber shaves running h. F665.1; soul in form of h. E731.5; why h. has short tail A2378.4.1; speaking h. B211.2.6; tame dog prefers food basin to fleeing h. J487; too cold for h. to build house in winter: must go without A2233.2.1; troll as h. G304.1.1.2; why h. is gray in summer A2411.1.4.4.1; why h. never drinks from rivers or streams A2435.3.12.1; why h. skips about A2479.2; witch in form of h. G211.2.7; witch transforms self to h. so as to suck cows D655.2.

Hare's food A2435.3.12; legs doubled up in punishment K581.2.1; magic stomach D1015.5.1. — Cause of h. hopping gait A2441.1.11; why h. ears are black *A2325.2; why h. lip is split *A2342.1; why h. nose is closed

during sowing season *A2335.2.4; quest for h. milk H1361.5; Santals eat h. entrails A1422.1.1; why ants do not live on h. back A2584.2.

Hares fearing death outrun pursuing dogs U242. — Dog alternately bites and caresses h. K2031; foxes desert h. when they foresee defeat by the eagle J682.1; king of h. B241.2.6; man lays bag by fencehole and all h. run into it X1114; two h. run into each other and are caught X1114.1; troll has h. in stable G304.3.2.4; why h. have cotton tails: deity rubs cotton on A2378.9.3; why men eat h. A1422.1.

Harem ladies recognize impostor king K1934.1. — Messenger to girl-captive in h. K1323.1.

Harlot, see **Prostitute.**

Harmful effects of meeting wild hunt E501.18ff. — Animal h. to holy person cursed A2231.7; avoiding things which are h. by nature J656; refusal to believe that friend h. P317.1.

Harming tree tabu C519.1. — Fairies h. men after enticing them F302.3.4.

Harmless. — Animal usually h. has horns B15.3.4; why animal is h. A2531ff.; magic object renders weapon h. *D1414ff.; magic writing on sword renders it h. D1414.2; salt sprinkled on fairy food renders it h. F384.1.2.

Harmony. — Philosopher instructs king on domestic h. J816.1.1; seek h. at home J1289.9.

Harness. — Plowing the field: horse and h. destroyed K1411; stretching, shrinking h. pulls wagon uphill X1785.1; trading only horse for h. J2085.1.1.

Harnessed. — Man h. and led to dance by witch G269.3; ogres h. to plow G675; wolf eats horses, is h. X1216.1.

Harp comes at owner's call D1649.2.1; music lullaby for snakes D1962.5; playing lures princess into forest K788.1. — Automatic figures on h. D1620.2.5; bride defeated in h. contest H332.1.3; fairy h. F245.1; heroine found in h. L111.2.5; hiding in h. K515.2; magic h. *D1231, (kills) D1402.22, (restores speech) D1507.7, (swine summoned out of) D1449.3; mouth-h. left by bed (token) H142; origin of h.: A1461.2.1; quest for living h. H1335; recognition through h. playing H35.1.1; sound of h. J1626; tick full of h. strings H1129.7; witch plays jew's h. K606.1.4.

Harps. — Playing nine mouth-h. at once F679.9.

Harper P427.10; as love messenger T55.9; puts mother asleep, lover visits maiden K1349.4. — Disguise as h. K1817.3; fairy h. F262.3.1, (enclosed in yew tree) F386.1.1; god as h. A465.2.0.1.

Harpies B52. — Man's food always seized by h. M435.

Harpooning contest won by deception K33. — Spirit h. sleepers F402.1.11.3.

Harrow. — Bluff: h. said to be hero's comb K1718.4; contours of land from hero driving h. A951.3; literal fool carries h. in his hand J2461.1.6; ogre induced to sit on reversed h. K1117.

Harrowing of hell V211.7.1. — Treasure to be found by man plowing with cock and h. with hen N543.2.

Hart eating earth-tree A878.3.2. — Prophetic h. B142.3.

Hartebeest. — Man transformed to h. D114.1.3; mantis transformed to h. D415.1.1.

Haruspices D1812.5.0.5.

Harvest-festival V70.4. — Farmer sleeps through h. time Q585.3; prayer for good h. V57.1; sacrifice at h. A1545.4; tabu to feast at beginning of h. C237; trolls help with h. F455.6.8.1; weeds spoil h. of rich men L482.2; why monkey has first fruits of h. A2433.3.19.1.

Harvested. — Spendthrift's uncut field already h. H586.4; why wheat must be planted one year, h. next A2793.2.1.

Harvesters. — Crow thinks h. are stealing his grain J953.7.

Harvesting contest K42; early for half crop J1932.6.

Hasty killing or condemnation *N340ff. — Avoid h. judgment J571; if you're too h. you won't arrive L148.1; over-h. toad X1862; thumbling born as result of h. wish of parents T553; too h. action forbidden C758.

Hat over eyes if ears cut off J2721. — Alleged bill-paying h. sold K111.2; boy with h. of butter X1153; burial service read into h. to prevent dead walking E431.1; captive throws his h. to lions who fight over it while he escapes K671; churchyard mould in h. prevents witchery D1385.11; devil in green clothing with h. G303.5.2.1; enemies shooting at decoy h. K631.3; fairy's sugar-loaf h. F236.3.3; giant carries man on h. brim F531.5.1.1.3; ghost scorches man's h. E542.4; holding down the h. K1252; magic h. *D1067.1; magic transportation by h. D1520.11; priest mistaken for h. J1763.1; revenant with h. of birch E422.4.1; symbolic interpretation of points on a bishop's h. H608.1; thumbling carried on h. brim F535.1.1.14.

Hats. — Fairies with belts and h. F236.3; removing h. tabu in otherworld C716; why husband and wife shall not exchange h. A1571.1.

Hatched. — Basilisk h. from cock's egg B12.1; birds h. from broken eggs repaired by skillful tailor have red line around necks F662.1.1; cobold h. from cock's egg, boar's testicle F481.0.1.1; helpful bird h. by hero B317.

Hatchel. — Man transformed to h. D257.

Hatchet. — Fairies return lost h. head F343.18; killing tiger by throwing h. into mouth K951.1.1.1.

Hatching. — Absurd ignorance concerning h. of eggs *J1902; numskull tries h. out calf from cheese J1902.2; other birds h. cuckoo's eggs A2229.5, A2431.2.1.1; task: h. boiled eggs H1023.1.

Hated. — Flight from h. husband R227.2; why animal is h. A2583.

Hateful or lovely child to be born first T548.1.1.

Hatred magically induced D1931; released among mankind A1388.1. — Husband's love becomes h. D1908.1; man pursued by h. of the gods M411.4; origin of h. A1388.

Hatter P454.
Haughtiness, punishment for Q552.19.5.
Haughty mistress makes extravagant demands of lover L431.1; punished Q4.
Hauling canoe over dead man's body causes resuscitation E607.3; enormous quantity in short time H1109.2.
Haunt. — Animal's characteristic h. A2433ff.; capture by waiting in enemy's h. K782.
Haunts of giants F531.6.2. — Devil's present h. G303.8ff.
Haunted, see also **Ghosts.** — Buildings h. by ghosts E280ff.; castle h. by demons F771.4.5; faithless lover h. by dead sweetheart E211; house h. to run owners out and leave it for servants to enjoy K336.1; husband h. by dead wife on second marriage E221.1; king's garden h. by witch H1191.2; place of great accident or misfortune h. by ghost E275; places h. by the devil G303.15ff.; staying in h. house as fear test H1411; "when Caleb comes" to h. house J1495.2; witch causes h. houses G269.5.
Hawk attacks hero's enemies B524.1.9; carries off queen's necklace, drops it by girl N698; carries man's hand F982.3; as culture hero A522.2.3; in earth-tree A878.3.4; flies away with geese on a line X1267.1; frightened at snipe's bill J2616; hard to hold by beak H659.2.1; lighting on man points out criminal B152.3; as messenger B291.1.10; persuades doves to elect him their king K815.8; as sky palace architect J2060.3; swims (lie) X1267.2; transformed to person D352.1; transformed to salmon D413.1. — Birds flee from cuckoo, who they believe will later become h. J645.1; buzzard hatched by h. ejected for fouling nest Q432.1; child with head of h. T551.3.2; creation of h. A1937; enmity between h. and hen A2494.13.10.3; flight of h. A2442.2.5; golden h. B102.1.1; why h. has forked tail A2216.5, A2378.5.2; why h. hovers over camp-fire: seeks grandmother A2275.5.2, A2471.3; helpful h. B455.4; how he would act if he were a h. J1391.4; literal fool strangles the h. J2461.1.6; man transformed to h. D152.1; reincarnation as h. E613.3; soul as h. seen in dream E732.9.
Hawks. — Food of h. A2435.4.6, A2435.6.6; why h. put heads of mice, etc. on pile of stones A2452.3; what h. are looking for A2471.7.
Hawthorn protects against witches G272.3; protects travelers D1385.23. — Fairies dance under h. trees F261.3.1.1; magic h. D950.13.
Hay fills empty lake with water D1549.3.6; transformed to horse D441.9.1; wagon and the gate J1411. — Bear on h. wagon thought to be the preacher J1762.2; coachman makes horses run by binding bundle of h. to shaft J1671; fairies dance in h. F261.3.5; fool sticks needle in h. wagon J2129.4; "painting" on the h.-cock K1013.2; selling h. which is not his K282.1; wisp of h. transformed (to bridge) D451.5.7, (to horse) D441.9.1.
Haymakers. — Fairies give h. dinner F343.17.
Hayrick. — Man and bear in h. B855.

Haystack asked to wipe dirty shoe Z41.7.1. — Drunkards war on h. X818; man throws carriage, horses, driver on h. F624.3.1.

Hazel rod kills snake D1402.10.2; — Ash becomes h. D451.1.1; goat who wouldn't leave h. bush Z39.1.1; magic h. D950.1.

Hazelcock's body made smaller *A2302.2.

Hazelnuts. — Magic h. D985.3; quest for the h. of ay, ay, ay H1377.3.

Head buried one place, body another V61.4; of corpse thrown on water to prevent return E431.9.1; cut off (to cure snakebite) X372.2, (and hung on tree) Q421.1.1, (and successfully replaced) E783.1, (by unseen sword in forest) F812.5; of decapitated person replaced backwards E12.2; falls off for lying to saint Q551.8.5; of giant F531.1.2ff.; is king of the body J1289.19; of murdered child becomes sun A1277.3; of murdered man displayed before his own house S139.2.1; retains life after being cut off *E783; separated from body to prevent return E431.7.2.1; shattered for breaking tabu C948.8; of slain man must not be moved C541.2; split as punishment Q451.13; taken off, other punishments not necessary J1293.2; transferred from one man to another *D711.1.1; used as ball S139.2.2.4.1; wagered N2.3.1; of beheaded witch mends if rubbed with salt G223. — Abbess puts priest's trousers on her h. K1273; amputated h. asks for drink E541.4.1; animal frightened by his own reflected h. K1715.1.1; animal with h. of bone B15.1.3; animal with one h., two bodies, six legs B15.7.11; animal unusual as to his h. B15.1; why some animals continually shake h. A2474; apple shot from man's h. F661.3; bad women because of h. exchanged with devil A1371.1; beautification by decapitation and replacement of h. *D1865.1; beast with human h. and shape of smith's bellows B92: beheaded man's h. laid at feet to prevent return E431.7; beheaded simpleton's h. replaced backwards (thus learns fear of death) J27; bird with golden h. B101.1; bird flies on h. of dupe's child K946; birth from person's h. T541.4; blindness cured by striking h. on tree F952.4; bringing enemy's h. as task H335.4.1; calf's h. transformed to death's h. D457.3; calf's h. in murderer's hand turns to corpse's h. Q551.3.3; chaste woman has conqueror cut off her h. T325.1; cuckold's knife cannot carve boar's h. H425.1; curse: h. to split in seven M431.9; cut-off h. prophesies D1311.8.2; cutting off h. at girl's desire H333.1; deity with animal's h. A131.3ff.; demon with pointed h. G342; devil in dragon's h. on a shield G303.8.10; devil's h. G303.4.1ff.; disenchantment by decapitation and replacement of h. D711.1; dog with human h. E423.1.1.2.2; dwarf has small body and large h. F451.2.1.3; fairies with gold crowns on h. F236.4; false dragon-h. proof H105.1.1; fate written on h. M302.2.1; fountain where saint's h. cut off D925.1.2; getting calf's h. out of pot J2113; ghost carries h. under arm E422.1.1.4; ghost as h. E422.1.11.2; ghost's h. downward unless summoned by king E389.1; ghost's flying h. attacks slayer E261.1.1; gigantic h. F531.1.2.0.1; giant thinks hammer-blow on h. is nut falling F531.5.4; god with cat's h. A131.3.1; god monstrous as to h. A123.4ff.;

goddess standing on h. supports earth A842.1; hero cuts off h. so won't be tempted by virgins T333.5; hero with deformed h. L112.3.1; hero's breath returns h. to headless horseman D1518.3; how many hairs are in the h.? H703; hanging for a thousand years h. downward over a fire of chaff Q522.6; having h. dressed before hanging J2174.3; horse's h. for extraordinary use F874; horse's magic h. D1380.3.1; human h. as weapon F839.4; indentions on rocks from h. of infant hero A972.5.1; "keep h. dry" J21.29; killing with enemy's h. D1402.23; lizard loses lawsuit: must bob his h. A2255.2; lover's h. put before adulteress at meals Q478.1.4; magic animal h. *D1011ff.; magic h. *D992, (of saint heals diseases) D1500.1.7.1.1; magic power of seeing Death at h. or foot of bed D1825.3.1; magic stone in animal's h. B722; man with bird's h. B55; man carries his h. under his arm F511.0.4; man cuts off own h. and eats it (lie) X1726.1; man with dog's h. B25.1; man without confessor like body without h. V20.1.1; man with deformed h. slays barbers K974; man so small he can put his h. through a mote in a sunbeam F535.2.4; man wagers he can run with his h. off J322.1; man's lip makes hood over h. F544.1.2; mole struck on h. as he steals fire: hence flat head A2213.5.1; monster's h. proves slaying H105.4; monster's returning h. G635.1; murder by crushing h. S116.4; murder by driving nail through h. S115.2.1; murdered man's h. causes calamity D1549.7; "never show your h. again": pot on head J2489.13; new race from stones (seeds) thrown over h. after deluge A1245.1, A1254.1; numskull gets h. caught J2131.5ff.; nut hits cock in h.: he thinks world is coming to an end (cumulative tale) Z43.3; oath taken on boy's h. H252.4; ogre monstrous as to h. G361ff.; ogre's h. cut off, hung above gate G512.1.2.1; old woman supports earth on her h. A842.2; oracular artificial h. *D1311.7.1; origin of animal's h. A2320ff.; otherworld h. emits stream F162.5.2; person consisting only of h. F501; person given animal h. D682.1; person unusual as to his h. F511ff.; person with (more than one h.) F511.0.2, (one eye in back of h.) F512.1.3; (wings on h.) F522.1; pestilence in form of h. F493.0.3.1; pieces of shattered god's h. are hills A962.8; price set on one's h. M208; prophecy: death by horse's h. M341.2.5; proud milkmaid tosses her h. and spills milk J2061.2; punishment for splitting h. and eating man's brains Q211.7; pursuit by rolling h. R261.1; "put it on my h." woman smothered J2465.7; putting h. under saint's cloak reveals reward in heaven D1329.1; question: did the man ever have a h. J2381; quest for Gorgon's h. H1332.3; reincarnation of h. as hill E649.1; resuscitation with misplaced h. *E34; revenant with half a h. E261.1.3; river flows from man's h. F715.1.4; ruler reproaches son for bringing enemy's h. W11.5.6; saint's severed h. speaks V229.22; scythe cuts man's h. off J2422; self-rolling h. D1641.7.1; self-returning h. *D1602.12, (of dragon) *B11.5.5; separable soul in hydra's h. E715.6; serpent with jewel in h. B101.7; seven tongues in a h. (riddle) H793; seven-headed witch defeated by

throwing egg at each h. G275.4; severed h. bites earth F1096.3; severed h. cannot be moved from helmet D1654.14; severed h. gives away thief J1149.8; severed h. of impious man in well causes water to become bitter part of each day F933.4; severed h. moves from place to place D1641.7; severed h. proves killing H106.2; severed h. regrows E783.2; sight of wild hunt causes swelling of h. E501.18.8; slain enemy's h. must not enter village C845.1; snake and turtle exchange h. for fangs A2247.2; soul in h. E714.3; severed h. reddens and whitens E783.3; speaking h. *D1610.5; spirit in form of horrible h. F401.5.1; spirit with half h. F401.4.1; singing h. D1615.7; standing on h. G269.26; as many stars in heaven as hairs in h. H702.2; stingy dead woman raises her h. W152.3; striking off donkey's h. to punish it J2113.1; substituted h. as execution proof K512.2.3.1; thief has his companion cut off his h. so that he may escape detection K407.1; touching chief's h. tabu C564.7; transformation by placing something on h. D596; transformation by sticking magic pin into h. D582; treasure from girl's h. D1454.8; visit to lower world h. first F109.1; walking on h. in otherworld F167.4; water falling on h. death omen J2311.1.3; weapon in h. causes sickness D2064.7; why babies have soft spots in h. A2875; why bird's h. is large A2320.5; why crab has no h. A2320.4; why mudhen's h. red A2320.3.1; why palm-rat has swollen h. A2320.7; why weaver bird's h. is small A2320.1.1; wife brings paramour husband's h. K2213.3.2.1; witch extraordinary as to h. G215.

Heads brandished to intimidate foe S139.2.2.1.6; placed on stakes for failure in performance of task H901.1, Q421.1; of slain advise hero E545.21; of slain enemies displayed P555.2.1.1; of slain piled up after battle P555.2.1; of thieves in casks cut off K312; of various people A1663. — Bridal couple's h. knocked together as they look in mirror T135.13; bringing animal h. H1154.0.1; child born with two h. T551.2; cult of h. V1.10.2; dead h. necessary to drinking C281; dwarfs with red h. and red caps F451.2.7.1; extraordinary h. act as living F1001; fatal game: putting h. in notches K865; fish with silver and gold h. B101.6; foreigners' h. exchanged with devils' A1610.1.1; giant's two h. H1174.1; goat's h. mistaken for human J1762.9; god with many h. A123.4.1; helpful vital h. N819.3; hero's dogs (horse) prevent dragon's h. from rejoining body B11.11.2; human h. in ogre's house smile, weep G461.1; indignities to h. of slain enemies S139.2.2.1; journey to Land of Men of H. only F129.1; monster with human h. on horns G361.1.1.1; mother cuts off h. of well to cure sick H583.4.3; origin of bald h. A1315.2; people in otherworld stand on their h. and pound yams with their h. F167.4; saint's bachall brings down mountain on h. of enemies D1549.4; severed h. of monster become birds E613.0.5; spirits without h. (or with h. under arms) F401.4; three h. of hair F555.5.1; trees with fruits like human h. F811.8; trees from lovers' graves resemble their h. E631.0.1.1; tree in hell made of living h. of the dead A671.2.3; troll

with many h. *G304.1.3; wild huntsmen with h. on backward E501.7.3; women adorning h. immoral below K2051.4.

Headache cure: removing eyes K1011.1; from dwarfs' cursing M424. — Bride pleads h.: groom retaliates with same plea later K2052.3; magic object cures h. D1502.1.

Headaches cured by Virgin Mary D2161.5.2.6.

Headdress. — Magic h. bears person aloft D1532.8.

Headdresses. — Live h. F827.1.

Headless animals *B15.1.1; body retains life E783.6; dog B15.1.1.1, E423.1.1.2.1, (ghostly) E521.2.2, E521.5.0.1; giant F531.1.2.1; horseman's head returned D1518.3; king, tailless tiger friends J876; ogre G361.3; person *F511.0.1; revenant *E422.1.1. — Devil in coach drawn by h. horses G303.7.3.3; fairy as h. woman F234.2.3; ghost as h. horse E423.1.3.3; magic identity of h. body D1819.3; witch in form of h. horse G211.1.1.1.

Headman. — Bonga made village h. F347.1.

Headwear, magic D1067ff.

Healed with his own medicine J1513. — Death respite until prisoner h. K551.15; dragon dips wounds in holy well, is h. B11.12.1.2; happy otherworld where dead are h. *E481.4.1; diseases h. by magic object D1500.1; saint miraculously h. V221.0.2; wounded soldiers h. by druid P427.5.1.

Healer. — Animal as h. B511; queen promises self to h. H346.1; woman fake h. marries then murders king K959.2.4.

Healer's payment: satisfaction at recovery K233.6. — Herbs grow from h. grave E631.3.

Healing, see also **Cure;** by animals B510ff.; by dwarfs F451.5.1.10; by fairies F344; pigskin B184.3.2.3; as reward Q161; sick as task H1199.2. — Accidental h. N640ff.; angel of h. A454.0.1; curse against wound's h. M431.5; every sick man practices h. H659.6.1; fairy grateful to mortal for h. F334; foolish imitation of h. J2412; giant has wound-h. balm F531.6.5.3; god of h. A454; husband attracted by wife's power of h. H151.8; life bought with promise of h. M234.4; magic h. grass D1500.1.4.1; magic h. power *D2161ff.; miraculous h. from passionate love T25; miraculous h. by saints *V221ff.; magic h. apples H1151.20; magic h. water H1151.21; man blinded in h. attempt N395; miraculous h. by Virgin V256; princess given to man for h. her H346; pseudo-magic h. objects sold K115; quest for h. (apple) H1333.3.1.5, (draught) H1324.2, (lantern) H1324.1, (water) H1321.2; saint h. enemy V441.1; sun's h. power A738.3.

Health disputes with Fortune, Intellect, Knowledge which is greatest J461.1.2; the most beloved H647.2; as most precious choice J232; as reward for drink Q145.1.1; test H1582. — Fast improves h. V73.2; magic object gives h. D1342ff.; transformation in h. D53; well-preserved brother gives h. secret H596.1.1.

Healthful. — Lies about h. atmosphere X1663.1.

Heard. — Dwarfs emigrate invisible but h. F451.9.6; soul striving to be h. E759.1.

Hearers aided by magic music D1359.3.1.1.

Hearing, see also **Overhearing;** bird cry good omen D1812.5.2.5; thunder on setting forth a good omen D1812.5.2.3. — Animal's h. A2428; contest in h. *K86; dead h. saint's bell E545.14; dragon h. child's cry B11.12.6; girl's heart breaks on h. lover kiss another F1041.1.1.2; headless persons without h. F511.0.1.2; insanity from h. strange sound D2065.2.1; magic h. D1827.1ff.; magic object affects h. D1332; not h. questions one doesn't wish to answer X441.1; person of remarkable h. F641ff.; magic object restores h. D1506; magic power of h. D1922; marvelous sensitiveness: fracture from h. man chopping wood F647.8.1; tabu: h. or listening C885.

Heart cremated to lay ghost E441.3; cut free, moves about in chest F1096.1; of dragon B11.2.9; of enemy eaten produces magic strength D1335.1.2; and liver of murderer torn out Q469.6; of man is deepest H643.1; might not stand winning mistress J2572; removed by magic D2062.1; successfully replaced E786; of unborn child renders person invisible D1361.8. — Adulteress caused unwittingly to eat lover's h. Q478.1; animal dies of broken h. F981.6; animal h. transformed D457.15; conception from eating woman's h. T511.6.1; compassionate executioner: substituted h. K512.2; death from broken h. F1041.1.1; disease to be cured by h. of monkey K961.1; disenchantment by eating enchanter's h. D763.1; doctor cures h. palpitation: stops breathing X372.1; eaten h. gives one the owner's qualities *E714.4.1; fairy replaces man's h. with h. of straw F281; giant with stone h. F531.1.6.10.1; girl's h. magically removed and fed to man draws her to him D1905.1; hardness of h. W155ff.; hound killed by tearing out its h. B17.1.2.2; impossible to burn witch's h. G275.3.2; iron bands around h. to keep it from breaking F875; key to house concealed in man's h. F1034.5.1; lamb (ass) without a h. K402, K402.3; magic bird h. *D1015.1.1, (eaten) D859.4.1; magic h. of animal *D1015.1ff.; magic human h. D997.1; magic object in whale's h. D849.5.1; man forced to eat dead father's h. goes mad G91.1; man vomits h. as punishment Q552.21; martyr with sign of cross on his h. V86.2; miser's h. found in his strong-box W153.1; monkey's h. left at home K544; monster's h. torn out F628.1.0.1; murder by hot iron through h. S112.2.1; murder by tearing out h. S139.6; parent's h. is hardest H637.1; person lives on after having h. cut free F1096.1; procuring dead husband's h. F81.1.1; pulling animal's h. out through log K952.3; remarkable h. F559.7; soul (life) in h. E714.4; spirit in h. F408.2; tabu to eat animal's h. C221.3.5; witch eats person's h. G262.2; with his whole h.: devil carries off judge M215; woman dies of broken h. after rivals kill each other T86.1.

Heart's ashes cast into river F932.7.1.

Hearts. — Ogre eats men's h. G312.6; person forced to eat relatives' h. S183.1; person of remarkable sight can see through h. of trees F642.3.1; eating of human h. as cure for insomnia D2161.4.13; power of flying from eating children's h. D2135.1.

Heartbeat. — Guilt detected by h. J1142.2.1.

Hearth abode of unpromising hero (heroine) L131; cleaned by angel D1683, V232.9; -god A411.4; extraordinary h. F893; familiar on magician's h. G225.0.5.1; fire issues from h. as man approaches H175.4; magic h. D1147; needle under h. causes death D2061.2.2.8.1; origin of domestic h. A1455.1; tabu to eat from cooking h. C219.4; water-spirits' h. of human skulls F420.2.5.

Hearths. — Stars as fires in ghosts' h. A761.4.

Hearthstones. — Bridal couple touch h. T137.2.1.

Heartlessness, see **Hardness of heart.**

Heartsease. — Why h. has red stripes A2772.3.

Heartsickness, magic D2064.0.2.

Heat and fury spread pestilence F493.4; prevents church theft D1389.2.1; produced by magic D2144.3; of saint's anger starts fire F1041.16.4; from stove without fire J1976; test H1511. — Alternate h., cold in hell A671.3.2; body with marvelous h. F686; burrowing swine h. ground B19.4.1; conception from h. of fire T535.1; contest in enduring h. H1542; contest of h. and cold D2144.2; excessive h. of otherworld beings F167.16; extraordinary body h. F593.1; god bores hole in hell to h. earth A141.3; goddess from earth's h. A119.2; holding in the h. J1942; magic cake protects from h. D1382.3; magic control of cold and h. D2144; magic h. melts enemies D2091.10; man created from h. A1262.1; person melts away from h. F1041.4; punishments by h. in hell Q566; returning from hell with h. F101.8; sun's h. dries out earth A733.5; sun's great h. A720.2; variations in sun's seasonal h. A739.4.

Heated. — Room h. by crowded corpses F686.2; souls of drowned in h. kettles in hell *E755.2.1.

Heath. — Dwarfs warm h. by underground fire F451.5.1.15.

Heathcock prefers home with hardships to travel in foreign lands J215.3. — Wedding of h. B282.15; witch as h. G211.4.3.

Heathen beats his god because of misfortune V381; city F767.1; to desert spot where saint lost tooth M364.5; king sets test for saint H527; prophesy coming of saint M364.7.2; swallowed by earth H1573.1.1. — Baptism of h. V332; conversion to Christianity because h. gods less powerful V331.1.3; covenant between h. and Israelites M201.0.2; devils dwell in h. idols G303.8.14; ground swallows h. idols F948.1; mother sells her child to h. sailors S328; punishment for taking h. wives Q243.4.

Heaven, see also **Otherworld, Paradise;** *A661; assured by burial in certain ground E754.3; connected to earth by navel string A625.2.1; and earth from egg A641.1; and earth touch each other A657.2; entered by a trick K2371.1; as God's throne A133.2.2; mother and earth father A625.1.

— Admission to h. as reward Q172; angels of death cannot bring soul to h. E754.2.2.1; animals understand language of h. B212.0.1; arrow shot to h. returns bloody F1066; banishment from h. for breaking tabu C955; bolt from h. kills animal F981.4; burning pillar reaching h. F774.2; chairs in h. H619.1; chariot from h. takes couple to sky A761.2; choice between life or h. V311.3; Christ's ascent to h. V211.9; creation of h. A610.2; cynic discusses h. J1442.8; dead and living go together to gate of h. E754.2.3; dead try to carry kettle from hell to h. A1433.0.1; deity ruler of lowest h. A307; demigods descend from h. A513.1; devil misportrays h. G303.9.7.4; devil teaches way to h. G303.9.4.6.1; devil's expulsion from h. G303.8ff.; distance from earth to h. H682.1; drinking as road to h. J1314; drunk woman thinks she's in h. X816; drunken man made to believe that he has been to h. and hell J2322; everyone buried in saint's soil to go to h. M364.11; eyes which can see h. D1820.3; fairy teaches way to h. F251.9; fairies depart to h. F388.1; fairies not good enough for h. F251.11; fairies in h. F215.1.1; fire carried from h. A1415.1.1; fire from h. F962.2, (as punishment) Q552.13; footstool thrown from h. F1037.1; gate as high as h. and huge as a mountain F776.1; gifts fallen from h. F962.0.1; ghost lives midway between h. and earth E481.5; giant with upper lip reaching h. F531.1.4.1; girls dancing in h. A661.4; giving money for those in h. J2326.1; god ascends to h. A171.0.2; god of h. A211; going to h. by holding divine elephant's tail J2133.5.2; hand from h. F1036; Hebrew as language of h. A1482.1; hero ascending to h. A566.2; heron wants no h. without snails U125.1; holy object falls from h. F962.12; how the Jews were drawn from h. X611; husband pursues fairy to h. F300.2; journey to h. *F11; journey to upper world by keeping thoughts continually on h. *F64; knight won't go to h. unless dogs there U134; land thrown down from h. A953; light as souls in h. A1412.2; lost soul given sight of h. E752.6; magic object assures going to h. D1588; magic object falls from h. D811.2; man admitted into h. but must not find fault *F13; man admitted to neither h. nor hell (becomes snipe) A1942.1, *Q565.1; man ejected from h. for folly of marrying twice T251.0.1; miser wants to enter h. with clothes on: gold sewn in W153.15; nine days' fall from h. to earth A658.1; nine nights' riding from h. to hell A658.1.1; object thrown from h. F1037; ocean the son of Earth and H. A921; peace in h. is sweetest H633.2; power of seeing whether dead go to h. or hell B161.4; priest may eat communion supper in h. J1261.2.3; promise of h. entices victim into box K714.2.1; provisions provided by messenger from h. D2105.2; quest for crown from h. H1261; rejoicing at arrival of rich man in h. E758; renouncing h. because companions not there V326; resurrected boys choose to return to h. E755.0.1; rewards in h. Q172.0.2; road to h. *F57; saint promises return from h. V229.2.13; saved soul goes to h. E754.2ff.; self-righteous tailor in h. expelled L435.3; sinner wanders between h. and earth E411.0.4; soul bound for hell given sight of h. E752.6; soul cannot enter h. till

body buried E750.0.1; soul leaves body to visit h. E721.7; souls carried to h. by doves E754.2.1; souls in h. *E755.1; storms in sixth h. A1130.2; thief tells pursuer that thief has gone to h. by way of a tree K341.9; threshing in h. H84.3; tree to h. A652.1; Two Sorrows of H. D1856.1.1; unchristened cannot enter h. E412.2.1; vision of chairs in h. V515.1.1; visions of h. V511.1; voice from h. testifies for accused H216.2; voices from h. F966; waters of h. prevented from engulfing earth A810.2.1; wife in h. by day, with husband by night E322.3; wife undertakes man's penances: also to go to h. for him? M292; wisdom from fool: h. refused J156.4.

Heavens A700—A799; break up at end of world A150ff. — Animals in h. B7; deity departs for h. A192.2.1; fairy music like that in h. F262.4; flood from deity stamping on h. A1015.3; highest world has twenty h. A651.1.0.1; magic arrow shakes h. D1549.1; man's voice shakes h. F688.1; seven h. A651.1.4; singing h. D1615.9; how many stars in the h.? H702ff.; stars as decoration for h. A763.2.

"Heaven key," origin of A2622, A2652.

Heavenly Academy F177; body as magic object D1291; books F883.1.6; help in battle D2163.2.1; hierarchy E755.1.1; lights A790ff.; maiden's magic power D1726.1; maidens not jealous T257.0.1; messenger brings food D2105.2; music caused by column under Lord's chair A661.0.2.1; voices proclaim hero's birth M311.0.4. — Ability to see h. beings D1825.3.4; artificial h. bodies F793; extraordinary behavior of h. bodies F961; looking at h. body tabu C315.2ff.; magic control of h. bodies D2149.6; magic object controls h. bodies D1546; riddles of h. distance H682ff.; skies reveal h. company F969.1; soul in form of h. body E741; worship of h. bodies V1.4.

Heavier. — Devil becomes h. G303.3.5.3.

Heaviest. — What is the h.? H645.

Heavy animal B870.1. — Giantess so h. boat sinks F531.2.13; object magically becomes h. D1687, *D2035; oath so h. it dries up stream M115.1.1; remarkably h. club F835.2.1; riddle: how h. is the earth? H691.2; sword so h. that hero must take drink of strength before swinging it F833.1.

Hebrew as language (of angels) V249.2.1, (of heaven) A1482.1. — Host wants to learn H. even at risk of forgetting his own language J344.2.

Hebrews. — Wisdom from H. J192.4.

Hebrides as otherworld F134.1.

Hecate as leader of wild hunt E501.1.8.3.

Hedge to catch sheep's wool J2060.2; to keep in moonlight J1796.1; protects person in magic sleep D1967.1. — Besieger scatters beads in protecting h. K2367; druid's h. prevents attack D1381.1; father puts h. around field H583.2.3; jumping over h. as suitor test H331.1.3.1; magic h. D945.

Hedgehog builds castle B191.5; and crab jump from boat after turtle

J2133.11; forces snake to suck out poison from raja B511.1.3; jumps into tiger's mouth L315.13. — Hans my H. C758.1; helpful h. B449.1; man-h. B29.8; marriage to person in h. form B641.5; revenant as h. E423.2.4; weaver prefers master with one h. J229.8.1; why h. draws himself up A2479.4; witch as h. G211.2.9.

Hedgehog's cry A2426.1.4; skin reward for good deed A2220.1, A2311.4.

Heeding not the past J311; persuasive person or thing forbidden *C810ff.

Heel. — Achilles' h. Z311; boring hole in h. as punishment Q451.2.0.2; cutting off h.-bone S162.4; girl hacks off her h. to get shoe on J2131.3.1.

Heels. — Devil has no h. G303.4.5.7; giant with h. in front F531.1.3.2.

He-goat, see also **Goat.** — Devil speaks with voice of h. G303.4.7; man transformed to h. D134.1; why h. has shaggy legs A2371.2.8.

He-goats. — Devil drives six h. G303.7.7.

Heidrun A661.1.0.2, B19.7.

Heifer as sacrifice V12.4.4.1.1.

Heifers impregnated by supernatural bull T539.4.

Height. — Bat rescues man from h. B542.1.2; curse given from a h. M413.1; ghost's strength waxes and wanes with h. of fire *D1836.1; insanity of princess dependent on h. of fire D2065.4; magic staves scale precipitous h. D1539.3.

Heightening. — Magic h. of mountain D2152.4.

Heimkehrsage N681.

Heir, see also **Inheritance;** to king finding bow, arrow D1812.5.2.9; of Linne J21.15, J1853.1.1. — Bargain with devil for h. M219.1; deceptive report of birth of h. K1847.1.1; first man to arrive after king's death to be h. P17.1; false h. K1923; impostor poses as h. K1938; marriage for a night to insure h. T156.1; miser appoints self his own h. W153.8; pretending to be corpse's h. K451.5; prophecy: birth of h. M369.7.2; tasks to determine king's h. H921.1; test to determine h. H1581; young h. too frank in celebrating his father's death J2358.

Heirs. — Magic object acquired by acting as umpire for fighting h. *D832; murderer punished: male h. die Q211.9.1; quarreling h. destroy entire property J2129.2.

Held, see also **Holding.** — Molten coin h. in devil's mouth G303.4.8.2; mountain h. up by strong man F623; person h. fast by magic object D1411, D1413ff.; ship h. back by strong man F637.

Hell, see also **Lower World, Underworld;** *A671ff.; -hounds accompany soul to lower world E752.5; as a monastery V118.0.1. — Account of punishments prepared in h. brings about repentance J172; artificial paradise and h. to punish and reward F705; beggar frightens lawyer into giving by telling him of all the lawyers in h. X312; broad path to h. F95.2; Christ's descent to h. V211.7; contacts on journey to h. tabu C542.1; creation of h. A610.2; dead try to carry kettle from h. to heaven A1433.0.1; death on beholding h. F1041.1.8; demons plaguing

souls in h. E752.1.2.1; descent to h. *F81; descent into h. to learn future M302.3; description of h. dissuades from suicide J628; devil abducts fiddler for h. G303.9.5.8; devil banished to h. A106.2.1; devil dies when he is fastened in door of h. by his beard G303.17.3.2; devil in h. G303.8.3; devil paints h. in glowing terms G303.9.7.4; devil retreats into h. amid thunder and lightning G303.17.2.5; devil's chair in h. made from thrown-away nail pairings G303.25.5; dragons live in h. B11.3.6; dream of all parsons in h. X438; drunken man made to believe that he has been to heaven and h. J2322; dwarf conducts shepherd to h. to collect debt from nobleman F451.5.1.14; eating in h. forbidden C211.2.2; fairies not bad enough for h. F251.11; fiddler in h. breaks strings, must return to earth for repair K606.1.3; god bores hole in h. to heat earth A141.3; hot weather from hole bored in h. A1137; husband chooses to go to h. rather than join shrewish wife in heaven T251.1.2.1; icy h. E481.7, E755.2.5; Jews drawn from heaven by clothes auction in h. X611; journeying to h. for receipt from judge J1289.11; lawyers punished in h. P422.1; looking into the pots in h. forbidden *C325; magic learned in h. D1721.1.1; man admitted to neither heaven nor h. A1942.1, *Q565; man in cold consoles himself thinking of rich men in h. J883.2; man in h. bargains about shrewish wife T251.1.2.2; masses release souls from h. V42; why no millers in h. X213; nine nights' riding from heaven to h. A658.1.1; parents descend to h. instead of sons P241; person from h. stresses religion's importance E367.1; power of seeing whether dead go to heaven or h. B161.4; punishments in h. *Q560ff.; quest to h. H1270ff., (for magic objects) D859.2; relieving souls in h. forbidden C741; release from h. as reward Q174; respite from h. Q560.2; saint's bachall overcomes beast in h. D1400.1.12.1; Satan created from h. fire G303.1.3.5; Satan punished in h. G303.17.3.5; smith punished in h. P447.4; soul leaves body to visit h. E721.7; souls in h. *E755.2ff.; spirit in h. must bathe people endlessly Q501.9; tailor punished in h. P441.3; threat to build a church in h. K1781; three things lead to h. Z71.1.4; twilight reflects fires of h. A1179.1.1; usurer punished in h. Q273.1; visions of h. V511.2; why no weavers in h. X251.1; witches punished in h. G275.11; woman satirists punished in h. M402.1.1.

Hells. — Series of h. E755.2.8.

Helldiver. — Why h. has flat stern A2356.2.10.

Hellebore, origin of A2662.

Helmet left for woman to quarrel with J552.4; shrieks D1610.24.2. — Bowl mistaken for h. J1772.5; child born wearing h. T552.5.1; magic h. D838.8, *D1101.4, (prevents baldness) D1389.8, (unpierceable) D1381.10.3; severed head cannot be moved from h. D1654.14.

Help in performing tasks H970ff.; in suitor tests F601.2; in wooing T66. — Animals h. man in contest K2; call for h. repeated as song J2417.1; child promised to devil for h. on road with broken wagon S225; devil's h. to man with robberies M212; devil called on for h. but man excuses

himself C12.1; dwarfs seek human h. F451.5.23; girl makes toilet and calls h. K551.5; luring victim by feigning need of h. K833; magic h. from falling D2166; man called for h. by animal B383; master's h. in theft J2136.5.6.1; person being robbed calls h. K432; plant blessed for h. at Jesus' birth A2711.1; refusal to accept h. until stories told P331; refusing h. to woman tabu C686.1; revealing animal's h. tabu C427; spirits' h. to mortal F403.2; spying on secret h. of angels forbidden C51.4.2; stealing from ogre a h. to friendly king G610.2; wise and foolish wish: h. in whatever one is doing J2073.1.1.

Helped. — Elder brother h. by youngest L31; man h. by animal to wealth and greatness *B580ff.; mother h. by monster child T550.1; mortal h. with labor by fairy F346; pretty sister h. by ugly L145.1; suitor h. with tasks by bride H335.0.1.

Helper in hiding treasure killed N595; steals object of quest K2036; summoned by calling his name D2074.2.4.3. — Angel as h. in battle V232; devil as h. *G303.22ff., (of robber refuses to let women's ornaments be stolen) M212.1; eating animal h. forbidden C221.2.1; foster father as h. P271.5; foster mother as h. P272.2; giant becomes victor's h. G510.3; looking at old woman h. as she eats forbidden C312.2.2; magic h. brings girl to hero's bed K1336; magic object summons h. D1421ff.; mother's brother as h. P293.2; ogre's relative as h. G530ff.; spirit in bottle as h. F403.2.2.4; sympathetic h. robbed K345; trickster poses as h. and eats woman's stored provisions K1983; wild man released from captivity as h. of hero G671; witch as h. G284.

Helpers *N800—N899; on quest H1233. — Deceptive eating (drinking) contest: relative h. K81.2, K82.2; demon's h. G302.8; race won by deception: relative h. *K11.1; succession of h. on quest H1235.

Helpful animal aids fugitives R243; animals B300—B349, K2; animals lost in wager N2.4; deeds of brownie F482.5.4; dwarfs F451.5.1; mountain-men F460.4.2ff.; underground spirit F450.1. — Attention drawn by h. animal's theft of food from wedding table: recognition follows H151.2; grains sorted by h. ants H1091.1; kinds of h. animals B400—B499; magic object found on grave of slain h. animal D842.3; magic strength from h. animal D1834; rescue from ogre by h. animals G552; services of h. animals B500—B599; stolen magic object stolen back by h. cat and dog *D882.1.1; tasks performed by h. forest spirits H973; transformation to act as h. animal D659.4; transformation by h. animals D684; treasure found in slain h. animal B100.1; witch overcome by h. dogs of hero G275.2.

Helpfulness. — Animal characteristics reward for h. A2223.

Helping. — Brothers h. each other P251.5.1; god as human h. men E605.2; gods h. those who help themselves J1034; mortals h. fairies F394; thieves not h. each other J2136.5.8; trolls h. men F455.6.8.

Helpless. — Why children are h. for so long A1361; magic object renders

person h. *D1410ff.; person or thing rendered h. D2072ff.; thief rendered h. by magic *K422.

Helplessness. — Victim enticed into voluntary captivity or h. K710ff.

Hemp. — Fairies turn h. into horses F241.1.7; magic h.-seed *D971.2; origin of h. A2684.2; swallow and h.-seed J621.1.

Hen, see also **Chicken;** complains that man eats her, but she eats ant U21.1; hitched to wagon B558.3; lays egg, mouse breaks it, etc. Z39.5; put in witch's hair to scratch while maid escapes G276.1. — Automatic h. and chickens of gold D1620.2.2; capon and h. J1269.6; cat offers to act as doctor for cock and h. K2061.7; cock and h. build pyre B599.1; cumulative tale (master to kill h.) Z32.4, (death of the little h.) Z32.2; dwarf with body like tailless h. F451.2.1.2; enemies of h. A2494.13.10, A2494.5.1, A2494.13.10.1; fox feigning illness admitted to h.-roost and kills hens K828.2; fox had rather meet one h. than fifty women J488; friendship of h. (and sparrow) A2493.34.1, (and duck) A2493.34; funeral procession of h. (cumulative tale) Z32.1; man honored above God: the dead h. J2215.3; long nose used as h. roost F543.1.2; numskull tries to wash black h. white J1909.6; overfed h. stops laying J1901.1; prayer over underdone h. J1342; prophetic h. B143.0.5; revenant as h. E423.3.6; soul in form of h. E732.3; swallow advises h. against hatching out serpent's eggs J622.1.1; treasure to be found by man who plows with cock and harrows with h. N543.2; wedding of cock and h. B282.21; why h. does not know how to steal A2455.4; why h. has no teeth A2345.8; why h. scratches in ground A2477.2; witch in form of h. G211.3.1.

Hens in mourning J1886. — Roast h. fly, heads to sky, tails to ground (lie) X1208.2.

Heptads P541.1.

Herald for chief's troop tabu C564.2.

Heralding. — Animal punished for not h. dawn A2236.5.

Herb, see also **Plant;** bath produces love D1355.17. — Magic h. *D965, (renders invisible) D1361.11, (saves girl from devil) G303.12.5.6; man made from h. A1256; quest for extraordinary h. H1333.2.3.

Herbs in ears as protection D1385.2.1; grow from healer's grave E631.3; as perfume F817.3. — Charm renders medicinal h. efficacious D1577.1; dwarfs know h. F451.3.12.1; magic food from h. D1030.3; magic h. D978; power in words, h., and stones J1581.2; snake heals mutilated maiden with magic h. B511.1.2; tabu to eat forbidden h. C224.2.

Hercules B11.11; fights with Death and rescues Alcestis R185; spins for his beloved K1214. — Bow and arrow of H. D1400.1.4.5; pillars of H. A984.

Herd which came from heaven B19.6; of cattle put into magic cup D491.1.1; of cattle transformed to wolves D412.2.1. — Buffalo h. aids trickster's theft K335.0.13; capturing deer from h. watched by giant (task) H1154.2; keeping four dogs in a h. (task) H1112.1; magic circle keeps h. enclosed D1446.5; magic compensates for loss of h. D859.6;

recognition of own cow in h. of twenty thousand H163; redheaded, white-starred h. C316.1.

Herds of sea monsters G308.3. — Fairies have h. of deer F241.5; herdsman threatens invasion with enormous h. K1784; Huldra tending h. F460.2.11; mountain-men drive off man's h. F460.4.4.6; why certain animals go in h. A2492; witches drive h. of deer G249.1.

Herding rabbits (task) H1112; wild animals B845. — Giant with tree for h.-stick G152.1; household spirit h. sheep F488.1; mountain-men as h.-girls' lovers F460.4.1.1.

Herdsboy. — Devil makes h. a priest M216.2.

Herdsman disguises as abbot and answers questions H561.2; to learn art of love T4.1; neglects his she-goats in favor of wild-goats J345.1; rears abandoned child S351.2; rescues abandoned child R131.3; slaughters animals entrusted to him K346.2; threatens invasion with enormous herds K1784. — Animal as h. B576.3; ascetic becomes h. V462.11; disguise as h. K1816.6; fairy as h. F271.6; giant h. G152, F531.6.17.5; poem taught to h. E377.1; remarkable h. F679.1; treacherous h. K2255; woodpecker from devil's h. transformed A1957.1.

Herdsmen give quest directions H1232.1. — Wild hunt powerless against h. E501.17.1.1.

Here as center of the earth H681.3.2.

Heresy punished Q225.1.

Heretic becomes tongue-tied Q551.7.1.1; loses debate with Christian V351.1; worried to death by fly Q415.8. — Devil saves h. from fire G303.22.13; wise man beats h. in debate K3.4.

Heretics V320ff.; repulsed by saint's sword D1400.1.4.1.1. — Demons burn h. at stake Q414.0.8.1.

Heritage, see **Inheritance.**

Herla as wild huntsman E501.1.7.1.

Hermaphrodite F547.2.

Hermaphroditic creator A12.

Hermes distributes wit L301.

Hermit, see also **Anchorite;** P426.2; asks for and receives princess's hand V316.1; curses, men die M411.8.2; explains anger a sin J153.2; fasting to death for fame E754.4; as helper N843; kills his own father, supposing him to be the devil K943; leaving his cell to become robber falls and breaks his neck Q226.1; having rebuked youth falls himself when exposed to the same sin U231; rescues abandoned child R131.10; unsuccessfully tempted by prostitute T331; wins argument with unbeliever V351.2. — Angel ceases to appear to self-righteous h. Q553.2; angel takes h. with him and does many seemingly unjust things J225.0.1; boys rescued from beasts by h. R169.2; chain tale: h. must get cat, cow, etc. Z49.12; devil as h. G303.3.1.8.1; devils leave h. who turns other cheek when struck G303.16.15; disappointed lover turns h. T93.2; dragon guards food of h. B11.6.5; "holy" h. surprised in amorous intrigue K2064; hut of h. at

border of otherworld F147.2; hyena leads h. from wilderness B380.1; magic power of h. *D1713; man becomes h. (after wife's death) T211.5, (when he realizes selfishness of his beloved's love) V472.1; nurse disguised as h. K1837.3; reward for austerities of h. Q34; saint as h. V226; self-righteous h. must do penance L435.1; three sins of the h. J485; woman disguised as h. R131.10.1.

Hero and Leander T83.

Hero A500—A599; abducted by loving witch R10.4; accidentally uses poisoned bath N332.1.1; assigns bride to another T141.3; born simultaneously with Christ T589.7.2; born by splitting mother's womb T584.7; buried as unknown in foreign country V69.2; catches hurled spear, kills serpent N654; contests with demons, using fighting animals B524.1.11; cursed to restlessness M455.1; eloping with king's fiancée treacherously slain K929.8; fights with fists alone J246.2; flies off on bird feathers B540.1; as giant's goatherd G462.1; goes north to fight trolls H945.2; granted wish to impregnate princess B375.1.1; as helper N838; kept from battle lest he be slain M341.2.18.1; killed fighting uncle P293.3; killed by ogre's medicines G347; kills hostile hound B17.1.2.2.1; kills ogress, wins her daughter G512.0.3; kills trouble-making strong men G512.0.1; kills witch G275.8; learns name only at first adventure J1730.1, T617.2; leaves bedmate treasure keys for son T645.4; licked by deer mother B635.3.1; locked up while father murdered R54; makes sun and moon from tree A717; as monster L112.1; not to swim in lake C615.2; overcomes devastating animal G510.4; overcomes giant lion B16.2.3; overcomes giant wolf B16.2.4; overcomes otherworld ruler F176; with rakshasi blood defeats rakshasa G369.1.2; rebuked by father P233.2; refuses to slay charioteers, women, or physicians W11.5.12; rescued by friend R169.5; rescued by his lady R161.0.1; rescues children from giant G551.3.1; requested to exhibit figure T55.6.1; returning from quest sent upon another T1241.1; searches for queen leaving message H1229.2; seeks his equal H1381.5; spared for his beauty F1088.1; spits twice at wife in recognition H186; substitutes false bride for father, then kills father K1094.1; takes fairy's wife F302.4.3; undertakes quest for vengeance H1228; unharmed by coiling serpent F1088.2; wins demon contest, disenchanted D785.1. — Abandoned daughter's son becomes h. S371; curse: h. not to stand sight of blood M438.2; destined h. N552.1, Z254; disagreeable tasks set h. H931.2; dragon saves h., rescues him from prison B11.6.1.2; eagle carries h. to safety D659.4.3; fairy rescues h. from battle F302.9; falsely accused h. sent on dangerous mission K2102; fly helps h. select weapons D659.14; gods prophesy about h. M301.16; gravel rises as h. enters lake F934.1; historic or romantic h. as leader of wild hunt E501.1.7; hospitality keeps h. away too long, wife abducted N391.0.1; lie: h. responsible for topography X958; lowly h. marries princess L101; magic animal used by h. in contest B195; magic helps h. win princess D1426.0.1; magic

wind transports h. D1524.9; mare brings h. back from land of no return F129.5.1; not laughing until h. arrives M151.7; primeval h. moves islands into their present position A955.3.2.1; prophecy: h. will be invincible M312.9; prophecy: h. to die early if wins fame M365.1; princess married to lowly h. Q485.1; rat digs passage to girl's chamber for h. B582.2.2; semi-divine h. granted free access to men's wives A591; shepherd as h. P412.1; star indicates location of newborn h. D1314.13; supernatural wives carry off h. F174; topographical features caused by experiences of primitive h. A901; transformation to protect h. D651.5; trees bear first buds to commemorate reign of primitive h. A2771.5; unpromising h. L100—L199, (as rescuer) R169.10, (last to try task) H991; ungrateful h. kills helpful animal B336; woman angers h., begs mercy for deer W133.2; wounded h. sheltered in peasant's house P411.3.

Hero's body taken to fairyland F323; career prophecy for baby M311.0.1; coming prophesied M394; corpse eaten in ritual G13.1; cross-eyes miraculously straightened F959.2; wife rescued R169.5.1. — Calamities at h. birth T583.2; crows announce h. coming to otherworld B143.0.8.1; disguised h. golden hair discovered H151.13; dwarf forced to do h. demands F451.3.2.1.1; dying h. request M257.1; earthquake at h. return F960.9; extraordinary occurrences at h. death F960.2; extraordinary phenomena at h. birth F960.1.2; giant shaves h. head, befouls it F531.5.12; hills from h striking earth A962.7; hills are loads from h. shoulders A962.10; lakes commemorate event in h. life A920.1.4; light around h. head F969.3.2; magic use of h. name D1766.7.2; man created from h. genitals A1263.6; milk drunk from h. skull gives strength M316; no sunrise at h. death F965.2.1; prophecy: h. birth at certain time M311.0.2; star signifies h. birth E741.1.1.2.

Heroes *Z200—Z299; dislike to kill sleeping people K959.2.2; seek greatest H1395. — Biblical h. as wise men J191.2; landing of returning h. prophesied M369.6; prophecies concerning fate of h. in battle M356.1.2; tabus of h. C566ff.; transformation to test h. D645.

Herodias as leader of wild hunt E501.1.8.1.

Heroine addresses groom as "tiger's son" H151.15. — Foundling h. L111.2; lowly h. marries prince (king) L162; menial h. *L113; orphan h. L111.4.2; tree bends only to h. D1648.1.1; unpromising h. L100—L199.

Heroism W33.

Heron as messenger B291.1.7; wants snails in heaven U125.1. — Ape pretends to louse h., but plucks out his feathers K874.1; color of h. A2218, A2411.2.5.2; falcon and h. eaten by wild boar recovered alive from his belly X1723.2; friendship between turtle and h. A2493.12; helpful h. B463.2; reincarnation as h. E613.9; ungrateful ape plucks feathers of rescuing h. W154.5.1.3; why h. has no nest A2431.2.2.

Heron's. — Crab cuts h. neck J631; hearing h. cry good omen D1812.5.2.5.2.

Herring as king of fishes B243.1.1.

Herring's bad odor A2416.7; eyes A2332.1.3, A2332.5.8.
Hesitation spoils lovers' rendezvous T35.4. — Disastrous h. J2183.
Hesperides. — Magic apple from garden of the H. D981.1.1.
Hewing way into house as obedience test H1557.5; way from prison R211.5.
Hibernating animals A2481. — Stork is man while h. in Egypt B775.
Hibichenstein associated with dwarfs F451.3.8.1, F451.4.4.1, F451.6.12.
Hidden fruit accidentally poisoned N332.7; paramour taken to own wife K1216; person sees robbers' treasure K439.10; soul (life) E712; wolf gives himself away by talking J2351.2. — Abandoned wife h. under a tub S445; bride h. in fairyland F322.4; children h. to avoid their execution (death) K515.1; children h. from murderous mother R153.2.1; culture hero h. A511.2.3; devil h. in corpse G303.8.15; dream shows where stolen girl h. D1810.8.2.1; eavesdropping wife h. in bushes killed unwittingly by husband N322.2; eyes h. as doctor passes graveyard P424.1; first husband kept h. A1279.1; fugitive magically h. by tree R311.1; genitals h. in body F547.3.5; girl h. by her hair spread on ground F555.3.1.1; hero h. and ogre deceived by his wife (daughter) G532; magic object tells where it is h. D1612.4; magic storm protects h. children D1393.3; magic wand locates h. treasure *D1314.2; monkeys from children h. by Eve A1861.1; paramour successfully h. from husband K1521; quest for h. princess H1381.3.7; rescuer h. by girl R182; return from dead to reveal h. treasure E371; riddle solved with aid of h. informant H573.1; robbers frightened from goods by h. man K335.1.6; sham wise man rewarded for finding horse he has h. K1956.2; sign over h. treasure "Here it is" changed to "Here it is not" J2091.1; suitor test: finding object h. by princess H322.1; sun h. at night A722.6; treasure to be found by hand that has h. it N543.1; treasure h. under the water N513; underworld people from children h. from God by Eve *F251.4; wisdom of h. old man saves kingdom J151.1; woman h. from lover R53.2.
Hide. — Air-castle: to sell h. of sleeping deer J2061.3; alleged oracular horse-h. K114.1.1; deceptive land purchase: ox-h. measure K185.1; devil writes down names of men on h. in church G303.24.1.3; future learned by sitting on h. D1812.3.1; ground opens and swallows h. F948.2; hero sewed up in animal h. carried by bird K1861.1; proud h. humbled J1476; rhinoceros exchanges his red h. for hippopotamus's black A2247.3; servant must keep horns and h. of slain cattle P622.
Hides. — Buffalo and cow exchange h.: hence bad fitting h. A2247.1; cows killed for their h. when large price reported K941.1; fresh h. spread on grass (girl slips up and is deflowered) K1339.1, (enemy slips and falls) K2352.1.
Hide-and-seek as bride contest H375.1. — Deceptive h. game K869.2.
Hiding in bag in order to be carried K1892.1; behind hero to trick enemy F601.4.1; in food in order to eat it K371; from ghosts E434.1,

E434.2; iron tabu C899.1; meat in clothing J1562.3; place speaks and betrays hider D1612.3. — Animals h. boy in belly to protect him B529.1; animal h. sun, causes eclipse A737.6; capture by h. (in foot baskets) K758, (in hollow tree) K763, (under screen) K752; chaste wife deceives suitors by h. them one at a time K1218.1; confederate h. fugitive K649.1; cuckold husband h. K1514.4.2; deception by h. weapons K818.4; devil gets into ark by h. in shadow of Noah's wife G303.23.1; devil h. in people's clothes G303.6.2.12; disenchantment by h. skin (covering) D721.2; dumbness as punishment for h. children Q451.3.1; entrance into woman's (man's) room by h. in chest K1342; escape by h. K515; foolishness of premature coming out of h. J582; god h. from sun A179.8; husband h. to kill paramour K1561.1; knockers h. miners' tools F456.1.2.1.2; king h. in ditch during battle P12.5.1; man in h.-box bought by girl's father K1342.1.1; marooned man h. himself in ogre's clothes outwits him K1616.2; men h. to conceal sins J1738.8; men h. from world-fire renew race A1038; moon h. her star children A764.1.2; nun hidden by abbess from pursuing knight betrays her own h. place to him V465.1.2.1; parts of body as h. place F1034.3ff.; prince first sees heroine as she comes forth from her h. box N712; revealing h. place to evil spirits J2367; secrets of animals accidentally overheard from tree h. place N451.1; spirit captured by h. stick and leg-wrappers F405.13; spirit h. articles F473.2.2; suitor test: h. from princess H321; sun h. A734; thumbling h. in small place F535.1.1.10; woman h. in wood stick D1393.1.1.

Hideous, see also **Ugly;** food at devils' feast G303.25.14.1; giant F531.1.0.2; husband of first parents A1279.1; man married to beautiful woman T268; person magically makes self seem beautiful D2031.4; youth becomes beautiful D682.4.2. — Devil in h. form G303.3.0.1; fairy in h. form F234.2.2; father with handsome son and h. daughter J244.1; magic herbs render h. D1337.2.2; magic object makes beautiful or h. *D1337ff.; man becomes h. D52.1; man grateful not h. as toad W27.1; trolls h. F455.2.2.

Hideousness. — Magic h. *D1870ff.

Hierarchy of gods A161; of heavens E755.1.1; of worlds A651.

High-born recognize equal rank J814.3; wages bring expensive living J342. — Building too h. a tower forbidden *C771.1; extraordinary effect of h. flight F1021.2ff.; gate as h. as heavens and huge as a mountain F776.1; horse jumps over h. wall F989.1; origin of h. sea waves A925.1; poor man wants h. office: made cook L427; short magistrate wears h. helmet X142.4; tree with coiling leaves three thousand miles h. F811.2.3.1; well shoots up h. F718.11; wolf tries to entice goat down from h. place K2061.4.

Highest ranking man in land to be sacrificed for good crops S263.1. — Deceptive wager: whose horse will jump h. K264.1; what is h. (riddle) H642.

Highway. — Do not leave h. (counsel proved wise by experience) J21.5; everything on h. belongs to public J1511.14.

Highwayman, see also **Robber, Thief.** — Boasting coward shown up by wife who masks as h. and robs him K1837.1.

Hildebrand, old K1556.

Hill, see also **Mountain;** lets fugitives pass D1552.8. — Captivity in hollow h. R45; carrying load up h. to roll it down J2165; changeling left on h. and thus banished F321.1.4.4; fairies' room in h. F221.3; giant builds h. home F531.6.6.2; giant thought to be a h. J1769.1; habitable h. F721.2; hero abandoned on high h. K1931.7; hero still alive in hollow h. A571.1; home of the gods inside of h. A151.1.1; illusory animal shapes on h-tops K1886.6; money left on h. to repay helpful mountain-men F460.4.2.2; otherworld under h. F141.0.2; reincarnation of head as h. E649.1; stove runs over h. D1641.3; strong man flattens h. F626.1; wild hunt appears by h. or mountain E501.12.5; wild hunt goes several times around a h. E501.14.4.

Hills from flapping of primeval bird A961.1; because sky asked earth to wrinkle up its feet A969.4. — Abode of dead in h. E481.3.1; helpful spirit warriors dwell in rocks and h. F450.1.1; king's seat on h. P14.10; mountains and h. from hero's angry striking of earth A962.7; primeval sea rolls back, leaves h. bare A816.3; trolls (fairies) live in range of h. F214; weeping h. F801.1; why it rains in h. A1131.0.2.

Hillside animal: two legs short X1381.

Himself. — Cursing h. M411.0.1; unable to hit man h., enemy kills foster brother P273.3; wooing emissary wins love for h. T51.1.

Hind, see also **Deer;** flees before the hounds U121.2. — Adventures from pursuing enchanted h. N774; horns of h. as snakebite antidote D1515.4.3; seeking h. seen in the woods ten years before (maiden) H586.2.1.

Hindmost. — Devil takes the h. G303.19.2.

Hindu drinks from Mohammedan's vessel V383.2.

Hindus. — Origin of H. A1611.6; why English more powerful than H. A1689.11.1.

Hinduism. — Absurdity of trying to convert king to H. J1536.2.

Hints. — Recognition from h. dropped by heroine as menial H151.5.

Hippogriff B42.1.

Hippopotamus. — Color of h. A2247.3, A2411.1.6.2; creation of h. A1872; giant h. B871.2.4; helpful h. B443.6; singing h. B214.1.11.

Hired men sing about bad food J1341.11. — Devil h. out as laborer G303.9.3.

Hireling deceives man J1114.1.

History. — Bird summarizes h. B122.6; recognition by telling life h. H11.1; temper lost from reading h. W185.3.

Hitched. — Horses h. both before and behind the wagon in otherworld F171.6.4.

Hitchhiker. — Ghost as vanishing h. E332.3.3.1.

Hitching-ring. — Strangers entertained by family to whose h. they happen to tie their horses P328.

Hitter. — Lie: remarkable h. X945.

Hive. See **Bee-hive.**

Hoarded game released A1421; gold stolen by spying K322; plants released A1423.0.1; seeds A1425.0.1.

Hobgoblin *F470ff.

Hobson's choice J201.

Hoe. — Bluff: plow as hero's h. K1718.5; magic h. *D1204; reincarnation of feet into h. E649.3; reincarnation of back into h. handle E649.3.1; self-digging h. D1601.16.1.

Hog, see also **Pig;** belongs to whichever place he goes of his own accord J1179.2; with broken leg keeps pea supply secret W151.6; goes to bath but wallows in the mud U123; with giant rib B871.1.2.1.1; good dead but not living H841.2; locked in church all week by mistake X415; refuses food from excommunicated men B259.3; rib as fairy gift F343.16.1; as sacrifice V12.4.3.1; with silver bristles H355.2; taken to roof to graze J1904.1; tired of his daily food W128.1; in Valhalla gives meat A661.1.0.3. — Bad women from transformed h. and goose A1371.3; creation of h. A1871, (incomplete since God has to go to a fire: cause of hog's round snout) A2286.1.1; devil rides on h., drives another G303.7.6; dog and h. dispute over their children P243.1; why h. has evil spirit A2287.1, A2523.1; why h. has good flesh A2221.1, A2381.1; fish as devil's h. G303.25.15.1; foolish bargain: horse for cow, cow for h., etc. J2081.1; friendship between goat and h. A2493.22; ghost of h. E521.5; giant h. B871.2.1; why h. grunts A2426.1.3; helpful h. B414, (wild) B443.5; why h. lives in sty A2433.3.6; man-h. B29.3; mountain-man in shape of h. F460.1.1.1; h. loses pancake in mud: still seeks it A2275.5.1; planting a h. in order to grow pigs J1932.4; revenant as woman riding h. E425.1.5; why h. roots in ground A2275.5.1, A2477.1; why h. has short snout A2287.1, A2335.4.1; soul as h. E731.12; speaking h. B211.1.4; why h. has "toes" on back of fore leg A2287.1.1, A2371.2; treasure-h. B101.2; trickster's sale involving tall h. K196.2; witch as h. G211.1.6.

Hog's forefoot cut off; woman's hand missing D702.1.2.

Hogs follow fairies F241.3; to be killed yearly C684.2; made to sleep in trees J1904.3; as mortgage collateral K231.5.2; in otherworld F167.11.2; root up gold for saint B562.1.1. — Children play at killing h. N334.1; compulsion to kill one of certain h. yearly C684.2; concert by h. J1675.5; eating dwarfs smack like h. F451.3.13.1; why h. inspect one another: seek pancake A2275.5.1, A2471.2; island made to appear to be h. back K1886.7.1; Jesus drives evil spirits into h. A2287.1ff.; lies about h. X1233; mice and h. let loose put elephant cavalry to flight K2351.3.

Holding what four things hardest? H659.2; wild huntsman's dogs E501.15.6.1. — Chastity ordeal: h. shaven and greased tail of bull H412.2; disenchantment by h. D721.4, (enchanted person during

successive transformations) D757; disenchantment made permanent by h. to a hair D793.1; magically h. on to sleigh D1413.3; trees created for h. earth together A857.3; turtle h. with jaws till it thunders B761; wild hunt avoided by h. (bread) E501.17.5.6, (plant) E501.17.5.7.

Hole in ground entrance to hell F92.5; in stone from warrior's weapon A972.5.6; to snake kingdom F92.7; from which treasure removed N563; of winds: stopper destroyed A1122.1. — Animal eludes bird watchman and escapes from h. R214; bride put in tree h. K1911.1.7; boring h. in boat to let water out J2119.4; childbearing queen puts head in h., fails to see issue K2115.0.1; cure by putting hair in tree h. D2161.4.18; coffin carried through h. in wall to prevent return of dead E431.4; communication of lovers through h. in wall T41.1; contest: jumping into ground (h. already dug and covered with boughs) K17.1; contest in pushing h. in tree K61; counting out pay: h. in the hat and hat over a pit K275; deceptive drinking contest: h. for water K82.1; deceptive eating contest: h. in bag *K81.1; drinking h. in pot lets gruel run out J2176.2; dupe lured into h. K737.1; escape by digging h. K615; female overpowered when caught in h. in hedge K1384; to find h. fool turns can about and lets oil run out J2127; fool digs h. in which to throw earth from excavation J1934; fool stops h. with money J1851.3.1; god bores h. in hell A141.3; hero pretends he pushed h. in wall: hole really bored before K1733.1; lioness caught in wall h. K771.1; magic by creeping through h. *D1795; magic water-h. D928; monster comes out of h. in evening G346.0.1; numskull sticks his head into h. of millstone J2131.5.4; ogre persuaded to go into h.: buried alive G512.4; people come up h. from underworld A682; porridge in the ice-h. J1938; rainbow lives in h. A791.8.1; recognition by h. burned in hand when woman removes glove H56.1; snake preserved in ark to stop h. with tail A2145.2; test of wife's obedience: finger in h. H473.1; theft through h. in house wall K315.2; visit to lower world through h. made by lifting clumps of grass F92.1.

Holes bored in enemies' boats prevent pursuit K636; in hills from gods' fights A964.1; in stones caused by piercing by saint's finger A972.3; trap those departing from straight path J95. — Absurd disregard of nature of h. X1761; cannibal sent for water with vessel full of h. K605; mats over h. as pitfall K735.1; people in otherworld pour water into tub full of h. *F171.6.2; stars are men peering through h. in sky A761.5; wind comes through h. in sky A1122.4; why certain leaves have h. in them A2763.

Holger Dansk asleep in mountain *D1960.2.

Holiday to last "until log burns out" K197. — Camel mistaken for religious h. J1738.7; witch's h. G247.1.

Holidays the year round J2231. — Knockers observe Jewish h. F456.1.2.3.3.

Holiness, see also **Holy;** of saint tames animal B771.2. — Saint's h. tested H257.

Hollow mountain *F131, F759.2; object used to cheat K499.2; tree as residence for hero F811.10.1; in tree shelters relics F979.7. — Boy in h. tree frightens woodchopper X1854.1; entrance to woman's room in h. artificial animal K1341; fairies have h. backs F232.1; fairyland under h. knoll *F211; king escapes through h. tree R311.2; lost wind found in h. tree: has been banished and is needed by men A1122.3; man in h. tree defends self from beasts X1854; otherworld in h. mountain *F131; treasure found in h. of tree N528.

Hollows. — Origin of h. A983.

Holly. — Riddle about h. H852.

Holmgang H1561.2.1; for bride H217.2; to decide gold's owner H217.3.

Holofernes K872.

Holy man (converses with dead) E545.7, (doesn't want sinner buried atop him) E545.9 (embraces man calling him ugly) J921, (emits light) F574.3, (finds lost object) D1810.0.3.2, (as helper) N848.0.1, (on quest) H1233.3; man's (diet during Lent) V73.6.3, (fall evil omen) D1812.5.14, (hair enormously long) F555.3.2, (touch disenchants) D782.1; men keep devils under control G515; object falls from heaven F962.12; person's birth painless T584.0.3; persons save one from the devil G303.16.11; spring restores sight D1505.5.4. — Animal characteristics: punishment for working on h. day A2231.3; animal curse for refusing to carry h. fugitive across stream A2231.7.2; animal leads cleric to h. place B563.4; bright star indicates birth of h. person F961.2.1; chastity tests of h. men H426; condemned soul saved by h. person E754.1.4; cure by h. man D2161.5.1; demon cannot hurt h. person G303.16.2.5; devil visible to one who walks in minister's h. shoes G303.6.2.4; diseases cured at h. man's birth D2161.6.3; disguise as h. man K1827; dragon makes bridge across stream for h. man B549.2; dwarfs emigrate because mortals desecrate h. day F451.9.1.11; extraordinary nature phenomena at birth (death) of h. person F960.1ff.; footprints of h. man still visible A972.1.3; four things prevent h. life Z71.2.6; learning art of love so as to become h. T4.1; heaven entered by slipping in along with h. person K2371.1.5; miraculous spring bursts forth for h. person F933.1; origin of plant from h. person's staff A2624; plants originate from experience of h. person A2620ff.; prince disguised as h. man R24.1; punishment for desecration of h. places (images) *Q222; punishment for opposition to h. person Q227; refugee entertained in h. place P322.3; repartee between h. man, king on religion J1289.10; resuscitation by h. man E121.5; reward for attendance on h. man Q38; reward for protecting h. fugitive *Q46.1; seduction by posing as h. man K1315.6; sham h. man K1961.1.5; sun darkened by death of h. person F965.2; tabu to look at h. objects C311.2; tree bows down to h. person D1648.1.2; do not trust the over-h. J21.18; uncharitableness to h. person punished Q286.1; wisdom from h. man J153.

Holy Family. — Leopards guide H. to Egypt B563.5.

Holy Ghost. — Nun claims her child is by H. J1264.6.

Holy Grail D1171.6. — Prophecy: hero to achieve H. M361.1; resuscitation by H. E64.5.1; vow to find H. M183.3.

Holy of holies. — Stream from under H. A941.7.3.

Holy land, see also **Jerusalem;** V317.1; not ravaged by deluge A1005.3. — Dragon guards H. B11.6.4; pilgrimage to H. V531.

Holy water V132; breaks fairy spell F382.2; destroys veil over well D1562.6; exorcises witch G271.2.2; gives magic knowledge D1810.6; as magic object *D1242.1.2; and mass prevent demons alighting on grave D1385.15. — Conception from drinking h. T512.3.1; devil chased by h. G303.16.7; man enabled to read baptismal service by washing in h. D1819.4.1; ordeal by h. H222.2; plenty of h. J2513; resuscitation by h. E80.4; saint's h. makes fairy vanish F379.4.

Homage. — King avenges lack of h. P12.12; tabu: refusing h. to saint's bell C94.8.

Home, see also **Abode, Dwelling;** of brownies F482.3; of dwarfs F451.4ff.; of Fortuna in otherworld N111.1.1; of giants F531.6.3; of the gods A151. — Ass is not at h. J1552.1.1; animal told to go h. J1881.2; better things at h. K1952.2; child unwittingly promised: "what you have at h." S242; choice: staying at h. with loving wife or going to tavern and having an unfaithful wife J229.1; curse for leaving h. Q556.3; disenchantment by sight of old h. D789.3; escape from h. R213; ghost asks to be taken h. E545.18; ghost vanishes when taken h. E599.8; ghost's bones brought h. from foreign soil E459.2; goat who would not go h. (cumulative tale) Z39.1; heathcock prefers h. with hardships to travel in foreign lands J215.3; husband (lover) arrives h. just as wife (mistress) is to marry another *N681; husband (wife) of supernatural being longs for old h. and visits relatives T294; magic flower opens dwarf h. F451.4.3.7; man marries fairy and takes her to his h. F302.2; new h. no escape from bad luck N250.2; prophecy of future greatness fulfilled when hero returns h. unknown N682; why rams live at h. A2433.3.7; resuscitation by returning corpse h. E138; sight of old h. reawakens memory and brings about return from otherworld *D2006.2; sleeping at one's own h. tabu C735.2.10; staying too long at h. forbidden *C761.2; strong hero sent from h. F612ff.; thief followed h. J1392.1; unpromising son leaves h. L133; unusual sight on road h. bad omen D1812.5.1.22; water-goddess's underwater h. F420.7.1; wife of supernatural husband must not see old h. C713.2.

Homes of fairies F220. — Fairies revenge for destroying h. F361.12; flood survivors' h. A1029.6.

Homecoming giant heard far away F531.3.8.3. — Adulteress kills h. husband K1510.1.

Homeland sinks beneath waves F944.2. — King helps take h. back N836.3; promise to bury father in his h. M258.3.

Homesickness. — Magic h. D2036.

Homocentaurus born after bestiality T465.3.

Homosexuality T463; punished Q253.2.

Hone. — Magic h. D1188.

Honest miller incomprehensible to baker X212. — Recognizing h. merchant J1661.1.9.

Honestly. — Luck only with h. earned money N143.

Honesty rewarded Q68.2; tests H1555. — Cynical retorts concerning h. J1370ff.; intemperance in h. J556; merchants try h. for a year and find that it pays J23; partnership of H. and Fraud: Fraud loses K1635; pretended h. to mulct victim K2054.

Honey collected, lightened tree springs back, kills K1112.1; as excrement of bees A2385.3; flows up high mountain (lie) X1547.2.1; from royal bee-hive H1332.7. — Air-castle: jar of h. to be sold J2061.1; attempts to take h. from jug X431.1; bees feed woman h. F561.6; bees leave h. on infant's lips B147.3.1.2; bees sting h.-thieves Q597.3; conception from eating h. T511.7.1; "don't require h. from strange country" J21.40; man in pit consoled by a drop of h. J861.1; covering with h. and exposing to flies Q464; drones dispute possession of h. J581.4; drop of h. causes chain of accidents N381; error was in the h. (bribed judge) J1192.2; frogs want to collect h. J512.15; getting h. from the wasp-nest K1023; giving away comb, eating h. K476.7; gold pieces in the h.-pot J1176.3; magic h. *D1037; magic healing h. D1500.1.29; man falls into jar of h. and is drowned N339.1; man hunting h. encounters lost maiden N785.1; milk and h. flow in land F701.1; new h. protection against ghosts E439.10; origin of h. A2813; palace surrounded by rivers of wine, rosewater, and h. F771.7; peasant leaves h. tree standing J241.2; riddle: always eat bread with h. H588.11; rainbow of h. F162.7; riddle about bees, h., and lion's carcass H804; river of h. F715.2.4, F771.2.4.1; river is transformed h. A934.11.4; rivers of h. in otherworld *F162.2.3; saint suckles with h. T611.5.1; sea of h. F711.2.5; shower of h. F962.6.3; water becomes h. D478.5; what is sweeter than h. (riddle) H671; wayward son tells mother h. is sweet J2497; wine becomes h. D477.0.1.2.

Honey-bees, see also **Bees.** — Creation of h. A2012.0.1.

Honeycomb. — Man wants roasted h. J1731.2.

Honeysuckle king of trees D965.0.1.

Honor W45; to be foster father to king's son P271.4. — Angels sing in h. of saint V234.1; envoys debate which due greatest h. W161.1; feasts to h. certain god A1541.2; man killed defending sweetheart's h. T326.2; mother-son incest to test his h. T412.3; mountains fight for h. F1006.1; quest to recover one's h. H1223.1; stranger thinks humiliating donkey ride an h. Q473.5.1; wit interprets unfavorable decision of court as doing him great h. J835; woman deceived into sacrificing h. K1353; woman sacrifices life for son's h. W28.2; worldly h. like shadow J152.6.

Honors. — High h. as reward Q113.0.1.

Honoring. — Angels h. mortal V241, h. saint V234.1; lion's precept on h. the woods J22.2.

Hood holds wine F866.7.1; renders invulnerable D1344.8.1. — Disguise with h. over face K1815.0.1; gigantic h. of serpent king B244.1.3; land purchase: as much as saint's h. covers K185.4.1; lawyer's h. and robe stolen K362.9; lip makes h. over head F544.1.2; magic h. *D1067.3, (enables person to pass under water) D1525.1; not naked but with h. on J2499.2.

Hoods. — Icy h. worn in hell Q567.1.

Hoodwinking dancers K826. — Means of h. guardian or owner *K330ff.

Hoof. — Ass's charter in his h. J1608; ghost horse's h. -beats E402.2.3; recognition through branding with h.-marks H55.1; springs originate from horse's h.-prints A941.1; why ass does not have cloven h. A2376.1.1.

Hoofs of devil's horses strike fire G303.7.3.5. — Animals' h. A2376; clods thrown up by horses' h. look like birds K1872.5.1; devil's abode is between h. of swine G303.8.7; devil detected by his h. G303.4.5.3.1; dragon's cloven h. B11.2.4.2; ghostly horse enters house and puts h. on breast of sleeper E281.2; horses' h. drop from heat F988.2; person with h. F517.1.6; thunder from h. of god's horses A1142.6.

Hooks, see also **Fishhook.** — Cutting h. to revenge father H591.3; self-suspension on h. under armpits Q541.4.

Hooked nose F543.1.3.

Hoop snake X1321.3.1. — Penance: carrying iron h. on head until it falls off Q521.3; pursuit of rolling h. leads to quest H1226.1.

Hoopoe's creation A1952; wedding B282.18. — Origin of h. crest A2321.2; shepherd transformed to h. still calls sheep (explanation of h. cries) *A2261.1.

Hooting. — Owl's h. (bad omen) D1812.5.1.27.1, (explained) A2427.3, (misunderstood by lost simpleton) J1811.1.

Hop-o-my thumb *F535.1.

Hope is most general H659.10.1. — Creditor has had his reward in h. of payment K231.7.

Hopping of animals explained A2441.1.0.1; of hare A2441.1.11; of raven A2441.2.1.

Horizon. — Sky-window at h. F56.3.

Horn, see also **Drinking-horn;** blows down wall D1562.3; fills with blood (life token) E761.1.2; of Roncevalles R187; will tell the tale on goat J1082.1. — Alleged resuscitating h. K113.7; animal with h. pointing to sky H312.8; creature with h. mounting to heaven H1331.7; elf-knight produces love-longing by blowing h. F301.2.1; gnats apologize for lighting on bull's h. J953.10; ghost summoned by h. E384.3; hidden man blows h., lovers flee K1271.1.4.2; magic h. (musical) *D1222, (stolen) D861.7.1, (has power over animals) D1440.1; man covered with h. F558; magic animal h. *D1011.1; merry-h. and angry-h. B501.1.1; old

king eats from h. F571.5; quest for lost h. H1386.1; respite from death until victim has blown on h. K551.3; stealing gold h. of three-horned ox H1151.7.1; three blasts on h. before sunrise to rescue prisoner from mound R112.1; wild huntsman blows h. E501.15.1.

Horns call out when girl tries to escape D1612.1.1; of dragon B11.2.5; on forehead *F545.2.2; grow on cuckold *H425.2; for summoning buffalo B501.1. — Animal h. bloom and bear man as fruit A1263.5; animal unusual as to his h. B15.3ff.; camel asks for h.: punishment, short ears A2232.1; cattle shed h. in grief B301.6.1; child with h. T551.3.4.2; conception from drinking elixir from goat's h. T512.1; cow with silver h. B101.8, H355.1; creator with two h. on head A18.2; curiosity satisfied: riding the ox's h. J2375; devil has h. G303.4.1.6; disenchantment by placing handkerchief between h. D777; earth rests on h. of bull A844.5; fairy h. heard by mortals F262.8; fawn, in spite of his fine h., runs from the dog U127; growth of ox h. F983.4; hare (jackal) makes h. of wax K1991; hind with golden h. B106.1; magic h. (grow on person's forehead) *D992.1; magic object causes h. to grow on person *D1375.1ff.; magic object removes h. from person D1375.2ff.; magic object returned in payment for removal of magic h. D895; man carried on goat's h. B557.1; man with h. B233; man pulls out devil's h. G303.9.6.1.1; monster with human heads on h. G361.1.1.1; mounds from h. cast by cattle A967.1; origin and nature of animals' h. A2326ff.; originally cock had h. A2326.2.3; person with h. F511.3; servant must keep h. and hide of his cattle that are slain P622; stag's h. borrowed from dog A2241.1; stag scorns his legs but is proud of his h. L461; stealing two h. of a savage bull (task)H1151.7; taming the bull by cutting off his h. J2107; why dog has no h. A2326.2.2; witch with h. G215.2; witch's h. discovered by lousing her *G253; wolf tied to cow's h. K1022.2.

Hornbill borrows tomtit's bill A2241.9; king of birds B242.1.3. — Man transformed to h. D153.3; why h. speaks through his nose A2423.1.5.

Horned god A131.6; snake B91.3; water monster B68. — Devil's cows one-h.: God makes them two-h. A2286.2.3; how h. viper got horns A2326.1.6; origin of h. serpent A2145.0.1.

Hornet. — Creation of h. A2013; remedy for h. sting D1517.1; soul in h. E715.3.3; spirit in h. form guards treasure F403.2.3.1.

Hornets sting opposing army B524.2.1. — Army of h. B268.8.1; bridegroom driven from bridal chamber by h. T171; bull's eye becomes h. D457.11.1; helpful h. B481.5; man who asks for good weather given a box of h. J2327; ornaments of h. F827.3; thieves directed to nest of h. K421.2.

Hornless cow B15.3.0.1. — Milk from the h. cow J1512.1; why some animals are h. A2326.2ff.

Horny. — Animal with h. skin B15.7.10.1; first man covered with h. substance A1281.1.

Horoscope taken by means of stars M302.4. — Choosing bride by h. T54.

Horrible sights in hell A671.2. — Revenant as h. female figure E425.1.6; spirits appear h. F401.5.

Horrifying. — Rescued person h. rescuers R188.

Horripilation F1041.2.

Horror. — Death from h. F1041.1.12.

Horrors. — Climax of h. (cumulative tale) Z46.

Horse, see also **Colt, Donkey, Mare, Mule, Stallion;** accidentally poisoned instead of master N332.2; bewitched G265.6.3; in blood up to knees E761.1.9; born of egg B19.3; catches thief K427.1; with crimson mane, green legs B731.2.1; dies after owner refuses large sum for him J21.26; drawn across ice, skin rubbed off J2129.7; enchanted so that he stands still D2072.0.2.1; executed for crime B275.1.1; exchanged by rider for food M225.1; fair forbidden C619.3; finds unknown person B151.1.1.0.3; -god A132.3.1; -goddess A132.3.2; with golden mane B19.5; hangs self D2061.2.8; helper on quest H1233.6.1; indicates election of emperor H171.3; jumps over high wall F989.1; -keeper rescues abandoned child R131.8.1; kicks up jewel B562.1.2; kicks murderer to death B591.2; kills another, owner forewarned J1141.1.12; kills dog with kick J2413.5; kills master's enemies B524.1.7; kneels before stolen sacrament V35.1.1; lies down when grain falls from load B159.2; lives from time of Adam A1881.0.1; made to appear as tree-trunk D2031.7; magically becomes immovable D1654.12; meat becomes mutton D476.3.3; as messenger B291.2.1; -nail stumps bewitch G224.13.1; painted different colors by thief K419.5; paramour B611.3; permits only certain rider H172.1; pulling ghost in cart goes mad E272.1; pushes sleep-thorn from master's head B511.3; pulled out of earth by magic D1399.1; recognizes false rider, throws him H62.2; recognizes transformed kol H62.2; refuses to carry one who speaks falsehood B133.4; replies to man's remarks B210.1; requests wolf to start eating at rear, kicks him to death K553.4; rescues children B540.2; as sacrifice V12.4.9; sewed in buffalo-hides F984.1; stands in blood to his knees (life token) E761.1.9; is the strongest (riddle) H631.1; as suitor B621.7; taught to live without food J1914; trade involving eating its excrement K198; transformed to another animal D412.4; transformed to object D422.1; transformed to stone D422.1.2; transports to fairyland F213.3; tried for crime B272.2.1; unable to draw evil dead man E411.0.3; unable to move enchanted wagon D2072.0.2.1.1; used by mortal under fairy spell changes to gray cat F234.4.1; wading in blood at Armageddon A1080.1; warns hero not to wash in water B521.1.1; weeps B301.4ff., B736.2, (for master's death) B141.2; that went like a ship J2481; in wild hunt breathes fire *E501.4.2.4; wins jumping contest for man B587.1; as witch's companion G225.2; withheld as sacrifice to a saint refuses to move K231.3.4; worship V1.8.2. — Air-castle: old woman thinks about h. she is finally to get from the sale of pail of milk J2061.2.1; alleged gold-dropping h. sold K111.1; alp rides h. sweaty at night F471.1.1.1; angry man kills his own h. by mistake

K942; arrow in leg of sun's h. A732.2.1; artificial flying h. D1626.1; ass envies h. in fine trappings J212.1; ass is jealous of the h. until he learns better L452; automatic statue of h. D1620.2.1; new backbone for h. made from a stick X1721.1; bear riding h. lets paws fall on horse's flanks J2187; bird-h. B41ff.; blacksmith's and h.-trader's dreams J1622; blade of grass transformed to h. D451.5.1; breaking h. as strength test H1562.6; bridling a wild h. (task) H1154.3.1; bull mistaken for h. J1759.4; bundle of wood magically acts as riding-h. D1523.3; cat transformed to h. D412.1.1; capture by tarring h. K741.1; capturing magic h. H1154.8; carrying the plow h. so as not to tramp up the field J2163; cleaning the h. K1443; clever, swift h. of fanciful origin B710.2; color of h. A2411.1.6.1; coming neither on h. nor on foot (task) H1053; creation of ass from proud h. A1882.1; creation of h. A1881; damages claimed for "lost" h. hidden by owner K251.4; deduction: h. drinks ass's milk J1661.1.5; devastating h. B16.1.3; devil in h. race G303.9.9.12; do not cross bridge without dismounting from your h. J21.7; deceptive contest in carrying a h. K72; deceptive sale of h. K134; deceptive wager: whose h. will jump highest K264.1; devil drives h. and wagon G303.7.3ff.; devil as h. G303.3.3.1.3; devil rides h. G303.7.1ff.; devil in the stable wrapped in h.-hide G303.8.12; difficult riding of h. as suitor contest H331.1; discourteous answer: why. h. is always eating A2231.1.1; "don't run h. down hill" J21.24; not to dismount from h. C521; do nothing but attend to the h. J2516.3; dragon becomes h. D419.1.2; dragon as modified h. B11.2.1.7; dragon from transformed h. B11.1.2; dupe believes h. will fly J2349.1; dwarf rides through air on wooden h. F451.6.2.2; entrance to maiden's room on flying h. K1346; escape by asking to die on a h. K551.6; escape on flying h. B542.2; escape from flying wooden h. R215.3; escape from lower world on h. F101.6.2, excuse for not staying on h. J1483.4; why h. has eye-like marks on forelegs A2262.1, A2371.2.7; fairy as h. F234.1.8; why h. has only two eyes A2286.1.2; A2332.2.1; fairy rides on h. F366.22; fairies ride mortal's h. at night F366.2; faithful h. B301.4ff., (to be abandoned) B842.1, (killed through misunderstanding) B331.1.1, (follows dead master to grave) B301.4; farmer kills anyone riding his h. L434; foal so heavy, h. not wanted J2212.8; fool advises buyer that the h. is worth little or his father would not sell it J2088.1; foolish bargain: h. for cow, etc. J2081.1; footless man outruns swift h. (lie) X1796.1; fourth h. must carry all J761.2; fugitive kills pursuer and takes his extraordinary h. to continue flight R233; ghost of h. *E521ff.; ghost rides h. E272.2, E581.2; ghostly h. enters house and puts hoofs on breast of sleeper E281.2; giant h. B871.1.5; giant so large he cannot be carried by a h. F531.2.7; giant who can find only one h. able to carry him F531.2.8; giant with h. head F531.1.2.4; giant ogre as h. G126.2; gnats think they have thrown h. down J953.6; god rides on wind-swift h. A171.1; golden h. B103; gorgon's blood becomes flying h. D447.3.2; great h. X1241.1; green h.

B731.2; guessing nature of devil's h. H523.1; hardhearted h. allows ass to be overburdened until it is crushed W155.1; hay transformed to h. D441.9.1; headless ghost rides h. E422.1.1.3.1; helpful strong h. caught B312.5; helpful h. *B401; hero kills h. to feed ravens B391.3; hostile h. B17.1.4; husband's slaying of h. tames wife T251.2.3; imagined refusal of h. loan tests friendship H1558.6; inciting h. tabu C857; if h. can pull one load he can pull two J2213.4; imprint of h. in rocks A972.4; king leads to victory by leaping h. overboard W32.1; kite tries to neigh like h. J512.2; land bargain: land surrounded by a h. in one day K185.7.1; laughing contest: dead h. winner K87.1; leading dead h. J2047; do not lend out your h. J21.10; loosing knots permits h. to return home D1782.3.2; lover's h. explained to husband: cow has foaled K1549.4; lover's gift regained: h. and wagon as gift K1581.2; magic h. *B184.1, (brings about mortal's death) K985, (hairs compel horse to follow) D1427.3, (made by carpenter) D853.1, (powerless after tabu broken) C942.2; magic power by crawling through ear of magic h. D1733.2; magic spell tames h. D1442.6.1; magic transportation from kick of h. D2121.9; man keeps h. in sleeve F1016.1; man helps h. against stag K192; man secure from devil on h. G303.16.19.1; man transformed to h. *D131ff., H62.0.1; man walks faster than h. F681.9; marriage to person in h. form B641.6; marvelously swift h. F989.17; mill h. when taken to war keeps going in a circle U137; mill gives birth to h. J1531.1.1; mouse transformed to h. D411.6.1; "my h. ten times better than best" J2217.1; mythical h. belonging to water-spirit B19.3.2; nag becomes riding h. D1868.1; Norse man-h. B21.1; numskull to die when his h. breaks wind three times J2311.1; numskull doesn't recognize his own h. J2023; oaths taken over severed pieces of h. M111; one-eyed man as appraiser of h. X122; one-footed h. draws chariot A136.2.2; plowing the field: h. and harness destroyed K1411; plowman to get h. for saying paternoster H1554.3; prince identifies marvelous disguised h. H62.3; prophetic h. B141.2; pursuer's h. stolen K341.4.1.1; quest for marvelous h. H1331.4; quest for wonderful, vicious h. H1363; race of ox and h. A2252.2; rainbow is rain-god's h. A791.7; rakshasa eats h. G369.1.4; recognition by overheard conversation with h. H13.1.1; recognizing a good h. by screwing ears F655.1; refusal to lend h. brings lawsuits J1552.3; reincarnation as h. E611.1; revenant as h. E423.1.3; riding h. kingship test H41.7; riding speckled h. credential test H242.1; riding, taming wild h. H1155.1; riddle about h. and rider H744; riddle: black h. and white h. chasing each other H722.2; runaway h. carries bride to her lover N721; sacred h. B811.1; saint's h. miraculously preserved H1573.3.2; sea h. B71; sea-riding h. transports to fairyland F213.3; seal transformed to h. D411.7.1; sham wise man hides h. and is rewarded for finding it K1956.2; six-legged h. B15.6.3.1.1; skillful smith shoes running h. F663.1; slander: woman as h.-eating thief K2127.2; speaking h. B211.1.3; spirit in form of h. F401.3.1; spring breaks forth where

fairy h. lies down A941.4.2; squirrel transformed to h. D411.1.1; staying in haunted house where h. carcass drops down chimney (fear test) H1411.1.1; stealing h. as task H1151.2, (troll's) H1151.9; stingy h. refuses ass little feed, though he promises much for later time W152.8; striped h. with purple mane, white feet B731.2.3; strong man lifts h. F624.1; suitor test: riding strong princess's h. H345.2; sword cleaves h. in two F628.2.10; where h. got his upper teeth A2241, A2345.1; tabu: touching h. C537.3; tabu: whipping magic h. C762.3; tame h. exchanged for vicious bullock K1456; task: capturing magic h. H1154.8; teaching h. to speak H1024.7.1, K491.2; test of strength: breaking spirited h. H1562.6; thief guards his pursuer's h. while the latter follows a false trail K346.1; thief pretends to show how h. can be stolen: rides it off K341.8; tournament won on borrowed h. K28; trading only h. for harness J2085.1.1; trained h. as harvester and hunter (lie) X921.3; transformation to h. by putting on bridle D535; tree grows out of h. and gives rider shade X1130.2.1; trickster pretends to ride home, steals h. K341.8.1; trickster steals h. from dealer K341.8.2; thief returns h. after using it K416.1; transformation to flying h. D657.2; transformation of h. by spurring D566.3; Trojan wooden h. K754.1; truth-speaking h. B133; two presents to the king: the beet and the h. J2415.1; ungrateful Jew steals Christian's horse W154.19; wild huntsman has his h. beaten E501.15.2; wild huntsman waters his h. *E501.15.7; wild huntsman's h. *E501.4.2ff.; wind serves Solomon as h. and carries him everywhere F963.1; wisp of hay transformed to h. D441.9.1; witch in form of h. G211.1.1; witch rides h. G241.3; witch transforms man to h. and rides him G241.2.1; witch's hair on h. become iron G265.3.1; winning h. race three times (suitor test) H331.5.3; woman exchanges h. for sack of bones J2099.1; woman killed by h. got through immoderate request Q582.6; wraith rides h. E723.7.7; youth trusts self to h. over which he has no control J657.1.

Horse's head for extraordinary use F874; image vivified D445.1; leg cut off and replaced *E782.4; magic head protects D1380.3.1; magic strength from hair combing D1835.2; neighing indicates important spot B155.4; sex organ provides money D1469.5. — Animal with h. body, hound's legs B14.2; body and hands human, head and ears h. B21.2; combat with h. sex organ F998; death respite until wolf reads h. passport K551.19; devil has h. foot G303.4.5.3; escape by reversing h. shoes K534.1; fairies plait h. mane, tail F366.2.1; fox waits in vain for h. scrotum to fall off J2066.1; ghormuhas; men's bodies, h. heads, cannibals B15.7.5; ghost h. hoofbeats E402.2.3; ghost as man with h. head E425.2.2; king asleep in mountain will awake when his h. shoes are worn down D1960.2.1; king induced to kiss h. rump K1288; magic h. rider immune D1381.30; man with h. mouth B213; origin of h. arched neck A2351.6; person with h. (foot) F551.1.2, (ears) F511.2.2, (head) F511.0.9.1; pins in h. heart release curse M429.2; prophecy: death by h.

head M341.2.5; punishment: tying to h. tail Q473.2; spring from h. urine A941.1.1; springs from h. hoof-prints A941.1; tying cat to h. tail K2383; water that has neither fallen from heaven nor sprung from earth (h. sweat) H1073; weapons from h. bones B338; why h. penis is long A2365.2.1.1; if witch grabs h. tail on bridge, man is safe from her G273.4.1; youth sees one and one-half men and a h. head H583.1.

Horses B802; become sick as punishment Q551.4.1; carry lost riders to safety B563.1.1; descended from heaven B811.1.1; determine road to be taken *B151.1.1; fail for slight to saint Q589.1; as fairy gifts F343.9.1; of the gods A155.2; hoofs drop from heat F988.2; knead dough (lie) X1241.2.3; mutilated to humiliate owner S175; as offspring of the devil G303.10.8; procured for boy at birth T602; refuse to remain with cursed owner B133.4.1; from sea serve man D2156.10; sent into enemy's camp to cause stampede K2351.6; spring at those unentitled to throne H71.10.4; travel between clerics without guidance B151.1.1.0.1. — Abused and pampered h. B316; artificially colored h. B731.2.2; birds frighten enemy's h., who throw riders K2351.5.1; blood-red h. draw devil's coach G303.7.3.5; breeding fine h. from an ass J1909.4; bringing as many h. are there are days in the year (task) H1117; clods from h. hoofs look like birds K1872.5.1; coachman makes the h. run by binding hay to the shaft J1671; curse: h. will die M471.3; dead person drives h. E582; demons race h. F419.1; devil stampedes h. G303.9.9.15; devil disappears in carriage drawn by four black h. G303.17.2.9; drawing asunder by h. Q416; driving h. over ashen yoke tabu C833.4; dwarfs have little h. F451.7.5; enemy h. captured by lion join forces and become friends J891; fairy gives man h., cattle, etc. F343.9; fairy kills mortal's hounds (h.) F369.3; flood caused by loosing fairy h. A1012.2.1; fairies' h. F241.1; farmer who trades h. with the devil is cheated G303.25.12; fire-breathing h. B742.3; frightened h. backed into enemy K2351.5; getting ninety h. H1154.2.1; ghosts visible to h. alone E421.1.2; hero's marvelous h. A524.1.2; immortal h. B19.3.1; infuriated h. kill driver B17.1.4.1; insects eat team of h. X1280.2.1; lies about h. X1241; lightning from heavenly h. striking hoofs A1141.3; magic bridle restrains all h. D1442.1; magic cloth leads owner to lost h. D1314.9; man tied to h., hounds set after Q415.1.2; man works h. to death, complains that borrowed one overeats W154.27; mountain-folk ride through air on h. F460.2.2; murder by trampling of h. S116.6; nine hundred h. draw strong man's chariot F639.12; ogress devours h. G312.7; people choose bows and arrows or guns and h. A1614.4.3; phantom coach and h. E535.1; people in otherworld hitch h. both before and behind the wagon F171.6.4; quest for the finest of h. H1308; race between wooden h. D1719.1.4; relics protect h. V144.2; repartee concerning runaway h. J1483ff.; resourcefulness test: find how old three h. are H506.1; spirit and h. F402.1.14; spirit rides, wears out h. at night F473.4.1; stealing h. from king H1151.13.3; stealing twelve h. out of stall (task) H1151.2; strong

man sent for wild h. F615.2.3; tabu: h. eating foreign provender C224.4; tabus concerning h. C884; telling their h. apart J2722; there are ten h.: why then when he is mounted only nine? J2031.2; three h. from dove's egg on last day A1091.1; thunder from hoofs of gods' h. A1142.6; various colored h. of brownie F482.4.1; waves as manes of sea god's h. A1116.1; wild hunt heralded by noise of h. E501.13.3; witch disguised as queen eats h. G264.3.1; witch rides h. at night *G265.3; wolf boasts of having eaten h. J2351.4.

Horses'. — Wild hunt throws h. feet on persons who see it E501.18.3.

Horseback journey to otherworld F159.2. — Death on h. F492; ghost on h. E332.3.1; hero feigns fear of h. K1777; journey to upper world on h. F66; old king cannot get on h. F571.6.

Horseblock. — Cast-forth wife must sit at h. of palace Q482.4.

Horseflesh, see **Horsemeat.**

Horsehairs. — Magic h. (when rubbed) compel horse to follow D1427.3.

Horsehead. — Reincarnation: man as h. E611.1.1; speaking h. *B133.3.

Horseheaded men reborn as money-lenders E605.8.

Horsehide. — Alleged oracular h. K114.1.1.

Horseman. — Automatic statue of h. D1620.1.2; copper h. indicates route *D1313.3; head restored to headless h. D1518.3.

Horsemen taken to be men on cattle J1766.1. — Children transformed into h. D98; impious h. swallowed up by earth Q221.4.3.

Horsemanship. — Parson's poor h. X443.

Horsemeat. — Tabu to eat h. C221.1.1.2, C756.4; penance for eating h. Q499.6; transformation: h. to mutton D476.3.3.

Horse-racing. — Demons' h. F419.1; origin of h. A1535.6.

Horseshoe brings good luck D1561.1.3; protection against witches G272.11. — Devil unable to enter house with h. over the door *G303.16.17; extraordinary h. F862; lost h. nail (cumulative tale) Z45, (brings train of troubles) N258; magic h. *D1286; woman with h. on one foot F551.1.2.1.

Horseshoes. — Countertask: making h. for cavalry from one needle H1022.2.1; fairies' horses have round h. F241; transformation to horse by wearing h. D535.1; witch as horse shod with h. *G211.1.1.2.

Horseshoeing. — Imitation of miraculous h. unsuccessful J2411.2.

Horseskin. — Magic h. D1025.7.

Horsewhips. — Origin of h. A1459.1.5.

Hose. — Magic adhesion to h. D2171.3.4; witch known by h. unbound on one leg G255.

Hospitable fire of his father is sought (bean merchant) H581.2; man impoverished by greedy guests W151.2.2; person saved from death Q151.3.

Hospital. — Harshness frightens h. patients K1955.1.2; recognition at h. H11.1.1.

Hospitality *P320ff.; of a citizen saves city from destruction Q152.1;

enforced on hero keeps him away too long N391.0.1; to incognito king rewarded K1812.4; rewarded Q45, (opposite punished) Q1; as a virtue W12. — Animal characteristics reward for h. A2222; customs of h. A1598; excessive h. causes chieftain to become poor Q42.1.3; execution escaped by invoking laws of h. J1183; fairy grateful for h. F332; fairy kills man refusing his h. F361.17.7; gods disguised as beggars test h. K1811.1; hero dispenses h. A547; inhospitable host punished for h. J1561.2; planting garden and offering free h. to all as penance Q523.5; quest as payment for h. H1219.7; sex h. T281; smith as lord of h. P447.3; test of h. H1564; trickster abuses h. K354; trickster feigns deafness and gets h. from miser K1981.1.

Hospitaller. — Disguise as h. K1825.4.

Host (person) entertains otherworld seeker F151.0.1; and guest P320ff.; imposes tabu C901.1.4; offers to send his guest a cask of the wine he has praised (verba honoris) M206.1; rebukes negligent servant J1573; robs guest K385; wants to learn Hebrew even at risk of forgetting his own language J344.2. — Bungling h. J2425; forgery dupes h. K455.8.2; luxury of h. rebuked J1566; magic object stolen by h. D861.1; suspicious guest forces h. to be killed in his stead K1611.2; treacherous h. K2294; winespilling h. rebuked J1511.5.

Host (sacrament) *V30ff.; put into beehive C55.3. — Devil disappears when given h. G303.16.5.2; devils worship h. G303.24.2; incredulity about h. confounded by miracle V33.1; princess must recover h. stolen by rat H1292.4.1; priest carries h. across stream J1261.2.8; punishment for desecration of h. Q222.1; sacred image appears on h. V39.5.

Host's. — Knight unsuccessfully tempted by h. wife T331.2; tabu to eat before h. house righted C231.4.

Hosts P320ff. — Phantom h. E500ff.; practical retorts: h. and guests J1560ff.; stolen sacred h. put into coffin, fill bag V35.2.

Hostage. — Prince imprisoned as h. P34; son gives mother as h. S21.3.

Hostages P533.1; buried alive S123.0.1; cursed M414.7; escape prevented as reward Q157; sacrificed S265.1. — Covenant confirmed by h. M201.6.

Hostel. — Forbidden h. C619.1.

Hostess who had no spoons J1561.4.1. — Virgin Mary supplies mead for unprepared h. V262.

Hostile animals B17; beasts B17.1; beings in otherworld F360.0.1; brides kill husbands in the bridal bed T173.2; brothers P251.5.3; dogs made friendly by having them fight common enemy, the wolf J145; twins T685.2. — Children abandoned by h. relative S322; giants h. to Christianity F531.5.8.1; keeping on good terms with h. gods J821; unworthy origin ascribed to h. tribes A1610.1.

Hostility. — Animal characteristics as punishment for h. at crucifixion *A2231.2ff.; prevention of h. by inspiring fear in enemy J623.

Hot rain F962.2.5; springs rise where Christ bathed his feet A942.1; weather from God boring hole in hell A1137. — Breasts h. enough to

cook on F546.5; chastity ordeal: holding h. iron H412.4.1; devil's money h. G303.21.3; dupe opens mouth, closes eyes: h. stones thrown in K721.1; dupe sits on h. iron K1074; dupe sits on h. stone K1032; fairies punish girl who pours h. water into their spring F361.5; flood from h. liquid A1016.2; fountain h. or cold as desired F716.3; god's throne becomes h. A152.9; lies about h. weather X1630; murder by h. object in mouth K951.1.1; murder by over-h. food S112.5; numskull feeds hens h. water so they will lay boiled eggs J1901.2; ogre killed by throwing h. stones into his throat G512.3.1; ordeal by h. iron H221.2; origin of h. springs A942; punishment: climbing h. rod Q469.2; red-h. floor protects city F767.2; red-h. meal forced on person S183.0.1; remarkably h. spear F834.1; saint invulnerable to red h. iron D1841.3.2.3; second lover burns paramour at window with h. iron K1577; sham-dead person tested by h. lead poured on hand H248.1; stream becomes h. in which saint performs his ascetic devotions F932.3; sun originally so h. all life threatened A727.1; sun's son too h. to hold A736.5.1; voice made rough by swallowing h. iron F556.1.

Hotel. — Lie: great h. X1035.

Hound, see also **Dog;** attack as valor test H1561.7; becomes lap-dog D412.5.2; of every color B731.6; flame of fire B19.4.4; of hell *A673; kills ogre's wife G519.1.1; strikes unique vulnerable spot N335.5. — Devil's h. G303.10.15; dog is h. by night, sheep by day B182.1.4, H1331.9; dog is h. by day, fire by night B182.1.5; fairy kills mortal's h. F369.3; fight between animal and h. pack B264.1; god battles h. of hell A1082.2.2; hostile dog (h.) B17.1.2, (killed by reaching through hollow log in its jaws and tearing out heart) B17.1.2.2; magic animal proof against h. D1841.7; magic boar drowns h. pack B184.3.1.1; magic whelp kills h. B182.1.3.1; pet h. killed, man dies of its blood Q582.4; quest for unknown h. H1383.1; saint's song silences h. D1442.5; savage h. guards door H1423.1; stealing king's h. H1151.13.4; venomous h. B776.3; whelp leaps through h. F916.2.

Hound's blood from magic spear D1404.2. — Animal with horse's body, h. legs B14.2.

Hounds must be followed C681.1; set after man Q415.1.2. — Chief's wolf-h. C564.3; forgetting leashes of h. bad omen D1812.5.1.21; giant's skull holds three h. F531.2.3.2; hell-h. accompany soul to lower world E752.5; hunter manages h. F679.5.1; wild hunt heralded by baying of h. E501.13.4.

Hour of grace used up in disputing J2183.4; has come but not the man M219.2.3. — Foreknowledge of h. of death D1812.0.1; sun changes h. F961.1.7.

Hours. — Bird calls out h. F989.3; canonical h. V48.

House appears overnight to shelter priest V229.21; -building learned from wasps A1445.2.2; burned down (cumulative tale) Z51.1, (with all inside) S112.0.2, (to rid it of insects) J2102.4, (to rid it of rats) J2103.3; burns

for no reason F473.2.4; crushed by magic D2099.3; destroyed by magic D2089.6; -door transformed to stone D471.2.1; where false judgment given slips down hill Q559.8; goes wherever owner commands F675.3; has neither eyes nor ears H583.8; of fairy F221; of my father with 150 lights and goat pen K1917.4; that Jack built Z44; to make house-spirit surrender booty F480.3.1; neither on ground nor in sky H1077; the old man was to build (cumulative tale) Z44.1; in otherworld F163.3; of saint filled with fragrance V222.4; seems afire K1889.1; spirit leaves after clothing gift F405.11; spirits F480ff.; transformed to stone D471.2; unlighted taken over by ghosts E593.3; without food or drink J2483. — Animal as guard of h. B576.1; animals keeping h. together; all goes wrong J512.7; bees caught in a sack which is opened in the h. J2131.2.1; blowing the h. in Z81; bodies of victims in front of ogre's h. G691; brownies live in h. F482.3.1; building iron h. overnight H1104.3; burning own h. for access to woman K1349.7; children wander into ogre's h. G401; criminal's h. burned down Q486.1; dead's h. of cloud E481.8.4; departing h. F1063; devil as h. G303.3.4.9; devil haunts h. G303.15.3; devil unable to enter h. with horseshoe over the door *G303.16.17; devil's grandmother keeps h. for him G303.11.4.1; devil's h. is visible on the way to hell G303.8.3.3; dog will not help build h.: must remain out of doors A2233.2; dupe burns h. because trickster reports high price paid for ashes K941.2; egg becomes h. D469.1.1; extraordinary h. *F771ff.; fairies build h. F346.2; fairies occupy peasant's h. F365.3; fairy h. disappears at dawn F221.1; fool roofs his h. on the inside J2171.2.2; fool whose h. is burning puts wood on the fire J2162.2; friendly ghost haunts h. E338.1; ghost laid by destroying haunted h. E451.8; ghostly horse enters h. and puts hoofs on breast of sleeper E281.2; ghosts haunt h. E281; gingerbread h. F771.1.10; if host does not return h. shall belong to the guest P326; husband in the chicken h. K1514.1; husband made to believe that h. has moved during his absence J2316; incombustible h. D1656.2; jinn kills occupants of his h. G307.3; kid perched on h. jeers at wolf J974; magic beautification of h. *D1867; magic h. D1133, (removed) D2136.9; magic object produces h. D1599.4; magic object taken from ogre's h. D838.1; man mistakes giant's glove for h. F531.5.2; means of entering h. or treasury K310ff; monkey pretends that his h. always answers him K1722; moon has h. A753.2; not to leave h. within ten days C755.1; not recognizing own h. converted to mansion J2316.1; objects keep h. together J512.7; ogre attacks intruders in h. in woods G475.1; ogre imprisoned in own h. G514.2; only fault with the h. J2236; peasant's h. P411.1.1; putting h. in order tabu C743; repairing the h. K1415; riddle on h. full of dead H831; robber-proof h. D2072.5; selling half his h. J2213.6; sham wise man does not know where his own h. is K1956.4; small niche in h. brings large price K182.1; snail grows and fills h. entirely F983.1; Socrates builds himself little h. J401.1; staying in haunted h. H1411; stream runs through h. F715.4; strong hero lifts

h. F624.6; sunlight carried into windowless h. in baskets J2123; tabu: being in h. with fire, weapon, dog C887; tabu to eat before host's h. righted C231.4; tabu: sleeping in h. lighted after sunset C735.2.4; too cold for hare to build h. in winter: must go without h. A2233.2.1; trickery to buy h. cheaply K1838; trickster appropriates host's h. K354; trickster pollutes h. so that he is left in possession K355; trumpet blown before h. of one sentenced to death P612; underwater h. F133.2, F725.3.3; victim burned in his own h. K812; victim lured into h. and killed K811; vow not to enter any h. before one's own M182; wild hunt avoided by keeping in h. with windows closed E501.17.5.3; wild huntsman's dog cannot be dislodged from h. it has entered E501.15.6.5.

Houses at border of otherworld F147; in lower world of dead E481.1.2; magically enlarged D488. — Acquisition of guest h. A1435.1; burning h. to sell ashes K941.3; fairies' h. F220; gods built h. A1402; jinns in ruined h. F499.3.3; wild hunt goes through h. when front and back doors are on a line E501.14.6; witch causes haunted h. G269.5.

Household articles act at command D1601.9; gods A411, (speak) A182.1.1. — Acquisition of h. implements A1446.5; animal as h. spirit B593; bewitched h. articles G265.8.1; entire h. dies same night F1099.1; jokers set h. at variance K2134.1; king slain by own h. P16.7; poltergeist malevolent h. spirit F473; magic h. articles answer for fugitive D1611.9; magic olive branch makes woman master in h. D1359.1.1.

Housekeeper. — Boy as h. for buffaloes N832.1; devil's grandmother is his h. G303.11.4.1; mysterious h. B537, N831.1; true bride as mysterious h. K1911.3.5.

Housekeeping. — Cows grateful for hero's h. B396.

Housemaid disguised as minister K1839.10.

House-pillars warn D1317.21. — Magic h. *D1149.3.

Housepost. — Man becomes h. D268.1; speaking h. D1610.30.1.

Housewife frightens away guests J1563.5.

Housework. — Grateful fairies do h. F339.3.1.

Hovel. — Noble person must live in h. Q485.

Hovering. — Angels h. over mortal V238.1; birds h. over battlefield F989.14; hawk loses grandmother: still h. and searching A2275.5.2; soul h. over body E722.2.8.2; spirits h. over battle F418.

Howe as home of (dwarf) E451.4.1.9, (troll) F455.1.1.

Howling of animal at night explained A2427. — Divination from dog h. D1812.5.0.9; dogs' h. as bad omen D1812.5.1.12.1; eaten magic dog h. from eater's belly D1619.2.1.

Huckauf *F472.

Huge, see also **Enormous, Gigantic, Large.** — Breaking h. rock to pieces (task) H1116; devil bound with h. chain G303.8.4.1; gate h. as mountain F776.1.

Hugh of Lincoln V361.

Hulls. — Man compelled to live on peas comforted by seeing a man once rich eating h. J883.1.

Hum. — Beetle demands return of gold from God: must h. A2231.11.

Human and animal offspring from marriage to animal B633; beings devoured, see **Cannibalism;** beings descended from seals B631.2; -dragon marriage B11.12.3.1; flesh eaten unwittingly *G60ff.; head used for divination D1311.8; helpers N820ff.; offspring from marriage to animal *B631; sacrifice S260.1; son of animal parents T566; sons of animal companions are friends P311.3. — Animal with h. eyes B15.4.4; animal in h. form recognized H48; animal substituted for h. sacrifice A1545.2; animals with h. emotions B773; animals in otherworld pass in and out of church and become h. beings *F171.5; animals or objects treated as h. J1850—J1899; animal uses h. speech B211ff.; animals with h. traits B200—B299; conception from eating parts of h. being T511.6; deity appearing before h. A189.6; deity in h. form A125; demons assume h. forms (to deceive) F402.1.4, (to revenge) D651.1.2; devil given animal instead of h. K219.6; devil's horse has h. feet G303.7.1.2.1; devil in h. form G303.3.1ff.; devils as h. beings voracious G303.3.0.2; dragon flies to nest with h. being B11.6.8; druids perform h. sacrifice P427.1.1; dwarfs seek h. help F451.5.23; dwarfs and h. beings F451.5ff.; eating of h. hearts as cure for insomnia D2161.4.13; fairies and h. children F310ff.; fettered monster in h. form A1072.1; first h. pair as creators A2.2; ghost haunts in h. shape E279.1; ghosts eat h. beings E541.2; giants marry h. beings F531.5.7; gods borne by h. woman A112.9; incarnation of a god: puts on h. form to help men E605.2; lotus transformed to h. hand D451.4.1; magic h. bodily members *D990ff.; mankind from h.-animal mating A1221.6; marriage to animal in h. form *B650ff.; offer to make pups born of woman in shape of hound h. D601; origin of h. sacrifice A1545.5; overheard h. conversation N455; partial transformation: animal with h. mind D682.3; parts of h. body furnish treasure D1454ff.; person substitutes for h. sacrifice K1853.2; pestilence in h. form F493.0.3; pisāca eats h. flesh G312.1; primeval h. pair A1270ff.; reincarnation in another h. form E605; relation of planets to h. life A787; revenant in h. form E425; spirit in h. form F401.6; star descends as h. being A762; sun as h. being A736; trees with fruits like h. heads F811.8; troll in h. form F455.2.5; why tigers eat h. flesh A2435.3.9.3; wild hunt throws h. flesh on persons who see it E501.18.2.

Humanity. — Objects attempt to destroy h. A1009.2.

Humble disguise K521.4.3, K1815; man asks aid of incognito king K1812.1.1; man miraculously saved from drowning Q151.5; rewarded Q4. — Incognito king helped by h. man K1812.1; king of h. lineage cannot be flattered J915; parents make selves h. before their son M312.2; proud ruler becomes h. L410ff.; transformation to h. man D24; wise man h. in death J912.

Humiliated lover J1251.1, K1214.1.1. — Princess h. for loathly marriage S322.1.4.

Humiliating owner by mutilating horses S175; penances Q523ff.; punishments Q470ff. — Deception into h. position *K1200—K1299.

Humiliation curse M438. — Seal of h. L11.1.

Humility J900—J999; rewarded Q66; as suitor test H313. — Devil spares abbot because of h. Q61.2; lightning strikes monk who despises h. Q552.1.1; magic depends on h. D1749.2; seven daughters of H. Z71.5.6.13.

Humming. — Ceaseless h. as punishment Q501.8; fools frightened at h. of bees J2614.1.

Hummingbird can see fowler's net but eagle is caught L333. — Industrious h. rewarded Q5.2.

Humor X (entire chapter); of discomfiture X0—X99; based on drunkenness X800—X899; of lies and exaggeration X900—X1899; of physical disability X100—X199; dealing with professions X300—X499; concerning races or nations X600—X699; concerning sex X700—X799; concerning social classes X200—X599; dealing with tradesmen X200—X299.

Humors. — Four h. Z71.2.3.

Hump. — Why animal has h. on back A2356.2.1, A2356.2.6, A2356.2.9; fairies remove hunchback's h. F344.1; giant with h. F531.1.6.11.

Humps. — Magic object causes h. to appear on back D1375.5.

Hunchback cured F953.1, (by fairies) F344.1; dwarf F451.2.1.4; healed as reward Q161.3; leads blind man N886.1; springs into fire, dies J1812.4.1. — Princess elopes with h. T91.6.4.3; three h. brothers drowned K2323; witch causes h. G269.11.1.

Hundred-handed giants F515.0.2.1; -headed serpent B15.1.2.10.2; league stride D2122.2; rajahs in love with one woman T27.3. — Alms to be returned h-fold J1262.5; city with h. palaces, gardens F761.1.1; cow makes a h.-fold return K366.1.1; eating h. onions J2095; monster with h. hands, h. palms on each, h. nails on each palm B15.7.15; prophecy: girl shall have h. lovers M345.1; surely saw h. wolves W211.2.

Hundreds. — Carrying h. of sheep across stream one at a time H1111; dwarfs come into the land by h. F451.3.14.1; person h. of years old F571.7.

Hundred-thousand. — Monkey becomes h. feet high D411.5.5.

Hung, see also **Hanged.** — Clothes h. on sunbeam *F1011.1; king h. between two fires K2213.15, Q414.5; stars h. in heavens as decoration A763.2; wolf h. by man B275.1.3.1.

Hungary. — Battle between lice of Strassburg and of H. X651.

Hunger cure J1606; in hell A689.3. — Faithful animal at master's grave dies of h. B301.1; food alone keeps off h. J712; magic object causes constant h. D1373ff.; magic object produces immunity from h. D1349.1; mice die of h. J1269.10; origin of h. A1345; starving colt fierce from h. J2214.10; tightening belt to counteract h. F1076; wager on whose h.

greater: man or beast? N73; wolf prefers liberty and h. to dog's servitude with plenty L451.

Hungry ghost reborn as jackal E694.1; ghosts haunt house seeking food E281.1; man eats fish intestines next morning J1606.1; old woman shakes, causes earthquakes A843; parson and porridge-pot X431. — Changeling always h. F321.1.2.2; coming neither h. nor satisfied (task) H1063; contract between h. god and untouchable M242.2; don't set h. guard over food J215.1.1; dwarf children are h. F451.3.5.3; fruit flies from h. man's reach Q501.2.1; mother drives away h. and compels the filled to eat H583.4.4; retorts from h. persons J1340ff.

Hunt for extraordinary animal F989.15. — Convening h. tabu C751.3; devil carries off h.-loving priest M219.2.4; king (prince) lost on h. has adventures N771; man on h. falls into ogre's (witch's) power G405; otherworld journey as h. F4; parents to abandon children on h. S345; skill in h. as suitor test H326.3; treacherous murder during h. K917; wild h. (see **Wild Huntsman** for analysis of this item) *E501ff.; wonderful h. (lie) X1110.

Hunter P414; beats dog which has grown old in his service W154.4; discovers girl being reared in cave N724; kills devil G303.16.19.20; mistakes louse for game J1759.2; reduced to ashes by power of heroine's chastity *D2061.2.5; rescues abandoned child R131.1; throws away what he catches and what he does not catch he carries with him (lice) H583.3; wants to be shown lion tracks, not lion himself W121.1. — Child born with weapon and game animal to be h. N121.1.2; devil as a h. in green G303.5.2.2; fairies give h. a dog F343.2; fisher and h. exchange catches for variety: soon return to original food U136; hero as mighty h. A526.2; lie: remarkable h. X1100; magic object from h. D823; one bird escapes as h. bends his bow: other remains and is shot J641.1; prophecy: success as h. M326, M369.10; skillful h. F679.5.

Hunter's ghost as nightmare F471.14; mass J2474; prey stolen D2087.2.

Hunters. — Beast seeks saint's help against h. B251.4.1.1; goddess protects animals from h. A189.12; jokes about h. X584, X1100; magic birds lure h. B172.6; Pleiades from h. marooned in sky A773.5; prophecy: h. will encounter boar M397; stag escapes h. to be eaten by lion N255.1; transformation to lure h. D659.10; women h. E501.3.10, F565, F565.4.

Hunting as animal's occupation A2452ff.; contest H1592, (won by deception) K30ff.; cry must be followed C681.1; fairy animal F241.0.1; a madness of kings P12.1; pig tabu C841.4; tabu in certain season C755.6; tabu on shortest day C636; of wild boar explained A1422.3; woman beaten, corpse's ankles tied E442.1. — Accidental success in h. N620ff.; devil destroys h. party with terrible wind G303.20.2; devil in disguise h. souls E752.1.1; devil dressed in h. clothes G303.5.5; devil gives luck in h. G303.10.7; devil h. lost souls G303.7.1.3; earl imprisoned for h. in king's forest Q433.10; enemies caused to lose sight while h. D2062.2.4; fairies h. human beings F368; ghost h. lost article E415.1; giant carries

prodigious h. prey F531.3.13.1; giant's h. F531.3.12; god of h. A452; infallible h.-dog B121.1.1; intercourse at h. season forbidden C119.1.3; lame man h. from wheel chair X143.1; magic h. collar *D1068.1; Milky Way a h. party A778.1; origin of h. A1458, (customs) A1520ff.; otherworld reached by h. F159.1; prince h. enters on quest H1222; sham prowess in h. K1968; tabu: h. in certain forest C614.1.0.2; trickster's greed while h. causes him to be deserted J2751; women not to participate in h. activities C181.2; wild huntsman wanders for h. on Sunday *E501.3.6.

Huntsmen. — Wild h. *E501.

Huntswoman. — Wild h. wanders for daughter's murder E501.3.10.

Hurling. — Playing in h.-match for corpses H1436; rock h. down hill slays enemy K914.2.

Hurting. — People magically continue h. themselves D2184.

Husband, see also **Bridegroom;** abandons wife to become ascetic V462.0.3; accepts children born buring long absence J2342.2; afraid of wife's paramour J2626.1; answers behind statue when wife wants to know how to fool him K1971.1; arrives home just as wife is to marry another *N681; assigns task to king stealing his wife H931.1.1; attracted by wife's power of healing: recognition follows H151.8; behind statue of saint advises wife to spin and weave K1971.4; becomes cannibal from eating wife's breast G36.1; concealed in wife's ear F1034.1; as cuckold K1500ff.; deceives wife with substituted bedmate K1844; digs up alleged treasure: wife taken K1388.1; discredited by absurd truth J1151.1.2; disguised as wife's relative K1839.13; disguised as woman answers wife's riddle with ten fingers H582.3; disguises as woman to spy on wife K1836.1; eats wife G77; eats wife's share of food W125.5; fondles second wife in presence of first as punishment for adultery Q484; forgiven for murdering wife: afterwards builds monastery Q171.1.1; follows witch G249.6; free from jealousy required M137.1; as God behind the tree forces his wife to confess adultery *K1971.5; ignored or discouraged by ghost wife E385.1; killed for having married against father's wishes K959.2.1; kills returning adulteress Q411.0.1; learns of wife's unfaithfulness by ring H94.0.1; loses willingness to die for mate H1556.4.5; magically forgets wife D2003.1; more merciful than blood relations P213; outwits adulteress and paramour *K1550ff.; persecutes wife S410ff.; poses as wife's brother K1919.1; pursues fairy wife to heaven F300.2; recognized by tears at sight of bird H14.1; refuses to believe wife unfaithful J2342; refuses to murder his wife for high honors (wife not so faithful) H492.1; rescues wife R151, (from burning to death) N658; resuscitated by cutting off wife's nose E165.2; has his strong servant substitute in bed with strong wife K1844.1; in seclusion during wife's pregnancy T583.10.1; shames wife's lover over kisses K1218.10; substitutes leaky vessel so that his wife and paramour are drowned Q466.1; tied to bed, wife's lover kills him K713.1.7; transformed to mouse to rescue wife R115.1; tricks poet into

slaying wife's lover K863.1; unwittingly instrumental in wife's adultery K1544; and wife *P210ff., (burn their mouths) J1478, (each receive money to bury the other) K482.1, (poison each other) K1613.2; to wife: "let him have what he wants" K1354.2.1. — Adulteress lures h. to his death K778.5; animal h. C36ff., (killed, wife throws self into pyre) B691, (provides animal food) B600.2; animal wins h. for mistress B582.1.2; adulteress outwits h. K1510ff.; adulteress pretends to faint when h. strikes her with rose K2051.2; beast-h. not to stay too long at home C713.3.1; to be beaten by deceiver of h. J1182.1; bride not to eat on journey to h. C232.1; burial of living h. or wife with dead spouse S123.2; cannibal h. *G81; continent h. and audacious water T315.2.1; crab shape of h. destroyed D719.2; cruel h. *S62; dangers to h. in bridal chamber T172; dead h. protests wife's second husband E221.3; dead wife asks h. go to spirit world E322.2.1; dead wife lives with h. until his death E322.6; dead wife haunts h. on second marriage *E221.1; departing h. assigns his wife tasks *H922; devil gives suspicious h. ring G303.9.7.3; devil-h. eats corpses G20.1; devil follows wife's curse, takes h. C12.5.7; disguised h. visits his wife K1813; not to eat food of transformed h. C243; eavesdropping wife hidden in bushes killed unwittingly by h. N322.2; fairy avenges herself on inconstant h. F302.3.3.1; fairy wife deserts mortal h. for repulsive lover F302.2.1; faithful h. T210.2; false bride fails when h. tests her K1911.3.3; false h. duped into entering jar J1172.3.1; fault-finding h. nonplussed J1545.3; first h. hideous, is hidden A1279.1; fox-h. lured off K341.29; future h. foretold M369.2.1; future h. met during magic sleep D1976.2; future h. revealed in dream D1812.3.3.9; which was most generous, h., robber, or lover? H1552.1; guest unaccompanied by h. slept with C119.2; heartbreak when former h. found alive F1041.1.3.7; henpecked h. returns home after hearing rooster crow J1811.4.1; heroine endures hardships with menial h. L113.1.0.1; impoverished h. begs from expelled wife L432.3; impoverished h. in wife's service recognized H152.2; imprisoned h. freed through wife's prayers V52.10; injured h. will not kill naked man P641; jealous h. T257, (kills innocent wife) N348; king rewards h. of woman spurning him Q87.1.2; kissing supernatural h. forbidden C121; lazy h. W111.4; leave of absence for obedient h. J2523; loathly h. god in disguise D733.3; loss of wife (h.) for breaking tabu C932; magic belt protects against h. D1387.3; magic hairs summon h. D1425.2; magic forgetting of wife when h. removes shirt she has given him D2004.6; man with unfaithful wife comforted when he sees jealous h. who carefully guards wife cuckolded J882.2; offending supernatural h. forbidden *C32ff.; olive branch insures fidelity of h. D1355.8; only h. of certain queen can rule P29.1; origin of code of conduct between h. and wife A1571; peace bought for h. M236; poor suitor makes good h. L143.2; predestined h. T22.3; prediction by bird

that girl will have dead h. M353; prophecy: death through future h. M341.2.12; property disposal rouses sham-dead h. J2511.1.1; quest for vanished h. H1385.4; resuscitation of wife by h. giving up half his remaining life *E165; retorts between h. and wife J1540ff.; not to reveal secret of supernatural h. *C421ff.; rose sheds petals when h. thinks of wife H1556.4.6; second h. ordered to return wife to first in pregnant condition J1173.1; seduction by masking as woman's h. *K1311; of seven wives each has h. one day T145.1.2; sham threat to evade h. K1771.6; stupid h. J1702; sun and moon as h. and wife A736.1.4.2; supernatural h. resumes true shape C32.1.2; supernatural h. takes wife to heaven F2.1; tabus for girl going to her h. C161; thief feigns pursuit by drunken h. K314; tiger-h. disenchanted D789.9; transformation to cure inconstant h. D662; transformed h. C32.1.1; twofold death of fairy's mortal h. C435.1.1.1; unexpected meeting of h. and wife N741; unfaithful h. loses magic wife C31.12; unrestricted intercourse between h. and wife A1352.1; when death comes wife points to h. K2065.1; whiskerless h. mistaken for lover in bed J1485.1; wife assigns h. tasks H934.1; wife betraying h. to father K2213.7; wife confesses for h. V29.5; wife flees h. R227; wife gives h. money to buy self genitals J1919.8; wife persuades h. he has cut off her nose J2315.2; wife reforms wayward h. J1112.1; wife rescuing h. from supernatural H923.1; wife tempts h. as another woman H1556.4.2.1; wife behind tree advises h. K1971.4.1, K1971.6.1; wife deceives h. with substituted bedmate K1843; wife in disguise wooed by her faithless h. K1814; wife persuades h. (to have a good tooth pulled) J2324, (that he is dead) J2311.0.1, (that house has moved during his absence) J2316, (that she has returned immediately) J2315, (that yarn has changed to tow) J2325; wish for h. realized (animal) C26, (exalted) *N201, (supernatural) C15; witch transforms h. into dog G263.1.4; woman deceived into sacrificing honor when ruler promises to release her h. K1353; woman devours her h. G11.6.4; woman dies of shame at seeing naked h. F1041.1.13.2; woman with more than one h. T146; woman as scorpion to punish h. E693.3; woman seeks lost h., entertains all travelers H152.1.1; woman subservient to h. A1571.2; woman substitutes for h. in combat K3.3; woman suckling h. R81.1.

Husband's hands tied, wife drowns K1652; love turns to hatred D1908.1; magic gift returns to him N212.1; return simulated, wife abducted K755.1. — Animals warn wife of h. danger B521.4; dead h. friendly return *E321; death from hearing of h. death F1041.1.2.2; faithless h. intrigue exposed K1271.3; forgotten fiancée reawakens h. memory D2006.1ff.; lost h. bones found among cannibals G691.4; lover sees mistress in h. father's house T35.5; magic sword protects woman from fairy lover in h. absence D1386.1; procuring dead h. heart F81.1.1; quest assigned by wife through appeal to h. love for her H1212.2; sham death to escape h. plot K522.3; transformation to h. form to seduce woman *D658.2; woman battles demons for h. soul E756.5.

Husbands. — All h. have perished on bridal night *T172.0.1; characteristics of wives and h. *T250ff.; gullible h. *J2301; hero chooses h. C566.4; hostile brides kill h. in the bridal bed T173.2; six short, fat h. married to fat, tall wives X151.1; tests for true h. H422; wager: h. able to do what wives tell them N13; wagers on h. N10ff.; woman with two h. is to be killed J1171.3.

Husking. — Bear h. millet B571.4.

Husks. — Replacing h. disguises grain theft K419.6.

Hussars. — Dwarfs mistaken for h. F451.6.2.3.

Hut becomes mansion D1867.1; for invalid to prevent noxious odor P661; transformed to palace D478.8. — Hermit's h. at border of otherworld F147.2; hero lives in h. L134; peasant's h. contrast to castle P411.1.1; stick becomes spirit h. D451.6.2; stone transformed to h. D452.1.1; wall of snow around h. in answer to prayer D2143.6.2.

Huts. — Grass h. as dwellings A1435.3; spirit h. V112.1.

Hvergelmir A661.1.0.4.

Hyades, origin of A775.

Hybrid animals A2382, B11—B14.

Hydra B15.1.2.8.1. — Poison of h. corrodes the skin F1041.5; separable soul in head of h. E715.6.

Hydrax. — Why h. has no tail A2235, A2378.2.5.

Hyena changes sex yearly B754.1.1; leads hermit from wilderness B380.1; poses as father, kills child K2011.1.3; with 365 different colors B731.14; turns into man D313.4. — Color of h. A2411.1.7.1; creation of h. A1834.3; devil as h. G303.3.3.2.9; helpful h. B435.6; man transformed to h. D113.5; mean person reborn as h. E692.2; reincarnation as h. E612.9; wedding of fox and h. B281.1; why h. stayed in burrow A2282, A2433.3.4; why h. has short left hind foot A2284.6, A2375.2.5.

Hyena's enemies A2494.3ff.; walk A2441.1.4.

Hyenas. — Army of h. B268.13.

Hymenoptera, creation of A2010ff.

Hymn drives away devils G303.16.2.4; prevents starvation D2105.1.1. — Devil sings h., becomes angel G303.8.1.2.1; magic h. *D1275.3, (assures heaven for person singing it) D1588.3, (effects prison escape) D1395.7, (protects) D1380.14.1, (protects against demons and vices) D1385.16, (protects against poison) D1383.4.1, (protects against poverty, death and dishonor) D1389.9, (protects from fire) D1382.7.1; magic results from singing h. D1766.9; origin of h. A1464.2; reward for writing h. Q35; saint writes h. to free self from wife T253.3; sight miraculously restored while poet writes h. F952.0.1.

Hymns V83. — Dwarfs dislike singing of h. F451.5.9.2; seas sing h. F931.12.

Hypnotic. — Magic sleep by h. suggestion D1962.4; snake's h. stare B765.14.

Hypnotised. — Person h. into believing himself transformed K1262.

Hypocrisy in confession: false shame over trivial sin V26; punished

Q267; of wife showing what she has done for her husband, but not what she has done for herself T263. — Detection of h. K2060ff.; doctor glad that all h. will have an end J171.2.3.

Hypocrite acclaimed as saint U116. — Blind tiger recognizes h. F655.2.

Hypocrites *K2000—K2099.

"I can't hear you" X441.1; "don't understand" J1802.1.

Ibexes. — Fairies own i. F241.5.1.

Ibis. — Riddle about i. H842.3.

Ibycus, Cranes of N271.3.

Icarus's wings melt F1021.2.1.

Ice bridge F842.1.2; controlled by magic D2144.5; flakes magically made small D491.4; forms while fish leaps from pool F935.2; transformed to grease D476.1.9. — Bear builds house of wood, fox of i. J741.1; bear persuaded to fish with tail through i. K1021; dupe forced on to thin i. drowns himself K893; flood from i. melting A1016.3; magic beads break i. jam D1549.11; magic i. D904; magic transportation on i. sheet D2125.2; man cuts i. with own head (lie) X1858; man falls through i. with his horse and wanders about on river bottom X1737.1.1; mermaid can pass through i. B81.8; mountain of i. F759.5; palace of i. F771.1.7; porridge in the i. hole J1938; pursuers tricked onto thin i. K893.1; rabbits freeze feet fast to i. at night X1115.1; revenant with i.-cold hands E422.1.3; sea of i. in otherworld F162.4.1; sea-scum becomes i. D469.4; sea turns to i. to permit flight D675; treasure found if one goes with one-night old colt onto one-night old i. N542.1; universe created from i. A623.

Ichneumon. — Helpful i. B433.3.

Ichor. — Gods have i., not blood A139.9.2.

Ichthyophages (people who live on fish) F561.2.

Icicles as firewood F962.9. — Dancers upon whom i. hang F572; saint's breath makes i. burn D1566.1.4.2.

Icy hell E481.7, E755.2.5.

Identical persons F239.2, H1381.3.5. — Adopted child i. with real one T678; culprit exposed to situation i. to one in which he sinned H1573.7.1; fairy women i. F239.2; friends i. in appearance F577.1; magic object to be chosen from among i. worthless objects K859.5; quest for woman i. with another H1381.3.5; recognition of transformed person among i. companions H161.

Identically. — Choosing princess from others i. clad H324; man does not know himself from another i. clad J2012.5; warriors i. equipped Z210.0.1.

Identification by cloth or clothing H110ff.; by a hair H75; by matching parts of divided token H100ff.; by ornaments H90ff. — Magic i. of headless body D1819.3.

Identifying rice in sack H522.3. — Ghost i. self E451.4.1; recognition by i. of property H19.1; trip to otherworld for i. dead F12.2.

Identity established, execution evaded N686; tests *H0—H199. — Boys

scolded to conceal i. K649.3; death result of mistaken i. N338; disclosing own i. forbidden C436; fairy dry in rain reveals i. F259.3; lover's gift regained: accidental discovery of i. K1581.4; magic knowledge of stranger's i. D1810.0.13; objects with mistaken i. J1770ff.; revealing i. of certain person forbidden C422; talking bed reveals king's i. N617; uncertainty about own i. *J2010ff.

Idiocy. — Pretending i. as protection J822.1.

Idiot thinks he's been dead twelve years J2311.11.

Idiot's magic power D1716.1.

Idle sons-in-law driven away by reducing food P265.1. — Devil writes down all i. words spoken in church G303.24.1.6.

Idleness begets woe J21.50. — Fool sleeps so as to avoid i. J2243.

Idol, see also **Image;** drinks milk D1633.1; opens to hide fugitive R325.2. — Alleged i. promises pay for book K1971.13; heathen beats i. because of misfortune V381; magic i. as chastity test H411.9.1; magic from stone i. D1726.2; marriage of girl to i. T117.4; naked i. considered poor J2216; punishment for beating i. Q222.5.6; saint's bachall defaces i. V356.3; Satan builds i. G303.9.1.14; speaking i. D1610.21.2; storm overturns i. F962.0.2; tabu: giving away i. C51.8.

Idols found on faces after saint's arrival V347. — Christian hero overthrows heathen i. V356; devils dwell in i. G303.8.14; ground swallows heathen i. F948.1; origin of i. A1544; worship of i. V1.11.

Idolators. — Branches turn to avoid i. F979.20; devil makes i. of believers G303.9.4.5.1.

Idolatry punished Q237; tabu C62. — Demons teach i. G302.9.8; love as inducement to i. T6; magic spring detects i. H251.3.9.1.

Ignorance. — Absurd i. J1730—J1749, (of animals' nature or habits) *J1900ff.; boy reared in i. of world T617; child confined to keep him in i. of life J147; feigned i. of person's identity K1792; ingratitude from i. W154.23; men not chosen for their i., else he should have reached heaven J911.1; ogre deceived by feigned i. of hero G526; repartee based on clerical i. J1263.1; seduction through i. of intercourse K1363; wise man acknowledges his i. J911.

Ignorant surpasses learned man L143. — Devils are i. of thoughts of men G303.13.1; only husband i. of wife's infidelity J2342.5; sheep and i. shearer J229.2.

Ignoring the unpleasant J1086.

Iguana persuades jackal to let him go K551.2.1. — Man becomes i. D197.1; oil sold to i. J1852.1.2; reincarnation as i. E614.5; why i. lives in stream A2433.6.4.

Ill-gotten. — Devil in each stone of church built with i. wealth G303.8.4.2; eagle carries off i. gain Q557.3.

Ill-mannered. — Dwarfs are i. F451.3.13.

Ill-omen. — Beast of i. B147.1.2ff.; bird of i. B147.2.1ff.

Illegible. — Curse makes books i. D2089.5.

Illegitimacy discovered by urinalysis F956.2. — Adulteress on deathbed reveals children's i. T238; boy twitted with i. seeks unknown (father) H1381.2.2.1.1, (mother) H1381.2.2.2.1; child not guilty of i. P526.2.

Illegitimate, see also **Bastard;** child exposed S312; children *T640ff.; son preferred to legitimate P233.4. — Father of i. child must walk in front of cross J1515.1; king must resign if begets i. son P16.2.1; lots cast to determine father of i. child N126.2; man as God behind the tree forces the girl to admit having an i. child K1971.5.1; murdered i. children as nightmares F471.1.3; Pleiades seven i. children A773.4.

Illicit sexual relations *T400—T499.

Illiterate pretends to be weeping over book K1795.

Illness, see also **Disease, Sickness;** from fear W121.8; feigned (to call physician paramour) K1514.11, (to cause child sacrifice) S268.1, (to bring about capture) K757, (causes death) Q591.1, (destroys magic) *D866.2, (to escape) K523, K1227.5, (by fox to enter hen-roost) K828.2, (to impose quest) H1212; (to go to mistress) K1569.3, (to learn secret) K2091, (to take life of helpful animal) *B335.2, (to seduce) K1326, K1339.3, K1393, (to surprise wife with paramour) K1553.1, (to test wife) H467.1, (by thief) K325 K411.1; (to woo hero) T55.5; from grief F1041.21. — Dream warns of i. D1810.8.3.1.1; extraordinary i. F1041.9; intercourse during i. tabu C119.1.1; origin of i. A1337.8; prayer that overbearing knight's i. be increased W185.2; quest assigned because of feigned i. H1212; water-spirits cause i. F420.5.2.12; witch causes i. G263.4.0.1.

Illogical use of numbers J2213.

Illuminating. — Self-i. stones in heaven A661.0.7.

Illusion dissipated by cross D2031.0.3. — Adultery presented as i. to husband K1518.1; deception by disguise or i. *K1800—K1899; extraordinary valley gives i. of earthly paradise F756.2.1; magic i. *D2031ff., (prevents raising treasure) N564, (as protection) D2031.6ff.; saint's i. deceives army D2163.7; unwitting murder because of insane i. N325; wizard gives i. man has been away twenty (forty) years D2012.2.

Illusions *K1870ff.; caused by magic object D1368ff.

Illusory, see also **Imaginary;** enemies K1883; light K1888. — Captor persuaded into i. punishment *K580ff.

Image, see also **Idol;** of animal vivified D445; of boy made of flowers comes to life D435.1.3; of child as substitute for one T677; of deceased comes alive E53.2; detects false oath H251.3.5; of God of Love sent to fetch bride T56.2; of horse will be vivified for only one person D445.1.1; in mirror mistaken for picture J1795; pierced with pins as love charm D1355.3.2; takes 1,000 men to carry it F855.4; transformed to person D435; of Virgin tries in vain to keep nun from leaving convent V265.1; of Virgin miraculously heals V256.2; of Virgin works miracles V268.5. — Ass who carried divine i. thinks people bow before him J953.4;

basilisk killed by seeing own i. B12.3; Christ's i. has broken his arm J1823.1.2; exorcism by injuring witch's i. G271.4.2; extraordinary i. F855ff.; god as an i. A139.8.6; hidden man behind i. gives unwelcome answer to suppliant: i. is blamed K1971.8; living person acts as i. of saint K1842; magic i. of animal relieves from plague D1586.1; man created in creator's i. A1212; man made from clay i. and vivified A1241.3; man worships devil's i. in order to secure advancement V55; mankind from vivified wooden i. A1252.1; murder by abuse of i. D2061.2.2.3; oracular i. *D1311.7; person cured by repairing i. that has the same deformity D2161.4.4; reincarnation of man to stone i. E648.2; recognition through i. H22; sacred i. miraculously appears on stolen sacrament V35.1.2; soul as i. E743.2; speaking i. D1610.21; sacred i. appears on host V39.5; sacred i. cannot be removed D1654.8.1; seeking wife to resemble i. T51.3.1; symbolism of church and i. H619.2; tabu: unseemly acts while carrying divine i. C56; tabu to throw away holy i. C94.6; temple about to be taken over by pagans saved by appearance of i. of the Virgin V344; test of god: when its i. is bound it frees itself H45; thief successfully claims that stolen i. has been given him by the saint himself K405.3; transformation to wooden i. C961.3.1; wooden i. frightens invaders K2346; wooden i. substituted for stolen child F451.5.2.3.1; wrestling match between fever, stone i. K12.4; youth gazing at own i. drowned N339.10.

Images *V120ff.; act as if alive *D1620ff. — Demons in stone i. exorcised D2176.3.3.1; gilded i. substituted for solid gold K476.4.1; misunderstanding concerning i. of Christ J1823.1; oracular i. occupied by spirits or priests who give the answers K1972; origin of religious i. A1544; spittle i. enable escape K525.10.

Imaginary, see also **Illusory;** debt and payment J1551. — King pays for i. weapon K499.7; lies about i. animals X1370; magician makes people lift garments to avoid wetting in i. river D2031.1.

Imagination. — Active i. W211; magic journey through power of i. D2121.3.

Imbolg. — Festival of I. V70.6.

Imitating witch with ointment in eye G242.8. — Dupe i. trickster's thefts is caught K1026; magic results from i. desired action D1782.1; tabu: i. god C51.5.

Imitation of animals cry to distract owner's attention from his goods K341.7; of cockcrow deceives devil G303.16.19.4.1; and the real pig J2232. — Animal characteristics from i. of other animal or object A2272ff.; cure by i. F957; fatal i. of how first man killed himself J2374; first poetry composed in i. of tones of hammer on anvil A1464.1.1; foolish i. *J2400—J2449; origin of death from unsuccessful i. of bad creator *A1335.2.

Immaculate Conception V312.

Immature. — Suitor finds girl i.; father protests she's already a mother J1279.3, U117.
Immediate death for breaking tabu C921.
Immediately. — Task: hatching eggs i. H1023.1.2.
Immersing. — Disenchantment by i. in water D766.1; transformation by i. D591.
Immersion. — Ascetic i. V462.8.
Immigrants repopulate Ireland A1006.6.
Immoderate request punished *A2232ff., Q3, *Q338.
Immolation S125; as punishment Q455ff.
Immortal animals B843; bird B37; fairies F259.1.4; giant F531.6.4.3; as helper N819.1; horse B184.1.8; serpent B91.7; sky A702.9. — God half i. A122; middle head of hydra i. B15.1.2.8.1; sight of mermaid bathing makes man i. B81.13.3; twin gods: one mortal, other i. A116.1.
Immortals, Land of F116.
Immortality D1850ff. — Belief in i. V311; druids teach doctrine of i. V311.0.1; fairies as sprites who have been given i. F251.5; fairies' food gives i. F243.5; magic drink gives i. to gods A154.1; magic food give i. to gods A153.2; magic object gives i. D1346ff.; quest for i. H1376.7; quest for plant of i. H1333.2.1; reincarnation origin as message of i. E600.1; request for i. punished by transformation into tree Q338.1; serpent given i. A1335.5; Solomon refuses water of i. for himself J369.1; tabu broken, i. lost C937.1; tabu to disbelieve in i. C61.2.
Immovability. — Magic i. of saints D1654.0.1.
Immovable fountain jet F716.4; object *D1654ff. — Animal rendered i. D2072.0.2ff.
Immunity from disaster as reward Q150ff.; to poison by eating poisons F959.6.2; from pestilence through kissing relic J762.1; from punishment for sin as reward Q171; from violent death as reward Q154. — Magic drug give i. from fire and iron D1344.2.1; magic i. (from fatigue) D1924, (from hunger and thirst) D1349.1; magic peach gives i. from age D1338.3.2, D1349.2.1; prophecy: i. from certain types of death M367.
Immunities of saints V228.
Immutable god A102.3.
Imp as witch's familiar G225.8.
Impalement as punishment Q461.
Impaling children on cleaning pretense K1461.3; enemies' heads S139.2.2.1. — Giant i. self on javelin K897.2.1.
Impatience W196.
Impenetrable breastplate D1381.10.1.
Imperfect god A102.18. — Recognition through i. disguise H151.6.2.
Impersonated. — Captive i. by rescuer R121.2; fugitive i. by magic object *D1611ff.
Impersonation. — Objects stolen by magic i. K359.5.
Impiety punished *A2231ff., *Q220ff.

Impious man's head embitters well F933.4. — Devil exhibits benovolence to i. people G303.22.5; devil plagues i. people Q220.1; devil in wagon drawn by two black horses carries off i. people G303.7.3.1; lake bursts forth to drown i. people A920.1.8.

Implement, see also **Tools.** — Animal characteristics from transformation of i. A2262ff.; chopping down tree with blunt i. (task) H1115; mountain-men leave broken i. for man to mend F460.4.3.

Implements bewitched G265.8.3. — Acquisition of household i. A1446.5; extraordinary i. F887; magic i. *D1170ff.

Important man quarrels with commoner J1141.8; and unimportant work J370ff. — Wealth is most i. J707.

Importunate lover (put asleep in street) Q473.4, (made ridiculous) K1213ff.

Impossible for cuckold's knife to carve boar's head H425.1; demand rebuked J1512ff.; for devil to eat in an inn G303.4.8.4; for devil to enter house with horseshoe over door *G303.16.17; for devil to take one who has read Pater Noster G303.16.2.1; for devil's unfinished work to be completed by human hands G303.14; for ogre to cross stream G638; for ogre to endure daylight G632; to please everyone J1041; quests H1371; to rid oneself of cobold F481.3; task assigned by plaintiff H919.4; tasks *H1010—H1049; tasks drive off fairies F381.11. — Castle revolving at night so that entrance is i. to find F771.2.6.2; comfort in the contemplation of i. pleasure J864; construction from i. amount of material (task) H1022; construction from i. kind of material (task) H1021; courage makes i. possible U243; devil cheated by imposing an i. task K211; death sentence escaped by propounding riddle i. for king (judge) to solve *H542; ghost laid by i. task E454; guests make i. demands J1563.2; land in which i. things happen *X1503; ogre sets i. tasks G465; punishment: performing i. task Q512; resuscitation i. after certain length of time E162; woman who asked for news from home gets i. answers J2349.4

Impostor acting as God in tree burned K1971.12; of low origin recognized by habitual speech H38.2ff.; punished *Q262, (by boiling in tar) Q414.1.1, (by burning) Q414.0.6. — Kingdom lost to i. P15.3; seduction by i. K1315; youngest daughter suspects i. L62.

Impostor's. — Girl takes i. place in marriage bed K1611.3.

Impostors. — Country of i. F709.3; marital i. K1910ff.; treacherous i. K1930ff.

Impostures K1900—K1999.

Impotence humiliates lover K1233; induced by magic T591.

Impotent husband gets substitute for virility test K1848.1. — Devil is made i. by confession G303.16.9; woman rids self of i. husband T271.1.

Impounded water *A1111.

Impoverished, see also **Poor;** fairy seeks fortune F393.3; husband begs from wife's new husband L432; husband recognized H152.2; lover

falsely accused of theft K401.3; man given high post N227; nobleman offers wife to ruler W11.7.1; overrich i. by gods L482.1.

Impregnated. — Brother said to have i. sister K2121.1; girl i. by god driven from home S12.5.1; goddess i. by wind A715.2; sneering princess i. by magic L431.3.

Impregnation, see also **Conception;** of princess by hero B375.1.1; of woman by shooting stars A788.3. — Child born of artificial i. exposed S312.4; miraculous i. T510ff.; unusual i. of animals B754.6.1.

Imprisoned, see also **Prison, Prisoner;** woman refuses to eat newborn child L71. — Animals help i. master B544.1; brother unjustly i. P251.5.5; children i. in grain pot S337; fairy i. in tree F386.1; ghost i. E459.4; gods i. A173.2; man i. by ogre G422; ogre i. in his own house G514.2, (cave) G514.2.1; proud king i. L416.1; rescuing i. princess as suitor test H322.2; souls of dead i. in tree E755.4.1; virgin i. to protect virginity *T381.

Imprisonment R0—R99; by magic D1417, D2177; of person under holy protection Q227.1.1. — Care against future i. J648; dream of future greatness causes i. L425; magic i. in cleft tree Q435; punishment: i. Q433ff., (in white-hot iron house) Q414.2.

Improvement. — King's i. of kingdom for sons J701.2; man never does work so well there is no room for i. J1073.1; servant's absurd i. of master's statements J2464.

Improvident mouse eats grain stored for famine J711.2.

Impudence punished Q326.

Inability to count J2030ff.; to dislodge dog of wild huntsman from house it has entered E501.15.6.5; to find object one is carrying J2025; to find own members *J2020ff.; of flesh of stolen animal to be cooked D1318.7.1.1; of horse to draw evil dead man E411.0.3; to move D5.1; of soul to go far from grave E722.3.1; of wild huntsman's dogs to pass over a grave E501.15.6.4.

Inaccessible city F767.

Inanimate objects (act as if living) F990ff., (blamed for theft) K419.9. — Devil in form of i. objects G303.3.4.

Inappropriate action from misunderstanding J1820ff.; entertainment repaid J1565.

Inauguration. — King's i. espousal to goddess P11.6.

Incandescent objects *D1645ff.

Incantation for testing guilt H245.1. — Adulteress covers husband's eyes during i. K1516.4; dream from i. D1812.3.3.3; magic sight overcome by i. D1822.1; storm raised by i. D2141.0.7; repeating i. continuously H1508.1; resuscitation by i. E73; sham recovery of goods by i. K1956.1.1; snake killed by own i. K1613.5; woman warns lover of husband by parody i. K1546.

Incantations. — Fishhook made without proper i. C221.4.2; husband sings i. about adultery K1556.1.

Incarnated. — Culture hero i. through birth from virgin A511.1.3; resuscitation by destroying i. object E29.4.

Incarnation of god: puts on human form to help man A184. — Newborn baby's tatoo tells of former i. T563.4.

Incense relieves from plague D1586.3; as sacrifice V12.10. — Ant collects i. for Christ A2221.4; magic i. *D1295, (summons genie) D1421.1.7.

Incest *T410ff.; accidentally averted N681.3; of devil's son and his mother G303.11.1.1; punished Q242; tabu C114; unwittingly committed *N365. — Allusive expression for gods' i. A1599.16; banishment to punish i. Q431.8.1; brother-sister i. A164.1, A1331.2, A1337.0.7, A2006, G37, M365.3, Q520.3, T415, T471.1; burning as punishment for i. Q414.0.3; child of i. exposed S312.1; children of i. sterile Q553.3.2; creation of animals as punishment for i. A1733; dog tells of i. B134.1.1; father-daughter i. M344.1, Q242.2, T411, *V132.1; flood as punishment for i. A1018.2; girl becomes cannibal because of brother-sister i. G37; holy water prevents a man from committing i. with his daughter *V132.1; insects from brother-sister i. A2006; magic lost through i. D1741.6; monstrous births from brother-sister i. A1337.0.7; mother falsely accuses son of i. with her K2111.5; mother lets daughter commit i. P232.2; mother dies of fright when she learns that she was about to commit i. with her son N383.3; mother-i. prophecy M344; new race from i. after world calamity A1006.2; paradise lost because of brother-sister i. A1331.2; prophecy: daughter shall commit murder and i. M345; riddle betrays i. H582.2.1; standing on pillar as penance for i. Q541.3.

Incestuous brother burned to charcoal D1865.2.1; first parents A1273.1; marriage arranged by trick K1377; youth reincarnated as root E692.6. —Girl flees i. brother R224; god from i. union A112.1; goddess of music from i. union A112.1.1.1.; tribe's i. origin sanctions intermarriage T131.5.1.

Inciting. — Fairy i. mortals to war F369.4.1; vision i. saint V513.1.

Inclinations. — Origin of evil i. A1384.

Inclosure during calamity preserves best types A1005.2.

Inclusa K1523.

Incognito, see also **Disguise;** king (given hospitality by enemy) K1812.14.1, (joins robbers) K1812.2, (helped by humble man) K1812.1; mistress T476, (overhears lover, leaves him) J2364; prince beaten J18; prophet as matchmaker T53.1; queen accused of killing child K2116.1.4.

Incombustible objects D1656ff.

Inconstant, see **Unfaithful.**

Incontinence of clergy J1264ff., V465.1; punished Q240ff. — Burning as punishment for i. Q414.0.3; discovery of abbot's (abbess's) i. brings permission to monks (nuns) to do likewise K1274; priest catches bishop in i. J1211.1.1; tabu: i. while treasure is being raised N553.1.

Inconvenience disregarded when booty is in sight J352. — Choices: small i., large gain J350ff.; man refuses cure which brings greater i. J343.

Incorrigible liar X909.1.
Incorruptible. — Dead body i. E182.
Increasing-decreasing paradox task H1075. — Carrying ever-i. burden up mountain H1114.2; miraculous i. of food D1652.1.0.1.
Incubus F471.2.
Incurable. — Curing i. ulcer H1199.2.2; lying is i. U235.
Incurables. — Mountebank cures i. F958.
Indecent. — Princess brought to laughter by i. show made in quarrel with old woman at well H341.3.1; wife in i. posture told to lock up shop J1545.5.
Indecision W123.
Indelible blood D1654.3.
Indentions on oak-leaves A2761.1; on plants from biting A2721.2.2, A2732, A2751.3.1; on rocks from prints left by man (beast) A972; in stem of reed A2751.3.1.
Indenture. — Identification by i. H102.
Index. — Chastity i. H430ff.; flame as miraculous i. *F1061; life i. *E760ff.; quest for life i. H1353.
India as otherworld F130.1. — Origin of tribes of I. A1611.4; women wear veils in I. A1599.3.
Indian says belongings safe, no white man near J1373. — American I. tribes A1611.1; ghost as I. E425.2.4; naked I. not cold: "me all face" J1309.1.
Indians chew spruce gum A1681.1; rescue children R131.20; sprang from legs of first man A1614.7. — Escape by overawing I. K547.2; hanging innocent oldster to appease I. J2233.1.1; woman alone makes I. think men are home K548.1.
Indication of desired place by magic object *D1314ff.; of road by magic object D1313ff.; of what is burning by color of flame F1061.2.
Indications of chastity H400ff.
Indifference bred by security U270ff.; of the miserable U150ff.
Indignity to corpse E235, E341.1.1, Q491.
Indispensible. — Banished minister found i. and recalled P111; deer, oppossum, and snake each render i. aid to man J461.4; smith honored by king as i. P447.5.
Indolent, see **Lazy.**
Indra carried by cock B552.3; controls fairies F252.1.2; sends down buffalo B184.2.3.3; separates the winds A1142.7. — Fairies come from I. kingdom F282.3; fairies dance before I. F261.3.7.
Indra's palace on Milky Way A151.6.1; tank F964.5, H1359.3.
Indus. — Plunge into I. tests valor H1561.10.
Industrial processes magically interrupted D2084. — Dwarfs emigrate because of i. development F451.9.1.4.
Industrious. — Lazy boy and i. girl matched T125; obedient and i. nun V461.1.

Industry rewarded Q5; test H1569.1; as tribal characteristic A1673. — Bride test: i. H382; reward for i. Q86; value of i. J1010ff.

Inedible substances transformed into edible D476.1. — Dwarfs given i. food F451.3.7.3; edible substance changed to i. D476.2.

Ineffable name of God A138, (magic) D804.

Inept child surpasses others L141.4.

Inequalities of fortunes among men A1599.8; of life U0—U99. — Origin of i. among men A1618.

Inexhaustible object *D1652ff.; purse furnishes money D1451ff.; treasure D2100.1. — Alleged i. bottle sold K117; deceptive eating contest: i. food K81.3; fairy gift of i. meat F348.5.1.1; house-spirit furnishes i. supply of food F481.2.2.

Inexorable fate N101.

Infallible article D1653ff. — Skillful tracker i. F677.1.

Infant, see also **Baby, Child;** allowed in river, drowns J2175.4; to be drowned spared by slaves K512.0.1; exposed to avoid fulfillment of prophecy M371; fed by bees B531.1; Jesus V211.1.8; marriages T143; picks out his unknown father H481; of slain mother cares for itself T612. — Father kills i. S11.4.4; girl child fed on i. boys' flesh to make her grow faster G77; indentions on rocks from head of i. hero A972.5.1.

Infants. — Baptism of i. V81.4; women, driven mad, devour their i. N325.2.

Infectious. — Priest's fear of i. disease repayed J1551.10.

Inference. — Wisdom (knowledge) acquired from i. *J30ff.

Inferno, see **Hell.**

Infertile, see **Barren.**

Infidel defies God to strike him with lightning Q552.1.8. — Monk seduces girl, kills her, and becomes i. V465.1.1.1.

Infidelity, see also **Adultery.** — Crown exposes i. of husbands H422.1; dog (bird) betrays woman's i. *B134.1, B131.3; girl disguised as man accused of i. K2113.1; goddess killed for i. Q246.1; husband refuses to believe wife's i. J2342; man falsely accused of i. K2114; object as token of i. discovered T247; satyr reveals woman's i B24.1; spirit reveals wife's i. F403.2.3.5; supernatural person reveals i. F345.2.

Infirm. — Magic power of the i. D1716.

Inflaming. — Women i. warrior's wounds K2014.

Inflated giant floats through air F531.6.17.2.

Information from dream D1810.8.2; about sought robbers reward for rescue Q53.2. — Angel gives soul i. E759.2; magic object gives supernatural i. *D1310ff.; oracular image refuses i. except to hero D1651.6.

Ingenuity. — Lie: remarkable i. X1012.

Ingratitude *W154ff.; punished *Q281. — Dwarfs emigrate because of mortals' i. F451.9.1.12.

Inhabitant of upper world visits earth F30ff.

Inhabitants of extraordinary castle F771.4ff.; of otherworld F167. — City's i. transformed to fish D692; gods as earth's first i. A1205.
Inhabited. — Castle i. by ogres F771.4.1; island in otherworld garden i. half by dead and half by living F162.1.2.5.
Inheritance. — Blood-test for i. H486.1; cat as sole i. N411.1.1; children substituted to gain i. K1847.1; king's son returns for i. division N699.2; modest i. best L223; oath broken: i. of earth lost M101.5; orphan deprived of his i. S322.0.1; sickle as only i. N411.2.1; thankless children think that chest of stones contains their i. P236.2.
Inherited. — Animals' characteristics i. X1202; friendship i. P310.4.1; magic object i. D816; magic power i. D1737; numskull destroys i. property J2461.1.8; trickster's ability i. by his daughter J1111.2; witch's power i. G224.9.
Inhospitable. — Father's deception of i. daughter J1561.5.
Inhospitality W158; punished Q1.1, Q292; repaid J1561; reproved enigmatically H594.
Initials recall forgotten wife D2006.1.9.
Initiation into witchcraft G286. — Mock i. for dupe K1286.
Injunctions of helpful animal disobeyed B341.
Injured husband will not kill naked man P641. — Numskull i. J2131.
Injuring yourself to insure your family's future J322. — Persons duped into i. each other K1080ff.; Satan i. man G303.20.8.
Injurious food with delusive sweet taste K1889.4.
Injury by deception K2382. — Accidental self-i. N397; curse: bodily i. M431; dead return to repair i. E345; death or bodily i. by magic *D2060ff.; fairy causes i. F362.4; fitting bodily i. as punishment Q583; marvelous sensitiveness: i. from rose leaves falling F647.3; pursuer deceived into self-i. K533.1.
Injuries. — Unintentional i. bring unfortunate consequences N385.
Injustice deadliest of monarch's sins P12.2; punished Q296. — Apparent i. chosen over greater wrong J225; justice and i. U10; small i. permitted rather than to cause troubles of state J221.
Ink transformed to light beams D454.14. — Saint throws i. bottle at devil D2176.3.3.3.
Inkwell. — Pouring water into i. proves that slave girl belonged to author J1176.1.
Inn at border of otherworld F147.4. — Day's journey from earth to heaven since there is no i. to stop at on the way H682.1.2; devil builds an i. for man G303.9.1.10; devil never eats in i. G303.4.8.4; guest at i. put in mistress's bed K1396; guests at i. thieves K365.2; magic object stolen by host at i. D861.1; princess (queen) compelled to keep an i. *Q481; recognition at i. where all must tell their life histories H11.1.1; "sleep not at i." J21.41.1; trickster reports lost money: searchers leave him in possession of i. K341.1; woman outwits landlord of i. K1837.5.
Inns. — Tabu: invading i. C856.2.

Innkeeper sells substitutes for wine, meat K476.3.1; sold hay by trickster K282.1. — Stingy i. cured of serving weak beer J1341.7; treacherous i. K2241.

Innkeeper's. — Devil woos i. daughter G303.12.1.

Innkeepers. — Thieving i. guilty of arson J1149.9.

Innocence. — Bird reveals suspect's i. B131.7; blood indicates guilt or i. *D1318.5; dry branches on grave blossom as proof of i. E631.0.5.1; irrevocable sentence carried out even when i. is proved M12; the guilty protests his i. and thus detected J1141.9; one-legged bird symbol of i. H619.5; primeval human pair live in i. A1270.1; tests of guilt or i. *H210—H239; test of i.: apple and gold offered H256.

Innocent girl sells her "love" and later receives it back K1362; made to appear guilty K2150ff.; man accidentally suspected of crime N347; man executed because he fits noose J2233.1; man hanged, island sinks into sea H252.5; person condemned for theft K401.2.3; person saved from hanging by saint R165.2; queen burned at stake Q414.0.7; woman accused of murder K2116; woman falsely incriminated K2112. — Blood of i. maiden as cure for leprosy D1502.4.2.1; dead father proves son i. E327.3; don't draw sword against the i. J21.2.3; each drop of i. blood turns to burning candle D1318.5.3; extraordinary phenomena at cruelty to i. F960.7; flame where i. murdered F1061.4; premature darkness at execution of i. F965.1.1; repeated attempts to seduce i. maiden T320.1; springs from i. king's blood A941.5.8; three i. children Z71.1.5; tree from i. man's blood E631.0.5; Virgin Mary defends i. accused V252.

Innocents. — Slaughter of i. to avoid fulfillment of prophecy M375.

Inquiry, see **Questioning.**

Inquisitive fools J2370—J2399.

Inquisitiveness punished *Q342.

Insane hero L116; man accidentally cured by blow on head N642; man burns heretic in his bed: restored to his senses as reward V321. — Adulteress pretends husband i. K1548; creditor falsely reported i. when he demands money K242; driving i. by keeping awake S191; fairies dance with youth till he goes i. F302.3.4.2; faithless wife drives husband i. T230.2; man falsely reported i. K1265; sight of dead woman spinning drives people i. E561.1; sight of wild hunt renders person i. *E501.18.6; tabu to violate i. woman C118.1; unwitting murder because of i. illusion N325.

Insanity for breaking tabu C949.1; as curse M452; causes death C928; from love T24.3; magically cured D2161.3.8. — Fairies cause i. F302.3.4.2, F362.2; magic i. *D2065ff.; magic object causes i. *D1367ff.; witch causes i. G263.7.

Insatiable. — Devil as i. queen G303.3.1.12.5; girl frightened by love becomes i. K2052.2.

Inscription accidentally seen saves hero R217; on forehead F545.2.3; of holy name aids resuscitation E174; on home of riddle solver: "I have

no care" H562; of name on article as ownership token H88; rots, devil claims debtor K231.12.1; on walls for condensed education J168. — Reading i. unique ability H31.11; treasure indicated by stone with i.: "Dig here" N535.

Inscriptions. — Equivocal i. at parting of three roads telling what will happen if each is chosen N122.0.1; origin of ogam i. A1484.1; proud i. sole remains of powerful king L413.

Inscrutable ways of providence J225.0.3.

Insect asks to be put in loosely-woven basket K581.6; army B268.8; as creator A13.3; grateful for being turned over B364.3; helps select magic object D859.5; inside jewel J1661.1.6; in murdered person simulates snoring K661.3; points out deity by settling where he is H162.1; swallowed by man comes out alive E32.1; transformed to another animal D415; transformed to object D424; transformed to person D380ff.; as witch's familiar G225.1; wedding B285. — Devil as i. G303.3.3.4; fairy as i. F234.1.16; marriage to person in i. form B643; origin of color of i. A2411.3; hair transformed to i. D447.1.2; man transformed to i. D180ff.; marriage to i. in human form B653; reincarnation as i. E616; separable soul in i. E715.3; soul in form of i. E734: witch as i. G211.5.

Insect's enemies A2494.14.

Insects teach wisdom J137; worry large animal to death L315.6. — Cause of walk of i. A2441.3ff.; creation of i. A2000—A2099; creator sent down i. to plant plants A2601; cutting down tree without scratching for stinging i. H1184; devastating i. B16.6; expensive means of being rid of i. J2102ff.; food of i. A2435.5ff.; giant i. B873ff.; haunts of i. A2433.5; helpful i. B482ff.; king of i. B246; kingdom of i. B224; language of i. B215.6; lies about i. X1280; markings on i. A2412.3; saint destroys disastrous i. D2156.6; sham dead tested by stinging i. H248.2; sounds of i. A2426.3; speaking i. B211.4.

Insensate. — Guilty confronted, become i. F1041.1.3.10.1.

Insensible. — Bath rendering one i. F872.6.

Inside. — City i. a tree F765; fish with larger fish i. X1154.1.1; fool roofs house on i. Z171.2.2; journey i. the earth F114; serpent i. man's body G328.1.

Inside out. — Garments i. exorcise will-o'-the-wisp F491.3.1.

Insignia. — Kingly i. worn only in battle P13.3.1; magic i. D1299.1; origin of family i. A1578; test of valor worthy for kingship: taking possession of royal i. H1561.5.

Insolence W187.

Insomnia. — Angel of i. A472.0.1; eating of human hearts as cure for i. D2161.4.13.

Inspection test for suitors H311.

Inspiration. — Divine i. for writing sacred books D1811.2.1; prevention of hostility by i. of fear in enemy J623.

Instinct. — Bridegroom learns power of i. from ducklings J64.

Instructing, see also **Teaching.** — Fairies i. mortals F345; man wins wife by i. her how to answer her mother's riddles H551.1; seduction by i. in marital duties K1315.7.1; vision i. saint V513.1.

Instructions for magic D806; of mother followed literally by daughter when she marries J555.1. — Disastrously following i. J2460.1; literal following of i. about actions J2461.1; numskull talks about his secret i. and thus allows himself to be cheated J2355; smith receives i. from underground spirit F450.1.2.

Instrument for unlawful work sticks to user Q551.2.5. — Ghost plays musical i. E554; giant plays musical i. F531.6.17.4; man condemned to lose his eye is allowed to choose the i. P511.2; musical i. causes magic sleep D1364.25; reincarnation as musical i. *E632ff.; resuscitation by withdrawal of wounding i. E21; prophecy: death by particular i. M341.2; waking from magic sleep by removal of enchanting i. D1978.3.

Instruments of torture transformed to lotus flowers D454.16. — Fairies' musical i. F245; magic musical i. *D1210ff.; self-playing musical i. D1601.18ff.

Insult repeated as harmless remark K1775; worse than wound W185.6. — Daughter overlooks i. of father proffering new husband K2052.4.3; man called rogue by noble man makes joke of i. J817.1; pulling a man's beard as i. P672; scalding punishment for i Q469.10.3.

Insults in pseudo-magic letter K115.1.2. — Dumb princess brought to speak by i. of shepherd H343.1; enduring i. to enter city gate H1553.3; "show me how to bear i." J1284.1; seeds rattling mistaken for i. J1812.1; words in foreign language thought to be i. J1802.

Insulted. — Dwarf is i. when scolded F451.3.6.1.

Integrity rewarded Q68. — Devil appears to persons ready to abandon their i. G303.6.2.5.

Intellect doesn't reach to heels; small men preferred J493; and Fortune, Knowledge, Health dispute which is greatest J461.1.2. — Human i. unable to conceive God A182.0.2.

Intelligence personified Z128.1; of various people A1667. — Luck or i. more powerful? N141; tasks performed through cleverness or i. H960ff.

Intelligent ship *D1310.3. — Alliances with the i. J685; dwarfs are i. F451.3.12; fool given i. wife T125.1.

Intercession of queen P21.1; of the dead for mortal E576.1. — Friend's i. saves man from execution P319.3; woman's i. for her accusers W11.5.9.1.

Intercourse, see **Sexual intercourse.**

Interest. — Giants repay loan with large i. F531.5.5; owner's i. distracted to steal goods K341; what is sweetest? one's own i. H633.4; woman enamored of unknown knight loses i. when she finds he is her husband T236.

Interested. — Beware of following i. adviser J758; executioner kept i. until rescue comes K555.

Interesting. — The valuable neglected for the i. J345.

Interior. — Devil in i. of earth G303.8.5; thieves disguised as i. decorators K311.7.

Intermediate future world *A693.

Intermittent river D915.4.

Internal markings of animals A2367.2; parts of plant A2755ff. — Magic i. organs (human) D997, (animal) D1015.

Interpretation of riddling remarks by girl at end of journey H586ff. — Misfortune from mistaken i. of prophecy N398.

Interpretations, symbolic H600ff.

Interpreter. — God uses i. to address women A182.3.0.4.

Interpreters. — Wasps as language i. K137.1.

Interrupted calculation J2035; cooking G475.1. — Industrial processes magically i. D2084; judicial combat i. by friends of loser H218.1; man i. each time he tries to eat something X12; mass i. by devil with pretended battle G303.9.9.2; trickster's i. feast revenged J1564.1.

Interrupting story reveals guilt J1177.0.1.

Intervention of gods in battle A172; of queen for condemned courtiers P21. — Husband's i. prevents wife's seduction H492.2.2.

Intestines, see also **Gut;** wagered N2.3.5. — Eating fish i. next morning J1606.1; exposed i. F1096.2; horse twists i. out of himself K1444; murder by twisting out i. S139.1; person lives on with i. exposed F1096.2.

Intimidating. — Brandished heads i. foe S139.2.2.1.6; sham warrior's boasting i. soldiers K1951.3.

Intoning. — Parson i. instructions to sexton as a part of mass X441.

Intoxicated, see also **Drunk;** father impregnates girl T411.2. — Animals become i. B299.3; creator i. A32.3.2.

Intoxicating drink's first use A1427.0.3; nurse to keep lovers' rendezvous T35.3. — Secret learned by i. dupe K1165.

Intoxication avoided by hole in cup K82.1.2; from magic food D1359.4. — Capture by i. K776; fatal i. K871; god of i. A481; resisting i. as suitor test H328.1.

Intruder. — Adulteress makes husband watch for i., meets lover K1514.10; owner burns i. in house K812.4.

Intruders. — Ghosts punish i. into ghost town E241; ogre attacks i. G475ff.

Invalid. — Hut for i. to prevent noxious odor P661.

Invasion as punishment Q429.2. — False report of impending i.: trickster paid to buy it off K1784.1; otherworld journey as i. F3; prophecies concerning i. M369.5.

Invasions. — Hero defends Ireland against i. A536.1.

Inventer of death machine uses it K1681.1. — Lie: great i. X1011.

Inventions. — Patriarchs because of long life made i. A1440.3.

Invested. — Blind man's stolen money i. by thief K1667.1.2.

Investigation. — "Don't do anything without i." J21.48.

Inviolable curse M415. — Guest's life i. P324.3.

Invisibility cap admits to woman's room K1349.10; of creator A11.1; of demons G302.4.2; of island F742. — Charm gives i. D1561.2.4; dragon's power of magic i. B11.5.2; escape from battle by magic i. K531; fairies lose i. F235.8; fairies seen by mortals lose i. F255.3; magic i. *D1980ff.; magic mist of i. *D902.1; seduction by wearing i. coat K1314; theft by coat of i. K324; theft by magic i. K359.1.

Invisible arrow F831.1; creator A11; devil G303.4.8.13; god A102.9; dwarfs at christening feast made to speak by brewing beer in egg-shell F451.5.17.1; echo A497.1; ghosts E421.1; guardians N810.1; hands aid task H986; man eats bread, owners quarrel K1883.6; objects D1655ff.; witches steal G266.1. — Devil appears i. among dancers G303.6.2.1; dupe persuaded that he is i. J2337; dwarfs made i by magic caps F451.3.3.8; dwarfs emigrate i. but heard F451.9.6; exorcising i. man D2176.6; fairy car i. F242.1.1; fairy horse i. F241.1.5; fairies i. F235.1; fairies' cattle become i. F241.2.2; flight on i. horse B184.1.6.1; ghost i. during day E452.2; giants can make selves i. F531.6.5.1; huldra i. F460.1.7; magic i. pig B184.3.2.1; magic object renders i. *D1361ff.; magic power to see i. creatures D1825.3; making an i. knot with an egg H1021.5; monster husband i. T118.1; trolls i. F455.5.1; why spirits are i. A2862; wild huntsmen i. *E501.9; witch i. G210.0.1.

Invitation to buy taken as offer of gift K247. — Accepting an i. tabu C744; deaf peasant and wedding i. X111.4; deceptive i. to feast J1577; man refuses fairy i., killed F361.17.7; symbolic i. to liberality H595.1.

Invitations. — Stingy man cancels i. W152.9.

Invited. — Fairy takes revenge for not being i. to feast F361.1.1; traveler i. into devil's wagon G303.7.1.2.2; until singer is i. to feast beer will not stop foaming C682.

Inviting. — Ogress i. boys to her house G414; penance: i. brahmin to dinner Q527.

Invoice. — Thieves' i. of stolen goods J2214.3.3.

Invoking deity A183.1. — Invulnerability by i. saint D1846.5.1.

Invulnerability reward for piety Q162; of witches G229.4. — Drug of i. T325.1; magic i. *D1840ff.; magic object gives i. *D1344ff.

Invulnerable berserk F610.3.1. — Dragon i. B11.12.1; escape by reporting oneself i. and overawing captor K541; magic i. horse B184.1.11.

Io transformed to cow with gadfly ceaselessly pursuing Q501.6.

Ireland as otherworld F130.3; repopulated by flood escapees A1006.5; — Ark sails to I. A1021.0.1; coming to I. tabu in peacetime C755.3; first convert to Christianity in I. A1546.3.1; first judgment in I. A1580.1.1; first woman in I. dies of grief F1041.1.2.2.2; five great roads of I. A994; "flame of fire" plague to destroy I M356.2; hero defends I. against invasions A536.1; nine wonders of I. Z71.6.3; no snakes in I. M318; one foot in I, one in Scotland K2319.1; origin of women in I. A1611.5.4.1; otherworld king in I. F184.1; preservation of life in I. during flood

A1005.1; stay in I. in return for magic shirt M226; three-fourths of men in I. die one night Z76.1; three worst things in I. Z71.1.15; vision of flames covering I. V515.1.3; why there are no snakes in I. A2434.2.3.

Irish saint as Virgin Mary V250.1; Solomon J1170.2; souls judged by St. Patrick E751.3. — Hero invents, teaches I. language A541.1; origin of I. language A1616.2; snakes will not cross I. earth B765.18.3; tribute slaves must not know I. P172; world-fire to punish I. A1031.1.

Iron axe becomes silver D475.3.4; in bamboo in deceptive contest K44.1; bands around heart to keep it from breaking F875; birds in hell A671.2.11; blessed by saint incapable of wounding D1674; boat F841.1.13; chains sever neck in contest H1562.7; created to punish cedar's pride A978.2; -eating tribe F561.8; first used for food A1432.1.1; forehead F545.2.4; -headed person F511.0.3.1; locks, doors around otherworld F148.5; magically disappears D2089.1; man F521.3.2; nail in witch's forehead G272.14; pillars steady the earth A841.3; powerful against fairies F384.3; tools become earth D479.2; tree F811.1.9; -winged locusts eat wheat crop B16.6.3. — Animal with hair of i. pins B15.7.10.2; animal with i. snout B15.5.2; arrow discovers i. pit D1314.1.6; bacon becomes i. D476.3.2; basket of things becomes i. D479.5; bath of molten i F872.5; bird with i. beak B15.7.13.1; boy born with one side flesh and one i. T551.4; boy forged from i. T544.2; breaking i. with wooden axe H1116.2; building i. house overnight H1104.3; captive hews through i. prison R211.5; chastity ordeal: holding hot i. H412.4.1; coffin with i. band E431.20; confinement in i. house to avoid prophecy fulfillment M372.1; contest in eating i. K63.1; crushing i. wall with fists F611.3.2.3; destruction of i. castle H1562.12; devil strikes man dead with i. bar G303.20.3; dwarf cave closed by i. doors F451.4.3.1; enemy lured into i. house, roasted K811.4; fairy's i. arms F231.1.1; garden warbler hears smith beat i.: learns his song A2272.1.3; ghost rides i. chest E581.5; ghost unlaid until hidden i. found E415.1.1; giant with i. nails F531.1.6.1.1; giant can be killed only with own i. club Z312.2; giant's i. weapons F531.4.5.1; hiding i. tabu C899.1; magic i. D1252.1.1; magic i. eaten D1721.5; magic i. measure D1470.1.47; magic drug gives immunity from fire and i. D1344.2.1; magic i. chain *D1251; magic i. glove gives strength D1335.3; magic i. rod causes waters to divide and close D1551.2; man proof against i., stone, and wood D1841.1; man with one side of i. F525.1.1; mice alleged to eat i. J1531.2; murder with hot i. S112.2, (in mouth) K951.1.1; oath on the i. K1115; ogre killed with own i. bar G519.2; ogre terrified by i. man K1756; ordeal by hot i. H221.2; origin of i. A1432.1; "painting" with a red hot i. K1013.3; penance: carrying i. hoop on head until it falls off Q521.3; penance: i. band forged round man's waist Q522.5; person vomits i. F1041.20; promise to be fulfilled when i. shoes wear out *M202.1; pulling i. bars through hole as strength test H1562.11; quest for magic i. rod H1342; remarkable thrower of i. F636.1; saint invulnerable to red hot i. D1841.3.2.3; shooting

through i. with arrow H1562.13; smith forges i. man, who helps him D1620.1.3; spear driven through i. plates F625.1; strong hero struck by smith from i. F611.1.12; strong man: breaker of i. F625; sun's i. weapons A739.9; throwing i. ball as suitor test H331.16.1; time measured by worn i. shoes *H1583.1; touching with i. forbidden C531; trustee claims that mice have eaten i. scales J1531.2; one twin eats other, body becomes i. T587.2.1; voice made rough by swallowing hot i. F556.1; vomiting i. F1041.20; wandering till i. shoes are worn out *Q502.2; why tortoise may be killed with i. spear A2231.7.3; witch with i. members G219.1; witch with i. teeth G214.2; witch's hair on horse becomes i. G265.3.1; working i. under sun tabu C842.1.

Irrational men as reincarnated animals E656.1.

Irreplaceable magic object D1661. — Wife saves father as only i. male P211.1.

Irresistible. — Hero's i. beauty spot A526.3; who are i.? meat, drink H659.20.

Irreverent young people punished by outraged old man Q283.

Irrevocable judgments M10ff.; king's promise M203. — Decree of gods i. A196.2.

Isaac. — Devils fear St. I. G303.25.2; sacrifice of I. S263.2.1.

Ishtar unveiled F85.

Island becomes canoe at will D632.1, D1524.4; created by magic D2153.1.1; of the dead *E481.2.0.1; inhabited by one woman F112.0.1.1; made to appear hog's back K1886.7.1; magically transported D2136.6; mistaken for dog J1771.5; in otherworld garden inhabited half by dead and half by living F162.1.2.5; of Promise F111.2.1; sinks for man's offense to saint Q552.2.3.2.3; sinks into sea F944.3; sinks into sea after innocent man hanged H252.5; split apart C984.8; to be towed by ships to new location J2287. — Abandonment on i. *S145; bird steals i. B172.11; captivity on i. R43; dragon lives in isolated i. B11.3.8; drunk man goes to the king and wants to buy an i. X812; escape from deluge on i. A1025; fairyland on i. F213; fairies battle for i. F277.0.2; fairies go to floating i. F388.2; flying i. F738; giant extends across whole i. F531.2.1.4; glass i. in otherworld F162.0.1.1; god's dominion over floating i. A179.2; gods' home on i. A151.3.2; hero still alive on i. A571.2; home of Fortuna on i. (in otherworld) N111.1.2; impostor abandons hero on i. K1931.6; lake bursts forth where i. is plowed out A920.1.9; looking on i. tabu C315.5; magic i. *D936, (moves at owner's wish) D1643.3; magic object found on an i. D849.3; magic object from otherworld i. D813.3; man on I. of Fair Women overcome by loving women F112.1; man (woman) transformed to i. D284; monastery on otherworld i. V118.1; no sun on druid i. F961.1.6; otherworld on i. *F134; quest to submerged i. H1287.1; refuge on an i. R316.1; saints bargain over i. ownership K185.13; stone becomes i. D452.1.8; storm appears to be i. D2031.17; storm breaks i. F962.1; tabu to land on gods' i. C93.8; tabu to point boat toward gods' i. C51.9;

treasures buried on i. N511.1.12; wandering i. F737; whale thought to be i. J1761.1; women tabu on i. C619.4.

Island's ownership determined by saint's staff D1524.1.2.1, K185.13.

Islands of birds F167.1.2.1; of the blest *A692; in sea of fire in hell A671.2.4.2. — Devil builds two i. in a lake G303.9.1.9; extraordinary i. *F730ff.; journey to otherworld i. F129.4; origin of i. A955; series of otherworld i. F134.0.1.

Isle of Man as otherworld F134.1. — Banishment to desert i. Q431.2.2; journey to I. of Laughter F111.1; journey to otherworld i. F129.4.

Israel. — Covenant between I. and God M201.0.1.1; creation on condition I. accept Tora A74.1; god as protector of I. A184.1; no snakes in I. M318.1; Satan fights I. G303.9.6.1.2.

Israel's — Paths open in sea for I. tribes F931.9.3.

Israelites feed on quail swarms F989.16.1. — Covenant between heathen and I. M201.0.2.

Italians. — Origin of I. A1611.5.2.

Itch. — Magic i. D2063.4; ointment producing i. X34; origin of i. A1319.10, A1337.5.

Itself, see also **Automatic, Self.** — Object sent to go by i. J1881.1; treasure opens i. N552.

Ivory bed F787.3. — Magic wishing i. tusk D1470.1.37.

Ixion lashed to wheel Q501.5.

Jabbering of magpie outside ark over drowned world A2542.1.1.

Jack and the Beanstalk F54.2; the Giant-killer G500—G599; o' Lantern A2817, F491. — House that J. built (cumulative tale) Z44.

Jackal as beast of ill-omen B147.1.2.4; boasting, falls, eaten by alligator L476; caught in bullock's carcass J2136.6.1; cheats other animals of elephant K171.0.3; comes to fireplace for food, burned K1032.1; demands camel's tongue K255.4; in elephant's carcass K565.2; escapes by asking for drink K551.17.2; escapes crocodile by false plea K551.23; escapes farmer by calling self king K547.4; escapes tiger's house K563.1; feigns holiness to seize rats K815.16; forces all animals to praise him W116.8; gets buffalo, tiger to kill each other: feeds on meat K1084.1.1; imprisoned in elephant's dead body K1022.1.1; inside carcass pretends his voice is God's K1973; as judge J1172.3.1; as judge comes late J1531.1.1; and king discuss husbands ruled by wives T252.2.2.1; leads lost men B563.4.1.2; as leopard cubs' nurse K2061.11; and leopard tie tails together J681.1.1; made king, howls at night, killed J512.13; makes horns of wax and poses as horned animal K1991; and man engage in flattery J814.3; ordered to take meat to lion's family takes it to his own K361.1; persuades deer to steal, informs on him K2037; persuades hyena to jump A2284.6; put head in anus of sham-dead camel K1036.1.1; realizes partridge too clever J423.1; refuses payment for being carried K233.5; released: grateful B375.10; rides on fox B557.13; as sham saint K1961.1.5.1; swallowed to drink water in elephant's belly K952.1.1; swung by tail, fears man J17.1; tooth as madness cure D1508.3; as trickster

J1117.1; tries to pose as peacock J953.14; tries to roar like lion J2413.8. — Why j. has black back A2218.2, A2356.3.2; camel and j. exchange food J512.11; clever j. covers up own inabilities J873.1; creation of j. A1834.2; elephant lets j. into stomach F929.1; enemies of j. A2494.5, A2494.5.1ff.; envious j. makes lion suspicious of bull K2131.2; friendships of j. A2493.11, (and elephant) M246.1.1, (and lion) A2493.30.1, (and tiger) A2493.11.3; helpful j. B435.2; hungry ghost reborn as j. E694.1; iguana persuades j. to let him go K551.2.1; jealous courtiers accuse j. of stealing lion's food K2141; king j. captured J951.5; lazy j. punished Q5.1; making j. laugh H1194.2; man becomes j. D113.4; marriage to j. B601.11; origin of j. B710.1; ox claims dogs chasing j. K1725.1; painted j. an outcast J951.4.1; prophetic j. B142.2; quick thinking saves j. J1662.1; reincarnation as j. E612.10; riddle about deaths of elephant, snake, and j. H803; struggles with j. free captive buried alive R212.1.2; tailless j. persuades others to cut off tails J758.1.2; wager: will j. howl or ass bray first? N92; why j. cries at night A2427.1; why j. has bare tail A2317.12.2; why j. has burnt tip on tail K581.5; why j. has short tail A2378.4.5; why j. may go everywhere A2434.1.5.

Jackal's head caught in blue dye pot: made king J2131.5.6; vanity punished Q331.21. — Barber's and j. common garden K171.8; crow tied to j. tail J2132.3.1.

Jackals enter pit to escape storm, killed K811.2; as judges P421.1; jump into well J1791.3.4. — Enemies buried alive, exposed to j. S123.6; houses to keep howling j. warm J1873.4; king of j. B241.2.9; marriage of j. and turtles F414.3; tiger settles argument for j. K555.3; why j. make noise at night A2479.3; why j. do not go in herds A2492.1.

Jackdaw, see **Daw.**

Jacob as man in the moon A751.10.2. — Riddle: who has had, here below, two names? (J.-Israel) H817.

Jacob's face on God's throne A152.8; sons throw hero into pit K1931.4.

Jaguar. — Ant-eater deceives j. K1721.2; color of j. A2411.1.1.2; creation of j. A1817; food of j. A2435.3.16; four-eyed j. B15.4.1.3; hero offspring of j. A511.1.8.2; heroes born from human wife of j. A511.1.4.3; human offspring of j. B631.7; man becomes j. D112.6; marriage to j. B601.15; speaking j. B211.2.2.2: strong man kills j. F628.1.1.3; two-headed j. B15.1.2.1.3.

Jaguars. — Tiger has family of j. B672.

Jailed, see **Imprisoned.**

Jailor. — Competition in friendship: prisoner and j. P315.1; tokens sent to j. as warrant of king's authority H82.1.

Jar of honey is to be sold (air-castle) J2061.1. — Child born in j. T561; coins concealed in j. J1655.3; deity animates j. beneath tree A199.1; escape from deluge in j. A1029.3; false husband duped into j. on woman's head J1172.3.1; getting melon out of j. resourcefulness test H506.8; greedy one gets stuck in j. W151.9; literal numskull drags j. on

string J2461.1.1; magic j. D1171.7.1; night kept in j. A1174.3.1; putting a large squash whole into a narrow-necked j. H1023.11; striking at reflection in j. J1791.7.1; tiger hides guests in j. K649.1.2; wolf puts head through j. handle K1022.7.

Jars. — Breaking j. to make weeping seem natural J1142.4.1.2; man dreams of j. of wealth N531.5.

Jasmine. — Quest for j. flower H1333.5.4.

Javelin. — Fairies drive iron j. through man's door F361.17.8; giant impaling self on j. K897.2.1; hurling j. as challenge P556.2; magic j. D1085.

Jaws. — Leaving j. at home to prevent quarrels F513.3; small animal grateful for release from j. of large one B371.

Jawbone cut from slain opponent P555.2.12. — Ass's magic j. D1402.3.4, D1472.1.24.2; water from j. D925.1.3.

Jay borrows cuckoo's skin A2241.6; in peacock's skin unmasked J951.2. — Color of j. A2411.2.1.8; creation of j. A1921; why j. is quiet at noon A2236.7.

Jealous co-wife kills woman's children S322.3; father kills daughter's suitors S11.4.1; father sends son to upper world on stretching tree *S11.2; husband T257, (kills bird to which wife falsely says she has been listening) Q587, (kills innocent wife) N348; king banishes son S322.1.5.1; mother casts daughter forth S322.2; and overhasty man kills his rescuing twin brother N342.3; queen dupes child-bearing one K2115.0.1; wife T257, (of god) A164.7, (makes merchant turn out queen) S463, (tells sister to look below: pushes her over cliff) K832.1; women mutilate attractive one S160.2; woman reborn as chilly E692.4. — Ass j. of horse, but sees horse later working in a mill L452.1; god j. of mortal A189.4; husband j. of wife who goes to confession is punished by the priest T257.4; ogre's wife j. G674; raven j. of partridge's way of flying W181.5; seduction by making woman j. K1368; sun's love for girl makes moon j. A736.7; tasks (quests) assigned at suggestion of j. (rivals) H911, (brothers) H912; vow never to be j. of one's wife M137.

Jealousy W181; punished Q301. — Death from j. F1041.1.9; first human killed out of j. A1297; fratricide through j. S73.1.2; friendship despite j. H1558.10; god's j. A194.3; goddess arouses heroes' j. K1093; husband free from j. required M137.1; origin of j. A1375.

Jeering at saint punished Q559.5.

Jennet. — Man transformed to j. D132.

Jephthah's vow S241.

Jericho. — Walls of J. overthrown by magic D2093.

Jerusalem, see also **Holy Land;** suspended in air F1083.0.1.3. — Pilgrimage to J. V535; prophecy: death in J. M341.3.1; signs before destruction of J. M369.5.1.

Jester comments on bid for queen's favors U66.1.1; disguises as prince K1839.4; punished G303.6.1.3, Q387; wins prince's pardon by clever remark J1181.3. — Clever j. J1124; sham execution fatal to j. N384.7.

Jesting punished Q387, (by appearance of devil) G303.6.1.3, G303.6.2.3.

Jesus, see **Christ.**

Jew claims he has burned up priest's counterfeit money J1511.10; refuses to be rescued from pit on Saturday J1613. — Devil carries J. to hell G303.9.5.7; devil as J. G303.3.1.15; discussion between priest and J. carried on by symbol H607.1; punishment of J. for apostacy Q232.2; ungrateful J. steals Christian's horse W154.19; Virgin Mary converts a J. V266; wandering J. Q502.1; washing J. as devil's task G303.16.19.3.3.

Jew's harp. — Witch plays j. K606.1.4.

Jews P715.1; bribe woman to steal host for them: miraculous manifestations V35.1; eating with heathen tabu C246.1; keep aloof from others A1689.13; protesting against marriage of Jewess and Christian are struck dumb V343; repaying devil with persons M211.4. — Christian traditions concerning J. *V360ff.; jokes concerning J. X610ff.; knockers as ghosts of J. F456.1.1.1, F456.1.2.3.2; pity for the poor J. J2383; seven whistlers are souls of J. who crucified Christ A1715.3; why J. don't worship idols A1544.0.1; why J. read, write from right to left: king's ugly name A1689.6; why J. smell bad: rubbed Christ's body with garlic A1662.1; why J. do not eat pork A1681.2.

Jewel found on donkey's neck N534.8; hidden in thigh F1034.3.4; present brings false accusation of theft K2104; responds to owner's voice D1651.13; for summoning animal's help B501.3; transformed to person D432.3. — Animal discovers j. B562.1.0.1; child born wearing j. T552.7; dragon with j. in head B11.2.14; fairyland quest for j. H1286.1; giant's enormous j. F531.4.6; hero will marry girl possessing certain j. H361; horse kicks up j. B562.1.2; identification by j. H93; insect inside j. J1661.1.6; luminous j. in animal's head B722.3; magic j. *D1071, (carried off by bird) D865, (heals wounds) D1503.6; (transports) D1520.29; mountain formed of a j. F752.3; playing marbles with j. H151.1.1; parrot recovers j. from sea B548.6; rabbi returns j. found with bought ass W37.3; serpent with j. in head B101.7; sham wise man sees j. hidden, gets reward K1956.2.1; sisters throw unique j. into lake: killed and thrown after it Q582.1; snake becomes j. D425.1.2; soul in j. E711.3; stone becomes j. D452.1.4; throwing away j. J2093.3; what is finest j.? H659.24; whispering announcement of finding lost j. K2095.1; woman gives j. for salad J2093.2; woman sells favors to obtain a j. T455.1; wearing unauthorized sacred j. forbidden C51.2.1.

Jewels, see also **Precious Stones;** aid in search for treasure D1314.8; float at new moon N513.6; of the gods A156.1; from hair D1454.1.2; magically shower from sky D2101.2; in otherworld streams F162.2.10; as reward Q111.7; as sacrifice V12.2; sold for trifle J2093.6; from tears D1454.4.2. — Animals with j. as ornaments F826.1; animals with members of j. B101ff.; beauty of j. admired, virtues neglected J264; birth with j. royalty sign H71.7.1; children as mother's j. T265; city of j. F761.4; clever ways of concealing j. J1655; deer of gold and j. possess-

ing life D1620.2.3; dissatisfied with gold, looking for j. J514.5; diving for alleged j. K1051.1; dwarfs possess j. F451.7.1; extraordinary j. F826ff.; father leaves sons three j. J462.3.1; "four j. of Tuatha Dé Danann" F244.1; fruits containing j. F813.0.1; girl's ghost lends j. E363.5.1; god's temple of j. A151.4.1; husband coveting wife's j. pretends he is giving them to deity K361.6; island's stones are j. F731.4; kite steals j. and thus saves condemned man B522.2; lover's gift regained: j. as gift K1581.6; man dissatisfied with gold looks for j., loses all J514.5; millstone preferred to j. J245.1; objects transformed to j. D475.4; palace of j. F771.1.5; power of excreting j. D1561.2.1; quest for castle of j. H1343; rain of j. F962.8.2; seduction by scattering j. K1332.1; serpent steals j., person accused N352.3; temple of j. F163.2.1.1, F773.3; trail of j. R135.0.3; treasure and j. in otherworld F166.1; tree with leaves of j. F811.2.2; underground palace of j. F721.5.1; wagon of j. F861.3; walls of j. in otherworld F165.3.2.

Jewel-box thrown away to test goddess's favor H1577.1.

Jewelry magically disappears D1641.14. — Magic ashes produce j. D1469.10; stealing j. from sleeping king and queen K331.7.

Jewess makes parents believe that she is to give birth to the Messiah but bears a girl J2336; must entreat Virgin to bear child T580.1.

Jewish automaton will not work on Saturday V71.1. — Origin of J. worship A1546.4; sixty thousand J. souls in heaven E755.1.4.

Jinn, see also **Genie;** G307; escapes bottle, kills captor N339.17; falls into boiling oil G512.3.4.

Jinns F499.3.

Joan, Pope K1961.2.1.

Job hears of successive misfortunes N252.

Jobs. — Men exchange j.: each thinks the other's is easier K1687.

Jockey. — Naked man imitating j. riding himself G269.21.3.

Jogi. — Disguise as j. K1827.2.

Jogi's. — Magic thread from j. garment D1400.1.18.

John the Baptist as first martyr V463.2; or John the Evangelist greater? J466.2. — Feast of J. A1002.1, V70.3.1.

John-crow. — Why j. has bald head A2317.11.

John Damascene V256.3.

John the Divine F451.5.9.4.

John the Evangelist J466.2.

John Henry: remarkable rock driller X991.

Joined. — God with two j. bodies A123.1.2; riddle: what are the two fixed, the two moving, and the two j.? H851; two persons with bodies j. F523.

Joining. — Mortal wins gratitude by j. in fairies' sport *F331; theft of money from fairies by j. unperceived in their game of money-throwing F351.1.

Joint creators A37; rescuers quarrel R111.7; rule of brothers P17.5. — Three j. depositors may have their money back when all demand it J1161.1.

Jointless bodies of bone F559.1; person F529.7.1.

Joke. — Accidental fatal ending of j. N334; man called rogue by nobleman makes j. of insult J817.1.

Jokes, see also **Humor;** X (entire chapter).

Joker playing dead killed N384.11.

Jokers set household at variance K2134.1.

Joking. — Preventing sisters-in-law from j. H1199.17.2.

Jonah as sacrifice S264.1; swallowed by whale F911.4, (riddle) H821. — Fish shows hell to J. F109.2.

Joseph and his Brethren N733.3; threatens to leave heaven when man who has always prayed to him is refused admittance V254.6; and Potiphar's wife K2111; places cup in sack of his brethren H151.4. — Brothers throw J. into pit K1931.4; crown of thorns given J. V211.1.6; dream (prophecy) of future greatness causes banishment of J. L425; origin of thorn tree from J. of Arimathea's staff A2624.1.

Joshua makes sun stand still D2146.1.1; as man in the moon A751.10.1.

Jotunheimar. — Giants in J. F531.6.2.0.1.

Journey to Avalon *F111; beyond seven seas Z71.5.2; to Land of Men of Heads only F129.1; to lower world *F80ff.; to otherworld *F0—F199; on Sabbath tabu C631.1; of soul to world of dead on reindeer E750.3; started too soon: evening star taken for morning J1772.7; to terrestrial otherworlds F110ff.; to underground animal kingdom *F127; to upper world F10—F79. — Animal accompanies man on j. B579.1; animals direct man on j. B563; animals go on j. *B296; branches as j. token H84.1; bridal j. to husband's home T137.6; day's j. from earth to heaven since Christ went to heaven in one day H682.1.1; dead tells of j. E374; deity accompanies mortal on j. A185.10; disenchantment by naked virgin undergoing frightful j. at midnight D759.3; "don't go alone on j." J21.36; eating on j. forbidden C232; fasting for prosperous j. V73.4; food compulsion on j. C675; hero directed on j. by princess J155.1; large boot-supply for j. H1231; magic aging by contact with earth after otherworld j. D1896; magic air j. from biting an ear D2135.2; magic j. D2121ff.; magic object protects from discomfort or accident on j. D1384ff.; modest request: present from the j. L221; numskulls go on j. J1711; objects go on j. F1025; prayer for j. to land of dead V52.9; rainbow spirit helps on j. F439.1.2; remaining on j. too long forbidden C761.1; riddling remarks of traveling companions interpreted by girl at end of j. H586ff.; soul goes on j. E721ff.; sledges turned in the direction of the j. J2333; start your j. early in the day: counsel proved wise by experience J21.19; tabu to rest on j. C731; turning back after beginning a j. forbidden C833.3; unborn child directs mother's j. T575.1.6.1; worn-out shoes as proof of long j. *H241.

Journeys. — Mountains from primeval j. of (a god) A962.3, (first man) A962.6; prophecies connected with j. M358; tabus for j. C833ff.; tabus connected with otherworld j. *C710ff.

Journeyman. — Devil helps j. win wager with master G303.22.8.

Jousting. — Knight j. with all comers P52.

Jove. — Saturn swallows stone instead of J. G11.0.1.1.

Joy. — Cure from excessive j. K1889.2; death from excessive j. F1041.1.5; fairy music causes j. F262.3.6; god's j. A194.4; magic object causes j. D1359.3; only j. felt in otherworld F165.6; quest for king's j. H1378.2.

Joys. — Good that all j. are mixed with sorrow J171.2.2.

Joyfully. — Woman saves herself from soldiers by receiving them j. rather than fearfully K2361.

Judaism. — Conversion to J. V336; power of J. tested H1573.4.1.

Judas Iscariot appears in sea E489.7; spills salt at Last Supper N131.3.1. — Tree on which J. hanged himself cursed A2721.5.

Judge *P421; frightened into decision J1195; of the gods A169.1; lenient to own son J1197; must yield bench after false judgment Q265.3; orders bride to consummate marriage T166; pays fine himself, tired of bickering J1179.9; put out of countenance J1212; reduces penalty, accused his son U21.5; saves one ear for other litigant J1289.8; sends fool back for rest of bribe money J2662; wants to know how the theft was committed J2372. — Animal as j. B274; bribed j. J1192ff., (punished) Q265.1; cat acts as j. between sparrow and hare K815.7; cynic as j. of wine J1442.5; deaf litigants and deaf j. misunderstand one another X111.14; death sentence escaped by propounding riddle j. cannot solve *H542.; druid as j. P427.6; drunk calls j. very wise J1289.12; fool as clever j. P192.2; God as j. of men A187.1; irrevocable judgment causes j. to suffer first M11; jackal as j. comes late J1531.1.1; king as j. P19.4.1; poet as j. P427.7.7; repartee with j. *J1280ff.; repartee on getting receipt from j. in hell J1289.11; ruler unable to intimidate j. rewards him Q54.1; saint made j. of doom Q173; skin of unjust j. stretched over a footstool J167; upright j. refuses bribe W35.2; why man picked as bullfight j. W35.1; with his whole heart: devil carries off j. M215; woman masks as j. and frees her husband K1825.3; youngest j. gives decision first P516.

Judge's bad-luck boots N136; humility, modesty J904; judgment affects fruit H251.3.10; temper leads to unjust death sentence W185.5. — Greasing j. palms J2475; killing fly on j. nose J1193.1; rascals pull of j. breeches and leave him exposed K1285.

Judges in the lower world A675; in upper world A669.1. — Seven thousand killed for stoning j. N340.2; why city with so many j. not destroyed? X332.

Judged. — Escape by debating which must be j. K622.1; judge not lest you be j. J571.6.

Judgment of Paris H1596.1; by testing love J1171. — Avoid hasty j. J571; child in mother's womb reveals unjust j. T575.1.1.3; death for unjust j. Q552.0.1; dream warns of error in j. D1813.1.2; false j. of distance in mountain area J2214.12; first j. in Ireland A1580.1.1; heroes seek j. as to which is greatest H1395; higher the office, heavier God's j. P16.1.3; house where false j. given slips down hill Q559.8; Last J. V313; laughing fish reveals unjust j. *D1318.2.1; magic object renders j. D1326; nature fruitless after false j. H243; stone bursts as sign of unjust j. *D1318.1.1; vision of j. V512; wise man follows fool against his better j. J1714.1; woman who has passed j. on girl who has a bastard is punished L435.2.

Judgments and decrees *M0—M99. — Clever or wise j. J1170ff.; image renders j. *D1621; irrevocable j. M10ff.; wise j. settle village quarrels J1170.1.

Judgment Day, see **Doomsday.**

Judicial combat H218. — Clever j. decisions J1170ff.

Judith and Holofernes K872.

Jug. — Child born in a j. T561; crow drops pebbles into water j. so as to be able to drink J101; disenchantment by weeping j. of tears J753.2; hero pitches giant j. F636.5; mending a broken j. (task) H1023.9; small j. of wine filled, large, not J1317; snake in j. bites would-be thief N332.3.2; test of curiosity: mouse in j. *C324, H1554.1; turning broken j. wrong side out H1023.9.1; woman duped into putting head in j. K714.5.

Jugs. — Carrying many water j. in one day as suitor test H331.10.

Juggler P483; promises to fly, escapes K1967. — Disguise as j. to enter enemy camp K2357.13; marvelous j. F698; transformation into j. D29.2.

Juice. — Fruit j. turns to blood D474.8; magic fruit j. D981.0.1; nuts yield purple j. F813.3.3; rejuvenation by j. of plant D1338.2.1.

July. — King's beard worth months J., August, and September H712.1.

Jump. — Disastrous j. to retrieve object J2146; magic horse makes prodigious j. B184.1.10; man boasts of his j. in Rhodes J1477; prodigious j. F1071, (tests strength) H1562.4.

Jumper. — Lie: remarkable j. X966; marvelous j. F684.

Jumping across river in one bound H1149.10; back from midair X1741.2; into the breeches J2161.1; contest won by deception K17; as chastity ordeal H412.7; over fire H1199.10; horse over palace H331.1.2.1; image D1639.6; over pit proves man's sex H1578.1.4.2; into the river after their comrade J1832; into river with treasure N513.1. — Animal characteristics from j. contest A2253ff.; dupe tricked into j. to his death K891; escape from ship by j. into sea R216.1; game killed by j. on it N622; horse j. over high wall F989.1; horse wins j. contest for man B587.1; magic power by j. into fire D1733.1; ogre j. on one's back *F472, G311; one animal j. through body of another F916; precocious hero j. across river F611.3.2.4; rejuvenation by j. over cliff D1889.11;

resuscitation by j. over E13; strong man j. across river F614.11; suitor contest: j. river on horseback H331.1.6; transformation by j. over D561; unsuccessful imitation of j. into fire unharmed J2411.6.

Jungle. — Centaur rescues man from j. B547.3; exposure in j. for refusing father's wishes S322.1.2.1; man from j. as cannibal G11.14; prince in love with girl exposed in j. T91.6.3.1; rat servants cut down j. B292.9.3; separation in j. N316; why man fears j. A1382.1; why squirrel stays hidden in j. A2433.3.9.1; why tiger lives in j. A2433.3.21.

Jupiter. — Origin of J. (planet) A782.

Jury. — Animal j. B276.

Jus primae noctis A1556.4, T161.

Just king brings good fortune to people P12.6.

Justice W35; and injustice U10ff.; of God A102.16; lacking in one-price city J21.52.1. — Animals ring bell and demand j. B271.3; Death preferred above God and J. J486; god of j. A464; god consults j. on his left A42.2; goddess of j. A464.1; origin of j. A1580.1; reign of peace and j. A1101.1.1.

Jutlanders. — Bees mistaken for J. J1762.5.

Kabonterken F485.

Kali. — Vow always to serve K. M177.2.

Kamar offers liquor to gods A1689.5.

Kangaroo. — Why k. has short front legs A2371.2.10.

Kangaroo-rat. — Why k. has white band around his body A2412.1.4; why tail of k. is not bushy A2317.12.1.

Karumba kills hero G347.

Kava. — Enormous k. F816.2; origin of k. plant A2686.3.1; why k. plant is gray A2751.4.6.

Keen. — Chariots, stones, weapons join in k. F994.2; horse joins in k. at hero's death B301.4.3.

Keeping first thing touched: ladder up to wealth K285; four dogs in herd (task) H1112.1; it if girl, sending it if boy T645.2; up a certain work all night (task) H1128. — Host as pledge for k. one's word V39.6; journey to upper world by k. thoughts continually on heaven *F64; mouse, bird and sausage k. house together J512.7; power of k. up all day what one starts D2172.2; wife k. half of money for shrine W152.17; wild huntsman punished for not k. fast day E501.3.5.

Kept. — Soul k. in object E711.

Kernel tries to escape death J1875.1.

Kernels. — Sun from fruit k. A718.3.

Kettenmärchen Z20ff.

Kettle borrowed from fairies and not returned F353; heating in hell for certain person Q561.2. — Alleged self-cooking k. sold K112.1; devil cooks folk in k. G303.25.4; as dwarfs emigrate each deposits coin into k. for mortals F451.9.4; first money from k. A1433.0.1; giant's huge k. F531.4.9; great k. X1031.1.1; hiding in k. K515.4; magic k. *D1171.3, (turns stones

to food) D1472.1.11.1; mosquitoes flying off with k. X1286.1.4; pot calls k. black J1063; refuge under k. R336; treasure buried in k. N511.18; treasure found in k. N525; wife refuses to take cover off k. T255.6.

Kettles. — Souls of drowned in heated k. in hell *E755.2.1.

Key in flax reveals bride's laziness H382.1; found in fish N211.1.2; to house concealed in man's heart F1034.5.1. — Bloody k. as sign of disobedience C913; disenchantment by finding k. D791.4; disenchantment by taking k. from serpent's mouth at midnight D759.1; duck recovers k. from sea B548.2.2.2; eighth k. awaits prince's rule C611.1.1; extraordinary k. F782.4; fish recovers k. from sea B548.2.2; golden k. F886.1; magic k. *D1176; penance: being locked in cellar and k. thrown into water Q544; question (on quest), where is the lost k.? H1292.6; task: recovering lost k. from sea H1132.1.2; thief copies k. by making wax impression K317; thief detected by psalter and k. H251.3.2; transformation: k. becomes bloody D474.1; troll in form of k. G304.1.2.2; wife to husband: "You have k." J1545.5.

Keys as protection against revenants E434.6. — Druid's "k. of wisdom" D1810.0.8.1; frog recovers k. from sea B548.2.2.1; hero leaves bedmate treasure k. for son T645.4; looking for k. to abbey J703.1; old and new k. (proverb) Z62.1; tricky animal secures treasury k. K341.18.

Keyhole. — Magic sight by looking through k. D1821.3.6; thumbling enters k. F535.1.1.11.1.

Keyholes. — Beautiful woman found in bed with man after he has plugged k. to keep elves out F304.3; witches go through k. G249.7.

Khijur. — Why k. leaves are long and narrow A2741.5.

Kick. — Magic transportation from k. of horse D2121.9.

Kicked. — Dragon k. in vulnerable spot B11.12.1.1; lecherous monk k. down stairs T322.1; man k. so hard he flies through air F1021.4; skeptic k. by sacrificed animal V346; wolf k. in mouth by ass who begs wolf to pull thorn out of foot before eating him *K566; wolf (lion) approaches too near the horse: k. in face K1121; youth made lame: had k. his mother J225.1.

Kicker. — Lie: remarkable k. X967.

Kicking. — Ass foolishly k. against pricks J833; man k. down mountain F626.2; punishment: k. to death by horses Q416.1; return from dead to punish k. of skull E235.5; strong man k. through door F639.5; witch k. helper into pit G269.1.1.

Kid perched on house jeers at wolf J974; puts tigress's cub in his place: she eats it K1611.5. — Man transformed to k. D134.3; well-trained k. does not open to wolf J144; Zodiac grows up: K. becomes Goat J2212.6.

Kidnapped woman escapes by asking for drink K551.17.1. — Miser k. W153.12; mortals k. by dwarfs F451.5.2.4; water-spirit returns k. man F420.5.2.2.1.

Kidnapping. — Echo k. men F443.1; fairies k. boy F325.1; missing girl saves man condemned for k. hero N692.1.

Killed game revives and flies away E161; man restored, invulnerable D1846.6; man can return to life E167. — Animal k. by magic object D1445; animals k. by strong man with own hands F628.1; husbands k. by brides in the bridal bed T173.2; child sold to be k. S210.2; creditor k. or driven away K235; faithful servant k. on quest P361.1.2; fairy k. by mortal F389.4; first human k. by his brothers A1297; ghost k. and thus finally laid E446; giant k. by strong man F628.2.3; goose that laid the golden egg k. D876; helpful animal k. (through misunderstanding) B331ff., (by hero's enemy) B335; king k. when old P16.3; love rival k. T92.10; magic animal k. B192; magic shows where person k. D1314.0.1; maiden enticed and k. by elf-knight F301.5; male children k. by Amazons F565.1.2; man not fated to die cannot be k. N146; man k. defending sweetheart's honor T326.2; man k. by snake in revenge B765.20; man must be k. with first blow C742.1; man plotting murder k. by Jesus (angel) J225.4; men k. by look of beautiful princess F574.1.3; ogre k. G512ff.; people k. by devil G303.20ff.; person unwittingly k. N320ff.; Red Riding Hood k. by wolf K2011; sham-dead k. by intended victim K311.1.1; slave k. P175; swallower k. from within F912; teller k. in own story Z13.2; victim lured by kind words and k. K815; witch k. G275.8.

Killer. — Lie: remarkable k. X955; prophecy: your k. will grow up in Braja M306.4; prophecy on your child's k. M306.5; prophecy: son to be k.; parents make him butcher M306.2; witch as k. G262.3.

Killers. — Would-be k. killed K1626.

Killing, see also **Slaying;** all earlier suitors H335.4.3; certain animals forbidden C841; children in cure attempt J2175.6; by deception K800; with Evil Eye D2071.2; ferocious beast (task) H335.3, H1161; giant's baby F531.5.14; if it is a girl T645.2.1; king tabu C563.6; by magic object D1402ff.; sacred beings forbidden C92; trees test H1522. — Abandoned children return, k. parents S366; accidental k. at sea bad omen D812.5.1.23; accidental k. or death M330ff.; advice on k. attacker J21.52.6; attempts at k. hero fail *H1510ff.; brother unwittingly k. brother N733.2; chain tale: animals k. each other provide meat Z43.6; cumulative tale: master refrains from k. hen, other animals Z32.4; deception into k. own family or animals K940ff.; devil tries to incite man into k. his wife G303.9.4.3; disenchantment by k. D712.9; dragon's breath k. man B11.2.11.2; dupe tricked into k. own children K1464; eighteen sisters k. one another P252.7; evil spirit cast out by k. E728.1.1; fairy k. man in revenge F361.17.7; fairies k. each other F259.1.1; faithless wife k. family K2213.3.1; father k. child S11.3; ghost k. man E247; ghost k. man in haunted house E281.0.1; girl k. man who threatens her virtue T320.2; god punishes man by k. his child A1335.15; hasty k. or condemnation *N340ff.; hero k. those who scorn him L156; husband k. unwelcome suitor K1551.1; husband k. wife's paramour K1561.1; husband and wife k. selves to avoid separation T211.3; innocent woman

accused of k. her new-born children K2116.1.1; lover k. rival brother T92.5; moon k. sun's children A736.1.4.1.1; mother k. child S12.2; promise not to kill on "any day": night k. K929.3; scorned lover k. successful T75.2; scorned woman prevented from k. man T72.3; shaving head compared to k. thousands H599.4; sister k. sister P252.1.1; stone from sky k. all but one couple A1009.3; strong hero sent from home for k. playmates F612.2; strong man k. lions F615.2.2; tabus for man-k. tiger, lion C549.1; witch k. person G269.10.1.

Killings. — Chain of k.: from bulbul to boy Z49.13.

Kiln. — Children abandoned in potter's k. S152.

Kin, see also **Relatives.** — Enormity of k. murder Q211.0.2; if I were not your next of k. E229.1.

Kind foster parents chosen rather than cruel parents J391; and unkind *Q2; words lure fish K815.14.1. — Choices between k. stranger and unkind relatives J390ff.; girl persuades father to marry k. widow S31.5; magic object renders k. D1354; peasant has k. words for daws but kills them K2090.1; suitor chooses k. girl H384.0.1; victim lured by k. words killed K815.

Kindling. — Magic k. of fire D1506.1, D2158.1; saint k. lamp without fire D2158.1.5.1.

Kindness W10ff.; rewarded Q40ff.; unwise when it imperils one's food supply J715; wins over enemies J26, L350.1. — Bride test: k. H384; devil repays k. G303.22.1; disenchantment by obedience and k. D731; loving k. of God A102.13; objects repay k. D1658.1.

Kine. — Fat and lean k. in (dream) D1812.3.3.5.1, (otherworld) F171.1.

King and abbot H561.2; absent hunting, angel holds mass V49.2; accepts criticism as patience test H1553.2; acquires wisdom after long sleep F564.3.3; accidentally finds maiden and marries her N711; advised to marry maid rather than widow J482; allows self to be killed to insure nation's triumph P711.9; asks for new trick H1182.2; assigns quest H1210.2; has amours with great men's wives so as to learn secrets from them J155.2; of animals *B240ff.; Arthur vows to watch at frightful place all night M156; asleep in mountain *D1960.2; assigns tasks to his unknown son H921; in the bath: years of experience in a moment D2012.1, L411; brought to sense of duty by philosopher J816.1.1; blows nose after giving to beggar: ruby appears V411.7; goes blind from overweeping F1041.3; breaks own tabu C901.4.1; breaks promise to care for a family M205.4; buried in deflected river's bed V67.3.1; buried in his war car V61.5; buys spendthrift's bed J1081.1; and clever youth H561.4; called baker's son since he has given the poet only loaves of bread J816.2; causes own men to be burned, killed K947; changes clothes with thief who steals his horse K346.1.1; cheats wounded chieftain in land grant K185.7.3; chooses personal troubles to help realm J221.2; chosen by test *H1574.3; covets subject's wife T91.6.2.0.1; cursed M414.5;

deceived about heir's birth K1847.1.1; defeated in repartee by boy H507.1.0.2; deflowering all twelve year old girls T161.0.1; demands subjects put milk in his cup J1391.7; of demons F402.2.1; descends sea to learn wisdom from fish J52.2; dies in tunnel to underground world J2137.7; in disguise K1812, (to learn subjects' secrets) N467; does not want daughter to marry T50.2; in dream advises take treasure from his grave N531.4; eaten, revived daily E155.6; exchanges riddles with rabbi H548.1; finding golden bow, arrow, lucky D1812.5.2.9; finds his children in floating casket H157; of fishes *B375.1, (eats subjects) K815.17, (prophesies hero's birth) B144.1; and fool look identical F577.3; forbidden to look at his son C319.1; forces follower onto throne: follower killed K1845.2; and foster son jump into sea F1041.16.7; of giants G156; given sleeping potion, beheaded by wife K873.1; of the gods A161.2; to have head pounded by strange queen M369.9; as helper N836; honors poet, critic J811.3; humble J912; imprisons all living creatures R9.6; improves kingdom for sons J701.2; of land under water F252.1.0.1; grows lean from fear of death U241; Lear judgment M21; lights first fire C751.1.1; loses ring while trying to learn art of stealing K341.8.4; lost on hunt has adventures N771; in love with lowly girl T91.6.2; made to change places with wronged subjects Q7; as magician D1711.7; makes peacock machine F675.1; may not marry anyone previously wed T131.7; and minister *H561.5; mourns vanished bride F1041.9.1.2; must cut off son's head to marry fairy H313.2; must summon ghost E389.1; neglected in exile, courted when regains throne U83; observes retaliation among animals and becomes just J52; orders own execution; believes will be king in next birth J1189.3; of otherworld F167.12; overhears girl's boast as to what she should do as queen N455.4; overlooks wife's unfaithfulness rather than to cause troubles of state J221.1; pardons thieves for confession J1198.1; participates in battle after he sees who is winning K2369.2.2; persuaded his desired ocean of milk is curdled J811.5; possessing one marvelous object sends hero on quest for another like it H1218; prefers poverty, primitive culture to civilization J245.2; pretends going in peace, really to battle K1774; as prophet M301.17; propounds riddles H540.3; prefers educated men as company J146.1; no priest's son J1827; punishes by killing one man in every house Q411.8; questions six doctors J171.2; refuses to exile gossipers J215.1.2; refuses fine tomb J912.2; refuses quarrel with bird J411.9.1; rejects crown and its cares J347.2; rescues abandoned child R131.11.2; restrained from hasty judgment J571.5; returns to rescue native country R191; saved in spite of self V523; searches for mate to marvelous object H1218; seeks prime minister who left him H1385.12; seeks bride only because counselors insist T64; seeks one richer than himself H1311.1; selected by cricket H162.2; selected by elephant's bowing to him H171.1; sends messenger to dead father H1252.4; sets sons task to determine heir

H921.1; for seven years Z71.5.4; and the cheap slippers J829.1; snake B765.22; speaking before druids tabu C402.1; speaks before people C402.2; strangles falcon when it kills eagle Q424.1; sulks until quest is accomplished H1212.3; takes off crown, licks spittle in penance Q523.9; takes subject's wife T481.5; tests gardener's obedience, plays thief H1557.6; told to seek harmony at home J1289.9; transformed to menial D24.1; transformed to parrot frees captured parrots R115; given three wheels to control his anger J571.2; traveling alone tabu C563.1; of trees A2777.2; tricked into sleeping with hag K1235; of underground kingdom F721.3.1; unwittingly killed N362; unwittingly shot by own order K1612.2; to be victorious as long as he rides muzzled gelding N125.3; weds common girl T121.8; weighs princess in chastity test H455; won't eat till gifts given W11.2.2; as wild huntsman E501.1.1; wooes through his daughter T51.2; of world of dead E481.9; for a year provides for future J711.3. — Absurdity of turning k. into brahmin J1293.3; animal parliament elects k. B236; why certain animal is k. A2547; animals dance for k. B293.0.1; animals make jackal k. J2131.5.6; army faces enemy rather than anger of their k. J216.1; banished youth becomes k. L111.1.1; bargain with k. of mice M244.1; bath in blood of k. as (cure for mange) D1502.5.1, (remedy) D1500.1.7.3.4; bird indicates election of k. H171.2; bird k. transforms quails to save them D666.1; borrowed fleet scares k. into giving daughter K1771.9; brahmin teaches k. J179.1; candle of k. lights itself H41.3; cannibalistic k. G11.7; "cease being a k. if too busy to hear me" J1284.2; clever answers to k. H561.4, H583; clever dealing with a k. J1675; contact with things belonging to a k. forbidden C501; conquering k. tricked, sleeps with princess's maid K1223.5; crow fat remedies k. F959.3.5; crown suspended over k. F828.1; cruel k. lured by execution invitation, killed K811.3; cruel k. slays brother, brother's son S11.3.5; death sentence escaped by propounding riddle k. cannot solve *H542; deduction: k. is a bastard J1661.1.2; devil k. G302.2.2; disguised k. (recognized by habitual speech) H38.1, (rewards rescuer from robbers) Q53.1, (taught courtesy by peasant) P15.1.1; disobeying the k. forbidden C64; dog made k. B292.10; don't give k. ruby cup J21.49; dragon-k. B11.12.5, (transformed to gust of wind) D429.2.1; dream warns k. of error D1813.1.2; druid's spells kill Christian k. D1402.13; drunk man goes to the k. and wants to buy an island X812; dwarf k. F451.4.5.1, (comes to surface every 500 years) F451.6.12, (lives in mill) F451.4.2.5, (prevents father from shooting son) F451.5.1.16, (has silver miner's torch) F451.7.4, (wears costly crown) F451.2.7.7; dwarf serves k. sleeping in mountain F451.5.1.8; dwarfs emigrate when their k. dies F451.9.1.15; eagle regains throne for k. B589.1; eater of magic bird-heart will become k. M312.3; eater of fruit to become k. M312.3.2; enigmatic conversation of k. and peasant H585; execution substitute thinks he will become k. of heaven K841.1; exiled k.

teaches ruler wisdom J55; fairy k. F252.1, (captive) F361.7, (with yellow hair) F233.5.1, (punishes ravisher of his daughter) F304.1; feigned ignorance not to reveal k. K1792.1; fiery sword between hostile k. and queen D2196; first of three sons to kiss his mother (earth) will be k. J1652; foolish k. J1705.4; foreign k. wages war to enforce demand for princess in marriage T104; Fortune's wheel turned by dead k. in mountain N111.3.1; freeing k. from magic doll H1196; frogs demand a live k. J643.1; garment fits only true k. H36.2; giants' k. F531.6.8.5.1; god gives k. advice A182.3.4.1; god as k. A137.10; god refuses k. a son on account of his many wars Q553.3.1; good luck leaves palace night k. is to die N113.3; no great knights because no great k. U211; harem ladies recognize impostor k. K1934.1; hawk persuades doves to elect him their k. K815.8; headless k. and tailless tiger as friends J876; heathen k. tests saint H527; husband assigns tasks to k. stealing his wife H931.1.1; imaginary clothes for k. K445; incognito slave becomes k. Q42.4; inhuman decisions of k. M2; jackal calls self k., escapes farmer K547.4; jackal made k., howls, killed J512.13; lake where blind k. plucks rushes A920.1.12; lamp prevents k. murdering queen D1381.29; letting k. starve S123.4; letting k. hear something that neither he nor his subjects have ever heard (task) H1182; lesson learned from example of k. in exile J55; greatest liar made k. of Schlaraffenland X905.2; line of kingship taken from k. defying saint Q494.1; lion as k. makes ass his lieutenant J421.1; lover masks as k. K1371.4.1; lowly boy becomes k. L165; lowly heroine marries k. L162; lowly successful hero invites k. and humbles him L175; loyalty to k. rewarded Q72.1; magic object received from dragon k. D812.7; magic poem causes k. to waste away D1402.15; man breaking oath to woman can't be k. M205.3; man fated to become k. does so despite breaking lucky tooth N101.4; man strikes k. saving his life N656; man before whom riderless car stops chosen k. H171.4; man buried alive with k. escapes from the tomb R212.1; munificent k. W11.2; oath concerning k. in act of marrying M192; old k. F571.5; one-eyed k. has rocks counted J1675.4; otherworld k. F184; oxen stop for k. H171.4.1; paper in hand which none but k. can remove D1654.11; parable on k. not leaving castle J97; parents murder all sons except one speaking of k. S311.1; peacock proves to be a bad k. J242.4; peasant surprised k. not larger J1742.4; pike helps Christ: made k. of fishes A2223.4; plagues during reign of wicked k. Q552.10.1; plot to make k. criminal: succession to be forfeit K1166; poor man happier than k. J1085.3; prophecy: child to become k. M311.4; praying before the K. of Kings J1269.7; two presents to the k.: the beet and the horse J2415.1; prophecy: man will become k. M314; prophecy: son of certain name to become k. M395; proud k. humbled L410.1; proud k. displaced by angel L411; queen aids lover to dispossess k. K2213.8; quest to avenge k. H1228.1; quest to k. for military aid H1224; quest for lost k. H1385.10;

quest for bride for k. *H1381.3.1; rainbow is transformed k.: lesser rainbow, his wife A791.5; red garment to show anger of k. Z141.1; repartee between k. and philosopher on destroying city J1289.10; riddle: how much is the k. worth? H711; riddle of k. and courtiers H731; riddle of k. surrounded by his nobles H825; robber helps k. N884.1; saint kills k. of cats F981.7; saint reforms vicious k. D2163.5.2; saint saves almsgiving k. from hell V229.15; Satan as k. G303.3.1.25; seat in which only fated k. can sit H41.9; seduction by posing as k. K1315.14; serpent-k. assigns tasks H939.4.1; sex hospitality to k. T281.2; sham dead k. jumps up, kills slave K911.4; shipwrecked men kill k. in revenge K913.1; silent man asks k. what can he say to fool J1714.5; silver k. F521.3.4.1, (with silver attendants) F576; slaying k. under holy protection Q227.1; sleeping k. abducted by fairies N661; sleeping k. in mountain as guardian of treasure N573; son frees father by bringing riddle the k. cannot solve R154.2.1; son of k. and son of smith exchanged K1921.1; son telling k. truth banished J551.6; stealing from a k. H1151.13; stealing from ogre to help a friendly k. G610.2; he who steals much called k. U11.2; stingy k. who will not hire soldiers defeated W152.6; stone roars under k. H171.5; stone screams under k. H71.10.6; sun as k. of earth and sky A731; symbolic wounding of k. Z182; tabu for k. to sleep after sunrise C735.2.3; tabu: people speaking before k. speaks C402.1.1; tabu: quarreling in house (presence) of k. C873; tact in reproving k. J816; to test favorite k. says that he is going to retire from the world J1634; treacherous k. K2246.1; thunder report of birth of k. F960.1.1.1; trickster goes around k., gets reward for encircling kingdom J1289.14; unjust k. compared to donkey H592.5; vanquished k. gives hero daughter T68.4; Virgin Mary supplies mead for unprepared hostess of the k. U262; vow to live, die with k. M161.3; vow not to eat until knowing if k. alive M151.6; vow to serve most generous k. M167; waves' roaring danger omen to k. D1812.5.1.24; what is strongest? k. H631.9; wild animal performs for k. B771.5; woman in disguise made k. K1837.8; woman drinks poison that son may be k. W28.1; woman, fake healer, marries k., kills him for kingdom K959.2.4; wounded k. fines would-be slayers Q211.8.1; youth in court for calling k. fool J1162.4.

King's capriciousness compared to ass in stream J1675.3; crown in well F166.4.1; curse M411.17; death prophesied M341.1.2.1; demands on winter guests P337; descendants indicated by stone D1311.16.1; downfall prophesied M342.1; enigmatic order to minister H587; example makes merchant wealthy N415; face ill-omened N119.3; magic power of sight D1820.2; preventives against assassination J634; promise irrevocable M203; race determined by magic stone *D931.0.2.1; son to die from thirst M341.2.2.6; son persuaded to woo father's bride, killed K1094; sons called kings P30.1; third son sacred V205.1; unique ability to occupy certain seat H41.9; vision of whelps, foster sons V515.2.1.1.

— Asking for k. daughter tabu C196; bird cut out from k. stomach J1842.3; courtier shields k. love affair J1211.3; crosswise spears test obedience of k. subjects H1557.5; demigod son of k. sister A511.1.3.1; demons carry off k. soul F402.1.5.1; disenchantment by maiden sitting at head of enchanted k. bed D759.7; druid attempts to shake k. faith H1573.1.3; dupe guards k. "litter" K1056; eagle seeks k. bride D647.2; exposed infant reared at strange k. court S354; fairy k. crown stolen F355; girl to be k. bride cloistered T381.0.1; hero takes refuge at k. court R331; holding k. sword makes one his inferior K1292; impostor poses as dead k. son K1952.4.1; Irish roads discovered at k. birth A994; magic knowledge of k. dream D1819.7; milk of two k. children protects hero in dragon fight D1385.14; mule as descendant of k. warhorse J954.1; outcast wife's castle like k. H153; philosopher spits in k. beard J1566.1; prophecy: k. grandson will dethrone him M311.1; quest for k. joy and woe H1378.2; rats gnaw k. saddle girths, cause defeat L316; retrieving k. falcon H1154.7.1; servant rescues k. children R169.4.2; slaying k. son to prevent father's death H1162.2; smith as k. grandfather P447.1; springs from innocent k. blood A941.5.8; stealing k. horse as he rides it H1151.2.2; stealing tray from k. bedside H1151.3.1; swearing on k. hand M116.0.1; taking k. place by changing dresses K1810.1.3; thief lies by k. bed, steals jewelry K331.7; thunder at k. birth F960.1.1.1; tokens sent to jailor as warrant of k. authority H82.1; vow not to fight k. relatives M166.5; tournament to avenge k. death P561.2; water for thieves in k. garden H1471.1.

Kings P10ff.; exchange forms and kingdoms for a year D45.1. — Betting contest between two k. N1.3; calumniators try to make friendly k. fight K1084.4; four k. try to save falcon N836.3; fur made from beards of conquered k. P672.1; guessing contest between k. H515; names of future k. foretold M369.4; origin of k. A1653.1; sacrifice so descendants may be k. W215.3; tabus of k. C563.

King Arthur's. — Indentions on rocks from K. dog A972.5.3; prophecy: end of Round Table for K. knights M356.5; symbolism of K. Round Table Z162.

King Hiram sends Solomon riddles H540.3.1.

King of Kings. — Fighting for K. J1164.

King Lear M21.

King-salmon. — Markings on k. A2412.4.2; why k. is thick around root of tail A2378.9.1.

Kingdom of demons G302.2.1; lost to impostor P15.3; as reward Q112.0.1; where seven rivers meet F715.8; well by day burns by night H1292.20. — Animal k. *B220ff.; extraordinary k. F707; half k. as wager N2.5.2; half of k. as reward Q112; origin of k. A1583; prophecy of downfall of k. M342; pygmy k. F535.6; tricky queen gets k. for her son K2213.11;

underground k. F721.3, (of animals) *F127; vow to destroy k. by austerities M193; whole k. as wager N2.5; wisdom of hidden old man saves k. J151.1.

Kingfisher. — Creation of k. A1951; marriage to k. B602.8; why k. lives in the air A2433.4.5.

Kingfisher's. — Origin of k. crest A2321.5, (beak) A2343.1.1; why k. beak is long A2343.1.5.

Kingly duty rewarded Q67. — Nature's fruitfulness proves k. right H1574.2; unknown prince shows his k. qualities in dealing with his playmates H41.5.

Kingship line taken away as punishment Q494.1; renounced to become ascetic V462.0.1; restored as reward for charity V434. — Achieving k. by bringing silk H1355.4; fratricide to gain k. S73.1.1; magic bird-heart brings man to k. D1561.1.1; magic fish (when eaten) brings man to k. D1561.1.1.2; parricide to obtain k. S22.1; test of valor worthy for k.: taking possession of royal insignia H1561.5

Kiss of forgetfulness D2004.2. — Betrayal by a k. K2021; death from joy of k. F1041.1.5.4; death by k. from God Q147.3; deserted wife asks for one last k. and chokes departing husband K951.0.1; disenchantment by k. D735; disguised wife makes husband buy k. K1814.4; dwarf stays away from house after maid tries to catch and k. him F451.5.19.1; escape by asking a last k. K551.10; fairy's k. fatal F302.3.4.1; fairy wins k. in game K786; fatal k. from dead E217; girl refusing lover final k. provokes rival to admit selling kisses K1275.1; god's k. causes painless death A185.6.1.1; heart breaks when girl hears lover k. another F1041.1.1.2; leper cured by saint's k. V221.3.1; lover given rump to k. *K1225; resuscitation by k. E65; soul leaves body after God's k. E722.2.12; spirit's k. fatal F402.1.11.4; transformation by k. D565.5; waking from magic sleep by k. D1978.5; witch's k. disfigures G264.2; witches k. devil's tail G243.1.1.

Kissed. — Dreaming of being k. by fairy J2345; living person k. by ghost E471; ox k. by patriarch on the lips A2221.5.1; pig k. by literal numskull J2461.2.1.

Kissing leper as curse M438.1; leper as punishment Q499.1.1; lover shamed by wife's husband K1218.10; the mother first J1652. — Adulteress prohibits k.: mouth loyal to husband K1595; brother first k. saint will be king P11.0.1; clever decisions concerning k. and rape J1174; cure by k. saint's letter V221.7; fairy k. man F302.3.4.1; father k. son while planning death S11.4.2; god k. mortal A185.6.1; magic results from k. *D1794; man dies from woman's k. T81.4; newborn child k. dying mother T585.6; ordeal by k. serpents H224.1; only k. in bed tests fidelity H1556.4.1; pig's licking mistaken for k. by sleeping man X31.2; princess k. ugly poet Q88.2; stealing money while k. it K378; tabu: k. C120ff.; vow against k. until father revenged M152.1.

Kitchen. — God of k. A411.2; great k. X1031.1; magic k. *D1141.1; queen is placed in k. and abused by butcher Q482.2.

Kite (bird) devours meat it is entrusted with J2124.1; as king of chickens J643.2; steals jewels and thus saves condemned man B522.2; tries to carry off so many partridges that he drops them all J514.1; tries to neigh like horse J512.2.— Creation of k. A1938; enmity between jackal and k. A2494.5.2; enmity of k. and crow A2494.13.2; helpful k. B455.5; lawsuit between owl, k. B270.1; man becomes k. D152.6; martens recover magic ring from k. B548.1.1; rhyme for summoning k. B501.2; wedding of eagle and k. B282.2.1; wind god as k. A139.8.4.

Kites, crows quarrel over wounded fox J581.5. — King of k. B242.2.3.

Kitten. — Deer steps on k. Z49.6.

Klabautermann F485.

Knapsack. — Devil cannot endure cross made by straps of k. G303.16.3.2; devil pounded in k. until he releases man K213.

Kneaded. — Serpent k. into dough H1407.

Knee. — Birth from k. T541.16; colored k. F548.1; person with black k. F548.1; sea as k.-deep H681.4.2; woman so old her chin reaches her k. F571.3.1.

Knees. — Afraid of his k. J2617; devil's k. backwards G303.4.5.6; indentions on rocks from k. of hero's enemy A972.5.4; giant with k. backwards F531.1.3.2; penance: crawling on k. Q521.1.1; person with k. backwards F517.1.5; witch's k. are beads G229.4.4.

Kneecaps. — Origin of k. A1312.1.

Kneeling. — Clothes of knight k. in mud before host as it passes miraculously kept clean V34.4; horse k. before stolen sacrament V35.1.1.

Knife accidentally kills girl N331.1.1; in bed as protection against witches G272.3; as childbirth precaution T582.4; drips blood (life token) E761.1.7.2; in ground exorcises spirit F491.3.2; leaps into hand of God's man H192.1; as tongue deceives ogre G572.2. — Alleged resuscitating k. sold K113.6; attempt to kill by throwing k. K2388; blade of grass transformed to k. D451.5.2; bleeding k. F991.1.1; bloody k. F1066.1, (left in innocent person's bed brings accusation of murder) K2155.1.1; breathing drives enemy on to k. D2061.2.9; cannibal sharpens k. to kill captive G83; child born with k. T552.5.3; child born carrying k. and calabash T552.3; compassionate executioner: k. with animal blood substituted K512.1.1; criminal detected by having child hand k. to him H211; cuckold's k. cannot carve boar's head H425.1; dupe persuaded to throw away his k. K1141; extraordinary k. F838; fairy k. stolen F361.2.4; fools try to use buffalo tongue as a k. J1971; giant killed with magic k. G512.1.1; golden wood for k. handle H1359.1; leaf becomes k. D451.8.2; life token: k. stuck in tree rusts (becomes bloody) E761.4.1; magic journey by throwing k. into whirlwind *D2121.8; magic k. *D1083, (carving)

*D1173; man will not lift k. to cut the rope about to hang him W111.1.2; obstinate wife: cutting with k. or scissors T255.1; ogre killed with k. G512.1; ogress with k. tail G510.5; penance: killing oneself with wooden k. Q522.2; precious k. as gift to helper Q114.1; recognition by k. H132; sheath and k. as analogy for mother and unborn child T579.1; sight of wild hunt causes one to stick axe or k. in foot E501.18.9; trickster gives a woman a k. to cut him a slice of white bread K344.1; whetting the k. K1418; wife's k. frightens off lovers K1569.6; witch with k.-like tail G219.8.2.

Knives on bridge to otherworld F152.1.6.1; as protection against revenants E434.7. — Bridge to otherworld covered with k. F152.1.6.1; deceptive game: throwing away k. K857; ladder of k. H225.1; oranges grow on tree-limb k. F811.7.2.2; snake killed by k. in animal he is swallowing K897.1; sound of clashing k. frightens tiger K2345.1; wounding by trapping with sharp k. S181.

Knife-holder. — Why catfish carry marks of k. A2261.3.1.

Knife-maker robbed by purse-cutting knife K341.8.3.

Knight *P50ff.; captured in pitfall K735.3; covers foal from storm Q51.1; dismisses devil in name of cross G303.16.3.5; disregards servant's insult J411.9; falsely accused of sedition K2126; feigns murder to escape city K579.6; jousts with all comers P52; pleads for fighting blasphemer J1164; ravishing nun captured Q244.2; saved from devil by friends G303.16.19.8; ungrateful for rescue W154.12.1; unsuccessfully tempted by host's wife T331.2; wants dogs in heaven U134; weds peasant girl T121.1. — Clothes of k. who kneels in mud before host as it passes miraculously kept clean V34.4; devil as a distinguished-looking k. G303.3.1.3; devil serves k. faithfully G303.22.10; devils appear to k. to try to call him from doing penance G303.9.4.5; fairy smith gives k. magic sword F343.3; hero in disguise of foolish k. rescues lady R169.1; king doubles reward to k. W11.12.1; lover disguised as other k. K1810.3; lover masks as k. K1371.4.1; madness from k. forsaking wife F1041.8.9; nearsighted k. mistakes own servant for enemy X124; nun hidden by abbess from pursuing k. betrays own hiding place to him V465.1.2.1; queen flees disguised as k. K1812.8.1; spendthrift k. Q42.1; sultan's daughter in love with captured k. T91.6.4.1; treacherous red k. K2265; uncharitable k. drives bargain even in giving alms: devoured by serpents V422; unknown k. R222; wronged k. conquers, pardons enemy W11.5.3; young k. substitutes for old K3.2.

Knight's. — Devil in fold of k. cloak G303.8.9.1; devil steals k. cloak G303.9.9.3.

Knights drink from huge nine-gallon cup F531.4.3; in wild hunt E501.2.1. — No great k. now because no great king U211.

Knighthood as reward Q113. — Garlic stalk as k. arms for servant J955.3.

Knitting. — Dead husband helps wife's k. E321.2.1; dead person k. E563; devil k. G303.9.8.1.

Knocked. — Bridal couple's heads k. together T135.13; dwarf carries his k.-off leg on his shoulder F451.6.13.

Knockers F456.1.

Knocking off single fruit from tree H1199.18. — Dead find no rest since someone is daily k. at grave E419.2; ghost k. E402.1.5.

Knoll. — Brownies live in k. F482.3.2; fairies loyal to mortal who owns their k. F336; fairyland under hollow k. *F211.

Knot. — Disenchantment by untying enchanting k. D765.2; magic k. *D1282.1; making an invisible k. with an egg (task) H1021.5; making a k. of spilled brandy (task) H1021.4.

Knots in grass mark underworld path F95.4; to be untied at childbirth T582.3. — Magic from loosing k. D1782.3; origin of k. in wood A2738, A2755.4; string with thirteen k. G271.10; transformation: handkerchief with three k. to (articles) D454.3.2.1, (animals) D454.3.2.2; why the saja tree has k. A2755.4.1; wind raised by loosing certain k. D2142.1.2.

Know. — Choice: do what you k. or learn to do something J483; devils do not k. or understand thoughts of men G303.13.1; Europeans k. more than natives A1667.1; how does priest k. about hell? J2221; "I don't k." thought to be a person's name J2496; I k. not how J1431; person does not k. himself J2012; all questions to be answered, "I don't k." C495.1; wise boy says, "I don't k." instead of "I know" J21.52.7.

Knowing. — Clever king k. everything in advance P12.7.

Knowledge, see also **Wisdom;** of animal languages B216; Fortune, Intellect, Health dispute which is greatest J461.1.2. — Acquisition and possession of k. J0—J199; cheating through legal k. K453; cripple healed by distributing k. H1292.4.3; eating magic salmon gives k. M315; hero's k.-giving member A527.2; learned man gave k. away H1292.2.1; magic charm gives k. D1310.6; magic sight from thumb of k. D1821.2; magic k. *D1810ff.; magic k. from touching "k. tooth" with thumb D1810.3; man with magic k. wins quest H1239.4; practical vs. theoretical k. J251; quest assigned because of hero's k. of animal languages H1214; recognition through common k. H10ff.; sacrifice for k. V17.5; saints have miraculous k. V223; salmon of k. F162.5.3, B124.1.1; sham wise man pretends k.: really overheard conversation K1956.7; supernatural k. from eating magic fish B162.1; tree of k. J165, (forbidden) *C621.1, (in otherworld) F162.3.5.

Kola. — Girls eat only k. nuts and tobacco F561.5.

Krishna plays cards with wives A164.3.1.

Kyffhäuser (king asleep in the mountain) *D1960.2, F451.5.1.8.

Kynanthropy D141.0.1.

www.ingramcontent.com/pod-product-compliance
Lightning Source LLC
LaVergne TN
LVHW040201080826
844660LV00001B/72